AMNESTY INTERNATIONAL REPORT 1997

This report
covers the period
January to December
1996

Amnesty International is a worldwide voluntary movement that works to prevent some of the gravest violations by governments of people's fundamental human rights. The main focus of its campaigning is to:

- *free all prisoners of conscience.* These are people detained anywhere for their beliefs or because of their ethnic origin, sex, colour, language, national or social origin, economic status, birth or other status – who have not used or advocated violence;

- *ensure fair and prompt trials for political prisoners;*

- *abolish the death penalty, torture and other cruel treatment of prisoners;*

- *end extrajudicial executions and "disappearances".*

Amnesty International also opposes abuses by opposition groups, including hostage-taking, torture and killings of prisoners and other deliberate and arbitrary killings.

Amnesty International, recognizing that human rights are indivisible and interdependent, works to promote all the human rights enshrined in the Universal Declaration of Human Rights and other international standards, through human rights education programs and campaigning for ratification of human rights treaties.

Amnesty International is impartial. It is independent of any government, political persuasion or religious creed. It does not support or oppose any government or political system, nor does it support or oppose the views of the victims whose rights it seeks to protect. It is concerned solely with the protection of the human rights involved in each case, regardless of the ideology of the government or opposition forces, or the beliefs of the individual.

Amnesty International does not grade countries according to their record on human rights; instead of attempting comparisons it concentrates on trying to end the specific violations of human rights in each case.

Amnesty International has around 1,000,000 members and subscribers in 162 countries and territories. There are 4,273 local Amnesty International groups registered with the International Secretariat and several thousand school, university, professional and other groups in over 80 countries in Africa, the Americas, Asia, Europe and the Middle East. To ensure impartiality, each group works on cases and campaigns in countries other than its own, selected for geographical and political diversity. Research into human rights violations and individual victims is conducted by the International Secretariat of Amnesty International. No section, group or member is expected to provide information on their own country, and no section, group or member has any responsibility for action taken or statements issued by the international organization concerning their own country.

Amnesty International has formal relations with the United Nations Economic and Social Council (ECOSOC); the United Nations Educational, Scientific and Cultural Organization (UNESCO); the Council of Europe; the Organization of American States; the Organization of African Unity; and the Inter-Parliamentary Union.

Amnesty International is financed by subscriptions and donations from its worldwide membership. No funds are sought or accepted from governments. To safeguard the independence of the organization, all contributions are strictly controlled by guidelines laid down by the International Council.

AMNESTY INTERNATIONAL REPORT

1997

Amnesty International USA
322 Eighth Avenue
New York, NY 10001
http://www.amnesty.org

First published 1997
by Amnesty International Publications
1 Easton Street, London WC1X 8DJ, United Kingdom

© Copyright Amnesty International Publications 1997

ISBN: 1-887204-11-3
AI Index: POL 10/01/97
Original language: English

Typesetting and page make-up by:
Accent on Type, 30/31 Great Sutton Street, London EC1V 0DX, United Kingdom

Printed by: John D. Lucas Printing Co., Baltimore, MD

Cover design: John Finn, Artworkers

Cover photograph: Liberian refugees on the freighter *Bulk Challenge*, May 1996
© AP/David Guttenfelder

All rights reserved.
No part of this publication may be reproduced,
stored in a retrieval system, or transmitted,
in any form or by any means,
electronic, mechanical, photocopying, recording and/or otherwise
without the prior permission of the publishers.

This report documents Amnesty International's work and its concerns throughout the world during 1996. The absence of an entry in this report on a particular country does not imply that no human rights violations of concern to Amnesty International have taken place there during the year. Nor is the length of a country entry any basis for a comparison of the extent and depth of Amnesty International's concerns in a country. Regional maps have been included in this report to indicate the location of countries and territories cited in the text and for that purpose only. It is not possible on the small scale used to show precise political boundaries. The maps should not be taken as indicating any view on the status of disputed territory. Amnesty International takes no position on territorial questions. Disputed boundaries and cease-fire lines are shown, where possible, by broken lines. Areas whose disputed status is a matter of unresolved concern before the relevant bodies of the United Nations have been indicated by striping only on the maps of the country which has *de facto* control of the area.

CONTENTS

Introduction/Refugees: Human rights have no borders	1
Campaigns and Membership/Speaking out against oppression	18
Death Penalty/No solution to crime	36
Work with International Organizations/	
International protection: consensus and compromise	43
Afghanistan (the Islamic State of)	63
Albania (the Republic of)	65
Algeria (the People's Democratic Republic of)	68
Angola (the Republic of)	71
Argentina (the Argentine Republic)	74
Armenia (the Republic of)	76
Australia	77
Austria (the Republic of)	79
Azerbaijan (the Azerbaijani Republic)	81
Bahamas (the Commonwealth of the)	82
Bahrain (the State of)	83
Bangladesh (the People's Republic of)	86
Belarus (the Republic of)	88
Belize	89
Bhutan (the Kingdom of)	90
Bolivia (the Republic of)	91
Bosnia-Herzegovina (Bosnia and Herzegovina)	92
Botswana (the Republic of)	95
Brazil (the Federative Republic of)	96
Bulgaria (the Republic of)	99
Burkina Faso	101
Burma (see **Myanmar**)	
Burundi (the Republic of)	102
Cambodia (the Kingdom of)	105
Cameroon (the Republic of)	108
Canada	111
Chad (the Republic of)	112
Chile (the Republic of)	116
China (the People's Republic of)	118
Colombia (the Republic of)	122
Comoros (the Islamic Federal Republic of the)	125
Congo (the Republic of the)	126
Costa Rica (the Republic of)	128
Côte d'Ivoire (the Republic of)	128
Croatia (the Republic of)	130
Cuba (the Republic of)	132
Cyprus (the Republic of)	135

CONTENTS

Denmark (the Kingdom of)	136
Djibouti (the Republic of)	137
Dominican Republic (the)	138
Ecuador (the Republic of)	139
Egypt (the Arab Republic of)	141
El Salvador (the Republic of)	144
Equatorial Guinea (the Republic of)	146
Eritrea	147
Estonia (the Republic of)	148
Ethiopia (the Federal Democratic Republic of)	149
France (the French Republic)	152
Gambia (the Republic of the)	154
Georgia	156
Germany (the Federal Republic of)	158
Ghana (the Republic of)	160
Greece (the Hellenic Republic)	161
Guatemala (the Republic of)	163
Guinea (the Republic of)	166
Guinea-Bissau (the Republic of)	167
Guyana (the Republic of)	169
Haiti (the Republic of)	170
Honduras (the Republic of)	173
Hong Kong	174
Hungary (the Republic of)	176
India (the Republic of)	177
Indonesia (the Republic of) **and East Timor**	180
Iran (the Islamic Republic of)	184
Iraq (the Republic of)	187
Ireland	190
Israel (the State of) **and the Occupied Territories**	191
Italy (the Italian Republic)	194
Jamaica	196
Japan	196
Jordan (the Hashemite Kingdom of)	198
Kazakstan (the Republic of)	200
Kenya (the Republic of)	202
Korea (the Democratic People's Republic of)	205
Korea (the Republic of)	206
Kuwait (the State of)	209
Kyrgyzstan (the Kyrgyz Republic)	210
Laos (the Lao People's Democratic Republic)	212
Latvia (the Republic of)	212

CONTENTS

Lebanon (the Lebanese Republic)	213
Lesotho (the Kingdom of)	217
Liberia (the Republic of)	218
Libya (the Socialist People's Libyan Arab Jamahiriya)	220
Lithuania (the Republic of)	222
Macao	223
Malawi (the Republic of)	224
Malaysia	224
Maldives (the Republic of)	226
Mali (the Republic of)	227
Mauritania (the Islamic Republic of)	228
Mexico (the United Mexican States)	228
Moldova (the Republic of)	232
Mongolia	233
Morocco (the Kingdom of) **and Western Sahara**	234
Mozambique (the Republic of)	236
Myanmar (the Union of)	237
Nepal (the Kingdom of)	241
Nicaragua (the Republic of)	242
Niger (the Republic of the)	243
Nigeria (the Federal Republic of)	245
Pakistan (the Islamic Republic of)	248
Palestinian Authority (areas under the jurisdiction of the)	251
Panama (the Republic of)	252
Papua New Guinea	254
Paraguay (the Republic of)	256
Peru (the Republic of)	257
Philippines (the Republic of the)	261
Portugal (the Portuguese Republic)	263
Qatar (the State of)	265
Romania	265
Russian Federation (the)	268
Rwanda (the Rwandese Republic)	270
Saudi Arabia (the Kingdom of)	273
Senegal (the Republic of)	276
Sierra Leone (the Republic of)	278
Singapore (the Republic of)	281
Slovakia (the Slovak Republic)	282
Somalia (the Somali Democratic Republic)	283
South Africa (the Republic of)	285
Spain (the Kingdom of)	289
Sri Lanka (the Democratic Socialist Republic of)	291
Sudan (the Republic of the)	293

CONTENTS

Suriname (the Republic of) 296
Swaziland (the Kingdom of) 297
Switzerland (the Swiss Confederation) 298
Syria (the Syrian Arab Republic) 300

Taiwan (the Republic of China) 302
Tajikistan (the Republic of) 303
Tanzania (the United Republic of) 305
Thailand (the Kingdom of) 307
Togo (the Togolese Republic) 309
Tonga (the Kingdom of) 310
Trinidad and Tobago (the Republic of) 311
Tunisia (the Republic of) 311
Turkey (the Republic of) 314
Turkmenistan 317

Uganda (the Republic of) 319
Ukraine 320
United Arab Emirates (the) 321
United Kingdom (of Great Britain and Northern Ireland, the) 322
United States of America (the) 326
Uruguay (the Eastern Republic of) 329
Uzbekistan (the Republic of) 330

Venezuela (the Republic of) 332
Viet Nam (the Socialist Republic of) 334

Yemen (the Republic of) 336
Yugoslavia (the Federal Republic of) 339

Zaire (the Republic of) 342
Zambia (the Republic of) 345
Zimbabwe (the Republic of) 346

APPENDICES

I	Amnesty International Visits 1996	351
II	Statute of Amnesty International: Articles 1 and 2	355
III	Amnesty International around the World	357
IV	International Executive Committee	360
V	Selected International Human Rights Treaties	361
VI	Selected Regional Human Rights Treaties	370
VII	Amnesty International's Declaration on the Role of Health Professionals in the Exposure of Torture and Ill-treatment	373
VIII	Amnesty International's Principles for the Medical Investigation of Torture and Other Cruel, Inhuman or Degrading Treatment	375
IX	Selected Statistics	378

INTRODUCTION

INTRODUCTION

Refugees: Human rights have no borders

A decade ago, there were some eight million refugees worldwide. Today, the number of refugees seeking protection from terrible human rights violations has almost doubled: to more than 15 million. Refugees are people who have fled their countries because they have a well-founded fear of persecution and cannot rely on their own governments to protect them. This is what distinguishes refugees from other migrants. Increasingly these people are evidence of the extent to which persecution, mass human rights violations and abuses arising out of civil war and other conflicts have erupted around the world during the 1990s, leaving refugees in their wake.

Most of the world's refugees are women and children. The majority of them have fled for the same reasons as men. Some refugees, however, have been forced to leave their homes because of human rights violations and abuses directed primarily or solely at women. Women from zones of conflict have fled areas where soldiers have systematically raped and sexually abused young girls and women. In Afghanistan, the states of the former Yugoslavia, Zaire and other countries, rape was used to terrorize civilians into flight. Women have also sought asylum abroad because of fear of persecution due to the status or activities of male

A Bosnian woman returns to her home village after four years as a refugee in the United Kingdom. Many go back only to find their homes completely destroyed.

INTRODUCTION

relatives, or because they have transgressed, or refuse to conform to, discriminatory religious, social or customary laws and practices. Some women have fled their countries to seek protection from the practice of female genital mutilation.

Women are not even safe once they have found refuge. In 1991, some 300,000 Somali refugees fled inter-clan fighting, famine and disease in their country. In 1996, some 170,000 Somali refugees were still living in Kenya. Most were housed in three camps in a remote area of the northeast, near the border with Somalia. Hundreds of Somali women were raped in these camps between April 1992 and November 1993. Although the majority of rapists were bandits, a number of women were raped by Kenyan soldiers or police. As far as Amnesty International is aware, to this day those responsible for raping or assaulting Somali refugees have not been brought to justice.

The growing number of refugees is neither a temporary problem nor the random product of chance events. It is the predictable consequence of human rights crises throughout the world. Often these crises were foreseen. In the two years before the outbreak of genocidal violence in Rwanda, a United Nations (UN) human rights expert warned that unless states took determined action, mass killings would follow. The international community not only failed to heed these warnings, but, when the massacres started in April 1994, withdrew the UN troops. Since then, refugee crisis has followed refugee crisis in the region, with millions of men, women and children suffering dislocation, terror, disease, starvation and death.

In Zaire, as many as 750,000 people were internally displaced in 1996, as a result of fighting between government troops and Zairian armed opposition groups. Many civilians were killed in the east of the country in October and November. In one incident in mid-November, members of the *Alliance des forces démocratiques pour la libération du Congo-Zaire* (AFDL), Alliance of Democratic Forces for the Liberation of Congo-Zaire, a Zairian armed group, massacred about 500 Rwandese and Burundian refugees and displaced Zairians. The massacre took place at the Chimanga refugee camp, about 60 kilometres south of Bukavu. Hundreds of refugees and Zairians had congregated around Chimanga camp, hoping to get assistance to cross into Rwanda. About 40 AFDL members arrived in four trucks and opened fire on the refugees, killing most of them. When a Zairian priest, Father Jean-Claude Buhendwa, protested, he was executed.

Tens of thousands of mainly Hutu refugees from Burundi were also living in eastern Zaire when the violence erupted. They had fled the civil war and ethnic violence which had escalated in Burundi ever since the October 1993 assassination of the country's first democratically elected president. Many were forced back to Burundi in late 1996 by Zairian armed groups, who handed them over to Burundi government forces at the border. Hundreds who returned, including women and children, were rounded up and

INTRODUCTION

Rwandese refugees in October 1996. Two years before the outbreak of genocidal violence in Rwanda, the UN was repeatedly urged by human rights organizations, as well as its own senior personnel, to take action to protect civilians from massacres. These appeals were not heeded. The UN member states allowed the situation to deteriorate and then, when mass killings began, withdrew almost all UN troops. More than two million Rwandans fled their country.

killed by the Burundian security forces near the border or in the capital, Bujumbura.

Decades of atrocities have set populations against each other in Africa's Great Lakes region. But the many disparate groups from Rwanda, Zaire and Burundi have one thing in common: they are in grave danger of continued human rights abuses and they are not getting from states and intergovernmental organizations the full protection which is due to refugees under regional and international treaties.

The refugee crisis in Europe also shows little sign of improvement. Its worst human rights disaster since the 1940s is far from being resolved. From 1991, as the former Yugoslavia fractured, systematic rape, mass murder and "disappearance" became commonplace. More than two million people in Bosnia and Herzegovina alone fled their homes, friends and livelihoods. Some found temporary refuge in Europe, others are still displaced within the country. One year after the peace agreement which brought an end to open conflict, there has been little real progress towards establishing the durably safe conditions which would allow refugees and displaced people to return to their homes.

INTRODUCTION

Mass human rights violations in the Middle East have forced countless people to flee their countries. September saw a new refugee crisis in the region when Iraqi government forces and the Kurdistan Democratic Party launched a joint attack on the Kurdish city of Arbil, then held by the opposition Patriotic Union of Kurdistan. At least 70,000 Kurdish refugees fled to Iran as the fighting spread to Sulaimaniya.

Thousands of Algerians have tried to seek refuge abroad to escape political violence which has resulted in more than 50,000 killings since 1992. Many of those killed have been members of the security forces and armed opposition groups killed in armed confrontation, but as the violence has spiralled out of control, civilians have increasingly borne the brunt of the carnage. More than 100 foreigners have been killed in Algeria, as a result of which European and other "northern" governments have advised their citizens against visiting the country because the Algerian authorities are unable to protect them. Tens of thousands of Algerians have been killed in the conflict, but these same governments often reject asylum-seekers' claims, arguing that they face no risk of serious human rights violations in their home country. This double standard has meant that asylum-seekers fleeing violence in Algeria have been unable to obtain the protection they need.

Bouasria Ben 'Othman, an Algerian asylum-seeker, paid the ultimate price when his right to asylum was violated. In July, the Belgian authorities forcibly returned him to Algeria, despite the clear risks he faced there. Four months later, the Algerian authorities informed the Belgian Government that he had been arrested on arrival in Algeria, released, then rearrested in mid-November while trying to cross the border into Libya. On 26 November, Bouasria Ben 'Othman appeared on Algerian television saying he was well and that people should stop asking about him. He died in detention one week later, allegedly as a result of torture. The Algerian police told his family that he had thrown himself out of a window.

The world responds: 'No refuge here'

The majority of the world's states have undertaken to accept and protect refugees fleeing persecution, by ratifying the 1951 UN Convention relating to the Status of Refugees (UN Refugee Convention) and its 1967 Protocol. However, more than 50 have not, and some of those sit on the Executive Committee of the UN High Commissioner for Refugees (UNHCR), the advisory body of the UNHCR. The Office of the UNHCR is the UN agency charged with protecting and assisting refugees.

Sudden mass movements of refugees often signal terror and human rights catastrophes. They should alert the international community to act swiftly to prevent further human rights tragedies and to develop coordinated strategies to protect and support refugees.

INTRODUCTION

An Albanian asylum-seeker arrives in Brindisi, Italy, in March 1991.

Instead, the 1990s have seen states take inadequate action to prevent the human rights violations which cause refugees to flee and at the same time evade their responsibilities towards refugees. Countries which proclaim the importance they attach to human rights simultaneously force men, women and children back into the arms of their persecutors by obstructing access to asylum procedures, misinterpreting the UN Refugee Convention definition of who is a refugee and forcibly returning those who are in need of protection.

The international regime that is supposed to protect refugees is in crisis. The UN Refugee Convention and its Protocol, which was designed to protect refugees fleeing persecution, often prove inadequate because many situations faced by refugees today are deemed to fall outside their terms. There is a gap in international protection for many of those who need it most. Many states have devised alternative legal categories in order to protect refugees, including "humanitarian status" and "*de facto* refugees". However, these categories are uncertain and usually mean that those in need of protection are given insufficient rights. The reasons why people flee their homes are becoming more complicated in a world beset by armed conflict, political instability and persecution of one nationality by another.

A further category of people forced to flee their homes and who do not benefit from effective international protection are the 25 to 30 million internally displaced, who have often fled for the same reasons as refugees, but have not crossed into another country.

The problems caused by inadequate protective measures are compounded by the fact that many states talk about the rights of refugees, while in practice devoting their energies to keeping refugees away from their borders, forcing them back into the arms of their persecutors and claiming that few who seek asylum are "real" refugees. States' commitment to offering asylum is dwindling, as is their political will to resolve the plight of desperate refugees, and minimal action is being taken to prevent the human rights violations which have caused people to flee their homes.

For more than four decades, UNHCR staff around the world have protected and assisted asylum-seekers, refugees and those in refugee-like situations. However, 1996 saw a marked deterioration in the level of international protection for refugees, as the political will of states dwindled in the face of very complex refugee movements. In December, the UNHCR supported the involuntary repatriation, after the first quarter of 1997, of certain categories of people to areas of Bosnia and Herzegovina where their nationality was in a majority. There is a risk that some of these people could be returned to areas where they have nowhere to live and where they may be at risk of further human rights violations or abuses. December also saw the UNHCR sign a joint statement with the Government of Tanzania endorsing the repatriation of hundreds of thousands of refugees from Tanzania to Rwanda without any opportunity for individuals to present reasons as to why they needed continuing protection. By the end of the year, some 5,000 of those who returned had been detained in Rwanda, where they had little prospect of justice. The fundamental guarantees of voluntary repatriation were no longer being upheld, and the silence of the international community in response to the mass return of refugees was remarkable. Only a few non-governmental organizations protested against this deterioration in refugee protection.

In a recent address to the Executive Committee of the UNHCR, Sadako Ogata, High Commissioner for Refugees, stated:

> *"One of the most difficult problems confronting my office in recent years has been the decline of asylum, even on a temporary basis. Many countries are openly admitting their weariness with large numbers of refugees and blatantly closing borders. Others are more insidiously introducing laws and procedures which effectively deny admission to their territory ... the threat to asylum has taken on a global character, affecting both the developing as well as the industrialized world."*

Increasingly, states are forcibly returning individuals to countries where their life or freedom is threatened – a practice known as *refoulement*. *Refoulement* is prohibited under Article 33 of the UN Refugee Convention and under other international instruments. The principle of non-*refoulement* is a fundamental one and is considered to be a norm of customary international law, which all states are obliged to uphold. Yet many states violate

INTRODUCTION

Rwandese refugees at the Rosumo Camp, Ngara, Tanzania. Refugees fled to camps in Tanzania to escape the human rights crises in Burundi and Rwanda – yet, in December 1996, the Tanzanian Government announced that within three weeks more than 500,000 Rwandese refugees would be repatriated. By the end of the year, most had been forced home.

this obligation and return refugees to countries where they are at grave risk.

In Sweden, at the end of 1996, Kaveh Yaragh Tala was awaiting the Aliens Appeal Board's ruling on his case, for him potentially a life or death decision. Kaveh Yaragh Tala is an Iranian citizen, who fled in 1990 after being tortured because of his involvement with the Peoples' Mojahedin Organization of Iran (PMOI), an armed opposition group. He made his way to Sweden and requested asylum, but his claim was denied, mainly because during the asylum process he had changed his story. His case was submitted to the UN Committee against Torture, which in December 1996 criticized the Swedish authorities' decision to return him, stating that this was a violation of Article 3 of the UN Convention against Torture and other Cruel, Inhuman or Degrading Treatment or Punishment. The Committee was of the opinion that complete accuracy can seldom be expected of victims of torture, that Kaveh Yaragh Tala had been tortured and that he would be at risk of further torture if he was returned to Iran.

Pauline, an asylum-seeker from Zaire, was also threatened with *refoulement* by the Swedish authorities. She had fled after being repeatedly raped in Kinshasa, in front of her children and while in detention, because of her political activities. The UN Committee against Torture opposed the *refoulement* of Pauline, and the Swedish Aliens Appeal Board, on re-examining the case, referred it to the Swedish Government for a decision. In November 1996, Pauline was granted refugee status.

Anna and Alexander, both ethnic Armenians and residents of the Chechen capital, Grozny, fled after being targeted because of their opposition to the Chechen authorities. On arrival in Moscow they were threatened by officers of the Russian special police force (OMON) because of their ethnic origin. They reportedly only avoided being forcibly returned to Grozny by paying bribes to OMON officers. They eventually obtained visas for Denmark and travelled to Copenhagen in December 1993, where they applied for refugee status. Their application was rejected in May 1996 by the Danish Refugee Appeals Board, which decided that they could be returned to the Russian Federation. The Appeals Board decided that the harassment and intimidation that Anna and Alexander would face if returned to the Chechen Republic was not sufficiently serious to warrant granting them asylum. Amnesty International members petitioned the Danish authorities, who granted Anna and Alexander humanitarian leave to remain in Denmark as Alexander was gravely ill.

A 31-year-old woman from Cameroon tried to apply for asylum in Romania, but was sent to Russia and then returned to Cameroon by the Russian authorities. She stated that she was involved with an opposition party in Cameroon, the Social Democratic Front, and had been detained several times between 1989 and 1996. In January, she learned that the security forces were again looking for her, so she went into hiding. In March, she fled to Romania, hoping to explain her position to immigration officials and to contact the UNHCR. In Bucharest airport, she was not even granted an interview, but was put on a plane to Moscow.

Iraqi refugee women in the Kermanshah Province of Iran weaving a carpet. At least 70,000 Kurdish refugees fled to Iran following fighting in northern Iraq between Iraqi government forces, the Kurdistan Democratic Party, and the Patriotic Union of Kurdistan.

INTRODUCTION

There are more than 90,000 refugees in camps in eastern Nepal, most of whom are from southern Bhutan. Many were forced to leave by the Bhutanese authorities in the early 1990s on account of their ethnic origin or political beliefs, amid unrest related to government policies on national integration and the application of a new Citizenship Act.

Russian officials also ignored her asylum application, refused to give her the telephone number of the UNHCR and, after keeping her in the airport transit zone for two weeks, forced her onto a plane going to Cameroon. She stated that she was detained as soon as she landed in Cameroon, and released after she signed a declaration that she would never again participate in political activity. Using all the money she had, she managed to escape again, with a transit visa to Belarus. She was believed to be in the Russian Federation, trying to submit an application for asylum.

In November 1996, the forcible return of 88 Colombian refugees, including 32 children, from Panama brought fears that more than 300 other refugees might suffer a similar fate. The refugees, peasant farmers and their families, had fled violence between left-wing guerrillas and right-wing paramilitary units in northern Colombia which has left scores of civilians dead and many others internally displaced. As soon as the Panamanian authorities became aware of their presence they contacted the Colombian Air Force to organize the refugees' return. The Colombian Air Force provided the aircraft in which they returned. Further repatriations were halted after international pressure and petitions from Amnesty International and other international non-governmental organizations.

At the end of the year, a group of 19 political activists of Vietnamese descent were forcibly removed from Cambodia to Viet Nam, despite the fact that prominent dissidents faced life imprisonment or even the death penalty for their peaceful opposition to the Vietnamese Government. The UNHCR in Cambodia attempted to intervene, but was ignored by the Cambodian authorities. The 19 were arrested and detained on arrival in Viet Nam. Their present situation is unclear.

The North clamps down

The world's richest countries host the minority of the world's refugees. While accepting in theory the principle of non-*refoulement*, in practice "northern" states return refugees by employing a variety of legal and administrative measures to obstruct and deter refugees from seeking asylum. Defenders of the rights of refugees have lost some of the battles over policy. They are now losing individual cases as "northern" states put their increasingly restrictive policies into practice. In many countries, public opinion is swayed by portrayals of genuine refugees as "bogus" economic migrants or as lacking in credibility.

"Northern" states avoid their obligations towards refugees by obstructing access. The measures used include rejection at the border, carrier sanctions, visa requirements that are impossible for asylum-seekers to fulfil, international zones in airports and interdiction at sea. For those refugees able to get into a country, the use of "safe third country" practices, "white lists", and readmission agreements result in refugees being sent to countries they may have travelled through, or to the country they fled. In Turkey, asylum-seekers have to register their claim within five days of entering the country. Asylum-seekers who failed to comply with the five-day rule have been returned to countries where they were at risk of serious human rights violations. Mehrdad, an Iranian citizen who was a member of the PMOI, spent 10 years in prison in Iran and was subjected to torture. He was released, but fled to Turkey in August 1995 because he feared rearrest. UNHCR recognized his asylum claim, but in April the Turkish authorities forcibly returned him to Iran for having failed to register his asylum claim within five days of arrival. On his return to Iran he was arrested and interrogated. Worldwide appeals on his behalf flooded in from Amnesty International members and other organizations. Mehrdad was eventually released after agreeing to return to Turkey and to send letters to the UN and human rights organizations criticizing the PMOI. Once in Turkey, he escaped from Iranian officials accompanying him and again sought asylum. He was eventually resettled in another country.

Some "northern" states off-load their obligations by sending asylum-seekers to a "safe third country". Sometimes the only connection the asylum-seeker has with the country is that their plane stopped to refuel there. Many "third countries" are far from safe; some do not adhere to the international refugee treaties, let alone have they established adequate mechanisms for dealing with asylum-seekers. One such country is Pakistan. Hundreds of thousands of refugees from civil war and mass human rights violations in Afghanistan have crossed the border

INTRODUCTION

Some of the 73 Afghan and Sri Lankan "boat people" on board the Norwegian freight ferry *Dana Baltica* after its arrival in Denmark on 1 August 1995. The ferry picked up the refugees from four dinghies in the Baltic sea.

to Pakistan in search of safety. However, many of them remained at risk there. Prominent Afghans living in Pakistan have frequently been targeted for assassination and abduction.

Mariam Azimi, an Afghan asylum-seeker, was forced to hide in a church in Norway with her two young children because the authorities did not believe her when she said it was unsafe for her to be sent to Pakistan. Already vulnerable by virtue of being an educated Afghan woman, she was in particular danger in Afghanistan because she had campaigned for women's rights. After receiving repeated death threats, she fled to Pakistan, where she continued her campaigning. She was again threatened by Afghan Mojahedin groups who operate in border areas in Pakistan. Attempts were made to kill members of her family and she was forced yet again to flee in fear of her life. She arrived in Norway with her two young children in search of asylum. The authorities rejected her claim on the grounds that it was safe for her to return to Pakistan. She went into hiding with her children to escape being forcibly repatriated.

Many "northern" states continue to impose carrier sanctions, whereby fines are imposed on shipowners and airlines that allow people without the required paperwork to board their craft. These sanctions can have terrifying consequences.

In May, three Romanian asylum-seekers who had stowed away on a container ship were left to drown off the coast of Canada after being forced off the Taiwanese ship *Mersk Dubai* into the sea. According to members of the ship's crew, they were given no life jackets, just pieces of styrofoam which were tied round their waists. The asylum-seekers did not have the proper papers, and the shipping company could have been fined $6,000 per person if the captain had landed them in Canada. A crew member said that he saw the stowaways pleading for their lives as the ship's officers forced them to climb down the ladder and into the ocean.

Immigration officials from "northern" countries have been dispatched to countries which produce large numbers of refugees to show airline staff how to spot passengers with suspect papers or motives. Airlines conduct pre-flight screenings at points of embarkation, especially at airports where potential asylum-seekers are expected. In Nairobi, Kenya, for example, Dutch and British immigration officials have trained airline staff in recognizing fraudulent travel documents. In several European Union member states, airline staff have the power to decide whether travel documents are genuine, despite the European Parliament resolution of 24 September 1995 that all asylum-seekers should have automatic and unfettered access to admission procedures, and that visa policies and sanctions on carriers should not be an impediment to such access. Measures which obstruct the entry of asylum-seekers, including visa requirements and carrier sanctions, are incompatible with the object and purpose of the international system for the protection of refugees. People fleeing persecution will often not be able to obtain the proper travel documents and may have no choice but to flee with false documentation.

Some states are trying to evade their responsibilities towards asylum-seekers while their claims are being assessed. A Zairian woman, Ms B., traumatized after being raped by state officials,

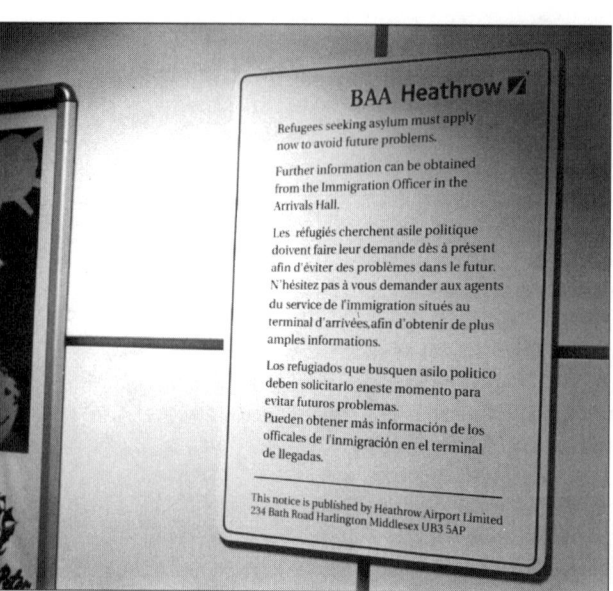

A poster at Heathrow airport in the United Kingdom, warning asylum-seekers that they should make their asylum claim immediately, without passing through immigration control.

arrived in the United Kingdom in February, hoping to find asylum. She arrived just a few days after a rule change which meant that only those who applied for asylum immediately at the port of entry were eligible to receive welfare payments while their claims were assessed.

Ms B. had been arrested in Zaire at a memorial meeting for her husband, who had been shot dead during an anti-government rally. In prison, she had been repeatedly raped by guards. A guard finally took pity on her and smuggled her out in a sack. Her family paid for her to travel to the United Kingdom via Belgium. She arrived in London by train and then went directly to the Home Office, some kilometres away, where she applied for asylum. She was subsequently denied any welfare payments on the grounds that she had not submitted her asylum application immediately on arrival at the port of entry. A legal challenge was made to the Court of Appeal, which in June ruled in her favour. One of the judges stated:

> "A significant number of genuine asylum-seekers now find themselves faced with a bleak choice: whether to remain here destitute and homeless until their claims are finally determined or whether instead to abandon their claims and return to face the very persecution they have fled."

This legal victory was short-lived. In July 1996, the British parliament passed legislation denying welfare payments to all those who failed to apply for asylum immediately on arrival and to people appealing against rejection of their asylum claim. However, in October a new High Court ruling required local government authorities to provide some assistance to asylum-seekers. In December, for the first time in 50 years, the Red Cross distributed food parcels in London. The recipients were destitute asylum-seekers.

In September, legislation limiting the social benefits available to immigrants and some refugees also came into force in the United States of America (USA).

The international community has agreed that states should normally avoid detaining asylum-seekers. However, in Europe and North America the use of detention has increased dramatically as states make strenuous efforts to deter and obstruct refugees from seeking asylum in their countries. In some countries, such as the USA and Austria, some asylum-seekers are detained as soon as they arrive and are held while their applications are processed. In many countries, refugees are held in the transit zones of international airports and then expelled. In others, specific groups of asylum-seekers are placed behind bars – for example, those whose applications are considered "unfounded". In a recent study, "Cell Culture", Amnesty International's United Kingdom Section examined the cases of 150 of 700 asylum-seekers detained in the United Kingdom and highlighted the

INTRODUCTION

A four-year-old Haitian boy is fingerprinted by a Haitian police officer after he and his family were returned to Haiti by the US Coast Guard. Between 1991 and 1994, thousands of Haitians were forcibly returned by the US authorities.

arbitrariness of detention of asylum-seekers in the country. Asylum-seekers are sometimes detained for years while they await a decision on their case, although they have committed no crime.

Australia has a policy of automatically detaining asylum-seekers who arrive without having first gained permission to enter. In March, Australian immigration officials refused to deliver letters sent by the government-funded Human Rights and Equal Opportunity Commission (HREOC) to Chinese "boat people" who, the Commission said, were held incommunicado at Port Hedland Detention Centre. The letters concerned a complaint about alleged human rights violations made on behalf of 34 Chinese adults and 12 children who had arrived by boat in February. The letters, which informed the detainees that the HREOC had begun an investigation into the alleged human rights violations, were not delivered on the grounds that the detainees had not themselves complained to the HREOC. In June, a Federal Court ordered the immigration department to pass on the letters. The government appealed against the decision and proposed legislation which would remove certain rights to legal advice for detained asylum-seekers and exclude them from scrutiny of their human rights situation, unless they made a formal request to the HREOC or the Ombudsman.

The arbitrary detention of asylum-seekers and refugees is punishment without crime. Depriving asylum-seekers of their liberty puts many in exactly the situation they fled to escape and makes it much more difficult for them to pursue their asylum claims.

Asylum-seekers in the USA are often held in remote locations, given inaccurate information about their status, and shackled hand and foot during asylum hearings; some have been held in cruel, inhuman or degrading conditions. Fauziya Kasinga was hit with a stick, sprayed with tear-gas and kicked at the detention centre where she was sent after seeking asylum in the USA. She had fled to escape female genital mutilation in her home country of Togo. When she arrived in the USA, she immediately asked for asylum and was taken to Esmor Detention Centre in handcuffs and shackles. Conditions in Esmor were harsh, with poor food, lack of heat, insect-infested bedding, filthy clothing and theft of detainees' belongings by staff. Fauziya, just 17 years old, was detained for more than a year in various detention centres. In April, she was finally granted asylum on the recognition that women fleeing persecution in the form of genital mutilation are refugees deserving international protection.

During 1996, there continued to be no further international clarification of standards for those refugees granted "temporary protection" on a group basis rather than refugee status in their own right. This denies them access to individual asylum procedures and to the rights associated with refugee protection. It also means that they can be sent home as part of a group to conditions which may remain dangerous for some individuals.

Some European states claimed that they limited the protection afforded to those fleeing the former Yugoslavia because of their inability to cope with a mass influx. There is no standard definition of what constitutes a mass influx, and in Europe only Germany and Sweden have admitted more than 100,000 refugees from the former Yugoslavia. The use of temporary protection in Europe represents a watershed in international refugee protection, as states have imposed a new protection standard which has not been agreed internationally.

In September, Germany unilaterally decided to embark on the forcible repatriation of refugees from Bosnia and Herzegovina, ending their temporary protection status. After the UNHCR statement, in December, that some categories of temporarily protected refugees could be returned to Bosnia and Herzegovina in 1997, it is likely that a number of other European governments will begin returning Bosnian refugees, although there is evidence that it is not yet durably safe for them to return.

The dilemma of the South

Governments in the South host 85 per cent of the world's refugees. In Africa alone there are five million refugees – one third of the world's total – and at least 16 million internally displaced people.

These countries are among the world's poorest, and yet they have been left to bear the enormous logistic, economic and environmental strains that result from mass flows of refugees.

Iran is a "refugee-producing" country, but for years it has hosted mass numbers of refugees. It still shelters more than two million, more than any other country in the world. For years it appealed to the international community for help, but its pleas were ignored. In the early 1990s, Iran's policies towards refugees changed. Today, asylum-seekers in Iran face rapidly deteriorating living conditions, and sometimes less than "voluntary" repatriation and *refoulement*.

Governments which host mass numbers of refugees have no secure mechanism by which to gain assistance. To make matters worse, aid is often pledged and then not given. Nevertheless, these governments are still obliged by international law not to forcibly return refugees to situations where their human rights would be in jeopardy.

"Southern" governments are increasingly acting against their long-standing traditions of hospitality towards refugees. They are coercing refugees to return to their countries of origin, using measures which include cutting food supplies and, as was the case in the mass expulsions of Rwandese refugees from Tanzania in December, the use of force.

Refugees from Liberia have been turned away by many western African states despite their desperate circumstances. Some three quarters of a million people have fled the country during six years of civil war, which escalated again in April after several months of peace. Bitter fighting broke out anew in the capital, Monrovia, and thousands of people were forced to take refuge in the compounds of foreign embassies in Monrovia. Thousands more bought tickets for ships that would take them away from the carnage. In the western African heat, men, women and children crammed into rusting freighters with little food or water and practically no sanitation. Numerous western African states, including Côte d'Ivoire and Sierra Leone, refused to let the refugees land, despite the appalling conditions on the boats, the desperation of the refugees and the pleas of UNHCR and other agency officials. In May, the Ghanaian Government allowed more than 3,000 refugees from one of the freighters, *Bulk Challenge*, to land.

In June 1996, 103 men of various African nationalities were deported from the Spanish city of Malaga and from Melilla, a Spanish enclave in northern Africa, after the authorities denied them access to refugee status determination procedures. Fifty of the Africans, including asylum-seekers, were deposited in Guinea-Bissau and were immediately detained in the Segunda Esquadra prison in Bissau, the capital, where several were beaten and otherwise ill-treated.

The recent measures which states in the North have taken to insulate themselves from refugees have meant that other parts of the world bear a heightened responsibility. Refugees who cannot reach western European states are increasingly seeking asylum in central and eastern European states, many of which are in a much weaker position to provide adequate protection.

INTRODUCTION

Sudanese refugees caught between government offensives and factional fighting carry all their worldly belongings on rafts of water hyacinths across a tributary of the Sobat river.

Refugee protection prevents human rights violations

Amnesty International works to prevent the human rights violations which cause people to flee their homes. It opposes the return of any person to a country where he or she would be at risk of serious human rights violations, such as imprisonment as a prisoner of conscience, torture, execution or "disappearance". This is the basis of Amnesty International's work for refugees. It is an important element of preventive human rights work – acting to prevent abuses, not just responding after they have occurred. Amnesty International calls on governments to ensure that their asylum procedures meet minimum international standards of fairness, impartiality and thoroughness. A corollary is that Amnesty International demands that no asylum-seeker is forcibly expelled without having had his or her claim properly examined. The organization also calls on governments to ensure that they do not expel someone to a country which may itself forcibly return refugees to danger.

Human rights activists campaigning on behalf of refugees face a dual challenge at the international level. They must uphold the protection provided by international refugee law in the face of growing efforts by governments to avoid and circumvent their obligations. They must also strive to ensure that as the world throws up new challenges to human rights, the system of international protection is extended to meet those challenges.

Speaking out against oppression

On 13 March, Amnesty International's China researcher and the organization's media director were stopped by Thai police as they tried to get into a taxi in Bangkok, Thailand's capital. They were on their way to a press conference to launch Amnesty International's campaign against human rights violations in China. A Thai policeman in plain clothes told them: "What you want to do is not possible." Over the next few months, Amnesty International members worldwide campaigned to prove those words wrong.

The two staff members were taken to a police station and held for two hours. They were released only after intervention by a Canadian Embassy official (the media director is a Canadian citizen). The Thai police claimed that they were checking their passports and that the two had attended the police station "voluntarily".

Later that day in Bangkok, Amnesty International members and activists from other Asian non-governmental organizations (NGOs) tried to deliver a report on human rights violations in China, entitled *No one is safe*, to the Chinese Embassy. They were stopped a few yards from the Embassy by about 80 Thai policemen in riot gear. The message from the Chinese authorities was clear: discussions about China's human rights record would not be tolerated – anywhere, by anyone, at any time.

These tactics of pressure and intimidation by the Chinese Government were used repeatedly around the world as the campaign gathered pace. In central Paris, 200 French police met about 150 Amnesty International members who were demonstrating during Chinese Premier Li Peng's visit to France. They were "peacefully detained" and later released. In Norway, members set up a roving "task force" of demonstrators to follow Chinese President Jiang Zemin during his tour of the country. His visit included a stopover in Oslo, where police rounded up the activists. Palden Gysatu, a Tibetan monk who had been tortured by the Chinese authorities, and Mo Lihua, a former Chinese prisoner of conscience, were among those held. Tension was heightened when Chinese bodyguards accompanying Jiang Zemin tried to enter the van in which Mo Lihua was being held. These events, after being reported by the national media, caused a public outcry, and the Chief of Oslo Police was subsequently forced to make a public apology.

Members in other countries experienced similar forms of intimidation. In Kathmandu, Nepal, on 18 March, more than one hundred members of Amnesty International's Nepalese Section,

CAMPAIGNS AND MEMBERSHIP

At the launch in Thailand of Amnesty International's Campaign on China, Thai riot police prevent Secretary General Pierre Sané from delivering Amnesty International's report on human rights violations in China to the Chinese Embassy in Bangkok.

along with a group of Tibetan activists, were arrested as they tried to march to the Chinese Embassy to deliver the report. The previous evening, three other Amnesty International members had been detained while collecting signatures and distributing material on human rights in China. The organization's international membership was mobilized – this time to free its own members – and by 21 March, all of them had been released.

The South Korean Section was also put under immense pressure to curb the activities it organized in support of the China campaign. Members were contacted on numerous occasions by their Ministry of Foreign Affairs after the Chinese Embassy made strong protests about the Section's plans to hold a concert in aid of Wei Jingsheng, a prisoner of conscience. The Section was asked to refrain from activities that could jeopardize relations between South Korea and China. The concert went ahead.

In Slovenia, the Chinese Ambassador was allowed to appear on prime-time national television to present China's official policy on Tibet. He was also granted three further broadcasts on the issue. The Slovenian Section issued a news release the next day outlining the organization's concerns in Tibet. This prompted an overwhelming response from the public: letters to the editor of the main daily newspaper condemned the television broadcast, and students drew up a petition for future broadcasts to be withdrawn.

The Slovenian Section also planned a demonstration outside the Chinese Embassy on 4 June, but the Interior Ministry refused permission for it to go ahead. The Slovenian Section issued another news release advising those invited to the demonstration not to attend, and, over the next three days, the news release made newspaper and television headlines and the Section was inundated with interview requests. On the morning of the third day, the members released the name of the government official responsible for banning the demonstration. Later that day permission was granted for the protest to go ahead, again attracting national media attention.

Despite these persistent moves across the world to silence the protests against China's human rights record, members were prepared to defend their right to speak out and the campaign thrived. Amnesty International delegations were sent to Bangkok, Tokyo and Hong Kong, taking the campaign's message to the heart of Asia, and sections worldwide were called on to take a wide range of actions, making it a very high-profile campaign.

Businesses were approached and asked to highlight their increasingly important role in the protection of human rights, and a businessman accompanied the organization's delegations to Hong Kong and Tokyo. The Internet was also used to spread information, and web surfers were contacted through various online networks. This involved people in debate and activity on an unprecedented scale, and many new and original ideas were incorporated into the campaign as a result. Chinese communities overseas also featured strongly in the campaign, and a great number of events were staged in Chinese areas of cities, such as Chinatown in London, United Kingdom.

Many imaginative and original activities were staged. In Australia, members erected "Walls of Hope" around the country, where people wrote messages in memory of the victims of Tiananmen Square. Members in Auckland, New Zealand, borrowed a tank from the Museum of Transport and Technology and parked it on one of the main squares. In Bermuda, the Section set up a mock prison in Hamilton and handed out fortune cookies with messages about Tiananmen inside. The Colombian Section sent a collage of flowers with a huge cut-out dove in the middle to the Chinese Embassy, while in France groups staged a massive "die-in" after transporting a model of the "Goddess of Democracy" through Paris.

For many Amnesty International members, the campaign for human rights in China was the most moving they had ever participated in, and a record number of members took part. The campaign culminated in a worldwide Lantern Festival at the end of September, organized to coincide with the Chinese mid-Autumn Festival. The words of a Chinese poem, "I hope people will think of each other for ever and enjoy the same moonlight – even if they are thousands of miles away", highlighted the themes of remembrance and loss. Activities were held in commemoration of those who had died and in remembrance of all those who remained imprisoned or who continued to suffer human rights violations.

Amnesty International's campaign against human rights violations in Turkey also took on a high profile this year. Launched in October, its aim was to persuade both the Turkish Government and the international community of the urgent need for a genuine guarantee of human rights protection for all people in Turkey. At the same time, the campaign sought to correct the many misrepresentations and untruths about Amnesty International's work disseminated over the years by various governments and widely broadcast by the Turkish media in an effort to discredit the organization's reports on human rights violations in the country and to portray Amnesty International as an "anti-Turkish" organization.

This issue was addressed by focusing on the international nature of the organization's work. For example, a pre-campaign speaking tour of Ankara, Istanbul and Mersin, which took place in May, included a former prisoner of conscience from China, a human rights activist from Western Sahara (who had "disappeared" in Morocco) and a US abolitionist lawyer working on death penalty cases in Alabama. The tour attracted impressive media interest and was extensively covered by the Turkish media.

This emphasis on international solidarity was central to the campaign, and on 26 October a delegation of Amnesty International section representatives from Pakistan, Taiwan and a number of European countries travelled to Istanbul to join relatives of the "disappeared" in Turkey in their weekly Saturday vigil. Representatives from organizations and families campaigning for the truth to be made known about the "disappeared" and "missing" in Bosnia and Herzegovina, Argentina and Lebanon also attended, and similar vigils and other actions were organized on the same day by sections and groups in many other countries.

A press conference and public meeting on the issue of "disappearances" in Turkey was attended by 200 people from more than 40 national and international newspapers, television and radio stations. Powerful testimonies from Bosnian, Argentine and Lebanese women were heard alongside the stories of their Turkish fellow-activists, and the Turkish media were quick to pick up on this truly international cry for truth and justice.

Other important campaigns which took place throughout the year included an action against police brutality in New York City, USA. In June, Amnesty International published a report, *Police brutality and excessive force in the New York City Police Department*, which described the results of an investigation by the organization into allegations of ill-treatment, deaths in custody and unjustified shootings by the police. Following its publication, Amnesty International delegates met the Police

Commissioner and other senior police officials to discuss the concerns raised.

With the collaboration and support of the organization's members in the USA, there was widespread media coverage and interest in the findings and, as a result, the US Section was able to develop new contacts with a wide range of community organizations in New York City and in other states. Most significantly, the report attracted widespread support from members of the racial and ethnic minority communities in New York City and others who had expressed concern about police brutality in recent years. Several police officers also contacted members of the delegation during the launch of the report to support its findings.

The other major action in the USA was one on the death penalty in the state of Georgia, planned to coincide with the Olympic Games in Atlanta. Amnesty International took advantage of the presence of the world's media in the city to highlight its concerns. Secretary General Pierre Sané launched Amnesty International's report, *The death penalty in Georgia: racist, arbitrary and unfair*, and also held a series of meetings with civil rights, business and black community leaders and with the Governor and the Attorney General of Georgia.

To complement this action, Amnesty International members from nine European countries and Mexico, along with family members of murder victims and of those on death row, organized an anti-death-penalty tour of Georgia, Mississippi and Alabama, supporting the work of other abolitionists and encouraging politicians, community activists and members of the legal profession to campaign against the death penalty. The tour delegates also presented a petition with nearly half a million signatures from all over the world calling on Georgia's Governor to declare a moratorium on all pending executions and to take steps to commute all death sentences in the state of Georgia.

The Chilean Section also stepped up its campaign against the death penalty in the country as parliament prepared to vote on a bill for its abolition. In collaboration with other NGOs, a "yellow ribbon" campaign was organized.

The campaign for an International Criminal Court

At the UN, in the lobby corridors of their home governments and through the international media, Amnesty International members continually reminded governments of their duty and responsibility to bring to justice the perpetrators of genocide, other crimes against humanity and serious violations of humanitarian law. The campaign made significant progress in December, when the UN General Assembly agreed to hold an international diplomatic conference in 1998 to adopt a treaty establishing a permanent International Criminal Court (ICC).

Amnesty International Week was devoted to campaigning on the ICC, and had been planned for a critical period in October, just before the UN Sixth Committee (legal matters) was due to

CAMPAIGNS AND MEMBERSHIP

During the Turkey campaign, Amnesty International brought relatives of the "disappeared" and "missing" from Argentina, Bosnia-Herzegovina and Lebanon to join the families of Turkey's "disappeared" during their weekly vigil in Istanbul. More than 20 Amnesty International members from around the world also joined the sit-down protest.

meet. Members from all over the world were mobilized, groups from some 40 sections sent lobbying letters to governments, experts organized visits to ministries of justice and ministries of foreign affairs, and many contacted governments in countries where there were no Amnesty International sections. In addition, 80,000 booklets and posters and 20,000 postcards were distributed, and campaigning activities such as petitions, street stalls, public meetings, discussions and radio and media work were extensively covered in the press and won widespread public support. (See also **Work with International Organizations**.)

Crisis response

Central Africa was hit by a new human rights crisis. Hundreds of thousands of people were in mortal danger in eastern Zaire as a consequence of fighting which broke out in September, and of the cycle of past and current violations in Rwanda, Burundi and Zaire. The international community focused on how to feed refugees and how to move them back to their countries of origin. In doing so they seemingly chose to overlook human rights.

Amnesty International members around the world participated in the *Amnesty International Week* campaign for a permanent International Criminal Court. Over 80,000 booklets *(right)* were distributed and governments were continually reminded of their duty and responsibility to bring the perpetrators of the worst crimes in the world to justice.

Amnesty International teams visited Zaire, Rwanda and other countries in the region to gather information, to present the authorities with the organization's information and obtain promises to respect human rights. Amnesty International members appealed to governments and international organizations to provide human rights protection for refugees and victims in the region.

Amnesty International also had to respond quickly to human rights crises in other parts of the world. Members lobbied governments and publicized the plight of civilians in Afghanistan after the *Taleban* forces captured the capital city of Kabul in September. The ensuing counter-offensive resulted in continual bombing and attacks on Kabul and the west of the country, forcing thousands to flee yet again. In Myanmar, where tension escalated between the State Law and Order Restoration Council (the ruling authority) and the National League for Democracy, hundreds were detained and Amnesty International worked to highlight concerns about their safety and publicized the names of those being held.

Members also responded quickly and effectively to events in many other parts of the world. The movement was spurred into action on Indonesia by the raid on the offices of the Democratic Party and the subsequent crack-down on freedom of expression and association. Work was carried out on the plight of refugees from Guinea-Bissau and Iran; members acted to counter the manipulation of information surrounding massacres after the coup in Burundi; the organization exposed the draft law that effectively legalized torture in Israel; it highlighted the risk of repatriating refugees to Bosnia and Herzegovina; and it responded to the reform of the military penal code in Colombia.

Action on military, security and police transfers

Throughout the year, Amnesty International continued to expand its actions to prevent international transfers of arms, security equipment and training from contributing to human rights abuses.

During the campaign on Turkey, sections in Europe and North America pressed their governments to stop transfers of military helicopters and military transport vehicles which were known to have been used to facilitate political killings, "disappearances" and torture by the Turkish armed forces. In November, the Turkish Government announced that it would no longer seek to purchase a number of military attack helicopters from the USA, costing about US$150 million, because the US Government was "stalling" the order to clarify their possible use in human rights violations. Sections also called on Belgian, French, German and Israeli companies to stop their negotiations to supply Turkey with licences to make assault rifles for the Turkish armed forces, and called for a complete halt to all electro-shock weapon exports to Turkey because of the incidence of electro-shock torture by Turkish police.

Amnesty International activists in a number of countries continued to raise concern about the international trade in electro-shock weapons used for torture and ill-treatment. In South Africa, members took part in a successful lobby for an official inquiry into the use of such weapons after a number of civilian commuters were killed or seriously injured in an attack using electro-shock batons at the Tembisa railway station in July. In the United Kingdom, further exposure of the trade of these weapons through third countries was an important part of the campaign to improve national legislation governing military and security equipment exports. In the USA, Amnesty International exposed the spread in the federal and state prison services of the use of a remote-controlled electro-shock belt for prisoners, and US members put pressure on their government to rectify the inadequate export controls on electro-shock weapons.

Once again, Amnesty International campaigned for governments worldwide to address the unprecedented human rights crisis in the Great Lakes region of central Africa, which escalated once more in October. As part of this effort, the organization lobbied the international community to stop all transfers of light weapons and related military equipment to the armed forces, militia and other armed groups in Burundi, Rwanda and Zaire, until it could be reasonably demonstrated in each case that such transfers would not be used to commit human rights abuses. The organization provided evidence to an International Commission

CAMPAIGNS AND MEMBERSHIP

of Inquiry appointed to investigate breaches of the UN arms embargo imposed on Rwanda on 17 May 1994. In an unpublished report in March 1996, the Commission found that arms had been transferred to the perpetrators of the genocide via Zaire by illegal arms traders with networks in Europe and southern Africa. Sections campaigned, often beside other NGOs, to persuade governments to cooperate with the Commission.

In November, an Amnesty International high-level mission to South Africa generated considerable publicity and, after concerted lobbying, helped persuade the government to suspend an arms contract with the Rwandese Government and launch a renewed effort to stop illicit arms trafficking to central Africa. Military procurement documents found by foreign journalists in eastern Zaire provided confirmation of secret arms flights involving United Kingdom and Nigerian traders delivering weapons and ammunition from Albania and Israel to Rwandese armed forces in eastern Zaire in mid-1994. Further action resulted from this discovery.

The inadequacy of human rights considerations in military and police training was also taken up in actions on Chad and Indonesia. In the case of Chad, the governments of France and China were questioned about the human rights content of the training they provided, and about procedures to select and monitor trainees in Chad, as well as the use of military and security equipment provided.

The action on Indonesia involved putting pressure on the British Government after an official audit report found that a program to train Indonesian police had not included respect for human rights, contrary to the declared aim. Arms sales and provision of military training to Indonesia continued to be the subject of lobbying. New contracts for light tanks and armoured vehicles were questioned publicly in Germany and the United Kingdom, and sections in Europe and the USA also questioned the transfer of attack helicopters, fighter jets and artillery to the Israeli armed forces following atrocities committed in Lebanon using such equipment.

Such specific cases were used to lobby for better national control on military, security and police transfers based on human rights criteria. These were linked with efforts to convince governments of the need for new international controls by the European Union and other regional intergovernmental bodies. Support was given to an initiative led by Dr Oscar Arias, the Nobel Peace Laureate, to develop an international code for the control of conventional arms.

Medical action

In May, Amnesty International launched an international action focusing on the role of health professionals in the exposure of human rights violations. The campaign was launched with a report, *Prescription for Change,* which highlighted the problems created by the lack of recognition of the importance of medical and forensic testimony.

The campaign urged support from professional associations and protection from governments, and publicized the fact that in many countries medical workers were being prevented, either overtly or through subtle pressure, from playing a protective role or from giving evidence in court. It also included examples of cases in which medical reports defending victims of abuses had been ignored.

During the campaign, Amnesty International's 11,000-strong network of doctors, nurses and other health workers spanning 35 countries began promoting two new sets of standards: the Declaration on the Role of Health Professionals in the Exposure of Torture and Ill-Treatment and the Principles for the Medical Investigation of Torture (see **Appendices** VII **and** VIII). Country reports on Brazil, India, Israel, Kenya and Turkey were also published in connection with the campaign.

Business outreach

A crucial part of many of the actions which took place during the year was the recognition of the increasingly significant role of businesses in the support and protection of human rights. In February, in New York, USA, Amnesty International held its first international meeting on relations with businesses, which established a network for the exchange of expertise and ideas. One of the recommendations from the meeting was to promote company "codes of conduct" based on universal human rights principles.

In Nigeria, after the execution of Ken Saro-Wiwa and eight other Ogoni people in November 1995, Amnesty International's activities around businesses intensified, including meetings between a number of sections and companies operating in Nigeria. Members in the Netherlands joined another NGO, Pax Christi, in issuing a joint memorandum entitled *The Challenge for Shell: Multinational enterprises can make an important contribution to the enjoyment of fundamental human rights*. In November, after a series of meetings with Shell representatives, Shell indicated that it was willing to insert references to human rights in its revised Statement of General Business Principles.

Amnesty International continued to call for Shell and other companies in Nigeria to put pressure on the government to improve the human rights situation. Specifically, the organization called on Shell to revise its "rules of engagement" for police seconded to work on company property, which fell far short of international standards. It also asked Shell to ensure that no weapons would be purchased or funded by the company for the Nigerian police where they might be used to commit human rights abuses.

Other countries in which Amnesty International focused on business outreach included Colombia, where British Petroleum was asked to respond to allegations about the relationship between members of its staff and people responsible for human rights violations, including torture and murder. In Myanmar, businesses and tourist companies investing in the country were approached about human rights abuses carried out in the development of tourist sites and infrastructure projects for gas and oil. The campaign on Turkey also focused on relations with businesses in the country. A meeting with an association which included 400 of the country's most influential business people took place.

Amnesty International also stepped up its work on the Asia-Pacific Economic Co-operation (APEC) meetings, attending the main forums in Manila, Philippines, and meeting with members of government delegations. The organization's message to the APEC community was simple: human rights and development must go hand in hand, and the business community in particular has a responsibility for these principles.

Women and children

Throughout the year, Amnesty International's work on women's human rights was expanded, with at least 37 sections committed to prioritize work on women. A women's page on the organization's worldwide web-site was set up by the Swedish Section.

The 1995 campaign for women's human rights continued into the first three months of the year and culminated on International Women's Day (8 March). Women's human rights were also central to the campaign on China. Many of the appeal cases and examples of human rights violations featured women, and the issue was raised at the Inter-Parliamentary Conference held in Beijing in September, one year after the UN Fourth World Conference on Women.

In April, Amnesty International held its first seminar on female genital mutilation (FGM) – a systematic attack on the human rights of millions of women and girls. The seminar, organized by the Ghanaian Section, was held in Bolgatanga, a remote town in the north of the country. The event marked the first step in a long-term international program aimed at raising awareness about the practice, which involves the surgical removal of parts or all of the most sensitive female genital organs.

Entitled "Working Together for Change – Stop FGM" and co-hosted by the Ghanaian Association of Church Development Projects, the meeting brought together some 50 representatives from a diverse range of NGOs in the northern regions of Ghana, where FGM is most prevalent. The seminar considered the practice from various perspectives, and included human rights, health, religious and legal dimensions. Discussions also covered the factors giving rise to FGM, as well as approaches to prevention, and survivors of FGM described the traumatic and far-reaching effects on their physical and mental health. Approximately 135 million females worldwide are genitally mutilated. It is common practice in 28 African countries, parts of the Middle East, Asia and

Members of Amnesty International Ghana arranged the organization's first-ever workshop on female genital mutilation. The two-day meeting was attended by Amnesty International delegates from seven African countries, as well as representatives from 41 non-governmental organizations in Ghana.

within certain immigrant communities in western countries as an age-old tradition to prepare girls for womanhood.

Political, community and religious leaders from the region joined with local health workers, teachers and women's rights activists in voicing a commitment to devising a national plan of action to eradicate FGM.

The seminar attracted widespread media coverage, featuring as the main news item on Ghanaian television as well as in several newspapers. News reports publicized the strong commitments made by local traditional leaders present at the meeting to work towards the elimination of FGM. The seminar also prompted unprecedented national discussion about the issue.

The fact that FGM is a cultural tradition in certain societies has not deterred the organization from asserting that the right of all women and girls to physical integrity is universal. The issue does, however, demand a sensitive approach that recognizes the links between FGM and other forms of gender-based abuse across cultures. It also requires Amnesty International to develop strategies and techniques which will empower rather than undermine efforts by those organizations and individuals best placed to tackle the issue at a grassroots level.

The seminar in Bolgatanga inspired programs on FGM by sections in other countries. At the end of the year, several west

African sections were planning workshops in conjunction with relevant NGOs in 1997.

Campaigning on children's human rights continued to attract attention, and was part of Amnesty International's continuing research and action. Amnesty International's children's rights advocates, who formed themselves into groups or networks in at least 28 sections, were actively involved in human rights promotion in their own countries based on the UN Convention on the Rights of the Child.

In February, in Cork, Ireland, the Irish Section hosted the second international meeting of the groups and networks working on children's human rights. The meeting made recommendations on how each group could expand its work on campaigning, promotional work around the issues of FGM, military, security and police transfers, and monitoring its country's obligations under the UN Convention on the Rights of the Child. A number of groups took on new Action Files and joined Regional Action Networks on children and juveniles.

On International Children's Day in November, an action was launched as part of the campaign on Turkey under the heading "No Security for Children". A special report was published and thousands of postcards were sent to the Turkish authorities regarding the illegal detention and ill-treatment of children and minors in jails.

Human rights defenders

The protection of human rights defenders continued to be a high priority for Amnesty International. The focus throughout the year was on Latin America, a region with a particularly long tradition of standing up for human rights in dangerous circumstances: over the last decade, hundreds of human rights activists have been assassinated or made to "disappear" for investigating and denouncing state violence and political killings. The repression continued in 1996: defenders were harassed or had their work curtailed through ostensibly legal channels – their writing was banned or censored, official restrictions denied them freedom of movement and the right to organize themselves or prevented them from representing victims. Defenders received death threats, their phones were tapped, their houses were watched, their families were intimidated. Many had to flee their countries.

Amnesty International could not function without the information and assistance provided by these brave men and women, and shares a responsibility with other international and national organizations to protect and support them. As a first step towards identifying and creating such collective protection mechanisms, Amnesty International convened an international conference in Bogotá, Colombia, which took place between 22 and 25 May. Some 75 people attended the conference, including Amnesty International staff and members, representatives from

Professor Noam Chomsky of the USA delivered the keynote address at the human rights defenders conference in Bogotá, Colombia. "For those who are dedicated to the protection of human rights," he said, "the task ahead is hard and challenging and of incalculable human significance."

© Semanario VOZ

12 other international human rights NGOs, legal and academic experts, and human rights defenders from 18 countries in the region. The Colombian Section participated in the organization of the conference itself, as well as carrying out a week of parallel campaign activities in and around Bogotá. The participants exchanged ideas and experiences through seminars, working groups and informal discussions, and emphasized the importance of promoting the right of all people to defend human rights.

The conference made a final Declaration of Principles on the Protection of Human Rights Defenders in Latin America which contained recommendations for a plan of action on legal mechanisms and intergovernmental organizations. It also made a series of concrete suggestions aimed at the immediate protection of human rights defenders at risk, the use of publicity in the defence of human rights and on cooperation between non-governmental organizations. The report of the conference was disseminated widely, both within the Americas region and beyond, and a follow-up meeting took place in Guatemala in September, organized jointly by Amnesty International and the Center for Human Rights Legal Action, a Guatemalan NGO. In December, Amnesty International went to Mexico City to launch a report and an action on human rights defenders in Mexico and Central America.

Conferences

An international conference on torture was organized on 6 October in Stockholm, Sweden, where a plan for worldwide action was launched. The conference was attended by some 120 participants from 50 countries and was organized by the Swedish Section with assistance from the Netherlands, British and US Sections. The "Plan of Action against Torture" stated that national NGOs should establish systems of vigilance so that any instance of torture would be detected and swiftly acted upon. It also recommended that special support be given to vulnerable social groups, raising their awareness of what constituted torture, and of their rights and how to defend them. An important part of the plan stated that respect for human rights should be inherent in professional policing, and that an international code of practice for the conduct of interrogation should be developed.

Amnesty International also organized an NGO forum in Manila, Philippines, in August as part of the campaign on China. The themes were not restricted to human rights violations in China; they covered the concepts of the universality and indivisibility of human rights throughout Asia and the Pacific region. The forum was hosted jointly with Forum Asia, a regional NGO. As more and more inter-regional meetings were being held by governments, the organization viewed joint activities and other forms of cooperation with NGOs worldwide as key elements for its future work.

Membership

During the year, the development of Amnesty International's youth membership was given a high priority. Thirty-eight sections informed the International Secretariat that they had a member of staff or volunteer with specific responsibility for building up a program of activities involving young people. In New Zealand, the number of Amnesty International school groups grew by 50 per cent in five months, after a member of staff was appointed to coordinate this work. Other youth programs in Australia, France, Mexico, South Africa, Sweden and Venezuela gathered energy and momentum during the year. The Venezuelan Section youth coordinator took on responsibility for building up programs for youth in other Latin American countries.

The first international youth festival on human rights was organized by the Philippine Section in January. Students, youth workers and young human rights activists from around the globe attended the conference in the mountain resort of Baguio. The festival aimed to establish links among Amnesty International's young members, and to serve as a venue where young people could respond to human rights challenges. The festival featured a week-long conference which explored topics from racial harmony to alternative lifestyles. Participants praised the

The Brazilian Section organized a series of innovative and eye-catching events on the day they launched their campaign on China. On a wall beside the Chinese Consulate, artists painted a mural demanding "justice, freedom and life in China" *(above)*, while Amnesty International supporters distributed campaign materials in the street. Two members of the Brazilian Section, together with a delegation including Brazilian writers, lawyers and business people *(left)*, presented the Chinese Consul with a copy of Amnesty International's report on China, *No one is safe*.

conference for enhancing their human rights awareness, creating new friendships, and starting debates destined to continue long after the meeting.

Human rights education

"To teach African people to recognize and uphold their rights is to extend to them a light with which to see and with which to move in the direction of freedom and justice."

These words were spoken by the Chair of Amnesty International's Ghanaian Section at the opening session of the first-ever meeting of the organization's human rights education coordinators in the Africa region. The meeting, held in June in Koforidua, Ghana, marked a particularly eventful year in the field of human rights education for the African sections. Delegates outlined and discussed a four-year strategy to develop this aspect of the organization's work, which has been consistently identified as a

CAMPAIGNS AND MEMBERSHIP

priority by the African membership. Later in the year, the Ghanaian Section embarked on an ambitious project to introduce human rights clubs in schools, while in South Africa, the Pretoria group set up a project, in conjunction with a local NGO, to provide human rights training for police working with street children in a suburb of the city. In Mauritius, plans were under way to target 17- to 20-year-old students in five separate colleges.

The Nigerian Section staged a children's theatre production at the University of Ibadan Arts Theatre, entitled "Children of Freedom". Issues such as inequality, freedom and human dignity were enacted through songs, poetry, mime and dance. Work also continued to produce story books on a variety of human rights themes with accompanying teachers' notes.

The Nepalese Section began a campaign in April aimed at putting pressure on the government to introduce human rights into the school curriculum. Government ministers and NGOs took part in a week-long program of seminars, during which it was agreed that the incorporation of human rights in the curriculum was indispensable for the future.

The Hong Kong Section continued with the education program it launched two years ago, working closely with major figures in the education system to encourage a greater profile for discussions on human rights in the classroom via incorporation of these issues in the curriculum. A survey was carried out which found that teachers desperately lacked materials and training, and as a result a resource library was established to provide access to both print and electronic media. A series of workshops was also set up to train teachers to become effective human rights educators. More than 400 teachers had been reached through this program by the end of the year.

The Israeli Section, in cooperation with an Israeli NGO, developed a program targeting deprived Israeli-Arab children between the ages of seven and 12, with university students acting as project facilitators. The project was set up to run initially in the Israeli-Arab sector, but there are plans to expand to the Jewish community.

The Americas region saw the development of a great many new projects, concentrating on liaising with educational establishments in order to design training programs and curricula for human rights education. The Argentine Section organized a number of activities, including an intensive workshop on "identity" in Villa Angela, attended by 90 children and some of their teachers. Publicity work incorporated slots on cable television and the development of a web-site. In Brazil, the National Program of Human Rights, opened by President Fernando Henrique Cardoso in May, formally recognized the role of the Brazilian Section in the training of police officers. During the year, the section developed work agreements with the government, NGOs and universities. In Mexico, a week-long summer school for teachers was held, and participants included the National Human Rights

The Gujar Khan group-in-formation in Pakistan during a procession to increase public awareness about human rights in China. During the campaign, the group also distributed campaign reports, organized a poster display and held information meetings in local schools and colleges.

Commission. As well as a variety of conferences and general workshops and training sessions, a theatre presentation was taken to 14 schools in the country. The Peruvian Section produced six new human rights guides for secondary schools, and, in cooperation with the Ministry of Education, ran a teacher training project for 21 schools. The US Section also produced some new teaching materials, including a resource book on children's rights. Its publication, *Human Rights for Young Children*, was translated and published in Arabic by Amnesty International's Palestinian groups.

In Hungary and the Ukraine, Amnesty International helped to organize several human rights education workshops aimed at teachers, educationalists and human rights activists which were run in conjunction with local organizations and trainers. The workshops were well attended, and a civics training program was under way in Szeged, Hungary, by the end of the year.

The final version of *First Steps*, a manual for teaching human rights designed for use in eastern and central Europe, was published and distributed in September. It was widely and enthusiastically received and there were plans to translate it into several languages and adapt it for use in other regions around the world.

The death penalty: no solution to crime

Despite continued progress towards worldwide abolition of the death penalty in 1996, there were alarming calls in different parts of the world for capital punishment to be reintroduced, expanded or more freely used. Such calls were largely linked to widespread public concern about rising crime rates, although no evidence emerged indicating that the death penalty would solve this problem. In some countries, officials said they wanted to abolish the death penalty but could not do so because of public opposition.

As part of its continuing campaign for the abolition of the death penalty as a violation of fundamental human rights, Amnesty International called on politicians to foster rational debate by making the facts about the nature of capital punishment and the invalidity of the deterrence argument known to the public.

Belgium abolished the death penalty for all crimes in August, giving legal form to a tradition of not using the death penalty which had lasted since 1863 except in two periods at the time of the First and Second World Wars. The Flemish and French-speaking branches of Amnesty International's Section in Belgium had worked for total abolition for many years through public information initiatives and by lobbying members of parliament.

Abolition in Belgium brought the number of totally abolitionist countries and territories to 58, more than twice the number it had been 15 years earlier. Fifteen other countries had abolished the death penalty for all but exceptional offences, such as wartime crimes, by the end of 1996. At least 27 countries and territories which retained the death penalty in law were considered abolitionist in practice, in that they had not executed anyone for 10 years or more or had made an international commitment not to carry out executions.

There was also progress in the ratification of international treaties providing for the abolition of the death penalty. Andorra ratified Protocol No. 6 to the European Convention for the Protection of Human Rights and Fundamental Freedoms (European Convention on Human Rights), which provides for the abolition of the death penalty in peacetime, bringing the number of states parties to 24. A proposal to create a further protocol to the Convention providing for the abolition of the death penalty in all circumstances (see *Amnesty International Report 1996*) was still before the Council of Europe's Committee of Ministers at the end of the year. Brazil ratified the Protocol to the American Convention on Human Rights to Abolish the Death Penalty, bringing the number of states parties to seven. Twenty-nine countries were parties to the Second Optional Protocol to the International Covenant on Civil and Political Rights, aiming at the abolition of the death penalty. A number of other countries had signed one or another of the protocols, indicating their intention to become parties.

Within the Organization for Security and Co-operation in Europe (OSCE), the Office for Democratic Institutions and Human Rights took the first steps towards developing a clearing house for information on the abolition of the death penalty in the OSCE area. Such action would help to fulfil the pledge made by states participating in the 1990 Copenhagen Meeting of the Conference on the Human Dimension of the Conference on Security and Co-operation in Europe (now the OSCE) to "exchange information within the framework of the Conference on the Human Dimension on the question of the abolition of the death penalty and keep that question under consideration".

In July, the UN Economic and Social Council (ECOSOC) adopted resolution 1996/15 on Safeguards guaranteeing protection of the rights of those facing the death penalty. The resolution, originally proposed by Austria, had been adopted by the UN Commission on Crime Prevention and Control on 31 May and forwarded to ECOSOC for its consideration. The resolution includes a call on UN member states "to ensure that officials involved in decisions to carry out an execution are fully informed of the status of appeals and petitions for clemency of the prisoner in question". This is designed to prevent a prisoner being executed even though an appeal is pending, ostensibly because the prison officials carrying out the execution were not aware of the appeal. The resolution also urges member states to apply effectively the UN Standard Minimum Rules for the Treatment of Prisoners "in order to keep to a minimum the suffering of prisoners under sentence of death and to avoid any exacerbation of such suffering". The UN Standard Minimum Rules for the Treatment of Prisoners include provisions on adequate food and exercise, and correspondence and visits with family, friends and lawyers. These provisions are under attack in many countries, and the conditions in which death-row prisoners around the world are housed often fall well short of UN standards.

In a study released in June, "Constitutional Prohibitions of the Death Penalty", Amnesty International reported that of the 57 countries which had then abolished the death penalty for all crimes, 24 had also prohibited the death penalty in their constitutions. Five other countries had constitutional provisions limiting the crimes for which the death penalty could be imposed. The study pointed out that in some legal systems, the constitution is the supreme law of the land; other laws must not conflict with it, and it is harder to amend than other laws. Enshrining the abolition of the death penalty in such a constitution is a way of solidifying abolition by establishing an additional legal basis which can serve as an impediment to any hasty attempt to bring back executions.

Alongside these positive developments in abolishing or restricting the scope of the death penalty, there were calls for the reintroduction, expansion or use of capital punishment in a number of countries. Most such calls were linked to public fears about rising crime rates, particularly in relation to drug-related and organized crime, as well as murder, rape, kidnapping and other violent offences. Such fears led to demands for action, sometimes extending to the public lynching of suspected offenders. Even in countries where there was no real evidence of an increase in crime, factors including sensationalistic media coverage of the issue left many people feeling threatened, and they reacted accordingly.

Calls for the death penalty came from members of the public, politicians and even heads of state. Officials in some countries organized public "consultations" or surveys which provided only the most superficial understanding of attitudes towards the death penalty. These "consultations" appeared designed to confirm general support for capital punishment without examining the reasons or the conditions for that support or the extent to which it would change if the public felt protected by genuine measures to combat crime.

In Belarus, President Alyaksandr Lukashenka organized a referendum on constitutional reforms in November which included a question on abolishing the death penalty. The referendum was opposed by the country's constitutional court and parliament and was criticized as illegal by the president of the country's central commission on elections and referendums. There were reports that sample ballots were available in polling stations, already marked in favour of the continuing use of the death penalty, the option favoured by President Lukashenka. As expected, the referendum produced a majority vote against abolition.

> 'We are determined that the death sentence will never come back in this country. It is not because the death sentence has been scrapped that crime has reached such unacceptable levels. Even if the death sentence is brought back, crime itself will remain as it is.'
> Nelson Mandela, President of South Africa

Some officials promoted the erroneous idea that the death penalty would reduce crime. In an August statement in which he announced the resumption of executions as part of a crack-down on violent crime, President Mohamed Taki Abdoulkarim of the Comoros said: "Anyone who knows that if he kills someone he will not escape the death penalty will think twice." The following month Ali Youssouf was publicly executed without recourse to appeal against his sentence. It was the first known execution in the Comoros since the country became independent in 1975.

DEATH PENALTY

Guatemala: Pedro Castillo Mendoza and Roberto Girón, convicted of the rape and murder of a child, were executed on 13 September by firing-squad. The double execution was witnessed by dozens of journalists and shown later that day on national television. Pedro Castillo, who was wounded in the first volley of shots, was eventually killed by a single shot to the head.

In South Africa, however, President Nelson Mandela responded to calls to reintroduce the death penalty by stating in September his determined opposition to reintroduction, and his conviction that levels of crime were not dependent on the existence or otherwise of this form of punishment.

In Guatemala, two men convicted of rape and murder were executed on 13 September, the first judicial executions in the country since 1983. An official of the *Misión de las Naciones Unidos para la verificación de derechos humanos en Guatemala* (MINUGUA), UN Mission for the Verification of Human Rights in Guatemala, had criticized the quality of legal representation in the trials of the two men. This criticism was denounced by members of the government and the judiciary and prompted accusations in the media that MINUGUA was interfering in the internal affairs of the country. Human rights defenders who opposed the executions were attacked in the press, where they were characterized as supporters of criminals and delinquents. Appeals for clemency from Amnesty International members around the world were denounced in the media as the work of a mercenary organization trying to discredit Guatemala internationally and to put pressure on a democracy to renounce its laws and give up its sovereignty.

In October, following the executions in Guatemala, the Legislative Assembly of neighbouring El Salvador adopted a constitutional amendment, proposed by the ruling party, the

Alianza Republica Nacionalista (ARENA), Nationalist Republican Alliance, to reinstate the death penalty for aggravated homicide, rape and kidnapping. Speaking in September, Juan Duch, parliamentary leader of ARENA, had said: "With this measure we can perhaps get it into the head of the criminal that he could be punished with the ultimate penalty." This constitutional amendment will only come into force if ratified by the new parliament, which will be elected in March 1997.

On 28 June, the Parliamentary Assembly of the Council of Europe adopted resolution 1097 (1996) reaffirming its opposition to the death penalty. The Parliamentary Assembly declared that any state joining the Council of Europe must introduce an immediate moratorium on executions and indicate its willingness to ratify Protocol No. 6 to the European Convention on Human Rights, thereby agreeing in effect that it would abolish the death penalty in peacetime.

In accordance with this position, the Council of Europe held a seminar on "Serious Crime and the Requirement of Respect for Human Rights in European Democracies" from 14 to 16 November in Taormina, Italy. It also held a seminar on the death penalty in Kiyv, Ukraine, from 28 to 29 November. These two seminars gave officials and members of parliament from all parts of Europe the opportunity to exchange ideas and perspectives on the death penalty and other penal matters with experts in criminology, penal policy, media communications and human rights.

Among the issues discussed at the seminars was the relationship between rising crime rates and the death penalty. Participants pointed out that crime is on the increase for myriad reasons that have nothing to do with the presence or absence of the death penalty. Poverty, social inequality, poor housing, unemployment, the disappearance of formal or informal methods of social control, and an expanding drug trade were all cited as factors contributing to criminality.

Professor Roger Hood, Director of the Centre for Criminological Research at Oxford University, United Kingdom, and author of a 1988 UN study on the death penalty, told the Kiyv seminar that there was no conclusive evidence that the death penalty reduces the rate of murder, and that none is likely to be forthcoming. "Looked at this way," he added, "the balance of the evidence definitely favours the abolitionist position."

Professor Hood also noted that: "Countries need not fear that a sudden and serious increase in homicides will occur if capital punishment is abolished: or to put it more correctly, that any increase in homicide that might occur will be related to the withdrawal of the sanction of death rather than to social and economic factors which push up crime".

The persistence of the popular belief that the death penalty will deter potential offenders more effectively than other punishments, despite the scientific evidence, indicates that the public is ill-informed about the causes of crime and how to combat it effectively, experts told the seminars.

The seminars also drew attention to the role that sensationalized reporting in the mass media plays in exacerbating public fear about crime. By portraying the world as a hostile, threatening place and blaming criminal behaviour for a degradation in the quality of life, the news media contributes to a hardening of public attitudes which can lead to attacks on the human rights of criminal suspects and offenders. The debate is posed as a competition of rights, where the rights of victims of crime are pitted against the "rights of criminals". This would amount to an attack on the principle, enshrined in international human rights instruments, that human rights apply to everyone without discrimination.

The seminars noted that abolition had taken place in many countries even when the majority of the population had been in favour of the death penalty. Yet there were no great public outcries when abolition occurred, and few genuine efforts were made to reverse it. This indicates that even in countries where support for the death penalty is strong, the public may still be willing to accept abolition. There is clearly a degree of complexity in public opinion about the death penalty which is not reflected in the polls.

Proponents of the death penalty often know little about how executions are or would be carried out, or about legal and other issues surrounding the use of the death penalty. Greater public knowledge and awareness might well produce a shift in attitudes. The Taormina seminar was told of an experiment carried out in 1990 by the Law Institute of the Ministry of Justice of Slovakia, in which 104 people were asked to complete a detailed questionnaire on capital punishment. After six hours of information sessions on death penalty issues, they filled in the questionnaire for a second time. While strong support for the death penalty was evident in the first set of questionnaires, attitudes had changed markedly by the time the participants were asked to fill them in again.

Participants in the two seminars called on governments to take the lead in educating the public about the death penalty and in particular, its failure to have any unique deterrent effect on crime. Although some governments have claimed that abolition must be delayed because of public opposition, members of parliament from several countries said they believed the public would accept abolition if governments took the lead in bringing it about.

In statements to the two seminars, Amnesty International acknowledged the role of public opinion but said that human rights considerations must be paramount. The death penalty violates fundamental human rights – the right to life and the right not to be subjected to cruel, inhuman or degrading punishment. Any attempt to reintroduce or to expand the use of the death penalty is an attack on human rights. "It is not possible for a government to respect human rights and use the death penalty at the same time", Amnesty International said.

During 1996, at least 4,272 prisoners were executed in 39 countries and 7,107 people were sentenced to death in 76 countries. These figures include only cases known to Amnesty International; the true figures are certainly higher. As in past years, a small number of countries accounted for the great majority of executions.

International protection: consensus and compromise

'Joint action' to protect human rights and the search for consensus

Action taken at the United Nations (UN) and other intergovernmental organizations has authority because states act collectively and put their combined weight behind decisions. Collective decisions can have a particularly powerful impact when reached by a consensus of up to 185 states. Such consensus has brought great legitimacy and authority to major human rights documents, such as those adopted at the end of the 1993 UN World Conference on Human Rights and the 1995 Fourth UN World Conference on Women, to human rights promotion and education programs and to human rights instruments adopted or welcomed without a vote by the UN General Assembly.

Consensus decision-making, however, is more problematic when intergovernmental bodies deal with human rights violations in particular countries. Consultation, negotiation and compromise among states are usual ingredients in the process of deciding joint action to end human rights violations in a country. The decision can have more political weight if it is accepted by a consensus of all states present. But it is crucial that the goal of such a process should not be the consensus itself. The duty of an intergovernmental body with a human rights brief is to help protect victims of human rights violations by holding states accountable to universally accepted standards. These are the human rights standards reaffirmed *by consensus* at the UN World Conference on Human Rights, where it was underscored that the international community has a right and a duty to hold any state accountable if it fails to respect these rights. Consultation and cooperation are desirable if and when they reinforce this accountability.

1996 saw a disturbing tendency, particularly at the UN Commission on Human Rights (the Commission), to seek concrete action against human rights violations only if all states agreed, sometimes including the violating state itself. But in the process of achieving a consensus, a proposal can be progressively weakened until it becomes devoid of content and significance, and actually undermines international standards. The search for consensus can allow a small minority of states to block effective action by intergovernmental bodies, often to protect their own perceived economic, political or security interests. This problem is compounded when states in the same regional grouping act to

WORK WITH INTERNATIONAL ORGANIZATIONS

Under the Charter of the United Nations, all member states are pledged to "take joint and separate action" in order to achieve "universal respect for, and observance of, human rights and fundamental freedoms for all without distinction as to race, sex, language, or religion".

protect one another because of intense pressure to maintain regional solidarity.

This chapter looks at how the drive for consensus decision-making, and for compromises with violating states below agreed international standards, hampered the work of the Commission in 1996, particularly the drafting of international instruments, aspects of the activities of the UN High Commissioner for Human Rights and some initiatives in regional organizations in Europe and Africa. At the same time, however, consensus in other fora helped to strengthen progress towards a permanent international criminal court and has given momentum to work on women's rights.

Evading accountability at the UN Commission on Human Rights

The 1996 session of the Commission displayed a particularly troubling preoccupation with seeking the consensus of all members. Following a strategy of "cooperation not confrontation", members of the Commission often weakened proposed actions by negotiating with, and seeking the agreement of, the state to be criticized. Like consensus decision-making, "constructive engagement" with violating states can be a useful tool for encouraging change in a country that is willing to change. At the Commission, however, it was sometimes used to conceal an ineffective, weak approach which protected members' own economic, political and security interests or enforced regional solidarity.

Prior to the session, Amnesty International urged states to tackle persistent, severe and systematic violations of human

WORK WITH INTERNATIONAL ORGANIZATIONS

rights in a range of countries, particularly in China, Colombia, Indonesia and East Timor, Nigeria and Turkey.

The Commission failed to respond adequately to the call by the 1995 General Assembly that it should give "urgent attention" to Nigeria. A strong proposal for the Commission to appoint a Special Rapporteur on Nigeria collapsed, partly because South Africa withdrew its support and no other African state was prepared to take the lead. In order to reach a consensus, the resolution was weakened, and finally called on Nigeria only to allow two thematic experts of the Commission to visit and investigate. By the end of the year Nigeria had failed to comply with even this softer approach. An emerging consensus over Nigeria at the 1996 UN General Assembly also broke down when Nigeria objected at the last minute, leading to the defeat of even a watered-down resolution.

> 'A hard look should be given [at] the laborious nature of consensus decision-making, which frequently rests on the lowest common denominator.'
> Ambassador Razali Ismail, President of the 51st Session of the UN General Assembly, 1996

In May, the UN Secretary-General released the report of a fact-finding mission he had sent at the request of the 1995 General Assembly. The human rights reforms promised by the Nigerian Government in reality failed to implement the basic measures recommended by the mission.

Proponents of consensus decision-making argued that states will more readily comply with a request from the Commission if they have participated in the decision to take such action. As this has not been proved in practice, the Commission should set up a way to evaluate state compliance, and be prepared to take a different approach when an agreed commitment is not honoured.

Prior to the 1996 session of the Commission, member states of the European Union had apparently agreed to lead the call for action on China. Within a few weeks the visit of Chinese Premier Li Peng to France and the offer of billion-dollar trade deals saw France and Germany lead a retreat which fragmented the European Union position. "European Union gagged by China with offers of trade deals", announced Amnesty International as the European Union vacillated and argued that "constructive engagement" was more likely to produce results in China than a critical resolution at the Commission. The resulting delays and uncertainties enabled China to win a procedural motion which blocked any vote on a resolution. China had used the same procedural ploy unsuccessfully in 1995.

In 1996, for a third consecutive year, members of the Commission negotiated with the Indonesian Government a weak statement on East Timor which was read out by the Chairman. The statement was silent on systematic human rights violations in Indonesia as a whole and on the Indonesian Government's

WORK WITH INTERNATIONAL ORGANIZATIONS

failure to comply with recommendations for change made by the Commission's own thematic experts. The Commission is not a forum for negotiating the facts of human rights violations and should base its action on the findings of its thematic experts.

Meanwhile, Turkey continued to be protected from any action on the part of the Commission by powerful regional allies with their own political and security interests at stake. This is despite the systematic torture and widespread extrajudicial executions, "disappearances" and arbitrary detention which have been documented by the UN's own expert bodies and mechanisms and the denial by the government of repeated requests by the Commission's thematic experts to visit the country.

Amnesty International had called for the appointment of a Special Rapporteur on Colombia, echoing a recommendation made by the Commission's thematic experts. Negotiations between Commission members and the Colombian delegation itself led only to an agreed statement from the Chairman. The statement does, however, emphasize the gravity of the situation, highlighting the persistence of impunity, extrajudicial executions, "disappearances", torture and the role of military courts. Together with the agreement to establish an office of the UN High Commissioner for Human Rights in Bogotá (see below), it sets out a framework against which to measure progress and may pave the way for stronger action in the future if necessary.

> 'Impunity is not only morally revolting and an insult to our sense of justice, it also strikes at the heart of governance by negating its very legitimacy.'
> José Ayala Lasso,
> UN High Commissioner for Human Rights

The UN High Commissioner for Human Rights fails to confront abusers

As José Ayala Lasso entered his third year as High Commissioner for Human Rights, he oversaw a potentially dynamic expansion in the use of different types of field presences, ranging from the provision of on-site training for international civilian police in Bosnia-Herzegovina to a new long-term office agreed for Colombia and growing monitoring operations in Rwanda and Burundi. However, the High Commissioner still consistently failed to confront gross human rights violations and was too eager to provide advisory services and technical assistance to governments which showed little willingness to implement changes.

Encouragingly, the High Commissioner began to elaborate in his public speeches the imperative of accountability of countries and individuals and the need to tackle impunity, which he described as "morally revolting and an insult to our sense of justice". It is unfortunate that this more forthright analysis has not been reflected in a willingness to confront the reality in particular countries; the High Commissioner failed to point out the seriously deteriorating human rights situation in Tunisia, during and after his visit there in June. Country visits by the leading human rights figure in the world cannot be primarily "promotional in nature", as he has suggested.

Quiet diplomacy and a conciliatory approach to governments might be important in certain cases, but they should be balanced with a greater willingness to confront governments publicly when necessary. A tough stance is needed if governments refuse to cooperate with the UN human rights machinery, when constructive dialogue does not lead to commitments and real change within a reasonable time or when a situation is deteriorating rapidly.

Where atrocities such as crimes against humanity and war crimes have been committed, the High Commissioner has a duty to take immediate action, including identifying the parties responsible and proposing an appropriate response to the international community. When the humanitarian and human rights crisis erupted in eastern Zaire in October, the High Commissioner's voice should have been heard as a champion of human rights protection and a guide in shaping action by the UN Security Council and other bodies (see below, Human rights in peacekeeping operations).

The High Commissioner did decide, however, to significantly increase the number of monitors in the Human Rights Field Operation in Rwanda. Amnesty International also called for such action as a way of helping to protect the hundreds of thousands of Rwandese refugees who returned to their country from eastern Zaire in November. In Burundi, the five staff of the High Commissioner could not operate effectively because of the appalling level of violence in the country and a government and armed opposition groups that prevented them from moving freely within the country. Amnesty International called for the High Commissioner to be more vocal about the grave situation in Burundi and to oppose any returns of refugees to the country. The organization also called for funds to expand the operation in Burundi, but only when the monitors are able to work effectively and unhindered.

The long delays before a small office was opened in the Zairian capital Kinshasa were overtaken by the crisis in the east of the country. Amnesty International called for branch offices to be set up in Goma, Bukavu and Kisangani to help protect the Zairian population as well as the remaining Burundian and Rwandese refugees. The three operations in the Great Lakes region will need secure funding for at least 12 months at a time and close coordination and integration.

Discussions with the Indonesian Government about the High Commissioner assigning one person with the UN Development Programme in Jakarta to provide advisory services to the government seemed to have stalled. In countries where the violations are gross and systematic, advisory services should be provided if the government demonstrates its willingness to implement changes and should usually be accompanied by monitoring functions explicitly accepted by the government. Unfortunately, neither the High Commissioner's visit to Indonesia in December 1995 nor the 1996 session of the Commission on Human Rights resulted in any firm commitments for change from the Indonesian Government. In November, an agreement was finally signed by the Colombian Government with the High Commissioner for the establishment of an office in Colombia which was expected to become operational in early 1997 and which could potentially contribute to addressing long-standing human rights problems in the country.

The High Commissioner launched a call for US$25 million in donations from governments to build up a new Fund for Human Rights Field Operations, as a way of overcoming the vagaries and delays involved in appealing for voluntary funding each time a new operation is proposed and the inadequacy of regular UN funding for the human rights program.

The High Commissioner oversaw a major reorganization of the UN Centre for Human Rights in Geneva. The reorganization should lead to the provision of more country and regional expertise, greater capacity for analysis of political and human rights trends and increased professionalism in supporting field operations. On this foundation the High Commissioner will need to build more effective strategies for improving respect for human rights in specific countries, drawing together the work of all parts of the UN system.

International experts, judges and parliamentarians

Members of parliamentary assemblies of some intergovernmental bodies showed during the year how their greater independence from the policies of their national governments and lesser reliance on the drive for consensus sometimes enable them to act more decisively than governments. In June, after an outcry by Amnesty International and other non-governmental organizations (NGOs), the Parliamentary Assembly of the Council of Europe condemned the Russian Federation and Ukraine for reneging on their commitment, made as a condition of joining the Council, to impose a moratorium on executions. The Assembly threatened to suspend their membership if executions continued. Although the moratorium is not yet in place, the tough stance has stimulated public and national parliamentary debate in both countries. This is in contrast to the 54-member Organization for Security and Co-operation in Europe (OSCE), where almost all decisions are made by consensus. The implacable opposition of the USA, supported principally by the United Kingdom, has blocked any progress in the OSCE towards abolition of the death penalty, despite overwhelming support for modest implementation of existing OSCE commitments to exchange information on the death penalty.

The UN and other intergovernmental bodies rely not only on political bodies, but also on a range of expert bodies and mechanisms to provide facts, objective analysis and recommendations on themes and countries.

Amnesty International criticized the Commission on Human Rights for continuing to ignore the often incisive work of the many thematic and country experts it has itself appointed and for failing to ensure that states implement the experts' recommendations. Amnesty International has also consistently called on the Commission to draw on the reports of the various UN treaty bodies which examine in detail whether states have implemented treaty obligations that they have freely undertaken. In July, the UN Human Rights Committee stated that it was "deeply concerned by the high number of extrajudicial executions" and other violations in Nigeria and called on the government to carry out a review of the legal framework. In November, the UN Committee against Torture showed how it could respond quickly by calling on Israel to explain the implications of an Israeli Supreme Court decision allowing the security services to use physical pressure during interrogations. When considering formal reports from some states parties during the year, such as the Russian Federation, the Committee against Torture made strong recommendations to prevent and end torture. But in other cases, such as that of Algeria, the Committee was timid in failing to confront the realities of endemic torture practices.

Since 1991, Amnesty International and other NGOs have submitted detailed evidence on torture in Egypt to the Committee against Torture, and have urged it to investigate. The Committee is able to carry out a confidential investigation if it receives reliable information indicating that torture is systematic in a particular country. In a major breakthrough in May, the experts used the Committee's power to issue a public statement after such an investigation. This was only the second time such a statement has been used, and it was issued as a last resort because the Egyptian Government had not allowed the Committee to visit the country. The experts concluded that "torture is systematically practised by the Security Forces in Egypt, in particular by State Security Intelligence".

Meanwhile, issuing its second public statement on Turkey in four years, the European Committee for the Prevention of Torture expressed in December its deep frustration at the failure of the government to tackle the "lip service" being paid by the police to official instructions prohibiting torture. "To attempt to characterize" the use of torture by police in Turkey "as one of isolated acts of the kind which can occur in any country ... is to fly in the face of the facts." "It is a common occurrence", the experts concluded.

If political bodies fail to act, victims can sometimes make individual complaints and seek redress from human rights commissions set up within the Council of Europe and the Organization of American States or from UN expert bodies such

WORK WITH INTERNATIONAL ORGANIZATIONS

In Bosnia and Herzegovina, the 55,000-member multinational military Implementation Force (IFOR) made no effort to search out and arrest people who had been indicted by the International Tribunal for the former Yugoslavia; arrests did not take place even when IFOR troops encountered known suspects.

© Rex Photos

as the Human Rights Committee and Committee against Torture. Human rights judges and independent UN experts are often guided more by the objective human rights standards found in treaties of which they are the guardians, and less by political considerations, than government representatives.

In a landmark case, *Chahal v United Kingdom*, in which Amnesty International made a written submission to the Court, the European Court of Human Rights found in November that the six-year attempt by the United Kingdom Government to deport Karamjit Singh Chahal to India was in violation of his right not to face torture if returned, a right which is protected by the European Convention for the Protection of Human Rights and Fundamental Freedoms (see **United Kingdom** entry). In *Akdivar v Turkey*, one of a series of cases being brought against Turkey by individual victims, the European Court of Human Rights ruled in September that Turkey had violated the rights of villagers whose houses had been deliberately burned down by state security forces in the southeast (see **Turkey** entry). It also found that the national remedies available to these victims were so ineffective that they were not obliged to exhaust them before lodging a complaint with the European Commission of Human Rights – an issue on which Amnesty International had made a written submission.

WORK WITH INTERNATIONAL ORGANIZATIONS

Human rights in peace-keeping operations

Amnesty International continued to work for effective human rights components in UN peace-keeping and other field operations and for the Security Council to mount its own field investigations in some situations so that it has hard facts, analysis and recommendations on which to base decisions.

When the Security Council was forced by the plight of hundreds of thousands of refugees in eastern Zaire to authorize an emergency, multinational military force (to be led by Canada) to assist in the delivery of humanitarian aid, Amnesty International argued that any such force should have a human rights dimension. This should have included making refugee and other camps in eastern Zaire safe for civilians by policing them and excluding combatants, reporting on human rights violations, and ensuring that the force did not participate in any repatriation of refugees to Rwanda or Burundi that was not completely voluntary. Although momentum for the intervention dissolved when hundreds of thousands of refugees returned to Rwanda in November, the force commander had set up a small civilian liaison team which included a legal and human rights adviser.

The Commission of Inquiry set up by the Security Council in 1995 to investigate reports of military training and arms transfers to the former Rwandese Government, based mainly in Zaire, reported three times. Amnesty International and other NGOs had campaigned for such an investigation and during the year provided it with information and called for the publication of its confidential October report. Amnesty International also continued to call for adequate resources for the Security Council-mandated International Commission of Inquiry into the assassination of President Melchior Ndadaye of Burundi in October 1993 and the subsequent massacres (see *Amnesty International Report 1996*). The Commission presented its final report in August (see **Burundi** entry).

> 'When global attention reaches a conflict at its height, a number of problems can occur and have. Acting at this point is the costliest and most dangerous way to intervene. It is also the least likely to succeed.'
> Kofi Annan, appointed UN Secretary-General in December 1996, writing in *Preventive Diplomacy: Stopping Wars Before They Start*

Amnesty International was dismayed by the silence of the UN Mission for the Referendum in Western Sahara (MINURSO) in the face of reports of torture, detention of prisoners of conscience, prolonged secret detention and forcible expulsion by Moroccan security forces in Western Sahara, even though the UN Secretary-General agreed back in 1993 that MINURSO "could not be a silent witness to conduct that might infringe the human rights of the civilian population". Amnesty International believes that MINURSO could make a difference if it honoured even the limited human rights functions set out in the Secretary-General's own Implementation Plan, if its mandate was broadened to include

WORK WITH INTERNATIONAL ORGANIZATIONS

investigating, reporting and acting on allegations of human rights violations and if the UN Civilian Police were fully deployed and active.

Following a visit to Angola, Amnesty International made a series of recommendations on the work of the Human Rights Unit of the UN Angola Verification Mission (UNAVEM III), which achieved some progress despite limited resources during the year. The Unit was urged, among other matters, to submit cases to the Angolan judicial system, improve the quality of investigation and reporting, make greater use of print, audio and visual media to explain its work to the public and involve Angolan civil society in the Unit's promotional work.

Working alongside the multinational military Implementation Force (IFOR) in Bosnia and Herzegovina that took over from the previous UN operation, the OSCE mounted its largest and most ambitious long-term mission to monitor human rights and elections. Regrettably, most of the mission's resources were devoted to election monitoring. Its efforts to protect human rights in Bosnia and Herzegovina suffered from fragmentation, lack of a clear, publicly available human rights budget and plan of action, insufficient experienced staff, poor training and a weakening resolve to provide political and financial support. Throughout the year Amnesty International also presented mounting evidence of violence and obstruction suffered by returning refugees and internally displaced persons and minorities in all areas (see **Bosnia-Herzegovina** entry). The freedom to return to one's home and freedom of movement, both guaranteed under the Dayton peace agreement, were not realized by the end of the year. However, the biannual OSCE Review Conference held in November in Vienna appeared undisturbed by such evidence when member states reviewed the work of the OSCE mission.

In June Amnesty International issued a 109-page report *Bosnia-Herzegovina: The international community's responsibility to ensure human rights*, which made extensive recommendations for improving the effectiveness of the human rights aspects of the international presence, including the OSCE mission. Amnesty International called on the High Representative to be required to implement a human rights plan. By the end of the year, as the 55,000-strong IFOR was succeeded by 35,000 personnel of the Stabilization Force (SFOR), the weaknesses in the human rights operation remained.

Building a consensus to strengthen international justice

Consensus helped to strengthen the substantial advances made in 1996 towards the establishment of a permanent international criminal court (see *Amnesty International Reports 1995* and *1996*). In a major breakthrough, and after intense pressure from NGOs around the world, the UN General Assembly decided to convene a diplomatic conference of governments in 1998, which is likely to take place in Italy. The conference should turn the draft

WORK WITH INTERNATIONAL ORGANIZATIONS

Amnesty International members in Benin, Côte d'Ivoire, Senegal and Togo campaigning for an international criminal court.

statute for the court into a treaty. If enough states then ratify the treaty, the court could be operating by the year 2000.

Speaking in May at Columbia University in New York, USA, the UN High Commissioner for Human Rights threw his support behind the early establishment of the court:

> "It is not a pleasant thing to admit, in what we think of as a civilized world, but there can no longer be any doubt that ... [a permanent international criminal court] is urgently needed ... So let the world now agree, that before the half-centennial of the Universal Declaration in 1998, we will establish, appoint, give authority to, and adequately fund a permanent international tribunal ... which will give judicial sanction to our commitment that there will be no more Auschwitzes, no more Ntaramas, and no more Srebrenicas."

The decision to convene a diplomatic conference in 1998 opened a new and difficult phase in the campaign for an international criminal court. Governments must not merely debate in theory the potential powers of a court and duties of states. They must negotiate and adopt an international treaty. There will be enormous pressure to weaken the statute for the sake of reaching agreement. But an effective international system of justice must not be sacrificed for the sake of consensus.

No state publicly opposed the creation of the court during the UN discussions, but it was clear to Amnesty International during six weeks of expert intergovernmental meetings in 1996 that fierce differences remain on key issues. These will have to be resolved in a further nine weeks of Preparatory Committee expert meetings in 1997 and early 1998. During the year Amnesty International developed further its recommendations for the draft

WORK WITH INTERNATIONAL ORGANIZATIONS

statute, to ensure it creates a just, fair and effective court. The court will probably have jurisdiction over genocide, other crimes against humanity and serious violations of humanitarian law. There is still opposition, however, to having a prosecutor who is independent, not subject to Security Council veto, with the power to investigate cases on her or his own initiative. All pre-trial, trial and appeal procedures must also be seen to meet the highest internationally recognized standards. Once set up the court will need long-term, secure financing by the UN.

Whether an effective system is created will depend partly on the strength of the worldwide NGO movement. Along with 80 other NGOs, Amnesty International contributed to the work of the New York-based NGO, Coalition for an International Criminal Court (CICC). The CICC facilitates exchange of information – particularly through an Internet website (http://www.igc.apc.org.icc/icc.new) and acts as a worldwide focal point for exchanges of ideas on campaigning work.

Amnesty International members throughout the world helped create a wave of public support for a permanent international criminal court: public seminars in Bangladesh, India and Nepal; a street action in Croatia; a call in Peru for church and women's groups, trade unions and academics to join a national coalition; petitions for parliamentarians to sign in Turkey and France; national radio and television coverage of a public seminar in Sierra Leone; a joint NGO appeal and an exhibition of Amnesty International material at a book fair in Morocco; meetings with diplomats in Latin American embassies in Argentina and media coverage in Kuwait. Hundreds attended a one-day conference in Turin in October organized by the Italian Section to hear speakers who included the UN High Commissioner for Human Rights and Amnesty International's Secretary General.

The International Criminal Tribunals for the former Yugoslavia and Rwanda (see **Bosnia-Herzegovina** and **Rwanda** entries) are part of the developing and interlocking system of international justice. Their success will help to address impunity in their respective regions as well as helping to build a consensus for the establishment of a permanent international criminal court. States must work together to ensure that these two *ad hoc* tribunals are just, fair and effective and receive the support they need.

Amnesty International repeatedly challenged the failure of IFOR in Bosnia and Herzegovina to fulfil the legal obligations of states under the 1949 Geneva Conventions and Security Council resolutions to search for, arrest and transfer to The Hague suspects indicted by the International Tribunal for the former Yugoslavia. IFOR, a powerful military force of some 55,000 troops, made no effort to search out such suspects or even to make arrests when troops repeatedly encountered them. In an open letter issued in March, Pierre Sané, Amnesty International's Secretary General, reminded states that "there cannot be a lasting peace in Bosnia and Herzegovina without justice".

In August, Amnesty International published a four-volume *International Criminal Tribunals: Handbook for government cooperation* which showed states how to cooperate with the two *ad hoc* tribunals. It removed the excuse of some states that they do not know how to enact legislation enabling their judicial, police and other authorities to cooperate with the tribunals or how to assist the tribunals to gather evidence, arrest suspects and transfer them to the tribunals. By the end of the year only 20 states had fulfilled their binding obligation to pass necessary legislation to cooperate with the International Tribunal for the former Yugoslavia and only 11 had done so for the International Tribunal for Rwanda.

Ten years of the African Charter

21 October 1996 marked the 10th anniversary of the African Charter on Human and Peoples' Rights. Commemorating the anniversary, Amnesty International said that the adoption of the African Charter "marked a point of departure for African states, and represented a formal commitment to human rights, although not a political will to address with any earnestness human rights violations in the continent."

The African Charter has significant shortcomings, with some guarantees falling short of international standards, and clawback clauses that allow states to curtail the rights of their people. The Organization of African Unity (OAU) should work towards amendment of key provisions. In the meantime, Amnesty International reiterated its call to the African Commission on Human and Peoples' Rights (the African Commission) to use its wide powers to interpret the African Charter in a progressive way, consistent with current international standards, in areas such as women's and refugee rights.

In a continent where many thousands of civilians have fallen victim to conflict in Algeria, Sierra Leone and Liberia, civil strife in Somalia, genocide in Rwanda and continuing massacres in Burundi and Zaire, to cite only a few situations, it is incumbent on African intergovernmental organizations to keep human rights at the heart of their political processes. Yet human rights have received scant attention at the meetings of the OAU Council of Ministers and Assembly of Heads of State and Government.

Amnesty International therefore welcomed the prominence given to the worsening situation in Burundi at the OAU Council and Assembly meeting in Yaoundé, Cameroon, in July. But although the Council expressed concern at the continuing atrocities in Burundi, it failed to make practical recommendations for action. Amnesty International called on the OAU to provide bold leadership and to ensure that peace initiatives include steps to protect human rights, investigate past violations and bring those responsible to justice. Only three weeks after the meeting, Major Pierre Buyoya led a coup in Burundi and massacres by government forces and armed groups continued unabated. Moreover, proposed action on Rwanda by the Council was frustrated by the continuing emphasis on consensus: a draft resolution expressing concern about the weakness of the judiciary and the imprisonment of tens of thousands of people was dropped in the face of objections from the Rwandese Government itself.

The African Commission – 11 experts charged with the formidable task of promoting human and peoples' rights and ensuring their protection in Africa – is grossly underfunded by the OAU, largely ignored by the Council and Assembly (although it could be mandated to undertake in-depth studies into serious or massive human rights violations) and suffers from poor working methods, a failure to concentrate on the most urgent countries and issues in Africa and a failure to follow up previous decisions such as resolutions to make on-site investigations.

However, the African Commission has made advances which give it the potential to make an important contribution to the protection and promotion of human rights in Africa. It has taken up an NGO proposal and appointed a Special Rapporteur on extrajudicial, summary or arbitrary executions who could be tackling endemic problems such as impunity. Unfortunately, more than two years since his appointment, no substantial work had been carried out. In 1996, a Special Rapporteur on prisons was appointed who could make recommendations to improve the appalling prison conditions in many African states. More states sent representatives to the two sessions of the Commission in 1996 to lobby the experts than in previous years, reflecting the anxiety of some states that the Commission will take action which exposes their responsibility for violations.

To its credit, the African Commission has allowed, unlike any other African intergovernmental body, maximum and intimate participation of NGOs in its work, although there were disturbing signs at the 20th Session of the Commission in Mauritius in October of attempts to restrict the role of NGOs. Amnesty International and other NGOs are willing to work with the experts to improve the Commission's effectiveness. At the October 1996 session, Amnesty International called on the Commission to undertake a critical review, with input from NGOs, governments and intergovernmental organizations.

Consensus decision-making threatens new international standards

Consensus decision-making seriously hampered the drafting of international human rights instruments during the year.

The UN draft Declaration on the Right and Responsibility of Individuals, Groups and Organs of Society to Promote and Protect Universally Recognized Human Rights and Fundamental Freedoms (draft "Declaration on human rights defenders"), has been under discussion for 12 years. This Declaration would make clear what rights human rights defenders, many of whom risk their freedom or even their lives to protect the rights of others, need in order to carry out their work freely. The Working Group of the UN Commission on Human Rights charged with elaborating the text made no significant progress during the 1996 session. As in 1995 (see *Amnesty International Report 1996*), a few states abused the concept of consensus to block the recognition of rights that are indispensable for the defence and promotion of human rights. Particularly disturbing has been the failure to recognize for defenders some of the rights and freedoms that make the defence of human rights possible, and are already guaranteed to all people – such as the rights to freedom of expression, association and peaceful assembly. Amnesty International called on the UN Commission on Human Rights, if it could not complete the draft Declaration at its next session, to appoint a Special Rapporteur on human rights defenders with a mandate to receive information and carry out investigations into the situation of human rights defenders, with the express aim of helping the Working Group resolve outstanding problems.

Similar problems were encountered in the drafting of an Optional Protocol to the UN Convention against Torture and Other Cruel, Inhuman or Degrading Treatment or Punishment (see *Amnesty International Report 1996*). Under this initiative an expert Sub-Committee of the UN Committee against Torture would inspect places of detention in states that have ratified the Protocol, identify practices and conditions which facilitate torture and other ill-treatment and enter into a confidential dialogue with the government on how to end torture. A working group of the UN Commission on Human Rights met in October for the fifth year. Although agreement was reached on a number of provisions, the elusive search for consensus threatened to undermine some of the core principles of an effective system. A small minority insisted that a state must consent to *each* mission by the proposed sub-committee before it can take place. Such a provision would render the Protocol useless: a state could ratify the Optional Protocol and then escape the basic obligation of having its places of detention regularly inspected by refusing to allow the Sub-Committee to carry out critical missions. Amnesty International set out this and other core principles in a document, *Draft Optional Protocol to the Convention against Torture: Developing an effective tool to prevent torture*.

New standards are proposed after a gap in protection is identified, in order to push forward international law and go beyond what states are already bound to do. However, consensus decision-making in the drafting of new instruments tends to maintain the status quo, or even threaten existing standards by agreeing to a lower level of protection. In both working groups Amnesty International sought to reaffirm fundamental principles on which the drafting should be based.

In 1996, an initiative was launched to develop a UN Convention on Forced Disappearance. In June, Amnesty International organized a meeting of NGOs and other experts to examine the text of a draft convention and discuss how it could contribute in practice to ending the phenomenon of "disappearances". Rapid progress was made when a member of a working group of the UN Sub-Commission on Prevention of Discrimination and Protection of Minorities tabled a draft text during its August session. After lively debate, the working group agreed that it should develop the draft text further next year, and will try to hold a workshop to which other experts and NGOs will be invited. Amnesty International hopes that input by NGOs and other experts at this early stage will build momentum behind a strong and innovative draft convention which builds on existing standards and on an understanding of how "disappearances" occur, and which is not subsequently derailed by the blocking tactics of a few governments.

Making the Beijing commitments a reality

The consensus of UN member states which stood behind the Beijing Declaration and Platform for Action adopted by the Fourth UN World Conference on Women in September 1995 (see *Amnesty International Report 1996*) is one example of how states speaking with a single voice have infused a document with legitimacy and authority. Building on cautious steps towards integrating human rights and women's rights, the UN made some advances towards implementing the recommendations made in Beijing. The UN Secretary-General appointed an Assistant Secretary General and Special Adviser on Gender Issues. The UN General Assembly supported the continuation of a working group of the Commission on the Status of Women which is drafting an Optional Protocol to the Convention on the Elimination of All Forms of Discrimination against Women. This would give women the right to make individual complaints about violations of the Convention by their government. Amnesty International is actively participating in this working group.

> **'Immediate action and accountability are essential if the targets are to be met by the year 2000.'**
> Beijing Declaration and Platform for Action

Considerable progress has been made in a short period, but much more needs to be implemented. The thematic and country experts of the UN Commission on Human Rights should be encouraged to devise strategies to ensure that they highlight the characteristics of violations to which women are particularly vulnerable as well as the measures needed to combat them. On-site investigations should include delegates with expertise in investigating violations against women, who should preferably be women, and female interpreters should be used when taking testimony from women about rape and other sexual abuse. During the year Amnesty International also worked for gender sensitivity in the future permanent international criminal court, including ensuring that investigators and prosecution staff have experience in cases involving sexual abuse and that such cases are prosecuted without unnecessary trauma for victims and their families.

A greater awareness in the UN Commission on Human Rights of the importance of a gender perspective has helped to underpin the work of the Special Rapporteur on violence against women. In 1996, the Commission gave specific attention to violence against women migrant workers, traffic in women and girls and violence against women in general. Coordination and integration of women's rights in the UN system should also be enhanced by further cooperation between the Commission on Human Rights and the Commission on the Status of Women.

What impact have the commitments made in Beijing had on the policies of governments within their countries? In *Women's Rights are Human Rights: Commitments made by governments in the Beijing Declaration and Platform for Action*, Amnesty International called on states to honour their promise to devise national plans of action to implement their new commitments. The plans should include ratification of human rights treaties, addressing impunity, creating and strengthening national human rights institutions, reviewing national laws, policies and practices and developing comprehensive human rights education programs.

COUNTRY ENTRIES

AFGHANISTAN

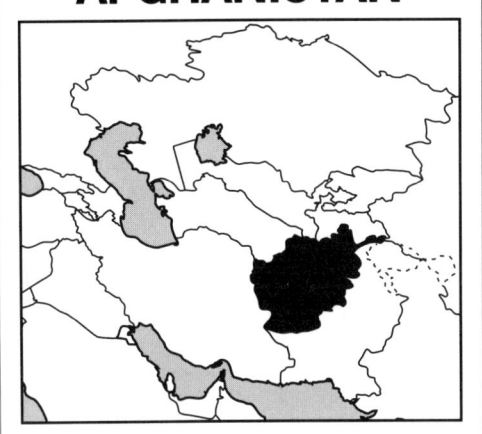

More than 1,000 people were held on account of their ethnic origin, their religious beliefs or their assumed political convictions. Many were believed to be prisoners of conscience. Thousands of women were physically restricted to their homes and scores of people were subjected to torture and ill-treatment for not obeying *Taleban* edicts. Dozens of civilians were killed in indiscriminate attacks against residential areas by warring factions. Scores of people were killed deliberately and arbitrarily. At least nine people were executed publicly, in several cases by stoning to death. Islamic courts passed sentences of death and amputation.

In June, Gulbuddin Hekmatyar, leader of *Hezb-e Islami* (Party of Islam), joined forces with the government of President Borhanuddin Rabbani, taking the office of prime minister.

For most of the year, Kabul, the capital, remained under road blockade and almost daily rocket attacks by the *Taleban* (religious students), an armed opposition group which controlled more than two thirds of Afghanistan. General Abdul Rashid Dostum, leader of *Junbesh-e Melli Islami* (National Islamic Movement), maintained control of the northern areas of the country.

On 27 September, the *Taleban* seized Kabul, ousting the government. They took former President Najibullah and his brother from a UN compound, where they had been taking refuge since April 1992, beat them severely and then hanged them from lampposts in the city centre. Mullah Mohammad Omar, leader of the *Taleban*, later exonerated their killers, saying that Najibullah deserved his fate. Armed groups opposed to the *Taleban*, including forces of the ousted government, Commander Ahmad Shah Masood, General Abdul Rashid Dostum and the Shi'a party, *Hezb-e Wahdat*, formed a new alliance called the Defence Council.

After the fall of Kabul, the *Taleban* advance was halted at the mouth of Panjshir valley, the stronghold of Commander Ahmad Shah Masood. *Taleban* militia attempted to cross the Salang tunnel but were stopped by the forces of General Dostum. Under military pressure, the *Taleban* withdrew from the positions they had captured north of Kabul. Opposition forces launched counter-attacks on Kabul and surrounding areas through sporadic air raids. A second front was opened in western Afghanistan where the *Taleban* held territory bordering the area controlled by General Dostum.

Days after the *Taleban* takeover of Kabul, the UN and other international agencies, including the International Committee of the Red Cross, evacuated some of their staff from the city. On several occasions, armed *Taleban* fighters carried out raids on premises and personal residences of UN officials in Kabul. The humanitarian work of the UN agencies and non-governmental organizations was severely curtailed by the *Taleban* authorities who did not permit women staff to participate in current programs outside the health sector. Several aid agencies, including Oxfam, suspended their programs when the *Taleban* stopped their female staff from working.

Attempts by the new head of the UN Special Mission to Afghanistan to bring about a negotiated settlement were frustrated by the warring factions' continued military confrontation. In October, the UN Special Rapporteur on Afghanistan, submitted a report to the UN General Assembly in which he urged all parties, *inter alia*, to respect the inherent right to life of every human being.

All armed groups held people on account of their ethnic origin, their religious beliefs or their assumed political convictions. Many of these people were believed to be prisoners of conscience. Several hundred people were detained by the *Taleban* in Herat and Farah provinces throughout the year because they did not obey religious decrees or because they sympathized or were suspected of sympathizing with the *Taleban*'s opponents. Many detainees appeared to be held as hostages; in some cases, they were released after paying bribes. Most were held incommunicado and family members found it difficult to trace them. Most detainees were held in prison but some were kept in metal transport containers.

In the days following their takeover of Kabul, the *Taleban* detained hundreds, possibly over 1,000 civilians, for allegedly sympathizing with the ousted president Burhanuddin Rabbani. On 10 October, *Taleban* members reportedly took away scores of young boys and men in raids on various mosques in Kabul. The *Taleban* told them that they would have to fight against forces loyal to the ousted government.

Thousands of women were physically restricted to their homes under *Taleban* edicts, which banned women from going to work or leaving the home unless accompanied by a close male relative. The women feared physical assault by *Taleban* guards. The edicts also banned girls from going to school. These restrictions were applied to different degrees in *Taleban*-controlled areas. At least 8,000 university students and tens of thousands of professional women in Kabul were affected.

Scores of women were beaten in the streets for not wearing a *burqa* (a garment covering the body from head to foot with a small, lace-covered opening for the eyes) or for exposing their ankles. In July, in the city of Farah, a woman named Turpeki was shot and injured by a teenaged *Taleban* guard for appearing in public. In October, a woman walking along a street in Kabul with her two children was whipped by *Taleban* guards with a car aerial because she had let her veil slip a fraction. In another incident, a married couple who had come from Samangan province to Kabul to visit friends were stopped in the market. One *Taleban* guard slapped the woman in the face while another beat her husband severely. They were accused of being "un-Islamic" for planning to buy cosmetics.

In October, two Afghan nurses were reportedly beaten with a tree branch by a *Taleban* guard for not wearing *burqas*. One of the women tried to run away. The guard forced her to the ground and held her between his legs while beating her with the stick.

Before the fall of Kabul, reports of women being raped by armed guards of the government of then President Rabbani continued to be received but in almost all cases the perpetrators remained unpunished. In one instance, five guards belonging to the forces of Commander Masood reportedly abducted a nurse from Nazwana Clinic in the Shahr Nou District of Kabul in January and held her for about a week, subjecting her to repeated rape.

Dozens of men were beaten in the streets by the *Taleban* and forced to attend Friday prayers in the mosque. Early in the year, over a dozen residents of Herat were beaten to punish them for anti-*Taleban* slogans on the walls of their houses. A number of prisoners died, reportedly while digging trenches in mined areas, or as a result of torture by the *Taleban*.

Journalists reporting human rights abuses against women were targeted. Two Argentine television journalists, together with their local interpreter and driver, were reportedly detained for about 24 hours by the *Taleban* in October. They told reporters in Buenos Aires, Argentina, that they had been held incommunicado by the *Taleban*, beaten with rifle butts and robbed of their equipment and papers. The two journalists were reportedly released after negotiations between UN officials and the *Taleban*, but their local interpreter and driver both remained in custody at the end of the year.

Indiscriminate rocket attacks on Kabul continued almost daily, with irregular intensity, for most of the year, as the *Taleban* laid siege to the city. At least nine civilians were killed and more than a dozen were injured in a *Taleban* rocket attack on 25 September. Bombs dropped from a *Taleban* plane on 24 October killed at least 20 people, mostly children, in the village of Kalakan.

The anti-*Taleban* alliance was also responsible for indiscriminate attacks on Kabul. In several instances bombs dropped from planes hit civilian areas of the city with no sign of military activity, killing several people. In November, three children were killed when anti-*Taleban* forces dropped two bombs on a residential area northwest of Kabul.

Civilians' houses were deliberately destroyed in the continuing conflict. On 22

October, at least 116 homes in the village of Sarcheshma, north of Kabul, were almost completely burnt out by the *Taleban* forces in retribution for the civilian villagers' failure to resist anti-*Taleban* forces.

Scores of people were killed deliberately and arbitrarily for supposed opposition to various factions. On 15 July, at least 30 young men were removed from Herat Prison and summarily executed. Several other mass executions reportedly took place in Herat. At least one man was reportedly killed deliberately and arbitrarily by the *Taleban* in early October in Kabul for not attending the mosque.

At least nine people were executed publicly. In February, an 18-year-old man alleged to have killed two *Taleban* guards was executed in public in Herat. Eye-witnesses observed that he had already been beaten close to death. He had reportedly been forced to sign a statement saying that he agreed with his death sentence. In the first executions in Kabul since 1992, three men convicted of murder were hanged in March, under President Rabbani's government. They included two members of the government armed forces.

Islamic courts passed sentences of death and amputation. In July, a man named Turiolai, and a young woman, Nurbibi, were stoned to death in the city of Kandahar. Turiolai had reportedly been involved in an affair with his father's widow, Nurbibi, for some years. On discovering the affair, the *Taleban* reportedly established an Islamic court which sentenced the couple to death by stoning. *Taleban* members threw the first stones and ordered bystanders to join in.

More than a dozen prisoners were subjected to amputations. Some of these were carried out after the victims had been sentenced by Islamic courts convened by the *Taleban* which often decided a dozen cases a day in sessions which took only a few minutes. There were reportedly no provisions for legal counsel or the presumption of innocence. Verdicts were final, with no mechanism for appeal. In April, the *Taleban* arrested Abduallah and Abdul Mahmood, two men from Uruzgan, on charges of theft. *Taleban* guards reportedly beat them severely, then cut off their left hands and right feet. The guards reportedly pressed red-hot iron plates against the wounds to stop the bleeding.

At the end of the year, about one million Afghan refugees were believed to be in Pakistan and about 1.4 million living in Iran.

Throughout the year, Amnesty International expressed concern about deliberate or indiscriminate attacks against residential areas of Kabul. In July, the organization visited Afghanistan for the first time in 14 years, meeting members of the government of Borhanuddin Rabbani in Kabul and the *Junbesh-e Melli Islami* of General Abdul Rashid Dostum in Mazar-e Sharif. The Amnesty International delegates raised cases of human rights abuses by government forces and armed opposition groups. They called on all parties to halt indiscriminate attacks on civilians and on the international community to work for human rights protection in Afghanistan. In November, Amnesty International published a report, *Afghanistan: Grave abuses in the name of religion*, detailing abuses in *Taleban*-held areas, including arbitrary and unacknowledged detention of civilians, torture and ill-treatment, deliberate and arbitrary killings, amputations, stoning and executions.

ALBANIA

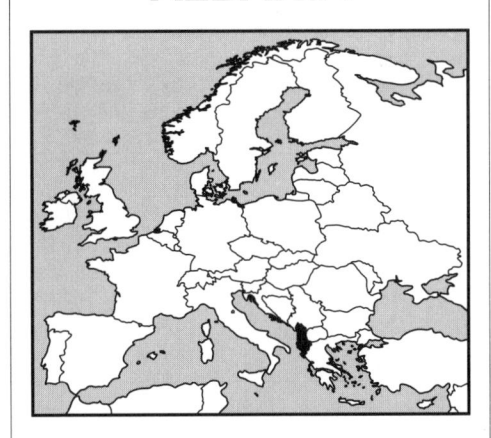

An opposition leader continued to be held as a prisoner of conscience. At least 14 prisoners of conscience, including journalists and opposition activists, were sentenced to between four months' and 15 years' imprisonment. Several hundred others were detained, usually for less than 48 hours, for non-violent political activity. Some political prisoners were denied a fair trial. Hundreds of people were

tortured or ill-treated by police. Eight men were sentenced to death; there were no executions.

The ruling Democratic Party won an overwhelming majority in national elections in May. However, the main opposition parties claimed there had been major election fraud and the Organization for Security and Co-operation in Europe (OSCE) criticized the conduct of the elections. In June, the OSCE suggested that new elections, "after a reasonable but limited period of time, under improved conditions and in the presence of international observers, would serve the interests of Albania." President Sali Berisha continued to assert that the elections had been free and fair.

In October, Albania ratified the European Convention for the Protection of Human Rights and Fundamental Freedoms and the European Convention for the Prevention of Torture and Inhuman or Degrading Treatment or Punishment.

Early in the year, more than 30 former senior communist officials, including former President Ramiz Alia, were detained for investigation on charges of "genocide" and "crimes against humanity". By the end of the year, 30 had been convicted, 10 of them *in absentia*, of "crimes against humanity" for their part in the administrative internment, under past communist rule, of relatives of imprisoned dissidents or of people who had fled the country illegally. The investigation of former President Alia and three others, suspected of responsibility for the killings of people who tried to flee the country in 1990 and 1991, and other crimes, continued.

An opposition leader continued to be held as a prisoner of conscience. Fatos Nano, the leader of the main opposition party, the Socialist Party (SP), was arrested in 1993 and convicted in 1994 (see *Amnesty International Reports 1995* and *1996*). In December, his sentence was reduced by six months by presidential pardon, reportedly leaving him 18 months to serve.

On 26 February, a bomb exploded in Tirana, the capital, killing four people and injuring 27 others. Later the same day, police arrested some 30 people, mostly journalists, at the offices of the independent newspaper *Koha Jone*, Our Time. All were released without charge within hours. Ylli Polovina, a freelance journalist, was also arrested on 26 February, but was detained until March, when Tirana district court convicted him of "incitement to violence", fined him and released him. The charge related to an article he had published three months earlier, in which he wrote about instability in the Balkans, and warned that corruption, "degraded politics" or a "peaceful putsch" might "explode" in Albania. The article did not appear in any way to incite violence.

Other prisoners of conscience included four men from Saranda. They had been arrested in September 1995, and charged with distributing leaflets describing President Berisha as a "spy" and demanding "America out of Albania". In March, Saranda district court found all four guilty of "distributing anti-constitutional materials"; Sulejman Mekollari, who was also found guilty of attempting to recreate the banned Communist Party, was sentenced to four years' imprisonment and Lirim Veliu to two years' imprisonment. Dilaver Dauti was sentenced to 30 months' imprisonment, but following conviction escaped from house arrest and fled the country. A fourth defendant received a suspended prison sentence. In September, four men were convicted by Tirana district court of seeking to recreate the banned Communist Party: Sami Meta was sentenced to 30 months' imprisonment, Timoshenko Pekmezi to two years' imprisonment and the two other defendants to a year's imprisonment each. No evidence was produced in court to support the prosecution's claim that they had advocated the use of violence to achieve power. Sami Meta and Timoshenko Pekmezi were released at the end of December by presidential pardon.

Idajet Beqiri, leader of an opposition party, the Party of National Unity (see *Amnesty International Report 1994*) was arrested in January. He was later charged, together with eight others – who had been senior communist officials – with "crimes against humanity". He was accused of having signed a proposal for the internment of four members of a family in 1985, when he was president of a district court. In September, the defendants were found guilty by Tirana district court. Idajet Beqiri was sentenced to 15 years' imprisonment. The charges against him, which he denied, appeared to be politically motivated, and serious violations of procedure undermined his right to a fair trial.

Other prisoners of conscience included four Jehovah's Witnesses from Berat who were imprisoned for between four and six months under Article 16 of the Military Criminal Code for refusing on religious grounds to perform military service. There are no provisions allowing conscientious objectors to perform alternative civilian service in Albania. Exemption is granted only to men who pay the state the equivalent of US$4,000, a sum beyond the reach of most. Three other Jehovah's Witnesses were placed under house arrest pending trial for refusing on religious grounds to do military service.

More than 20 men were arrested in October on suspicion of involvement in political killings, bombings and bank robberies. They included Klement Kolaneci, the son-in-law of Albania's former communist ruler, Enver Hoxha. On at least two occasions, in October and November, his lawyers complained that in violation of national law their access to him had been severely restricted. There were unconfirmed reports that the other defendants had also been denied unrestricted access to their lawyers.

In the run-up to the elections, many of the several hundred opposition activists or supporters who were briefly detained by police were ill-treated. In many cases they were engaged, or suspected of being engaged, in peaceful activities such as attending party rallies, writing slogans or putting up party posters. Journalists writing for the opposition or independent press were also detained and beaten or threatened with legal proceedings. In February, Fatos Veliu, a journalist for *Koha Jone*, was physically assaulted and injured by the police chief in Saranda, after he had written an article critical of the local police. Also in February, Behar Toska, an unemployed former police officer, was arrested and severely beaten and injured by police in Tirana who accused him of having been paid by SP leaders to write anti-government slogans on walls.

Police violence against the opposition culminated on 28 May, two days after the elections, when a demonstration in Tirana's main square in protest at alleged election fraud was violently dispersed. Police beat demonstrators, including opposition leaders, women and the elderly, as well as some bystanders and local and foreign journalists. Almost 100 people testified in writing about the ill-treatment they had suffered. Arben Imami, leader of the Democratic Alliance Party, was among some 20 opposition leaders who were arrested. He stated that he was beaten and kicked by state security police before being released later the same day. A medical report noted severe bruising to his head and body and a broken tooth. After the demonstration had been dispersed, Bardhok Lala, a journalist, was forced into a van by men who appear to have been state security officers and driven to a lake near Tirana, where he was forced to undress, beaten and subjected to a mock execution. His injuries were so severe that he had still not fully recovered by the end of the year and continued to receive treatment abroad. A parliamentary commission was later formed to investigate allegations of violence in connection with the elections, and the Tirana Prosecutor's Office started two investigations. By the end of the year, no police officer had been charged or tried in connection with the alleged ill-treatment, but the authorities stated that seven officers had been dismissed for "incompetence".

There were also reports of cases in which police beat detainees in incidents which did not have a political context. For example, in September, Ismail Hoxha, a miner from Krasta, was severely beaten by police after an argument in a village bar. He was taken to hospital two days later in a coma with a fractured skull and subsequently underwent surgery in Tirana.

Five men were sentenced to death for murder. Two of these sentences were commuted to imprisonment on appeal, as were death sentences imposed in May on three former communist officials convicted of "crimes against humanity". There were no executions.

Amnesty International published two reports, *Albania: detention and ill-treatment of government opponents – the elections of May 1996* in September, and *Albania: A call for the release of prisoners of conscience* in November. In these reports and in other appeals the organization called on the authorities to release prisoners of conscience and stressed its concern at the failure on the part of the government to bring to justice police officers responsible for ill-treating or torturing detainees. Amnesty International also called for political prisoners to be granted a fair trial.

ALGERIA

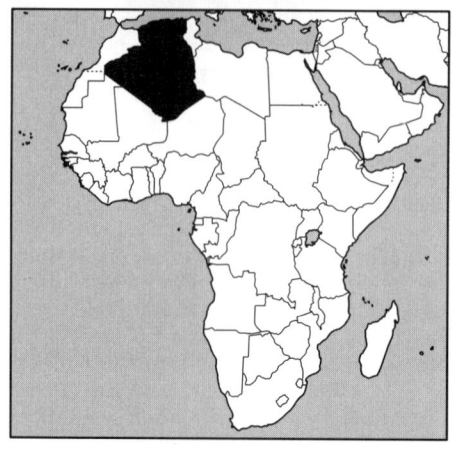

Thousands of people were killed by the security forces and government-backed militias, hundreds of them being extrajudicially executed. Hundreds of civilians were deliberately and arbitrarily killed by armed opposition groups, both in targeted attacks and indiscriminate bomb explosions, and others were abducted and killed. Hundreds of people, among them prisoners of conscience and possible prisoners of conscience, were arrested and charged with security offences. Scores of political detainees arrested since 1992 continued to be held without trial. Trials of individuals accused of "terrorism" fell short of international standards for fair trial. Torture and ill-treatment of detainees continued to be widespread, especially during secret detention after arrest. Beatings and other ill-treatment in prisons were increasingly reported. Hundreds of people arrested by the security forces during the year and in previous years remained unaccounted for. Hundreds of death sentences were imposed, most of them *in absentia*. More than 600 people sentenced to death in previous years remained on death row. No judicial executions were known to have been carried out.

A conference aimed at solving the political crisis was convened by President Liamine Zeroual in September. It was boycotted by some of the main political opposition parties. The *Front islamique du salut* (FIS), Islamic Salvation Front, which had been included in similar initiatives in previous years, was excluded.

A new Constitution, which gave increased powers to the President, was passed by referendum in November. The official results of the referendum were disputed by the majority of the opposition parties, the news media and other observers. Legislative and local elections were announced for 1997.

The state of emergency imposed in 1992 (see *Amnesty International Report 1993*) remained in place, but the curfew, which had been in place in various provinces, was lifted in February.

Responsibility for individual killings and attacks was increasingly difficult to establish as the patterns of conduct of the security forces, government-backed militias and armed opposition groups were often similar. The security forces often operated in plain clothes, used ordinary cars and refused to show arrest warrants or identify themselves, while armed opposition groups at times wore uniforms and posed as members of the security forces.

In November, the UN Committee against Torture considered Algeria's first periodic report and expressed concern at allegations of increased torture, extrajudicial executions and "disappearances". The Committee also recommended that the UN Convention against Torture and Other Cruel, Inhuman or Degrading Treatment or Punishment be published in the Algerian official gazette.

Thousands of people were killed by the security forces. Many were killed in armed confrontations, but hundreds were extrajudicially executed when they posed no threat to the lives of members of the security forces. Some were killed in their homes, in front of their families, or in detention. Extrajudicial executions were reportedly often used as an alternative to arrest. According to eye-witnesses and to members of the army, security forces, and government-backed militias, individuals known or suspected of belonging to, or having links with, armed opposition groups were often extrajudicially executed after they were captured or when they could have been arrested. Victims of extrajudicial executions reportedly included civilians, relatives of members of armed opposition groups and others who were suspected of having cooperated with these groups, either willingly or under threat. Government-backed militias, which defined themselves as "*groupes d'auto-*

défense" ("self-defence groups"), or "*patriotes*" ("patriots"), were increasingly involved in counter-insurgency and security operations, either acting on their own initiative or in conjunction with the army and security forces, and were responsible for widespread deliberate and arbitrary killings. Such groups received arms and ammunition from the army and security forces, but did not appear to be subject to any chain-of-command control or accountability to the authorities.

Four young men – Khelifa and Benyoucef Bokreta, Benyoucef Belhadj-Bouchaib and 'Adelkader Gouasmi – were reportedly extrajudicially executed outside their homes in January in Dawadji, Djelida area, in the province of 'Ain-Defla by *gardes communaux* (communal guards).

Boumedienne Ould-Sa'adi, a 16-year-old high-school student, was reportedly extrajudicially executed in January after being arrested by security forces at his school in Algiers. His family later found his bullet-ridden body in the morgue; they had not been informed of his death.

In May, four brothers and their 84-year-old father were killed, reportedly by members of the security forces, in their home in the suburbs of Algiers in front of their mother, wives and sister. The family reported that they were asked by the security forces to sign a declaration stating that their relatives had been killed by "terrorists".

Scores of civilians were reportedly killed in bombings and heavy artillery attacks by the security forces on houses and villages where armed opposition groups were believed to be hiding. In February, several civilians were reportedly killed in Laghouat when the security forces attacked an area of the city where armed groups, who had taken civilian hostages, were hiding.

Armed opposition groups, which defined themselves as "Islamic groups", deliberately and arbitrarily killed hundreds of civilians and non-combatants. Many of the victims were killed in targeted attacks, including civil servants, journalists, employees of state companies, teachers and artists. Scores of others died in indiscriminate attacks such as bomb explosions.

In May, Boubekeur Bellik, president of the Algiers *Délégation exécutive communale* (Communal Executive Delegation), a body appointed to replace elected mayors after the FIS was banned in 1992, and Ahmed Tayeb, head clerk, were shot dead by unidentified gunmen.

In some cases, armed opposition groups abducted civilians before killing them. In September, the singer Boudjem'a Bechiri, known as "Cheb 'Aziz", was found dead in Constantine two days after being abducted by an armed group.

Foreign nationals, including members of the Christian religious community, continued to be targeted by armed groups. Seven French Trappist monks, one of whom was 82 years old, abducted in March from a monastery in the Medea region, were found dead in May. The *Groupe islamique armé* (GIA), Armed Islamic Group, claimed responsibility for the abduction and killing of the monks and for other killings.

In the second half of the year there was an increase in the number of bomb explosions; the GIA claimed responsibility for a number of such attacks. Scores of civilians were killed. For example, in October at least 10 civilians were killed, including women and children, and more than 70 injured, when a bomb exploded in a market in the town of Kole'a.

Hundreds of people were arrested on charges of "terrorism" and other security offences. Hundreds were released without charge, but several hundred remained detained awaiting trial at the end of the year. Among them were prisoners of conscience and possible prisoners of conscience, including journalists detained for publishing information deemed to undermine state security. Chawki La'amari, journalist and cartoonist with the daily *La Tribune*, was arrested in July for drawing a cartoon featuring the Algerian flag. He was tried on charges of insulting the national flag and given a three-year suspended prison sentence. The director and the editor of the newspaper also received suspended prison sentences of one year and six months, respectively, and the newspaper was closed for six months.

The 12-day legal limit for incommunicado detention was routinely breached. The security forces systematically held detainees in secret detention, often for prolonged periods, and refused to acknowledge their detention. In July, Rachid Mesli, a human rights lawyer, was abducted at gunpoint by a group of unidentified armed men who stopped his car, in which his five-year-old son and a relative were also travelling. The authorities refused to acknowledge his detention for over a week. During secret detention he was reportedly beaten and otherwise ill-treated and threatened with death. He was subsequently charged with having links with armed opposition groups and was detained awaiting trial at the end of the year.

Beatings and other ill-treatment were increasingly reported in prisons. In September, several detainees were reportedly beaten and otherwise ill-treated in El-Harrache prison in Algiers. No inquiry was known to have been carried out by the end of the year.

Scores of people arrested in previous years remained detained without trial at the end of the year. They included 'Abdelkader Hachani, a leading FIS figure, detained since January 1992, Nadir Hammoudi, an engineer, detained since October 1992, and 'Ali Zouita, a lawyer, detained since February 1993.

Trials of individuals accused of "terrorism" and other security offences continued to violate international standards for fair trial. The courts routinely disregarded allegations by defendants that their confessions, which they retracted in court, had been extracted under duress.

Reports of torture and ill-treatment of detainees in secret detention centres were widespread. Bouasria Ben 'Othman, an asylum-seeker deported from Belgium in July, died in secret detention in December, allegedly as a result of torture. The authorities said that he had thrown himself out of a window. There had been no investigation of his death by the end of the year. In most cases torture was reportedly used to extract information and confessions from detainees during secret detention, which often lasted for weeks or months. The most commonly reported methods included: the *"chiffon"*, where the detainee is tied to a bench and a cloth is placed in the mouth through which a mixture of dirty water and chemicals is poured causing choking and swelling of the stomach; electric shocks to sensitive parts of the body; tying a rope around the detainee's penis and/or testicles, causing swelling of the genitals; suspension in contorted positions; cigarette burns; and beatings. For example, a 16-year-old boy arrested in August on charges of having links with armed groups was reportedly subjected to the *"chiffon"* method, having his genitals tied with a metal wire, electric shocks and beatings during secret detention. He remained detained awaiting trial at the end of the year.

Hundreds of people who "disappeared" after arrest in the course of the year and in previous years remained unaccounted for and some were reported to have been killed. Kamel Chorfi-Khelil, an engineer who was reportedly arrested in June and later seen in the Châteauneuf detention centre, remained "disappeared" until October, when he was reportedly extrajudicially executed. Allaoua Ziou, Djamaleddine Fahassi, Mohamed Rosli, Brahim Cherrada, Mohamed Chergui, Yamine 'Ali Kebaili, and 13 others who "disappeared" after their arrests in 1993, 1994 and 1995 (see Amnesty International Report 1996), remained unaccounted for. The authorities denied that some of these "disappeared" had ever been arrested, and stated that others had been killed by the security forces in armed confrontations, or had been abducted and killed by "terrorists". However, the authorities failed to provide substantive information as to the precise circumstances of these deaths, and in some cases the information contradicted reports from other sources, including official sources. They also failed to explain why the families had not been informed of their relatives' deaths. According to the authorities, Saghir Bouhadida, who "disappeared" after arrest in June 1995 (see Amnesty International Report 1996), was killed during a security force operation aimed at arresting him and other members of an armed group. No clarification was provided as to why his family had not been informed of his death at the time.

'Ali Belhadj, a FIS leader arrested in 1991 and sentenced to 12 years' imprisonment in 1992, remained "disappeared". He was reportedly last seen in mid-1995 in a secret detention centre in the Tamanrasset desert region in the south of the country.

No investigations were known to have been carried out into cases of deaths in custody and extrajudicial executions during the year and in previous years. In April, the authorities stated that Fouad Bouchelaghem, who had been arrested in June 1994 and was reported to have been extrajudicially executed in July 1994 (see *Amnesty International Report 1995*), had been shot dead by the security forces in detention while attempting to escape. No further details about the circumstances of his death or clarification as to why his family had not been informed were provided.

Hundreds of death sentences were reportedly imposed during the year, many of them *in absentia*, but the exact number was not made available. According to official figures issued during the year, 336 death sentences, 277 of them *in absentia*, had been imposed in 1995. More than 600 detainees sentenced in previous years, many after unfair trials, remained on death row. No judicial executions were reported during the year, and the moratorium on executions announced in December 1993 remained in force.

In November, Amnesty International issued a report, *Algeria: Fear and silence – a hidden human rights crisis*. This included recommendations to the Algerian authorities to investigate human rights violations committed by the security forces; to bring to justice those responsible; and to take concrete measures to prevent further violations, including disbanding all government-backed militias. The organization also called on armed opposition groups to end the killing and abduction of civilians. Most of the concerns contained in the report had been raised with the authorities in a confidential memorandum in 1995. No response was received to this memorandum or any other communication. The Algerian Government failed to respond to Amnesty International's requests to send a delegation to discuss its concerns with the authorities.

ANGOLA

A prisoner of conscience was detained, then given a suspended prison sentence. Scores of suspected supporters of the União Nacional para a Independência Total de Angola (UNITA), National Union for the Total Independence of Angola, including possible prisoners of conscience, were detained for short periods. There were reports of severe beatings and other ill-treatment by police and soldiers. Unarmed civilians were reported to have been deliberately killed by government soldiers. UNITA was responsible for gross human rights abuses including torture and executions.

The implementation of the peace agreement, concluded in Lusaka in November 1994 (see *Amnesty International Reports 1995* and *1996*) between the government of President José Eduardo dos Santos and UNITA, led by Jonas Malheiro Savimbi, and monitored by the UN Angola Verification Mission III (UNAVEM III), lagged far behind schedule. UNITA retained control of much of rural Angola, and cities remained overcrowded with displaced people afraid to return to their villages. A "special status" for Jonas Savimbi – a requirement of the Lusaka Protocol – remained undecided after UNITA rejected the offer of one of two vice-presidential posts. The Government of National Unity and Reconciliation had not been established by the end of the year.

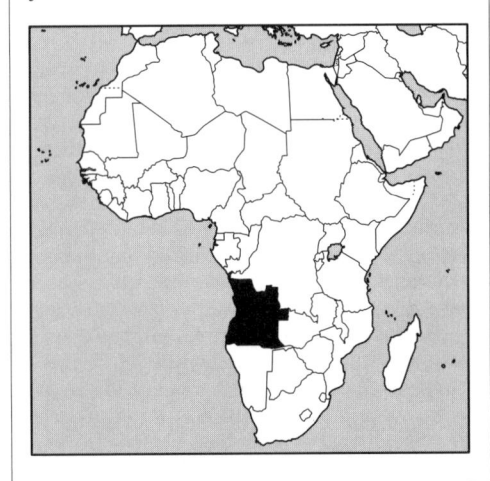

The quartering and demobilization of UNITA's 63,000 troops was not completed until October. Of those encamped, an estimated 30 per cent were civilians captured to make up the numbers. More than 13,000 people deserted the camps. UNITA was reported to be concealing large quantities of military material and thousands of soldiers in northern Angola and in its police force. By the end of the year very few UNITA troops had been demobilized or integrated into the army and police force. By December, 4,000 of UNITA's estimated 5,000 police had been moved to quartering areas. The government's 5,000-strong paramilitary Rapid Intervention Police were confined to barracks. In August, the disarming of civilians commenced; police collected a variety of weapons, including mines and rocket launchers, which were stored under UNAVEM III supervision.

An amnesty law was passed in May in favour of those who had committed military and security crimes. The government released 379 prisoners arrested in the context of the conflict and UNITA released 170 people, including four South Africans (see *Amnesty International Report 1996*). The fate and whereabouts of hundreds of people arrested after the war resumed in late 1992 remained unclear (see *Amnesty International Reports 1994* to *1996*).

The Human Rights Unit within UNAVEM III compiled two reports documenting cases of human rights abuses and making recommendations for remedial action by the Joint Commission set up to implement the peace agreement. The April report indicated that neither the government nor UNITA had responded adequately to the Unit's recommendations. A second report was produced in mid-December.

As a result of delays in implementing the peace process, some 300,000 refugees in neighbouring countries were not repatriated, although several thousand returned to Angola independently. An estimated million or more displaced persons, including some 40,000 people in Jamba, UNITA's former headquarters in southeastern Angola, were unable to return to their homes.

Despite the peace agreement, there was little security for ordinary citizens. Unemployment, poverty and corruption contributed to high levels of violent crime. Poorly paid, ill-disciplined police and soldiers were also involved in crimes. Tension in Luanda, the capital, rose in May as the cost of living escalated. Demonstrations were banned and paramilitary police were deployed in the city. In June, a new Prime Minister, Fernando França Van Dumem, was given the task of stabilizing the economy. Import controls were introduced and over a thousand illegal immigrants, mostly traders from other African countries, were deported.

Fighting continued in Cabinda, which is separated from the rest of Angola by a strip of Zairian territory, between government forces and the three armed factions of the separatist *Frente da Libertação do Enclave de Cabinda* (FLEC), Cabinda Enclave Liberation Front. In August, after months of bilateral talks with the government, the three factions agreed on a joint platform for peace negotiations.

Evidence of killings carried out in previous years came to light in July in Soyo, Zaire province, when a mine clearance team discovered the remains of at least 60 people, apparently victims of deliberate and arbitrary killings. Local residents said that the victims were probably people abducted during UNITA's occupation of Soyo in 1993 and 1994, but UNITA denied responsibility for the killings. By the end of the year no forensic or judicial investigation had been carried out to determine the identity of the victims or the perpetrators.

One prisoner of conscience was held briefly and tried for exercising his right to freedom of expression. Father Konrad Liebscher, a German Roman Catholic priest, was arrested in Luanda in May while distributing posters asking why people did not enjoy rights such as clean water and freedom of expression. The posters invited people to alert those in authority by demonstrating peacefully. The Luanda municipal court sentenced him to one month's imprisonment, suspended for two years, for carrying out a demonstration without official permission. By the end of the year the Supreme Court had not considered Konrad Liebscher's appeal against his conviction or the prosecution's appeal against the suspension of his sentence.

Scores of people suspected of supporting UNITA, including possible prisoners of conscience, were detained for short periods. About 60 suspected UNITA sympathizers were briefly detained in Uige City in May. They had previously been detained without charge or trial for six weeks in late 1995 and, on the grounds that the prison was full, held in 15 containers without adequate ventilation or sanitary facilities.

There were reports of severe beatings and other ill-treatment by government soldiers and police, sometimes as they were carrying out arrests or searches and sometimes while the police themselves were committing crimes. For example, officers of the Rapid Intervention Police assaulted and robbed women at Senga market, Uige province, in June.

Government police and soldiers carried out killings which appeared to be extrajudicial executions. In none of the following cases were the perpetrators known to have been brought to justice by the end of the year. A police officer shot dead a young street vendor in a busy street in Luanda in June. Also in June, a policeman beat a pregnant woman to death in a market in Uige City. The motive for these killings was unclear. A woman was killed in Cabinda City in May in what may have been an extrajudicial execution when soldiers and police, in retaliation for the murder of a policeman, drove about firing indiscriminately into the crowd. According to reports, some police and soldiers were arrested but had not been brought to trial by the end of the year. António Casimiro, a television cameraman, was reportedly extrajudicially executed in Cabinda City in October after security personel broke into his house. The motives for the killing were unclear but he had earlier reported receiving threats, apparently in connection with his work.

Those responsible for apparently politically motivated killings which occurred in 1995 had not been brought to justice by the end of 1996. Domingos Hungo, Governor of Bengo province, was shot dead and two of his bodyguards were injured in Luanda on New Year's Eve, 1995. Initially both the government and UNITA said they suspected a political motive. Suspected perpetrators were arrested but none were brought to justice. The results of investigations into the killings of Ricardo Melo, a journalist (see *Amnesty International Report 1996*), in January, and of Adão da Silva, UNITA's Provincial Secretary for Luanda and a former high-ranking government police officer, in July, had not been published by the end of the year.

UNITA continued to hold prisoners. Of the thousands of people who remain in Jamba, hundreds of civilians had been taken there as prisoners. In 1996, as in previous years, some managed to escape. There were dozens of reports of people being detained on suspicion of being government spies or supporters.

UNITA forces were responsible for torture. In Uige province in June, a man was severely beaten for trying to stop a UNITA soldier raping his wife. In the quartering areas, where UNITA was responsible for discipline, soldiers were publicly caned for theft and other offences. Beating on the sexual organs was reported in Nduko quartering area in Zaire province. Other methods of torture included the use of whips with several thongs, each with a pebble tied to its tip, and severe beatings on the hands. Costa Afonso Rangel, a government municipal official in Bocoio, Benguela province, was allegedly beaten on the head with an iron bar in January by UNITA soldiers whom he had accused of stealing cattle. Amnesty International received new information that the torture of João André Lina had not resulted in his death as previously reported (see *Amnesty International Report 1996*). He was crippled after being subjected to *candambala*, a severe beating by two men armed with sticks who each hit him 50 times on the back.

UNITA continued to sentence people to death for both political and non-political offences in accordance with its internal regulations and military law, but details were difficult to obtain. In one case, in February, two UNITA soldiers accused of killing someone they considered to be a "witch" were executed at Mbanza Congo airport in Zaire province. Information came to light during the year about executions carried out in previous years. In September 1994, João Lourenço Madalena and José António Cristina were executed in Nkama Nsoke village, Zaire province, after being convicted of collaborating with a government reconnaissance group. There were unconfirmed reports that two people had been executed in October 1995 just before a stay of execution was ordered as the result of an appeal by Alioune Blondin Beye, the head of UNAVEM III; the lives of eight others, on whose behalf Alioune Blondin Beye had also appealed, were spared (see *Amnesty International Report 1996*).

Armed FLEC factions carried out human rights abuses. In January, the *Frente para a Libertação do Enclave de Cabinda–Forças Armadas de Cabinda*, Cabinda Enclave Liberation Front–Cabinda Armed Forces, abducted three South Africans and a national of São Tomé and Príncipe who were working for a gold-mining company in Buco-Zau. The four were released in March, reportedly after a ransom was paid.

Amnesty International published two reports in April and October. *Angola: The Lusaka Protocol – what prospect for human rights?* examined the observance by the government and UNITA of the human rights provisions of the Protocol. *Angola: From war to ... what? No reconciliation without accountability* called for the establishment of mechanisms to provide additional protection for human rights after the withdrawal of UNAVEM III.

Two Amnesty International delegates visited Angola in June and July and met government officials, representatives of UNAVEM III and non-governmental organizations and other individuals. In August, the organization issued a memorandum containing comments and recommendations concerning the work of the Human Rights Unit, which was welcomed by the head of UNAVEM III. The organization also appealed to the government to ensure that perpetrators of human rights violations were brought to justice, but received no response.

ARGENTINA

One prisoner of conscience remained imprisoned. There were reports of torture and ill-treatment of detainees in police stations. Investigations into past "disappearances" made little progress, although new legal proceedings were initiated. Dozens of killings by police in circumstances suggesting possible extrajudicial executions were reported. Demonstrators were beaten and otherwise ill-treated by police.

In February, Argentina ratified the Inter-American Convention on the Forced Disappearance of Persons.

In September, the newly-created constitutional body of Buenos Aires, in charge of drawing up the statutes under which the capital city will be governed, amended the Buenos Aires police by-laws. The new legislation removes federal police powers to arrest, interrogate and detain suspected offenders for up to 30 days without bringing them before a judge. The new police regulations, incorporating these guarantees, had not been approved by the end of the year.

In its report to the UN Commission on Human Rights, the Working Group on Enforced or Involuntary Disappearances observed that the Argentine State was obliged to conduct investigations thoroughly and impartially "for as long as the fate of the victim of enforced disappearance remains unclarified", in accordance with the provisions of the UN Declaration on the Protection of All Persons from Enforced Disappearance.

One prisoner of conscience remained in jail at the end of the year. Fray Antonio Puigjane, a 68-year-old Franciscan friar, was arrested in the wake of an armed attack in January 1989 by members of the *Movimiento Todos por la Patria* (MTP), All for the Fatherland Movement (see *Amnesty International Reports 1990* to *1993*). Fray Antonio Puigjane, a leading member of the MTP, had denied any knowledge of the attack and had not participated in it. In October 1989, he was sentenced to 20 years' imprisonment on the basis of unsubstantiated allegations that he was aware of and contributed to the attack. At the end of the year, his case was pending before the Inter-American Commission on Human Rights of the Organization of American States.

Incidents of torture and ill-treatment of detainees in police stations were reported. In February, Leandro Oliva and his female companion, a minor, were arrested by a police patrol in Buenos Aires after cannabis was reportedly found in his possession. In his complaint, filed before the Human Rights Under-Secretariat in the Ministry of the Interior, Leandro Oliva stated that while on his way to Police Station No. 5 he was subjected to torture, including being burned with cigarettes. In the police station, he stated that he and his companion were handcuffed, beaten, and threatened with the same fate as Walter Bulacio, a youth who died in police custody in 1991 (see *Amnesty International Report 1996*). In March, Clarisa Andrea Lencina filed an official complaint against two police officers of Police Station No. 3 at Berazategui, Buenos Aires Province. She stated that she had been subjected to beatings, near-asphyxiation and other physical abuse on the two occasions when she was detained in February and March.

Fernando Pérez Ferreira, a student, was arrested in July in San Carlos de Bariloche, Neuquén Province. According to the legal complaint filed by his parents, he was severely beaten during the seven hours of his detention. Three police officers were reportedly suspended from duty and a police inquiry was announced.

In July, 11 young people were arrested in Buenos Aires by armed police in civilian clothes. The youths were taken to Police Station No. 21 in Buenos Aires where they were allegedly beaten. Some were held incommunicado for 17 hours and interrogated about their attendance at a public meeting organized by *Hijos por la Identidad y la Justicia contra el Olvido y el Silencio*, Children for Identity and Justice against Oblivion and Silence, a group formed by children of the "disappeared". A complaint relating to this incident was filed, but no inquiry was known to have been initiated.

Little progress was made in investigations into past "disappearances", although new information came to light from neighbouring countries regarding collaboration in the past between their security forces and the Argentine military government in carrying out human rights violations. In May, a former Uruguayan navy captain, Jorge Tróccoli, stated that nationals from both countries had been arrested and made to "disappear" by Uruguayan and Argentine security forces personnel (see **Uruguay** entry). In July, the Paraguayan Supreme Court released to the Argentine authorities files on the arrest in Paraguay and subsequent "disappearance" of Argentine nationals Alejandro Logoluso, Dora Marta Landi and José Nell in 1977 (see **Paraguay** entry). The police record of their arrest stated that the three were handed over, with two Uruguayan prisoners, to members of the Argentine and Uruguayan security forces. Their whereabouts remain unknown.

Two other investigations into the cases of three foreign nationals – French nuns Alice Domon and Léonie Duquet, and Dagmar Hagelin, of joint Swedish/Argentine nationality – who "disappeared" in Argentina in 1977, were reopened in March and June respectively by the Argentine Appeals Court. The investigations had not concluded by the end of the year.

Legal initiatives on cases of Italian and Spanish nationals who "disappeared" in Argentina were undertaken by courts in their respective countries. In May, an Italian judge ordered that the investigation continue into the cases of more than 70 Italians and Argentines of Italian origin who "disappeared" in Argentina during the period of military rule. In September, a Spanish High Court judge summoned more than 100 members of the Argentine security forces, including members of former military juntas, to testify in the cases of 300 Spanish citizens who "disappeared" in Argentina between 1976 and 1983.

In February, the government agreed to pay compensation to the families of Adolfo Argentino Garrido, Raúl Baigorria and Pablo Cristian Guardatti after their cases had been submitted to the Inter-American Court of Human Rights of the Organization of American States. The three men "disappeared" between 1990 and 1992 in Mendoza after detention by members of the provincial police (see *Amnesty International Reports 1993* and *1994*). The provincial government agreed to the appointment of an independent commission to investigate the fate of the three men.

Dozens of killings by police in circumstances suggesting possible extrajudicial executions were reported and led to investigations in some cases. In February, Alejandro Mirabete was shot by two police officers in civilian clothes in Belgrano, a district of Buenos Aires. He died at Pirovano Hospital after nine days in a coma. The police officers had shot Alejandro Mirabete when he ran away after they requested his identification papers. Initial claims by police authorities that Alejandro Mirabete was armed and had been wounded while struggling with the police were contradicted by eye-witnesses, who subsequently reported that they had been harassed and threatened with death. A police officer was arrested and charged with manslaughter.

Throughout the year widespread demonstrations against government policies were forcibly dispersed by the police, who beat and ill-treated demonstrators. In

February, a student demonstration in the city of La Plata, Buenos Aires Province, was dispersed with rubber bullets and tear-gas by police officers, some of whom were reportedly wearing hoods and driving unmarked vehicles. Several journalists were beaten with truncheons, and Hernán Ramos, a television cameraman, was seriously injured when he was hit by rubber bullets fired at point-blank range by police officers in civilian clothes.

In February, Amnesty International wrote to the federal and provincial authorities urging a full and independent inquiry into the incidents in La Plata. In April, the provincial Security Secretary replied that 11 police officers had been temporarily suspended from duty and that a police investigation into the incident had been initiated. No findings were known to have been made public by the end of the year. In July, Amnesty International wrote to the Minister of Government and Justice of Corrientes Province asking for a prompt, thorough and independent investigation into the killing of Pedro Salvador Aguirre. The Minister replied that two police officers had been suspended from duty. He also stated that an investigation into the killing had been initiated, but no findings were known to have been made public by the end of the year.

Throughout the year, Amnesty International urged the government to clarify the fate of victims of past "disappearances". Amnesty International repeated its calls for the immediate and unconditional release of Fray Antonio Puigjane.

ARMENIA

Over 40 political prisoners faced criminal proceedings that appeared to fall short of international fair trial standards. Allegations of ill-treatment of detainees and army conscripts continued. At least four men were sentenced to death. There were no executions.

In April, the UN Committee against Torture considered Armenia's initial report under the provisions of the Convention against Torture and Other Cruel, Inhuman or Degrading Treatment or Punishment. The Committee welcomed the integration of prohibitions against torture into the new Constitution adopted in 1995, but recommended, among other things, that torture be mentioned in penal law as a crime in itself and be clearly defined, and that measures be taken to guarantee that no one could be expelled or extradited to other states where they were in danger of being tortured. It asked that reports of ill-treatment of detainees, denied by Armenian delegates at the session, be investigated and the results communicated to the Committee.

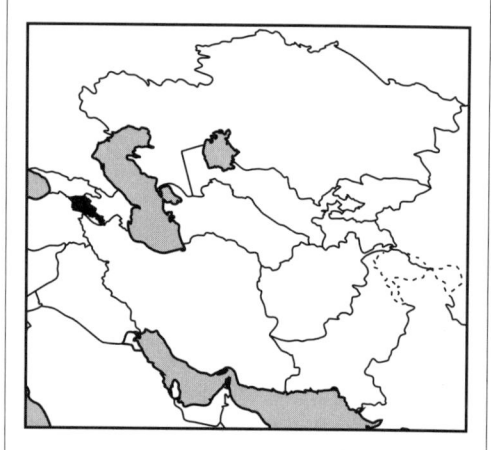

Presidential elections in September returned President Levon Ter-Petrosyan for a further term. The suspension of the opposition Armenian Revolutionary Federation (ARF) continued (see *Amnesty International Report 1996*) and they did not field a candidate. Opposition parties disputed the election results, and reports suggested that over 100 people were detained for short periods, and many beaten, after protests by supporters of opposition candidate Vazgen Manukian became violent.

The trial concluded in December of 11 men accused of crimes in connection with their alleged membership of a secret group within the ARF named *"Dro"* (see *Amnesty International Report 1996*). Three men – Arsen Artsruni, Armen Grigorian and Armenak Mujoyan – were sentenced to death, amid continuing allegations that proceedings fell short of international standards for fair trial.

Similar claims were made in the case of senior ARF member Vahan Ovanessian (see *Amnesty International Report 1996*) and 30 others, accused of attempting to stage an armed coup. At their trial, which opened in April, a number of defendants alleged that they had been forced to sign confessions and had been denied full and proper access to a defence lawyer of their choice, especially in pre-trial detention. Manvel Yeghiazarian alleged that he had been assaulted during his arrest in July 1995 and interrogated while still suffering from concussion, bruising and fractured ribs. Other defendants alleged that their families had been threatened. In spite of such allegations, no confessions in this or the so-called "*Dro*" case were known to have been ruled inadmissible.

Dozens of people were said to have been beaten following the disputed presidential elections. For example, four female staff from a non-governmental organization said that they were kicked and beaten with rifle butts by uniformed men who entered their office and confiscated equipment. A member of parliament who was present, Aramazd Zakarian, was reportedly attacked, detained, and again beaten at a police station. He was transferred to hospital two days later with injuries said to include facial cuts, a fractured skull and a broken rib.

Reports emerged that army conscripts had been beaten by, at the instigation of, or with the knowledge of senior or non-commissioned officers, and those responsible rarely brought to justice. Amayak Oganesyan was said to have been struck on the head with a spade and knifed in the ribs by a sergeant after joining a unit in June 1995. He was reportedly denied medical treatment for his injuries and threatened with further violence if he complained. After further beatings Amayak Oganesyan was transferred to hospital, where he was reportedly again beaten. He was eventually transferred to a civilian hospital and discharged from the army, diagnosed as suffering from lymphosarcoma. Amayak Oganesyan's father lodged a complaint about his son's treatment in August 1995, but by March 1996 had received no substantive response from the authorities.

At least four men were sentenced to death, making a total of around 17 men on death row at the end of the year. There were no executions, as President Ter-Petrosyan personally opposed the death penalty, but no death sentences were known to have been commuted.

Amnesty International urged the authorities to conduct a judicial review of the so-called "*Dro*" case, and called for all reports of ill-treatment to be investigated comprehensively and impartially, with the results made public and those responsible brought to justice. In May, the Minister of Defence denied any involvement by military personnel in attacks on religious minorities the previous year (see *Amnesty International Report 1996*) but did not indicate what substantive investigations, if any, had taken place into the allegations.

Amnesty International continued to call for all pending death sentences to be commuted.

AUSTRALIA

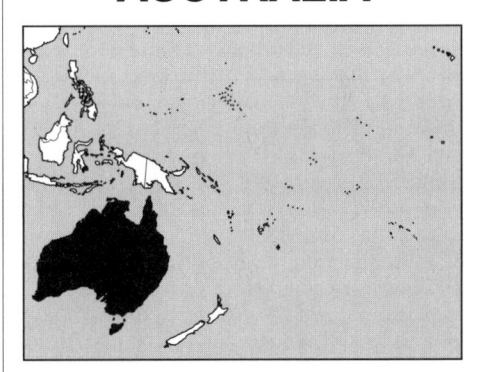

A political activist was imprisoned; he was a prisoner of conscience. Alarmingly high rates of death in custody of Aboriginal people raised concerns about ill-treatment. Australia's policy of mandatory detention of asylum-seekers who arrive without proper documentation continued to infringe the country's obligations under international law.

A National-Liberal Party coalition under Prime Minister John Howard replaced the Labor government in federal elections on 2 March. In negotiations on a "Framework Agreement" with the European Union the new administration refused to agree to a binding clause on the respect of "basic human rights as proclaimed in the Universal Declaration of Human Rights".

In January, the Tasmanian State Government announced plans to increase the maximum penalty for private homosexual acts between consenting male adults from 21 to 25 years' imprisonment. Following state elections in February, these plans were dropped. In June, the Tasmanian Legislative Council voted against a bill aimed at bringing the Criminal Code into line with Australia's international human rights obligations (see *Amnesty International Reports 1993* to *1996*). At the end of the year the High Court had not decided on a submission made by gay activists in November 1995 to determine whether the disputed sections of the Criminal Code subjected homosexuals to arbitrary interference with their privacy and were therefore inconsistent with federal laws protecting sexual privacy. Amnesty International remained concerned that the law allows for the imprisonment of prisoners of conscience, solely on the basis of their sexuality.

In February, political activist Albert Langer was sentenced to 10 weeks' imprisonment for breaching a court injunction ordering him to stop advocating an alternative but legally acceptable way of filling in federal election ballot papers. He was a prisoner of conscience. On 7 March a Federal Court reduced his sentence to three weeks' imprisonment. By the end of the year no decision had been made on a bill introduced in October to repeal section 329A of the Commonwealth Electoral Act 1918 which provides for up to six months' imprisonment for anyone who publicly encourages voters to fill in ballot papers other than in the way prescribed by Parliament.

Although they make up two per cent of the population, Aborigines accounted for more than 20 per cent of all deaths in custody. At least 17 Aborigines died in custody or during police attempts to detain them.

There were numerous reports of physical ill-treatment, harassment or intimidation of Aboriginal people by law enforcement officials. In the Northern Territory, an Aboriginal woman suffered treatment which Amnesty International considered to be cruel, inhuman or degrading in January when police held her in custody for more than 15 hours after she complained of having been raped by two men. Police justified her detention with their discovery of an outstanding warrant for her failure to appear in court on a minor charge. Despite instructions by senior police officers to treat her primarily as a complainant in a rape case rather than as a suspect, officers delayed her medical examination, which recorded internal injuries, and discouraged a counsellor sent by the doctor from seeing her. She was brought to court in the rain, locked in the uncovered cage of a police van. During an Ombudsman investigation into her complaints police officers reportedly justified her treatment on the grounds that she had been better cared for in the lock-up than she would have been in her "primitive" Aboriginal community home. The Speaker of Parliament ruled against publishing the Ombudsman's findings.

In February, charges were dropped against six police officers who took three Aboriginal boys, aged from 12 to 14, from central Brisbane to an industrial wasteland 14 kilometres outside the city to "reflect on their misdemeanours". Police had detained the boys in a shopping mall after 3am on 10 May 1994, but did not charge them or take them to a police station. The boys told a Criminal Justice Commission of Inquiry that the police officers had threatened them with torture and drowning in a nearby river and then left them to find their way home in the dark. During committal court hearings of the case against the officers, the boys were reportedly intimidated by the police officers' lawyers and were wrongly addressed as "defendants" by the magistrate.

There were developments in two cases from previous years involving the ill-treatment of non-Aboriginal Australians. In June, a parliamentary committee called for an independent judicial inquiry into the death of Stephen Wardle who died at East Perth Police Station in Western Australia within hours of his arrest in February 1988 (see *Amnesty International Report 1996*). The state government told Amnesty International in November that it would not initiate an inquiry into the case.

In October, two police officers in Perth, Western Australia, faced charges of perjury and assault after allegedly ill-treating Geoffrey Young and then claiming he had injured himself in a fall. Geoffrey Young alleged that in June 1994 police had twice punched him in the face and kneed him in the stomach after they learned that he had been to a nightclub frequented by homosexuals. In September, the state parliament voted against proposed legislation to prohibit discrimination on the grounds of sexuality.

Australia's policy of mandatory detention of asylum-seekers who arrive without proper documentation continued to infringe the country's obligations under international law. Since 1989 more than 800 children, among them more than 70 babies born in detention, had spent up to two years in detention. International standards stress that, in view of the hardship which it involves, the detention of asylum-seekers should normally be avoided and should only be used in specific, exceptional cases.

In March, the Department of Immigration refused to deliver letters sent by the Human Rights and Equal Opportunities Commission (HREOC) to asylum-seekers who the Commission said were held incommunicado at Port Hedland detention centre, informing them of an investigation into alleged violations of their human rights. In June, the Federal Court ordered the Department to pass letters from HREOC to the detainees. Two weeks later the government introduced a bill in Parliament to remove immigration officers' obligations to inform unauthorized asylum-seekers of their legal rights and to exclude them from independent scrutiny under human rights legislation governing HREOC and the federal Ombudsman. Asylum-seekers often do not know, and are not informed of, their rights under Australian and international law to interpreters, legal assistance and communication with refugee assistance agencies.

In February, Amnesty International called for the immediate and unconditional release of Albert Langer. In March, an Amnesty International delegation visited Australia to investigate violations of human rights in the context of the over-representation of indigenous Australians in the criminal justice system. Delegates met prisoners, victims of alleged human rights abuses and their relatives, and held discussions with local organizations, senior police, prison officers, government officials and ministers.

Amnesty International repeatedly expressed concern about Aboriginal deaths in custody and urged the federal and state governments to increase efforts to address the factors giving rise to abuses against Aborigines in prison and police custody. It called upon the new Federal Government to demonstrate its stated intention to make the issue of Aboriginal deaths in custody a priority and recommended that all investigations into deaths in custody should be based on the UN Principles on the Effective Prevention and Investigation of Extra-Legal, Arbitrary and Summary Executions.

In October, the organization released a report, *Australia: Too many open questions – Stephen Wardle's death in police custody*, expressing concern that Stephen Wardle had suffered from lack of care amounting to cruel, inhuman or degrading treatment, with fatal consequences. The organization also highlighted the lack of independence in previous investigations into his death and called for a thorough and fully independent judicial inquiry.

Amnesty International wrote to the Tasmanian Government and to each member of the Legislative Council calling for the Tasmanian Criminal Code to be brought into line with Australia's international human rights obligations. In February and July, the organization published two reports on its concerns about the Tasmanian legislation.

AUSTRIA

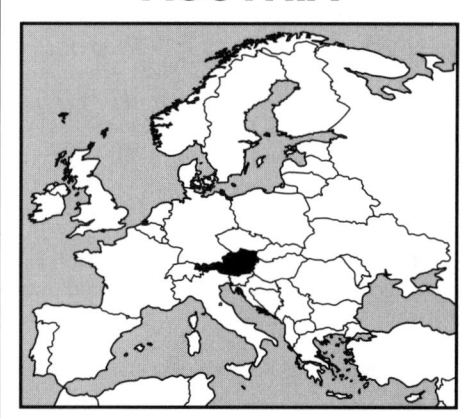

There were allegations of ill-treatment of detainees by police officers.

In October, the Government published the report of the European Committee for the Prevention of Torture and Inhuman or Degrading Treatment or Punishment on its visit to Austria in September and October 1994. The Committee reported receiving, during its visit, "a considerable number of allegations of ill-treatment of persons by the police", some of which "amounted to torture". The Committee repeated the main conclusion of its previous report, published in 1991, that people detained by the police are "at serious risk of being ill-treated", and made extensive recommendations to remedy the violations.

In December, parliament passed an amendment to the Law on Alternative Service increasing the length of alternative service from 11 to 12 months. The length of military service remained unchanged at eight months. The new legislation, effective from 1 January 1997, continued to impose time limits on the period within which conscientious objectors are able to submit applications for alternative service.

In October, Peter Zwiauer was charged with "failing to comply with a call-up order", an offence punishable by up to one year's imprisonment. His application to perform alternative service had been rejected in October 1994 because it had not been submitted within the required time period. His appeal against the decision was turned down and he was ordered to report for military duty in May.

There were allegations of ill-treatment of detainees by police officers. Sabine Geisberger alleged that following a drugs raid on her apartment in Vienna in November 1995, a police officer dragged her by the hair, threw her in a corner and repeatedly kicked her in the genitals. A medical examination the next day reported bruising to the rim of her pelvis, left thigh, and genitals.

In March, Peter Rosenauer alleged that officers at Lambach police station banged his head against a wall three times, kneed him in the testicles and struck him on the shoulders with a baton following his arrest at a demonstration. The detainee stated that he received no medical attention at the station, or at Wels Detention Centre to which he was transferred later the same day. A medical report stated that Peter Rosenauer had a bruised right eye, swelling on the back of his head and pain in the shoulders, wrists and right testicle. On the day of his release, Peter Rosenauer was charged with resisting arrest and assault. A court acquitted him of the charges in June.

In April, Violetta Jevremović alleged that she and her husband, Nicola – both Roma – were beaten by police officers who had come to their Vienna flat to arrest her husband. According to Violetta Jevremović, the officers beat her husband and turned on her when she asked them what he had done. Medical records showed that Violetta Jevremović suffered bruising of both elbows, the left wrist, right hand, right thigh and left ankle, and swelling on the head, upper jaw and upper lip. Both Violetta and Nicola Jevremović stated that police officers subjected them to racist verbal abuse and asked them when they were "finally going to go home". (They had been living in Austria for 16 years.) In September, Violetta Jevremović went on trial for resisting state authority and assault.

In February, three officers were charged with assaulting Emad Faltas, an Egyptian national, at a Vienna railway station in 1995 (see *Amnesty International Report 1996*). Emad Faltas suffered three broken ribs and cuts and bruises to his arms, stomach and face following his arrest in a case of mistaken identity. In April, a court acquitted the three officers. According to press reports, the trial judge ruled that "even schoolchildren have to be sometimes kept in check by their teachers". An appeal by the Public Prosecutor's Office against the judgment was rejected in November.

In October, Wolfgang Purtscheller's complaint of ill-treatment was rejected by the Vienna prosecuting authorities (see *Amnesty International Report 1996*).

In February, Amnesty International urged the authorities to investigate the alleged ill-treatment of Sabine Geisberger promptly and impartially, to bring to justice those found responsible and to provide compensation for her injuries. In July, the organization was informed that a judicial investigation into the allegations was in progress.

In June, Amnesty International expressed concern to the authorities that while the police complaint against Peter Rosenauer had been dealt with promptly, his own complaint appeared to have made little progress. In October, the organization was informed that Peter Rosenauer's complaint of police ill-treatment had been rejected because it "was not possible to clarify the exact origin of [his] injuries". In response to allegations that the detainee had been denied medical treatment, the authorities replied that the local physician whom the officers telephoned was on a house call and could only come in an emergency.

Also in June, Amnesty International called upon the authorities to investigate the alleged ill-treatment of Violetta Jevremović. In August, the organization was informed that her allegations of ill-treatment and racist verbal abuse were the subject of an "extensive investigation".

In November, Amnesty International informed the authorities that if Peter Zwiauer was imprisoned for refusing on conscientious grounds to perform military service, the organization would consider him to be a prisoner of conscience and would call for his immediate and unconditional release. Amnesty International also expressed concern that the draft proposal to amend the Law on Alternative Service took insufficient account of the fact that people's conscientiously held beliefs could change over time. In December, the Minister of Defence informed Amnesty International that Peter Zwiauer was obliged, under Austrian law, to complete his military service.

AZERBAIJAN

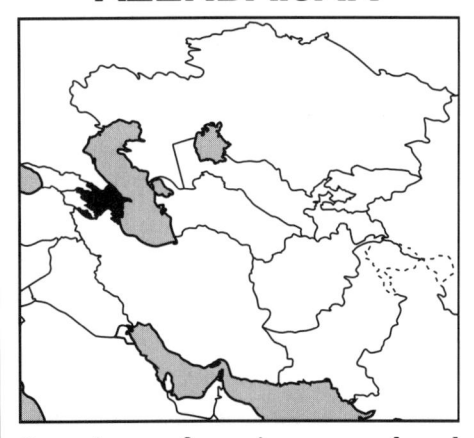

One prisoner of conscience was released on health grounds, and his trial postponed. Several possible prisoners of conscience were reportedly detained in connection with the Karabakh conflict solely because of their ethnic origin. Reports of torture and ill-treatment in detention continued, and at least one detainee was said to have died as a result of his injuries. The scope of the death penalty was restricted. At least 41 death sentences were passed. At least nine death sentences were commuted. No executions took place.

President Heydar Aliyev met the Armenian President in October as efforts continued to resolve the situation in the disputed Karabakh region (see *Amnesty International Report 1996*). In May, to mark the second anniversary of a cease-fire in the region, over 100 people, described variously by the different sides as either hostages or prisoners of war, were exchanged by Azerbaijan, Armenia and the self-proclaimed Nagorno-Karabakh Republic.

In August, Azerbaijan acceded to the UN Convention against Torture and Other Cruel, Inhuman or Degrading Treatment or Punishment.

Prisoner of conscience Tofiq Masim oglu Qasimov, a prominent opposition figure arrested in September 1995 on a charge of complicity in a failed coup attempt, was released pending trial in February, suffering from reactive psychosis. The charge related to a March 1995 rebellion by a special police unit in the capital, Baku (see *Amnesty International Report 1996*). The trial of Tofiq Qasimov and two co-defendants opened in May, but in June Tofiq Qasimov's case was separated from that of his two co-defendants on medical grounds. It had not resumed by the end of the year. In September, Tofiq Qasimov's co-defendants received long prison sentences.

Reports continued of the detention of civilians in connection with the Karabakh conflict solely because of their ethnic origin (see *Amnesty International Report 1996*). Asmik Ignoyan, an elderly Armenian, was reportedly detained in Nakhchivan in February, and held for three months after an unsuccessful attempt to exchange her for three Azerbaijanis captured during fighting. She was released during the May exchange of prisoners. At least six other civilians of Armenian origin were reportedly detained after the May exchange. They included a woman, Larissa Kirakosian; a 17-year-old girl, Irina Kachaturian; and a 15-year-old boy, Armen Nersisian. All were said to be detained at a special holding camp in Gobustan.

There was no news of 17-year-old Zaven Ramazyan, an ethnic Armenian reportedly held hostage since 1994 by a private individual with the knowledge of the authorities (see *Amnesty International Report 1996*).

Reports of torture and ill-treatment in pre-trial detention continued; at least one detainee was said to have died as a result of injuries inflicted by law enforcement officials. As in previous years, verification remained difficult owing to restrictions on access to detainees. Isa Yasar Tezel, a Turkish journalist detained in April, was allegedly beaten by police officers while held at the main police headquarters in Baku. He was released in June. Kenan Gurel, an Austrian businessman of Turkish origin charged with Tofiq Qasimov in connection with the unsuccessful March 1995 rebellion by police (see above), is said to have been beaten in January during pre-trial detention at investigation-isolation prison No. 1 (Bayilov). As a result of his injuries he suffered from severe headaches and insomnia. He was sentenced to 15 years' imprisonment in September.

Ilgar Samedov died from injuries sustained at investigation-isolation prison No. 3 (Shuvelyan) in Baku, where he had been taken following deportation from Ukraine on 14 June on a charge of drug possession. The following day, he was taken to the prison hospital at Beyukshore suffering from serious injuries to the head and body, and on 29 July he died there. Ilgar Samedov's father, Adil Samedov, had applied several times to the investigating official for permission to visit his son in hospital, but had been refused. It is alleged that the death certificate recorded the cause of death as a blow to the head by a blunt instrument, and that photographs taken in the morgue showed evidence of beatings. The authorities attributed his death to injuries sustained while attempting suicide.

An investigation was held into the 1995 death in custody of Rafiq Shaban oglu Ismayilov (see *Amnesty International Report 1996*). The district court found the acting head of the police department guilty in connection with Rafiq Shaban oglu Ismayilov's death, but he benefitted from an amnesty passed in May. However, following a Supreme Court ruling, the case was referred back for reinvestigation.

In May, parliament voted to reduce the number of crimes carrying a possible death sentence from 33 to 12, and to exempt from the death penalty men aged over 65.

Official statistics recorded that 41 death sentences were passed during the year. According to official statistics, five death sentences were commuted in April, and four ethnic Armenians under sentence of death were released under the exchange of prisoners negotiated in May. No executions took place; according to official sources the last execution took place in 1993.

Amnesty International sought further information on several possible prisoners of conscience, and continued to call on all parties to the Karabakh conflict to release anyone held hostage, or held solely because of their ethnic origin. The organization urged that all allegations of ill-treatment by law enforcement officials be investigated promptly and impartially, with the findings made public and any perpetrators identified brought to justice. It also welcomed moves to limit the scope of the death penalty, but throughout the year urged the authorities to commute all pending death sentences and to take steps towards complete abolition.

BAHAMAS

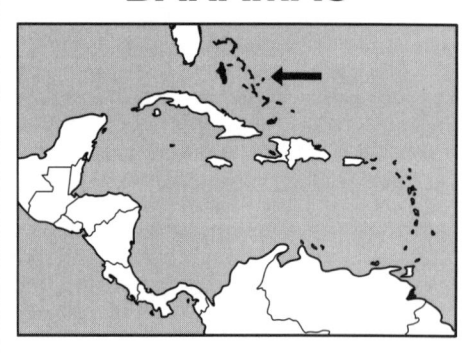

Two people were hanged in the first executions to be carried out for 12 years. At least seven new death sentences were imposed; four prisoners had their death sentences commuted. More than 30 prisoners remained under sentence of death.

Thomas Reckley, sentenced to death for murder in 1990, was hanged in March. He was the first person to be executed in the Bahamas since 1984. His execution went ahead despite a 1993 decision given in a Jamaican case by the Judicial Committee of the Privy Council (JCPC) in London, the final court of appeal for the Bahamas, that execution after a delay of more than five years would be presumed to constitute inhuman or degrading punishment and therefore grounds for commutation (see *Amnesty International Report 1996*). The JCPC turned down an application for a stay of execution on the day he was hanged, without giving reasons. Dwayne McKinney, sentenced to death in 1992, was also hanged in March. Warrants for the execution of five more prisoners were signed during the year but all received stays of execution pending further appeals.

At least seven people were sentenced to death for murder. Four prisoners had their death sentences commuted. In October, the JCPC commuted the death sentences on Dwight Henfield and Ricardo Farrington in a ruling likely to affect other capital cases in the Bahamas. Dwight Henfield's death sentence had been commuted by the Bahamas Supreme Court in 1995 (see *Amnesty International Report 1996*) but was reinstated by the Bahamas Court of Appeal in April 1996, following a governmental appeal. In October, the JCPC overturned the appeal court's ruling on the ground that to execute Dwight Henfield after nearly seven years' delay would constitute inhuman punishment.

The JCPC dealt with the case of Ricardo Farrington in the same decision. Although Ricardo Farrington had been on death row for only three years and four months, the JCPC ruled that a shorter time-span than the five years given in its 1993 decision was sufficient to render an execution in the Bahamas inhuman or degrading punishment. This was established on the basis that in the Jamaican case the JCPC had taken account of the time required to lodge an application with the UN Human Rights Committee under the (First) Optional Protocol to the International Covenant on Civil and Political Rights, a procedure not available to defendants in the Bahamas. The JCPC set a guideline of three and a half years within which the appeal process in the Bahamas would be expected to be completed, and held that Farrington, who was nearing this limit, should also benefit and have his death sentence commuted.

Two further prisoners had their death sentences commuted in July by prerogative of mercy.

More than 30 other prisoners remained on death row at the end of the year.

Following the execution of Thomas Reckley and Dwayne McKinney, Amnesty International wrote to the government expressing deep regret at this retrograde step. It called for all death sentences to be commuted.

BAHRAIN

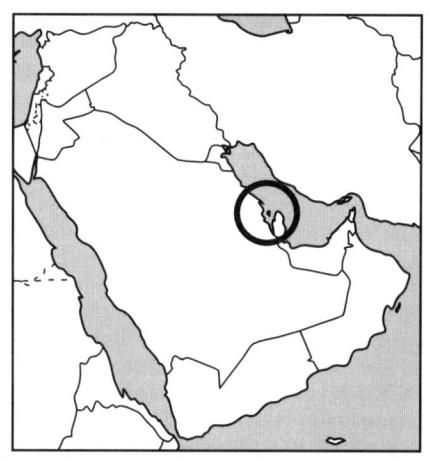

Several hundred people, among them prisoners of conscience, were arrested in connection with demonstrations demanding the restoration of democratic rights. Most were held incommunicado for months without charge or trial. At least 150 people received unfair trials before the State Security Court. Torture was widely reported, and an increasing number of women and children were ill-treated. At least one person died in custody, apparently as a result of torture, and four people were reportedly shot or beaten to death by members of the security forces. Three people were sentenced to death and one person was executed, the first execution in nearly 20 years. Bahraini nationals suspected of opposition political activities continued to be banned from entering the country.

The widespread protests and unrest which began in December 1994 (see *Amnesty International Reports 1995* and *1996*) continued throughout the year. Protesters called for the restoration of democratic rights and for the release of political prisoners. The security forces carried out mass arrests, particularly in the Shi'a Muslim districts of Bani Jamra, Sitra, Jidd Hafs and al-Sanabes, in response to demonstrations protesting against the government's closure of mosques where clerics had called for political and economic reforms. Many of the demonstrations were peaceful, but some escalated into violent clashes with police and security forces. There were at least five bomb attacks on restaurants, business centres and banks that left seven

Bangladeshi and four Bahraini nationals dead. In March, the Amir, Shaikh 'Issa bin Salman Al Khalifa, issued a decree referring all cases of suspected arson and other violent offences to the State Security Court, whose procedures violate internationally recognized standards for fair trial. In October a new *Majlis al-Shura* (Consultative Council), a government-appointed body with no legislative powers, was formed with 10 additional members. The Amir announced an extension of the Council's powers, but by the end of the year the Council's powers had not been widened.

An unknown number of prisoners of conscience were detained during the year. Shaikh 'Abd al-Amir al-Jamri, 'Abd al-Wahab Hussain 'Ali and Hassan Mushaim'a were detained in January along with five other prominent Shi'a Muslim religious and political leaders. Most had been arrested in 1995 and released without charge or trial after about six months (see *Amnesty International Report 1996*). The eight detainees remained held in solitary confinement at the end of the year with limited access to relatives, but no access to lawyers.

Three men who participated in the preparation of a petition in 1994 calling for democratic reforms (see *Amnesty International Report 1995*) were detained; all were prisoners of conscience. Ahmad al-Shamlan, a Sunni Muslim lawyer, was detained in February. He was acquitted by the State Security Court in May of possessing and distributing literature containing false information about the government and released. Ahmad Mansur 'Ali Ahmad was arrested in February and held incommunicado for two months, and Sa'id al-'Asboul, a civil engineer, was detained in April for eight days. Both were released without charge or trial and no reason was given for their arrest.

In March, 10 women were arrested, apparently because of their relationship to male political prisoners and their involvement in public protests. Among them was Muna Habib al-Sharrakhi whose husband, Muhammad Jamil 'Abd al-Amir al-Jamri, was sentenced in 1990 to 10 years' imprisonment for offences including membership of an unauthorized organization (see previous *Amnesty International Reports*). Also among them was Zahra Salman Hilal whose husband, Ahmad Mahdi Salman, was detained without charge or trial for 18 months and then charged in June with membership of *Hizbullah* (see below). The women, all prisoners of conscience, were released without charge or trial after having been held incommunicado for periods ranging from several days to 10 weeks.

Mahdi Rabi', a journalist, was sentenced in April to six months' imprisonment after an unfair trial before the State Security Court for possessing and distributing false information aimed at harming state security. He was a prisoner of conscience.

By the end of the year, over a thousand political detainees were believed to remain in prison. Most were administratively detained under a law which permits the Minister of the Interior to detain individuals for renewable periods of up to three years. The law allows for a petition challenging the detention every six months, but many people were held without official orders and were detained for several months without any judicial review.

More than 100 minors were reportedly detained for varying periods; most were arrested after demonstrations or school sit-in strikes. Many were released without charge after a few days; all were denied access to relatives or lawyers. Among them were Yasser 'Ammar, aged seven, who was arrested with Al-Sayyid Majed al-Sayyid Hassan and 'Ali Mahdi Mahmud, both aged eight, and held for several days for alleged insolence to police during demonstrations in January. At least 12 minors were tried in connection with the protests and convicted during the year, but no details on their cases were available by December.

Scores of people were arrested over several weeks, starting in June, in connection with an alleged Iranian-backed plot to overthrow the government. The authorities announced that the suspects were members of *Hizbullah*, an unauthorized group. Most were held incommunicado in Jaw and al-Qal'a prisons, and some were reportedly tortured during interrogation. By December, none of the estimated 55 detainees who remained held had been tried.

At least 150 people were tried and sentenced by the State Security Court following the Amir's decree in March referring all cases of suspected arson and other violent offences to this court. Defendants were denied access to lawyers until they appeared in court; tried *in camera*; had no right to appeal the sentence to a higher court; and were convicted mainly on the basis of their uncorroborated confessions. Such confessions were often reportedly extracted under torture. Custodial sentences ranged from three months to life imprisonment. In July, four defendants, Khalil Ibrahim Khamis, Qambar Khamis Qambar, 'Abdullah Ibrahim Khamis and Muhammad Ridha al-'Attar, were sentenced to life imprisonment for their part in a fire-bomb attack on a restaurant in Sitra in March which resulted in the death of seven Bangladeshi nationals. Another defendant in the same case was sentenced to 15 years' imprisonment and three others were sentenced to death (see below).

There were numerous reports of routine and systematic torture and ill-treatment to extract information from detainees during the initial weeks of their detention. Methods included severe and sustained beatings, suspension by the limbs, sexual abuse and threats of execution. Women and female students were increasingly subjected to cruel, inhuman and degrading treatment. In March, over 25 women, including high-school students, were arrested in connection with protests which erupted after the execution of 'Issa Ahmad Qambar (see below). They were held incommunicado for up to a month and ill-treated. Safiyya Yusuf 'Ali Darwish, Nawal 'Ali 'Abbadi and Ahlam 'Abd al-'Aziz Salman 'Ali, all aged 18, were reportedly stripped to their underclothes by female security officers and kept standing for up to four hours at a time during interrogation. Some of them were also deprived of sanitary facilities and food for more than 24 hours. There were also reports that the students were threatened with rape by male officers. All 25 women were released without charge or on bail. Safiyya Darwish and Nawal 'Abbadi were later tried and received suspended sentences of six months and one year respectively.

In August, one detainee died in custody, apparently as a result of torture. The body of al-Sayyid 'Ali al-Sayyid Amin al-'Alawi was handed over to his parents four days after his arrest, reportedly bearing marks of torture. A British forensic expert who examined photographs of the body found marks suggesting that he died suddenly while suspended face downwards with his wrists bound. No investigation into his death was known to have been carried out.

At least four people, including a woman, died after being shot or beaten by members of the security forces in what may have been extrajudicial executions. Fadhel 'Abbas Marhoun died in May after being shot by members of the security forces during a reportedly peaceful demonstration in the district of Karzakkan. Also in May, 'Abd al-Amir Hassan Rustum was knocked down by a police car chasing demonstrators in the village of al-Daih. Police then reportedly beat him with rifle butts and batons. He died of his injuries at home two days later. In July, Zahra Ibrahim Kadhem died after members of the security forces beat her and shot her with rubber bullets in the face and back at close range when she tried to prevent them from arresting her son in the village of Bani Jamra. No investigation was known to have been initiated into these deaths.

Three people were sentenced to death after unfair trials before the State Security Court in July. They were 'Ali Ahmad 'Abdullah al-'Usfur, a civil servant; Yusuf Hussain 'Abd al-Baqi, a teacher; and Ahmad Khalil Ibrahim al-Kattab, employed in an aluminium company. They had been convicted of carrying out a fire-bomb attack in March which killed seven people (see above). In October, the Court of Cassation, which under Bahraini law must review all death sentences, ruled that it had no jurisdiction over State Security Court sentences. At the end of the year, all three remained on death row.

One person, 'Issa Ahmad Qambar, who had been sentenced to death in 1995 (see *Amnesty International Report 1996*), was executed in March by firing-squad in the first execution in Bahrain in almost 20 years.

During the year, at least seven Bahraini nationals were banned from entering the country. They included non-violent opponents of the government who had been expelled or had left voluntarily and students who had spent time abroad, especially in Iranian theological centres. Yasser Mirza Ahmad 'Abdullah was kept with his wife at Bahrain airport for four days when he tried to return from Iran in February. They were forbidden to contact their families or friends in Bahrain and sent to the United Arab Emirates.

At least nine Bahraini nationals, among them political opponents who had fled the country, were arrested in June in the United Arab Emirates and forcibly returned to Bahrain (see **United Arab Emirates** entry). By December, three of them were known to remain held without charge or trial, including Ja'far Hassan Sahwan and Ghazi Radhi al-'Abed. Another Bahraini national, Jamil 'Abd al-Ghani 'Abdullah, was forcibly returned from Kuwait in May; he was detained for one week before being released without charge.

Amnesty International continued to appeal to the government to release prisoners of conscience, carry out independent investigations into reports of torture of detainees and into killings by members of the security forces, and ensure that detainees were brought before courts which comply fully with international standards for fair trial. Throughout the year, the organization repeated its proposal to send a delegation to Bahrain on a fact-finding visit and to hold talks with government officials. The government responded by rejecting Amnesty International's findings but failing to address specific cases or concerns. The government did not grant Amnesty International access to Bahrain.

In April, Amnesty International submitted information about its continuing concerns in Bahrain for UN review under a procedure established by Economic and Social Council Resolutions 728F/1503 for confidential consideration of communications about human rights violations.

In July, Amnesty International issued a report, *Bahrain: Women and children subject to increasing abuse*, which described a growing pattern of detention without charge or trial of women and children and the cruel and degrading treatment of women in detention. It also contained recommendations to the government. The government responded by challenging the credibility of the report, but did not address the organization's concerns.

BANGLADESH

Dozens of prisoners of conscience were detained after a series of opposition strikes and demonstrations. They were held without charge or trial for several weeks under special legislation. There were at least 13 deaths in custody reportedly as a result of torture. One woman was believed to have "disappeared". At least 14 people were reportedly extrajudicially executed by the police. Courts sentenced two people to death. No executions were reported.

February elections, boycotted by the major opposition parties, were won by the ruling Bangladesh National Party (BNP), led by the then Prime Minister Khaleda Zia, but with a low turnout.

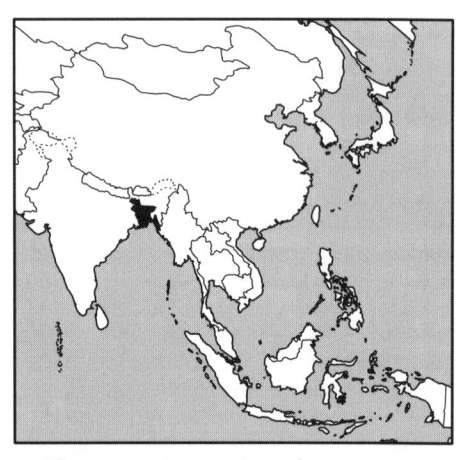

The campaign against the government continued, and was at times violent. Dozens of political activists were killed and hundreds more injured in clashes between opposition and government supporters. In March, the Constitution was amended to allow for parliamentary elections under caretaker governments. The BNP government resigned and a caretaker government was appointed. Fresh elections were called in June. The Awami League won the majority of seats and its leader, Sheikh Hasina Wajid, was sworn in as Prime Minister. Former Chief Justice Shahabuddin Ahmed was elected President.

In November, parliament repealed the Indemnity Ordinance, which had granted immunity from prosecution for those involved in the assassination of the first President of Bangladesh, Sheikh Mujibur Rahman, and members of his family, in a military coup in August 1975. Several former army officers and a former state minister were arrested in connection with the killings.

In October, the government announced the establishment of a National Committee on the Chittagong Hill Tracts to find a lasting solution to the conflict there, but no major breakthrough in talks between the government and tribal representatives was reported. A periodically extended cease-fire was broken on several occasions throughout the year.

Dozens of prisoners of conscience were among hundreds of people detained under the Special Powers Act, which allowed for detention without charge or trial for an indefinite period. Senior Awami League politician Begum Motia Chowdhury was arrested with five opposition activists in February following a three-day strike. She was detained for several weeks until the High Court declared her detention unlawful.

The charges against Taslima Nasrin, the feminist writer charged with outraging religious sentiments, were not dropped (see *Amnesty International Reports 1995* and *1996*). As in previous years, court hearings were adjourned.

Tens of thousands of people were arrested throughout the year during a police operation to recover illegally held weapons. Many were not informed of the grounds for their detention, and most were released uncharged after days or weeks as the police could not substantiate charges against them. Some of those arrested for alleged possession of firearms were tortured.

At least 13 prisoners reportedly died in custody following torture. Hundreds more were subjected to beatings. In October, a man died reportedly after being beaten by police in a village in Sylhet district. He and a number of others had protested against the arrest of a fellow villager. Two police officers involved in the beating were suspended, but no criminal charges were brought against them.

Police frequently beat anti-government demonstrators, and journalists covering demonstrations. In January, police reportedly beat scores of students during a raid on the Jagannath Hall student residence at Dhaka University. In February, police punched and kicked several journalists who attempted to photograph police shootings and beatings.

At least seven incidents of rape in custody by security forces were reported. In October, four policemen reportedly raped a 17-year-old girl in a police station in Chittagong while she was held in custody overnight. They were arrested after a medical report established evidence consistent with rape, and detained while the police reportedly initiated an investigation. The trial of three police officers charged with the rape and murder of 14-year-old Yasmin Akhter in 1995 (see *Amnesty International Report 1996*) began in October but had not concluded by the end of the year.

Kalpana Chakma, a tribal women's rights activist, reportedly "disappeared" in the Chittagong Hill Tracts in June. Security personnel reportedly took her from her home. A government-appointed commission of inquiry had not reported its findings by the end of the year and her whereabouts remained unknown.

At least 14 people were believed to have been extrajudicially executed. Ten were killed in March when the paramilitary Bangladesh Rifles opened fire on anti-government demonstrators in several districts. No official inquiry to establish responsibility for these killings was carried out. Four people were killed in August when police in Bogra opened fire on crowds during two days of unrest between government and opposition supporters. An inquiry commission was set up, but had not reported its findings by the end of the year.

At least two people were sentenced to death, both of them for murder. No executions were reported.

The armed opposition group *Shanti Bahini* (Peace Force) reportedly abducted and killed 28 woodcutters in Rangamati district in September following a dispute over tariffs demanded by *Shanti Bahini* on the collection of timber.

Amnesty International appealed to the successive governments of Bangladesh to release all prisoners of conscience and to drop the charges against Taslima Nasrin. It also called for the fate and whereabouts of Kalpana Chakma to be established and for the institution of impartial and independent inquiries into all reports of human rights violations. In February, Amnesty International issued a report, *Bangladesh: Beating and arbitrary detention of religious minority students*. No substantive response was received from the authorities during the year.

BELARUS

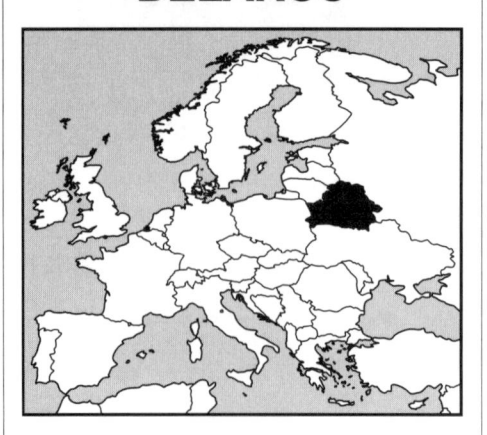

Two prisoners of conscience were detained in April. There were reports of ill-treatment of demonstrators by law enforcement officials. At least 24 people were executed.

In April, President Alyaksandr Lukashenka signed an agreement on closer integration with Russia which provoked a wave of protests and demonstrations. In the context of growing political unrest, the President held a referendum in November on amending the Constitution in an attempt to increase his constitutional powers over parliament, which he won overwhelmingly. In response to a question put forward during the referendum, only 17.9 per cent of people voted in favour of abolishing the death penalty.

Vyacheslav Sivchyk, secretary of the opposition Belorussian Popular Front (BNF), was arrested on 26 April, with 11 other BNF activists, during a police raid on the organization's headquarters. Yury Khadyka, another prominent BNF member, was arrested on the following day near his home. The arrests followed a rally in Minsk on 26 April, organized to commemorate the 10th anniversary of the Chernobyl nuclear disaster, during which participants denounced the President's policy of closer ties with Russia and a crack-down on trade unions and the opposition press. Most were released after a few days, but Yury Khadyka and Vyacheslav Sivchyk were charged with "instigating mass disorder", for allegedly having organized the rally. If convicted, they face up to three years' imprisonment. They were released pending trial in May.

There were reports of alleged ill-treatment of demonstrators by law enforcement officials. Regular police and special police forces reportedly beat and otherwise ill-treated a number of participants in the 26 April rally. On 30 May, police clashed with nearly 3,000 demonstrators who picketed the presidential administration building in Minsk. According to witnesses, police beat protesters who were demanding, among other things, that legal proceedings against Vyacheslav Sivchyk and Yury Khadyka be dropped. Reports stated that up to 84 protesters were detained for up to 15 days. About 50 of the demonstrators were hospitalized for injuries allegedly inflicted by the police during the clash. Some 20 people were reportedly injured by police in a similar incident on 17 November when police wielding riot shields beat demonstrators with truncheons and arrested more than 10 people during a peaceful demonstration against the President called the "March of Silence".

At least 24 people were executed during the year, according to official statistics. They included Igor Mirenkov, who had been sentenced to death in August 1995 for premeditated aggravated murder (see *Amnesty International Report 1996*). He was executed in June after the President rejected a request for clemency. New official statistics on the use of the death penalty, released in September, stated that 20 people had been sentenced to death in 1990, 40 in 1994, and 46 in 1995. In January, the government informed Amnesty International that Igor Yurevich Kopytin's death sentence had been overturned by the Supreme Court and substituted by 15 years' imprisonment (see *Amnesty International Report 1996*).

Amnesty International called for the immediate and unconditional release of prisoners of conscience Vyacheslav Sivchyk and Yury Khadyka. The organization also called on the government to investigate allegations of ill-treatment by law enforcement officials. It also called on the President to commute all pending death sentences and continued to urge total abolition of the death penalty.

BELIZE

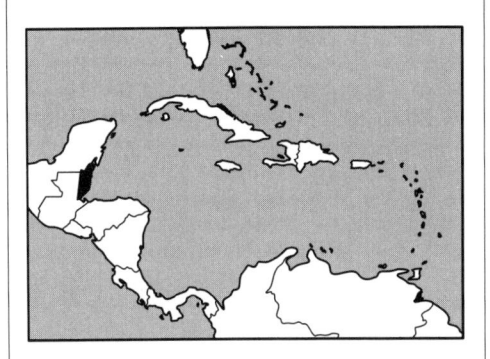

One person was sentenced to death and seven others remained under sentence of death. Three people had their convictions or death sentences quashed on appeal. No executions were carried out.

In June, Belize acceded to the International Covenant on Civil and Political Rights.

Dean Tillett was sentenced to death for murder in May. His appeal to the Belize Court of Appeal was heard in October and the Court's decision was pending at the end of the year.

Seven others sentenced in previous years remained on death row. They included Rupert Burke, who was convicted of murder in 1995, Adolph Harris and Marco Tulio Ibañez (see *Amnesty International Report 1996*). At the end of the year, Rupert Burke was awaiting the outcome of his appeal to the Belize Court of Appeals. Adolph Harris' petition for leave to appeal to the Judicial Committee of the Privy Council (JCPC) in London, the final court of appeal for Belize, was dismissed in November. A constitutional appeal on his behalf was pending in the Supreme Court at the end of the year. Marco Tulio Ibañez' appeal to the JCPC was also pending at the end of the year.

Another death-row prisoner, Wilfred Lauriano, was awaiting the outcome of his petition to the JCPC for leave to file a constitutional motion at the end of the year. In another capital case from Belize the JCPC ruled that the Supreme Court, in its 1995 ruling on Wilfred Lauriano's appeal, had incorrectly attempted to limit the JCPC's jurisdiction in granting leave to appeal on capital cases (see *Amnesty International Report 1996*).

Pasqual Bull, who received a last-minute stay of execution in August 1995 (see *Amnesty International Report 1996*), was granted leave to appeal to the JCPC in March; the full hearing of his appeal was pending at the end of the year. Herman Mejia, who had also received a last-minute stay of execution in August 1995 (see *Amnesty International Report 1996*), was refused leave to appeal to the JCPC in March. Nicolás Antonio Guevara's appeal to the JCPC was dismissed in February.

In March, a constitutional appeal on behalf of Pasqual Bull, Herman Mejia and Nicolás Antonio Guevara was dismissed by the Chief Justice in the Supreme Court of Belize on the grounds that it was of a "frivolous and vexatious nature". The Belize Court of Appeal quashed the Supreme Court's ruling in June and remitted the applications to the Supreme Court for a full hearing of the appeal. However, in July the Chief Justice ruled that the Court of Appeal had acted in error in sending the case back to the Supreme Court. In October, the Court of Appeal overruled this decision and sent the case back to the Supreme Court. The hearing on the merits of the constitutional appeal was pending in the Supreme Court at the end of the year. The grounds for this appeal included a claim that the conditions under which death-row prisoners were kept constituted inhuman and degrading treatment or punishment and as such were a violation of the Constitution. Conditions in Hattieville Rehabilitation Centre, where all prisoners under sentence of death were held, were reported to be insanitary and grossly overcrowded.

Early in the year, the Belize Court of Appeal overturned the death sentence on Anthony Bowen (but not the conviction for murder) as he had been under the age of 18 at the time of the offence (see *Amnesty International Report 1996*).

In March, the JCPC allowed an appeal on behalf of Alfred Codrington (see *Amnesty International Report 1995*) and referred the case back to the Court of Appeal. The Court of Appeal, after examining his claim that his trial counsel was ineffective, ordered a retrial. At the retrial Alfred Codrington was convicted of manslaughter and sentenced to 20 years' imprisonment. The JCPC also allowed an appeal by Lindsberth Logan, quashing his murder conviction and substituting one of manslaughter, and referred the case back to the Court of Appeal. The Court imposed a 20-year prison sentence.

In March, the JCPC allowed an appeal by Ellis Taibo (see *Amnesty International Report 1996*), ruling that it was doubtful there had been enough evidence for a murder conviction at the original trial and ordering the Court of Appeal either to retry Ellis Taibo or to release him. He was released in May 1996 after nearly four years on death row.

BHUTAN

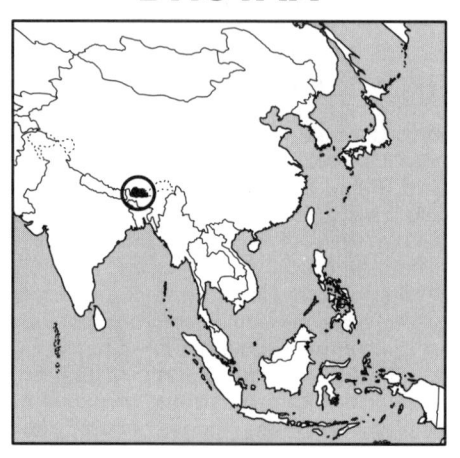

A prisoner of conscience spent his seventh year in prison. Fifty people, most of whom were of Bhutanese origin living in refugee camps in eastern Nepal, were briefly detained by police while attempting to cross the border at Phuntsholing.

In April, a seventh round of talks between the Governments of Bhutan and Nepal took place in Kathmandu on the fate of more than 90,000 people living in refugee camps in eastern Nepal, most of whom were Nepali-speaking people from southern Bhutan. The process of joint verification of the status of the people in the camps agreed by the Governments of Bhutan and Nepal in April 1994 was further delayed (see *Amnesty International Reports 1994* and *1995*). By the end of September, over 100 more people had left southern Bhutan to seek asylum in Nepal (see *Amnesty International Reports 1995* and *1996*). Hundreds of camp residents participated in peaceful marches and a cycle rally in northeast India aimed at publicizing their plight. Hundreds of them were detained by the Indian authorities but later released (see **India** entry). Several incidents of armed robbery in southern Bhutan were attributed by the government to people returning to Bhutan from the refugee camps in Nepal.

Delegates of the UN Working Group on Arbitrary Detention visited the country in April and May to check, among other things, on the implementation of the 15 recommendations made after their 1994 visit (see *Amnesty International Report 1995*). The Working Group reported that its recommendations had generally been implemented but urged that a new Code of Criminal Procedure should be adopted and that the institution of the *jabmi* (a person conversant with the law) be strengthened.

Tek Nath Rizal, a prisoner of conscience, spent his seventh year in prison (see *Amnesty International Report 1994*). The UN Working Group had earlier decided that his detention was not arbitrary. After visiting the country, the Working Group declared that he had been arbitrarily detained for the period from his arrest in November 1989 until his appearance before the court in December 1992, but added that his detention since that time was not arbitrary.

Fifty people, most of whom were of Bhutanese origin living in refugee camps in eastern Nepal, were arrested in August by the Royal Bhutan Police when they tried to cross the border from India to Bhutan at Phuntsholing. They were detained overnight at a local administrative office in Phuntsholing and then taken to the Indian national highway in Jalpaiguri district where they were released, some by being pushed out of moving vehicles.

In July, the government reported that 89 people had been imprisoned under the National Security Act. When the UN Working Group visited Bhutan in May, it was reported that 153 political prisoners were serving sentences at Chemgang detention camp, while 52 were detained at Thimphu prison.

Amnesty International continued to appeal for the release of Tek Nath Rizal and for fair trials for political prisoners.

BOLIVIA

A prisoner of conscience was detained for 42 days. Trade unionists and peasant leaders were repeatedly detained for short periods. There were reports of ill-treatment by police during arrest and in custody. A military conscript received disciplinary punishments amounting to torture. Investigations into human rights violations against political prisoners documented in previous years remained unresolved.

Throughout the year there were widespread strikes and protests, some of them violent, against the economic and agrarian reforms of the government of President Gonzalo Sánchez de Lozada. Scores of peasants and trade unionists were arrested in La Paz, the capital, and Cochabamba and Potosí Departments during and after these demonstrations. At least 13 people were killed in disputed circumstances during confrontations with the security forces. They included a police colonel and nine miners and peasants killed during mine occupations in Potosí Department in December.

Manuel Morales Dávila, a 69-year-old lawyer and president of the *Comité de Defensa del Patrimonio Nacional*, National Heritage Committee, was arrested in March in La Paz after he publicly criticized President Sánchez de Lozada's policy of "capitalization" – which some see as privatization – of *Yacimientos Petrolíferos Fiscales Bolivianos* (YPFB), the state-owned oil and gas company. He was taken to San Pedro prison, held incommunicado for five days and charged with sedition and contempt of presidential authority. He was released on bail after 42 days in detention. He was a prisoner of conscience.

Trade union leaders were repeatedly detained, in most cases briefly, in what appeared to be a pattern of harassment to exert pressure on trade unions to support government proposals. In April, four peasant leaders, including Alejo Véliz and Luis García, Secretary General and Press Officer, respectively, of the *Federación Sindical Única de Trabajadores Campesinos de Cochabamba*, Cochabamba Peasant Workers' Trade Union, were arrested without warrant in Cochabamba one day before a demonstration was due to take place during a Summit of Ministers from the European Union and "Rio Group" of Latin American countries. Their place of detention was unknown for two days. Three of the men were subsequently released without charge. Alejo Véliz was charged with incitement to commit crimes. He was released in May, but legal proceedings against him were continuing at the end of the year.

There were several complaints of ill-treatment of people by the police during arrest and in custody. In April, 78 people were arrested by police in La Paz after a demonstration in protest against the "capitalization" of the YPFB and in support of demands for salary increases by the *Central Obrera Boliviana*, Bolivian Labour Confederation. The arrests were reportedly carried out violently and without warrants. Two men, Mario Andrade Peñaloza and Adrián Monzón, sustained serious head injuries. The 78 were held for several days at the *Criminalística*, the police centre for criminal investigations, in one cell 24 metres square. Sanitary conditions were poor and the detainees had to take turns sitting and sleeping. All were later released without charge.

There were reports that peasants were ill-treated during police operations. For example, in September, Modesto Peña Jiménez reportedly required hospital treatment for injuries sustained during his arrest by members of the *Unidad Móvil para el Patrullaje Rural*, Mobile Rural Patrol Unit, in the locality of Chipiriri, Cochabamba Department, during a police operation to forcibly eradicate coca-leaf crops. The same month, seven peasants publicly complained that they had been ill-treated by the police during their arrest in La Paz following a police raid on the neighbourhood of Villa Fátima. One of them, Eulogio Mamani Tapia, was reportedly taken to the *Hospital de Clínicas*, a state-run teaching hospital in La Paz, to be treated for his injuries.

A military conscript received disciplinary punishments amounting to torture. In September, Wilson Pucho Alí, a conscript in the Bolivian Air Force, was reportedly tortured by three officers and two civilians at the El Alto Air Force barracks because he had misplaced his rifle. According to public complaints made by the *Asamblea Permanente de los Derechos Humanos de la distrital de El Alto*, El Alto Permanent Assembly for Human Rights – a local non-governmental organization – Wilson Pucho Alí was kept in chains for a week and tortured by being hung upside-down, immersed in water, beaten with a stick and subjected to mock executions. He was reportedly taken to the Military Hospital with extensive bruising and fractured ankles.

The authorities failed to clarify numerous cases of human rights violations committed between 1989 and 1993 against political prisoners accused of participating in armed uprisings (see previous *Amnesty International Reports*). The alleged violations, which included extrajudicial executions, torture, ill-treatment and denial of defence counsel, had been extensively documented by the Human Rights Commission of the Chamber of Deputies (see *Amnesty International Report 1996*).

Amnesty International appealed to the authorities to investigate all reported cases of human rights violations and to bring to justice those responsible. Amnesty International delegates visited Bolivia in April and presented the organization's concerns to national and departmental authorities. The organization requested information about any investigations initiated into the deaths in previous years of at least three conscripts in army barracks in Santa Cruz Department and called for the immediate and unconditional release of Manuel Morales Dávila.

In a report published in September, *Bolivia: Awaiting justice – torture, extrajudicial executions and legal proceedings*, Amnesty International reiterated its concern about human rights violations against political prisoners in previous years and at the failure of the authorities to adopt the findings and recommendations of the investigation undertaken by the Human Rights Commission of the Chamber of Deputies. The organization urged the government to ratify the UN Convention against Torture and Other Cruel, Inhuman or Degrading Treatment or Punishment, and the Inter-American Convention to Prevent and Punish Torture.

BOSNIA-HERZEGOVINA

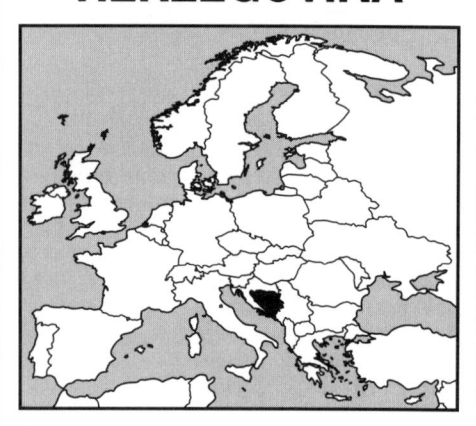

Dozens of prisoners of conscience and possible prisoners of conscience were detained in the Federation of Bosnia and Herzegovina (the Federation) and the Republika Srpska (RS) for weeks or months on account of their nationality; some were hostages. Some detainees were tortured or ill-treated. Displaced people and refugees were deliberately prevented, because of their nationality, from visiting or returning to their homes by violent attacks and the deliberate damage to, or destruction of, hundreds of houses. Members of minorities, particularly Muslims, were forcibly expelled from their home areas by violent attacks or threats. A small number of people "disappeared". At least one death sentence was passed.

As a result of the implementation of a comprehensive cease-fire in October 1995, and the signing of the General Framework Agreement on Peace (the peace agreement) in December 1995, there was no armed conflict during the year. The military peace-keeping force, Implementation Force (IFOR), led by the North Atlantic Treaty Organization (NATO), was deployed quickly. However, the civilian organizations and functionaries mandated to oversee the implementation of the civilian aspects of the peace agreement – such as the Organization for Security and Co-operation in Europe (OSCE), the High Representative, Carl Bildt, and the UN International Police Task Force (IPTF) – which were all involved in human rights monitoring, lacked resources and were slow to deploy their missions. In December, IFOR was replaced by a smaller NATO-led peacekeeping force, the Stabilization Force.

Tension remained high between the authorities in the two entities created under the peace agreement, the Bosniac- or Muslim-Croat Federation and the RS. There was also significant tension between the Muslim and Croat authorities within the Federation.

Despite the parties' general compliance with the military aspects of the peace agreement, little progress was made towards implementing those aspects relating to human rights, such as freedom of movement and the right of displaced people and refugees to return to their homes. Few people were able to return, and most people moving outside areas where their nationality was in the majority were only in transit. The UN High Commissioner for Refugees (UNHCR) believed that up to 250,000 refugees or displaced persons returned during the year. However, most of these people returned to areas where they belonged to the majority nationality.

Amnesty laws applying to people who had "served in enemy armies" or had committed other crimes connected with the war, excluding war crimes, were passed in the Federation in February and in the RS in June. In the Federation, desertion and draft evasion were included in the amnesty law, but both acts were specifically excluded from the law in the RS.

The International Criminal Tribunal for the former Yugoslavia (the Tribunal) issued further indictments for crimes committed in Bosnia-Herzegovina. These included an indictment against three Bosnian Muslims and one Bosnian Croat for crimes perpetrated against Bosnian Serbs in a detention camp in 1992. However, the vast majority of indictments were issued against Bosnian Serbs for crimes perpetrated against Bosnian Muslims.

In December, in the Tribunal's first conviction, Dražen Erdemović, a Bosnian Croat and former member of the Bosnian Serb Army, was sentenced to 10 years' imprisonment. He had pleaded guilty to participating in the shooting of an estimated 1,200 Bosnian Muslim men captured near Srebrenica in July 1995.

The Bosnian Serb and Bosnian Croat authorities, and the Governments of Croatia and the Federal Republic of Yugoslavia (FRY) failed to arrest people indicted by the Tribunal in areas under their control (see **Croatia** and **Yugoslavia** entries). Governments contributing to IFOR also failed to ensure that their troops fulfilled their obligations under international law to search for and detain individuals suspected of grave breaches of international humanitarian law. Despite an expressed NATO policy that IFOR troops would at least detain people suspected of war crimes if they encountered them, on many reported occasions IFOR troops encountered people indicted by the Tribunal, but did not arrest them. On other occasions they deliberately avoided such encounters. However, several people indicted for, or suspected of, war crimes were arrested by the Bosnian authorities in the Federation and by the governments of Germany and Austria and transferred to the Tribunal. The FRY transferred one suspect, Dražen Erdemović. Despite reports that others were at large in Croatia, the authorities only arrested Zlatko Aleksovski, who had been indicted for crimes against Bosnian Muslims in 1993. He had not been transferred to the Tribunal by the end of the year. Only seven of those indicted for crimes committed in Bosnia-Herzegovina were in the custody of the Tribunal at the end of the year. In October, the FRY authorities arrested and charged one man in connection with the abduction of around 21 people from a train at Štrpci in 1993 (see *Amnesty International Report 1994*).

In September, national elections were held under the new Constitution. Municipal elections scheduled for the same day were postponed to 1997 by the OSCE amid evidence of massive manipulation of registration procedures for absentee voters, which was mainly attributed to the *Srpska Demokratska Stranka* (SDS), Serbian Democratic Party. Numerous incidents of violence in all areas against opposition candidates and their supporters were reported during the run-up to the elections, and the opposition in all areas complained of other forms of discrimination such as lack of access to the media. The main nationalist parties, the SDS, the *Hrvatska Demokratska Zajednica*, Croatian Democratic Union, and the Muslim *Stranka Demokratske Akcije*, Party of Democratic Action, retained power in the elections. The former President of the Republic, Alija Izetbegović, was elected the first chairperson of the collective presidency under the new Constitution.

A range of human rights violations occurred in most areas of the country throughout the year. Dozens of prisoners were held by all sides without charge or trial; many were possible prisoners of conscience. Most were held because of their nationality and were detained as they travelled through an area controlled by another nationality. The prisoners were frequently offered for exchange or exchanged, making them hostages, and their detention was a deterrent to those seeking to exercise the freedom of movement set out in the peace agreement. The authorities frequently failed to notify international organizations, particularly the IPTF, about detainees and denied access to some of them, in violation of the obligations undertaken by the parties to the peace agreement.

Among the detainees were Father Tomislav Matanović, a Bosnian Croat Roman Catholic priest, and his elderly parents, who had been detained by police in August 1995. The RS authorities acknowledged that they were detained, but failed to give reasons for their detention, the place of their detention or to ensure their release. Others detained during the year included a Bosnian Croat man who was arrested by the RS authorities near Priboj in February. He was reportedly made to sign a blank piece of paper which was used for a false confession to war crimes and he was then offered for exchange. Both men were released in December. In July and September, four Bosnian Serb men went "missing" on roads near Sarajevo in two separate incidents. The Federation authorities denied knowledge of the detention of the four men until October, when international organizations found them imprisoned in Sarajevo. The authorities admitted that they had been detained and they were released shortly afterwards. In June, four Bosnian Serbs were detained by Bosnian Croat police close to the Inter-Entity Boundary Line near Glamoč, in the Federation, where they had driven to inspect their former homes or places of work. The men were taken to a police station in Glamoč but were concealed for 11 days from IPTF officers and IFOR soldiers who sought to visit them. International agencies were only able to gain access to them after they had been transferred to a prison in Mostar. The men were released in a prisoner exchange in July. In all these cases, the available information indicated that the detainees were prisoners of conscience.

Some detainees were tortured or ill-treated in detention. Seven Bosnian Muslim men who were detained near Zvornik, in the RS, in May were reportedly beaten severely in detention in Bijeljina in order to extract confessions. In August, a Bosnian Muslim, Hasan Kovačević, died in custody in a police station in Banja Luka. According to the post-mortem examination, he had sustained fractured ribs, most likely as a result of beatings he received in custody.

Displaced people trying to visit or return to their homes, particularly Muslims to the RS or to Bosnian Croat-controlled areas of the Federation, were frequently obstructed and physically attacked on many occasions. For example, in late April, when a large group of Muslims attempted to visit their village near Doboj in the RS, local Serbs attacked them, but the RS police who were present did little to restrain the attackers. Two Muslims were killed and others injured when they ran into a minefield while attempting to flee. Many other attempts to return, including some by Bosnian Serbs who wished to visit their homes in Bosnian Croat-controlled areas of the Federation, were obstructed by road-blocks, demonstrations or police officers who refused to guarantee people's safety.

Although some of the pilot projects sponsored by UNHCR to ensure the return of Muslims and Croats within the Federation succeeded, key projects such as the return of 200 Muslims to the Bosnian Croat-controlled town of Stolac failed as a result of obstruction and violence by the Bosnian Croat authorities.

In October and November, actions to prevent the return of displaced people included the widespread destruction, as punishment because of their nationality, of the houses which people, mostly Muslims, were to repair and wished to return to. For example, on one day in October, 94 Muslim-owned houses were destroyed in the RS. All were reportedly on a list of houses which displaced people wished to visit which had been passed to the authorities by UNHCR. Bosnian Serbs' and Muslims' houses in several Bosnian Croat-controlled towns in the Federation were also destroyed. Some Croats' houses in Muslim-controlled areas of the Federation, such as Bugojno, were also reportedly damaged.

Some 60,000 Serbs fled the suburbs of Sarajevo before these were transferred from the RS to the Federation between January and March under the peace agreement. Most fled because of fears for their safety, caused by propaganda from the RS authorities and the deliberate harassment of those unwilling to leave by gangs of Bosnian Serbs. Following the transfer, Serbs who remained were subject to harassment, including beatings and arson, by Bosnian Muslims. The Federation police failed to provide adequate protection for them in the period immediately following the transfer.

There were also frequent reports of forcible expulsions of members of the minorities who remained in other areas. Between April and June, there were frequent reports of violent attacks by armed men against Muslims in their homes in villages near Teslić in the RS. At least 94 people left for the Federation, apparently as a direct result of harassment. From September, UNHCR organized the evacuation of at least 100 Muslims from the Vrbanje suburb of Banja Luka after RS police failed to protect them from violent attempts to evict them from their homes.

There were frequent reports of Muslims and Serbs being evicted from their homes in Bosnian Croat-controlled west Mostar. The victims were forced to seek shelter in Muslim-controlled east Mostar.

Some information came to light on the fate of the "missing" and "disappeared" during the year, mainly as a result of exhumations of mass graves, new witness testimony and tracing operations by the International Committee of the Red Cross. Around 6,000 people, mainly Bosnian Muslim men, were still reported "missing" from Srebrenica (see *Amnesty International Report 1996*). The exhumations and new testimony from Dražen Erdemović (see above) reinforced fears that most of them had been deliberately and arbitrarily killed.

A small number of new "disappearances" occurred during the year. For example, at least two Bosnian Serb prisoners of war who were seen in detention in Zenica by fellow prisoners in January remained unaccounted for after the release of their fellow prisoners; the Federation authorities had offered no information on their whereabouts by the end of the year.

At least one death sentence was passed during the year, despite a commitment by Bosnia-Herzegovina under the peace agreement to implement Protocol No. 6 to the European Convention for the Protection of Human Rights and Fundamental Freedoms concerning the abolition of the death penalty. In March, Ivan Stjepanović, a Bosnian Croat, was convicted in a court in Banja Luka in the RS of involvement in the killing of eight Bosnian Serb civilians in 1992. He was later released in a prisoner exchange.

Amnesty International addressed the authorities, governments and organizations involved in the implementation of the peace agreement on a variety of concerns during the year. In March and April, the organization appealed to governments contributing to IFOR to fulfil their obligations under international law to search for and arrest individuals suspected of war crimes. In June, Amnesty International issued a report, *Bosnia-Herzegovina: The international community's responsibility to ensure human rights*, which made extensive recommendations, including one for a comprehensive human rights action plan.

BOTSWANA

There were continued reports of ill-treatment and torture by police. A paramilitary police officer was convicted of the 1995 killing of a demonstrator. One man, charged with having homosexual relations and briefly detained as a prisoner of conscience in 1995, appealed against laws criminalizing homosexuality. One man sentenced to death in 1995 was awaiting execution at the end of the year. Two people under sentence of death had their sentences commuted.

Amnesty International continued to receive reports of widespread torture and ill-treatment by police of criminal suspects, particularly those involved in the theft of cars and diamonds. In January, for example, police allegedly assaulted Percy Mutambo Dzike, a Zimbabwean national arrested on suspicion of aiding and abetting an escape. He suffered serious bruising. Further cases of police ill-treatment were reported in September.

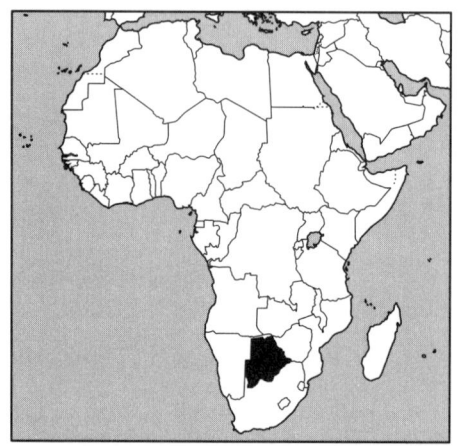

A member of the Special Support Group (SSG), a paramilitary police force, was convicted of manslaughter in June and sentenced to 12 years' imprisonment, reduced on appeal to an effective three-year sentence. The SSG officer fatally shot Binto Moroke in February 1995 during an attempt to arrest him in connection with rioting in Mochudi town (see *Amnesty International Report 1996*). In June, the government indicated that it would not charge a police officer who shot and paralysed an alleged car thief in September 1995. In October, the High Court awarded damages to the widow of a man shot dead by police in 1993.

The High Court of Botswana postponed until 1997 a hearing to determine whether Sections 164a and 167 of the Botswana Penal Code, which criminalize homosexual activity, violate the rights to privacy and freedom of association. The appeal was made in the case of a man who had been detained for three weeks in 1995 as a prisoner of conscience and charged, together with another man, with "unlawful carnal knowledge". The other man pleaded guilty in 1995 to a lesser charge and was sentenced to pay a fine (see *Amnesty International Report 1996*).

One man sentenced to death in 1995 was awaiting execution after the Appeal Court confirmed his death sentence in February. Gaolatile Kwae had been convicted of killing his ex-girlfriend's four children in 1995.

Two men convicted of murder and sentenced to death had their death sentences set aside in Appeal Court decisions. Joseph Kgaodi, convicted of killing his nephew in 1993, had his death sentence commuted to life imprisonment in January. Boiki Mohkolo, convicted of killing his girlfriend in 1995, had his death sentence commuted to a 15-year prison term.

In December, Amnesty International wrote to President Quett Masire, expressing concern about specific reports of torture by police and asking for clarification of the policing role being undertaken by members of the security forces. No reply had been received by the end of the year.

BRAZIL

Hundreds of people were killed by police and death squads in circumstances suggesting extrajudicial executions. Several people, including one prisoner of conscience, were detained or sentenced *in absentia* for their activities in campaigning for land reform. Torture was reported to be widespread in police stations, and conditions in police stations and prisons remained harsh.

In May, President Fernando Henrique Cardoso launched Brazil's National Human Rights Program, which included measures which, if implemented, could reduce impunity for human rights violations. However, by the end of the year, Congress had passed only one significant legislative reform from the Program. Jurisdiction for intentional homicide by on-duty military police was transferred from military to civilian courts, although the military police retained responsibility for investigating these crimes and determining intentionality. Subsequently, several high-profile human rights cases were transferred from military to civilian courts.

In July, the UN Human Rights Committee examined Brazil's first report on implementation of the International Covenant on Civil and Political Rights. The Committee expressed concern that "members of the security forces implicated in gross human rights violations enjoy a high level of impunity that is incompatible with the Covenant" and that "measures taken to ensure the implementation of Covenant rights in all parts of the federation remain ineffective and inadequate". The Committee strongly recommended that "all complaints of misconduct by members of the security forces be investigated by an independent body and not by the security forces themselves".

In August, Brazil ratified the Protocol to the American Convention on Human Rights to Abolish the Death Penalty.

Hundreds of people were killed by police and death squads in circumstances suggesting extrajudicial executions. In April, military police surrounded a group of 1,500 peasants connected to the Landless Rural Workers Movement (MST) who were demonstrating for land reform by blockading a road in Eldorado de Carajás, Pará state. Police fired on the crowd and demonstrators, who responded by throwing staves and stones. After the initial confrontation, military police apparently targeted individuals for extrajudicial execution. Nineteen peasants were killed and over 60 wounded. Autopsy reports indicated that 12 had been shot in the head, two at close range, and that seven died from lacerations, indicating that they had been struck with their own farm implements after being overpowered. Official investigations revealed that military police destroyed evidence, obstructing the investigation. In June, all 155 military police who participated in the operation were charged with homicide, but not suspended from duty. Little attempt was made to identify those responsible for individual extrajudicial executions, or to protect witnesses. State compensation for the victims' families was approved.

There were other violent incidents in Pará state. Gilvam Alves da Silva was one of four squatter peasants abducted on 20 August from the São Francisco estate, near Marabá, and interrogated by armed men about a land occupation there. The next day the four men were shot in the head and left for dead outside the estate. Gilvam Alves da Silva survived by pretending to be dead. The other three were believed to have been killed although their bodies were not recovered. Amnesty International was concerned at a pattern of impunity in such killings of landless peasants by gunmen reportedly hired by local landowners.

In September, Neire Reijane dos Santos Guimarães, a women's rights activist investigating census fraud in Mãe do Rio, Pará state, was shot dead in her home. She and her husband, a former member of the state legislature, had received death threats related to their political activity in the region.

In July, military police extrajudicially executed Raimundo Brandão and seriously wounded Augustinho Brandão and Nicolau Brandão – all three Shanenawá Indians – in Feijó, Acre, after they embraced a non-indigenous child known to them. Amnesty International sought government action to halt violent attacks on indigenous communities, after a decree (1775/96) in January changed procedures for demarcating indigenous land. In November, 76 Kitathaurlu Indians were tied up and beaten by armed trespassers illegally logging and mining on the Sararé reserve in Mato Grosso, with the acquiescence of local politicians. Although alerted to the armed incursion in March, the federal authorities only took action to protect the indigenous group in December. In November, three Yanomami Indians were reported killed by miners in Roraima state. The authorities had cut their protection for the Yanomami in March. Although an operation to remove miners illegally prospecting in the Yanomami indigenous reserve was approved, it was not implemented during the year. In December, five miners were sentenced *in absentia* to 20 years' imprisonment each on a charge of genocide for the killing of at least 12

BRAZIL

Yanomami Indians in July 1993 (see *Amnesty International Report 1994*).

Police-backed death squads continued to act with impunity in many states. Federal Police agents were sent to Acre in July, after public prosecutors alleged that the state police Special Operations Team was acting as an extermination squad and had extrajudicially executed scores of criminal suspects. In June, an associate of a man suspected of murdering a military policeman had his limbs and genitals severed and his eyes gouged out before being killed; his son was burned to death. In Amazonas, over 25 killings and "disappearances" of criminal suspects between January and May were attributed to a death squad, known as "The Firm", made up of police and former police operating in the state capital, Manaus.

In October, Francisco Gilson Nogueira de Carvalho, a human rights lawyer working with the Centre for Human Rights and Collective Memory (CDMP), was shot dead outside his home in a suburb of Natal, capital of Rio Grande do Norte state. Since May 1995, he had been assisting a special commission of state prosecutors investigating killings of criminal suspects attributed to a death squad known as the "Golden Boys" operating within the state civil police (see *Amnesty International Report 1996*). Prior to his killing, federal police protection had been suspended. Other members of the CDMP, six state prosecutors and a police investigator were allegedly named on a "death list".

In Rio de Janeiro, the number of fatal shootings of criminal suspects rose sharply following a November 1995 state Decree offering large pay rises to police agents involved in acts of "bravery and fearlessness". The Secretary of Public Security for Rio de Janeiro made repeated public statements endorsing a "shoot first, ask questions later" policy. Although the Rio de Janeiro authorities claimed that fatal shootings occurred only during armed confrontations, in some cases the circumstances suggested that victims had been extrajudicially executed. In January, Edval Silva and Fábio Gonçalvez Cavalcanti were killed in the shanty town of Vigário Geral. According to eye-witnesses, three hooded men shot Edval Silva dead. They then tortured Fábio Gonçalvez Cavalcanti, pulling out some of his teeth with pliers, before shooting him in the face and throwing him onto a railway line. The authorities claimed that both youths had been killed by military police in a confrontation and no further investigation was undertaken.

Gunmen charged with, or convicted of, killings of rural trade unionists continued to escape from custody, apparently with police acquiescence. In July and November, however, a father and son, convicted in 1991 of the assassination of rubber tappers trade union leader Francisco (Chico) Mendes, in 1988 (see *Amnesty International Report 1989*), were recaptured, having escaped from custody in 1993. In September, two men were convicted of the assassination in 1985 of Nativo de Natividade de Oliveira, a rural workers' trade union president, in Carmo do Rio Verde, Goiás state (see *Amnesty International Report 1986*).

Three trials were held in Rio de Janeiro in connection with the Candelária massacre of July 1993 (see *Amnesty International Report 1994*) in which seven street children and one youth were killed. In April and November, two military policemen were sentenced to 309 and 261 years' imprisonment (the first sentence was reduced to 89 years on appeal). In December, a civilian, a military policeman and a military police officer were acquitted. There was concern that all the evidence about the massacre may not have emerged during these trials.

In September, the bodies of the victims of the Vigário Geral massacre, in which 21 shanty town residents were killed in September 1993 (see *Amnesty International Report 1994*), were exhumed after it was discovered that not all bullets had been removed from their bodies as evidence at the time of the original autopsies. Forty-five military police continued to face charges in connection with the massacre.

In October, charges were brought by a civilian court against 22 Rondônia state military police for involvement in the killing of 10 peasants in Corumbiara in August 1995 (see *Amnesty International Report 1996*). An eleventh peasant, Darli Martins Pereira, last seen in military police custody in August 1995, remained "disappeared".

Land reform activists continued to be arrested and charged with "forming a criminal band". Diolinda Alves de Souza (see *Amnesty International Report 1996*),

Felinto Procópio, Laércio Barbosa and Claudemiro Marques – all members of the MST – were detained from 25 January to 12 March on a charge of "forming a criminal band" for supporting land occupations in São Paulo state. Diolinda Alves de Souza was a prisoner of conscience. The federal Higher Court of Justice ordered their release, ruling that the charge of "forming a criminal band" was not appropriate for activities related to land occupations and campaigning for agrarian reform. Nevertheless, such charges continued to be brought against agrarian reform campaigners. In July, a Franciscan priest, Frei Anastácio Ribeiro (see *Amnesty International Report 1996*) was sentenced to four years and 10 months' imprisonment, together with six other members of the Church Land Commission, for campaigning for agrarian reform in the state of Paraíba. The sentences against all seven were overturned on appeal in October.

Reports of torture in police custody were widespread and conditions of detention remained harsh in police stations and prisons. Several thousand convicted prisoners continued to be held with remand prisoners in police stations because of prison overcrowding. In January, several detainees were beaten while suspended by the knees and wrists from an iron bar at the Robbery and Theft Police Station in Campo Grande, Mato Grosso do Sul. They were then returned to severely overcrowded cells and received no medical attention for their injuries.

In August, José Wilson Pinheiro da Silva lost an eye as a result of beatings by military police while being taken to the Fifth police district in Fortaleza, Ceará. According to the police Ombudsman in São Paulo state, reports of torture increased in São Paulo during the second half of the year. In August, nine youths were held incommunicado and tortured for several weeks on suspicion of involvement in killing two people in a bar in São Paulo. They were released without charge. In July, the Federal Congress voted compensation for the family of José Ivanildo Sampaio Souza who died after being tortured in federal police custody in Ceará state in October 1995 (see *Amnesty International Report 1996*).

A Special Commission on Disappearances, inaugurated in January, awarded compensation to the families of 136 people who the authorities acknowledged had died after "disappearing" in custody during the period of military rule in the 1970s (see *Amnesty International Report 1996*). The Commission also examined 150 cases of deaths at the hands of the security forces during this period and decided that 107 incidents had taken place in official custody and were the responsibility of the state, and that relatives should be duly compensated.

Amnesty International sought full investigations into cases of human rights violations. The organization conducted an on-site investigation of the Eldorado de Carajás massacre, sent observers to the first trial related to the Candelária massacre, and held meetings with the government to present its recommendations for a National Action Plan on Human Rights. During the year, the organization published several reports, including *Brazil: Human rights violations and the health professions*, which called for better medical documentation of human rights abuses, and for the independence of forensic services from the police.

In July, the organization submitted its concerns on human rights violations in Brazil to the UN Human Rights Committee.

BULGARIA

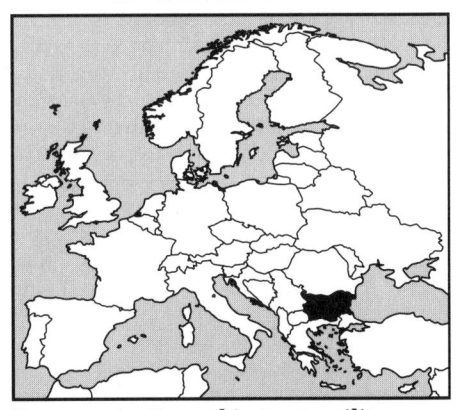

One conscientious objector to military service was imprisoned and four men were detained for exercising their right to freedom of expression; all were prisoners of conscience. There were widespread reports of torture and ill-treatment by law enforcement officials. Many of the victims were Roma. At least five people reportedly died as a result of ill-treatment or torture. Shootings by police officers in disputed circumstances resulted in at least three deaths. Seven people were sentenced to death. No executions were carried out. An asylum-seeker was returned to Tunisia, where he was detained and tortured.

In November, Petar Stoyanov, the candidate of the main opposition group, the Union of Democratic Forces, was elected President. The government of the ruling Bulgarian Socialist Party was facing growing criticism for failing to resolve serious economic problems and widespread corruption in state institutions, including the police force.

Four people detained in violation of their right to freedom of expression were prisoners of conscience. In February, in Smolyan, Valentin Hadzhiev and Mitko Shtirkov, both journalists, were arrested and detained for 24 hours for publishing articles in which they stated that a local prosecutor was a former police officer who had been dismissed from the force for taking bribes. They were charged with defaming a public official in the press, but had not been brought to trial by the end of the year.

In July, in Sandanski, two police officers arrested Georgi Stoev and Andon Andonov as they were putting up leaflets announcing an assembly of the *Obedinena makedonska organizatsiya "Ilinden"* (OMO "Ilinden"), United Macedonian Organization "Ilinden". Police officers reportedly slapped and punched them during questioning at the police station. They were released without charge the following day.

In September, Dian Dimitrov, a conscientious objector to military service, began a 10-month prison sentence for evading military service. Although the right to alternative service is guaranteed by the Constitution, a separate bill to regulate alternative service had not been adopted by the end of the year. Dian Dimitrov was a prisoner of conscience.

There were daily reports of torture and ill-treatment by police officers. In September, two senior police officers in Harmanli were suspended from duty following an incident in which at least two men were severely beaten.

Many victims of torture or ill-treatment by police were criminal suspects, but an increasing number appeared to have been the targets of random violence by police officers. In March, Anton Mitkov Dimitrov, a 14-year-old student, was walking to his home in Sliven when he was stopped by three police officers, one of whom beat him with his truncheon and kicked him in the knees and groin. He was then handcuffed, taken to the police station and shortly afterwards released. He was examined by a doctor, who noted bruising on the nape of the neck and on his left wrist. In April, Zlatka Asenova Gikova was punched in the face several times and hit on the back by an off-duty police officer at a bus stop in a Sofia suburb. A medical certificate noted cuts and bruising on her mouth, temple and the back of the head. In May, Ivan Todorov was reportedly beaten in a Sofia park by a plainclothes police officer following an identity card check. When Ivan Todorov started to run, the officer shot him twice. A police press statement claimed that the officer had acted in self-defence.

As in previous years, many of the victims of alleged ill-treatment were Roma. Seventeen-year-old Angel Zubchikov died in hospital in January, the day after he was arrested in Razgrad on suspicion of theft and taken to the police station. An autopsy reportedly established that his death resulted from a brain haemorrhage following a blow to the head. After his parents took the body home, they observed other injuries, including broken ribs, which were photographed by a local journalist. The police claimed that Angel Zubchikov had fallen and hit his head on a kerb. An investigation was initiated, but no results had been made public by the end of the year.

At least four other people died in detention, apparently as a result of torture or ill-treatment. Among them were Filip Kunchev, who died in July in the Eighth Precinct in Sofia, where he had been detained in the course of a criminal investigation, and Hristo Bekirski, detained in Plovdiv on suspicion of murder, who died in September following an operation to determine whether he had suffered internal injuries. Hristo Bekirski had reportedly been severely beaten with truncheons by police officers, following an escape attempt in which he injured two guards. In July, two police officers of the Eighth Precinct in Sofia were charged as accomplices in the murder of Ivan Benchev. In April, Ivan Benchev had been beaten to death following his release from this precinct, by men reportedly incited to the act by the police officers.

There were several cases of police shootings of unarmed people which resulted in death. In April, a police officer in Sliven shot and killed Hristo Hristov, who was reportedly stealing electric cable from a shaft. The police officer was found guilty of manslaughter and sentenced in September to one year of corrective labour. In July, in Lesura, a major in the military police shot and killed Kancho Angelov and Kiril Petkov, unarmed soldiers who had left their unit without permission. An investigation was initiated by the military prosecutor but the major responsible for the killings had reportedly not been suspended from duty.

Seven people were sentenced to death. A moratorium on executions, imposed in 1990, remained in force.

In July, an asylum-seeker was sent back to Tunisia, where he was held incommunicado for six days and later subjected to torture during interrogation by the police.

In March, Amnesty International expressed concern to then President Zhelyu Zhelev about the detention of the two journalists in Smolyan and about the law under which they were charged, which appeared to restrict the right to freedom of expression. In June, Amnesty International published a report, *Bulgaria: Shootings, deaths in custody, torture and ill-treatment*, which described in detail some of the cases which had been reported to the organization since 1993, including seven deaths in custody in suspicious circumstances, three incidents in which six people were shot by police and 17 cases of torture and ill-treatment involving dozens of victims. The organization made extensive recommendations regarding investigations into reports of such violations.

In July, Amnesty International urged the Minister of the Interior not to deport the Tunisian asylum-seeker. In September, the organization expressed concern to Prime Minister Zhan Videnov about the detention of OMO "Ilinden" activists and urged him to initiate investigations into further reports of shootings, deaths in custody and torture and ill-treatment. In October, Amnesty International called for the release of Dian Dimitrov.

The authorities wrote to Amnesty International in July and September providing information about investigations into 16 cases of deaths in custody, torture and ill-treatment. In October, Amnesty International published a report describing the government's response and the organization's outstanding concerns.

BURKINA FASO

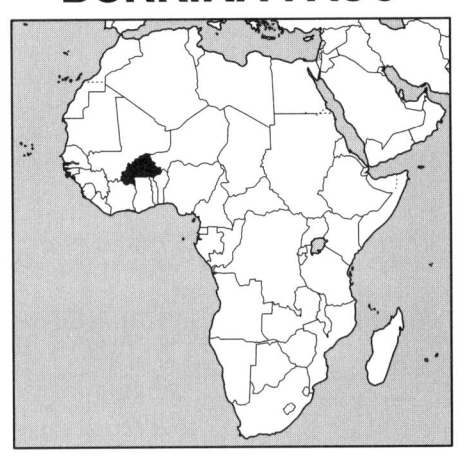

A prisoner of conscience was released. Students were briefly held without charge. Soldiers charged with disciplinary offences may have been prisoners of conscience. Detainees and prisoners were reportedly tortured and ill-treated. Official inquiries into seven apparent extrajudicial executions and the killing of two students by the security forces in 1995 had not concluded by the end of the year.

Prisoner of conscience Ernest Nongma Ouédraogo, Secretary General of the *Bloc socialiste burkinabè* (BSB), Burkinabè Socialist Bloc, an opposition political party, was released in January. He had been sentenced to six months' imprisonment in August 1995 for insulting the Head of State after a statement by the BSB executive committee, claiming that President Blaise Compaoré had accumulated personal wealth through fraud, was published in a newspaper (see *Amnesty International Report 1996*). Ernest Nongma Ouédraogo was singled out because of his opposition to President Compaoré. In mid-January, he was granted special permission to leave prison for one month, shortly before his prison sentence expired.

Dozens of students were arrested following protests in March, May and December. In early December, some 20 students from the *Centre universitaire polytechnique de Bobo-Dioulasso*, University and Polytechnic Centre of Bobo-Dioulasso, were arrested; all were subsequently released without charge, some after being held for more than two weeks. Two students, a Cameroonian and a Chadian, both recognized as refugees in Burkina Faso, were to be expelled to other countries in western Africa.

Twenty-five soldiers of the presidential security service were arrested in Ouagadougou in October. The authorities described the arrests as a preventive security measure because of breaches of military discipline. Following investigation by the gendarmerie, the soldiers were charged with indiscipline. It appeared that some may have been arrested solely because of their close association with Chief Warrant Officer Hyacinthe Kafando, formerly responsible for the presidential security service, who was reportedly opposed to plans for restructuring the army and, in particular, the presidential security service. The soldiers were initially held at the *Conseil de l'Entente* building in Ouagadougou; some were later transferred to military barracks in different parts of the country. Chief Warrant Officer Kafando, also charged with indiscipline, was abroad at the time of the arrests.

The release of all 25 soldiers was officially announced on 18 December, but had not been independently confirmed by the end of the year. On 24 December, Sergeant Arzouma Ouédrogo died in what military authorities described as a road accident. However, the exact circumstances of his death remained unclear. The *Mouvement burkinabè des droits de l'homme et des peuples*, Burkinabè Movement for Human and Peoples' Rights, a non-governmental human rights organization, requested an official inquiry into his death, but the authorities had not responded by the end of the year.

There were reports of torture and ill-treatment of detainees and prisoners. Following disturbances at the University of Ouagadougou in March, about 20 students were arrested by police. Some were beaten with truncheons at the time of their arrest. They were taken to the *Sûreté nationale*, the criminal investigation department of the police, where they were stripped and again beaten before being released later the same day. Thirty-five people were arrested in early May in Ouagadougou and Bobo-Dioulasso during demonstrations by student nurses and midwives of the *Ecole nationale de santé publique*, National School of Public Health. Some were beaten by police at the time of their arrest; one woman suffered a fractured jaw as a result. Some of the detainees were charged with breach of the peace but all were released three or four days later. Reports were received that prisoners at the Ouagadougou prison, the *Maison d'arrêt et de correction de Ouagadougou*, were punished by beatings. No action was known to have been taken against those responsible.

An official investigation was initiated into the apparent extrajudicial executions in 1995 of seven men from the village of Kaya Navio, Nahouri Province, but its findings had not been made public by the end of the year. The men died after being detained by forces of the *Centre national d'entraînement commando*, National Centre for Commando Training, based in Pô, following a confrontation between villagers and gendarmes in February 1995 (see *Amnesty International Report 1996*).

An official investigation into the killing of two school students during a demonstration in 1995 had not concluded by the end of the year. Blaise Sidiané, aged 18, and Emile Zigani, aged 14, were shot dead by security forces in May 1995 at Garango, Boulgou Province, during a demonstration (see *Amnesty International Report 1996*).

Amnesty International wrote to the authorities, seeking clarification of the basis of the charges against the 25 soldiers arrested in October.

BURUNDI

Tens of thousands of people were victims of political killings by government forces and by Hutu and Tutsi armed groups. More than 6,500 people, virtually all Hutu, were held in detention without trial. About 150 people were convicted after trials which did not conform to international fair trial standards, and more than 80 were sentenced to death. Torture was reported to be systematic. At least 24 detainees were summarily executed. Hundreds of people "disappeared" and were feared killed. Among them were Burundi refugees forcibly returned from eastern

Zaire. Burundi forcibly returned refugees to Rwanda.

The civil war escalated between the Tutsi-dominated security forces and armed opposition groups led by members of the majority Hutu ethnic group. The largest armed Hutu group was the *Forces pour la défense de la démocratie*, Forces for the Defence of Democracy, the armed wing of the *Conseil national pour la défense de la démocratie*, National Council for the Defence of Democracy. Hundreds of thousands of people were forced to leave their homes in search of safety, either in camps and rural settlements within Burundi, or in Zaire and Tanzania as refugees.

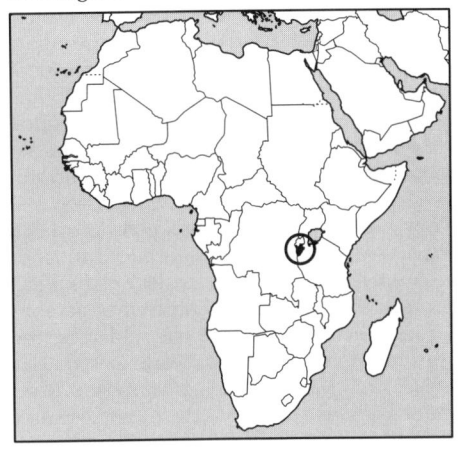

By June, the escalating violence prompted the Heads of State of Tanzania, Rwanda, Zaire, Uganda and Ethiopia to propose sending a combined force of troops from various African countries to help restore security. This decision aroused considerable opposition within Burundi, and on 24 July, President Sylvestre Ntibantunganya was ousted in a military coup. He had led a transitional government in which the Hutu-dominated *Front pour la démocratie au Burundi*, Front for Democracy in Burundi, which won elections in 1993, shared power with Tutsi-dominated opposition parties.

A former President, Major Pierre Buyoya, was declared President. He suspended the National Assembly and all political parties. The new government was not recognized by the international community, and the Organization of African Unity (OAU) and neighbouring countries reacted by imposing trade sanctions. In September, the government reinstated the National Assembly and political parties, but the sanctions remained in place and Burundi was excluded from regional discussions on the crisis which erupted in eastern Zaire that month.

Thousands of refugees fled to Rwanda, Zaire and Tanzania in the first eight months of the year. Tanzania, which had closed its border with Burundi in 1995 (see *Amnesty International Report 1996*), allowed some further refugees to enter. When fighting broke out in eastern Zaire in September, more than 140,000 Burundi refugees found themselves trapped between armed conflict and starvation. At least 100,000 fled from refugee camps in eastern Zaire, many of them forced back by Tutsi-led armed groups to Burundi (see below). An unknown number died; some refugees were targeted by Tutsi groups in Zaire, some were caught in the cross-fire and others succumbed to disease, hunger and thirst.

A UN commission of inquiry into the October 1993 coup attempt and subsequent massacres published its report in July, after many delays (see *Amnesty International Report 1996*). The commission had earlier expressed concern about lack of security for its personnel and about inadequate resources. The report was criticized for confining itself to a narrow mandate and failing to address issues of impunity.

Tens of thousands of people were killed during the year by the security forces, by Tutsi groups acting in collusion with government forces, and by armed Hutu opposition groups. Often it was difficult to establish who had carried out particular killings. As well as the many people massacred solely because of their ethnic origin, the victims included prominent members of the majority Hutu community, church leaders, teachers and students, journalists, foreign aid workers, Rwandese refugees in Burundi and Burundi refugees returned from Zaire.

The civil war entered a new phase in March, when armed groups extended their attacks from the northern provinces and around Bujumbura, the capital, to the southern provinces. The number of unarmed civilians who died continued to rise. Nearly 500 people were killed in the first two weeks of April by government forces or armed groups. In May, there were reports of massacres in which at least

1,200 people lost their lives, and by June more than 1,000 people were dying each week. After the 24 July coup, the killings escalated even further. More than 6,000 people were reported to have been killed in various parts of Burundi in the three weeks after the coup. The return of exiled Hutu fighters who had been based in and around refugee camps in eastern Zaire led to a further upsurge of violence in Burundi towards the end of the year.

Massacres by government soldiers and armed Tutsi civilians were reported throughout the year. Most of the victims were Hutu. In one incident on 3 May, at least 300 people were killed by soldiers in Kivyuka market.

On 25 July, Tutsi students killed 30 Hutu fellow students at an agricultural college while the security forces surrounded the building. Some students were burned to death. Those killed included Fabien Buyana and Valérie Nimbesha. Ten other students "disappeared".

On 29 July, soldiers killed around a hundred people, including women and children, in Giheta, Gitega province. Those too weak to run away were drowned in the nearby Ruvyironza river. Among the dead were Veronica Cishikaye and her three children.

Between 27 July and 10 August, at least 4,050 unarmed civilians were extrajudicially executed by government forces in Gitega province. Most were shot dead after being rounded up by soldiers who came to their villages, ostensibly to obtain information about rebel movements.

Thousands of refugees were forcibly returned to Burundi by Tutsi-led Zairian rebels in November and December. Hundreds of the returned refugees were massacred by Burundi government forces. In one incident on 22 October, at least 400 returnees from Zaire were rounded up by soldiers at Muramba Seventh Day Adventist Church, Cibitoke province. The adult males were then shot dead or bayoneted to death. Also killed were Juliette, a former headmistress of Rukana primary school, and her son, Abasi; Hosana Gushima, a former teacher at the Munyika primary school; and Annika, a teacher at Rugombo secondary school.

Hutu armed groups also deliberately and arbitrarily killed unarmed civilians. For example, 16 civilians were killed on 23 February when armed Hutu attacked the town of Buganda in Cibitoke province. A further 30 people were killed three days later when a Hutu group using automatic weapons attacked a camp for displaced people. In another incident on 3 May, an armed group killed four patients and a guard during an attack on a hospital in Bujumbura. Fifty-one people were reportedly killed by Hutu rebels at Butezi displaced people's camp in May.

More than 6,500 people, almost all Hutu, were held in a number of detention centres around the country. At least 2,600 of them were accused of involvement in massacres, or of belonging to Hutu armed groups. Most were held without charge or trial. Among them was a group of about 16 people arrested on 18 February after a shoot-out near Gasenyi, where there is a camp for displaced Hutu. When the local people heard shots being fired, they followed instructions to go to a position held by government soldiers. There, about 60 men of fighting age were arrested and accused of being members of armed groups. They were taken to the headquarters of the *Brigade spéciale de recherche* (BSR), Special Investigation Brigade, where 15 continued to be held at the end of the year.

A military court ruled in March that soldiers charged in connection with the October 1993 murder of President Melchior Ndadaye had no case to answer and should be released (see previous *Amnesty International Reports*).

A series of unfair political trials was held from February onwards. At least 150 people, all Hutu, were tried in connection with killings of members of the Tutsi ethnic group. None had legal representation: virtually all Burundi's lawyers are Tutsi and they refused to represent the defendants. The accused had no opportunity to call witnesses in their defence or to cross-examine prosecution witnesses. Over 80 people were sentenced to death, including Firmat Niyonkenguruka, a former secondary-school director. There were demands, mainly from Tutsi government employees, for the death penalty to be imposed and, although the Supreme Court had not yet responded to the defendants' appeals, a government minister agreed to consider this punishment. On 9 August, Firmat Niyonkenguruka and five others were moved to a special isolation cell, prompting fears that they would be tortured or executed.

Information received by Amnesty International gave grounds for fears that Michel Nziguheba, a journalist arrested in March and still held on unknown charges at the end of the year, might not receive a fair trial.

Torture in custody was reported to be systematic, and the Tutsi-dominated judiciary failed to investigate detainees' torture allegations. Almost all suspects held at the BSR were subjected to torture or ill-treatment, including beatings and enforced kneeling on sharp objects.

At least 24 detainees were summarily executed during the year. Three were shot dead in Mpimba prison in Bujumbura in December.

Hundreds of people "disappeared" during the year, including Gerols Mupenda Watu, an engineer in Bujumbura, who was abducted from a government building on 7 August, apparently by a militia acting with the collusion of the security forces.

On 27 July, at least seven people "disappeared" after reportedly being abducted by security forces in Kanyosha, near Bujumbura. They were said to have been on a list of people sought by the security forces.

Tens of thousands of refugees returned to Burundi from Zaire after war broke out in late September. A number of them were summarily executed by Burundian security forces. At least 50 men of fighting age who had returned from Zaire were reported killed in Bujumbura on 8 November. Hundreds more "disappeared" from Gatumba transit camp near the border, and were feared killed.

In July, Burundi forcibly expelled 15,000 Rwandese refugees from northern Burundi to Rwanda. At the end of August, Burundi repatriated about 80,000 Rwandese refugees who had been living in camps in the north of the country. The return was officially described as voluntary, although heavy pressure was applied and at least three refugees were killed, apparently by government troops, before the others agreed to go.

Amnesty International repeatedly appealed to all political and military leaders in Burundi to respect human rights. It called on them to publicly instruct those under their command to stop killing unarmed civilians and to disarm and bring to justice anyone accused of such killings. The organization also called on the government to stop forced repatriation of Rwandese refugees. In February, Amnesty International published a report, *Rwanda and Burundi: The return home – rumours and realities*, which described the situation of more than a million refugees from Rwanda and Burundi and the risks facing them if they were to return home. In June, the organization published *Burundi: Armed groups kill without mercy*, which highlighted killings by armed groups, and in August a further report, *Burundi: Leaders are changing, but human rights abuses continue unabated*, documented continuing government massacres.

Amnesty International issued an appeal to the OAU on 26 July, in the aftermath of the coup, calling on it to mobilize the international community to prevent further massacres of defenceless civilians in Burundi.

After the outbreak of war in eastern Zaire, Amnesty International drew attention to the fate of over 100,000 refugees from Burundi in its appeals to the parties to the conflict and to the international community (see **Zaire** entry). In November, it published *Burundi: Refugees returned to danger*, which described continuing killings of civilians and massacres of returned refugees.

CAMBODIA

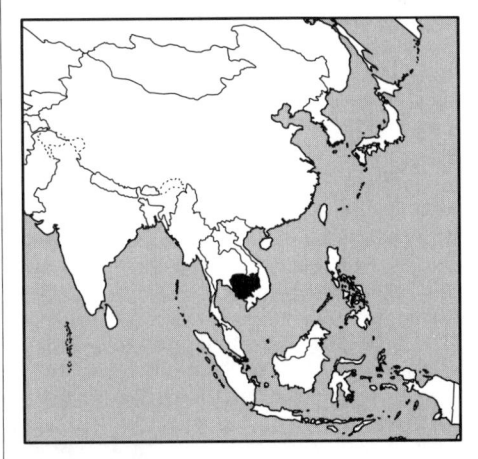

Two prisoners of conscience were imprisoned and subsequently pardoned; a third was released without charge. At least nine people were sentenced to prison terms following unfair trials. Dozens of people, including at least five political prisoners, were tortured and ill-treated in police custody. At least four people died as a result of torture. At least 27 people, including six children, were extrajudicially executed. Twenty-two people were arrested and deported to a neighbouring country where they were at risk of human rights violations. An armed opposition group committed grave human rights abuses, including deliberate and arbitrary killings of civilians.

Civil war between the Royal Cambodian Armed Forces and the National Army of Democratic Kampuchea (NADK) – the armed wing of the Cambodian National Union Party (CNUP), formerly the *Partie of Democratic Kampuchea*, commonly known as the Khmer Rouge – continued throughout the year, with fierce fighting in February and March. The CNUP split in August, and the breakaway faction which controlled parts of the northwest of the country formed a new political group, the Democratic National Union Movement (DNUM). Ieng Sary, leader of the DNUM, received a royal pardon in September. He had been Foreign Minister and Deputy Prime Minister in Cambodia from April 1975 to January 1979, during which time the Government of Democratic Kampuchea (GDK) was responsible for gross violations of human rights, including the torture and extrajudicial execution of hundreds of thousands of civilians. Ieng Sary had been sentenced to death *in absentia* after an unfair trial on charges relating to human rights violations during the period in which the GDK was in power. The request for a royal pardon had been made by the two Prime Ministers, Prince Norodom Ranariddh and Hun Sen, and supported by a majority of National Assembly members.

Attempts throughout the year by prominent government critic Sam Rainsy to gain legal status for his political party, the Khmer Nation Party (KNP), were frustrated by the government, and provincial party workers were harassed by the authorities. A new law on nationality was passed by the National Assembly in August which discriminates against certain ethnic minorities.

In February, the UN High Commissioner for Human Rights visited Cambodia and signed an agreement with the government extending the presence of the UN Centre for Human Rights in Cambodia for two years. The UN Secretary-General's Special Representative on the situation of human rights in Cambodia submitted a report to the UN Commission on Human Rights in February, condemning government and NADK abuses. In November, the Special Representative submitted a report to the UN General Assembly.

Two prisoners of conscience, Chan Rotana and Hen Vipheak, both newspaper editors and senior members of the KNP, were jailed briefly before being pardoned. In June, the Supreme Court upheld the conviction and sentence of Chan Rotana, former editor of *Samleng Yuvachen Khmer* (Voice of Khmer Youth). Chan Rotana had been convicted in 1995 on charges of "disinformation" in connection with an article published in his newspaper and sentenced to one year's imprisonment and a heavy fine (see *Amnesty International Report 1996*). In October 1995, the Appeals Court had upheld the conviction and sentence without a new trial, despite the fact that the prosecution had altered the charge to one of "defamation". Chan Rotana was freed by royal pardon after serving seven days of his sentence. Hen Vipheak, former editor of *Serei Pheap Thmey* (New Liberty News), was jailed in August after the Supreme Court upheld his conviction for "disinformation" and the sentence of one year's imprisonment and a heavy fine. He was freed by royal pardon shortly after starting his sentence. No one was brought to justice for the violent attack on the *Serei Pheap Thmey* office in 1995 (see *Amnesty International Report 1996*).

Heng At, a prisoner of conscience detained in Kampong Cham province (see *Amnesty International Report 1996*) was released without charge in January.

At least nine people were sentenced to prison terms after unfair trials. Prince Norodom Sirivudh, who had been detained in November 1995 on suspicion of plotting to kill Second Prime Minister Hun Sen and was exiled to France following an intervention by King Norodom Sihanouk, was tried *in absentia* and sentenced to 10 years' imprisonment in February. He was convicted on charges of conspiracy and illegal possession of weapons, following a trial which fell short of international standards for fair trial. Before the trial his wife and children, who live in Cambodia, received telephone death threats. Prince

Sirivudh remained in exile at the end of the year.

Eight people who were arrested in December 1995 on suspicion of having links with the outlawed NADK (see *Amnesty International Report 1996*) were brought to trial in August. Their trial, which appeared to be politically motivated, fell short of international standards for fair trial. Six men were found guilty of involvement in organized crime and each sentenced to one year's imprisonment, despite the lack of evidence to substantiate the charges. One man was found guilty of illegal possession of weapons, and another, a former journalist, of "disinformation"; both were sentenced to eight months' imprisonment. A ninth person arrested with the group was released without charge.

Torture and ill-treatment in police custody were reported in many parts of the country. At least five people arrested in Battambang province in the first half of the year on suspicion of having links with the NADK were tortured. In June, Lam Han, who speaks only Vietnamese, was arrested on suspicion of theft and tortured by police in Battambang province. She was threatened with death and beaten on the legs by three policemen over a two-day period, while detained in a cell with no toilet facilities. She was denied food and water, and was injected by a policeman with an unknown substance which made her lose consciousness. Evidence of the injuries sustained by Lam Han at the police station was not accepted by the judge and she was convicted and given a one-year prison sentence on the basis of confessions obtained under torture in a language she did not understand. No action was taken against the policemen.

Evidence also emerged during 1996 of the detention and torture in September 1995 of a 13-year-old girl arrested on suspicion of theft who was reportedly tortured with an electric baton by a military policeman and an army officer in Kampong Thom province. The two men involved had not been brought to justice by the end of the year.

At least four people died following torture. In February, Ry Sarith was arrested by policemen and military police in Prey Veng province on suspicion of robbery. He was interrogated at the local police station, after which a military police captain reportedly handcuffed him and beat him to death. In May, Tong Sophara was arrested without a warrant by military police in Siem Reap province on suspicion of car theft. He was taken to their headquarters, stripped naked and detained in a basement room, where he was found dead the following day. The official report into his death stated that Tong Sophara had committed suicide by hanging. However, serious inconsistencies in the report led to an order from the civilian authorities to exhume the body, which was found to have a broken arm, rib and tooth, and burns, bruises and puncture wounds. Those responsible had not been brought to justice by the end of the year.

At least 27 people were extrajudicially executed. In May, Thun Bun Ly, a prominent KNP worker and newspaper editor, was shot dead by two men, one of them in uniform, as he was riding pillion on a motorcycle taxi near his house in Phnom Penh. Half an hour before his death he had telephoned a friend and said he was frightened as he had been followed home from KNP leader Sam Rainsy's house. Later that day, municipal police came and removed two bullets from Thun Bun Ly's body. A Ministry of the Interior official came in the afternoon and removed the third bullet. The whereabouts of these pieces of evidence were never disclosed. The manner of killing and the removal of the bullets mirror the case of Nuon Chan (see *Amnesty International Report 1995*). Thun Bun Ly had been appealing against a prison sentence for articles he had published in his newspaper, *Oddomkete Khmer* (Khmer Ideal). No one had been brought to justice for the killing by the end of the year.

In May, two villagers, So Saly and Phan Samoun, from Svay Rieng province, were arrested, beaten and executed in front of local villagers and policemen by a group of military police who accused them of robbery. One was shot in the head eight times. No prosecution had been initiated against any of the officers involved by the end of the year. In June, Seng Voeun was arrested by military policemen and police officers in Takeo province on suspicion of armed robbery. He was publicly stripped and beaten while protesting his innocence. The officers then shot him four times and, when he still refused to confess, shot him dead. In spite of a request by the Minister of Justice for action to be taken, those responsible had not been apprehended by the end of the year.

In September, six children were killed and six others injured when a soldier in Krang Kontro village fired a rocket into a group of children at an ice-cream stall. Four soldiers, who were also injured, then fired their weapons at villagers and forced them to leave the children and assist the soldiers first. The perpetrator had not been arrested by the end of the year, and no action had been taken against the surviving soldiers. The unit commander was reportedly taken into military custody.

Twenty-two people were arrested and deported to Viet Nam, where they were at risk of human rights violations. They included three ethnic Vietnamese men, two of whom were born in Cambodia and had Cambodian identity documents, who were arrested and deported in March. The Cambodian Ministry of the Interior claimed that the men were linked to an illegal organization, the Free Viet Nam Movement, which aimed to overthrow the Vietnamese Government. At the end of the year, one man remained in custody in Viet Nam (see **Viet Nam** entry). Nineteen people of Vietnamese descent were deported in December because of their alleged involvement in an organization calling for political change in Viet Nam. Their fate and whereabouts in Viet Nam were unknown at the end of the year.

The NADK committed grave human rights abuses, including deliberate and arbitrary killings. In June, more than 80 civilians working on logging concessions were abducted by an NADK unit in Kampot province. Fourteen of the hostages were executed with axes by the NADK soldiers. Some 35 others were released and delivered ransom demands to family members for the remaining hostages. There were reports that NADK soldiers were also responsible for a massacre of villagers on the Tonle Sap lake, some of whom were ethnic Vietnamese. The fate and whereabouts of a British man and his Cambodian translator who were taken hostage in March remained unknown.

In May, Amnesty International published a report, *Kingdom of Cambodia: Diminishing respect for human rights*, detailing human rights violations during the previous year, cataloguing the lack of government action on cases of human rights violations and describing NADK abuses.

The organization called for the immediate and unconditional release of prisoners of conscience and expressed concern at the killing of Thun Bun Ly and the deportation of the three men in March. In September, Amnesty International sent an open letter to the King and members of the National Assembly, reiterating the need for accountability for past gross human rights violations and urging that full investigations be undertaken and those found responsible brought to justice. The King issued an open letter in response, in which he explained that as a constitutional monarch it was his duty to follow the wishes of the government, but that he would support any international tribunal which brought senior Khmer Rouge leaders to justice. Amnesty International wrote to the Prime Ministers in November, calling for action to be taken to protect the villagers of Krang Kontro from the soldiers who had killed their children. There was no response from the government to Amnesty International's many appeals on individual cases.

CAMEROON

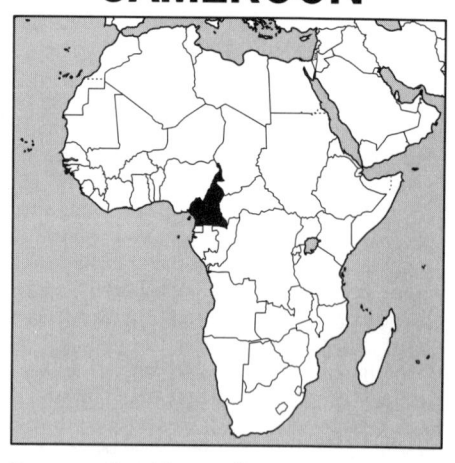

Dozens of critics and opponents of the government, including journalists and members of opposition political parties, were arrested; some were convicted and imprisoned. Most were prisoners of conscience. Torture and ill-treatment of detainees and prisoners remained routine. Many prisoners died because of harsh prison conditions amounting to cruel, inhuman or degrading treatment. An opposition politician was killed by a traditional ruler's personal force; no action was taken against those responsible.

A revised Constitution was promulgated in January. However, the amendments retained extensive presidential powers and did little to strengthen the independence of the judiciary. Local government elections took place in January. Although President Paul Biya's party, the *Rassemblement démocratique du peuple camerounais*, Cameroon People's Democratic Movement (CPDM), controlled a majority of local authorities, opposition parties – including the Social Democratic Front (SDF) and the *Union nationale pour la démocratie et le progrès* (UNDP), National Union for Democracy and Progress – made important gains, particularly in major towns. A subsequent government decree nominated government representatives to replace elected mayors in 20 significant authorities, including those held by opposition parties; protest demonstrations resulted in arrests and at least five deaths.

Opposition parties called for an independent electoral commission to oversee legislative and presidential elections scheduled for 1997; this was rejected by the CPDM.

In April, fighting broke out between the armed forces of Cameroon and Nigeria over a long-standing border dispute in the Bakassi peninsula. Intergovernmental organizations sought to mediate between the two countries.

Twelve Rwandans accused of participation in the genocide in Rwanda in 1994 were arrested in March and April. The International Criminal Tribunal for Rwanda requested in June that four be extradited but President Biya had not authorized their extradition by the end of the year; all 12 remained held.

Nine journalists were tried on criminal libel charges and sentenced to prison terms, although most were not imprisoned. Several others were held for short periods without charge. Newspapers were suspended. Some judicial procedures against journalists were marked by serious irregularities; prosecutions appeared to be attempts to inhibit criticism of prominent government members, their close associates, or government policies. In May, Vianney Ombe Ndzana, publisher of the newspaper *Génération*, was sentenced to five months' imprisonment and a fine for libel following publication of an article accusing a company director of professional misconduct; the court also ordered the suspension of *Génération*. Vianney Ombe Ndzana was not imprisoned, but in August he was seriously injured in an assault by unidentified armed men in Yaoundé. The following month, Nicolas Tejoumessie, editor of the weekly newspaper *Challenge Nouveau*, was abducted by four men claiming to be members of the security forces. He was taken some 30 kilometres outside Douala and severely beaten. In October, the Douala Court of Appeal convicted Pius Njawe, editor-in-chief of *Le Messager*, and a colleague, Eyoum Ngangué, of insulting the President and members of the National Assembly. The charges related to an article in December 1995 about draft constitutional amendments presented to the National Assembly. Initially only fined when the case was first heard in February, they had their sentences increased to fines and prison terms: Pius Njawe received six months and Eyoum Ngangué one year. Pius Njawe was imprisoned in the Central Prison, New Bell, Douala, where he was denied access to his doctor and medical treatment. He was conditionally released after 17 days. Eyoum Ngangué had not been imprisoned by the end of the year. Paddy Mbawa, publisher of the *Cameroon Post*, was released in August after a year's imprisonment for libel and publishing false information (see *Amnesty International Report 1996*). However, several similar cases against him were still pending. Four journalists associated with *Le Nouvel Indépendant* and *Le Front Indépendant*, established when *Le Nouvel Indépendant* was temporarily suspended, were detained in November and December; all were subsequently released without charge.

Seven UNDP members held since 1994 were sentenced to 10 years' imprisonment in March and remained imprisoned in Maroua Central Prison, in Far-North Province. Their appeal against conviction and sentence had not been heard by the end of the year. Another defendant was sentenced *in absentia* to 15 years' imprisonment and eight others received three-year suspended sentences. Twenty-eight UNDP members had been arrested and charged with complicity in various offences following clashes in Maroua in July 1994 (see *Amnesty International Reports 1995 and 1996*). There was no evidence of individual responsibility for any criminal act against those convicted. They were prisoners of conscience.

Officials and members of other opposition parties, in particular the SDF, were intimidated, arrested and detained. Six SDF members arrested in Mbanga, Littoral Province, during the January elections were charged with public order offences; they were conditionally released in August. In March, dozens of SDF members and supporters were arrested in Limbe, South-West Province, following demonstrations against the appointment of government representatives to replace elected mayors; 32 were held in administrative detention in Buea for six weeks, despite a court order that they be released. In June, shots were fired by security forces at the home of SDF Chairman John Fru Ndi in Bamenda, North-West Province. Also in June, Joseph Lavoisier Tsapy, a lawyer and SDF local government leader in Bafoussam, West Province, was abducted and held for four days by unidentified men, apparently members of the security forces; and Ndang George Achu, an SDF official in Santa, North-West Province, was held for two weeks under legislation introduced in December 1990 which allows administrative detention without safeguards against arbitrary imprisonment.

Suspected government opponents were frequently held longer than the 72 hours allowed by law before being referred to a judicial authority or released. In May, up to 30 striking teachers were arrested in Bafoussam; two women were reportedly seriously injured during beatings by the security forces. Most were released without charge after a week, but four trade union officials were charged with public order offences.

In June, up to 200 striking students at the University of Yaoundé were arrested. The arrests followed violent confrontations between students and security forces, and also a vigilante group known as *auto-défense* operating with the acquiescence of the university authorities and the security services. University buildings were burned and a university lecturer was assaulted. Most of the students were released shortly afterwards, but others remained held, in various places of detention, by police, the *Centre national d'études et de recherches* (the security police) and special units of the security forces. They were held until mid-July before being charged and conditionally released. Further arrests of students accused of provoking continuing unrest were made in October. Several students were detained overnight at the university by members of *auto-défense*, and were then transferred to the Ministry of Defence; all visits were refused for a week. They were later charged with public order offences. None had been tried by the end of the year.

At least three people arrested in 1995 during the collection of signatures for a referendum on independence for Cameroon's English-speaking provinces, organized by the Southern Cameroons National Council, remained held without charge in the Central Prison in Yaoundé, known as Nkondengui Prison, throughout the year (see *Amnesty International Report 1996*).

The case against four members of the Mbororo Social and Cultural Association was dismissed by a court in Bamenda in September, after their trial on charges of defamation and abuse was repeatedly adjourned because the complainant failed to appear in court. The charges related to tracts critical of an influential landowner and businessman who was also a prominent CPDM member (see *Amnesty International Report 1996*). However, the same charges were brought two months later and the trial was adjourned until early 1997.

In northern Cameroon, traditional rulers known as *lamibe* continued to illegally detain political opponents with the tacit approval of the government and to operate unofficial prisons in residences of the *lamido* and local dignitaries. At least seven men, two of them held since 1992, remained held on the orders of the *lamido* of Rey Bouba, North Province, a prominent supporter of the CPDM (see previous *Amnesty International Reports*). Some of those detained were reported to have died in detention as a result of ill-treatment and neglect.

Torture and ill-treatment of both political detainees and criminal suspects by the security forces remained routine. Beatings of detainees, who were often stripped, held in severely overcrowded cells and denied sanitary facilities, were common. Torture and ill-treatment of students arrested in June and October included beatings to the head, buttocks and feet, and electric shocks to the genitals. A student died in June, apparently after being stabbed and beaten during a confrontation between students and members of the security forces and *auto-défense*. No action was taken against those responsible.

Although prosecutions of those responsible for torture and ill-treatment were rare, in July a police inspector was convicted of assault and fined. The victim, a woman arrested in 1995, sustained serious injuries after being beaten, punched and kicked (see *Amnesty International Report 1996*).

Prison conditions throughout the country, and particularly in more isolated areas, remained extremely harsh and amounted to cruel, inhuman or degrading treatment. Severe deficiencies in food, sanitation and medical care resulted in a high mortality rate. For example, at the prison in Mantoum, West Province, and at New Bell prison in Douala, several deaths a week were reported. Seriously ill prisoners were denied medical treatment. Prisoners were punished by being tied up, suspended upside down and beaten; others, including prisoners under sentence of death at Tchollire II prison, North Province, were permanently shackled.

A UNDP National Assembly member from Mayo Rey, North Province, died after being attacked by men acting on behalf of the *lamido* of Rey Bouba. Haman Adama Daouda, another UNDP politician and their delegation were attacked with sticks, knives and machetes while campaigning for the elections in January; Haman Adama Daouda subsequently died from head injuries. No action was taken against those responsible.

At least five people were reported to have died in incidents where excessive force appeared to have been used by the security forces. The victims included a criminal suspect shot while held at a gendarmerie headquarters in Douala in March.

Courts continued to pass death sentences and more than 100 prisoners remained under sentence of death. No executions took place.

Amnesty International called for the release of SDF members arrested in March; their subsequent release was confirmed in a response from the Minister of Justice. The organization also called for the release of imprisoned UNDP members. It called for the release of Pius Njawe and other detained journalists and urged that no journalists be imprisoned solely for their professional activities. Amnesty International urged that students arrested in June and October be protected from torture and ill-treatment; it called for safeguards to protect all prisoners and detainees from torture and ill-treatment and for impartial investigations into reports of torture, in order to bring those responsible to justice.

CANADA

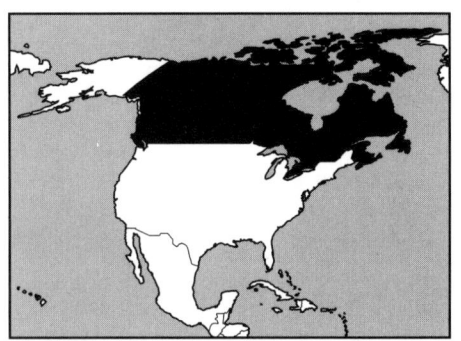

A Tamil refugee remained detained under legislation falling short of international standards. Two men faced extradition to the USA on charges which could carry the death penalty. A police officer was charged in connection with the possible extrajudicial execution of a Chippewa Indian protester in 1995, but there was no progress on the investigation into a death in custody in 1995.

Manickavasagam Suresh, a Tamil refugee from Sri Lanka, detained in October 1995 on the grounds that he "has or will engage in terrorism", remained held under section 40(1) of the Immigration Act, the provisions of which fall short of international standards for fair trial. Under this legislation detainees are not provided with full information on the reasons for their detention and are therefore deprived of an effective opportunity to defend themselves. There was also concern that Manickavasagam Suresh could be returned to Sri Lanka, where he might face human rights violations.

In July, the Minister of Justice and Attorney General agreed to the extradition of two Canadian citizens, Atif Ahmad Rafay and Glen Sebastian Burns, to Washington State, USA, to face charges of capital murder. The Minister failed to seek assurances from the US authorities that the death penalty would not be imposed, despite an agreement between the two countries allowing him to do so. At the end of the year the two men were awaiting the outcome of appeals against the Minister's decision. In 1994, the UN Human Rights Committee found that Canada had violated its obligations under the International Covenant on Civil and Political Rights when it extradited Charles Ng to California, USA, where he faced a capital murder charge, without first obtaining assurances that he would not be sentenced to death (see *Amnesty International Report 1995*). In October, the Minister of Justice agreed to allow the extradition of Rodolfo Pacificador to the Philippines to face murder charges. The Minister obtained assurances from the authorities in the Philippines that Rodolfo Pacificador would not face the death penalty if convicted.

In July, an Ontario Provincial Police officer was charged with "criminal negligence causing death" in connection with the shooting of Dudley George in circumstances suggesting he may have been extrajudicially executed. The trial was scheduled to take place in April 1997. Dudley George, a member of the Chippewa Indian tribe, was shot dead in September 1995 during disturbances that followed the occupation of Ipperwash Park, Ontario, by protesters claiming the land as Indian. Police opened fire on a bus that had been driven at police officers who were allegedly beating one of the protestors. The 15-year-old driver of the bus was wounded and Dudley George, who, according to witnesses, was standing some distance from the vehicle, was killed. Earlier in the day Dudley George, who had made statements critical of the police, had been threatened by police officers.

Michael Akhimen, an asylum-seeker from Nigeria held in detention in the Celebrity Inn Immigration Holding Center in Toronto, died of diabetic ketoacidosis after receiving inadequate medical attention in December 1995. A coroner's inquiry made recommendations to prevent future unnecessary deaths of asylum-seekers in similar circumstances. The recommendations are currently being considered by the Department of Citizenship and Immigration.

In May, the Court Martial Appeal Court overturned a severe reprimand given to an officer of the Canadian Airborne Regiment, members of whose unit were involved in the torture and death of a Somali youth during the 1992 to 1993 mission to Somalia (see *Amnesty International Report 1995*). The officer, the highest-ranking officer to be sentenced in the affair, had his sentence increased to three months' imprisonment and was dismissed from the military. Another soldier, sentenced to 90 days' imprisonment and demotion for negligence, subsequently had his sentence increased to one year on appeal. The Regiment has since been disbanded for its part in the torture and deaths of Somali citizens.

In October, the Chief of Defence Staff resigned amid allegations that documents pertaining to the incident were altered by military officials. A Commission of Inquiry began an investigation into these allegations as well as alleged abuses by the regiment during its mission to Somalia, including an incident where soldiers fatally shot a Somali man at close range in March 1993. The inquiry continued at the end of the year.

In June, Amnesty International wrote to the Minister of Justice, the Attorney General and the Premier of Ontario seeking further information about the investigation into the shooting of Dudley George. No detailed reply was received. Amnesty International also expressed concern about the continued detention without trial of Manickavasagam Suresh.

CHAD

Dozens of suspected opponents and critics of the government, some of them prisoners of conscience, were detained without charge or trial. One prisoner of conscience was convicted after an unfair trial. Torture, including rape, and ill-treatment were widespread; several people may have died under torture. One person died in custody apparently as a result of harsh prison conditions. Four members of an armed opposition group arrested in Sudan "disappeared" after being forcibly returned to Chad. Scores of people were extrajudicially executed. Armed opposition groups were reportedly responsible for grave abuses.

Armed opposition groups remained active, particularly in the south, west and east of the country, and launched sporadic attacks against the Chadian armed forces. Conflict, however, was on a lesser scale than in previous years. The security forces continued to carry out human rights violations during counter-insurgency operations. In January, a conference hosted by President Omar Bongo of Gabon failed to effect a reconciliation between armed opposition groups and President Idriss Déby.

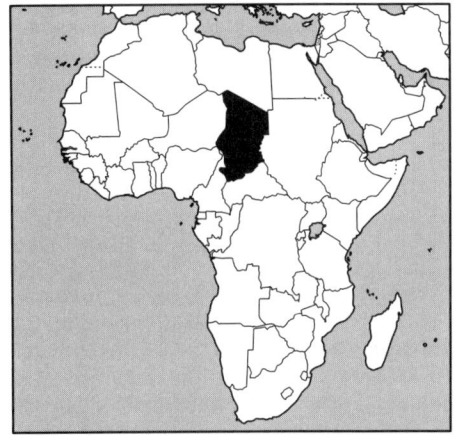

A new Constitution was approved by referendum in March. In July, President Déby began a second five-year term in office after defeating General Abdel Kader Kamougué in the first ever presidential elections. The *Union des syndicats du Tchad*, Federation of Trade Unions of Chad, was suspended for one month for calling for a boycott of the second round of voting, alleging irregularities in the first round. Several human rights groups were threatened with suspension by the Minister of the Interior when they also contested the results of the first round. Legislative elections scheduled for November, which would have ended the period of transition initiated after the 1993 *Conférence nationale souveraine*, Sovereign National Conference, were postponed until 1997.

A prisoner of conscience was convicted after an unfair trial. In March, Delwa Kassiré Koumakoye, former Prime Minister of the transitional government and President of the opposition party *Rassemblement national pour la démocratie et le progrès*, National Rally for Democracy and Progress, was arrested and sentenced following an unfair trial to three months' imprisonment for illegal possession of weapons. The arrest and conviction appeared to have been motivated by a desire to prevent Delwa Kassiré Koumakoye from standing in the presidential elections. His bodyguard, arrested at the same time, was released without charge or trial after 18 days. He claimed to have been tortured (see below). Maître Issa Hassan Goffa, a court clerk, was arrested and held for one day for supplying a copy of Delwa Kassiré Koumakoye's police record, a document necessary for him to submit his candidature.

Scores of political prisoners, many of whom may be prisoners of conscience, remained in detention without charge or trial, and arrests of possible prisoners of conscience, including human rights activists and leaders of political parties, continued.

Tohnel Doumro, an employee of the *Secours catholique pour le développement*, Catholic Development Aid, was arrested in November and held at the gendarmerie in Bousso for "collaborating with the enemy". Mahamat Abdelhaq, President of the *Association tchadienne pour la défense des droits de l'homme*, Chad Association for the Defence of Human Rights, was arrested in December and held at Abéché on suspicion of having links with the armed opposition *Front national du Tchad*, Chad National Front. At the end of the year both had been transferred to the gendarmerie in N'Djaména; neither had been formally charged.

More than 20 political prisoners arrested in previous years were still in detention. They included Benoît Djebongoum, Samuel Dingambaye and Célestin Ndoubaye, who had been arrested in the two Logone regions between July and October 1995, on suspicion of collaborating with the *Forces armées pour la République fédérale* (FARF), Armed forces for a Federal Republic, and the *Mouvement pour la démocratie et le développement* (MDD), Movement for Democracy and Development, armed opposition groups which receive support in the area. They appeared to have been arrested simply because of where they lived. Since their transfer to N'Djaména, in October 1995, and subsequently to Faya Largeau, there had been no official confirmation of their whereabouts. They were believed to have been kept chained together in groups of four and beaten during their detention. It was learnt that Mahamat Dare and Mahamat Sokou, also arrested in 1995 in the Logone district, died in detention later that year as a result of ill-treatment and inadequate diet.

A number of prisoners of conscience and political prisoners were released uncharged. Many of those arrested during the year were held for several days.

In March, at the time of a referendum on the adoption of the Constitution, Mayo Kebi, the head of the *Ligue tchadienne des droits de l'homme*, Chadian Human Rights League, in Bongor, was arrested and held for several days for asking a village headman to follow the instructions of the *Commission électorale nationale indépendante* (CENI), Independent National Electoral Commission. He was released without charge.

In July, Ngarlégy Yorangar Le Moïban, leader of the opposition party *Front d'action pour la République*, Action Front for the Republic, was arrested and held for two weeks at Bebédjia, Logone Oriental, where he was campaigning in the second round of the presidential elections on behalf of General Kamougué, leader of the *Union pour le renouveau et la démocratie*, Union for Renewal and Democracy. He was subsequently transferred to the gendarmerie's National Section for Investigation in N'Djaména. He was released after two weeks without charge. Following his release he was reported to have received a number of threats from members of the security forces.

In August, at least 13 N'Djaména University students were arrested following a demonstration to demand payment of grants. They were held for periods of up to eight days before being released without charge.

In October, Hadge Awatif, whose husband Mamadou Bisso was extrajudicially executed in January 1992 by the Chadian armed forces, was detained for a few hours at the ANS headquarters in N'Djaména for offering her condolences to Bichara Digui's family (see below).

Two Tama tradesmen and tribal chiefs, arrested in September 1995 by the *Agence nationale de sécurité*, National Security Agency, the counter-espionage service, which has no legal powers of arrest or detention, and transferred subsequently to the *Renseignements généraux*, General Intelligence Service, in N'Djaména, were released in February without charge or trial. They had been accused of financing the *Armée nationale tchadienne en dissidence* (ANTD), Dissident Chadian National Army, an armed opposition group.

In March, seven people from the two Logone regions of southern Chad, including high-school students Guillaume Ngarmadji, Joseph Morgoutoum and Alain Natimbaye, were released without charge or trial. They had been arrested in July 1994 on suspicion of belonging to an armed opposition group, the *Comité de sursaut pour la paix et la démocratie* (CNSPD), Committee of National Revival for Peace and Democracy. Despite peace agreements, known as the Bangui II Accords, concluded in August 1994 between the CNSPD and the Chadian authorities, and despite two amnesties which should have led to their release, these seven people were held for more than 18 months. There had been no official confirmation of their whereabouts.

There were continuing reports of torture and ill-treatment by members of the armed forces; torture was often used to extract confessions. New methods included submerging detainees in the River Logone in sacks. The discovery of several mutilated and unrecognizable bodies in the River Logone in June suggested that such torture sometimes resulted in death. No investigation was known to have been carried out as a result of the discovery. Former prisoners of conscience reported that they were tied to a vehicle in the "*arbatachar*" position, where the arms are painfully tied behind the back (see *Amnesty International Report 1996*), and dragged for a kilometre along the banks of the Logone river. Women and girls reported that they had been raped by the armed forces. Between September and December, three young girls were raped by members of the armed forces in Ngalaba, Logone Oriental.

Bachaïn Massingar, Delwa Kassiré Koumakoye's driver, who was arrested in March, was subjected to torture and ill-treatment, including threats and mock executions, to force him to incriminate his employer.

In March, members of the security forces, claiming to be in pursuit of FARF members, fired on civilians at Goré village market, Logone Occidental. At least 11 people, including two children, were seriously injured. Rimoumbubue Diallo, aged 13, had an arm and leg amputated as a result of injuries he sustained; Benjamin Bjekoungaye's femur was fractured by a bullet; and several others, including Jacqueline Djenon, received bullet wounds requiring lengthy hospitalization.

Prison conditions continued to be harsh, sometimes amounting to cruel, inhuman and degrading treatment. Severe overcrowding appeared to be common. In March, Mbaïlassem Gédéon, a former soldier suspected of being a member of an armed opposition group, who was arrested by gendarmes from the Moundou rural prefecture without the knowledge of the public prosecutor, was found dead at the Moundou criminal investigation brigade. The Public Prosecutor informed his superiors that Mbaïlassem Gédéon had apparently suffocated as a result of the heat in an overcrowded cell. The judicial authorities had not opened any investigation by the end of the year, nor had any action been taken against the men on guard duty at the time.

In April, new information came to light about the "disappearance" of Alyo Bouka, a member of the CNSPD arrested in July 1994 in Logone Occidental. Confirmation was received that he had been held for 24 days in the military quarters outside Moundou brewery and transferred by Hercules C 130 plane to N'Djaména. He was last seen in November 1994 at the *Camp des martyrs* prison in N'Djaména after he had confessed to being a CNSPD member.

In August, four members of armed opposition groups, the *Conseil national de redressement*, National Council for Recovery, and the ANTD, "disappeared" after being forcibly returned to Chad. They were among several members of Chadian armed groups arrested in El Généina, Sudan, by members of the Sudanese security forces and reportedly transferred to N'Djaména by the ANS. None has been seen since.

Bichara Digui, a member of the opposition *Rassemblement pour la démocratie et le progrès*, Rally for Democracy and Progress, was shot in August by three unidentified men, believed to be members of the security forces, as he returned to his home in N'Djaména. Moussa Brahim, his driver, was seriously injured. Members of the security forces who were nearby did not intervene. A few months before his death, Bichara Digui, who had been detained previously without charge or trial for over a year, had revealed that since his release in December 1994, he had been summoned on a number of occasions to interviews with the Chadian authorities, including the President and the presidential staff, where he had reportedly been threatened with death on account of his past links with Abass Koty Yacoub, extrajudicially executed in 1993 (see *Amnesty International Report 1994*). No investigation had been carried out into Bichara Digui's death by the end of the year.

In November, the Director General of the National Gendarmerie signed an order instructing members of the gendarmerie to extrajudicially execute persons caught in the act of committing a crime. In the following weeks scores of people were extrajudicially executed, including five people in Gaoui, and nine in Mayo-Kebbi, suspected of theft. In November, members of the *Garde nationale et nomade du Tchad*, Chad National Nomadic Guard, extrajudicially executed Ngarmadjim Raphaël following mass arrests when a member of the Guard died in a fight.

In February, the death sentences passed in August 1994 on Daoud Ahmat Chérif, Awat Abdou and Yacoub Issaka were reported to have been commuted to life imprisonment. Daoud Ahmat Chérif and Awat Abdou had been sentenced to death for murder, and Yacoub Issaka for an attack on Gninguilim market-place which caused 64 civilian deaths. In August, on the occasion of his investiture, President Déby commuted all death sentences passed in 1994 and 1995 to life imprisonment. No new death sentences were reported to have been passed.

Armed opposition groups were responsible for human rights abuses, including hostage-taking. In June, during the presidential elections, four men were abducted in Ngara, Lake prefecture, by MDD forces. The four, including Soumaïne Adam Moustapha, a member of the CENI, were reportedly collecting ballot boxes. They were apparently taken over the border to Nigeria, where they were handed over to the authorities in November, and eventually returned to Chad in December. FARF members were reportedly responsible for the execution of the chief of Tilo village, Mondji Laokoura, in December.

There were reports of human rights abuses, including rape, carried out by armed opposition groups in previous years. In June 1995, four girls had been raped by

FARF members as they returned to their village in Logone Occidental.

Amnesty International delegates visited Chad in April to investigate reports of human rights violations, particularly in the south of the country, and met members of human rights organizations and senior government and military officials. The delegates called on the authorities to release prisoners of conscience, condemn torture, open independent and impartial inquiries into cases of torture and extrajudicial execution and to adhere to the international human rights treaties ratified by Chad in 1995. Despite generally acknowledging the violations documented in Amnesty International's reports, government and military officials did not seem willing to open impartial investigations into human rights violations committed by the security forces.

Also in April, Amnesty International submitted information about its concerns in Chad to the UN Commission on Human Rights under the confidential 1503 procedure.

In October, Amnesty International published a report, *Chad: A country under the arbitrary rule of the security forces with the tacit consent of other countries*, which documented human rights violations by the security forces and abuses by armed opposition groups carried out since 1995. Amnesty International also expressed concern to foreign governments, particularly France and China, that military, security and police transfers had contributed to human rights violations in Chad.

CHILE

Unresolved cases of past human rights violations continued to be closed by military and civilian courts, but a military petition to end all investigations of past violations was rejected. A prisoner of conscience was detained briefly. There were reports of torture of detainees by members of the security forces. One death sentence was passed and subsequently commuted.

In April, the Senate rejected constitutional reforms proposed by the government in 1995, which had included changes in the law governing the structure of the Armed Forces, amendments to alter the composition of the National Security Council and reductions in the terms of office of nine Senators appointed by General Augusto Pinochet. A revised proposal for legislation to curtail judicial proceedings and restrict investigations into "disappearances" which occurred under the 1973 to 1978 military government, known as the "Figueroa-Otero Bill", remained "frozen" in the Senate at the end of the year (see *Amnesty International Report 1995*).

A bill proposing the abolition of the death penalty was brought before the Senate but was still awaiting a vote at the end of the year.

Courts continued to close investigations into cases of "disappearance" and extrajudicial execution which occurred between 1973 and 1978. During the first half of the year, civilian and military courts closed 21 cases involving 56 victims; the Amnesty Law of 1978 was applied in several of these cases. In most cases, lawyers acting for the victims' families filed appeals against the courts' decision. One such case concerned Carmelo Soria Espinoza, a UN official of dual Chilean-Spanish nationality who was abducted and killed by members of the security forces in 1976. In June, a Supreme Court judge classified the crime as "homicide" and closed the case under the Amnesty Law. As a state party to the UN Convention on the Prevention and Punishment of Crimes against Internationally Protected Persons, including Diplomatic Agents, Chile is obliged to make crimes against people protected under the treaty punishable by penalties which take into account their grave nature. In August, the Supreme Court upheld the June verdict, pronouncing the case closed.

In August, the *Corporación Nacional de Reparación y Reconciliación*, National Corporation for Reparation and Reconciliation – the government agency created in 1992 to pursue complaints of past human rights violations (see *Amnesty International Reports 1993* to *1995*) – presented a report to the government confirming a further 899 cases in which human rights violations had occurred. The Corporation's mandate expired at the end of the year.

In October, the Military Prosecutor General petitioned the Supreme Court to instruct all appeal courts and judges to close, under the Amnesty Law, hundreds of cases of human rights violations which occurred during the 1973 to 1978 military government. The Supreme Court rejected the petition at the end of October, thereby re-establishing the judges' authority to decide on cases within their jurisdiction.

A prisoner of conscience was briefly detained in October. Gladys Marín, Secretary General of the Communist Party, was arrested and held at the women's prison in Santiago, the capital. She was charged under National Security Legislation with the "slander" (*injuria*) of General Augusto Pinochet, Commander-in-Chief of the Army. The charge stemmed from a speech Gladys Marín gave at the "Memorial to the Detained-Disappeared and Extrajudicially Executed" in which she reportedly described General Pinochet as a "blackmailer" and a "psychopath who came to power through deceit, treason and crime". The charge was subsequently dropped and she was released after two days.

More than 20 cases of torture and ill-treatment by members of the security forces were reported to the General Director of the uniformed police (*carabineros*) and the General Director of Investigations by national non-governmental organizations.

In July, Alfredo Alegría Saavedra, Wilson Pérez Melgarejo, Rufino Pérez Abayay and a pregnant woman, Ana Ayala Medina, were arrested by members of the *Investigaciones* (civilian police) and taken to the First Police Station in Viña del Mar v Region. They said they were kept blindfold, handcuffed and chained to a wall, deprived of food and water for three days and denied access to toilets. They were reportedly beaten on the face and stomach, and tortured by having electric shocks applied to the temples; the men were also given electric shocks to the genitals. Ana Ayala Medina subsequently miscarried. All four were taken to hospital, but reportedly were not examined by a doctor. They were released without charge after a few days. No investigation was known to have been initiated.

Also in July, Cristina Poblete Cerda was taken from her home by the *Investigaciones*, who reportedly slapped her on the face and pulled her by the hair. She was taken to the First Police Station in Viña del Mar where she was allegedly kept blindfold, tortured with electric shocks and subjected to sexual harassment. She was subsequently released without charge.

In January, the UN Special Rapporteur on torture, who visited Chile in August 1995, issued a report endorsing the recommendations made by the UN Committee against Torture in 1994 (see *Amnesty International Report 1995*). The report cited a pattern of police ill-treatment of detainees and the Special Rapporteur urged the government to bring provisions for incommunicado detention into line with the Body of Principles for the Protection of All Persons under Any Form of Detention or Imprisonment. The Special Rapporteur also recommended prohibiting the blindfolding of detainees and ensuring that all detainees had prompt access to medical examination by an independent physician.

In May, Cupertino Andaur Contreras was sentenced to death by the Santiago Appeals Court. He had been found guilty of raping and killing a nine-year-old boy in December 1992. In August, the Second Chamber of the Supreme Court confirmed the death sentence. The death sentence was later commuted to life imprisonment by presidential pardon.

Five political prisoners were still facing possible death sentences in trials before the military courts at the end of the year (see *Amnesty International Report 1996*).

In March, an Amnesty International delegation visited Chile to present the authorities with a report, *Chile: Transition at the crossroads – human rights violations under Pinochet rule remain the crux*. The report analysed legislative proposals before the Chilean Senate aimed at curtailing investigations into past human rights violations. It called for the investigations to continue and for those responsible to be brought to justice. In August, an Amnesty

International observer attended the concluding phase of the appeal hearing in the case of the "disappearance" and killing of Carmelo Soria. During the year the organization called on the Chilean Government to repeal the 1978 Amnesty Law on the grounds that it contravened international human rights standards.

In July, Amnesty International appealed for Cupertino Andaur to be granted clemency and repeatedly urged that the death penalty be abolished. In October, the organization urged the President of the Supreme Court to reject the military petition to close investigations into past human rights violations. In November, Amnesty International wrote to the Minister of Justice urging the immediate and unconditional release of Gladys Marín.

CHINA

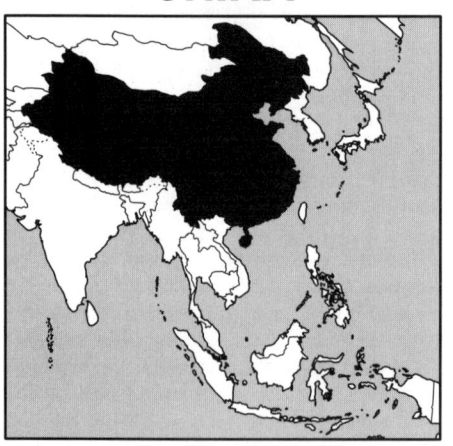

Hundreds, possibly thousands, of suspected opponents of the government were arrested during the year, while thousands of political prisoners detained in previous years remained imprisoned. Many were prisoners of conscience. Some were sentenced after unfair trials. Others were administratively detained without charge or trial. Torture and ill-treatment continued to be widespread, in some cases resulting in death. Mass summary executions were carried out. At least 6,000 death sentences and 3,500 executions were recorded during the year, but the real figures were believed to be much higher.

In March, the National People's Congress (NPC) adopted a new Administrative Punishment Law and amendments to the Criminal Procedure Law, which introduced new protections for detainees and of defendants' rights. In March, the NPC also repealed legislation providing for summary trials in death penalty cases, effective from January 1997. A new Martial Law was adopted, providing for the suspension of constitutional rights during a state of emergency.

Despite the legal reforms, numerous instances of arbitrary and summary justice were recorded. An anti-crime campaign, known as "strike hard", which was launched by the authorities in April and accompanied by a crack-down on suspected nationalist opponents and religious groups in Tibet and Xinjiang, was marked by mass summary trials and executions on a scale unprecedented since 1983. Outbreaks of violence by armed opposition groups were reported in Xinjiang during the crack-down.

Hundreds, possibly thousands, of suspected dissidents and opponents of the government, including prisoners of conscience, were detained during the year. Some were sentenced to prison terms after unfair trials, others were held under various forms of administrative detention. They included human rights and pro-democracy activists, members of religious groups not approved by the state, and members of ethnic groups who sought greater autonomy or religious freedom.

Political dissidents who addressed petitions to the authorities were immediately arrested. They included Wang Donghai and Chen Longde, pro-democracy activists from Zhejiang province who were detained in May after issuing a petition calling for the release of political prisoners; Wang Hui, the wife of prisoner of conscience Zhou Guoqiang, who was detained in September in connection with an open letter calling for help for her husband who was in poor health; and Liu Xiaobo, a leading dissident who was detained in October after co-signing a letter calling for political reforms. Wang Hui was released in October. Wang Donghai, Chen Longde and Liu Xiaobo were assigned terms of three years' "re-education through labour".

"Re-education through labour", a form of administrative detention imposed by local government committees without charge or trial, was increasingly used to arbitrarily detain dissidents for up to three years in labour camps. Liu Xiaobo's administrative sentence was imposed a few hours after his arrest, in breach of the safeguards for a fair and public hearing guaranteed by the new Administrative Punishment Law which had come into force one week before his arrest. Others assigned three years' "re-education through labour" included Liu Nianchun, a labour activist from Beijing detained since 1995 (see Amnesty International Report 1996).

Members of religious groups not approved by the state continued to be detained. Scores of Roman Catholics and Protestants were arrested in various provinces. In Anhui province, for example, 14 Roman Catholics were detained in April, and many beaten, after petitioning local officials for the return of church property. Eleven of them were subsequently released, but Dong Yimin, Zhang Zhongxiao and Zhou Guang'e reportedly remained in detention. There was no news of them at the end of the year. In May, up to 5,000 troops, supported by armoured cars and helicopters, reportedly surrounded the village of Donglu, Hebei province, to prevent Roman Catholics from attending an annual pilgrimage there. Several people were arrested, including Hu Duo and Wei Jingkun, both Roman Catholic priests, and Zhang Dapeng, a lay leader who had been imprisoned previously for peaceful religious activities. Others were placed under house arrest or subjected to severe restrictions. Up to 80 Roman Catholics were also reportedly arrested in Jiangxi province in November.

A crack-down on suspected nationalists and religious groups in Tibet was carried out during the "strike hard" anti-crime campaign. Early in the year the authorities had ordered the closure of monasteries in Tibet which had "political problems". In May, enforcement of a ban on photographs of the Dalai Lama led to clashes between government officials and monks at the Ganden monastery. Several monks were injured when security forces intervened; one reportedly later died of his injuries. The monastery was closed and up to 90 Ganden monks and novices were reportedly detained or "disappeared" in the following days. At least 15 were reportedly still detained at the end of the year and 45 others remained unaccounted for. Between May and October, a political "re-education" campaign carried out in Tibetan monasteries by official propaganda teams resulted in the arrest of at least 15 monks and the expulsion of many others from several monasteries. Those arrested included Ngawang Tharchin, who was reportedly imprisoned for three years in October for arguing with officials during a political lecture at Drepung monastery, and Tenchog Tenphel, who was arrested during a "re-education" session in September at Sakya monastery, southwest of Shigatse, and died in a local prison two weeks later. Police reportedly said he had committed suicide, but there was no inquest into his death. Lay Tibetans suspected of supporting Tibetan independence were also arrested, although few cases were publicly reported. They included five Tibetans accused of calling for Tibet's independence who were sentenced to up to five years' imprisonment at a public rally in Shigatse in May.

A similar crack-down on suspected Muslim nationalists, alleged "terrorists" and those accused of "illegal religious activities" was carried out in the Xinjiang Autonomous Region. Those jailed included Abduvahit Ahmedi, a Uighur accused of writing "reactionary" material "seeking to split the motherland", who was sentenced in May to three years' imprisonment for "counter-revolutionary incitement". According to official sources, 2,773 suspected "separatists", alleged "terrorists" and ordinary criminal suspects were arrested in Xinjiang between the start of the "strike hard" anti-crime campaign in April, and early June. The authorities did not indicate how many were held on political grounds and denied claims by exiled Uighur opposition leaders that 18,000 Muslim nationalists had been arrested in Xinjiang between May and July.

A crack-down on religious groups in Xinjiang resulted in the closure of "illegal" mosques and Koranic schools; the confiscation of "reactionary" or "illegal" religious materials; and, according to unofficial sources, up to 180 arrests. Those held included Aisha Awazy, a local people's representative for Kezhou, who was arrested in June in Akto county for "long-standing illegal religious activities". His fate was unknown at the end of the year. In July and August, 19 religious schools were closed and 98 people detained during a large-scale police operation against "illegal" religious schools near Hotan city in southwest Xinjiang. An official later claimed that the 98 were held for a "re-education" course, but, according to unofficial sources, by October 12 of them had been sentenced to terms of detention or imprisonment, 15 were still being held for investigation, 68 had received "administrative punishments" and three had been released. The crack-down on religious groups was continuing at the end of the year.

Thousands of political prisoners detained without trial or convicted after unfair trials in previous years remained imprisoned. They included many prisoners of conscience serving long sentences for their part in the 1989 pro-democracy movement and others jailed for the peaceful expression of their beliefs. Hada and Tegexi, two ethnic Mongol intellectuals detained in Inner Mongolia since December 1995 for promoting the concept of autonomy for China's ethnic minorities, were charged in March with "counter-revolutionary" offences. They were sentenced in December to 15 and 10 years' imprisonment respectively. Over 600 political prisoners were believed to remain in prison in Tibet. In July, prisoner of conscience Ngawang Sangdrol, a Tibetan nun held in Drapchi prison in Lhasa, reportedly had her sentence doubled to 18 years' imprisonment for shouting "Free Tibet" while undergoing punishment for a breach of prison rules.

Several prisoners of conscience were released on completion of their sentences. They included Fu Shenqi and Zhang Xianliang, both detained in Shanghai since 1993 (see Amnesty International Report 1994), who were released in April and June respectively; and Tong Yi (see Amnesty International Report 1995), who was released in October.

Political trials continued to fall far short of international fair trial standards; verdicts and sentences were routinely decided by the authorities before trial. For example, prisoner of conscience Wang Dan, a student leader during the 1989 pro-democracy protests, was sentenced in October to 11 years' imprisonment after being convicted of "conspiring to overthrow the government". The charge, brought against Wang Dan after he had been illegally detained without charge for nearly 17 months, was based on accusations that he had "endangered state security" by writing articles critical of the government which had been published overseas, receiving financial assistance from abroad, and having contacts with dissidents in China and abroad. Despite prior official statements that the trial would be public, foreign journalists and independent observers were excluded and no witnesses were called during the four-hour trial. Wang Dan's appeal against the verdict and sentence was rejected by a high court in November after a 10-minute hearing.

Torture and ill-treatment of detainees and prisoners held in detention centres, prisons or labour camps remained widespread, in some cases resulting in death. In March, information came to light about Wang Jingbo, a factory worker in Beijing, who was reportedly beaten to death while in police custody in late November 1995. An autopsy showed he had 12 broken ribs and had suffered a brain haemorrhage. Police claimed that he had been beaten by other prisoners. No judicial investigation into his case was known to have been carried out. In mid-August, prisoner of conscience Chen Longde (see above) was reportedly kicked, punched and beaten with an electric baton by a prison officer at the Luoshan labour camp in Zhejiang province, and jumped from a third-storey window in order to escape the beating. He suffered serious injuries, including hip and leg fractures, and was hospitalized. He was reportedly beaten to make him "acknowledge his guilt". The continued use of torture by police to speed up confessions was acknowledged in November by the official newspaper *Guangming Daily* in an article denouncing increasing corruption among the judiciary.

Prison conditions were often harsh, with inadequate food and medical care, and many prisoners suffered from serious illnesses as a result. Prisoner of conscience Kelsang Thutob, a Tibetan monk serving an 18-year prison sentence at Drapchi prison in Lhasa, was reported to have died in prison in July owing to lack of medical care. No investigation into his death was known to have been carried out. Medical parole, which is possible under Chinese law, was rarely granted to political prisoners. One prominent prisoner of conscience, Chen Ziming, was released on bail for medical treatment in November, but placed under virtual house arrest. Previously paroled in 1994, he had been sent back to jail in 1995 to serve the rest of his sentence (see *Amnesty International Report 1996*). According to his family, he had received no medical treatment after returning to prison despite suffering from cancer and needing continuous medical care.

The death penalty continued to be used extensively. At least 68 criminal offences, many of them non-violent, were punishable by death. At least 6,000 death sentences and 3,500 executions were recorded by Amnesty International, but the true figures were believed to be far higher.

The number of executions increased dramatically after the launch of the "strike hard" anti-crime campaign in April. Well over 200,000 arrests and at least 2,500 executions were believed to have been carried out within the first four months of the campaign. Most of those executed were summarily tried following official instructions to the judiciary to speed up prosecutions and trials and to impose "severe" punishments, including the death penalty. The state media publicized arrests and executions daily.

Across the country, groups of people were executed immediately after mass rallies and public trials held "to pronounce" death sentences. Some such "trials" were held jointly by several courts. In Gansu province, for example, 14 people were executed on 16 May immediately after being sentenced to death at a "joint open trial" held by two courts in Lanzhou. Some people were executed days after the crimes were allegedly committed. In Jilin province, for example, three men were executed on 31 May, seven days after their arrest for allegedly committing a robbery on 21 May. Their trial, sentencing, as well as the hearing of the appeal lodged by one of the three men, and the review and approval of the three death sentences by a high court, all took place between 24 May and 28 May.

Prisoners condemned to death were paraded in public at mass rallies, some in shackles and with ropes around their necks. Zheng Jian, a condemned prisoner who had attempted to commit suicide by jumping from a two-storey building, was reportedly taken on a stretcher onto the stage of a mass rally in Shenzhen, where his sentence was announced, and then carried to the execution ground. He was among 62 people executed on 30 October in three cities in Guangdong province.

Amnesty International repeatedly urged the Chinese authorities to release all prisoners of conscience; ensure fair trials for other political prisoners; take steps to stop torture and executions; and review the use of the death penalty. In March, Amnesty International launched an international campaign to draw attention to continuing massive human rights violations in China and published a report, *China: No one is safe – political repression and abuse of power in the 1990s*. The government did not respond to requests for representatives of the organization to discuss human rights concerns with authorities in China. Amnesty International published 10 other reports during the year including: in May, *China: State secrets – a pretext for repression*; in June, *China: Repression in the 1990s – a directory of victims*; and in July, *Religious repression in China* and *Women in China: Detained, victimized but mobilized*.

In September, an Amnesty International delegation attending the 96th Inter-Parliamentary Conference in Beijing held informal talks with Chinese representatives at the Conference.

In March, Amnesty International raised its concerns on China in statements at the UN Commission on Human Rights. Yet again, discussion on a draft resolution was halted by the adoption of a procedural motion to take no action.

In May, the UN Committee against Torture examined China's second periodic report and made a number of recommendations. These included the enactment of a law defining the crime of torture in terms consistent with the definition provided in the UN Convention against Torture and Other Cruel, Inhuman or Degrading Treatment or Punishment; the establishment of a comprehensive system to investigate complaints of ill-treatment effectively; changes in the methods for carrying out executions, improvements in prison conditions, prompt access to legal counsel for detainees, as well as to their families and to a medical doctor, and measures to ensure the independence of the judiciary.

COLOMBIA

More than 1,000 civilians were extrajudicially executed by the security forces and paramilitary groups operating with their support or acquiescence. Many victims had been tortured. Human rights activists were repeatedly threatened and attacked. More than 120 people "disappeared" after detention by the armed forces or paramilitary groups. "Death squad"-style killings of people regarded as "disposable" continued in urban areas. Several army officers were charged in connection with human rights violations, but many others continued to evade accountability for thousands of extrajudicial executions and "disappearances" in recent years. Guerrilla groups were responsible for numerous human rights abuses, including scores of deliberate and arbitrary killings and the taking and holding of hundreds of hostages.

In April and May, under provisions of the state of emergency, the government issued Decree Laws 0717 and 0900 providing for the creation of "Special Public Order Zones". Designated zones were placed under the direct authority of regional military commanders with additional powers to enforce public order. In July, the Constitutional Court ruled that three of the provisions of these decrees were unconstitutional, including the obligatory registration of residents and preventive detention. Nevertheless, the armed forces continued to exercise these powers in the more remote areas of the country. The state of emergency introduced in November 1995 was lifted in July, as required by the Constitution, but emergency measures remained in effect for a further 90 days.

In August, the government introduced a constitutional reform bill which, among other things, would grant certain judicial police powers to the military and would remove the Constitutional Court's control over the declaration of states of emergency, thereby increasing the likelihood of extended periods of emergency rule and the suspension of constitutional guarantees. The Senate Chamber of Congress added a number of provisions to the constitutional reform bill designed to eliminate civilian judicial and disciplinary controls over the armed forces. Other Senate proposals included the reintroduction of administrative detention and the relegalization of paramilitary forces by creating a civilian "national militia" to act as an auxiliary force to the military. Congress gave the bill a partial preliminary approval in December.

The long-running armed conflict spread and intensified. More than 1,000 people were killed as a result of combat during the year. In August and September, the *Fuerzas Armadas Revolucionarias de Colombia* (FARC), Revolutionary Armed Forces of Colombia, and the *Ejército de Liberación Nacional* (ELN), National Liberation Army, launched military offensives on a scale unprecedented in recent years. At least 200 people died as guerrilla forces attacked economic and military targets. In August, FARC guerrillas took Las Delicias military base on the border between Caquetá and Putumayo departments in southern Colombia. Dozens of soldiers were killed and injured and 60 soldiers were captured. Despite intense negotiations to secure their release, the soldiers remained in captivity at the end of the year.

Between July and September, strikes and mass demonstrations were staged by peasant farmers in the departments of Caquetá, Putumayo and Guaviare. The demonstrations had been called to protest against the destruction of coca plantations. The security forces' response frequently involved excessive use of force; at least 12 unarmed civilians died and scores of protesters and journalists were seriously injured. The demonstrations ceased when the government agreed a program of voluntary eradication and crop substitution.

Paramilitary organizations, declared illegal in 1989, continued their territorial expansion through military offensives characterized by widespread human rights violations. Torture, political killings and "disappearances" of civilians by these groups escalated dramatically in several areas of the country, including the departments of Antioquia, Chocó, Cesar, Sucre and North Santander. Paramilitary forces frequently acted under the direction, or in complicity with the Colombian armed forces. In April, a group of heavily armed men entered bars in the La Paz, Tigrito and Borbollón districts of the town of Segovia, Antioquia department. They forced those inside to lie face down, and shot dead 15 people, including four teenagers, and injured another 15 people. The drivers of one of the vehicles commandeered by the paramilitary, "disappeared". Although local civilian authorities informed the police and military authorities when the attack began, the security forces took no action. In May, an army captain attached to the Bomboná Battalion of Brigade XIV was arrested when judicial investigations established that he had assisted the gunmen to travel to Segovia. Following the attack, Segovia and neighbouring Remedios were declared "Special Public Order Zones". Despite increased military presence, paramilitary threats and attacks against Segovia's residents continued throughout the year. The April attack bore many similarities to the massacre of 43 Segovia residents in 1988, which remained unresolved despite evidence that armed forces' personnel were responsible (see Amnesty International Report 1989).

The government's failure to take action to halt paramilitary abuses was starkly illustrated by events on the Bellacruz ranch, Cesar department, in northern Colombia where peasant farmers were persecuted for several months by a paramilitary group operating in complicity with the Colombian armed forces. In March, more than 280 families were forcibly expelled from the Bellacruz ranch by a paramilitary group operating on behalf of a family which claims ownership of the land. Several peasants were beaten and otherwise ill-treated during the eviction and their homes were burned. In the months following the eviction, at least eight of their leaders were killed and five were made to "disappear" by the paramilitary forces. Despite numerous official guarantees that the evicted families could safely return, no action was taken by the authorities to execute arrest warrants against paramilitaries responsible for the killings or to remove them from the Bellacruz ranch.

Civilians continued to be the principal victims of the conflict between guerrilla forces and army-backed paramilitary groups in the Urabá region of Antioquia department. Most attacks were directed against civilians presumed to support rival armed groups, although children were also among the victims. In August, paramilitary forces reportedly decapitated 12-year-old César Augusto Rivera in front of scores of school children in Apartadó, Urabá, who were assembled for a peace meeting to be addressed by Apartadó's mayor.

Human rights defenders faced a growing campaign of harassment, intimidation and violent assaults. In October, Josué Giraldo Cardona was shot dead in the presence of his two young daughters by an unidentified gunman outside his home in Villavicencio, Meta department. Josué Giraldo, President of the *Comité Cívico por los Derechos Humanos en el Meta*, Meta Civic Committee for Human Rights, and an activist with the legal left-wing *Unión Patriótica* (UP), Patriotic Union, had received repeated death threats in recent years which he attributed to members of the Colombian armed forces (see *Amnesty International Report 1996*). The Inter-American Court of Human Rights issued a resolution requiring the Colombian Government to adopt urgent measures to protect the life and physical integrity of Josué Giraldo's family and other members of the Meta Civic Committee; to guarantee that they would not be persecuted or threatened by state agents; and to investigate the murder of Josué Giraldo and other acts against members of the Meta Civic Committee and to punish those responsible.

More than 120 people "disappeared" after being detained by the security forces or paramilitary groups. In rural conflict areas, paramilitary forces were responsible for scores of "disappearances" of civilians suspected of being guerrilla sympathizers. In October, paramilitary gunmen raided the community of Media Luna, municipality of San Diego, Cesar department. Six people, including an eight-year-old boy, were killed outright. Seven others were abducted. One was later found dead, bearing signs of torture. The other six, including a 13-year-old boy, remained "disappeared", with two other inhabitants of Media Luna who were seized in the nearby town of Valledupar. A paramilitary group left graffiti in the town identifying themselves as members of the *Autodefensas Campesinas de Córdoba y Urabá* (ACCU), Peasant Farmer Self-Defence Group of Córdoba and Urabá, and threatening other residents. At least 15 close relatives of guerrilla commanders were kidnapped and held hostage by ACCU paramilitary forces. In public statements, ACCU said the relatives would only be released when the FARC and the ELN released their hostages (see below). At least five of the relatives remained in captivity at the end of the year.

The killing of so-called "disposables" by police-backed "death squads" and urban militias linked to armed opposition groups continued in many cities and towns. Victims included vagrants, petty delinquents and drug dealers. In July, the Regional Ombudsman based in Manizales, Caldas department, publicly called on the police to investigate the deaths of more than 80 people in the first six months of the year in the town of Chinchiná, in circumstances suggesting they were victims of "social cleansing".

Investigations by the Human Rights Unit of the Attorney General's Office into illegal paramilitary activities led to criminal charges against more than 200 people, including several members of the armed forces. In October, retired army General Farouk Yanine Díaz was arrested and charged in connection with the creation of paramilitary groups responsible for widespread human rights abuses in the central Magdalena Medio region in the 1980s. An imprisoned paramilitary leader, who confessed to responsibility for several hundred political killings in the Magdalena Medio region in the late 1980s, testified that General Yanine Díaz had orchestrated paramilitary activity in the area and tacitly approved human rights violations such as the torture and killing in 1987 of 19 merchants suspected of collaborating with guerrilla groups. In November, the military justice system was granted jurisdiction over the case. Military courts have persistently failed to impartially investigate and bring to justice members of the armed forces responsible for human rights violations.

In September, two members of the army's Brigade IX were arrested and charged in connection with the killing of UP Senator Manuel Cepeda Vargas in August 1994 (see *Amnesty International Report 1995*). Twenty-seven members of the army, including three officers, were formally charged by a military court in October in connection with the murder of 13 peasant farmers in Riofrío, Valle de Cauca department, in October 1993 (see *Amnesty International Report 1994*).

In November, the Procurator Delegate for Human Rights announced that during the previous 15 months his office had imposed disciplinary sanctions, including 50 dismissals, against 126 military and police personnel for violations of human rights. In the same period, the Procurator Delegate had opened more than 600 cases against members of the security forces involving 1,338 victims of massacres, torture and "disappearance".

Guerrilla groups continued to commit grave human rights abuses including deliberate and arbitrary killings. In response to the continuing paramilitary offensive in Urabá, FARC guerrillas killed dozens of suspected paramilitary supporters. In May, 16 people, including six women, were killed when the FARC attacked the villages of Pueblo Bello and Alto de Mulatos, Urabá. The victims were taken from their homes and shot or hacked to death with machetes.

Marden Betancur Conda, a leader of the Paez indigenous community of Jambaló, Cauca department, was killed in August by presumed members of the Cacique Calarcá unit of the ELN which had publicly accused him of organizing army-backed vigilante squads in the area. Five Paez indians, who were tried under the community's traditional laws for complicity in the killing, were sentenced to 60 lashes, later commuted to exile from the community.

At least 500 people were kidnapped and held hostage, principally by the FARC and the ELN. Victims included landowners, industrialists, business people and foreign nationals. Some were released after ransoms were paid or other demands met. However, others were killed when ransoms were not paid or during escape attempts. According to eye-witnesses, 65-year-old Isaac Durán Blanco was shot dead in August when he tried to escape a kidnap attempt by members of the ELN and the

Ejército Popular de Liberación (EPL), Popular Liberation Army, near La Esperanza, Norte de Santander department. Some of his relatives subsequently received death threats from the EPL. Other kidnap victims were held hostage for more overtly political motives, either to pressurize the authorities to accede to guerrilla proposals or to demand publicity for guerrilla policies. Local officials, including several mayors, accused by armed opposition groups of corruption were kidnapped and held hostage and subjected to "popular trials" of their administration. Juan Legarda Noguera, Mayor of Ricaurte, Nariño department, was released by the ELN after 63 days in captivity. He reported having been subjected to a "popular trial" because of alleged irregularities in his administration. At least 12 other mayors were kidnapped and held hostage during the year.

Amnesty International raised its concerns about Colombia at the 52nd session of the UN Commission on Human Rights. These were addressed in a statement by the Chairman of the Commission about endemic violence, violations of the right to life, "disappearances", torture and impunity; the need to strengthen the civilian judicial system and to exclude crimes against humanity from military jurisdiction; and insufficient government efforts to implement the recommendations of UN thematic mechanisms. The Commission asked the UN High Commissioner for Human Rights to establish a permanent office in Colombia mandated to help the authorities develop policies and programs for the promotion and protection of human rights, to observe violations of human rights in the country, and to submit analytical reports to the High Commissioner. After several months of negotiations between the Colombian Government and the High Commissioner, an agreement for the establishment of the office was signed in November. However, the office was not functioning by the end of the year.

An Amnesty International delegation, led by the organization's Secretary General, visited Colombia in May and hosted an international conference on the protection of human rights defenders in Latin America. The conference appealed to the Organization of American States to adopt a declaration on the right to defend human rights and called on governments to adopt effective protection mechanisms for human rights defenders. Amnesty International's delegates met President Ernesto Samper, government ministers and victims of human rights violations and their relatives. Amnesty International urged the government to honour its commitments to ensure respect for human rights, to conduct thorough, independent and impartial investigations into all extrajudicial executions and "disappearances", to bring those responsible to justice in civilian courts and to dismantle paramilitary organizations. Amnesty International appealed to opposition groups to end deliberate and arbitrary killings and to release all hostages.

COMOROS

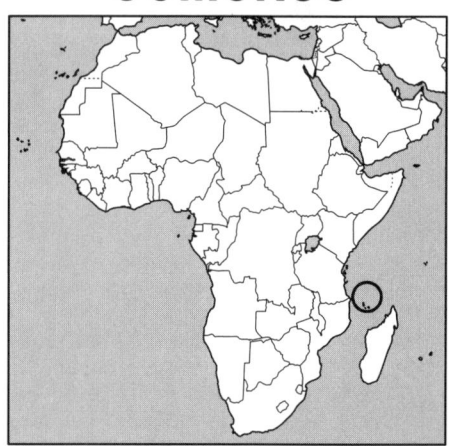

The first judicial execution since 1975 was carried out in September. At least four people remained under sentence of death at the end of the year.

President Mohamed Taki Abdoulkarim was elected in March. His election marked an end to a transitional government which was installed in October 1995 after government troops led by French mercenary Bob Denard overthrew President Said Mohamed Djohar in September 1995. The coup was defeated by French government troops.

Although President Djohar had been reinstated as President without executive powers, he was banned from standing as a candidate in the presidential elections in February.

Soon after his election, President Mohamed Taki announced that people convicted of murder could be sentenced to death under Islamic law. The announcement reportedly followed public concern about a rise in the murder rate. Some politicians denounced the decision as politically motivated.

Legislative elections in December were boycotted by opposition political parties. Nearly all seats in the National Assembly were won by a coalition party, the *Rassemblement national pour le développement*, National Union for Development, which supports President Mohamed Taki.

In October, a new Constitution was adopted by referendum. The Constitution upholds the principles of the UN Charter, the Universal Declaration of Human Rights and the African Charter on Human and Peoples' Rights. Although the Constitution guarantees freedom of expression and assembly, it also provides for the dissolution of political parties which fail to obtain at least two representatives in the National Assembly. While stating that all people are equal before the law and that there will be no discrimination on grounds of sex, origin, race, ideological convictions or religion, the Constitution nevertheless provides for the creation of an Islamic council, known as the *Conseil des ulémas*, Council of the Ulemas, to advise the National Assembly on the conformity of laws with Islamic principles.

At the end of November and beginning of December, five members of opposition political parties were arrested after the authorities accused them of involvement in burning ballot boxes. According to reports, they may have been arrested for criticizing the political system. They were released within days without charge or trial.

Ali Youssouf was executed by firing-squad in September. He had been convicted of murder in August by a criminal court. He did not have legal counsel during the trial and was denied the opportunity to appeal against his conviction or sentence; judges of the *Cour de Cassation* (Appeal Court), had not then been appointed by the National Assembly. This was the first judicial execution carried out since 1975.

At least four people remained under sentence of death at the end of the year. They included Saidali Mohamed (also known as Rodin), who was sentenced to death in December.

In September, Amnesty International condemned the execution of Ali Youssouf and appealed to President Mohamed Taki to commute all death sentences. The organization urged that all suspects charged with capital offences be given access to legal counsel.

CONGO

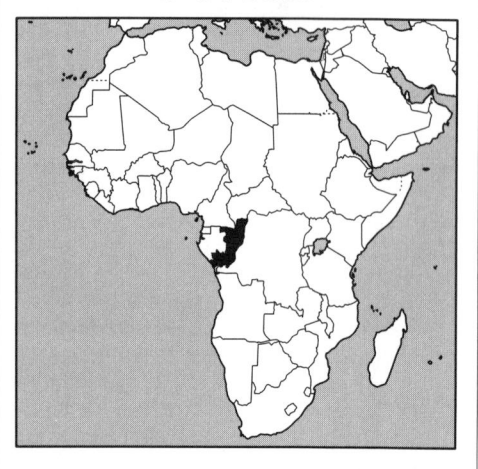

Critics of the government, and trade unionists were imprisoned; some of them appeared to be prisoners of conscience. A refugee was threatened with death by a member of the security forces. Several people were killed by members of the security forces in suspicious circumstances. Prison conditions continued to be so harsh that they constituted cruel, inhuman or degrading treatment.

Although there was relative stability during the year, sporadic incidents of political violence continued to be reported (see previous *Amnesty International Reports*). Between 14 and 19 February, there was a mutiny among former members of a disbanded militia allied to the ruling *Mouvance présidentielle*, Presidential Tendency, who demanded that they be paid and their position regularized. The mutiny reportedly left five people dead and 37 injured. Following the mutiny, up to 2,500 former members of pro-government militias were recruited into the army.

For the first time, the 19 members of the Supreme Court were elected by the National Assembly and Senate. Of the 19, 12 were associated with the *Mouvance présidentielle*, and five with the opposition *Mouvement congolais pour la démocratie et le développement intégral* (MCDDI),

Congolese Movement for Democracy and Integral Development, led by Bernard Kolélas.

A law passed by the National Assembly in late 1995 (see *Amnesty International Report 1996*) which restricted journalists and limited freedom of expression was finally approved by the Senate.

In February, four trade unionists from the state-owned Post and Telecommunications company were sentenced to four months in prison and a fine for their role in a strike over the privatization of the company. There were reports that they had been ill-treated in custody.

A pattern of arrests and harassment of government critics and potential electoral opponents emerged during the year, ahead of presidential elections scheduled for July 1997.

In May, Colonel Casimir Buissa Matoko, a close friend of former President and opposition leader Denis Sassou Nguesso, was arrested at Brazzaville airport. He was accused of possessing seditious documents. According to reports, the documents included human rights publications and information about the 1992 elections. He was held incommunicado without charge for two weeks at the airport, before being transferred to a civilian prison.

In September, Colonel Matoko and another supporter of Denis Sassou Nguesso, Gabriel Longombe, were convicted by a Brazzaville court of endangering the security of the state. Neither of the defendants had been charged with the offence, nor had the charge been raised during the trial. Colonel Matoko was also convicted of illegal possession of arms. He was sentenced to two years' imprisonment with one year suspended. Gabriel Longombe was stripped of his civil rights and prohibited from living in Brazzaville for two years. Both men lodged an appeal, which had not been heard by the end of the year.

In September, another supporter of former President Sassou Nguesso was arrested. Pierre Otto Mbongo, a businessman, was arrested without a warrant by around 50 armed soldiers. He was detained for seven days at a Border Police station, then taken to Brazzaville central prison after a committal order was issued by a judge. When he arrived at the prison he was immediately taken to an undisclosed location, where he was held incommunicado. Although he required medical care for gout and hypertension, he was not allowed to see his doctor. On 12 December, he was moved to another place of detention at the request of his doctor.

A leading member of a local refugee organization received death threats from the security forces and escaped an assassination attempt. Emmanuel Cole, President of the *Association des réfugiés du Congo*, Association of Refugees in Congo, was threatened by a member of the *Direction pour la surveillance du territoire*, Department of Territorial Surveillance, on 30 March. Two days later he was shot at from a passing car as he walked along the street. He had been detained for a month in 1995 and allegedly tortured.

A number of people died at the hands of members of the security forces. On 24 January, three people were reported to have been killed and a number injured in clashes between trainee soldiers and civilians at Nyaki which followed the death of a trainee soldier. It was not known whether there was any investigation into the deaths. There were no investigations into extrajudicial executions and other human rights violations perpetrated in previous years (see *Amnesty International Reports 1995* and *1996*).

Prison conditions continued to be so harsh that they amounted to cruel, inhuman or degrading treatment. Lack of food, inadequate hygiene and overcrowding led to severe malnourishment among prisoners and a high incidence of tuberculosis, malaria and AIDS.

Amnesty International expressed concern about the incommunicado detention of Colonel Casimir Buissa Matoko and was assured by the authorities that he had been given access to a doctor as well as to his lawyer and members of his family. The organization urged the authorities to investigate the irregularities surrounding his detention and trial and to take steps to ensure that such breaches of procedure did not recur. Amnesty International sought assurances regarding the safety of Emmanuel Cole and other refugees and that the threats against him and attempt on his life would be investigated.

COSTA RICA

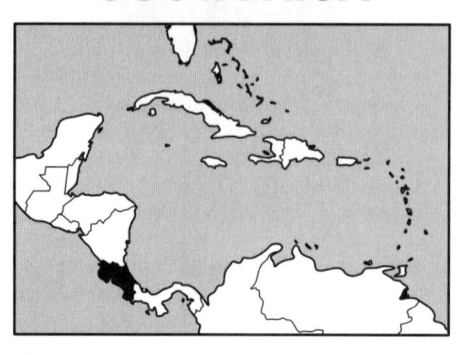

There were reports of ill-treatment and excessive use of force by police officers and armed security guards against peasants involved in land disputes. A refugee in Costa Rica was allegedly intimidated by members of the Honduran security forces.

In June, Costa Rica ratified the Inter-American Convention on the Forced Disappearance of Persons.

Throughout the year there were widespread demonstrations against privatization measures and the government's economic austerity plans. In the city of Puerto Limón, during riots against the privatization of port services in August, three people were reportedly killed and nearly 80 were injured.

There were continued reports of ill-treatment and excessive use of force by police and armed security guards operating under licence of the Ministry of Public Security during land evictions. In May, 80 members of the civil guard and several armed security guards evicted 200 peasants who were occupying a farm, "Dieciocho de Abril S.A." in Sarapiquí, department of Heredia. During the eviction, three peasants were shot and injured: Juan Víctor Víctor was injured when a bullet hit him the abdomen, and René Rojas Ferrogino and Dennis Zambrana were wounded by pellets. Some peasants were allegedly beaten after their detention by members of the civil guard. Carlos Rangel Mendoza was reportedly beaten repeatedly in the face after being handcuffed.

Reina Xiomara Zelaya, a refugee living in Costa Rica, was reportedly intimidated by members of the Honduran security forces. Reina Xiomara Zelaya fled Honduras in February after her former husband, Florencio Caballero, testified in front of national and international agencies to having worked between 1979 and 1984 as an interrogator for the Honduras military intelligence unit, Battalion 3-16. The battalion was entrusted with the task of investigating political suspects and carrying out their abduction, detention, torture and murder.

Reina Xiomara Zelaya had fled Honduras with her three young daughters after receiving death threats and had been granted asylum in Costa Rica. Between August and December, she and her daughters were intimidated in Costa Rica on a number of occasions, allegedly by members of the Honduran security forces. Amnesty International repeatedly urged the Costa Rican authorities to guarantee the safety of Reina Xiomara Zelaya and her daughters and to investigate the death threats (which she continued to receive in Costa Rica), and to bring those responsible to justice. However, no effective action had been taken by the authorities by the end of the year.

In June, Amnesty International wrote to the Minister of Public Security requesting a thorough and independent investigation into the reports of excessive use of force by members of the civil guard and armed security guards during the eviction from the farm "Dieciocho de Abril S.A.", and calling for those responsible to be brought to justice. Amnesty International also urged that all necessary measures be taken to ensure that such incidents were stopped, including the training of the security forces in the UN Code of Conduct for Law Enforcement Officials and the Basic Principles on the Use of Force and Firearms by Law Enforcement Officials. No reply had been received by the end of the year.

CÔTE D'IVOIRE

Three prisoners of conscience were released at the end of the year. At least 100 people arrested in 1995 and 1996, including possible prisoners of conscience, remained detained without trial. There were reports of ill-treatment by the security forces. Some 10 officers and an unknown number of soldiers held incommunicado since November 1995 on suspicion of plotting a coup were punished or cleared of all charges in November. More

than 200 criminal prisoners and six political prisoners died in detention in Abidjan and Gagnoa as a result of extremely harsh conditions. **One person was sentenced to death but there were no executions.**

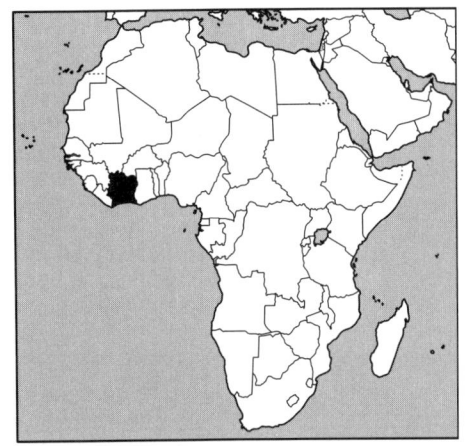

The political unrest that followed the presidential elections in October 1995, and led to the arrest of dozens of opposition party supporters including possible prisoners of conscience, had subsided by the beginning of the year.

A publisher and two journalists from the newspaper *La Voie*, all prisoners of conscience, received presidential pardons and were released at the end of the year. One of the journalists, Freedom Neruda, was arrested in January and sentenced to two years' imprisonment. The others, Aboudrahmane Sangaré, Deputy Secretary General of the *Front populaire ivoirien* (FPI), Popular Ivorian Front, and Director of *La Voie*, and another journalist, Emmanuel Koré, had received the same sentence in December 1995. All three were convicted of insulting President Henri Konan Bédié in an article which suggested that his presence brought bad luck to a football team. In August, the three prisoners had refused a presidential pardon because it was conditional on their withdrawing their appeal to the Supreme Court.

Some 20 people, including possible prisoners of conscience, sentenced to terms of imprisonment after the October 1995 events were released in August following a presidential pardon. They had been prosecuted under a law passed in 1992, but not previously invoked, under which anyone who calls or leads a gathering is held accountable for any violence that occurs, even if he or she did not personally incite or use violence (see *Amnesty International Report 1996*). A number of other detainees held in connection with the October 1995 events were provisionally released or had their sentences reduced on appeal, but at the end of the year at least 100, including possible prisoners of conscience, remained detained without trial on charges under this law.

At the beginning of the year, there were further arrests linked to the events of October 1995. In January, 11 people were arrested in Guiberoua, in the west. They were charged with looting camps belonging to the Baoulé ethnic group, of which President Konan Bédié is a member, during the October 1995 election period when ethnic tension developed between Baoulé villagers and the majority ethnic group, the Bétés, to which Laurent Gbagbo, leader of the opposition FPI, belongs. By the end of the year, at least 80 Bétés remained in detention without trial in Gagnoa in relation to the October events.

Student activists belonging to the *Fédération estudiantine et scolaire de Côte d'Ivoire* (FESCI), Ivorian Federation of Students and School Pupils, continued to face harassment by the security forces (see *Amnesty International Report 1996*). Two press conferences held by FESCI in May and in August at Youpougon University in Abidjan were broken up by members of the security forces who beat and otherwise ill-treated the students, some of whom were briefly detained. In December, four FESCI leaders were arrested and held incommunicado for four days. They were charged with incitement to violence, although there was no evidence to substantiate the charges. All of them appeared to be prisoners of conscience, detained solely because of their membership of FESCI.

Some 10 officers and an unknown number of soldiers, arrested in November 1995, were held incommunicado for most of the year. They were accused of plotting a coup. In November, some were released after receiving 16 months' suspension from duty, others were cleared of all charges and seven were dismissed from the army and remained in prison awaiting trial. According to some sources, these soldiers were arrested because they obeyed their Chief of Staff, who was reportedly reluctant to use the army to maintain order during the turbulent October 1995 elections.

During the year, more than 200 criminal prisoners held at the *Maison d'arrêt et de correction d'Abidjan* (MACA), the main prison in Abidjan, died apparently as a result of gross medical neglect, poor hygiene and malnutrition. Six opposition party supporters died during the year after several months of detention without trial in the MACA and in the Gagnoa prison. They had been arrested in the wake of the October 1995 demonstrations. Some 5,000 prisoners were held in the MACA, around a third of whom had been awaiting trial for several years.

In July, André Ossey Ayékoué was sentenced to death after being convicted of three murders, but had not been executed by the end of the year. The legislation passed by parliament in 1995 to extend the scope of the death penalty (see *Amnesty International Report 1996*) had not been promulgated by the President and no executions were reported.

In May, Amnesty International published a report, *Côte d'Ivoire: Government opponents are the target of systematic repression*, in which it expressed concern at the prolonged detention without trial of more than 200 government opponents and at the conviction of dozens of them under a law introducing the concept of joint responsibility. The organization also called for the immediate release of all the prisoners of conscience including the two journalists and the publisher of *La Voie* newspaper.

CROATIA

Journalists were prosecuted for publishing articles critical of the authorities. Scores of prisoners, mostly Croatian Serbs, tried for crimes connected with the armed conflict in former Yugoslavia may have received unfair trials. There were reports of soldiers and civilians taking part in ill-treatment and deliberate and arbitrary killings of elderly Croatian Serbs in the Krajina. Military and civilian police ill-treated civilians, including human rights defenders and refugees, or failed to protect them from ill-treatment. The fate of around 5,000 people, Croats and Serbs, who "disappeared" during the war remained unclear. The authorities obstructed the return of Croatian Serb refugees and ill-treated and forcibly returned Bosnian Muslims to Bosnia-Herzegovina, where they faced ill-treatment (see Bosnia-Herzegovina entry).

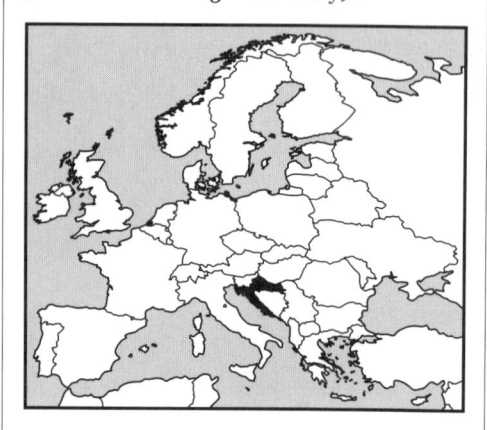

In January, the UN Security Council established the UN Transitional Authority in Eastern Slavonia, which was to oversee the peaceful reintegration of the territory which remained under rebel Serb control after the Croatian military actions of 1995 (see *Amnesty International Report 1996*).

Political tension between the government and opposition continued throughout the year as a result of President Franjo Tudjman's refusal to accept opposition nominations for the Mayor of Zagreb after the opposition's victory in the October 1995 municipal election in the city.

In April, the Criminal Code was amended so that when the President or certain other public figures were "slandered" the State Prosecutor would be obliged to initiate criminal charges, with a possible custodial sentence. The authorities harassed the independent media, using such methods as the arbitrary application of tax and other regulations.

In July, the Organization for Security and Co-operation in Europe established a mission to provide "assistance and expertise" in, among others, the field of human rights.

Croatia enacted implementing legislation in April to enable cooperation with the International Criminal Tribunal for the former Yugoslavia. The authorities arranged the voluntary surrender to the Tribunal of one of those indicted and arrested another, who had not been transferred to the Tribunal's custody by the end of the year. However, the Tribunal complained of the authorities' refusal to secure the arrest of Bosnian Croat suspects residing in Bosnian Croat-controlled areas of Bosnia-Herzegovina.

Amnesty laws applying to individuals (mainly Croatian Serbs) who participated in the armed conflict against Croatia (see *Amnesty International Reports 1992* to *1996*) were passed in May and September. The second law was enacted after pressure from the UN as the first was restricted only to residents of the eastern Slavonia region. About 100 people were released as a result of amnesties, although a number were immediately rearrested for war crimes which were not covered by the amnesty laws.

In October, Croatia and the Federal Republic of Yugoslavia established full diplomatic relations. Croatia was admitted to the Council of Europe in November after twice being refused admission earlier in the year because of concerns about human rights. In November, Croatia signed the European Convention for the Protection of Human Rights and Fundamental Freedoms and its Protocol No. 6 concerning the abolition of the death penalty, and the European Convention for the Prevention of Torture and Inhuman or Degrading Treatment or Punishment.

In September, two journalists, Viktor Ivančić and Marinko Čulić, of the independent weekly *Feral Tribune* were acquitted of "slandering" or "insulting" the President. The charges, which carried a possible custodial sentence, had been brought under the amended Criminal Code. An appeal against the acquittal was outstanding at the end of the year. The editor of another weekly, *Nacional,* was prosecuted in April for "spreading false information" after his paper suggested that poor equipment had caused a plane crash in which a US government official was killed. They all remained at liberty during the proceedings.

A series of trials were held on charges relating to the armed conflict in former Yugoslavia. Charges included "armed rebellion" and war crimes. Those accused only of the former were granted amnesties.

The authorities failed to provide adequate protection for elderly Croatian Serbs who had remained in the Krajina after the military offensive of 1995 (see *Amnesty International Report 1996*). They were threatened and attacked by both civilians and soldiers – in some cases with explosives, rocket-propelled grenades or incendiary materials. Two elderly Croatian Serbs were reportedly killed in such incidents in June and August and several others were seriously injured. Those responsible were reported to include uniformed Bosnian Croat soldiers. The police, some of whom reportedly complained of inadequate resources early in the year, were criticized for failing to prevent incidents and for ineffective investigations.

The authorities made little progress in investigating human rights abuses against Serbs in the Krajina in 1995 and prosecuting those responsible. The government reported large numbers of investigations and trials which it claimed answered demands placed upon it to act to protect the remaining Croatian Serb population in the Krajina under UN Security Council Resolution 1019 (1995). However, the information it provided was incomplete and failed to confirm that the majority of human rights abuses had been investigated or that suspects had been brought to justice and punished where found guilty.

In one of the few trials for serious criminal acts committed against Croatian Serbs in the Krajina, eight Croatian soldiers were acquitted at a trial in Zadar in July of the killing of 16 Croatian Serb civilians in the villages of Varivode and Gošić in August and September 1995. The judge reportedly complained of serious deficiencies in the investigations by the authorities and some of the defendants claimed that they had been beaten or otherwise ill-treated in order to extract confessions. Two of the defendants were found guilty of a murder and an attempted murder respectively in other villages in proceedings which were held concurrently with the above trial. They were sentenced to six years' and 18 months' imprisonment respectively.

Activists in human rights or humanitarian organizations and journalists who were repeatedly subject to human rights abuses were not adequately protected by the authorities. For example, the summer house of Ivan Z. Čičak, President of the Croatian Helsinki Committee for Human Rights, was attacked by a bomb in July while he and relatives were in occupation. No one had been brought to justice for the attack by the end of the year. In other cases, human rights activists and journalists were threatened and physically attacked.

Military police were responsible for ill-treating civilians, including a conscientious objector. The military and military police also failed to protect civilians from violence perpetrated by serving soldiers, former soldiers, or others purporting to represent the military authorities. Most of these incidents were associated with attempts to evict people illegally from apartments which soldiers or ex-soldiers wished to occupy as part of a tacit policy on the part of the authorities. Cases of ill-treatment by police were also reported.

Some progress was made towards resolving cases of people who had "disappeared" in previous years as mass graves were exhumed by both the Croatian authorities and the Tribunal, and exchange of information with the Federal Republic of Yugoslavia increased. However, at the end of the year there were still around 5,000 missing persons.

Fear for their safety, and bureaucratic obstacles imposed by the Croatian authorities, meant that during the year few Croatian Serb refugees returned to Croatia and fewer still to their homes. Estimates varied, but it appeared that no more than 10,000 to 15,000 of the 200,000 Croatian Serb refugees who fled the Krajina in 1995 were able to return to Croatia during the year. Many of them did not return to their homes in the Krajina.

Amnesty International addressed the authorities on a variety of human rights concerns during the year, including the forcible return of Bosnian Muslim refugees to Bosnia-Herzegovina and their reported ill-treatment by Croatian police; the prosecution of journalists for exercising their right to freedom of information; ill-treatment by police and military personnel; and the lack of adequate protection from the authorities for human rights defenders and members of national minorities. In many cases the authorities responded, but failed to address fully Amnesty International's concerns.

CUBA

Scores of people were arbitrarily detained for short periods or subjected to persistent harassment. Several were tried and imprisoned as prisoners of conscience or confined to specific areas of the country. At least nine people were forced into exile. Some 600 other prisoners of conscience and several hundred political prisoners remained in prison. Trials in political and death penalty cases fell far short of international fair trial standards. There were reports of ill-treatment in police stations and in prisons. There were reports that unarmed civilians were shot dead by law enforcement officials in disputed circumstances. At least seven people were under sentence of death, but no executions were reported.

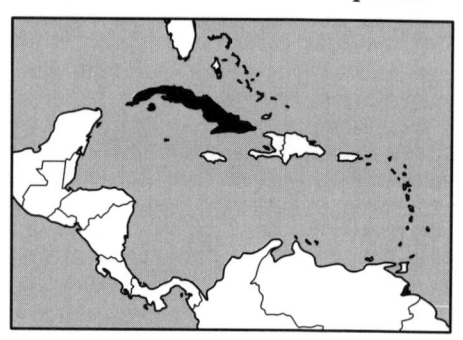

The crack-down by the government of President Fidel Castro, begun in late 1995, on the *Concilio Cubano*, Cuban Council, continued in 1996. The *Concilio Cubano*, a loose coalition of unofficial groups of various kinds including political groups, human rights defenders, lawyers and women's organizations, had been established in October 1995 to work for political change through peaceful means (see *Amnesty International Report 1996*). A national meeting of the *Concilio Cubano* planned for February was banned by the authorities and between mid-February and mid-March scores of *Concilio Cubano* activists, including most of the national leaders, were detained (see below).

In February, four people were killed when the Cuban Air Force shot down two small planes flown by members of *Hermanos al Rescate* (Brothers to the Rescue), a Cuban exile group set up to rescue "rafters" trying to escape Cuba by sea and based in Florida, USA. The Cuban Government claimed that the planes had entered Cuban airspace without authorization and that warnings had been given before they were shot down. It said that this and previous incursions were provocative and criticized the US authorities for failing to take steps to prevent them. Following a protest by the US Government, the UN Security Council called on the International Civil Aviation Organization (ICAO) to investigate the incident. The ICAO investigation, the conduct and results of which were disputed by the Cuban Government, concluded that the two planes had been shot down without warning in international airspace. The UN Security Council subsequently "condemned the use of weapons against civilian aircraft in flight" without specifically naming Cuba, but also reminded all states of their duty "to take appropriate measures to prohibit the deliberate use of civilian aircraft ... for purposes that are incompatible with the aims of the Chicago Convention [the 1944 International Civil Aviation Agreement]".

In response to the shooting-down of the planes, US President Bill Clinton signed the Helms-Burton Act which extended the US trade embargo on Cuba, in place since 1962, by seeking to take action against foreign companies investing in Cuba. The US Government also urged other governments, the vast majority of whom strongly opposed the Helms-Burton Act because of its extraterritorial nature, to join it in seeking other "concrete measures to promote democracy in Cuba". In November, the UN General Assembly again overwhelmingly condemned the US embargo.

The Cuban Government continued to resist international pressure to take any significant initiatives on political or human rights matters and accused the US Government of interference in its internal affairs and of funding opposition groups. The Cuban Government continued to deny access to the country to the UN Special Rapporteur on Cuba, despite a resolution adopted by the UN Commission on Human Rights calling on the government to allow him to visit.

Scores of people were arbitrarily detained during the February round-up of *Concilio Cubano* activists. Most were released after a few hours or days. However, at least four people were tried and convicted on politically motivated charges; they were prisoners of conscience. They included Leonel Morejón Almagro, a lawyer and national delegate of the *Concilio Cubano*, who was initially sentenced to six months' imprisonment for "resisting authority", but had his sentence increased on appeal to 15 months' imprisonment after a further charge of "disrespect" was added.

Dozens of members of unofficial groups were again detained for short periods in July and early August and warned not to attempt to organize protests or commemorations on 13 July, the anniversary of the sinking of the *13 de Marzo* tugboat in 1994 in which some 40 people died (see *Amnesty International Report 1995*). Aída Rosa Jiménez of the *Movimiento de Madres Cubanas por la Solidaridad*, Cuban Mothers' Solidarity Movement, was threatened with imprisonment if she went to church on 13 July, and Isabel del Pino Sotolongo, President of *Seguidores de Cristo Rey* (Followers of Christ the King), was threatened with several charges after being detained for displaying photographs of the victims of the tugboat disaster and distributing leaflets containing quotes from the Bible.

Several dissidents had their freedom of movement restricted. In June, Nestor Rodríguez Lobaina and Radames García de la Vega were arrested in Havana, the capital, and charged with "disrespect" and "resistance", reportedly because of their attempts to organize a movement for university reform in the city. They were sentenced respectively to 12 and six months' "restricted liberty" as well as confinement to their home towns in eastern Cuba for a period of five years. The sentence was imposed before they could lodge an appeal. By the end of the year the appeal hearing had still not taken place. Other activists, including independent journalists and human rights defenders, were banned by police from travelling to certain places within Cuba or were refused permission to travel abroad to attend conferences.

Pressure on dissidents and political prisoners to go into exile increased. Throughout the year, dozens of dissidents, including members of independent press agencies, were threatened with long-term imprisonment if they did not give up their activities or leave the country. Rafael Solano, Director of *Habana Press* (see *Amnesty International Report 1996*), and Eugenio Rodríguez Chaple, President of the *Bloque Democrático José Martí*, José Martí Democratic Block, both of whom were arrested in the February crack-down and held for several weeks under investigation on several charges including "associating with others to commit a crime", were released in April. While in detention and again upon release, both men were put under pressure by the Department of State Security to leave the country. Both eventually left Cuba for Spain, in May and July respectively, under threat of imprisonment if they did not do so. Both were warned not to try to return to Cuba.

Roxana Valdivia Castilla, President of the press agency *Patria*, left Cuba, as did Mercedes Parada Antúnez, one of the four national deputy delegates of the *Concilio Cubano*. Both had been subjected to months of harassment and threats of imprisonment if they did not do so. Yndamiro Restano Díaz, a former prisoner of conscience and founder of the *Buró de Periodistas Independientes de Cuba* (BPIC), Cuban Independent Journalists' Bureau, (see *Amnesty International Reports 1994* and *1995*), who left Cuba in 1995, was prevented from exercising his right to return.

Prisoners of conscience Luis Grave de Peralta Morell and Carmen Arias Iglesias, and political prisoner Eduardo Ramón Prida, were given early release from prison on condition that they went into exile. They were released in February through the mediation of a US congressman and left for the USA with assurances that their families would be able to join them. However, by the end of the year the immediate family of Luis Grave de Peralta Morell had not been permitted to leave Cuba, despite having reportedly fulfilled all necessary requirements.

In November, prisoner of conscience Rubén Hoyos Ruiz was released on condition that he left Cuba. He had been sentenced to six years' imprisonment in 1990 for disseminating "enemy propaganda". While in prison, he was given an additional two-year sentence for showing disrespect to President Castro.

Some 600 prisoners of conscience and several hundred other political prisoners were believed to remain imprisoned. Prisoner of conscience Domiciano Torres Roca (see *Amnesty International Reports 1994* and *1995*), arrested in 1993 and serving a three-year sentence for "enemy propaganda", was released two weeks before the completion of his sentence.

Detention and trial procedures in all political cases and in criminal cases involving a possible death sentence continued to fall far short of international fair trial standards, particularly with regard to the right of access to defence counsel. The defence lawyer who represented Leonel Morejón Almagro (see above) reportedly had access to his client and to details of the case only hours before the trial hearing. The lawyer was fined after the trial for having asked "irrelevant political questions".

According to testimony received during the year from a man detained during the 5 August 1994 demonstration in Havana (see *Amnesty International Report 1995*), he and 33 others were tried for "dangerousness" in September 1994 in a collective trial lasting 20 minutes in El Pitirre Prison. He had had no access to a lawyer and no contact with his family and was assigned a lawyer by the state only at the time of the hearing. None of the accused were allowed to speak in their own defence.

In a welcome and unusual move, the Minister of Justice called on the People's Supreme Court to review the sentences passed on possible prisoner of conscience Juvencio Padrón Dueñas and three others (see *Amnesty International Report 1996*). He and two of the others had been sentenced to death for murder in September 1995 but had subsequently had their sentences commuted on appeal to 30 years' imprisonment. The review was requested on the grounds that serious irregularities had taken place both during investigation of the case and during the first trial hearing. Amnesty International had previously received reports that incriminating statements admitted as evidence during the trial had been obtained under duress and believed that the charges against Juvencio Padrón Dueñas may have been politically motivated. There had been no news of the outcome of the review by the end of the year.

There were reports of ill-treatment at the time of arrest and during pre-trial detention in State Security facilities and police stations, as well as in prisons. Nestor Rodríguez Lobaina and Radames García de la Vega (see above) were reportedly beaten in a Havana police station following their arrest and had visible injuries on their faces at the trial hearing. When they attempted to complain about their treatment at the hearing, one of them was again beaten in the courtroom by a State Security official while handcuffed.

Frequent reports continued to be received of beatings, sometimes with blunt instruments such as lengths of hosepipe, in many prisons and work camps, in some cases resulting in serious injury. In June, some 120 youths aged between 14 and 20 held in Valle Grande Prison went on hunger-strike to protest about the failure of the prison director to take action following their complaints that guards systematically beat and kicked them for reasons such as failing to stand in line for meals correctly. It was not known whether any official action was taken as a result of the protest.

Prison conditions were generally very poor with frequent reports of insufficient food and medical attention and poor sanitation. Although such conditions may have resulted partly from general shortages in the country, there were frequent indications that food and medical attention were withheld as a form of punishment.

Prisoners who protested about their treatment or refused to obey prison rules were kept in punishment cells, sometimes with no light or furniture, for weeks or months at a time, often on reduced rations and without access to medical attention. José Miranda Acosta, serving a 12-year sentence for "terrorism", was reportedly held in an underground punishment cell in Pinar del Río Provincial Prison (known as "Kilo 5½") for over two years and deprived of family visits for his refusal to wear prison uniform and follow the "re-education" program. He was transferred to the Special Maximum Severity Prison in Camagüey (known as "Kilo 8") in September; no further news of the conditions in which he was being held had been received by the end of the year.

Further reports were received of shootings by law enforcement officials in disputed circumstances, in some cases resulting in deaths. Iván Agramonte Arencibia died in May in Havana after reportedly being shot in the head at point-blank range by a police officer while handcuffed. Reports were received of shootings, in most cases fatal, by security officials between 1994 and 1996 of people attempting to steal food or cattle from state-run farms. No information was received regarding action taken against officials responsible for such shootings.

At least seven men were under sentence of death, but no executions were reported. In April, Humberto Real Suárez, one of seven members of a Cuban exile group who had illegally entered the country in October 1994, was sentenced to death for killing a man at the time of his arrest. His appeal to the People's Supreme Court was pending at the end of the year. At least six other men were reported to be on death row, two awaiting a decision of the Council of State, which is the final arbiter in capital cases, and four pending appeal to the People's Supreme Court. All had been convicted of rape or murder.

Throughout the year Amnesty International appealed to the authorities to release prisoners of conscience; to guarantee all Cubans the right to freely exercise their civil and political rights in accordance with the Universal Declaration of Human Rights; to ratify the International Covenant on Civil and Political Rights; and to commute all death sentences. The organization also expressed concern about the practice of forcing dissidents into exile abroad and called on the authorities not to arbitrarily prevent anyone from exercising their right to return to Cuba. On the second anniversary of the July 1994 tugboat sinking, the authorities were again urged to conduct an independent investigation into the incident and to stop harassing those seeking to protest peacefully or commemorate the event. No replies were received from the authorities.

CYPRUS

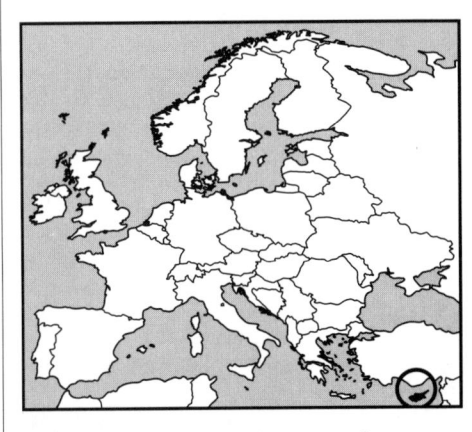

A Greek Cypriot civilian was beaten to death while a Turkish Cypriot police officer failed to intervene. Two unarmed Greek Cypriot civilians were shot dead by Turkish Cypriot soldiers. A journalist was shot dead in an alleged politically motivated killing in the Turkish Cypriot-administered part of the island. Jehovah's Witnesses continued to be imprisoned for refusing on grounds of conscience to perform military service.

In August, Tasos Isaak, a Greek Cypriot, was beaten to death in the UN buffer zone by Turkish Cypriots or alleged members of the Turkish organization Grey Wolves. Video footage showed a Turkish Cypriot police officer watching Tasos Isaak being beaten without intervening. Violence erupted when Greek Cypriots protesting against the division of Cyprus tried to force their way through the buffer zone. Tasos Isaak was beaten unconscious with clubs and stones after becoming trapped in barbed-wire barricades. He died soon afterwards from severe head injuries.

On 14 August, during a demonstration following Tasos Isaak's funeral, Solomos Solomou, also a Greek Cypriot, was shot dead by Turkish Cypriot soldiers as he tried to pull down a flag on the Turkish Cypriot side of the buffer zone.

In October, Petros Kakoulis, a Greek Cypriot, was shot dead by Turkish Cypriot soldiers when he wandered into the buffer zone. According to his son-in-law, who was with him, six Turkish Cypriot soldiers approached Petros Kakoulis who immediately raised his arms in a gesture of surrender. The soldiers fired at him, reportedly shooting again at close range after he had fallen to the ground. An autopsy carried out by Turkish Cypriot doctors reportedly found that Petros Kakoulis died of a single gunshot wound. However, a second post-mortem examination carried out after his body was returned to his relatives found two other gunshot wounds.

In July, Kutlu Adalı, a journalist living in the Turkish Cypriot-administered part of the island, was shot dead outside his home. He had reportedly received death threats after criticizing the presence in Cyprus of Turkish troops and the policy of encouraging citizens of Turkey to live in Cyprus. Reports suggested that the Turkish Revenge Brigade was responsible for the killing.

The alternative "unarmed military service" provided for conscientious objectors remained punitive in length (42 or 36 months as against 26 months of ordinary military service) and is suspended during periods of emergency or general mobilization. At least 18 members of the Jehovah's Witnesses religious group were imprisoned during the year for refusing to perform military service. Those called up for the first time received 26-month sentences, while reservists received sentences of seven or eight months' imprisonment. All were prisoners of conscience.

In August, Amnesty International called on the UN to establish an effective commission of inquiry to investigate "disappearances", "missing" persons and deliberate and arbitrary killings in Cyprus arising out of the events of 1963 to 1964 and 1974. The organization called on President Glafkos Clerides and Rauf Denktaş, the leader of the Turkish Cypriot community, to support the establishment of such a commission.

Also in August, Amnesty International asked Rauf Denktaş what steps had been taken to investigate the killing of Kutlu Adalı and urged that prompt, thorough and impartial investigations be carried out into the killings of Tasos Isaak and Solomos Solomou. The organization called on President Clerides, Rauf Denktaş and the UN peace-keeping forces to take all appropriate measures to ensure that no such incidents happened in future. Rauf Denktaş responded that the events which led to the death of Tasos Isaak were provoked when "Greek Cypriots tried to force their way through the UN buffer-zone at various points" in "direct threat to the rights and security of Turkish Cypriots". In November, Rauf Denktaş responded that an investigation into the death of Kutlu Adalı continued but that no charges had been brought in connection with the killing. Also in November, the authorities responded to Amnesty International's call for an investigation into the killing of Petros Kakoulis, stating that the matter was being dealt with by an internal inquiry.

DENMARK

There were allegations of ill-treatment by police officers.

The UN Human Rights Committee examined Denmark's third periodic report in October. It expressed concern at the methods of crowd control employed by the police and made a number of recommendations, including further training of the police in methods of crowd control and the handling of offenders, reconsideration of the use of dogs in crowd control, revision of regulations concerning the length of pre-trial detention and solitary confinement, and measures to ensure the direct application of the International Covenant on Civil and Political Rights in domestic law.

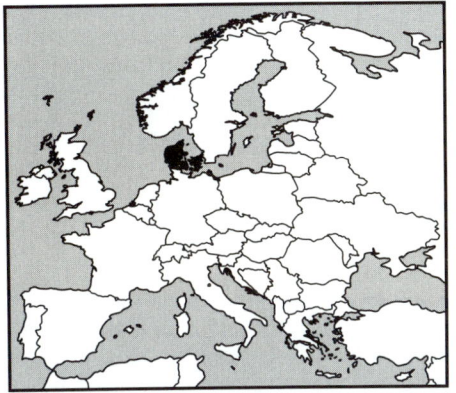

Some people alleged that they were ill-treated by police officers, including being lifted and dragged by handcuffs. There were also reports of police dogs used in crowd control biting people.

Veronica Ngozi Ugwuoha, a Nigerian national, alleged that she was ill-treated and subjected to racist abuse in July by police officers after they arrested her. While being restrained by police she sustained a fractured leg and a split kneecap. She also alleged that she had been denied medical attention for several hours while in detention. At the end of the year, her allegations were being investigated by the Regional State Prosecutor for Copenhagen.

Information came to light that Dung Chi Nguyen, a Vietnamese national, had reportedly been ill-treated in April 1995 during the course of his arrest. Eyewitnesses stated that, although handcuffed, he had been repeatedly beaten with batons by plainclothes police officers both before and after he lay on the ground. The prosecution authorities did not bring criminal or disciplinary charges against the police officers involved. In May, however, the new regional police complaints board found that the police officers had acted improperly by hitting Dung Chi Nguyen with batons while he lay handcuffed on the ground.

A new investigation into the events surrounding the shooting and wounding of at least 11 people during demonstrations in Nørrebro, Copenhagen, in May 1993, had not been completed by the end of the year (see *Amnesty International Reports 1994, 1995* and *1996*). This latest investigation, initiated by the Ministry of Justice in May and consisting of an independent panel of three people by the Minister of Justice after consultation, was also examining previous investigations into the incident.

Amnesty International expressed concern to the government about the allegations of ill-treatment made by Veronica Ngozi Ugwuoha and Dung Chi Nguyen. The organization also requested to be kept informed about the government's implementation of the recommendations made by the UN Human Rights Committee.

DJIBOUTI

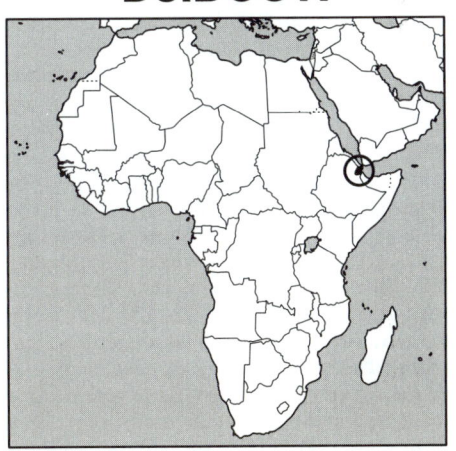

Five former senior officials were imprisoned, as prisoners of conscience, for six months for criticizing the government. Numerous teachers were briefly detained during peaceful demonstrations. Several Ethiopian government opponents were deported to Ethiopia and imprisoned.

In August, five dissident former officials of President Hassan Gouled Aptidon's government and ruling party, the *Rassemblement pour le progrès populaire* (RPP), People's Assembly for Progress, were convicted of defaming the Head of State and sentenced to six months' imprisonment, heavy fines and deprivation of their civil rights for five years. They had issued a press communique in May criticizing the President for acting undemocratically. Three were members of parliament, former ministers and senior

RPP officials – Moumin Bahdon Farah, Ahmed Boulale Barre and Ali Mahamed Houmed – and the other two were Ismail Guedi Hared, former director of the President's cabinet, and Abdillahi Guirreh, a former RPP official. They were prisoners of conscience. The lifting of their parliamentary immunity was contrary to normal procedures and their trial by the Court of Appeal was also unusual. They later went on hunger-strike for some days in Gabode prison until their conditions of imprisonment were improved. In November, the Supreme Court upheld their convictions.

In January, some 200 school-teachers were detained during a peaceful demonstration against the government's education policies. They were released after two days and charges brought against teachers' union leaders were dropped. Fourteen teachers were briefly detained in December, also in connection with a peaceful demonstration.

Seven Ethiopian government opponents were arrested in August and forcibly deported to Ethiopia, where they were detained without charge or trial by the authorities (see **Ethiopia** entry). They included Girmay Moges Newaye-Mariam, a refugee; Muhyadin Muftah, a leader of an armed Afar opposition group; and members of the Ogaden National Liberation Front.

Amnesty International appealed to the authorities urging the release of the five prisoners of conscience. The organization protested at the forcible repatriation of a refugee and other Ethiopian government opponents who were subsequently imprisoned in Ethiopia.

DOMINICAN REPUBLIC

One prisoner of conscience, held despite judicial orders for his release, escaped from prison and remained at liberty at the end of the year. There were reports of ill-treatment, both of prisoners and of Haitians detained pending deportation. The authorities reopened the investigation of a 1994 "disappearance". At least nine people were shot dead by police in disputed circumstances.

In June, Leonel Fernández Reyna of the *Partido de la Liberación Dominicana*, Dominican Liberation Party, was elected President. Former President Joaquín Balaguer had agreed to step down following allegations of fraud in the 1994 presidential elections.

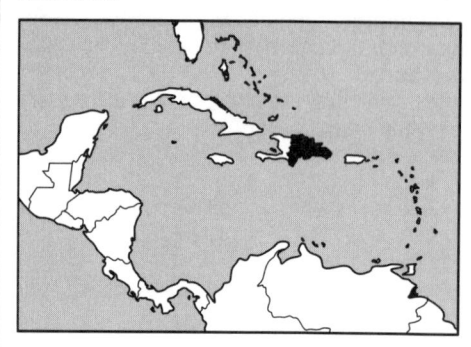

In September, prisoners in La Victoria Prison, where 90 per cent of the 4,000 inmates were held on remand, rioted in protest at delays in bringing their cases to court, at poor prison conditions and at the practice of holding minors with adult prisoners. The three-day riot, which left one prisoner dead in disputed circumstances, ended when 30 of the more than 300 minors in La Victoria were released and a commission drawn from the police force, the courts and the prison authorities agreed to study prisoners' demands.

The police continued to refuse to comply with three judicial decisions ordering the release of prisoner of conscience Luis Lizardo Cabrera, a political activist who was arrested in 1989 for alleged involvement in a bombing (see previous *Amnesty International Reports*). On 24 December, Luis Lizardo Cabrera escaped from prison, and he remained at liberty at the end of the year.

There were reports of torture and ill-treatment. In August, four prisoners held at Plan Piloto police station in the capital, Santo Domingo, were reportedly tortured by being hanged by the arms for several hours, and being beaten with a baseball bat while having a plank of wood placed between their bound hands and feet. The District Attorney reportedly initiated an investigation but no findings had been published by the end of the year.

In May, several Haitians were reportedly ill-treated by the army during a deportation campaign in which thousands of Haitians, including citizens of the Dominican Republic, were rounded up and deported.

Six employees of the Monte Llano sugar-cane plantation were arrested and charged with the kidnapping and ill-treatment of 40 Haitians who had been driven away and beaten by security guards in September 1995. By the end of the year, no one had been brought to justice for the beating of a group of Haitians by army personnel in December 1995. Five of the victims were later killed when the bus transporting them back to Haiti overturned (see *Amnesty International Report 1996*). Their bodies were reportedly buried without having been identified. The Director-General of Migration is reported to have stated that his department was not involved and that the deportations were army initiatives.

In October, the authorities reopened the investigation into the 1994 "disappearance" of Narciso González (see *Amnesty International Reports 1995* and *1996*) after the Inter-American Commission on Human Rights of the Organization of American States gave the government 30 days to clarify his fate. The Secretary of State for the Armed Forces and about two dozen other high-ranking army officers were dismissed after being implicated in the case. At least nine military and police officers were summoned for questioning in connection with the investigation which had not concluded by the end of the year. There were fears for the safety of Narciso González' wife and two other human rights activists campaigning on the case after they reportedly received threats.

At least nine people were shot dead by police in disputed circumstances, three of them in two separate incidents over two days. In October, two police officers shot dead two men in Ciudad Agraria after one had allegedly left a bar without paying for his drinks. The following day, in another suburb of the capital, two police officers reportedly shot dead, without warning or apparent motive, a young man who had been released from prison a week earlier. Investigations were reportedly initiated in some of these cases and in at least three of them the police officers involved were arrested.

Amnesty International continued to call for the immediate and unconditional release of Luis Lizardo Cabrera and for those responsible for the "disappearance" of Narciso González to be brought to justice.

ECUADOR

Seven prisoners of conscience arrested in 1993 were released. Numerous cases of torture continued to be reported. At least two people were killed in circumstances suggesting that they may have been extrajudicially executed. Hundreds of human rights violations committed during previous years remained unresolved.

Constitutional reforms approved in 1995 came into effect in January, including provision for the establishment of a *Defensoría del Pueblo*, Office of the Ombudsman. However, by the end of the year the Office of the Ombudsman had yet to come into operation.

Following elections in July, Abdalá Bucaram Ortiz took office as President on 10 August. Days later, the new government decreed a country-wide state of emergency. The decree made provision for mobilizing the military and the police to combat widespread corruption and crime.

In September, the National Congress set up a special commission to investigate allegations made public by former policeman Hugo España. According to these allegations, a police "death squad" had been responsible for the torture, "disappearance", and extrajudicial execution of suspected members of an armed opposition group, *Alfaro Vive, Carajo!* (Alfaro Lives, Damn it!) (see *Amnesty International Reports 1985* to *1992*). Some victims had been buried in unmarked graves in a police precinct in Pusuquí, near Quito, the capital, and close to the Cuenca–Girón highway. The authorities visited the sites but, in the absence of precise locations, did not order excavations.

Also in September, the Ministry of Government and Police established the *Comisión Verdad y Justicia*, Truth and Justice Commission, to investigate unresolved cases of human rights violations which had taken place since 1979, when military rule ended. By the end of the year the Commission was reported to have received information on almost 300 such cases. The Commission investigated reports of unmarked graves in the Fumisa police precinct, near the town of Quevedo, province of Los Ríos, said to contain the remains of scores of peasants who had died under torture or been summarily executed during the 1970s. Both the congressional and Truth and Justice commissions were expected to publish their findings in 1997.

In September, President Bucaram announced that he was seeking the opinion of Roman Catholic Church leaders concerning his proposal that the Constitution be amended to allow the death penalty for the rape and murder of children. Following a rejection of the proposal by church leaders, the government announced preparation of a bill to allow the castration of those who rape children.

Seven agricultural workers arrested in 1993 in connection with an armed attack against Ecuadorian forces patrolling the river Putumayo were released in September (see *Amnesty International Reports 1995* and *1996*). They were prisoners of conscience. Their release followed a ruling by the Supreme Court of Justice which overturned the convictions and sentences handed down to the seven defendants in February by the Napo Criminal Court. However, the judicial authorities failed to bring to justice those responsible for the torture of the seven, and of four other peasants detained with them but released in 1995.

Numerous cases of torture by police officers were reported. For example, in January, Patricio Vaca, a cobbler, was detained in the city of Quevedo on suspicion of having information about the killing of a policeman. According to reports, Patricio Vaca was taken to a building where he was blindfolded, handcuffed, and repeatedly punched and kicked. He was later transferred to a cell in the *Oficina de Investigación del Delito*, Office for the Investigation of Crime, where members of the *Grupo de Operaciones Especiales*, Special Operations Group, allegedly placed a hood over his head into which gas was pumped, and beat and kicked him.

In July, a judge ruled that there was no conclusive proof against three policemen and two civilians implicated in the detention and death under torture of Vicente Muñoz Ruiz (see *Amnesty International Report 1996*), and ordered their release.

At least two people were shot in circumstances suggesting that they may have been extrajudicially executed. In February, Pedro Pablo Armas, a Quito-based taxi driver, stopped his vehicle while his passenger loaded the boot. According to reports, a policeman whose vehicle the taxi was obstructing approached Pedro Armas, hit him in the face, drew a gun and shot him dead. The policeman was reportedly dismissed from the force but later readmitted.

In September, five police officers conducting an anti-drugs operation broke into a house in the district of La Tola, Quito. According to the police, José Miguel Manrique Morales, a 16-year-old student, was accidentally shot by one of the police officers during a struggle. However, a witness claimed that a policemen took him to a back yard and deliberately shot him. He died hours later. A judicial warrant ordering the policeman's detention was reportedly obstructed by police authorities, who claimed jurisdiction over the case. By the end of the year a High Court had yet to rule whether the case was to be referred to the jurisdiction of the civilian or police courts.

Hundreds of cases of human rights violations in previous years remained unresolved. These included the deaths of at least 25 men, women and children shot by police during a mass protest by workers and their families at the Aztra sugar mill in October 1977 (see *Amnesty International Report 1978*); the torture, "disappearance" or extrajudicial execution over a four-year period by members of the police and armed forces of scores of people suspected of belonging to *Alfaro Vive, Carajo!* (see *Amnesty International Reports 1985* to *1989*); and the torture of four Colombian refugees in a military establishment in August 1995 (see *Amnesty International Report 1996*).

In July, the Consuelo Benavides case was formally admitted by the Inter-

American Court of Human Rights following a submission to the Court by the Inter-American Commission on Human Rights (see previous *Amnesty International Reports*). By the end of the year the Court had yet to hear the case.

In July, the government wrote to Amnesty International rejecting "the claims made [in *Amnesty International Report 1996*], in so far as there exists a clear difference of perceptions between the facts and the unfounded claims made in the report". The communication referred to several cases included in the report, but failed to respond to Amnesty International's specific concerns.

In July, Amnesty International wrote an open letter to President-elect Bucaram urging his government to outline a plan of action for the protection and promotion of human rights. In the letter the organization appealed for the immediate and unconditional release of the prisoners detained in connection with the Putumayo incident. Amnesty International also urged the President-elect to ensure that urgent measures were taken to end Ecuador's pattern of impunity; to prevent torture and ill-treatment; to reject all proposals to reintroduce the death penalty; and to put into practice domestic and international human rights standards.

In September, Amnesty International publicly welcomed the establishment of the Truth and Justice Commission and urged the authorities to ensure that the Commission was able to carry out its mandate successfully.

EGYPT

Seven prisoners of conscience were sentenced to three years' imprisonment and 53 others, tried by the Supreme Military Court in 1995, continued to serve prison sentences. Thousands of suspected members or sympathizers of banned Islamist groups, including possible prisoners of conscience, were held without charge or trial; others were serving sentences imposed after grossly unfair trials before military courts. Torture and ill-treatment of political detainees continued to be systematic. At least 45 people were sentenced to death, including four *in absentia*, and at least 14 people, including eight sentenced in previous years, were executed. Armed opposition groups committed grave human rights abuses, including deliberate and arbitrary killings of civilians.

A state of emergency introduced in 1981 (see previous *Amnesty International Reports*) remained in force.

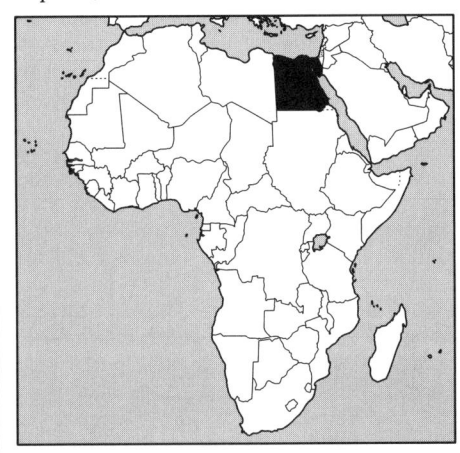

In May, the UN Committee against Torture issued a report which concluded that "torture is systematically practised by the Security Forces in Egypt, in particular by State Security Intelligence...". The Committee noted with concern that "no investigation has ever been made and no legal action been brought against members of the State Security Intelligence since the entry into force of the Convention [UN Convention against Torture and Other Cruel, Inhuman or Degrading Treatment or Punishment] for Egypt in 1987". It urged the Egyptian Government to "make particular efforts to prevent its security forces from acting as a State within a State, for they seem to escape control by superior authorities".

Violent clashes continued between armed opposition groups and the security forces, especially in Upper Egypt, resulting in dozens of casualties on both sides.

Thirteen prominent members of the Muslim Brothers were arrested in April. They included former members of parliament, university lecturers and engineers. In May, President Hosni Mubarak issued a special decree referring their case to a military court. The defendants were charged with membership of an illegal organization which "aims to overthrow the regime and to suspend the Constitution". However, the prosecution failed to provide substantive evidence to demonstrate that the defendants had committed any recognizably criminal offence. In June, the Supreme Military Court sentenced seven of the defendants to three years' imprisonment. They were prisoners of conscience. Among those sentenced were Mohammad Mahdi 'Akef, a 68-year-old former member of parliament; Dr Mahmoud 'Omar al-'Arini, a 72-year-old lecturer in the Faculty of Agriculture at the University of al-Azhar; and Dr 'Abd al-Hamid al-Ghazali, a lecturer in the Faculty of Economics at Cairo University. One defendant, 'Abd al-Adhim 'Abd al-Magid al-Maghribi, received a one-year suspended prison sentence and five others were acquitted.

The 53 prisoners of conscience sentenced to up to five years' imprisonment by the Supreme Military Court in November 1995 (see *Amnesty International Report 1996*) continued to be held in Mazra'at Tora Prison. One of them, 'Abd al-Rahman 'Abd al-Fattah 'Abdallah Mohammad, President of the Teachers' Syndicate in Fayyum, died in October reportedly as a result of a blood clot for which he allegedly did not receive anti-coagulant medication or other medical treatment while in prison. He was transferred to Qasr al-'Aini Hospital in Cairo, but reportedly died on arrival. No investigation was reported to have been carried out into his death.

Hundreds of people were arrested on political or religious grounds during the year. In September, 10 alleged members of the Muslim Brothers were arrested in Bani Sueif and accused of distributing leaflets critical of government policies and inciting the population to demonstrate. They were all released in November. In October, 57 alleged members of a Shi'a group were arrested and accused of planning to influence public opinion by propagating the Shi'a doctrine and having links with Iran. They were still detained at the end of the year. Also in October, Mohammad Wagdi Mohammad Durra was arrested at his home in Tanta and allegedly tortured. According to reports, he was arrested in connection with his conversion from Islam to Christianity and the charges against him reportedly included "propagating ideas" and "belittling religions". A prisoner of conscience, he was released in December.

Thousands of suspected members or sympathizers of banned Islamist groups, including possible prisoners of conscience, arrested in previous years, continued to be held in administrative detention, without charge or trial, under emergency legislation. For example, Gihan Ibrahim 'Abd al-Hamid, who was arrested in November 1994, continued to be administratively detained, despite numerous release orders issued by the courts. She was allegedly interrogated in connection with her contacts with the wife of a suspected Islamist activist said to have been killed by the police in a shoot-out in November 1994. Gihan Ibrahim 'Abd al-Hamid, whose husband was serving a 15-year prison term, was held in al-Qanater al-Khairiya Prison (women's section) at the end of the year.

At least 49 lawyers remained in detention at the end of the year. Some were held without charge or trial; others had been tried and acquitted by military and (Emergency) Supreme State Security Courts, but continued to be detained. Mu'awwadh Mohammad Youssef Gawda, who was arrested in May 1991, continued to be detained without charge or trial despite at least 21 release orders from the courts. He had reportedly been tortured on a number of occasions at the headquarters of the State Security Investigations Department (SSI). At the end of the year he continued to be held in Istiqbal Tora Prison.

Torture of political prisoners continued to be systematic, particularly in the SSI headquarters in Cairo, SSI branches elsewhere in the country and in police stations. The most common methods reported were: electric shocks, beatings, suspension by the wrists or ankles, burning with cigarettes, and various forms of psychological torture, including death threats and threats of rape or sexual abuse of the detainee or female relatives. Lawyers, the Bar Association and local human rights groups lodged hundreds of complaints of torture with the Public Prosecutor's Office. No information was made available regarding any investigations into the allegations. Amal Farouq Mohammad al-Maas was arrested in July and held at an SSI building in al-Marsa, Cairo, for 10 days. She was allegedly subjected to electric shocks on various parts of the body; slashed with a knife on her legs, back and arms; and beaten. She was believed to have been arrested because she had earlier lodged a complaint against two SSI officers whom she alleged had tortured her in April 1993 when she was first arrested in connection with her husband's activities. In August, Ahmad Mohammad 'Abd al-'Adhim Higazi died in the headquarters of the SSI in Cairo, reportedly as a result of torture. He and at least 50 others, including Sayyid 'Abbas Sayyid, Taha Mansour, Sa'eed Taghour, Hisham Mohammad 'Abdu and 'Abd al-Hamid Mahmoud Qutb Khalil, had been arrested in July and reportedly accused of membership of an illegal armed group, *Talai' al-Fatah* (Vanguards of the Conquest), and preparing to overthrow the regime. They were all held in the SSI headquarters in Cairo and allegedly subjected to torture including beatings, electric shocks, suspension in contorted positions and burning with cigarettes.

The death penalty continued to be used extensively. At least 45 people were sentenced to death, including four *in absentia*; seven of them were civilians sentenced by a military court after an unfair trial and 10 others were sentenced by (Emergency) Supreme State Security Courts, which allow no appeal. At least 27 people were sentenced to death by criminal courts for murder and at least one for drug-trafficking. At least 14 people, including eight people sentenced in previous years, were executed. In June, six people were executed. They had been sentenced to death by the Supreme Military Court in Cairo in January in the case known as *al-'Aidoun min al-Sudan* (Returnees from Sudan). They were reportedly members of *al-Gama'a al-Islamiya* (Islamic Group) and were charged with, among other things, plotting to overthrow the regime, threatening peace and national unity through the use of violence and illegally importing weapons and ammunition into the country. Death sentences passed by military courts are subject only to review by the Military Appeals' Bureau, a body composed of military judges which is not a court, and ratification by the President. All death sentences were confirmed by the Bureau and the President.

Armed opposition groups continued to commit gross human rights abuses, including deliberate and arbitrary killings of civilians. Bomb and firearm attacks were carried out by banned Islamist groups, particularly *al-Gama'a al-Islamiya* and *al-Gihad* (Holy Struggle). At least 70 unarmed civilians were killed by armed men believed to be members of *al-Gama'a al-Islamiya*. In February, eight civilians, including six Coptic Christians, were killed by two armed men, believed to be members of *al-Gama'a al-Islamiya*, in the village of al-'Uthmaniya in Asyut governorate. Eighteen Greek tourists, including 14 women, were killed outside a hotel in Cairo by four armed men in April. *Al-Gama'a al-Islamiya* claimed responsibility for the killings. A 68-year-old retired guard, Mahmoud 'Abd al-Hakim 'Abd al-Nasser, and his two sons – Mur'i, a teacher, and Redha, a farmer – were shot dead by armed men believed to be members of *al-Gama'a al-Islamiya* in August in the village of Nawai near Mallawi in Minya governorate.

Dr Nasr Hamed Abu-Zeid remained under threat of death from *al-Gihad* (see *Amnesty International Report 1996*). In August, the Court of Cassation in Cairo upheld the June 1995 Court of Appeal's ruling that he had insulted the Islamic faith through his writings and that he and his wife should divorce. In September, the Giza Court of Emergency Matters ordered "a suspension of the execution" of the ruling made by the Court of Appeal in June 1995. An Islamist lawyer appealed against the new ruling, but in December a court upheld the September ruling. Dr Nasr Hamed Abu-Zeid and his wife, Dr Ibtihal Younis, had left Egypt at the end of 1995.

Amnesty International repeatedly appealed to the authorities to release all prisoners of conscience and called for the immediate implementation of safeguards to stop torture and ill-treatment of detainees, and for urgent, thorough and impartial investigations into all allegations of torture. The organization criticized the long-term detention without charge or trial of political detainees and called for an end to trials of civilians before military courts and for all political prisoners to be given fair trials. It also called for all death sentences to be commuted and for the abolition of the death penalty.

In July, Amnesty International published a report, *Egypt: Indefinite detention and systematic torture – the forgotten victims*, which focused on the government's use of administrative detention, systematic torture and the death penalty as well as on killings and other human rights abuses by armed opposition groups. In response to the report, the authorities denied that there were any prisoners of conscience held in Egyptian prisons and stated that those held in long-term administrative detention, including those mentioned in Amnesty International's report, were a threat to society and would resume their "terrorist" activities if released. The state of emergency was, according to the authorities, being used only in connection with crimes relating to "terrorism" and drugs. While the response noted the prohibition of torture and ill-treatment of prisoners under Egyptian law, it failed to address the systematic use of torture in practice. The authorities failed to respond on the specific cases raised by Amnesty International, and gave no indication that investigations were being carried out into past violations, or that any steps had been taken to prevent human rights violations.

Amnesty International strongly condemned deliberate and arbitrary killings of civilians by armed opposition groups, calling on them to put an end to such killings, and to stop issuing death threats.

EL SALVADOR

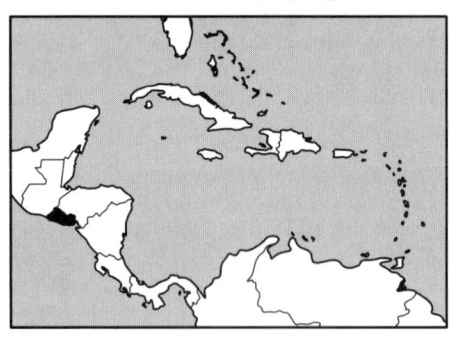

Dozens of people were killed in circumstances suggesting extrajudicial executions. Death threats against human rights defenders continued. A human rights worker was the victim of an attempted abduction. There were reports of torture and ill-treatment by the police of people in custody. The death penalty was reintroduced for certain crimes.

In June, El Salvador ratified the UN Convention against Torture and Other Cruel, Inhuman or Degrading Treatment or Punishment.

In November, the Legislative Assembly approved a revised Penal Code which reinstated so-called extrajudicial confessions. Such confessions can be made to, among others, members of the National Civil Police when a judge is not available, and are admissible as evidence in court. Although the confessions are subject to certain rules, their reinstatement caused concern because of their past association with the use of duress and torture.

The mandate of the UN Mission for El Salvador, which monitors compliance with the 1992 peace accords, was extended to the end of 1996. Its operations, however, were reduced and in May it was renamed the UN Verification Office.

In a report covering the period between May and June, the UN Secretary-General reiterated calls for implementation of the recommendations made in 1994 by the *Grupo Conjunto para la investigación de grupos armados ilegales con motivación política*, Joint Group to Investigate Politically Motivated Illegal Armed Groups, in view of new violent incidents, similar to those which characterized the period of armed conflict.

Dozens of people were killed in circumstances suggesting extrajudicial executions. There were fears that "death squads" were responsible for several killings during the latter part of the year.

In April, two youths aged 15 and 16 and a young man were killed in Agua Caliente, Quezaltepeque, department of La Libertad, by six men dressed in black uniforms, with their faces covered and carrying M-16 rifles and grenades. Brothers Jairo and Carlos Hernández Cornejo were hanged from a tree, with their hands tied behind their backs and their thumbs tied together, a method widely used by the army and paramilitary groups during the armed conflict. No one had been brought to justice for the killings by the end of the year.

In October, Francisco Antonio Manzanares Mojaraz, a member of the *Frente Farabundo Martí de Liberación Nacional*, Farabundo Martí National Liberation Front, was shot dead in Colonia Satélite de Oriente, department of San Miguel, by eight heavily armed men wearing bulletproof jackets. Francisco Manzanares was unarmed. Eye-witnesses were later threatened by unknown persons, and feared for their safety. Francisco Manzanares had reported to the *Policía Nacional Civil* (PNC), National Civil Police, in late September that unidentified men were watching his house and asking about his activities. Police authorities claimed that Francisco

Manzanares was involved in extortion and that the operation in which he was killed was part of the police investigation. An investigation by the authorities into the killings was still in progress at the end of the year.

Human rights defenders, members of non-governmental organizations, indigenous people, journalists and political figures were victims of human rights violations.

Members of the *Asociación Nacional Indígena Salvadoreña* (ANIS), Salvadorean National Indigenous Association, received death threats on several occasions during the year. In January, five unidentified men came to the house of a member of ANIS in the community of Las Hojas, Sonsonate, and threatened to kill Adrián Esquino Lisco, chief of the Nahuat, Lenca and Maya indigenous community. In May, his son, Mario Cruz Crespín Esquino, escaped an attempt on his life, reportedly by members of the *Batallón Jaguar,* Jaguar Battalion, a paramilitary group. An investigation into the incident by the Human Rights Procurator's Office was continuing at the end of the year.

In June, a newly formed clandestine group calling itself *Fuerza Nacionalista Roberto D'Aubuisson*, Roberto D'Aubuisson Nationalist Force, issued death threats, which were published in a national newspaper, against a group of public figures, including Monsignor Gregorio Rosa Chávez, Auxiliary Bishop of San Salvador; Francisco Elías Valencia, a newspaper editor; and Victoria Velásquez de Avilés, National Human Rights Procurator. The group issued at least two other threats.

Members of the *Centro para la Promoción de los Derechos Humanos "Madeleine Lagadec"*, Madeleine Lagadec Human Rights Centre, also received death threats. In August, the Centre's offices in San Salvador received an anonymous note warning that they would be burgled and staff members killed. In September, Eliezar Ambelis, a human rights worker at the Centre, received a death threat, and in October he escaped an attempted kidnapping by unidentified masked men who tried to bundle him into a car. Later the same day, threats were received by the Centre's offices in San Salvador and Santa Clara. A few days later the Santa Clara offices were burgled. These actions were believed to be in response to the Centre's community work and its campaign against the extension of the death penalty.

In November, the Human Rights Procurator stated that she had been subjected to harassment and death threats since May 1995. On one occasion, unidentified individuals had threatened to rape and kill her four daughters. The threats had followed public statements she had made denouncing the criminal activities of clandestine armed groups acting in a manner similar to "death squads" active during the armed conflict in the 1980s.

There were many allegations of torture and ill-treatment by the PNC. In January, a young man arrested by the PNC in Soyapango was beaten with a metal bar and threatened with a knife by a police officer. In February, a man detained in Jiquilisco was so severely beaten that he required hospital treatment.

In October, the Legislative Assembly approved a motion proposed by members of the ruling *Alianza Republicana Nacionalista*, Nationalist Republican Alliance, reintroducing the death penalty for kidnapping, aggravated homicide and rape. The death penalty had been abolished in 1983 for all but exceptional crimes in time of international war. This legislation, which comes into force only if ratified by the new assembly to be elected in March 1997, infringes international instruments to which El Salvador is a party, such as the American Convention on Human Rights.

Amnesty International expressed concern at the threats against members of ANIS, the Madeleine Lagadec Human Rights Centre, church leaders, the Human Rights Procurator, journalists and others, and called on the government to guarantee their safety, investigate the threats and bring those responsible to justice.

In October, Amnesty International called on the government of Dr Armando Calderón Sol to carry out a thorough investigation into the killing of Francisco Manzanares. The organization also called for protection to be accorded to witnesses.

Amnesty International called on members of the Legislative Assembly to oppose the proposal to reintroduce the death penalty. Following the approval of the proposal, the organization expressed its deep regret at the decision taken by the Legislative Assembly.

EQUATORIAL GUINEA

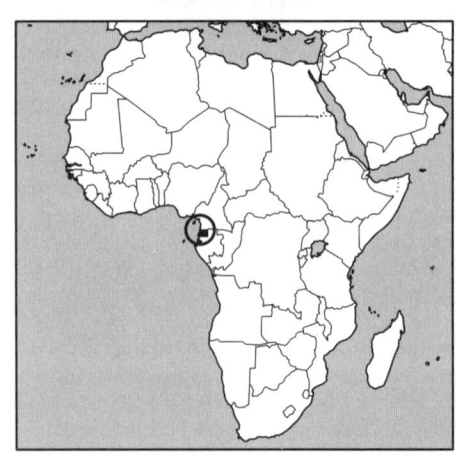

Scores of suspected government opponents were briefly detained without charge or trial. At least 150 of them were prisoners of conscience. Many of them were tortured or ill-treated.

President Teodoro Obiang Nguema was returned to power in elections in February. There was no secret ballot, and political opponents of the government were subjected to various restrictions and intimidation. The members of the *Plataforma de Oposición Conjunta* (POC), Joint Opposition Platform, boycotted the election after the government dissolved the POC and banned its presidential candidate, Amancio Gabriel Nse.

In April, the UN Commission on Human Rights examined the report of the UN Special Rapporteur on Equatorial Guinea, who had visited the country in 1995 (see *Amnesty International Report 1996*), and called upon the government to end arbitrary arrests and torture. The Special Rapporteur, whose mandate was extended for another year, visited Equatorial Guinea again in December and was due to present a further report in 1997.

At least 150 prisoners of conscience were detained during the year because of their peaceful political activities or beliefs. They were held for short periods without charge or trial; most were tortured or ill-treated and denied medical treatment for their injuries. At least 60 were arrested during the pre-election period. They included Genoveva Nchama, information secretary of the *Unión Popular*, Popular Union, who was arrested in January for criticizing irregularities in the electoral roll such as omitting names of people in areas where the opposition was strong. She was reportedly beaten and held in a cell with 10 men. Vitorino Bolekia, the first democratically elected Mayor of Malabo, the capital, and a member of the *Alianza Democrática Progresista*, Progressive Democratic Alliance, was arrested in February. Santiago Obama and Celestino Bacale, the President and the Foreign Relations Secretary of the *Convergencia para la Democracia Social* (CPDS), Convergence for Social Democracy, were also detained along with two other councillors. All five were severely beaten with electric cables, including on the soles of the feet.

A Roman Catholic priest, Father José Luis Engono, was arrested and ill-treated in late January in Mbini, a town in the mainland region of Rio Muni. At about the same time, three Roman Catholic seminarists and a catechist were detained briefly in Bata, the Rio Muni regional capital, and at least one, seminarist José Carlos Esono, was tortured. The authorities apparently suspected them of involvement in opposition political activities.

CPDS members were frequent targets for arrest. Amancio Gabriel Nse and Pedro Ndong Mbale were arrested in March at a road-block outside Niefang, Rio Muni region. They were carrying a letter written by Celestino Bacale concerning party strategy. They were transferred to a police station in Bata, where Pedro Ndong Mbale was released without charge shortly after arrival. Amancio Gabriel Nse was held for several more days and tortured.

Celestino Bacale was rearrested in April, held for a few days in Malabo and questioned about the letter. He was then held in Bata for three days in a police station before being released uncharged. In November, he was detained for five days and charged with insulting President Obiang Nguema. He was forbidden to leave Malabo pending trial by a military court. By the end of the year the trial had not begun.

Benita Nchama was arrested in Acurenam, Rio Muni region, early in May and detained in Bata for about six weeks for possessing a copy of the CPDS newspaper, *La Verdad*, before being released without charge.

Francisca Nzang Ebasi was detained for a few days with her 10-day-old baby in Nkimi, Rio Muni region, in May, after her husband, Alberto Ngomo Mfumu, the first democratically elected Mayor of Nkimi and a member of the *Partido del Progreso* (PP), Progress Party, went to complain to the central government authorities in Malabo about interference in council affairs by the local government representative. Alberto Ngomo Mfumu had himself been briefly detained on at least two occasions earlier in the year.

Norberto Esono, a PP member and Niefang town councillor, was detained for 12 days at Niefang police station in May and accused of holding illegal meetings. While held he was severely beaten on the head and body and sustained a broken leg. Basilio Ava Eworo, Vice-President of the PP, was held for a few days in Malabo in September and accused of holding an unauthorized meeting. All three were released without charge.

In November, 11 soldiers were sentenced to prison terms ranging from four to 13 years in Malabo after an unfair trial. They reportedly faced charges of attempting to overthrow the government. They were tried before a military court which uses summary procedures that curtail the rights of the defence. There is no right of appeal against conviction or sentence imposed by military court. Few details about the proceedings in this case were available.

Amnesty International repeatedly expressed concern to the government about the detention and torture of political prisoners and called for the release of prisoners of conscience. The organization sought further information about the trial of 11 soldiers in November. The government did not respond.

ERITREA

During the year scores of political prisoners were detained without charge or trial. Over 100 political prisoners detained in previous years remained in detention without charge or trial. Scores of detainees who had been held since 1991 were secretly tried and sentenced to prison terms after unfair trials. The fate of at least a dozen people who "disappeared" in 1991 and 1992 remained unknown. There were fears that some may have been extrajudicially executed.

President Issayas Afewerki's Government continued to face armed opposition from the Sudan-based Eritrean Islamic *Jihad* group. Eritrea was also involved in a territorial dispute with Yemen over the Hanish Islands in the Red Sea, in which the French Government sought to mediate.

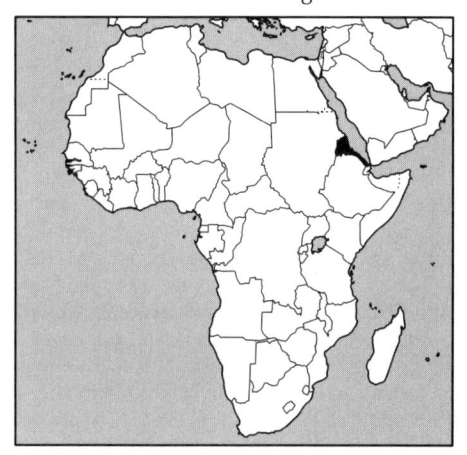

Conscription remained in force (see *Amnesty International Report 1996*) with no provision for conscientious objection. Members of the Jehovah's Witnesses religious group remained without citizenship rights (see *Amnesty International Report 1996*).

There was no independent press. A new press law enacted in June proclaimed the freedom of the press but provided for penalties, including imprisonment, for offences which could include exercising the right to freedom of expression.

No opposition organization was permitted. The People's Front for Democracy and Justice (PFDJ), formerly the Eritrean People's Liberation Front (EPLF), remained the only permitted political party. The first draft of a constitution for Eritrea, containing restrictions on the right to form political parties, was approved by a parliament consisting mainly of PFDJ officials.

Eritrea was one of only two African states not to have ratified the African Charter on Human and Peoples' Rights.

Information came to light that a group of people from the Jaberti community detained without charge or trial for some two years had been released by early 1996 (see previous *Amnesty International Reports*).

During the year scores of political prisoners were detained without charge or trial. There were reports of arrests of suspected government opponents linked to the Eritrean Islamic Jihad group and the different Eritrean Liberation Front (ELF) groups. Several Sudanese nationals were detained on suspicion of passing information to the Sudanese authorities about a Sudanese opposition organization operating from Eritrea. Over 100 political detainees, including possible prisoners of conscience, were believed to be held without charge or trial, many incommunicado and some since 1991 when the EPLF came to power.

Scores of Eritrean former members of the Ethiopian security forces and civilian administration who had been detained in 1991 were secretly tried by military tribunals in early 1996. The charges were not disclosed, but may have included human rights crimes. They did not receive fair trials and had no right to legal representation or appeal. Many were sentenced to long prison terms.

The authorities continued to deny that at least a dozen people who had been abducted from Ethiopia and Sudan in 1991 and 1992 were in their custody, which increased fears that some might have been extrajudicially executed.

Amnesty International called for all political detainees to be given fair and prompt trials or to be released. The organization expressed concern about the secret trials of former officials, but received no reply. It urged the government to allow all detainees access to their families and to lawyers, and renewed its calls for investigations into "disappearances".

ESTONIA

At least four men were sentenced to death and at least nine other prisoners were believed to be on death row at the end of the year, three of them having spent over three years in isolation.

In April, Estonia ratified the European Convention for the Protection of Human Rights and Fundamental Freedoms without its additional Protocol No. 6 which abolishes the death penalty in peacetime. Estonia had signed the Convention and its Protocol No. 6 in May 1993, when it became a member of the Council of Europe, and therefore, under international law, may not carry out executions pending a decision on ratification. In June, the Parliamentary Assembly of the Council of Europe called upon Estonia to abolish the death penalty "as soon as possible". In November, Estonia ratified the European Convention for the Prevention of Torture and Inhuman or Degrading Treatment or Punishment.

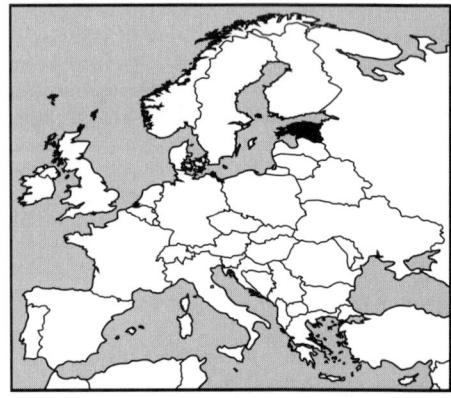

In December, parliament adopted an amendment to the criminal code allowing courts to impose life imprisonment as an alternative to the death penalty. A proposal to abolish the death penalty was rejected.

Three prisoners – Andrean Ojala, Albert Solodov and Oleg Borisov – were sentenced to death in February for robbery and murder. An appeal against their sentence was reportedly rejected in May. At least 10 other prisoners were believed to be on death row at the end of the year, three of whom had spent over three years in isolation and were still awaiting the outcome of appeals for clemency submitted to President Lennart Meri in 1993 and 1994. Amnesty International believes that prolonged isolation could have serious effects on the physical and mental health of the prisoners and might constitute cruel, inhuman or degrading treatment or punishment.

Amnesty International appealed to the authorities to abolish the death penalty and commute all pending death sentences, and expressed concern about the prolonged isolation in which death-row prisoners were held. In June, the Deputy Prosecutor General responded that prisoners on death row were isolated for their own protection. He also informed the organization that the prison authorities had submitted an appeal to the National Court for commutation of the death sentence passed on death row prisoner Vladimir Botchko. In October, Amnesty International urged the authorities to explore ways of alleviating the effects of isolation on death-row prisoners without compromising their security, and requested information on the progress of the appeal on behalf of Vladimir Botchko. In November, the organization was informed by the Chairman of the National Court that no such appeal had been filed.

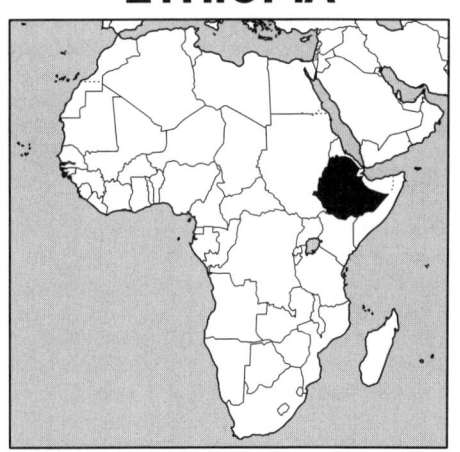

ETHIOPIA

Hundreds of critics and opponents of the government were arrested, including prisoners of conscience. Some were brought to trial and sentenced to prison terms, but most political trials had not been completed by the end of the year. Most political prisoners were detained without charge or trial. The trial continued of 46 former government officials charged with genocide and crimes against humanity, but some 1,800 other former officials remained in detention without charge or trial. There were further reports of torture of government opponents and "disappearances" and extrajudicial executions by the security forces, particularly in areas of armed conflict. At least 13 death sentences were imposed, but there were no reports of executions.

Prime Minister Meles Zenawi's government, established in 1995 after a four-year transitional period, continued to face armed opposition in some regions. Fighting continued between government forces and the Oromo Liberation Front (OLF) in the Oromo region and the Ogaden National Liberation Front (ONLF) in the Somali region in the east. Anti-government violence by other groups continued. In August, September and December, government forces attacked the bases in Somalia of *Al-Itihad,* an Islamist organization which claimed responsibility for bombings in Ethiopia. Judicial reorganization, involving extensive dismissals of federal and regional court judges, seriously undermined the legal rights of political prisoners.

Ethiopia was one of only two African states not to have ratified the African Charter on Human and Peoples' Rights.

Dozens of journalists were arrested in Addis Ababa, the capital, and held for investigation, in some cases for several months, before being charged and tried or granted bail. Seventeen were still held at the end of the year because of articles they had published, none of which advocated violence. They were prisoners of conscience. Most of the 17 were held without charge or trial, but three were tried and sentenced to terms of imprisonment. In March, Terefe Mengesha of *Roha* magazine was jailed for one year, shortly after completing a one-year prison term for a similar offence, and Solomon Lemma of *Wolafen* magazine was jailed for 18 months. They were both arrested because of articles reporting on armed opposition and were charged under the Press Law with "publishing false information in order to incite war and unrest".

Several hundred people suspected of supporting or belonging to the OLF were detained without trial. Among those arrested in February was Olana Bati, a lawyer, and previously a prisoner of conscience on several occasions. He was detained without charge for seven months in the town of Nekemte; he was finally hospitalized after repeated denial of medical treatment, and released. Two Oromo singers, Baharsitu Obsa and Shabbe Sheko, were arrested in February in Dire Dawa and Goba in Bale region. Hailu Tarfassa Tasse, an employee of the Ethiopian Evangelical Mekane Yesus Church, was detained in May. They were still held without charge or trial at the end of the year.

In some incidents the security forces arbitrarily detained hundreds of suspected government opponents. Most of them were released after some weeks of investigation, but others were held for longer periods without being brought to court. Scores of Somalis, including Roda Ibrahim, working in Somaliland for a British development agency, and Mohamed Osman, working in Angola for a Canadian relief agency, were detained without charge for some months after a hotel bombing in Addis Ababa in January for which *Al-Itihad* claimed responsibility. Mohamed Yusuf Ahmed, a UN consultant, was detained in January during a round-up of scores of Sudanese residents in Addis Ababa after a diplomatic clash between Ethiopia and Sudan. He was held for four months without charge. Abdi-Deq Shirreh Farah was one of several Somalis who were detained without charge or trial after an attempt to assassinate a government minister in July, for which *Al-Itihad* also claimed responsibility.

Scores of suspected ONLF members were detained in the Somali region of Ethiopia. In January, scores of people were arrested, including Abdi Ismail, a former district governor. In July, shortly after the announcement of an alliance between the OLF and the ONLF, Ali Bashe Abdi and Riyale Hamud Ahmed and 10 other members and former members of the regional parliament, were arrested in Jijiga and Dire Dawa. Elected as members of the ONLF party, they appeared to have been detained on suspicion of involvement in recent ONLF armed opposition. Most were still held incommunicado, without charge, at the end of the year, and there were fears for their safety.

In March, Abate Angore, an official of the Ethiopian Teachers' Association (ETA), and Kebede Desta, an official of the Retired Teachers' Association, were arrested shortly after the ETA had criticized government action against it and the detention and killing of scores of its members. Abate Angore was released without charge after two months but redetained in September and still held without charge at the end of the year. Taye Woldesmiate, ETA chairman and a former university professor, was arrested in May on his return to Ethiopia from Europe. He was held incommunicado until July when he and five others, including Kebede Desta, were charged with organizing violent anti-government activity in a clandestine group, the Ethiopia National Patriots' Front, a charge which he denied. The trial of all six, who were possible prisoners of conscience, started in October and continued at the end of the year.

Hundreds of suspected government opponents arrested in previous years continued to be detained. The trials of some, who were possible prisoners of conscience, proceeded slowly and were not completed by the end of the year. The trial in Ziwai of 285 members of the OLF who were detained in 1992 made little progress. The trial of Professor Asrat Woldeyes, chairman of the All-Amhara People's Organization, and 31 others for conspiracy to carry out armed rebellion had not concluded by the end of the year (see *Amnesty International Report 1996*). Sheikh Mohamed Awel Reja, Vice-President of the Supreme Council of Islamic Affairs, and Mohamed Abdu Tuku, an engineering lecturer, were among 31 Muslim leaders on trial on a similar charge in connection with a violent disturbance at the Anwar mosque in Addis Ababa in 1995 (see *Amnesty International Report 1996*). Bayera Mideksa, an Oromo pharmacist held beyond his release date as the prosecutor sought an increase in his sentence, and Mengesha Dogoma, a southern politician charged with criminal violence but not yet tried, had both been in prison since 1992.

Hundreds of other political detainees arrested in previous years remained in detention without charge or trial throughout the year. They included Ahmed Mohamed Hussein (known as "Makahil"), a former Vice-President of the Somali region detained in Addis Ababa in 1995, and Hassan Ali Omar, Mayor of Shilabo, both thought to be detained for their suspected ONLF connections. Several suspected Ethiopian People's Revolutionary Party (EPRP) members, including Lemma Haile – arrested in Addis Ababa in 1993 – and hundreds of OLF suspects, including Bogalech Tolosa and her sister, Bizunesh Tolosa – arrested in Nazareth in August 1995 – remained in custody without charge (see *Amnesty International Report 1996*). Scores of local government opponents arrested and tortured in Shakicho district in southwestern Ethiopia in November 1995 remained in detention. Seven Ethiopians were forcibly returned to Ethiopia from Djibouti in August, including Girmay Moges Newaye-Mariam, a refugee and former member of the Tigray People's Liberation Front (TPLF); Muhyadin Muftah, a leader of the armed opposition Afar Revolutionary Democratic Unity Front; and Hussein Ahmed Aydrus and five other ONLF supporters (see **Djibouti** entry). They were detained on arrival in Ethiopia. Three other ONLF supporters, including Abdullahi Haliye, were deported from Somaliland in October and detained by the Ethiopian authorities (see **Somalia** entry).

Some political prisoners were released, including Sissay Agena, a journalist, whose one-year sentence expired in late 1996, and Said Hassan and three other EPRP members who had been detained since 1992 after being forcibly returned to Ethiopia from Sudan. Martha Arera, arrested in late 1995 with three other staff of the Oromo Relief Association (ORA), which was closed down by the government, were released in June without charge. Ahmed Mohamed, the ORA representative in Dire Dawa who "disappeared" after being arrested in Dire Dawa in February, was released in October. Mohamoud Muhumed Hashi, a former university lecturer detained in 1994 for alleged ONLF connections, was released in mid-1996.

The trial of 46 members of the former ruling Provisional Military Administrative Council (known as the *Dergue*) continued with lengthy adjournments during the year (see *Amnesty International Report 1996*). The Special Prosecutor presented evidence of extrajudicial executions ordered by the *Dergue*, including the killing of Emperor Haile Selassie in 1975 and of his former ministers and of EPRP members. Some 1,800 other former officials of the government of Mengistu Haile-Mariam (who is now in exile in Zimbabwe) accused of similar crimes remained in detention without charge. They included Mammo Wolde, a former Olympic athlete, Alemayehu Teferra, a former university president, Aberra Yemane-Ab, an opposition leader who had returned from exile, and Mekonnen Dori, a southern opposition politician and former vice-minister in the post-1991 Transitional Government.

Reports were received of torture by the security forces while interrogating suspected government opponents. Suspected members of the OLF and ONLF were particularly targets of torture. Hussein Ahmed Aydrus and Abdullahi Haliye were allegedly tortured after being returned from Djibouti and Somaliland respectively (see above). Political prisoners were held in harsh conditions, particularly in regional prisons and unofficial secret interrogation centres, and two of them (see above) – Taye Woldesmiate and Aberra Yemane-Ab (detained since his return from exile in the USA in 1993) – were kept permanently chained in Addis Ababa Central Prison.

There were further reports of "disappearances" of government opponents abducted by gunmen believed to be members of the security forces. Among those who remained "disappeared" at the end of the year was Kumsa Burayu, an Oromo journalist, who "disappeared" in Addis Ababa in January.

The fate of dozens of other people who "disappeared" after the overthrow of the government of Mengistu Haile-Mariam remained unknown. Among them were OLF suspects Mustafa Idris and Yoseph Ayele Bati; Hagos Atsbeha, detained by the TPLF in 1988; Deeg Yusuf Kariye, an ONLF journalist; and Tsegay Gebre-Medhin and other EPRP officials (see *Amnesty International Report 1996*).

There were numerous reports of extrajudicial executions by the security forces, particularly in the areas of armed conflict in the Oromo and Somali regions. Ebissa Adunya, an Oromo singer killed at his home in Addis Ababa by soldiers in August, appeared to have been extrajudicially executed on suspicion of supporting the OLF.

No investigations were known to have taken place into allegations of torture, "disappearance" or extrajudicial execution.

Three members of an Egyptian Islamist organization – Abdulkarim al-Naji Abdelradi, Al-Arab Sadiq Hafiz and Safwat Hassan Abdelghani – were sentenced to death in September after a six-month trial *in camera*. They were convicted of attempting to assassinate Egyptian President Hosni Mubarak in Addis Ababa in June 1995 and of killing two Ethiopian police officers. Their appeal to the Supreme Court had not been heard by the end of the year. At least 10 other people were sentenced to death by regional courts. No executions were reported of any people condemned to death since 1991.

An Amnesty International delegate visited Ethiopia in May to observe the *Dergue* trial and examine other judicial proceedings against government opponents. In July, Amnesty International published a report on the trial and the detentions of other former officials, *Ethiopia: Human rights trials and delayed justice – the case of Olympic gold medallist Mammo Wolde and hundreds of other uncharged detainees*. Amnesty International expressed concern that the *Dergue* trial was proceeding so slowly and criticized the delay in charging the other detainees.

Throughout the year Amnesty International appealed for the release of prisoners of conscience and for fair and prompt trials of other political detainees. The organization again called for urgent and impartial investigations into "disappearances" since 1991 and allegations of torture and extrajudicial executions by the security forces. It urged the government to abolish the death penalty, not to apply the death penalty in the trials of former officials, and to commute death sentences. The government did not respond to any of these appeals.

FRANCE

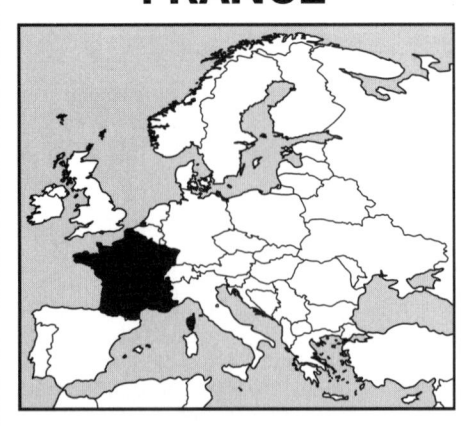

Criminal proceedings were under way against conscientious objectors to the national service laws. There were reports of shootings, killings and ill-treatment, sometimes accompanied by racist insults, by law enforcement officers. There were long delays in the judicial investigations of such cases and it was evident that, in some instances, there was a lack of thoroughness in the conduct of the inquiries. In some cases from previous years officers were brought to justice.

The government maintained the severe policy on immigration and border control of the previous year. In August, the *Office central pour la répression de l'immigration irrégulière et de l'emploi des étrangers sans titre* (Ocriest), Central Office for the Suppression of Illegal Immigration and Unauthorized Employment of Foreigners, was formed in the Ministry of the Interior. There were further mass expulsions of illegal immigrants and the government announced its goal of repatriating 20,000 such people annually.

The major security operation to combat attacks by armed groups, codenamed "*Vigipirate*", continued. It had been launched in September 1995 following a wave of bombings (*see Amnesty International Report 1996*). In December, a bomb in a suburban train exploded at Port-Royal station in central Paris, killing four people and injuring nearly 100.

In June, the Council of Ministers adopted the legislative proposal of the Minister of Justice to introduce radical reforms to the courts' handling of the most serious criminal cases. This proposal would entitle parties in trials at first instance in the present Court of Assizes to appeal for review by a higher court on grounds other than the purely legal aspects of the case. In addition, for the first time, juries in the Court of Assizes would be required to state in writing the grounds for their decisions.

The UN Special Rapporteur on extrajudicial, summary or arbitrary executions, in his 1996 annual report, regretted that France had not replied to his questions on reported shootings and killings by law enforcement officers, but welcomed the proposed judicial reforms in criminal cases.

There was still no right to claim conscientious objector status during military service and the alternative civilian service available to recognized objectors remained, at 20 months, twice the length of ordinary military service. In November, the government approved a draft bill proposing the total suspension by 2002, via a phasing-out process commencing in 1997, of compulsory national service. It would be replaced by a compulsory five-day citizenship course (*rendez-vous citoyen*) for both males and females, and voluntary military and civilian services. Parliament was due to consider the bill in 1997.

During the year, criminal proceedings continued to be opened against conscientious objectors who refused to conform to the national service laws, with the exception of Jehovah's Witnesses, for whom the experimental arrangements introduced under a Ministry of Defence directive of 1995 remained in force (see *Amnesty International Report 1996*). The criminal proceedings resulted in prison sentences, sometimes suspended. However, throughout the year there were no reports of conscientious objectors entering prison and thus becoming prisoners of conscience, as those sentenced to periods of detention remained at liberty while awaiting the outcome of appeals lodged with higher courts.

There were further allegations of ill-treatment and shootings and killings of unarmed people by law enforcement officers during the year.

In January, Etienne Leborgne, a Paris taxi driver born in Guadeloupe, was stopped by police officers at Roissy airport for a time-clock check. He tried to escape the police check as his clock was over the limit and, in the process, injured one of the officers.

Three days later a team of police in plain clothes succeeded in blocking and immobilizing his taxi with him inside. Two shots were fired, shattering the windows. One of the officers then went up to the taxi and shot Etienne Leborgne through the head at close range. The officer claimed that he fired because he saw the driver reaching into the glove compartment, which allegedly contained a tear-gas canister. A judicial inquiry into Etienne Leborgne's death was opened and his mother lodged a judicial complaint alleging murder and complicity to commit murder against the officers.

Allegations of ill-treatment by law enforcement officers were sometimes accompanied by reports of officers using racist insults. In April, Abdelkrim Boumlik, a 16-year-old minor of Moroccan origin who was visiting his family in Soisy-sous-Montmorency, was beaten and subjected to racist abuse by two police officers. One of the officers was a plainclothes member of the *Brigade anticriminalité* (BAC), Anti-Crime Brigade. Abdelkrim Boumlik had been riding on a motorcycle with a 15-year-old friend without a helmet, contrary to French law.

In a formal judicial complaint, Abdelkrim Boumlik claimed that the officers chased him and his friend, kicked and punched them and beat them with truncheons. The officers then attempted to throw him into a lake. Both boys were then handcuffed and ordered to kneel on the floor of the officers' car where they were racially abused and threatened.

The two boys were taken to Enghien-les-Bains police station and held in cells until the following morning. The police claimed that they tried to contact Abdelkrim Boumlik's parents without success. However, the parents dispute this. Neither a lawyer nor the public prosecutor's office was informed of his detention. After nearly 12 hours' detention Abdelkrim Boumlik was allowed to leave. A medical certificate from the local hospital recorded injuries consistent with his allegations.

Judicial inquiries into many cases of shootings, killings and ill-treatment by law enforcement officers remained open after many years.

In April, the Ministry of Defence informed Amnesty International that a reconstruction of the facts had finally been carried out in January in the inquiry into the death of Ibrahim Sy, a young man who was a passenger in a stolen car fired on by gendarmes near Rouen in 1994 (see *Amnesty International Report 1995*). The inquiry had still not been completed at the end of the year.

In August, a gendarme who shot and killed Franck Moret in 1993 was sent for trial in the *Tribunal correctionnel* (Correctional Court). Franck Moret was shot while he was in his car with his fiancée in the Drôme department. The families of both young people filed a judicial complaint alleging murder. The officer claimed to have acted in self-defence. In February, two and a half years later, the investigating magistrate finished her inquiry but there was a further delay of six months while the authorities considered which court should try the case. In August, it was sent for trial to the lower court, which sits without a jury, and the party representing the families appealed for it to be transferred to the higher Court of Assizes.

The inquiry was still open, after three years, into the fatal shooting of a young man of Algerian descent in Saint-Fons, near Lyon. Mourad Tchier, who was unarmed, was shot in the back while reportedly trying to escape. The case has been characterized by procedural irregularities and continual delays. The reconstruction of the facts by the magistrate was only held two years after his death.

Despite long delays, some officers were finally brought to trial during the year. In January, an officer of the BAC intervention squad was found guilty of assault and battery of Didier Laroche in 1994 (see *Amnesty International Report 1995*). He had been punched, kicked and hit with a truncheon, sustaining a fractured nose and various injuries to his eyes, face, chest, knees and thighs. The officer was given a four-month suspended prison sentence and fined. The conviction was appealed.

In February, the Paris Court of Assizes sentenced an officer to eight years' imprisonment on a charge of assault and battery leading unintentionally to death. Makomé M'Bowole, a 17-year-old Zairian, had been arrested in 1993 in connection with a suspected petty theft of cigarettes. He had been questioned at Grandes-Carrières police station with two others, even after the prosecutor's officer ordered his release to his parents because he was a minor. However, reportedly, the parents could not be found (see *Amnesty International Reports 1994 and 1995*). The officer admitted producing his weapon to intimidate the teenager, who he said was shouting and had insulted him. The officer stated at the time: "I wanted to frighten him". He claimed that the gun went off accidentally when the teenager tried to grab his hand. Forensic evidence, however, showed that Makomé M'Bowole was killed by a shot at point-blank range from the gun pressed against his temple.

In May, Douai Court of Appeal reduced the sentence of a police officer convicted of involuntary homicide. Rachid Ardjouni, a 17-year-old of Algerian origin, was shot in the back of the head and killed. He was reportedly lying face downwards on the ground at the time and the officer was drunk (see *Amnesty International Reports 1994 to 1996*). The Court amended the original 24 months' imprisonment, increasing the period of suspension from 16 to 18 months and reducing the damages and financial compensation awarded to the family of the deceased. In an exceptional decision, it overturned the Correctional Court's sentence that the conviction should be entered on the officer's criminal record (*casier judiciaire no. 2*). The officer will, therefore, be allowed to continue to serve in the police, and to carry arms.

Amnesty International continued to express concern that, because of its punitive length, civilian service did not provide an acceptable alternative to military service. The organization was also concerned that there was still no provision for conscientious objection developed after joining the armed forces and reiterated its belief that conscientious objectors to military service should be able to seek conscientious objector status at any time.

Amnesty International sought information from the authorities about the progress of investigations into incidents of shootings, killings and ill-treatment.

In April, an Amnesty International delegation held talks with the Minister of Justice and leading government officials from the Ministries of Defence and the Interior. The delegation referred to the detailed recommendations made in its October 1994 report (see *Amnesty International Reports 1995* and *1996*) and, in particular, the need to reduce the excessive length of proceedings involving law enforcement officers and unwarranted delays in the investigation process. Amnesty International also expressed concern that the special powers available under certain laws to the gendarmerie allowed them to use firearms in situations where the police were forbidden to do so. The delegation stressed that French law should conform to international recommendations. The Minister of Justice described this legislation, in particular the decree of 1943, as "null and void", but at the end of the year it was still in use. The delegation received assurances that police training would be improved and information regarding plans for improving the administration of justice.

GAMBIA

At least 28 people who appeared to be prisoners of conscience were detained for most of the year. At least five prisoners of conscience were arrested and held without charge or trial for brief periods. At least three members of the security forces continued to be held without trial. Two other possible prisoners of conscience "disappeared". Previous cases of suspected extrajudicial executions had still not been investigated.

In August, a new Constitution was adopted following a national referendum. While claiming to reintroduce the rule of law under a civilian government, it granted members of the Armed Forces Revolutionary Council (AFPRC) total immunity from prosecution. The Constitution allowed for derogation of fundamental rights and freedoms during a state of public emergency, without specifying the criteria for such a derogation. The death penalty was retained.

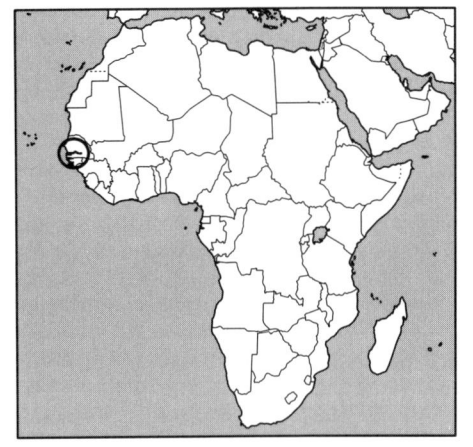

Soon after the Constitution was adopted, the ban on political activities, in force since the July 1994 coup, was lifted. However, a decree was passed which disqualified former President, Sir Dawda Kairaba Jawara, former Vice-President Saihou Sabally and all former ministers of the People's Progressive Party (PPP) from contesting any political office. Two pre-coup opposition parties were also banned from participating in both the parliamentary and the presidential elections. The penalty for contravening this decree was life imprisonment or a fine of one million *dalasis* (approximately US$100,000). A separate decree gave the Minister of the Interior and the security forces wide powers of arrest and detention, in some instances for 90 days, without any right of legal challenge by the detainee.

The presidential election in September, contested by four candidates, was won by Captain Yaha Jammeh, Chairman of the AFPRC. The promised transition to civilian rule was due to be completed by parliamentary elections scheduled for January 1997, after which the new Constitution adopted in August was due to come into force.

At least 28 people who appeared to be prisoners of conscience were held for most of the year. About 25 alleged supporters of the banned PPP, who had been arrested and detained in October 1995 (see *Amnesty International Report 1996*) were released in October and November, after 13 months in detention. Most of them had not been charged, and those who were had the charges against them dropped.

Three other leading figures from the previous government, Omar Jallow, Hussainu Njie and Mamadi C. Cham, also arrested in October 1995, were released in September, after almost 12 months' detention without formal charges or trial. The police had reportedly tried to bring charges of treason against them, but they were never brought to court.

At least five prisoners of conscience, including four journalists and a trade unionist, were arrested and held without charge or trial for brief periods. S.B. Danso, a journalist from the *Daily Observer* newspaper, was held for 24 hours by the National Intelligence Agency (NIA). Paa M. Fall, a trade unionist, was detained for about three weeks without formal charge or trial.

At least three former members of the security forces, arrested in July 1994, and whose trial had been repeatedly adjourned, continued to be held (see *Amnesty International Reports 1995* and *1996*). They were possible prisoners of conscience. Pa Sallah Jagne, former Inspector General of Police, Ebrima Chongan, his deputy, and Kebba Dibba, Assistant Superintendent of Police, were tried in April and acquitted on various counts of stealing from the state while serving as government employees. Days later new criminal charges were brought against them. The magistrate who had acquitted them was dismissed. They remained in detention at the end of the year.

The whereabouts of two possible prisoners of conscience, believed to have been held incommunicado at Jangjangbureh prison, were unknown. The authorities continued to deny that they had been arrested and detained. Ousman Sillah, a youth leader, had been arrested in late 1995 and Lamin Waa Juwara, a former opposition member of parliament, was arrested in February. He had been arrested twice in 1995 for defying the government's ban on political activities (see *Amnesty International Report 1996*).

No investigations were carried out into previous cases of suspected extrajudicial executions. These included the death in custody of Captain Haidara, the death of Finance Minister Ousman Koro Ceesay and the deaths of at least 13 military personnel at the time of the alleged coup attempt in November 1994 (see *Amnesty International Report 1996*).

No death sentences were known to have been passed, and no executions were known to have taken place.

Amnesty International repeatedly called on the Gambian authorities to release prisoners of conscience, end incommunicado detention and investigate possible extrajudicial executions. It also called on them to reconsider their position on the death penalty. Amnesty International delegates who visited the Gambia in January met the Minister of Justice and discussed a number of human rights issues of concern to Amnesty International, including the death penalty. Before the referendum, Amnesty International made public its concerns about the lack of human rights safeguards in the draft Constitution. During the year Amnesty International published *The Gambia: Erosion of human rights safeguards continues* and *The Gambia: A new constitution – revised draft still threatens human rights*. In December, the organization called on the Gambian Government to protect human rights during the parliamentary elections scheduled to take place in January 1997.

GEORGIA

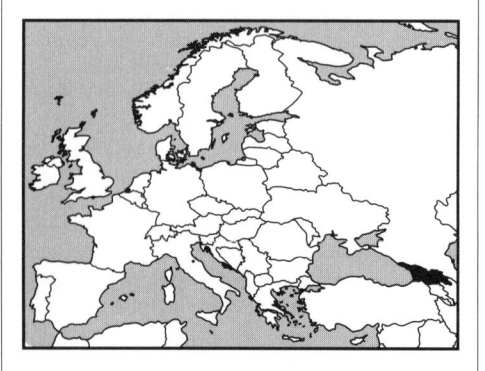

At least six political prisoners were sentenced after proceedings which appeared to fall short of international fair trial standards. Allegations of torture and ill-treatment in detention continued. One man died after reportedly being beaten by police officers. At least six people were sentenced to death; the real figure was thought to be higher. At least 50 others remained on death row, but no executions took place. An official moratorium on executions was declared in December. In the disputed region of Abkhazia dozens of people were reportedly detained because of their ethnic origin. At least one person was awaiting execution. Around 200,000 ethnic Georgians displaced by the conflict continued to face obstacles to their return.

The situation in Abkhazia remained tense. The mandates of both the UN Observer Mission in Georgia (UNOMIG) and the peace-keeping force from the Commonwealth of Independent States were renewed, but talks on the political future of the region remained deadlocked.

Progress was made, however, regarding the self-proclaimed territory of South Ossetia. In May, both sides signed a memorandum pledging to reject the use or threat of force or persecution based on ethnic origin, and in August President Eduard Shevardnadze met the leader of the South Ossetian authorities.

The post of Public Defender, established to monitor the defence of human rights and freedoms (see *Amnesty International Report 1996*), had not been filled by the end of the year.

In November, the UN Committee against Torture considered Georgia's initial report under the provisions of the Convention against Torture and Other Cruel, Inhuman or Degrading Treatment or Punishment. Georgia's report admitted that torture continued in places of detention, that law enforcement agencies did not always ensure proper investigation of such violations, as a result of which those responsible frequently went unpunished, and that conditions in many penal institutions were degrading. The Committee against Torture expressed concern about the volume of complaints of torture, particularly related to the extraction of confessions; the failure to investigate promptly claims of torture and to prosecute alleged offenders; the grossly inadequate conditions in places of detention; and the unwillingness of many law enforcement officers to respect the rights of people under investigation and prisoners.

In December, President Shevardnadze announced an official moratorium on executions, and parliament voted to reduce the number of capital offences from 13 to seven.

Six political prisoners were convicted in June after a trial which appeared to fall short of international fair trial standards. Their confessions did not appear to have been ruled inadmissible, although all alleged that they had been obtained under physical duress. Zviad Sherozia, for example, claimed that he was hung by the feet and beaten and had a grenade forced into his mouth. Badri Zarandia was sentenced to death, while his co-defendants received various terms of imprisonment.

Allegations of torture and ill-treatment in detention continued. In August, an official of the Prosecutor-General's office stated that police officers had frequently tortured detainees, including by giving them electric shocks. Later that month the trial opened in Tbilisi of the former deputy head of the Tbilisi police anti-drug department and four co-officers. They were accused of, among other things, using electric shocks on suspects.

In December, David Amashukeli died after being arrested on suspicion of drug abuse. Doctors at the drug examination centre where he was taken reportedly stated that he had been so severely beaten they were unable to carry out tests for drugs. He was then taken to hospital in Tibilisi but was pronounced dead on arrival. Three police officers were reportedly arrested in connection with the incident.

At least six people were sentenced to death during the year, but the real figure was thought to be higher. No executions were carried out. Around 50 men were believed to be under sentence of death at the end of the year.

Dozens of Georgians were allegedly detained by Abkhazian police forces solely on grounds of their ethnic origin. In one incident 20 Georgians were said to have been detained in the village of Dikhazurgia, Gali district, after a mine exploded under a vehicle driven by Russian peacekeeping forces. Thirteen were reportedly released after a ransom was paid. The others were released over the following three weeks.

At least one man remained under sentence of death in Abkhazia. Ethnic Georgian Ruzgen Gogokhiya had been convicted in 1995 of terrorist acts against civilians (see *Amnesty International Report 1996*). In May, the *de facto* Abkhazian authorities informed Amnesty International that he had the services of a lawyer throughout the trial, had an appeal pending before the Supreme Court of Abkhazia, and in addition had the right to petition for clemency.

Many of the estimated 200,000 ethnic Georgians displaced by the conflict in Abkhazia continued to face obstacles to their return, on what appeared to be grounds of their ethnicity and suspected political sympathies. In July, the UN Security Council again condemned the continued obstruction by the *de facto* Abkhazian authorities of the voluntary return of refugees and displaced people.

Amnesty International called for a judicial review of the case of Badri Zarandia and his co-defendants and a full, prompt and impartial investigation into all allegations of torture and ill-treatment in custody, with the results made public and any perpetrators identified brought to justice. It appealed for all death sentences to be commuted, and for immediate moves to ensure that all those sentenced to death had the right to appeal to a higher court.

Amnesty International urged the *de facto* Abkhazian authorities to ensure the security of all residents, regardless of ethnic origin, and sought further information on the cases of all Georgians still allegedly detained on ethnic grounds. Amnesty International also expressed concern at reports that Abkhazian police officers had demanded money for the release of some prisoners and asked what steps had been taken, if any, to investigate those allegations. The organization urged the *de facto* Abkhazian authorities to commute all death sentences, including that imposed on Ruzgen Gogokhiya, and sought further information on the application of the death penalty. Amnesty International also urged the *de facto* Abkhazian authorities to take all appropriate and timely measures to ensure the voluntary return of refugees and displaced people, under conditions in which their safety, and the safety of those who had already spontaneously returned, would be guaranteed.

GERMANY

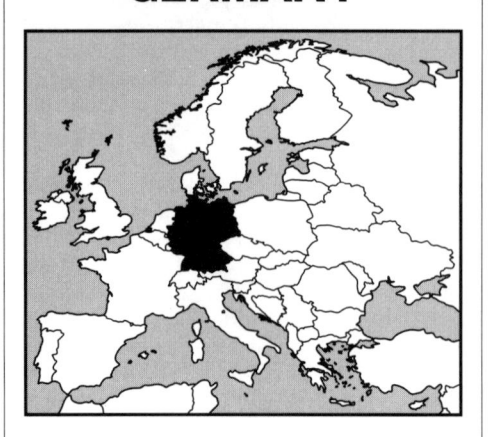

There were further allegations of ill-treatment of detainees by police officers.

In February, the results of a study, *The Police and Foreigners*, commissioned by the ministers of internal affairs of the 16 German federal states, were published. The report concluded that the problem of police abuse of foreign nationals concerned more than "just a few isolated incidents". A similar conclusion reached by Amnesty International in its May 1995 report, *Germany: Failed by the system – police ill-treatment of foreigners*, had been rejected at the time by the German authorities (see *Amnesty International Report 1996*).

In November, the UN Human Rights Committee met to consider Germany's fourth periodic report on its compliance with the International Covenant on Civil and Political Rights. In its concluding remarks the Committee expressed its concern at "instances of ill-treatment of persons by the police". The Committee also criticized the lack of any "truly independent mechanism for investigating [such] complaints" and recommended the establishment of "independent bodies" for this purpose.

There were further allegations of police ill-treatment of foreign nationals, including asylum-seekers, and members of ethnic minorities.

Ahmet Delibas, a Turkish national, alleged that two police officers repeatedly punched him in the face while in the back of a police car following his arrest outside a club in Hamm in North-Rhine/Westphalia in October 1995. According to witnesses, Ahmet Delibas showed no signs of injury when he was placed in the car with his hands secured behind his back. The detainee himself reported that when he arrived at the police station he was so dazed that he was unable to walk. Medical evidence showed that Ahmet Delibas had suffered serious injuries to his face, including a fractured cheek-bone, and separate fractures to both eye-sockets. He later underwent two operations on his face. In August, two officers were charged with assaulting Ahmet Delibas.

In January, Mohamed Z., a Moroccan citizen, alleged that a police officer punched and kicked him and struck him on the head with his torch after stopping him in central Frankfurt. Mohamed Z. was arrested and taken to a police station where, according to the detainee, the same officer placed him in a cell, made him undress and kicked him in front of two other officers. According to medical evidence Mohamed Z.'s injuries included multiple bruising and cuts to his head which required stitches. The police authorities brought a complaint against Mohamed Z. for resisting state authority.

Aliu B., a 16-year-old asylum-seeker from Sierra Leone, alleged that he was slapped by police officers and by a police doctor following his arrest at Bremen railway station in April. He was taken to a police station, where, he alleged, two officers held him down while the doctor forced a tube into his nose in order to administer an emetic. Aliu B.'s nose began to bleed and he was violently sick. After being made to wipe up his vomit he was reportedly thrown out of the station and collapsed in the station yard. Amnesty International believes that the forcible administration of emetics to detainees for non-medical reasons amounts to cruel, inhuman or degrading treatment.

In July, Mustafa K., a German national of Turkish origin, alleged that he was beaten, kicked and subjected to racist insults when he protested to Berlin police officers searching his flat. Medical reports recorded that Mustafa K. had suffered multiple bruising of the face and body, abrasions and vomiting. The police officers involved issued a complaint against Mustafa K. for attempted assault and resisting state authority.

In February, Mathias Brettner was tried on charges of offering for sale copies of the document "Police officers who make you vomit". In the document the Bremen-based non-governmental organization Anti-Racism Office accused the Bremen police of racist practices, including the physical ill-treatment and arbitrary arrest of blacks. Mathias Brettner was charged under section 130 ("Incitement of the people") of the German Criminal Code, which carries a penalty of up to five years' imprisonment. He was found guilty and fined. In September, his conviction was overturned on appeal.

Decisions were reached by prosecuting and judicial authorities on a number of cases of alleged ill-treatment by police in previous years.

In January, the Bremen authorities rejected a number of complaints of ill-treatment brought by black African detainees against Bremen police officers and doctors (see *Amnesty International Report 1996*). The detainees had alleged that they were forcibly given emetics, verbally threatened or physically ill-treated when they refused to cooperate, and subjected to racist abuse.

In January, a Berlin court ruled that there was insufficient evidence to convict two officers charged with ill-treating Vietnamese asylum-seeker Nguyen T. in June 1994 (see *Amnesty International Report 1996*).

In February, a court acquitted three officers of ill-treating Lutz Priebe in a Hamburg police station in August 1989. The court concluded that it was no longer possible to clarify what had actually happened almost six and a half years after the event (see *Amnesty International Report 1996*).

Also in February, Hidayet Secil's complaint of police ill-treatment was rejected by the Baden-Württemberg authorities (see *Amnesty International Report 1996*). A subsequent appeal against the authorities' decision and a request for a judicial review of it were both denied.

In May and June, two Hamburg police officers were tried on charges of assaulting Oliver Neß, a journalist, at a demonstration which he was covering in May 1994 (see previous *Amnesty International Reports*). Oliver Neß had alleged that officers hit him repeatedly in the kidneys, pelvis and chest with their batons and deliberately and violently twisted his foot while he was on the ground. Oliver Neß's injuries included multiple bruises and abrasions and torn ankle ligaments. In its findings the court rejected one of the accused officer's claims that Oliver Neß had been an "agitator" at the demonstration, and established that the officer had threatened the journalist and violently brought him to the ground in order to "teach a lesson" to demonstrators. The second officer who, according to the court's findings, had twisted Oliver Neß's foot in an effort to turn him over onto his back, was found guilty of causing bodily harm to the detainee through negligence. Both officers were fined. The court was unable to attribute any of Oliver Neß's other injuries to the actions of either officer.

In July, the highest court in the federal state of Berlin ordered a retrial of three police officers accused of assaulting Iranian student Habib J. in December 1992 (see *Amnesty International Report 1996*). The officers had been found guilty of the offence in September 1994 but their convictions had been overturned on appeal. In ordering a retrial the Higher Regional Court described the appeal court's findings as "contradictory and full of holes".

Throughout the year Amnesty International expressed concern to the authorities about fresh allegations of ill-treatment brought to its attention and called for them to be investigated promptly, impartially and thoroughly. In most cases the organization received confirmation from the authorities that investigations were in progress.

In February, Amnesty International expressed concern to the Bremen authorities that the prosecution of Mathias Brettner was inconsistent with Germany's obligations under Article 19 of the International Covenant on Civil and Political Rights and Article 10 of the European Convention for the Protection of Human Rights and Fundamental Freedoms, both of which instruments guarantee the right to freedom of expression. The organization informed the authorities that if Mathias Brettner was imprisoned for offering the document "Police officers who make you vomit" for sale, Amnesty International would adopt him as a prisoner of conscience and would call for his immediate and unconditional release. In March, the Bremen Ministry of Justice described Amnesty International's action as "outrageous".

Also in March, Amnesty International expressed concern to the Baden-Württemberg authorities that the investigation into

Hidayet Secil's alleged ill-treatment may not have been impartial, in contravention of Article 12 of the UN Convention against Torture and Other Cruel, Inhuman or Degrading Treatment or Punishment. The organization's criticism was rejected by the authorities the same month.

In May, Amnesty International expressed concern to the Bremen authorities that some of the complaints of ill-treatment which had been rejected by the prosecuting authorities the previous month did not appear to have been investigated thoroughly and impartially. In July, Amnesty International was informed that two investigations which the organization had criticized had been reopened following appeals by the complainants.

In February, Amnesty International published a report, *Federal Republic of Germany: The alleged ill-treatment of foreigners – an update to the May 1995 report*.

GHANA

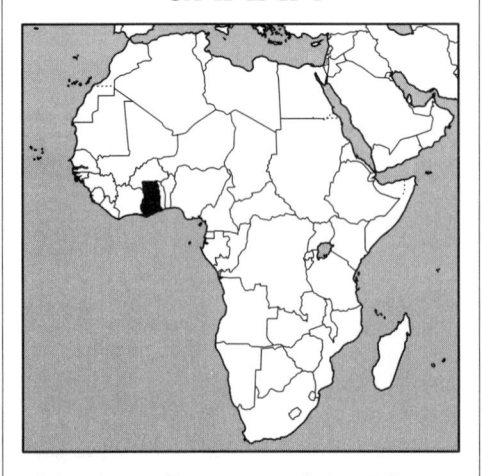

Three journalists arrested in February were possible prisoners of conscience. At least 13 political prisoners arrested in previous years, some of whom may have been prisoners of conscience, remained imprisoned at the end of the year. One death sentence was known to have been passed.

In December, President J.J. Rawlings, Head of State since 1981, won the presidential elections and his party, the National Democratic Congress, won a majority of parliamentary seats.

In February, Tommy Thompson and Ebenezer ("Eben") Quarcoo, publisher and editor respectively of the *Free Press* newspaper, and Kofi Coomson, editor-in-chief of the *Ghanaian Chronicle*, were detained for more than a week after their newspapers accused government officials of involvement in illegal drug dealing to finance the purchase of arms. They were charged with publishing a report "likely to injure the ... reputation of Ghana or the Government", an offence punishable by up to 10 years' imprisonment, and released on bail to await trial. By the end of the year, the Supreme Court had not ruled on a legal challenge to the constitutionality of the legislation under which they were charged, on the grounds that it contravenes the human rights provisions of the 1992 Constitution.

At least six political prisoners arrested in 1994 and charged with treason (see *Amnesty International Report 1995*) remained imprisoned at the end of the year. They included Karim Salifu Adam, a former soldier and leading member of the opposition New Patriotic Party. His trial before a specially appointed High Court began in May 1996 and had not concluded by the end of the year. In a statement to the Court, he said the charges had been fabricated by the security police, the Bureau of National Investigation (BNI), because he had refused a financial inducement to implicate opposition leaders and neighbouring governments in a fictitious coup conspiracy, and that he had been beaten severely. He said that, after he refused to cooperate, he was moved to a flooded cell and tortured for six days.

Five men – Sylvester Addai-Dwomoh, Kwame Alexander Ofei, Kwame Ofori-Appiah, Emmanuel Kofi Osei and John Kwadwo Owusu-Boakye – arrested in September 1994 and charged with treason (see *Amnesty International Report 1995*), remained imprisoned. No trial date had been set by the end of the year.

At least seven political prisoners tried in the 1980s before the Public Tribunal, a special court which was not independent of government control and which allowed no right of appeal or appeal only to another government-appointed court, remained imprisoned. Despite doubts about the fairness of their trials, their convictions could not be challenged because of the Transitional Provisions of the 1992

Constitution granting legal immunity for any action by the outgoing military government of Flight-Lieutenant (now President) J.J. Rawlings.

In May, Nana Akwasi Agyeman, the singer known as "Gemann", was sentenced to death for murder by the High Court in Accra. His appeal had not been heard by the end of the year. There were no executions.

The authorities allowed more than 3,000 refugees on the ship *Bulk Challenge* to land in Ghana in May after it had been turned away by other countries. The refugees were fleeing renewed killing and fighting in Liberia's civil war.

Amnesty International appealed to the government not to force refugees on the *Bulk Challenge* to return to Liberia.

GREECE

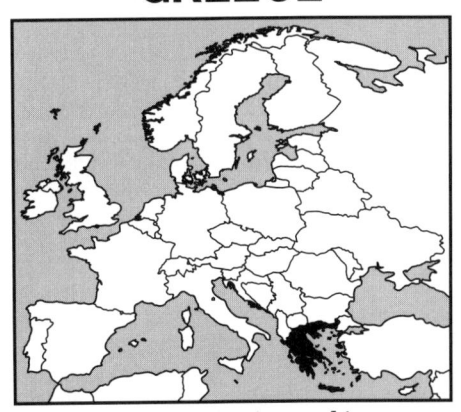

About 350 conscientious objectors to military service on religious grounds were imprisoned. All were prisoners of conscience. Legal proceedings continued in the case of 10 people prosecuted for peacefully exercising their right to freedom of expression. Hundreds of people detained following a demonstration were reportedly not given a fair trial. There were further reports of torture and ill-treatment. One person died in police custody in disputed circumstances. People were shot by police and military forces in disputed circumstances.

In January, Andreas Papandreou, leader of the *Panellinio Sosialistiko Kinima* (PASOK), Panhellenic Socialist Party, resigned as Prime Minister owing to ill health. Kostas Simitis, who succeeded him as Prime Minister, was elected leader of PASOK in June and called for early elections in September, which his party won.

There was no progress towards the introduction of an alternative civilian service for conscientious objectors to military service. About 350 Jehovah's Witnesses were serving prison sentences of up to four years for refusing to perform military service on religious grounds.

Legal proceedings continued against 10 people who had been prosecuted for exercising their rights to freedom of expression or religion. In March, Hara Kalomiri was sentenced to three months' imprisonment in Thessaloniki for "founding and operating a place of private worship for a Buddhist community in Chalkidiki without government permission". Hara Kalomiri remained free pending an appeal hearing. In May, Archimandrite Nikodimos Tsarknias was acquitted in Edessa on three charges of "impersonating a priest" (see *Amnesty International Report 1996*). Professor Georgos Roussis and actor Vassilis Diamantopoulos were tried in Athens in May for statements made during a television talk show, two days after clashes took place during a demonstration at Athens Polytechnic University in November 1995. They had defended calls for changes in society and publicly condemned the violence of police officers who beat a 16-year-old boy during his arrest. Although they were acquitted, an appeal against the verdict on Georgos Roussis was ordered. In October, the appeal court confirmed the acquittal. The appeal hearings of six members of the *Organosi gia tin Anasingrotisi tou Kommounistikou Kommatos Elladas*, Organization for the Reconstruction of the Communist Party of Greece, due to take place in July 1996, were postponed until July 1997.

There were allegations of irregularities in the trials of people arrested in connection with the November 1995 demonstrations at Athens Polytechnic University. More than 500 people had been detained by the police and charged with offences including disrupting public order and destroying a symbol of the state. The defendants were divided into groups of up to 40 and tried by different courts. The verdicts and sentences ranged from acquittal to 40 months' imprisonment, sometimes suspended. Both at the pre-trial and trial stages, the proceedings were in many respects not conducted in accordance with international human rights standards and Greek law. The families of those arrested were not immediately informed of the arrests and the location of detainees; detainees were not promptly notified of the charges against them and in some cases were not brought promptly before a judge. Defendants were not able to cross-examine prosecution witnesses at the trial and the prosecution failed to present, nor did the court cite, evidence of individual responsibility in support of the convictions.

There were further allegations of torture and ill-treatment of detainees by police and prison officials. There were numerous reports of beatings in police custody, which in one case resulted in death. At about 1am on 14 January police officers from Vyrona police station, Athens, detained Lütfi Osmance, a Greek national, who was reportedly drunk, vomiting and suffering from stomach pains. At 8am Lütfi Osmance was taken to hospital, but discharged. The prosecutor of Athens Criminal Court ordered him to be remanded in custody. In the evening, Lütfi Osmance was found dead in a cell at Vyrona police station. According to the autopsy report, Lütfi Osmance's head and face bore marks of beating. He had ruptured blood vessels and bruises around his right eye and an open wound on his right eyebrow, injuries which had not been observed by the hospital doctor who had examined him that morning. In October, the office of the Prime Minister referred the case to the Ministry of Public Order.

In February, police raided a Roma camp in Aspropyrgos, near Athens, ostensibly in search of five men wanted for criminal offences. Members of the Special Anti-Terrorist Forces, wearing balaclavas and flak jackets and armed with knives and automatic weapons, reportedly stormed into the camp, slashed open tents and pointed pistols at people's heads. They swore at, kicked and beat Roma whom they had ordered to lie on the ground. An investigation into the incident was believed to have been ordered in March.

In August, attacks took place against members of the Turkish minority in Komotini, apparently provoked by the killing of two Greek Cypriots in Cyprus on 11 and 14 August (see **Cyprus** entry). Emine Inceyizli, aged 70, and Saliha Cansız, aged 60, were severely injured when a group of bikers attacked them and other members of the Turkish minority while police reportedly stood by.

In October, Mohamed Farhank Amin, an Iranian refugee living in Germany, and his friend were allegedly ill-treated by seven police officers, one of them in civilian clothes, in a park in Neos Kosmos, Athens. The two men were grabbed by the hair, had their arms locked behind their backs and were hit on the face, legs and genitals before being taken to Nea Smyrni police station. There, Mohamed Farhank Amin was further beaten until he lost consciousness.

There were reports of shootings by police and military forces in circumstances which appeared to indicate unwarranted and excessive use of force. In January, during an operation to round up Albanian illegal immigrants in Skala, Oropos, an unarmed Albanian was shot dead by police officers while attempting to escape. According to the police, one officer fired in the air to frighten the escapee. Another officer then also took out his gun and while jumping over a ditch lost his balance. A bullet from his gun hit the Albanian in the back, killing him. An investigation into the killing was believed to have been ordered.

Amnesty International called on the authorities to release all conscientious objectors to military service and to introduce legislation on conscientious objection which fully reflected international recommendations. The organization called on the authorities to drop all outstanding charges against Archimandrite Tsarknias and Hara Kalomiri.

In March, Amnesty International delegates observed two trials of people charged in connection with the demonstrations at Athens Polytechnic University. The organization called upon the authorities to hold new trials in accordance with international standards and to ensure effective implementation of international human rights standards at all stages of the proceedings in all criminal cases.

Amnesty International urged the authorities to investigate all allegations of torture and ill-treatment, and shootings by law enforcement officials in disputed circumstances, and to bring to justice those responsible, but it had received no substantive response by the end of the year. In October, Amnesty International published a report, *Greece: Unfair trials of people arrested at Athens Polytechnic University.*

GUATEMALA

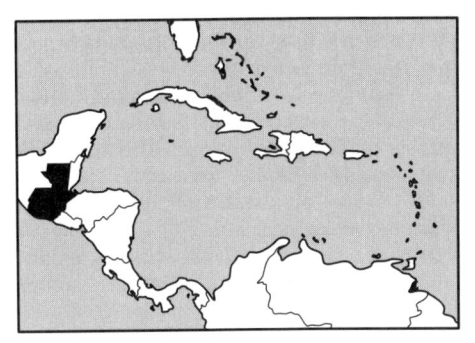

Members of the security forces and government-backed armed groups were allegedly responsible for more than a hundred extrajudicial executions and scores of cases of torture, ill-treatment and "disappearance" for short periods; hundreds of people received death threats. Victims included street children, journalists, lawyers, public prosecutors and witnesses, trade unionists, human rights defenders, priests and land activists. Little progress was made in investigating thousands of past and present human rights violations. Two men were executed by firing-squad when the death penalty was applied in Guatemala for the first time in 13 years.

In January, a new government took office under President Alvaro Arzú Irigoyen. In his inaugural speech, the President recognized the need for the state to fight impunity in order to fulfil its duty to protect human rights.

In June, Congress approved new legislation enabling cases of human rights violations perpetrated by members of the army to be transferred from military to civilian courts.

The government and the armed opposition Guatemalan National Revolutionary Unit agreed a cease-fire in March. UN-brokered peace negotiations between them continued throughout the year, and a final peace agreement was concluded at the end of December.

In August, the demobilization began of more than 300,000 members of the government-backed armed groups, or civil patrols, which had been responsible for gross human rights violations such as "disappearances", torture and extrajudicial executions during the 1980s and 1990s. Although civil patrol members were allegedly demobilized, cases of death threats against people who refused to join the civil patrols continued to be reported.

Criminal violence escalated. Scores of kidnappings for extortion, involving members of the security forces and, in some cases, members of armed opposition groups, were reported.

In April, the UN Commission on Human Rights passed a resolution expressing concern that serious human rights violations persisted in Guatemala and situations of impunity continued to exist. It also expressed concern at the lack of progress made in investigating cases of human rights violations. These concerns were reiterated in statements and reports by the *Misión de las Naciones Unidas para la verificacion de derechos humanos en Guatemala* (MINUGUA), UN Mission for Guatemala, and the UN Independent Expert on Guatemala. MINUGUA's mandate was extended to the end of the year and the UN Independent Expert was asked to submit a new report on the human rights situation in Guatemala to the UN Commission on Human Rights in March 1997.

In December, the Guatemalan Congress approved a Law of National Reconciliation, which recognized the right to reparation for victims of human rights violations and charged the Commission for Historical Clarification with establishing "the historic truth about the armed conflict". Following concerns raised by Amnesty International and other local and international organizations, the final text of the law was amended so that immunity from prosecution would not apply in cases of forced "disappearance", torture and genocide. Amnesty International remained concerned that members of the security forces responsible for extrajudicial executions could still be granted immunity from prosecution.

Members of the security forces and government-backed armed groups were allegedly responsible for more than a hundred extrajudicial executions.

Information came to light regarding the involvement of new vigilante groups, acting in collaboration with members of the security forces, in the killing of members of juvenile gangs and petty criminals. The victims had been shot point-blank in the head, and the bodies, frequently with the hands tied, showed signs of stabbing and torture. Gilmar Fernando Miculux Tuctuc, detained in Guatemala City on 26 July 1995, was found dead the next day with six bullet wounds in his body. He had been detained by members of the *Guardia de Honor*, military guards, who interrogated him about criminal activities in the area and then handed him over to a vigilante group, *Los guardianes de la noche*, night vigilantes. Investigations into his killing during 1996 were obstructed by members of the armed forces, who refused to hand over crucial information to MINUGUA.

There were reports of killings of street children by members of the security forces. Sixteen-year-old Ronald Raúl Ramos was beaten and then killed in September by a member of the *Guardia de Hacienda*, Treasury Police, in Tecún Umán, department of San Marcos. According to witnesses, the police officer shot Ronald Raúl Ramos in the forehead with a rifle. Investigations were initiated by the Public Ministry but by the end of the year no one had been detained

A pattern of intimidation against journalists reporting on human rights, impunity and the involvement of the security forces in corruption and organized crime emerged during the first six months of the year. In February, Estuardo Vinicio Pacheco Méndez, a journalist with *Radio Sonora*, was abducted by four men and drugged. He was held for around four hours, during which time he was beaten, kicked, burnt on the chest with cigarettes and the soles of his feet were cut. His assailants told him he was only being released as a warning to other journalists. The abduction was apparently motivated by Estuardo Vinicio Pacheco's investigations into alleged criminal activities of members of the security forces. He continued to receive death threats after his release and fled the country shortly afterwards.

Efforts by judges, lawyers, prosecutors and witnesses to break the legacy of impunity by bringing members of the armed forces to account for their actions met with systematic resistance, manifested in killings and death threats. Otto Leonel Hernández, a witness to the abduction and killing of Lucina Cárdenas in November 1995, allegedly perpetrated by members of the security forces operating in collaboration with criminal gangs, was kidnapped in June in the city of Quelzatenango and tortured for six days before being released. In March, a member of the armed forces had been charged and detained in connection with the killing of Lucina Cárdenas.

Witnesses and prosecutors involved in investigations into the Xamán massacre (see *Amnesty International Report 1996*) were also subjected to harassment and threats. In March, the then Attorney General, Ramses Cuestas, acknowledged that state prosecutors from the Public Ministry were receiving three or four death threats every month and were frequently attacked. MINUGUA investigated similar allegations and reported that in one case, a prosecutor who had been threatened was later killed. Another prosecutor was forced to leave the country after receiving death threats.

Two investigators from the Public Ministry were killed in May on a road to the Salvadoran border, in an area frequented by members of the security forces allegedly involved in organized crime. Their deaths were believed to relate to investigations they were conducting into the possible involvement of members of the security forces in murders on the same road of a Salvadoran citizen and son of a Salvadoran parliamentarian in April, and of a Russian diplomat in May.

In November, attorney Abraham Méndez García left the country temporarily following a series of death threats. He was in charge of investigations into the killings of newspaper owner Jorge Carpio Nicolle and three others (see *Amnesty International Report 1994*).

Trade unionists were also targeted for attack. In September, two unidentified men shot at Víctor Hugo Durán, Secretary General of the *Sindicato General de Trabajadores de Guatel "22 de Febrero"*, "22 February" General Trade Union of Guatel Workers, as he was driving between Guatemala City and Villanueva. He escaped unharmed. The next day, unidentified gunmen sprayed bullets at Víctor Hugo Durán's house in the municipality of Villanueva. Two weeks later, three other members of the same trade union were threatened. Víctor Hugo Durán and his fellow trade unionists were campaigning against the privatization of Guatel, the public telecommunications company, which has historic links to military intelligence.

Many human rights defenders were also subjected to harassment and intimidation. In May, María Tuyuc Velásquez, a member of an indigenous women's organization, the *Coordinadora Nacional de Viudas de Guatemala*, National Coordinating Committee of Widows of Guatemala, was seized outside the organization's offices by a man in plain clothes who repeatedly beat, threatened and sexually assaulted her. A few days earlier, several unidentified men attempted to kidnap two other members of the same organization, Josefa Ventura and Sebastiana Hernández. The organization believed these attacks and threats related to a public march organized as part of their campaign in support of conscientious objection to military service.

In June, members of the community of Todos Santos in the northern department of Huehuetenango were threatened by two civil patrol commanders who interrupted a community gathering, accusing all the people present of being guerrillas and drawing up a list of their names. The commanders had apparently mistaken the community gathering for a meeting of a newly formed human rights committee.

More than 10 people, including members of the security forces, were killed in the context of violent land disputes. Land activists and members of the Church assisting those involved in land disputes were subjected to death threats and harassment by members of the security forces and private guards. Father Daniel Joseph Vogt received persistent death threats because of his community work in Rubelpec, municipality of El Estor, department of Izabal. Other members of the parish were also threatened and accused of being guerrillas. In another case in March in San Roque, Génova, Quelzatenango, more than 60 bullets were fired at the house of Raúl Juárez López, a land activist working with the *Coordinadora Nacional Indígena y Campesina*, National Indigenous and Peasant Coordinating Committee, by a group of individuals who allegedly included members of the military intelligence unit, the G-2.

Little progress was made in clarifying the extrajudicial execution of tens of thousands of Guatemalans during the army's counter-insurgency campaign of the late 1970s and early 1980s, or in bringing those responsible to justice. In August, the first case of its kind to reach the courts was suspended after the accused civil patrol members reportedly requested amnesty under Decree Law 08-86 (see *Amnesty International Report 1987*). The case concerned the massacres in Agua Fria, El Quiché department, and Rio Negro, Baja Verapaz department, in 1982, in which at least 240 people were killed.

Government officials continued to obstruct efforts to exhume the bodies of victims of human rights violations buried in mass graves. New estimates calculated a total of more than 500 graves. At least 27 legal complaints concerning clandestine cemeteries in Rabinal, Baja Verapaz, were lodged with the Public Ministry between 1994 and 1995. Of those reported, only a few had been excavated by the end of 1996. In no case had exhumations led to the trial of those responsible for authorizing, planning or carrying out the killings. Those conducting exhumations were also subjected to death threats and intimidation.

Further information came to light regarding the involvement of the US Central Intelligence Agency (CIA) in past human rights violations in Guatemala. In a report published in June, the US Intelligence Oversight Board (IOB) alleged that in the early 1990s Guatemalan CIA agents had ordered, planned, or participated in serious human rights violations such as extrajudicial execution, torture and kidnapping, and that the CIA's headquarters, the Directorate of Operations, had been aware of these crimes. The report confirmed that Guatemalan CIA agents had also engaged in acts of intimidation and concealment of human right violations. In the case of US nun Diana Ortiz *(see Amnesty International Report 1990)*, no new information was provided by the IOB because the case was allegedly still under investigation.

The first legal executions in more than 13 years took place in September. Pedro Castillo Mendoza and Roberto Girón were executed by firing-squad for the rape and murder of a child in April 1993. The executions were shown on national television and included images of the prisoners being shot in the head after the firing-squad's first volley failed to kill one of them.

Amnesty International repeatedly called on the Guatemalan authorities to carry out full and impartial inquiries into past and new human rights violations.

This call was reiterated in two memoranda submitted to the government in August, expressing concern about an amnesty law or any other measure which might grant impunity to the perpetrators of gross human rights violations. The memoranda also expressed concern about the ambiguity of the mandate of the Clarification Commission which was expected to begin work on looking into human rights violations once the peace negotiations had concluded (see *Amnesty International Report 1995*). By the end of the year Amnesty International had received no reply to either memorandum.

Amnesty International delegates visited the country on three occasions, collecting testimonies from victims and witnesses to human rights violations, and holding meetings with government officials.

In July, Amnesty International appealed to President Alvaro Arzú Irigoyen to commute the death sentences of Pedro Castillo Mendoza and Roberto Girón.

GUINEA

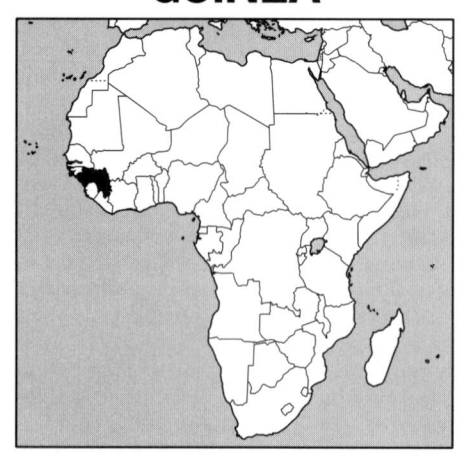

Possible prisoners of conscience were among trade unionists, journalists and opposition supporters detained. A trade unionist and six journalists were detained during the year. Five opposition party members were arrested and held without charge or trial. Twenty-eight opposition party supporters were tried in connection with a strike in 1995. They had allegedly been tortured and ill-treated in detention. The Supreme Court confirmed six death sentences passed in 1995. No executions were reported.

In February and March, armed revolts led by the army erupted twice in the capital city, Conakry, leaving hundreds wounded and scores dead. In February, a pay dispute turned into a revolt against President Lansana Conté. Mutinous soldiers surrounded and shelled the presidential residence. Scores of members of the armed forces were subsequently arrested. In March, shooting broke out again when dozens of soldiers were charged with treason in connection with the February mutiny. Again, scores were arrested. Some were released in August, but dozens remained in detention charged with treason.

In July, President Conté appointed a new government, the majority of whose members belonged to the President's party, the *Parti de l'unité et du progrès*, Party of Unity and Progress. The President appointed Sidia Touré as Prime Minister.

In January, Thierno Ismaïl Diallo, a trade unionist, was arrested in Télémélé and held for three days without charge. He was accused by the local military authorities of having led strike action by teachers from his region in December 1995. Thierno Ismaïl Diallo was also the member responsible for the Télémélé branch of the *Organisation guinéenne des droits de l'homme*, Guinean Organization for Human Rights.

Souleymane Diallo, Director of *Lynx*, a satirical newspaper, was arrested in March and released after 20 days in detention. The authorities had accused him of falsifying documents because he had not published the full text of a presidential decree fixing the pay scale for members of the armed forces. Although a court ordered his release on the grounds that no crime had taken place, the prosecutor overruled the decision and he remained detention for five more days.

Thierno Sadou Diallo and Siaka Kouyaté, editor-in-chief and editor, respectively, of the weekly newspaper *Le Citoyen*, were arrested in June for publishing an article concerning the theft, during the February mutiny, of a diamond belonging to President Conté. They were held at the *Maison d'arrêt* in Conakry until their trial in July on a charge of insulting the Head of State, and were then released conditionally before being sentenced to a fine. The newspaper was suspended for two months.

Foday Fofana, a Sierra Leonean journalist working for *Reuters* and *British*

Broadcasting Corporation (BBC) radio, was arrested in November when he pointed a microphone at President Conté. He was tried for assault two weeks later and sentenced to two weeks' imprisonment.

Ismaël Bangoura and Louis Célestin Espérance (an Ivorian national), the Director and Managing Editor, respectively, of *L'Oeil* newspaper, were arrested in December following the publication of an article about the collapse of the government. Louis Célestin Espérance was released after two days but Ismaël Bangoura was still in detention at the end of the year.

In October, Bandjou Oulen Oularé, Secretary General of the Faranah branch of the opposition *Rassemblement du peuple de Guinée* (RPG), Guinean People's Rally, was arrested. He was detained on the orders of the General Secretary in the office of the President, reportedly because the police commissioner "dreamed" that Bandjou Oulen Oularé overthrew the Head of State.

Four other members of the RPG, Saloum Cissé, Madame Keita (née Bintoubé Camara), Louceni Condé and Mamady Diaby, were arrested in November and December. All four were still held without charge at the end of the year.

Amadou II Diallo and some RPG supporters arrested in previous years remained in detention. Amadou II Diallo, who had been arrested in October 1992 and charged with attempting to assassinate the Head of State (see *Amnesty International Report 1996*), had still not been tried at the end of the year. Twenty-eight RPG supporters who had been arrested in September 1995 in Nzérékoré, Guinée Forestière, when the opposition launched a strike known as *"ville morte"* (dead city) (see *Amnesty International Report 1996*), were tried in October. Only two received prison terms. Moussa Traoré was sentenced to three years' imprisonment for disseminating information about the strike. Aboubacar Cissé was sentenced to five years' imprisonment for the lynching of a member of the security forces. Five others held until the trial were released, but did not appear to have been tried.

All those tried stated that they had been beaten at the time of their arrest. Some received as many as 64 truncheon blows; some had been subjected to electric shocks. During the first four months of their detention they were shackled and chained together in groups of eight.

Information emerged about the death in custody of Fallo Kouayaté in November 1995. He had apparently been arrested in November 1995 and accused of helping someone who wished to avoid an arranged marriage to escape, although no formal charges were brought against him. He died as a result of beatings and torture in detention. No independent inquiry into the death was known to have taken place.

In January, the Supreme Court confirmed the death sentences imposed on six people in 1995. Five of them had been convicted on charges of murder, attempted murder, complicity in murder, armed robbery and criminal association. The sixth person, Sekou Bangoura, had been convicted of murder, having thrown a grenade into a bar, causing the death of three people. One of those under sentence of death, Djibril Koly Koné, died of illness in November. No executions were known to have taken place.

GUINEA-BISSAU

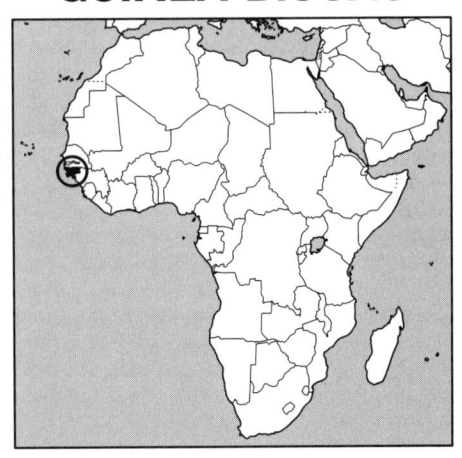

Dozens of people were tortured and ill-treated by the police. One person was killed and others were injured when police opened fire during a violent demonstration. One person was extrajudicially executed. A human rights worker and a journalist received threats of physical harm after criticizing government policies.

Torture and ill-treatment by police were reported on a regular basis in all parts of the country. The government of President João Bernardo Vieira took no action to investigate these reports.

The victims included members of a group of 50 foreign nationals from Cameroon, Liberia, Nigeria and other African countries forcibly expelled from Spain as illegal immigrants in June and detained in the capital, Bissau. Most of them were beaten by members of the Rapid Intervention Police on arrival at the airport. They were taken to the Second Squadron police detention centre where many of them were again beaten. Japhy Sul, a Nigerian, alleged that he was beaten on the head with a gun. One man said his hand was broken. Another had teeth knocked out. After being held incommunicado for about two weeks the detainees were allowed to leave the prison during the day. Beatings continued to be reported until mid-August. In August, after six of those detained, all nationals of the neighbouring Republic of Guinea, were ordered to leave the country, the remaining 44 men went on a hunger-strike, which lasted a total of eight days, in protest at their treatment.

In September, one person was killed and several others were injured by the Rapid Intervention Police during a demonstration, by the foreign nationals and Guinea-Bissau sympathizers, which turned violent. Police shot into the crowd, killing Naruna Ahire Uwaifo, a Nigerian, and wounding another Nigerian, David Adekoro Damolekun, in the arm. Two other men, Femi Singleton, a Nigerian, and Soulemanou Zakari, a Cameroonian, were badly beaten by police and reportedly sustained black eyes, bruised faces and lacerations on their backs. Cesaltine Leila Choaib, an elderly woman who lived near the prison and who had befriended the detainees, was also arrested. She was made to undress, beaten and kicked and then released without charge.

In mid-October, the remaining 20 Nigerians were each given money and driven to the Gambia where they were expected to fly back to Nigeria. Twenty-two of the foreign nationals were repatriated in December. One, a Rwandan, remained in Guinea-Bissau at the end of the year.

A parliamentary commission set up in October to examine the government's handling of the case of the 50 foreign nationals had not published its findings by the end of the year. There was apparently no judicial investigation into the alleged torture and the death of Naruna Ahire Uwaifo.

In June, a police officer extrajudicially executed João Manuel Nhamai Figá in Bandim, Bissau. The victim had been running to escape arrest for non-payment of a small debt but fell into a ditch where the police officer shot him three times in the stomach. The judicial police initiated an inquiry which had not concluded by the end of the year. The *Liga Guineese de Direitos Humanos* (LGDH), Guinea (Bissau) Human Rights League, wrote to the government to express concern but received no response.

Critics of government policy sometimes received threats of physical harm. In January, Amine Saad, Secretary General of the *União para Mudança*, Union for Change, lodged a complaint with the Procurator General alleging that he had received a death threat from a senior government official in December 1995. The procuracy had not examined the complaint by the end of the year. Fernando Gomes, President of the LGDH, received threats of physical harm in May after the LGDH issued a press statement expressing concern that the Prime Minister had assaulted a number of citizens. In October, the director of a privately owned radio station announced that the father of Ladislau Stanislau Robalo, one of the radio station's reporters, had been told by government officials that his son would be badly beaten if he did not stop telling "lies" about the Prime Minister and the government. After the announcement the government reportedly assured the journalists that their right to freedom of expression would be respected.

Amnesty International expressed concern about threats against the physical safety of Fernando Gomes. It also asked the government about alleged human rights violations by government ministers. The organization called for inquiries into reports of torture and ill-treatment and into the deaths of Naruna Ahire Uwaifo and João Manuel Nhamai Figá. It urged the government to ensure that any of the 50 foreign nationals who wished to apply for asylum be granted a full and fair review of their cases. The government had not replied by the end of the year.

GUYANA

Two men were hanged in the first executions for more than five years. More than 15 people remained under sentence of death. At least one new death sentence was imposed. There were reports of torture and ill-treatment by police and of police shootings of suspects in disputed circumstances. A former soldier in the Guyanese army was charged with the 1980 murder of a leading opposition figure. Inquests were still pending in the cases of three men who died in police custody in 1993 and 1994.

Two men were hanged in the first executions since 1990. Ayube Khan, sentenced to death for murder in 1991, was hanged in February. Rockliffe Ross, sentenced to death for murder in 1992, was hanged in June, while an application – alleging that his rights under the International Covenant on Civil and Political Rights had been violated – was still pending before the UN Human Rights Committee in Geneva. The day before the execution, the Committee had faxed the government asking it not to carry out the execution while the application was under examination. Following the execution, the Attorney General said that the government had not received the Committee's request in time.

In May, the Court of Appeal confirmed the death sentences on Abdool Yasseen and Noel Thomas. The Court dismissed a constitutional motion which claimed that their protracted detention on death row awaiting execution amounted to cruel and inhuman punishment. In the same month, they were granted a stay of execution pending a further appeal to the same Court.

At least one new death sentence was imposed.

There were reports of torture and ill-treatment by police and of police shootings of criminal suspects in disputed circumstances. Eye-witnesses stated that Jermaine Wilkinson, a suspect in a burglary case, who died in May in a Georgetown hospital, had been beaten on the head and body with the butt of a gun by a police officer, who then shot him and dragged him to a police vehicle. An initial manslaughter charge against the officer was later changed to one of murder. An appeal by the officer against the murder charge was believed to be pending at the end of the year.

In August, Kamal Khan was reportedly shot in the penis by two detectives while detained in New Amsterdam police station. The officers were later reported to have been charged in connection with the incident.

In June, Gregory Smith, a former soldier in the Guyana Defence Force, was charged with the 1980 murder of Walter Rodney, leader of the opposition Working People's Alliance. An application for Gregory Smith's extradition from French Guiana was still pending at the end of the year.

Inquests had reportedly still not taken place into the deaths in custody of Ricky Samaroo, Joseph Persaud and Shivnarine Dalchand (see *Amnesty International Reports 1994* to *1996*), although the government had stated in 1995 that the necessary documents had been submitted to the Coroner's court.

Amnesty International wrote to the Guyana authorities expressing deep regret at the executions of Ayube Khan and Rockliffe Ross and appealing for commutation of all death sentences. An Amnesty International observer attended the hearing of the constitutional motion in the cases of Abdool Yasseen and Noel Thomas.

In October, Amnesty International wrote to the Minister of Home Affairs to express concern at increasing reports of police shootings and torture or ill-treatment of people held in custody. The letter cited, among other cases, those of Jermaine Wilkinson and Kamal Khan, and referred to a list of more than 50 cases of alleged torture or ill-treatment by the police, police shootings and deaths in custody during 1995 and early 1996, which had been presented to the Police Commissioner by the Guyana Human Rights Association in June. Amnesty International urged that all reports of killings by police in disputed circumstances, deaths in custody and complaints of torture or ill-treatment be fully and impartially investigated with the results made public. It also called for police guidelines on the use of force and firearms to be brought into line with international standards.

HAITI

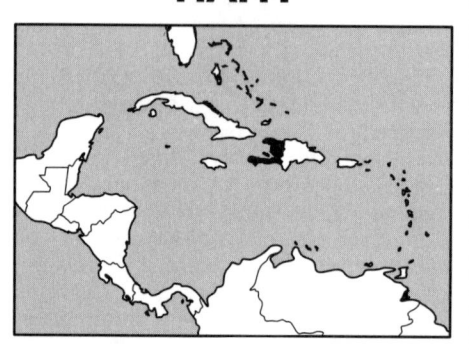

Little progress was made in bringing to justice those responsible for human rights violations committed under previous administrations, although investigations continued into several cases. There were increased reports of torture and ill-treatment by police, in some cases resulting in death, and of shootings by police, in some cases fatal, in circumstances suggesting excessive use of force or extrajudicial execution. There were allegations that two government opponents may have been extrajudicially executed.

In February, René Préval, a candidate for the *Lavalas* political movement, took over the presidency from Jean-Bertrand Aristide who had been constitutionally barred from serving a second term.

The UN Mission in Haiti, renamed UN Support Mission in Haiti (UNSMIH) in July, had its mandate extended for what was intended to be the last time by the UN Security Council until 31 May 1997, with the possibility of a further final two-month extension. The joint Organization of American States/UN International Civilian Mission in Haiti (MICIVIH) was mandated by the UN General Assembly to remain in the country until 31 July 1997 with the possibility of a further extension to the end of the year.

In what was considered by the authorities to be a deliberate destabilization campaign, acts of violence – including armed robberies, kidnappings and the murder of at least eight off-duty police officers – escalated in the second half of the year. Former soldiers were alleged to be responsible for the violence. On 16 July, Claude Raymond, a general and cabinet minister under former President François Duvalier, was arrested for "terrorist and subversive activities". Four days later André Armand, a former army sergeant and leader of a retired soldiers' pressure group, was killed by unknown assailants after publicly alleging that former army members were plotting to assassinate President Préval and former President Aristide.

In mid-August, police arrested 19 people, including former soldiers, suspected of attempting to destabilize the country, 17 of them at the offices of the *Mobilisation pour le développement national* (MDN), Mobilization for National Development, a political party. They were detained at the police headquarters in Port-au-Prince, the capital. On 19 August, some 30 men armed with grenades and automatic weapons attacked the police headquarters where the 19 were held, killing one bystander and wounding one policeman. Despite the arrival of the police and UN personnel, those who carried out the attack escaped. The following day, Antoine Leroy and Jacques Florival, both leading members of the MDN, were shot dead by unidentified gunmen in the capital. There were allegations, so far unsubstantiated, that the US-trained presidential security unit was linked to their killings. The US Government dispatched diplomatic security personnel to be based at the National Palace and UNSMIH also increased its presence there. President Préval announced the reorganization of the presidential security unit and two of its senior members were suspended. An investigation into the killings of the two MDN leaders was opened by police (see below).

In September, further arrests took place in connection with the alleged plots against the government. Arrest warrants were also issued against MDN leader Hubert de Ronceray, who shortly afterwards was reported to be in the USA, and Prosper Avril, a former army general who ruled Haiti between 1988 and 1990.

In September, police reportedly found an arms cache and evidence of plans to assassinate government officials at the home of Emmanuel Constant, former leader of the paramilitary organization *Front pour l'avancement et le progrès d'Haïti* (FRAPH), Front for the Advancement and Progress of Haiti, who had fled to the USA in December 1994. Two men were arrested at the scene, including a former army sergeant. By December, some 34 people reportedly remained in detention on suspicion of plotting against the authorities and engaging in other related activities, but had not been brought to trial.

In February, the *Commission nationale de vérité et de justice*, National Commission of Truth and Justice, set up in March 1995 to report on the most serious human rights violations committed between 29 September 1991 and 15 October 1994 under the *de facto* military government of General Raoul Cédras, submitted its report to then President Aristide. The report, which was published in September, documented abuses allegedly perpetrated by military and paramilitary personnel against 8,650 people, including 333 cases of "disappearance", 576 cases of extrajudicial execution, 439 cases of attempted extrajudicial execution and 83 cases of rape. The names of those responsible, where known, were included in an unpublished appendix which the National Commission recommended should be handed over to the relevant judicial authorities so that, where possible, those concerned could be brought to justice. The report contained a series of recommendations on judicial reform and compensation for victims, as well as recommendations concerning cases of rape and other forms of sexual violence against women. The UN Commission on Human Rights urged the Haitian Government to implement the report's recommendations. However, by the end of the year no specific steps had been taken to implement them.

A MICIVIH report, dated May 1996, analysed the continuing weaknesses of the justice system and put forward recommendations on reforms needed to strengthen it. Lack of resources and trained personnel, as well as fear of reprisal and lack of coordination between the different authorities involved, were among the problems highlighted. In August, the Minister of Justice presented a judicial reform bill to the National Assembly addressing some of the recommendations made in the MICIVIH report. The bill was still under consideration at the end of the year.

Little progress was made in bringing those responsible for past human rights abuses to justice. Several of those suspected of having ordered or participated in human rights violations under previous governments remained abroad. In April, the authorities in the Dominican Republic arrested Michel François, former police chief and member of the *de facto* military government who was convicted *in absentia* in 1995 for his involvement in the extrajudicial execution of Antoine Izméry in 1993 (see *Amnesty International Report 1996*), and Frank Romain, a former mayor of Port-au-Prince, whose extradition had been sought in 1989 in connection with the 1988 massacre at St Jean Bosco Church in La Saline (see *Amnesty International Report 1989*). They were deported to Honduras where they were granted political asylum. Former FRAPH leader Emmanuel Constant, who had been in detention in the USA pending deportation to Haiti since 1995 following a request from the Haitian Government for his extradition (see *Amnesty International Report 1996*), was released in June and remained in the USA. He had publicly admitted while in detention that he had been in the pay of the US Central Intelligence Agency (CIA) at the time of the military government and was reportedly released as a result of a secret deal with the US authorities in which he agreed to drop a civil suit he had been intending to bring against them for "wrongful incarceration".

The US Government transferred the 160,000 documents seized from Haitian army headquarters and the FRAPH offices in October 1994 to its embassy in Port-au-Prince, reportedly after having removed the names of US nationals from them. The documents were widely believed to contain crucial information relating to human rights violations committed by both the military and FRAPH under the military government, including the possible collusion of the US Government in such activities. The US authorities agreed to hand the documents over to the Haitian Government on condition that the safety of any Haitian nationals mentioned in the documents was ensured. However, the Haitian Government refused to accept the documents unless they were returned in their original form.

In May, two former soldiers were sentenced to seven years' hard labour after a trial in Mirebalais for the torture of Faniel Glosy in 1993.

In July, a jury acquitted two men of involvement in the 1993 extrajudicial execution of former Justice Minister Guy Malary (see *Amnesty International Reports 1994* and *1996*). Only two of a reportedly large number of eye-witnesses to the assassination were prepared to testify in court. According to reports, some jury members showed open support for the defendants while one claimed he had been offered a bribe to acquit them. An appeal by the prosecution against the acquittal was rejected by the Court of Appeal on the grounds that it was not lodged within three days as required under Haitian law. However, the two defendants remained in detention under investigation on other charges. Others suspected of involvement in the same case, including the former *attaché* (civilian auxiliary working with the army) unexpectedly released from detention in 1995 (see *Amnesty International Report 1996*), remained at liberty. In October, the US-based Center for Constitutional Rights made public an internal CIA memorandum, which it had obtained under subpoena in the course of a lawsuit brought against FRAPH by Haitian citizen Alerte Belance (see *Amnesty International Report 1996*), indicating the possible involvement of members of FRAPH, including Emmanuel Constant, and military leaders in the extrajudicial execution of Guy Malary.

The trial of several people accused of involvement in the massacre of some 50 people in Raboteau, Gonaïves, in 1994 (see *Amnesty International Reports 1995* and *1996*), which had been scheduled to take place in September, was postponed.

There was an increase in reports of torture and ill-treatment by police, in some cases resulting in death. A MICIVIH report on the police noted that 86 cases of torture and ill-treatment were reported in the first five months of the year. It found that most of the victims were suspected of armed robbery, belonging to armed criminal gangs, or having killed police agents. Some reportedly alleged that they had been subjected to electric shocks in a police station. Others were reportedly beaten with fists, pistol butts, batons and other blunt instruments, sometimes while blindfolded.

The MICIVIH report found that 20 people had died and 30 others were injured between January and May as a result of shootings by members of the newly-established *Police nationale d'Haïti* (PNH), Haitian National Police, and that in several cases the circumstances suggested "excessive use of force or summary execution".

At least eight people died in Cité Soleil on 6 March. The PNH alleged that the deaths occurred in the course of an exchange of gunfire between police and armed civilians. However, eye-witnesses alleged that some of the victims were shot inside their homes and MICIVIH observers found that six of them had been shot in the head, probably at point-blank range. A police investigation into the incident had produced no results by the end of the year.

Four men held in police custody at the Croix des Bouquets police station, after allegedly attacking the home of a PNH agent, died between 20 and 24 June. One had been shot and one bore signs of torture. One policeman was charged with murder and 17 others were disciplined in connection with the case.

In the second half of the year, several dozen police were suspended or dismissed from the force and about nine were charged with criminal offences believed to relate to human rights violations.

Several people, including known government opponents, were killed in disputed circumstances, but only in the cases of Antoine Leroy and Jacques Florival (see above) were there any specific allegations, albeit not publicly substantiated, of official involvement. A police investigation into the killing of Jacques Florival and Antoine Leroy was reported to be under way at the end of the year. There was no progress in investigations into disputed killings that had occurred during 1995, including that of lawyer Mireille Durocher Bertin (see *Amnesty International Report 1996*).

In January, Amnesty International published a report, *Haiti: A question of justice*. While welcoming the reforms so far implemented by the government to strengthen respect for, and protection of, human rights, the organization expressed concern at the slowness of the justice system in bringing to justice those responsible for human rights violations committed both before and after October 1994. Amnesty International urged the government to take immediate measures to speed up judicial reform and called on the international community to continue supporting the government's efforts to build institutions that would guarantee respect for human rights, and to assist efforts to bring to justice those responsible for past human rights violations.

HONDURAS

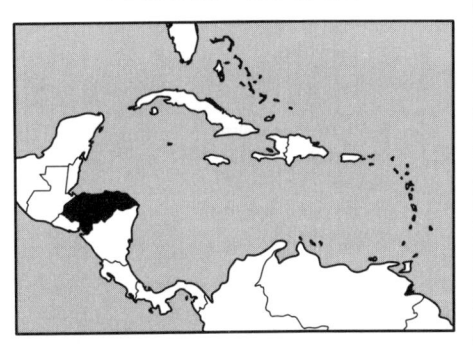

Further steps were taken to bring to justice those responsible for some past human rights violations, although there was little progress in other cases. Human rights activists continued to be subjected to intimidation, including death threats and bomb attacks. There were reports of torture and ill-treatment. At least five people were killed in circumstances suggesting extrajudicial execution.

A series of bomb attacks throughout the year against the judiciary, government buildings and President Carlos Roberto Reina, was linked by the National Human Rights Commissioner to human rights violations under investigation in the courts. In December, Congress approved the transfer of the Public Security Force (FSP) to civilian control (see *Amnesty International Report 1994*).

In July, Honduras ratified the Inter-American Convention on the Forced Disappearance of Persons and in December it acceded to the UN Convention against Torture and Other Cruel, Inhuman or Degrading Treatment or Punishment.

In June, 13 army and police officers were charged in connection with the "disappearance" and killing of Adán Avilés Fúnez and Amado Espinoza Paz in Choluteca in 1982. One of the accused gave himself up to the authorities but was later provisionally released pending trial. The other 12 went into hiding. At the end of the year judicial proceedings were continuing. The remains of Adán Avilés Fúnez and Amado Espinoza Paz had been exhumed and identified in Choluteca in November 1995. At least three of the 13 officers had been charged in 1995 in connection with the temporary "disappearance" of six students in 1982 (see *Amnesty International Report 1996*).

Two military officers sentenced for the rape and killing of Riccy Mabel Martínez (see *Amnesty International Report 1992*) had their sentences revoked by the Appeals Court. Following a lengthy judicial process, the Court found that the guilt of the convicted military officers could not be proved. The case was pending judicial review by the Second Criminal Court at the end of the year.

On 5 January, the First Appeals Court ruled that military and police officers charged with past human rights violations should benefit from an amnesty law passed in 1991 (see *Amnesty International Report 1992*). However, on 19 January, the Supreme Court of Justice overturned that decision, leaving the way open for the case against the 13 officers to proceed. In July, the Supreme Court ruled that military officers charged with human rights violations could remain in preventive detention in military barracks instead of civilian detention establishments.

There was little progress in other cases against military officers involved in human rights violations. Investigations continued into the "disappearance" in 1982 of lawyer Nelson Mackay Chavarría, whose remains were exhumed in December 1994 (see *Amnesty International Report 1995*). In January, arrest warrants were issued against high-ranking military officials in connection with his "disappearance" and death. At least one of those involved was also charged in connection with the "disappearance" and killing of two people in Choluteca and the temporary "disappearance" of six students in 1982. None of those charged had been detained by the end of the year.

In November, the remains of two people were exhumed in southern Honduras. The exhumations were initiated by the Special Prosecutor for Human Rights and the *Comité de Familiares de Detenidos Desaparecidos en Honduras* (COFADEH), Committee of Relatives of the Disappeared in Honduras, a non-governmental human rights organization. Definitive identifications were pending at the end of the year. The remains of at least three other victims exhumed during 1995 were awaiting definitive identification at the end of the year.

Relatives of the "disappeared" and other human rights activists were subjected to intimidation. Members of the non-governmental *Comité para la Defensa de los Derechos Humanos en Honduras* (CODEH), Committee for the Defence of Human Rights in Honduras, and of COFADEH, as well as staff in the office of the National Human Rights Commissioner, received death threats throughout the year. In March, two Public Ministry prosecutors were threatened with death by a member of the FSP under investigation for murder. During July, Leo Valladares Lanza, National Human Rights Commissioner, received a series of death threats. In October, following allegations by Dr Ramón Custodio, President of CODEH, that people responsible for a bombing campaign were connected to the military, bombs exploded in two clinical laboratories owned by him.

In February and October, the government threatened to cancel the legal status of the *Casa Alianza Honduras*, Covenant House of Honduras, a non-governmental organization working with street children in the capital, Tegucigalpa, and campaigning for children to be held separately from adults in Honduran prisons.

There were reports of torture and ill-treatment. At least 26 prisoners were tortured or ill-treated by prison guards.

In January, four members of the FSP raided a house in San Pedro Sula and reportedly beat and raped a 14-year-old girl in front of her relatives, who were threatened with death if they reported the abuses. No investigation was known to have been carried out by the end of the year.

During June and July, at least five former members of the disbanded *Dirección Nacional de Investigaciones* (DNI), the investigative branch of the FSP, were killed in circumstances suggesting extrajudicial execution. One of the victims, René Orellana, had been due to give evidence before a court in Choluteca about a murder reportedly carried out by members of the DNI in 1994. He was shot dead in June.

Information came to light about the "disappearance" in October 1995 of Dixie Miguel Urbina Rosales in Tegucigalpa, following his detention by members of the FSP. Despite repeated appeals to the authorities by human rights organizations and his relatives to investigate his whereabouts, at the end of the year Dixie Urbina remained "disappeared".

Amnesty International issued a report in March, *Honduras: Continued struggle against impunity*, describing developments which took place during the second half of 1995, including the exhumations initiated by human rights organizations and the Special Prosecutor for Human Rights, and judicial proceedings against military personnel. Amnesty International called on the government to support judicial proceedings against those charged in cases of past human rights violations.

Amnesty International appealed to the authorities to take measures to guarantee the safety of human rights defenders and of members of the judiciary and governmental agencies involved in clarifying cases of human rights violations; to investigate all cases of harassment and death threats against them, and to bring those responsible to justice. In February and October, the organization called on the government to ensure the necessary conditions for the *Casa Alianza Honduras* to continue their activities without impediment.

HONG KONG

Uncertainty continued over the future implementation of the Bill of Rights and international standards. There was concern over the legality of a new, unelected legislative body due to take office in 1997. Thousands of Vietnamese asylum-seekers who were detained pending return faced harsh conditions of detention.

In December, former businessman Tung Chee-hwa was selected as Chief Executive of the Hong Kong Special Administrative Region (SAR), to be set up in July 1997 when China resumes sovereignty over the territory. He was selected by the 400-member Selection Committee made up of Hong Kong citizens, under rules established in 1990 when the Basic Law of the Hong Kong SAR was adopted by China.

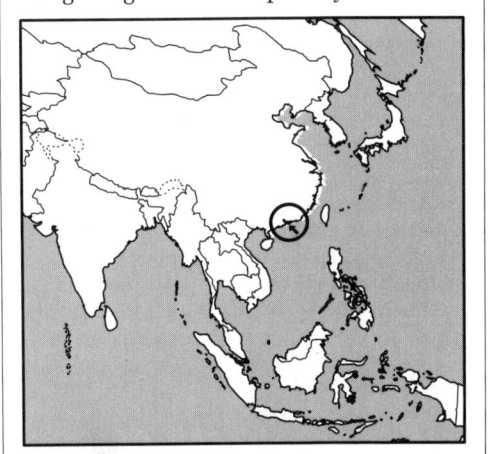

Also in December, the Selection Committee nominated the members of the Provisional Legislature. This is to replace the existing Legislative Council (Legco) as the first legislative organ of the Hong Kong SAR. The Chinese Government considers that the 1992 electoral reforms which led to a widening of the electorate made the subsequent elections to the Legco incompatible with the Basic Law. However, as the Basic Law made no provision for a non-elected Provisional Legislature, the compatibility of the Provisional Legislature with the Basic Law continued to be debated throughout the year. A number of political parties and professional groups expressed opposition to the Provisional Legislature, which they considered illegal. Others showed support for it by joining the Selection Committee. The Committee designated 51 of its own members to join the 60-seat Provisional Legislature. They included most of the 33 members of the current Legco who had sought membership of the new body, as well as a number of pro-China personalities who had failed to gain seats in Legco in 1995.

There were fears that the Provisional Legislature might amend laws to restrict the scope of human rights safeguards. In 1995, the Preliminary Working Committee, an advisory body set up by China, had stated that aspects of Hong Kong's Bill of Rights Ordinance, which enshrines in Hong Kong domestic law most provisions of the International Covenant on Civil and Political Rights (ICCPR), were contrary to the Basic Law. The Committee had suggested that legislation which had been abolished or amended to ensure consistency with the Bill of Rights be reinstated in its original form, which might restrict the exercise of certain fundamental rights (see *Amnesty International Report 1996*). In December, legislative amendments were debated by Legco, defining the scope of the offence of treason, as required of the Hong Kong SAR under the Basic Law. The Chinese authorities criticized the amendment and indicated that the Provisional Legislature could abolish it and replace it with another definition of the offence.

In September, Qiao Xiaoyang, Vice-Chairman of China's National People's Congress (NPC), was reported to have stated that Hong Kong courts might have no jurisdiction over members of the People's Liberation Army (PLA) stationed in Hong Kong. In December, a law on PLA troops in Hong Kong was adopted by China's NPC. It suggested that Chinese law would govern the activities of PLA troops in Hong Kong after a state of war or "turmoil" was declared. It also made PLA officers committing offences in Hong Kong virtually immune from prosecution under Hong Kong law, except for offences committed while off-duty, although these could be difficult to define in practice.

In October, the UN Human Rights Committee considered the supplementary report of the United Kingdom on implementation of the ICCPR, which it had requested in 1995 (see *Amnesty International Report 1996*). The Committee expressed regret at the failure of the Hong Kong Government to set up a Human Rights Commission, and called on the British Government to present a further report covering the period up to 30 June 1997. The Committee also reiterated its call on the British and Chinese Governments to ensure that the obligation to report on the implementation of the ICCPR is fulfilled after that date.

In September, five labour activists, including Wong Ying-yu and Mung Siu-tak, were convicted of disturbing the peace and ordered to pay fines. They had taken part in an unauthorized demonstration in January demanding better safety conditions for workers in toy factories set up in China and other countries by Hong Kong companies. The five appealed against their convictions, arguing that their activities were legal under the Bill of Rights. Their appeal had not been heard by the end of the year.

More than 6,000 Vietnamese asylum-seekers, most of whom had been denied refugee status following a flawed refugee determination procedure, were still in detention at the end of the year. Most faced forcible return to Viet Nam. About 15,000 people who had been denied refugee status were forcibly returned to Viet Nam during the year, or chose to return under a voluntary repatriation scheme. The conditions in which the asylum-seekers were detained deteriorated as some social services were withdrawn. Conditions at Victoria Prison, part of which was used as a holding centre for Vietnamese asylum-seekers awaiting imminent return, were reported in September to have seriously worsened, with severe overcrowding and insufficient hygiene provisions. In the same month, lawyers applied for a judicial review of the legality of the detention of Vietnamese asylum-seekers, but no ruling had been made by the end of the year. The forcible return of Vietnamese asylum-seekers was speeded up towards the end of the year, as the authorities attempted to complete all returns before the July 1997 hand-over of the territory.

An Amnesty International representative visited Hong Kong in May and September to study the human rights implications of the transition to Chinese sovereignty. In December, Amnesty International issued an open letter to the Chief Executive designate, summarizing the organization's concerns in the light of the territory's return to Chinese rule. It urged him to commit himself publicly to maintaining and implementing the Bill of Rights and all provisions of the ICCPR.

HUNGARY

There were reports of ill-treatment of detainees by police officers. One detainee was kept in prolonged isolation. Non-European asylum-seekers were denied adequate legal protection.

In February, the government authorized publication of the report of the European Committee for the Prevention of Torture and Inhuman or Degrading Treatment or Punishment on its visit to places of detention, primarily in the Budapest area, in November 1994, together with the government's response. The Committee stated that it had heard numerous allegations of ill-treatment by the police and concluded that persons deprived of their liberty in Budapest run a not inconsiderable risk of ill-treatment. The Committee also concluded that living conditions in a hostel where illegal immigrants were detained (see *Amnesty International Report 1993*) were inhuman and degrading and constituted a significant risk to the physical and mental health of the detainees. The government agreed with most of the findings and accepted the recommendations. The Kerepestarcsa Community Hostel was closed and more appropriate accommodation provided.

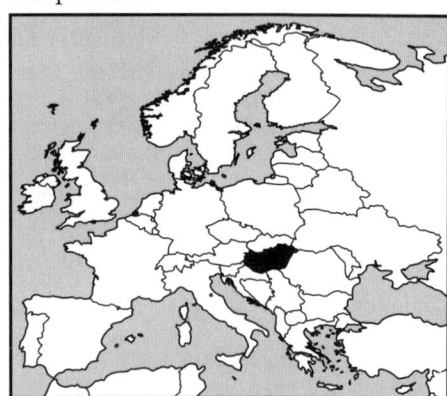

There were new allegations of police ill-treatment. In May, Hamodi Ahmed was reportedly assaulted by police officers outside a Budapest restaurant. The officers pushed him against the wall, handcuffed his arms behind his back and beat him. Later, at the Fifth District Police Station, Hamodi Ahmed was kicked by five or six other officers. The following morning he was released without charge from the Central Police Station, to which he had been transferred, and received hospital treatment for his injuries. His complaint to the prosecutor was reportedly dismissed on the grounds that it was not possible to establish the identity of the police officers involved, who, according to the results of the investigation, did not use excessive force.

In the same month, also in Budapest, István Nagy was detained when he criticized a police officer who had allegedly shouted at an old man for crossing the road too slowly. István Nagy was taken to the Eighth District Police Station, where he was reportedly hit in the face, beaten and kicked. He was later admitted to Erzsébet Hospital, where he was treated for three days for a ruptured ear-drum and injuries to the chest and spleen. István Nagy filed a complaint with the prosecutor and an investigation was in progress at the end of the year.

In January, Christopher Kwaku was detained in Budapest Police Headquarters for illegal entry into Hungary. He was held in virtual isolation for over 10 months after a medical examination established that he was HIV positive. In November, he was released into the custody of a local human rights organization. Amnesty International believes that prolonged isolation may have serious effects on the physical and mental health of detainees and may constitute cruel, inhuman or degrading treatment or punishment.

Hungary operates a geographical limitation to the 1951 UN Convention relating to the Status of Refugees, under which it does not recognize non-European refugees. Consequently, non-European asylum-seekers are in danger of being returned to a country where they face serious human rights violations. In June, brothers Anthony Zakaria Laki and Samuel Lado Zakaria, two Christians from Sudan, arrived in Hungary from Damascus, Syria, and sought asylum at Budapest Airport. Both men were returned to Damascus, where they were arrested on arrival and detained before being sent back to Sudan in September. Their subsequent fate and whereabouts were unknown.

In September, Amnesty International urged the Minister of the Interior to arrange a comprehensive medical examination of Christopher Kwaku in order to assess the effects of prolonged isolation on his health. The Minister replied that Christopher Kwaku's isolation had been recommended by medical experts and that he was receiving appropriate medical assistance to "alleviate his psychologic complaints arising from the separation". Amnesty International further questioned the decision to detain Christopher Kwaku in isolation, particularly in the light of the recommendation of the European Committee for the Prevention of Torture and Inhuman or Degrading Treatment or Punishment to the Hungarian Government

that HIV-positive detainees who are well should not be segregated.

Amnesty International expressed concern to the authorities that the two brothers from Sudan had been refused effective and durable protection in Hungary.

In December, Amnesty International expressed concern about new allegations of ill-treatment and requested information about the results of investigations.

INDIA

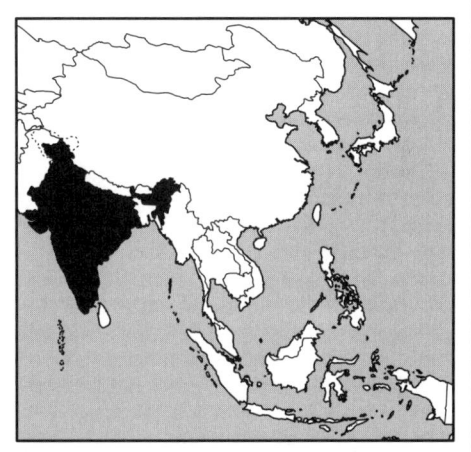

Thousands of political prisoners were held without charge or trial. Torture, including rape, and ill-treatment were endemic throughout the country, leading or contributing to at least 200 deaths in custody. Prison conditions amounting to ill-treatment were common. "Disappearances" continued. Hundreds of people were reportedly extrajudicially executed by the security forces; human rights defenders continued to be targeted. At least two people were judicially executed and at least 30 were on death row. Armed opposition groups committed grave human rights abuses, including deliberate and arbitrary killings of civilians and hostage-taking.

In June, the United Front, a coalition of regional and national parties led by Prime Minister H.D. Deve Gowda, formed a government with the support of the Congress Party, following the brief tenure of a Bharatiya Janata Party (BJP) government, led by A.B. Vajpayee after general elections in April and May. The new government committed itself to ratifying the UN

Convention against Torture and Other Cruel, Inhuman or Degrading Treatment or Punishment. In September, state assembly elections were held in Jammu and Kashmir, ending nine years of central rule. The successful National Conference Party promised to establish a human rights commission to investigate allegations of human rights violations committed in the previous seven years and a committee to review the cases of political detainees.

The government continued to face violent attacks by armed opposition groups in Jammu and Kashmir, throughout the northeastern states and in some other parts of the country, including Andhra Pradesh. In some areas former members of armed opposition groups – so-called "renegades" – apparently acting with the connivance of the security forces, reportedly carried out killings, abductions and rapes.

Preventive detention provisions remained in force in national legislation, including the National Security Act, and in state-specific legislation, including the Jammu and Kashmir Public Safety Act and the Tamil Nadu Goondas Act. The Criminal Law Amendment Bill, proposed in 1995 as a replacement to the lapsed Terrorist and Disruptive Activities (Prevention) Act (TADA), was not enacted and hundreds remained in detention under the TADA (see *Amnesty International Report 1996*). Other special legislation remained in force, including the Armed Forces (Special Powers) Act – which gives the security forces the right to shoot to kill with virtual impunity – and the Disturbed Areas Act. Judicial review of these statutes had been pending in the Supreme Court of India since 1980.

Such legislation was criticized by the National Human Rights Commission (NHRC), established in 1993, which continued initiatives to raise public awareness of human rights and reported on human rights violations in several states, although its recommendations were not binding. Despite giving discretionary powers such as awarding compensation, the mandate of the NHRC remained limited in relation to human rights violations committed by the armed forces, effectively excluding the areas where there was violent opposition activity.

Thousands of political prisoners were detained without charge or trial under special legislation – such as the TADA, the Armed Forces (Special Powers) Act and the Disturbed Areas Act – which lacked vital legal safeguards.

In March, the government disclosed that more than 42,000 people were detained pending trial under the TADA. However, following a Supreme Court directive ordering the release on bail of various categories of detainee, the government revised the figure in December to 2,000. The National Security Act was used in July to detain Narayan Reddy during a protest in Gopalpur, Orissa State, against the decision to build a steel plant in the area. It was used throughout the year to detain people suspected of involvement in armed opposition in the northeastern states.

A number of reports were received about the use of false charges to quell dissent. In October, 16 women, including three juveniles, protesting against the Miss World Contest in Bangalore were detained for 17 days, after reportedly being beaten in police custody, on a false, non-bailable charge of causing damage by fire.

At least 1,500 Nepali-speaking people from southern Bhutan living in refugee camps in eastern Nepal, were arrested in West Bengal between January and April during a series of peaceful marches in the border region aimed at presenting a petition to the King of Bhutan (see **Bhutan** entry). Of these, 791 remained detained for over two months, before being released without charge in July.

Refugees arriving in India from Afghanistan, Myanmar and Sri Lanka were detained under the Foreigners Act, which regulates the entry of aliens into India but makes no provision for refugees.

Torture, including rape, and ill-treatment were endemic throughout the country. Victims included suspected political activists, criminal suspects, people from underprivileged sections of society and those defending their economic and social rights. Torture was used to extract information from common criminal suspects and to humiliate and degrade detainees.

Firoz Ahmed Ganai, a suspected member of an armed opposition group, was arrested in November 1995 in Sonawar, Jammu and Kashmir, and tortured while in the custody of the Border Security Force. He subsequently suffered kidney failure and had to have his leg amputated. In January, the government claimed that his leg became gangrenous after he fell and fractured it in heavy snow. Despite medical reports stating that the kidney failure may have been a result of torture, no investigation was carried out.

Husband and wife Parkash Singh and Nirmal Kaur from Nabha, Patiala, were taken into custody by the Punjab police in April on suspicion of possessing drugs. They were both stripped and beaten with fists and sticks. Wooden rollers were rolled over the muscles in their thighs. They were released on bail and filed a complaint of torture with the Punjab and Haryana High Court. It had not been heard by the end of the year.

In May, Rajesh, a 14-year-old rag-picker from Kerala, was illegally detained and tortured by police who denied that he was in their custody. Pins were reportedly inserted under his nails, his head was banged against the wall and he was beaten on the soles of his feet. No inquiry appeared to have been ordered into his torture and illegal detention. In July, police entered a village in Uttar Pradesh inhabited predominantly by *dalits* (members of a socially and economically disadvantaged group determined by caste hierarchies) at midnight in search of a suspect. A female relative of the suspect was beaten, stripped and pinned to the ground by a police officer in front of the villagers. Police later threatened to rape her if she attempted to lodge a complaint.

Villagers, including women, were beaten by police in June in Mithini and Khairi villages in Uttar Pradesh. They had been arrested during a protest to defend their land from being bulldozed as part of the expansion of a thermal power project funded by the World Bank.

At least 200 people were reported to have died in the custody of police, security forces and prison officials, many following torture. The figure may be higher; the NHRC recorded 159 deaths in custody in the first three months of 1996. For example, in August, Gopalappa, an unemployed man, died in police custody in Karnataka. A post-mortem report found that his spleen had ruptured as a result of a blow to the stomach.

Although the number of cases of torture and death in custody in which compensation was awarded increased – in a number of cases on the recommendation of the NHRC – there were few convictions. In a rare example, two police officers were fined and sentenced in August to one year's imprisonment for the torture of Archana Guha in Calcutta in 1974, after a 20-year legal battle by her brother. Both officers appealed to the High Court, but the outcome was not known at the end of the year.

Both the NHRC and the Supreme Court spoke of the harsh conditions in which most prisoners were kept. The NHRC proposed changes to the India Prisons Act, reporting that some prisoners were kept in shackles for long periods. The Supreme Court called on the prison authorities to end torture and overcrowding.

"Disappearances" continued and the fate of hundreds of people who "disappeared" in previous years remained unknown. In Manipur, Laishram Bijoykumar – whose brothers had reportedly been members of an armed opposition group – was taken from his house late at night in June, reportedly by soldiers in civilian clothes. Reports suggested that he was being held in an army camp in Manipur. A *habeas corpus* writ was filed in the High Court in Guwahati and there were widespread demonstrations against his "disappearance". However, the army continued to deny that he was in their custody, and his whereabouts remained unknown at the end of the year

In August, the Central Bureau of Investigation submitted an interim report into allegations that police in Punjab had extrajudicially executed hundreds of young men and disposed of their bodies. The report found that at one site alone 934 unidentified bodies – presumed by human rights groups to be those of "disappeared" young men – had been cremated between 1990 and 1995. The Bureau completed its inquiry into the abduction of Jaswant Singh Khalra, a lawyer and human rights activist from Punjab who "disappeared" after filing a petition in the Supreme Court about the cremation grounds (see *Amnesty International Report 1996*). The inquiry concluded that he had been taken by the police. His whereabouts were unknown.

Hundreds of people were reportedly extrajudicially executed by members of the security forces. In March, the tied and mutilated body of Jalil Andrabi, Chairman of the Kashmir Commission of Jurists, was found in the Jhelum river, near Srinagar, in Jammu and Kashmir. Three weeks earlier he had been detained by members of the Rashtriya Rifles who were accompanied by unidentified armed men. Investigations into his abduction and death continued in the High Court in Jammu and Kashmir.

In September, in the State of Andhra Pradesh, Dr Ameda Narayana, a doctor practising in an area where the government faces armed opposition, was reportedly shot dead by members of the police.

Reports were received that harassment, abduction, rape and deliberate and arbitrary killings perpetrated by so-called "renegades" in Jammu and Kashmir, and by other such groups, in Assam and other states, were carried out with the support of the security forces. Parag Kumar Das was killed by suspected former members of the armed opposition group United Liberation Front of Assam (ULFA), known as SULFA (surrendered ULFA), acting on behalf of the state authorities. Parag Das's son, Rohan Das, aged eight, was injured in the shooting.

At least two people were judicially executed and at least 30 were sentenced to death or remained on death row.

Armed opposition groups committed grave human rights abuses, including torture, deliberate and arbitrary killings of civilians, and hostage-taking. In May, following public threats that anyone participating in the elections would be killed, armed opposition groups in Jammu and Kashmir killed several election candidates. The victims included a Congress leader, his wife and two children who were killed in Rajauri, and election officials who were blown up in a bus in Dada.

In January, Amnesty International expressed concern at the quashing of the Srikrishna Enquiry, a judicial inquiry into allegations of police killings during the riots in Bombay in 1992 and 1993 (see *Amnesty International Reports 1993* and *1994*). The inquiry was subsequently reinstated in May 1996 during the brief tenure of the BJP government. In February, Amnesty International published a report, *India: Harjit Singh – in continuing pursuit of justice*, which documented the virtual immunity from prosecution for human rights violations afforded by the operation of the legal process.

In March, a report, *Amnesty International and India*, provided a detailed summary of the organization's concerns in India, particularly in relation to legislation and the legal process.

In April, Amnesty International sent an open letter to all political parties on the occasion of the general elections, setting out its human rights concerns. The organization issued a number of appeals to the security forces and armed opposition groups in Jammu and Kashmir, calling for human rights to be respected in the election period. Concerns were raised about attacks on political leaders and their detention under house arrest, death threats against civilian electoral officials and harassment of journalists and human rights defenders.

In July and August, Amnesty International delegates were granted access to India to conduct research for the second time in 16 years and held talks with government officials, members of the NHRC and numerous human rights activists. In September, the organization published a report, *India: Human rights abuses in the election period in Jammu and Kashmir*, which had been submitted to the Indian Government during the visit. The report detailed abuses by the security forces, "renegade" and armed opposition groups, and recommended, among other things, the disarming and disbanding of "renegade" groups. The government dismissed the report as containing "baseless and absurd allegations", while acknowledging inquiries instituted into the killing of Jalil Andrabi and Ghulam Rasool Sheikh.

In July, Amnesty International called for the release of the five foreign hostages held since July 1995 in Jammu and Kashmir (see *Amnesty International Report 1996*).

INDONESIA AND EAST TIMOR

At least 137 prisoners of conscience were detained. Nine were sentenced to prison terms and at least 20 others were on trial or awaiting trial at the end of the year. Hundreds of people, including possible prisoners of conscience, were arrested and held briefly without charge or trial. At least 208 political prisoners sentenced in previous years, many of them prisoners of conscience, remained imprisoned. At least 187 political prisoners received

prison sentences after unfair trials. Torture of detainees, including juveniles, was common, and in several cases resulted in death. At least one person was believed to have "disappeared" in East Timor; dozens of people were killed by members of the security forces in suspicious circumstances. Previous cases of "disappearances" and extrajudicial executions remained unresolved. At least 26 people remained on death row at the end of the year. There were no executions. An armed opposition group committed human rights abuses including deliberate and arbitrary killings and hostage-taking.

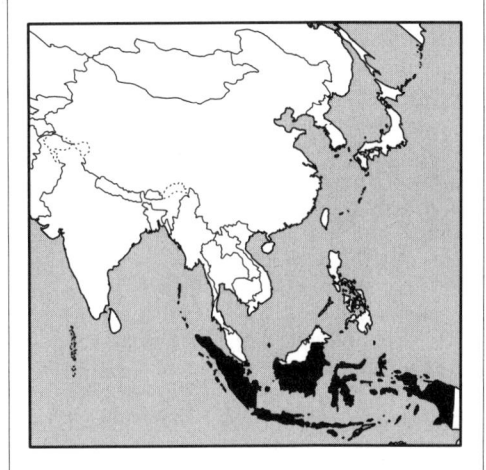

The government faced continued armed opposition from groups seeking independence in East Timor, Irian Jaya and Aceh. Access by international and domestic human rights monitoring organizations to East Timor and parts of Indonesia continued to be restricted.

In March, the Chairman of the UN Commission on Human Rights made a statement, which was accepted by the member states of the Commission, reiterating concern about the human rights situation in East Timor and calling on the Indonesian Government to implement undertakings contained in previous Chairman's statements, including the release of East Timorese detained in connection with the 1991 Santa Cruz massacre in Dili. Also in March, in his report of a visit to Indonesia and East Timor in December 1995, the UN High Commissioner for Human Rights called on the government to grant international human rights non-governmental organizations full access to Indonesia and East Timor; to repeal the Anti-subversion Law; to grant clemency to individuals detained in connection with the Santa Cruz massacre; and to continue the search for the dead and "disappeared" in the massacre.

In July, the human rights situation in Indonesia deteriorated sharply when the Jakarta headquarters of the Indonesian Democratic Party (PDI), occupied by supporters of ousted party leader Megawati Sukarnoputri, was raided by hundreds of police and alleged supporters of a government-backed rival faction of the PDI. Following the raid and subsequent riots, the government launched a crack-down on opposition groups. In September, the authorities announced restrictions on election campaigning during 1997, including increased police powers to ban campaigning activities they considered to be a threat to public safety.

Investigations by Indonesia's National Human Rights Commission (*Komnas HAM*) revealed evidence of human rights violations, including "excessive behaviour" by the military leading to the deaths of three students during protests in Ujung Pandang in April. In October, *Komnas HAM* released a report on the raid on the PDI headquarters and the riots which followed, which blamed the riots on the violence with which the raid was conducted. *Komnas HAM* reported that five people were killed during the raid or riots, 149 were injured and 23 were missing. *Komnas HAM* opened an office in Dili, East Timor, in October and announced its intention to open an office in Irian Jaya.

At least 137 prisoners of conscience, including human rights and political activists, were detained during the year. Nine were sentenced to terms of imprisonment and at least 20 were on trial or awaiting trial at the end of the year.

At least 108 people were arrested during a crack-down on peaceful opposition activities following the raid on the PDI headquarters in July. Most were released without charge, some after being held incommunicado for weeks in military custody, but 12 were charged with subversion or under legislation which prohibits "spreading hatred" against the government. They included several members of a left-wing political organization accused by the government of instigating the riots. Their trials began in December.

Muchtar Pakpahan, an independent trade union leader, was arrested in July after attempting to arrange a meeting between a foreign journalist and an eye-witness to the raid on the PDI headquarters. His trial, on a charge of subversion, began in December. In November, the Supreme Court reimposed on him a four-year prison sentence it had quashed in May 1995 (see *Amnesty International Report 1996*).

In July, three labour activists were arrested and later charged with subversion for their involvement in a peaceful labour demonstration in the town of Surabaya. Their trials began in December. In October, two men, Andi Syahputra and Dasrul, were arrested at a printing house in Jakarta for their alleged role in printing an independent magazine, *Suara Independen*. Andi Syahputra was charged with "insulting the President" and "expressing feelings of hostility, hatred or contempt toward the government".

In May, Sri Bintang Pamungkas, a politician, was sentenced to 34 months' imprisonment for "insulting the President" in remarks he was alleged to have made during a seminar in Germany in 1995 (see *Amnesty International Report 1996*). In June, he lodged an appeal against the sentence, but in December it was announced that the sentence had been upheld.

In November, Danang Kukuh Wardoyo, sentenced to 20 months' imprisonment for his alleged role in disseminating an unlicensed publication in September 1995, was released. Two journalists convicted with him remained in prison.

At least 22 East Timorese prisoners of conscience were serving prison sentences of up to life imprisonment. They included six East Timorese convicted of "publicly expressing hatred towards the government" during a pro-independence demonstration in Dili in February and sentenced to one year's imprisonment. In May, Jose Antonio Belo was released after 17 months' imprisonment for his role in a peaceful pro-independence demonstration in January 1995 (see *Amnesty International Report 1996*). Eleven people tried and convicted for their alleged role in the same demonstration were expected to be released in early 1997.

Hundreds of people, including peaceful political activists, were subjected to short-term detention and harassment by the security forces. Four men from Irian Jaya were arbitrarily detained in Jakarta and held incommunicado for up to nine days before being released without charge. The four appeared to have been arrested in connection with peaceful protests in Jakarta concerning Irian Jaya. At least 300 East Timorese were believed to have been arbitrarily detained, including five men who were arrested in November because they were thought to have publicized information about the killing of two civilians by the military in September.

At least 208 political prisoners, many of them prisoners of conscience, continued to serve sentences of up to life imprisonment, imposed in previous years after unfair trials, for alleged links with armed secessionist movements in East Timor, Irian Jaya and Aceh, and with Islamic and political activism. At least 14 prisoners convicted for their alleged role in a 1965 coup attempt, remained imprisoned; many were prisoners of conscience and all were imprisoned after unfair trials. All were elderly and most were suffering from serious ill health. Five had spent more than 25 years on death row, including former parliamentarian Sukatno.

At least 187 political prisoners were sentenced, many reportedly after unfair trials, to prison terms of up to 10 years. They included 115 people sentenced to up to four months and three days' imprisonment for refusing to disperse from the PDI headquarters in Jakarta during the raid in July. All 115 were believed to be supporters of ousted PDI leader Megawati Sukarnoputri. In Irian Jaya, at least 31 men were tried for their alleged role in disturbances which took place in March in Abepura, Irian Jaya. The men received sentences of up to one year's imprisonment. In August, six men were sentenced to prison terms ranging from two to 10 years in Merauke, Irian Jaya, for an armed attack in which an Indonesian soldier was killed. They were reportedly pressurized by the authorities not to appeal against the sentences. In East Timor, 21 people were imprisoned for their alleged role in disturbances in Baucau, East Timor. All 21 were believed to have been tried without legal representation and to have been denied information about the scheduling of their trials, which resulted in them having inadequate time to prepare their defence.

There were numerous reports of torture and ill-treatment by the security forces.

Five people arrested outside a church during disturbances in Abepura, Irian Jaya, were reportedly taken to a security post and kicked, hit and slashed with a knife by soldiers before being released without charge the following day. Three East Timorese were hospitalized after being severely beaten by members of the security forces when they were expelled from the German Embassy in Jakarta, where they had attempted to seek asylum. The three were promptly arrested by soldiers waiting outside the Embassy who beat and kicked them. The three men were reportedly detained for two days before being released without charge.

Torture and ill-treatment of criminal suspects were also commonplace and sometimes resulted in death. In October, Tjetje Tadjudin died in police custody after he had apparently told police that he believed members of the Indonesian Armed Forces were involved in a robbery to which he had been a witness. The post-mortem reportedly demonstrated that Tjetje Tadjudin died from injuries consistent with torture. A police lieutenant was arrested in October in connection with his death.

"Disappearances" continued to be reported. Despite a police inquiry announced in February 1995, there was no information about the fate of five men believed to have "disappeared" after they were arrested in Dili in January 1995.

Dozens of people were believed to have been killed by the security forces in suspicious circumstances. In August, Faud Muhammad Syafruddin, a journalist, was severely beaten by two men after publishing articles about local government corruption; he died three days later. There were allegations that local government officials may have been involved in Faud Muhammad Syafruddin's death, and in November *Komnas HAM* announced that his death was linked to his publication of controversial articles.

Several East Timorese were reportedly killed by members of the security forces in suspicious circumstances. In September, two men were reportedly shot by soldiers as they stopped at a military check-point on a road to the East Timorese town of Viqueque. In November, *Komnas HAM* announced an investigation into their deaths.

Many killings and "disappearances" in previous years remained unresolved. In February, a military court sentenced four soldiers to prison terms of between one and three years in connection with the killing of three civilians in the village of Hoea in Irian Jaya in May 1995. However, 13 other killings and four "disappearances" in the same area of Irian Jaya, confirmed by *Komnas HAM* in September 1995, were not investigated by the authorities. The authorities did not initiate investigations into the fate of the estimated 270 people killed and 200 others "disappeared" during the 1991 Santa Cruz massacre in East Timor, despite being urged to do so by the UN Commission on Human Rights and the UN High Commissioner for Human Rights.

At least 26 people remained on death row at the end of the year, including five political prisoners who had been under sentence of death for over 25 years. No executions were carried out.

An opposition group committed human rights abuses including hostage-taking and summary executions. In January, the Free Papua Movement (OPM) took 26 people hostage in Mapunduma village, in the Baliem Valley area of Irian Jaya. Several of the hostages were released, but 11 Indonesians and foreigners were only released after a military operation in May. Two of the Indonesian hostages were believed to have been killed by the OPM during the release operation.

Amnesty International repeatedly appealed for the immediate and unconditional release of all prisoners of conscience, for the review of cases of political prisoners imprisoned after unfair trials, and for urgent steps to be taken to end torture, extrajudicial executions and the use of the death penalty.

Amnesty International published reports in July, *East Timor: Going through the motions*; in August, *Indonesia: The 1965 prisoners – how many more will die in jail?*; and in November, *Indonesia: Arrests, torture and intimidation – the government's response to its critics*.

In a statement to the UN Commission on Human Rights in April, Amnesty International included reference to its concerns in both Indonesia and East Timor. In an oral statement to the UN Special Committee on Decolonization in July, Amnesty International described its concerns about extrajudicial executions, torture and other human rights violations in East Timor. In

January, Amnesty International called on the OPM to release 13 people taken hostage in Irian Jaya.

IRAN

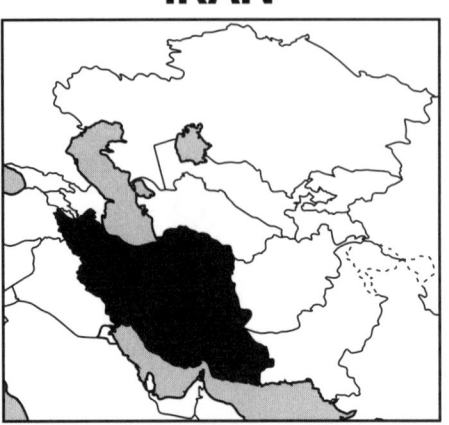

Thousands of political prisoners were held during the year, including prisoners of conscience. Some were held without charge or trial; others were serving long prison sentences after unfair trials. There were continuing reports of torture and ill-treatment. The judicial punishments of flogging and amputation were implemented. Several "disappearances" and suspected extrajudicial executions were reported. At least 110 prisoners were executed, including political prisoners, some after unfair trials.

The government, headed by President 'Ali Akbar Hashemi Rafsanjani, continued to face armed opposition from the Iraq-based Peoples' Mojahedin Organization of Iran (PMOI) and organizations such as the Kurdistan Democratic Party of Iran (KDPI), Arab groups in Khuzestan, and Baluchi groups in Sistan-Baluchistan.

In July, Iranian forces attacked KDPI bases in northern Iraq following reports of attacks by KDPI members on Iranian forces inside Iran. In September, following fighting between rival Kurdish factions in northern Iraq (see **Iraq** entry), tens of thousands of Kurdish refugees fled to Iran.

In December, riots broke out in Bakhtaran (formerly Kermanshah) province following the death in disputed circumstances of a Sunni religious leader, Molla Mohammad Rabi'i. Several people, including a police officer, reportedly died and an unknown number were arrested.

In March and April, two rounds of elections took place for the fifth Islamic Consultative Assembly (ICA), Iran's Parliament. Arrests were reported following demonstrations in Tabriz after a local candidate was disqualified. Scores, if not hundreds, of people, including 32 women, were reportedly held at the end of the year. It was not known if they had been tried.

In May, the ICA passed an amendment extending the *moharebeh* (enmity towards God) clause of the Penal Code to include espionage, punishable by a mandatory death sentence. Thousands of prisoners were believed to have been executed under this clause since 1979. It was not clear if the law had come into force by the end of the year. In July, the revised fifth book of the Penal Code (Law on *Ta'zirat*) came into force. Its provisions appeared to allow the possibility of imprisonment for the peaceful exercise of political or other beliefs while dozens of offences were punishable by flogging.

In January and February, the UN Special Rapporteur on freedom of expression and the UN Special Representative on the Islamic Republic of Iran visited the country. In April and August, the UN Commission on Human Rights and the UN Sub-Commission on Prevention of Discrimination and Protection of Minorities adopted resolutions condemning human rights violations in Iran (see *Amnesty International Report 1996*).

Prisoners of conscience held during the year included Dhabihullah Mahrami, a Baha'i accused of apostasy. He was sentenced to death in January, but the sentence was overturned on appeal by the Supreme Court. He remained detained at the end of the year, apparently awaiting a fresh trial on the same charges before a different court. In August, another Baha'i, Musa Talibi, was sentenced to death for apostasy. He had been arrested in June 1994 in Esfahan and sentenced to 10 years' imprisonment, reduced to 18 months on appeal. Following an appeal by the prosecution, the Supreme Court referred the case to a Revolutionary Court which sentenced Musa Talibi to death. At least 10 other Baha'is were also held at the end of the year, including Bihnam Mithaqi and Kayvan Khalajabadi whose death sentences were confirmed by the Supreme Court in February (see *Amnesty International Report 1996*). Information was received about the detention of Christians, apparently on account of their religious activities or beliefs. For example, the Reverend Harmik Torosian, of the Assembly of God Church in Shiraz, was reportedly detained in November 1995 and released in late 1995 or early 1996, possibly after being forced to agree not to proselytize nor to allow people of Muslim background to attend his church.

Possible prisoners of conscience included religious figures and their followers. At least three Grand Ayatollahs – Hossein 'Ali Montazeri, Sayed Sadeq Rouhani and Sayed Hassan Tabataba'i-Qomi – were said to remain under house arrest, apparently on account of their opposition to certain government policies. At least eight followers of Grand Ayatollah Shirazi and their relatives were arrested during the year, in addition to at least 21 arrested in 1995 (see *Amnesty International Report 1996*). Most had been released by the end of the year, but at least six remained held without trial. Charges against 11 of them included: forming and belonging to an illegal organization; forgery; helping people leave the country illegally; insulting the Leader of the Islamic Republic of Iran; and disseminating false information. In December, Sheikh Makki Akhound, a follower of Grand Ayatollah Shirazi, arrested in 1994 and sentenced to three years' imprisonment and flogging, apparently in connection with his association with the Grand Ayatollah, was released early (see *Amnesty International Reports 1995* and *1996*). Ayatollah Ya'sub al-Din Rastgari, a close associate of the late Grand Ayatollah Shariatmadari, was arrested in February. He was held incommunicado for several months and reportedly tortured. He was released in December and believed to have been placed under house arrest.

Former Deputy Prime Minister 'Abbas Amir Entezam, another possible prisoner of conscience arrested in December 1979 and sentenced to life imprisonment on charges of espionage, continued to be held in a guarded, government-owned house in Tehran (see *Amnesty International Report 1996*), although he was regularly allowed to leave for short periods.

Hundreds of political prisoners were reportedly held on charges such as espionage and membership of armed groups. Their fate was rarely known. In September the authorities announced that 41 people in West Azerbaijan had been arrested over the previous five months on suspicion of offences including espionage and "propagating pan-Turkism". The arrest of over 200 "counter-revolutionaries" was announced at the same time. They may have included at least 22 members of the KDPI who were reportedly arrested in August, following attacks by Iranian military forces on KDPI bases in northern Iraq (see above).

Other political prisoners were serving long prison terms after unfair trials. They included supporters of the PMOI; at least 10 members of the *Mohajerin* movement (followers of Dr 'Ali Shari'ati); members of left-wing organizations such as the *Tudeh Party*, *Peykar*, and factions of the Organization of People's Fedaiyan Guerrillas of Iran; supporters of Kurdish groups such as *Komala* and the KDPI; and supporters of other groups representing ethnic minorities such as Baluchis and Arabs.

Several amnesties were declared during 1996, but no details of those released were made available by the authorities.

As in previous years, political trials fell far short of international fair trial standards (see previous *Amnesty International Reports*). Trial hearings were often held *in camera* and, despite official assurances to the contrary, detainees were still reportedly often denied access to legal counsel.

Reports of torture or ill-treatment of prisoners and detainees continued to be received. Most, if not all, of the detained followers of Grand Ayatollah Shirazi were reported to have been tortured. Methods were said to include beatings; burning; prolonged enforced standing; detention in confined spaces; suspension, sometimes from a rotating ceiling fan; exposure to severe cold; shackling the arms in painful positions; and prolonged sleep deprivation.

At least two people reportedly died in custody, possibly as a result of torture or ill-treatment. Kazem Mirza'i, reportedly detained without trial since mid-1994, and Sulayman Ghaitaran, reportedly arrested in August, died in June and September. Both were members of the KDPI. No independent investigations were known to have been carried out into these deaths.

The judicial punishments of flogging and amputation remained in force. In August, the first amputations reported since 1994 took place when six recidivist thieves had their fingers amputated. Other convicted thieves were reportedly forced to watch. Sentences of flogging were reported for a wide range of offences, including some which appeared to relate to the right to freedom of expression. In January, 'Abbas Maroufi, the editor of *Gardoon* magazine, was sentenced to 35 lashes and six months' imprisonment, reportedly after conviction for "publishing lies", insulting the Leader of the Islamic Republic and publishing poems deemed "immoral". The sentence of flogging was not known to have been carried out by the time 'Abbas Maroufi left the country in March.

"Disappearances" were reported, both inside and outside the country. Faraj Sarkouhi, a magazine editor, "disappeared" in November for about seven weeks while on his way to Germany. The Iranian authorities maintained that he had left the country, but other sources – including a letter attributed to Faraj Sarkouhi himself – indicated that he was held in secret detention and tortured. No information was received about the fate of 'Ali Tavassoli who went missing in Azerbaijan in 1995 (see *Amnesty International Report 1996*).

Several people, including a Christian priest, several Sunni leaders and writers, were killed both inside the country and abroad in circumstances suggesting they may have been extrajudicially executed by agents of the Iranian Government. For example, Molavi Ahmad Sayyad, a Sunni Muslim leader of Baluchi origin, died in unclear circumstances after being arrested at Bandar Abbas airport in January on his return from the United Arab Emirates. His body was found outside the city five days later. He had previously been arrested in 1990 and apparently detained without trial for five years on account of his religious beliefs and perceived close relationship with the Saudi Arabian Government.

In February, two Iranian nationals, Zahra Rajabi, a member of the National Council of Resistance of Iran (NCRI), and Abdolali Moradi, an NCRI supporter, were killed in Turkey. Reza Mazlouman, a former Deputy Minister of Education under the Shah, was killed at his home in France in May. In September, Mojtaba Mashhadi, a French national of Iranian origin, was reportedly sentenced in France to seven years' imprisonment for having given information on opponents of the Iranian Government to the Iranian intelligence service, apparently for use in planning their killings. Also in September, the trial began in Turkey of a man accused of killing 'Ali Akbar Ghorbani, a PMOI member killed in Turkey in 1992 on the orders of the Iranian authorities (see *Amnesty International Report 1993*).

The threat of extrajudicial execution extended to many Iranian nationals abroad, as well as to non-Iranians such as British writer Salman Rushdie whose killing had been called for in a *fatwa* (religious edict) in 1989.

There was a significant rise in the number of executions reported during the year. At least 110 people were executed, some in public, more than twice as many as reported in 1995. As in previous years, the real number of executions was believed to be considerably higher than was publicly reported.

Death sentences continued to be imposed on political prisoners after unfair trials. For example, in July, Hedayatollah Zendehdel, a businessman, Abolghasem Majd-Abkahi and 'Alireza Yazdanshenas were sentenced to death. They were among six men brought to trial in January, about seven years after their arrest, on a wide range of charges including espionage, economic sabotage and working to restore the former imperial family. In his report, the UN Special Representative on Iran stated after observing one session of their trial that he "was left with the impression that the judge was clearly not a neutral third party between the prosecution and the defence". All were believed to have been executed by the end of the year.

Political prisoners executed in 1996 reportedly included Salim Saberniah, Mustafa Ghaderi, Rahman Rajabi, Molla Ahmad Khezri and Majid Sulduzi (see *Amnesty International Report 1996*). In June and July, two men and two women were stoned to death in Oromieh and Shiraz after conviction for adultery and murder. Also in June, 12 Dervishes were reportedly hanged in Hamadan for allegedly setting up "centres of corruption".

Amnesty International sought clarification about the fate of detainees and detention procedures from several opposition groups including the NCRI, *Komala* and the KDPI.

Amnesty International repeatedly called for the immediate and unconditional release of prisoners of conscience and for the review of cases of political prisoners held after unfair trials. It urged investigation of reports of torture, sought information about the fate of people said to have "disappeared" and called for investigations into possible extrajudicial executions. It appealed for cruel judicial punishments and death sentences to be commuted and urged against the extension of the death penalty. The government responded to some inquiries. However, in most cases there was insufficient information to allay the organization's concerns. Amnesty International published reports in August and October, highlighting the case of a prisoner of conscience, the resumption of amputations and the rise in the number of executions.

Amnesty International delegates continued to be denied access to the country for research or government talks.

IRAQ

At least 100 members of opposition groups were extrajudicially executed and hundreds arrested when government forces entered Kurdish-controlled northern Iraq. Hundreds of people were executed during the year. Hundreds of suspected government opponents, including possible prisoners of conscience, were reportedly detained without charge or trial. Tens of thousands arrested in previous years remained held. Trial and pretrial procedures for political detainees fell short of international standards. Torture and ill-treatment of detainees and prisoners remained widespread. The fate of thousands of people who had "disappeared" in previous years remained unknown. Human rights abuses continued in areas of Iraqi Kurdistan under Kurdish control. They included arbitrary arrests, incommunicado detention of suspected political opponents and executions.

Economic sanctions on Iraq, imposed by a UN Security Council cease-fire resolution in 1991, remained in force. Two "air-exclusion zones" over northern and southern Iraq continued to be imposed. In May, Iraq agreed to the implementation of a UN Security Council resolution allowing it to sell oil worth US$2bn every six months and to use the proceeds for humanitarian purposes. The agreement began to be implemented in December. Humanitarian relief continued to be distributed on a reduced scale under the terms of a UN-sponsored Memorandum of Understanding.

At the end of August, Iraqi government forces entered Arbil, located within the northern "air-exclusion zone", in conjunction with forces of the Kurdistan Democratic Party (KDP), taking control of the city and ousting forces of the Patriotic Union of Kurdistan (PUK). Within days, US forces responded by launching missile attacks on military targets in southern Iraq and, together with allied forces, extended the southern "air-exclusion zone" up to the 33rd parallel. The Iraqi Government announced that its forces would withdraw to their previous positions, but in December Iraqi army units, together with intelligence and security personnel, remained stationed in the vicinity of Arbil. The government also announced the lifting of the economic embargo it had imposed on the Kurdish-controlled region in October 1991.

Following armed clashes in September, PUK forces retreated from most areas under their control in Arbil and Sulaimaniya provinces, which fell under KDP control. In October, PUK forces launched counter-attacks and regained control of these regions, with the major exception of the city of Arbil, and called for a negotiated settlement. During these clashes human rights abuses were committed by all sides and an estimated 70,000 people fled to neighbouring Iran. Talks between the KDP and PUK with the aim of finding a durable solution to their differences began in Turkey in October, under US Government auspices, and were continuing in December. A cease-fire agreement was implemented and no major armed clashes were reported by the end of the year.

In January, the government announced that the judicial punishments of amputation and branding (see *Amnesty International Report 1995*) had ceased and would be abolished by law. In March, President Saddam Hussain reportedly ordered an end to the practice of ear amputation for army desertion and the release of hundreds of army deserters and draft evaders. In August, the Revolutionary Command Council (RCC), Iraq's highest executive body, reportedly issued Decree 81, abolishing the judicial punishments of ear amputation and branding for army desertion.

In March, a new 220-seat parliament was elected. All 160 ruling *Ba'th* Party candidates were elected; the remaining 60 seats were filled by pro-government, non-affiliated candidates. A further 30 deputies were appointed to represent the Kurdish areas.

In September, the government announced an amnesty for all Kurdish political opponents, excluding those convicted of espionage, embezzlement of state funds, premeditated murder or rape.

In March, the UN Commission on Human Rights adopted a resolution condemning "the massive and extremely grave violations of human rights for which the Government of Iraq is fully responsible" and extended for a further year the mandate of the UN Special Rapporteur on Iraq. A resolution adopted by the UN Sub-Commission on Prevention of Discrimination and Protection of Minorities in August welcomed, as in previous years, the Special Rapporteur's proposal for the setting up of a human rights monitoring operation for Iraq, but such an operation had not been set up by the end of the year.

Hundreds of people were executed during the year. At least 96 members of the opposition Iraqi National Congress (INC) and four members of the Iraqi National Turkman Party were executed by government forces following their capture in Qoshtapa, near Arbil, in August. Among the victims were Lieutenant Ra'ad 'Umar al-Khalidi and Fahd Muhammad Sultan. Hundreds of suspected government opponents, including possible prisoners of conscience, were also arrested in Arbil. They included members of the INC and the Iraqi Communist Party, suspected members of Turkman and Islamist parties and other non-Kurdish political opponents. They were said to be detained in government-controlled areas but their fate and whereabouts remained unknown.

At least 12 Iraqi army officers were reportedly executed for objecting to orders to intervene in the take-over of Arbil. They included Brigadier General Adham al-'Alwani, Major Jihad 'Abd al-'Aziz al-'Alwani and Major Faisal 'Abd al-Hamid al-'Issawi.

Several political prisoners were said to have been executed, among them Duraid Samir Jihad al-Khayali and Jihad Samir Jihad al-Khayali, executed in May in connection with anti-government demonstrations in al-Ramadi province in 1995 (see *Amnesty International Report 1996*). They were reportedly subjected to torture prior to execution.

More than 120 army officers believed to be connected to the opposition Iraqi National Accord, were executed following an alleged coup attempt against President Saddam Hussain in June. Among those executed were several high-ranking officers, including Major-General 'Abd Mutlaq al-Jibburi, Major Fawzi Karim al-Hamdani and Colonel Riyadh Talib Jassem. Up to 300 had been arrested but the fate and whereabouts of those detained remained unknown.

In February, Lieutenant-General Hussain Kamel al-Majid and his brother, Lieutenant-Colonel Saddam Kamel, both sons-in-law of President Saddam Hussain, who had fled to Jordan in August 1995 (see *Amnesty International Report 1996*), were killed within days of having returned to Iraq after reportedly being pardoned. Their father, a brother and three other relatives were also killed. The government announced that the killings constituted an act of revenge by other members of the al-Majid family, but it was widely believed that the killings had been carried out with the acquiescence of the President. There was no investigation into the killings and no one was brought to justice.

Hundreds of suspected government opponents, including possible prisoners of conscience, were arrested during the year and remained held without charge or trial. Relatives of detainees were arrested on the basis of family links. In some cases relatives of suspected political opponents who fled abroad were said to be under house arrest. About 2,000 people arrested in 1995 following demonstrations in al-Ramadi province (see Amnesty International Report 1996) continued to be held without charge or trial, as were tens of thousands more arrested in previous years. Following an assassination attempt in December on 'Uday Saddam Hussain, the President's eldest son, hundreds of arrests were reportedly carried out in Baghdad and other cities. The fate and whereabouts of those arrested remained unknown.

Trials of political detainees continued to be held *in camera*, using procedures which did not meet internationally recognized standards for fair trial. Defendants had no access to defence counsel and appeared before special *ad hoc* security courts, usually headed by a military or security officer. It was not possible to ascertain the number of political detainees tried during the year.

Physical and psychological torture and ill-treatment of detainees and prisoners remained widespread. Methods of torture reported included beatings, electric shocks to the tongue and genitals, suspension from a rotating fan, burning the skin using heated metal implements or sulphuric acid, and rape. Some prisoners were said to have been flogged before their release.

The fate of thousands of people who had "disappeared" in previous years remained unknown (see previous Amnesty International Reports). Among the victims were seven brothers of the al-Hashimi family who "disappeared" following their arrest in Baghdad in October 1980. In May, the authorities released Nadia Muhammad al-'Anaizi, a Kuwaiti national who was among an estimated 625 Kuwaiti and other nationals arrested by Iraqi forces during the occupation of Kuwait in 1990 and 1991 and believed to remain held in Iraq. In September, the Iraqi Government announced that it had set up a committee to determine the fate of "Iraqis and Kuwaitis missing since the 1991 Gulf war". The committee, said to be composed of members of parliament, lawyers, members of an Iraqi human rights organization and the Iraqi Red Crescent, was to establish offices throughout Iraq to gather information about those missing. It was not known by the end of the year whether this took place.

Serious human rights abuses were carried out in the Kurdish-controlled provinces by the two main political groups, the KDP and PUK. Members of smaller political groups were among those targeted for arrest, prolonged incommunicado detention and torture or ill-treatment. They included members of the Iraqi Workers' Communist Party, the Kurdistan Farmers' Movement and the Surchi clan (see below).

In May, two unarmed members of the Assyrian Democratic Movement (ADM), Samir Moshi Murad and Peris Mirza Salyu, were killed in 'Ain Kawa, near Arbil, by Kurdish students allegedly associated with the PUK. The ADM members were reportedly intervening to settle a dispute between Kurdish and Assyrian students when they were deliberately shot. Although PUK leaders condemned the killings, no one was brought to justice (see below). In June, at least 10 people were reportedly killed in armed clashes when KDP forces attacked members of the Surchi clan in the village of Kalakin, north of Arbil. Among the dead were two women and Hussain Agha Surchi, head of the Association of Kurdish Clans.

It was not known whether death sentences had been imposed by courts operated by the KDP and PUK in Iraqi Kurdistan during the year, nor whether any passed between 1992 and 1994 had been carried out (see previous Amnesty International Reports). In October, 59 KDP members were reportedly executed in the town of Rania after their capture by the PUK. They included Shukri Hussain Diab and Mustafa Hassan 'Uthman. In September, four PUK members were said to have been executed in Sulaimaniya after their capture by the KDP. Among them were Amjad Haji Khaled and Fa'iq Tawfiq. Up to 17 other PUK detainees were reportedly executed in October in various areas under KDP control.

Amnesty International continued to raise serious human rights violations with the government, including the detention of prisoners of conscience; arbitrary arrests and incommunicado detention of political suspects and their relatives; unfair and secret trials; the widespread torture and ill-treatment of prisoners and detainees; "disappearances"; and executions. In April, the organization published a report, *Iraq: State cruelty – branding, amputation and the death penalty*, documenting cases of ear amputation, hand amputation and branding of the forehead. It also raised concern at the widening of the scope of the death penalty to cover at least 18 new offences. Amnesty International urged the government to officially abolish the penalties of amputation and branding. It also called on the government to provide compensation for victims or for families of victims of human rights violations, to commute all outstanding death sentences and to ratify the UN Convention against Torture and Other Cruel, Inhuman or Degrading Treatment or Punishment. In August, the authorities responded by noting that RCC Decree No. 81 ended the practice of ear amputation and branding for army desertion. However, no copy of the decree was made available.

In August, Amnesty International welcomed the release in May of Nadia Muhammad al-'Anaizi and called for the release of all remaining Kuwaiti and other nationals held in Iraq since the end of the Gulf war.

During the year Amnesty International expressed its concern to Kurdish political leaders about human rights abuses committed by their respective parties, including arbitrary arrests, incommunicado detention and unlawful killings. In July, Amnesty International raised with the PUK the cases of two ADM members killed in 'Ain Kawa in May (see above). The PUK told the organization that an investigation into the killings was initiated but that the main perpetrators had fled to government-controlled areas. In September Amnesty International raised with the KDP, among other things, reports that at least 100 members of opposition groups were executed by Iraqi Government forces in August in Arbil, reportedly with the complicity of KDP forces, following door-to-door searches for suspected opponents. In its response the KDP stated that Iraqi intelligence personnel had been responsible for human rights violations committed during the capture of Arbil. It denied allegations that it had assisted the Iraqi forces in committing the violations, and stated that efforts were being made to implement the recommendations submitted in Amnesty International's report, *Iraq: Human rights abuses in Iraqi Kurdistan since 1991* (see *Amnesty International Report 1996*). By the end of the year, none of the Kurdish political groups had responded substantively to Amnesty International concerning the allegations of human rights abuses contained in the report.

IRELAND

Some people arrested in connection with the killing of a police officer alleged that they were ill-treated in police custody.

It was reported that 18 people were arrested in Limerick as part of a police investigation into the killing of *Garda* (police) Detective Jerry McCabe on 7 June; three of them were charged. Jeremiah Sheehy was arrested on 9 June and subsequently charged with membership of the Irish Republican Army (IRA) and firearms possession. It was reported that when Jeremiah Sheehy was transferred to prison after being charged, the prison guards noted his injuries and insisted that he first be taken to a hospital to record these. It was subsequently reported that the file of the police investigation into the alleged ill-treatment had been submitted to the Director of Public Prosecutions.

John Quinn was arrested on 9 June and subsequently charged with IRA membership and possession of ammunition. At the court hearing on 12 June his lawyer stated that John Quinn had received a number of injuries to the head and body while in custody at Henry Street *Garda* Station in Limerick and that he was suffering from periods of unconsciousness and memory loss as a result. John Quinn had been taken to hospital four times between 9 and 12 June.

Some of those who were released without charge also complained that they had been subjected to physical and psychological ill-treatment while in police custody. A human rights researcher reported that she was threatened with arrest while interviewing some of these people.

In October, Amnesty International urged the government to carry out a full and independent inquiry into all these allegations, and to make public the findings of the inquiry. The organization also expressed concern about the apparent lack of adequate safeguards to prevent the ill-treatment of people held in police custody and during interrogation, including the recording of such interviews and the presence of lawyers during interrogations.

The lack of effective safeguards to prevent the ill-treatment of people held in police custody was also highlighted in a letter Amnesty International wrote to the government in March. The government replied that it was reviewing the provisions regulating detainees' rights to legal assistance and that the electronic recording of interrogations was being pilot-tested at four police stations. In response to Amnesty International's concerns about the effectiveness of the police complaints procedure, the government replied that it was satisfied that the *Garda Siochána* Complaints Board was operating satisfactorily but was reviewing the composition and the operation of the Board in line with recommendations made by the European Committee for the Prevention of Torture and Inhuman or Degrading Treatment or Punishment in its report published in 1995.

ISRAEL
(STATE OF)
AND THE OCCUPIED TERRITORIES

At least 1,600 Palestinians were arrested on security grounds by the Israeli authorities. At least 600 Palestinians and five Jewish Israelis were administratively detained during the year. Prisoners of conscience included at least three conscientious objectors. Other political prisoners included at least 65 Lebanese nationals – including 22 who were held without charge or trial, or after the expiry of their sentences. At least 1,000 Palestinians received trials before Israeli military courts, whose procedures did not meet international fair trial standards. A total of 1,155 Palestinian prisoners were freed in the context of peace agreements, but more than 3,500 others, including 2,000 sentenced to prison terms in previous years, remained held at the end of the year. Torture and ill-treatment of Palestinians during interrogation continued to be systematic and officially sanctioned. At least 80 Palestinians, including 60 civilians were killed by Israeli forces, some in circumstances suggesting extrajudicial executions or other unlawful killings. At least seven houses were destroyed as punishment. Palestinian groups opposed to the peace process carried out deliberate and arbitrary killings of at least 56 Israeli civilians.

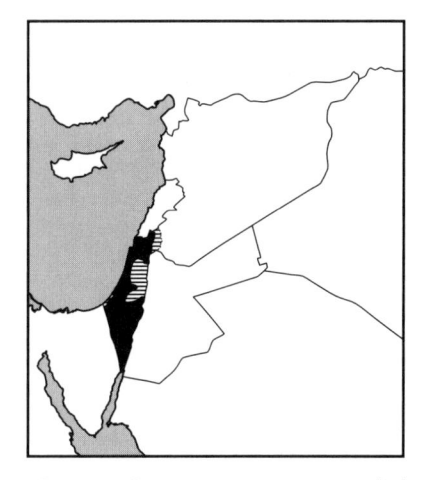

The Israeli Government amended a draft bill which might have legalized torture (see *Amnesty International Report 1996*) and in February withdrew for further consideration a bill which offered impunity to the General Security Service (GSS). In March, an international summit conference was called in Sharm al-Shaikh to oppose "terrorism" following attacks by Palestinian suicide bombers in February and March (see below).

In April, the Israeli Government under Prime Minister Shimon Peres launched a military operation on Lebanon named "Grapes of Wrath" during which Israeli forces unlawfully killed Lebanese civilians (see **Lebanon** entry).

In May, Binyamin Netanyahu, leader of the *Likud* Party, was elected Prime Minister. He formed a government in June in the newly-elected *Knesset* (parliament) based on an alliance between *Likud* and religious parties.

ISRAEL AND THE OCCUPIED TERRITORIES

The implementation of the next stage of the peace accord (the 1995 Oslo II accord) between the Palestinian Authority and Israel, which was to involve Israeli withdrawal from part of Hebron, was delayed after suicide bombings and again delayed after the new government was formed.

The Israeli authorities continued to make extensive use of border closures, confining Palestinians to the Gaza Strip and to Areas A and B of the West Bank (areas over which the Palestinian Authority had joint or exclusive jurisdiction according to the Oslo II accord). Palestinians living in Area B in the West Bank were liable to arrest and detention by both the Israeli and Palestinian security services. Under the new government, existing Israeli settlements in the West Bank were expanded. Attacks continued to be carried out on Palestinians by armed Israeli settlers and on settlers by armed Palestinians.

At least 1,600 Palestinians were arrested on security grounds, including more than 1,000 people arrested after the suicide bombings in February and March.

Renewable administrative detention orders of up to one year were served on more than 600 Palestinians, including prisoners of conscience and possible prisoners of conscience. Administrative detainees were held without charge or trial. Appeals, which took place several weeks after detention and in which the evidence against the detainee was consistently concealed, were frequently boycotted by detainees. Prisoners of conscience included Wissam Rafidi, a journalist, who was arrested in August 1994. Ahmed Qatamesh, said to be a senior official of the Popular Front for the Liberation of Palestine, also remained detained throughout the year; at the end of the year he was serving his seventh administrative detention order, having been continuously detained since 1992 (see previous *Amnesty International Reports*). Five Jewish Israelis from Israeli settlements in the Occupied Territories were also administratively detained for up to two months. They included Aryeh Friedman, accused of being a danger to state security, who was arrested in January and released in March.

Prisoners of conscience included at least three conscientious objectors to military service. For example, Eran Avizkar, a pacifist, was arrested in October and sentenced to 45 days' imprisonment.

Other political detainees held during the year included more than 65 Lebanese nationals imprisoned in Israel. At least 12 Lebanese nationals taken prisoner in South Lebanon during the year were transferred to Israel. They included three Lebanese nationals and one person with dual Israeli and Lebanese nationality abducted in South Lebanon in February and secretly detained in Israel until they were brought to trial in Haifa in October on charges which included conspiring with the enemy. Twenty Lebanese nationals, who had been taken from Lebanon and held in Israel for up to nine years without trial or held beyond expiry of their sentences, continued to be detained. Shaykh 'Abd al-Karim 'Ubayd and Mustafa al-Dirani, abducted from Lebanon in 1989 and 1994, respectively, were held incommunicado, without access to the International Committee of the Red Cross, in an unknown place of detention. In February, the then Israeli Deputy Minister of Defence told Amnesty International that they were being held pending information as to the whereabouts of Ron Arad, an Israeli airman missing in Lebanon since 1986 (see *Amnesty International Reports 1994* to *1996* and **Lebanon** entry).

At least 130 prisoners remained held without charge or trial at the Khiam detention centre in an area of South Lebanon controlled by Israel and the South Lebanon Army (see **Lebanon** entry).

At least 1,000 Palestinians were brought to trial before military courts on charges such as stone-throwing or membership of illegal organizations, and moved to Israel or Area C of the West Bank (areas over which Israel retained sole jurisdiction under the Oslo II accord). These trials, which accepted confessions allegedly extracted by torture or ill-treatment as the main evidence for a conviction, did not meet international standards for fair trial.

A total of 1,155 Palestinian prisoners were released by Israel in January in the context of peace accords between Israeli and the Palestinian Authority. However, more than 3,500 Palestinians, including about 260 administrative detainees and 2,000 people sentenced to prison terms in previous years, remained in prison for security offences at the end of the year.

Torture and ill-treatment of Palestinians continued to be systematic and officially sanctioned by secret guidelines allowing the GSS to use "moderate" physical and psychological pressure. The ministerial committee charged with overseeing the GSS continued to give three-month dispensations allowing the use of "increased physical pressure", the meaning of which remained secret. Violent shaking (*tiltul*) was also allowed with the authorization of the head of the GSS (see *Amnesty International Reports 1995 and 1996*).

A number of High Court decisions allowed the use of physical force against detainees suspected of having information about armed attacks. 'Abd al-Halim Belbaysi said he was subjected to violent shaking, sleep deprivation for up to three days while handcuffed, hooding with dirty sacks, and was made to jump up and down from a crouching position. In January, after he confessed to helping suicide bombers who had caused the death of 21 Israeli nationals in 1995, the High Court of Justice overturned an injunction imposed in December 1995 forbidding the use of physical force. In November, similar injunctions were overturned in two other cases, including that of Muhammad 'Abd al-'Aziz Hamdan, who said he had been hooded with a filthy sack, deprived of sleep for long periods and violently shaken three times.

In June, the Ministry of Justice announced that an interrogator who had shaken 'Abd al-Samad Harizat, who died as a result of violent shaking in April 1995 (see *Amnesty International Report 1996*), had been acquitted on most counts by a disciplinary court and returned to his post. He was said to have been convicted of "not carrying out his duty", but no information was given as to what this entailed.

Mordechai Vanunu remained held in solitary confinement for his 10th successive year (see previous *Amnesty International Reports*). Avraham Klingberg, a 78-year-old physician held since 1983 on charges of spying for the former Soviet Union, was refused a reduction of his 20-year sentence on health grounds (see *Amnesty International Reports 1994 to 1996*).

At least 80 Palestinians, including 60 civilians, were shot dead by Israeli forces. Some were shot in armed clashes; others were killed in circumstances suggesting extrajudicial executions or other unlawful use of lethal force. Yahya 'Ayyash, an engineer said to have made suicide bombs, was killed with a booby-trapped mobile telephone in January. The killing was said to have been carried out by the GSS; the Israeli Government neither accepted responsibility nor denied involvement. In September, 65 Palestinians (including 37 members of the Palestinian security forces), 16 Israelis (all members of the security forces) and one Egyptian national were killed when Israeli security forces opened fire on demonstrators and some members of the Palestinian Security forces returned fire. The Israeli forces used helicopter gunships which on some occasions reportedly shot at crowds. Palestinians unlawfully killed included 'Ayman al-Dakaydak, Ibrahim Ghanem and Jawad Bazalamit, who were shot with rubber bullets or live ammunition outside the al-Aqsa Mosque in Jerusalem in circumstances where the lives of the security forces were not in danger.

The security forces continued to enjoy virtual impunity for past human rights violations. In November, four members of an undercover unit of the Israeli Defence Force were each fined one agora (about half a US cent) for "negligently causing the death" in 1993 of Iyad Amali, a passenger in a car which had stopped at a checkpoint.

In March, the Israeli army carried out the punitive destruction of at least seven houses of Palestinians accused of involvement in suicide bombings. Among them was the house in Rafat village of the wife of Yahya 'Ayyash; he had been killed in January. Other houses were sealed.

Palestinian groups opposed to the peace process carried out deliberate and arbitrary killings. Armed attacks by such groups resulted in the deaths of at least 70 Israeli nationals, including at least 56 civilians. A total of 59 people were killed in Jerusalem and Tel Aviv and outside Ashkelon in February and March by four suicide bombers belonging to *Hamas* and Islamic *Jihad* (see **Palestinian Authority** entry).

In February, an Amnesty International delegation met members of the Israeli Government, including the Minister of Justice and the Deputy Minister of Defence. Throughout the year, Amnesty International condemned human rights violations, including torture and unlawful killings, and called for the release or fair trial of administrative detainees. In July,

Amnesty International published a report, *Israel/Lebanon: Unlawful killings during operation "Grapes of Wrath"*; in August it published, *"Under constant medical supervision": Torture, ill-treatment and the health professions in Israel and the Occupied Territories*, which expressed concern about the role of medical professionals in interrogation centres where detainees suffer torture.

In an oral statement to the UN Commission on Human Rights in March, Amnesty International stressed that sustained peace and security could only be built on the basis of respect for human rights. In November, the UN Committee against Torture invited Israel to submit a special report on the implications of the High Court of Justice decision the same month allowing the use of physical force.

Amnesty International condemned the deliberate and arbitrary killing of civilians by armed opposition groups and called on such groups to respect fundamental principles of humanitarian law.

ITALY

There were further allegations of ill-treatment by law enforcement officers, and numerous prison officers were involved in criminal proceedings relating to alleged torture and ill-treatment of prison inmates in previous years.

Reform of existing legislation governing conscientious objection to compulsory military service, under consideration by successive legislatures since 1988 (see *Amnesty International Reports 1989* to *1996*), had still not received final parliamentary approval by the end of the year. The bill before parliament in 1996, substantially similar to the texts of previous bills, included proposals to broaden the grounds on which conscientious objector status might be granted but did not recognize the right to claim conscientious objector status during military service.

There were further allegations of ill-treatment by law enforcement officers; many concerned people of non-European ethnic origin and were often accompanied by reports of racist insults. In February, Grace Patrick Akpan, a medical student of Nigerian origin, lodged a complaint alleging that two police officers who stopped her for an identity check in Catanzaro, Calabria, verbally abused and physically ill-treated her on the street, in their car and in a police station, where her requests for medical assistance were refused. She stated that when she informed them that she was an Italian citizen married to a *carabiniere* officer and that her identity papers could be retrieved from her nearby apartment, they told her that a black woman could not be an Italian citizen and radioed the police station to say they were bringing in a prostitute. She was released from custody after a police inspector from the Foreigners' Bureau, a relative, confirmed her identity. Within hours she was admitted to hospital where she remained for two weeks receiving treatment for a neck injury and various cuts and bruises. The police accused her of refusing to identify herself and of striking and scratching one of the officers. In December, the police officers were committed for trial on charges of threatening and causing serious bodily harm to Grace Patrick Akpan, while she was ordered to stand trial for refusing to identify herself to a public official, for insulting and resisting police officers and for causing one of them bodily harm.

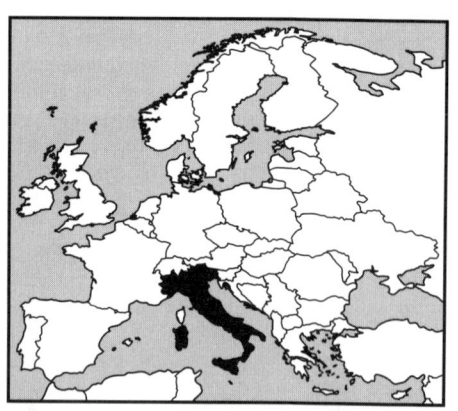

Some official investigations into alleged ill-treatment appeared to lack thoroughness. In March, Edward Adjei Loundens, a Ghanaian citizen normally resident in Denmark, alleged that he had been detained overnight and subjected to an unprovoked physical assault by around seven police officers at Leonardo da Vinci international airport, near Rome, while in transit between Denmark and Ghana in December 1995. In a written account of the incident, which he lodged with Italian diplomatic authorities, he stated that one police officer head-butted him and others beat him, some using their guns, in the stomach and on his side. He claimed that other travellers witnessed the assault but were threatened with a gun when they tried to intervene. He suffered various injuries, including the dislocation of a facial bone, which resulted in disfigurement and reduced hearing in his right ear, affecting his career as a professional musician. His allegations were supported by a medical certificate issued in Ghana in January and by photographs, showing marked facial swelling, apparently taken at Leonardo da Vinci airport by a Polish traveller who had witnessed the assault.

In June, the Public Security Department of the Ministry of the Interior stated that, as his name was very similar to that of a Ghanaian citizen who was the subject of an expulsion order from Italy, the police had detained Edward Adjei Loundens in order to carry out a full identity check. This confirmed that he possessed a valid transit visa. The Department said that the attitude of the police had been "marked by the utmost institutional propriety, thus necessarily ruling out any racial prejudice or violent and oppressive behaviour". However, the Department failed to explain how it had investigated the allegations of ill-treatment and gave no indication that any steps had been taken to obtain evidence from the Polish traveller, whose name and address were available, or from friends who travelled with Edward Adjei Loundens and saw him immediately before and after his detention, or to obtain further forensic evidence from doctors who examined him in Ghana and Denmark.

There were developments in some criminal proceedings relating to cases of alleged ill-treatment by law enforcement officers in previous years.

Voghera's Public Prosecutor asked the competent judge to dismiss Ben Moghrem Abdelwahab's complaint that *carabinieri* officers had ill-treated and racially insulted him, and forced him to sign an unread statement at gunpoint in September 1995 (see *Amnesty International Report 1996*). Ben Moghrem Abdelwahab contested the Prosecutor's request and asked the judge to order further relevant inquiries, including interviews with friends and hospital doctors who saw him immediately after his release from custody.

However, in September, the judge endorsed the Prosecutor's request and dismissed the complaint.

A judicial investigation into the complaint of ill-treatment lodged by Salvatore Rossello against *carabinieri* officers in Barcellona Pozzo di Gotto, Sicily, in June 1995 (see *Amnesty International Report 1996*), had not concluded by the end of the year. In the course of the investigation the *carabinieri* accused him of insulting them at the time of arrest. However, in August the judicial authorities apparently ruled that there were no grounds for bringing such a charge and dismissed the *carabinieri*'s complaint.

A number of criminal proceedings relating to alleged torture and ill-treatment by prison officers, dating back as far as 1992 and subject to many delays, were still open. There was concern that the investigation into the alleged ill-treatment of Marcello Alessi in December 1992 had not been conducted either promptly or impartially. The trial hearing of a San Michele prison officer charged with causing him bodily harm did not open until October – almost four years after the complaint had been lodged. Marcello Alessi was ordered to appear as a defendant at the same hearing to answer a charge of insulting the officer during the December 1992 incident. However, in May 1994 he had already been tried and sentenced to six months' imprisonment for insulting the officer and using violence against him during the December 1992 incident. The 1994 trial, which apparently failed to call witnesses on Marcello Alessi's behalf or take into account all available evidence, was the result of a complaint lodged by the prison officer some 24 hours after Marcello Alessi had lodged his own. The hearing of Marcello Alessi's appeal against the 1994 sentence was postponed from November to January 1997.

In March, some 65 prison officers and the former prison director went on trial in connection with the alleged systematic ill-treatment of inmates of Secondigliano prison (see *Amnesty International Reports 1994* to *1996*). The result was not known at the end of the year. The opening of the court hearing in the trial of six other Secondigliano prison officers, indicted on various additional charges in connection with the alleged ill-treatment, was apparently delayed owing to the enormous backlog of cases pending before the Naples Tribunal. There was still no news concerning the outcome of a judicial investigation opened into the alleged ill-treatment of inmates of Pianosa Island prison in 1992 (see *Amnesty International Reports 1993* to *1996*).

Amnesty International sought information from the authorities about the progress and outcome of criminal investigations into allegations of torture and ill-treatment. In October, in response to the organization's inquiries about the steps taken to investigate Edward Adjei Loundens' allegations, the Ministry of Justice stated that it had referred the case to Rome Public Prosecutor's Office. Amnesty International also expressed concern about the conduct of judicial proceedings relating to the alleged ill-treatment of Marcello Alessi. At the opening of the scheduled court hearing in October, the judge ordered further investigation into the circumstances of the case and adjourned the hearing to December 1997.

JAMAICA

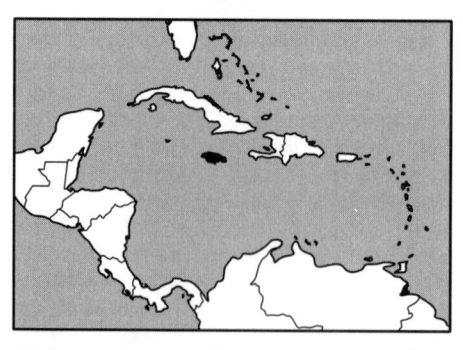

At least two people were sentenced to death and at least 61 others remained under sentence of death. There were no executions. One person was killed by police in disputed circumstances.

In July, the UN Human Rights Committee found that Jamaica had violated the rights of Rickly Burrell under the International Covenant on Civil and Political Rights (ICCPR). Rickly Burrell had been killed by prison guards in 1993 while under sentence of death (see *Amnesty International Report 1994*). The Committee found that the killing was in violation of Article 6 of the ICCPR, which states: "No one shall be arbitrarily deprived of his life". The Committee also found that Rickly Burrell's rights under Article 14 of the ICCPR had been violated, in that he was "not effectively represented on appeal" by legal counsel; his appeal lawyer had stated in court that the grounds for the appeal against his conviction and death sentence were without merit.

In August, in a ruling on the case of death-row inmate Errol Johnson, the chairperson of the UN Human Rights Committee criticized Jamaica for having refused for the previous 10 years to comply with its obligations to report under article 40 of the ICCPR. This had prevented the Committee from considering whether the death penalty was being applied in accordance with the strict limits imposed by the ICCPR.

At least two new death sentences were imposed, of which one was later rescinded. Elvis Martin was sentenced to death in January, and Kevin Mykoo in February, both for murders committed in 1995. In October, the Court of Appeal overturned Elvis Martin's conviction, finding that the judge had failed to adequately direct the jury. At least 61 prisoners remained under sentence of death but no executions were carried out.

In October, Keith Francis was killed by police officers in disputed circumstances. Police claimed that Keith Francis had been shot dead in an exchange of gunfire with the police; according to several eyewitnesses, police officers shot him after he had been captured and disarmed.

In November, Amnesty International wrote to the Minister of National Security and Justice asking for information on the shooting of Keith Francis and to be informed of the outcome of any official investigations. No reply had been received by the end of the year.

In December, Amnesty International wrote to the authorities asking that no executions be carried out.

JAPAN

Conditions of detention for all prisoners remained harsh, often amounting to cruel, inhuman and degrading treatment. Reports persisted of ill-treatment of prisoners and of foreign nationals detained at border points. Ninety prisoners remained under sentence of death. Six prisoners were executed.

Prime Minister Murayama Tomiichi resigned in January and was replaced by Hashimoto Ryutaro, leader of the Liberal Democratic Party (LDP), one of three parties in the ruling coalition. General elections in October gave the LDP enough seats to form a minority government, still led by Hashimoto Ryutaro, without entering into a coalition but with outside support from its former coalition partners, the Social Democratic Party of Japan and the New Party Sakigake. The new LDP cabinet pledged itself to a program of administrative reform, particularly in economic affairs. The Minister of Justice, Matsuura Isao, stated that his priority would be to fight corruption.

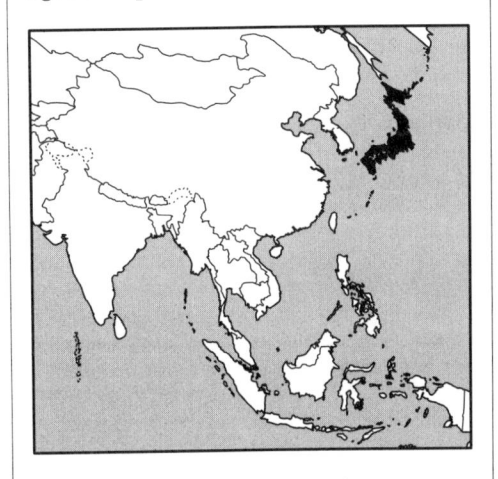

In February, the UN Special Rapporteur on violence against women published a report on the government's responsibility towards so-called "comfort women" – women forced into prostitution by the Japanese army during the Second World War. About 200,000 women, mostly from east and southeast Asia, were subjected to sexual slavery during the war. The Special Rapporteur's report called on the Japanese Government to acknowledge moral and legal responsibility for human rights violations against these women, to apologize, to provide compensation and to bring to justice those responsible for the recruitment and ill-treatment of the women. The government strongly criticized the Special Rapporteur's report and stood by its 1995 decision not to use state funds to pay compensation. In August, a private fund which had been set up in 1995 at the government's instigation (see *Amnesty International Report 1996*) started to send payments to some of the women. Most of them refused to accept the payments, continuing to criticize the government's refusal to accept moral and legal responsibility.

Conditions of detention remained harsh and humiliating for all prisoners, and often constituted cruel, inhuman or degrading treatment. Among other rules, prisoners were not allowed to look at or speak to each other except during short rest periods, and were forbidden to speak to guards unless invited to do so. Minor infringements of the rules could lead to weeks in solitary confinement, where prisoners were often forced to sit still in a specified position for hours on end. Punishment could also involve solitary confinement in "protective cells" with padded walls, in which prisoners had to wear, sometimes for days on end, special belts which prevented them from moving their arms. Lawyers reported that more than 100 prisoners had initiated lawsuits claiming government compensation for alleged ill-treatment and excessively humiliating or harsh treatment. In September, a prisoner was awarded compensation by the Kumamoto District Court for the "mental pain" he suffered when the Kumamoto Prison authorities refused him permission to mail more than one letter per month to his daughter. In October, the parents of a man who died in a "protective cell" in July initiated legal proceedings for compensation, on the grounds that his human rights had been violated. The detainee, who was serving a two-month sentence for a driving offence, died a few days after being put in a "protective cell" in Hamada, Shimane Prefecture, reportedly as a punishment for being "noisy and violent". The outcome of the proceedings was not known by the end of the year.

Foreign nationals alleged that they were ill-treated while detained at border points pending expulsion. In October, a Danish national of Iranian origin was reportedly detained at Narita Airport, near Tokyo, when a border control official questioned the authenticity of his Danish passport. When he refused to sign a statement admitting that he was carrying forged documents, he was reportedly slapped, beaten about the head with a heavy cardboard roll and kicked in the legs by an immigration officer. He was also forced to pay a "fee" for staying in the transit area where he was detained. He was held for 24 hours and then deported to Malaysia.

Six people were executed during the year; all had spent more than 10 years awaiting execution and claimed that they were not informed of their right to the assistance of a lawyer during pre-trial interrogation. In July, Ishida Mikio was executed in Tokyo, and Yoshiaki Sugimoto and Yokoyama Kazumi in the southern city of Fukuoka. Ishida Mikio had been sentenced to death in 1982 for robbery and murder; his sentence was confirmed by the Supreme Court in 1988. He had unsuccessfully sought a retrial, claiming, among other things, that he had been given no access to a lawyer in the early stages of his pre-trial detention. Yoshiaki Sugimoto and Yokoyama Kazumi had also been sentenced to death in 1982. In December, Hirata Mitsunari, Imai Yoshito and Satoru Noguchi were executed in Tokyo. The new Minister of Justice broke with a tradition of secrecy by acknowledging that he had signed the warrant of execution concerning the three men hanged in December. However, no prior notice of the execution was given to the lawyers or relatives of the prisoners.

Ninety prisoners remained under sentence of death at the end of the year, including some 52 whose sentences were confirmed by the Supreme Court. Four prisoners had their death sentence commuted to life imprisonment during the year. Three death sentences were passed by district courts during the year, but they had not been confirmed by the Supreme Court by the end of the year.

Amnesty International expressed regret at the execution of the six men in July and December and criticized the secrecy surrounding the death penalty.

JORDAN

Five prisoners of conscience arrested in previous years continued to be held. Hundreds of people, including prisoners of conscience, were detained for political reasons during the year, among them more than 500 people arrested after violent anti-government protests in August. Political detainees were held incommunicado in prolonged preventive detention for up to 40 days. More than 100 political detainees were sentenced to prison terms, some after unfair trials before the State Security Court. Reports of torture and ill-treatment, particularly of detainees arrested for common law offences, continued. One person died in custody, allegedly after torture or ill-treatment. At least nine people were executed and 21 others were sentenced to death. At least five asylum-seekers were sent back to countries where they were at risk of torture.

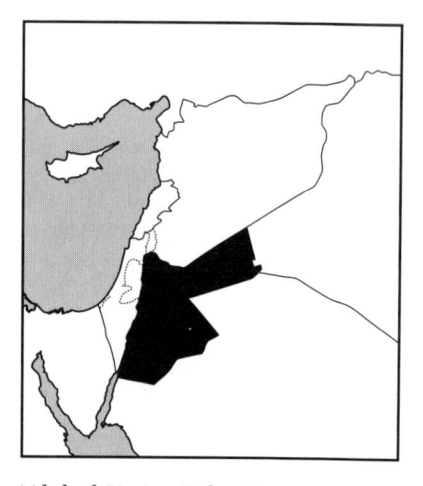

'Abd al-Karim Kabariti was appointed Prime Minister in February by King Hussein bin Talal. He promised to "respect human rights and the freedom of the press". In August, demonstrations and riots against a doubling of the price of bread took place in Krak, Tafileh, Amman, the capital, and other towns.

A total of 107 detainees were released in royal amnesties in November and December.

Prisoners of conscience who remained in prison during the year included 'Ata' Abu'l-Rushta, spokesperson for the *Hizb al-Tahrir fi'l-'Urdun* (LPJ), Liberation Party in Jordan, a party seeking to re-establish the Islamic Caliphate, was sentenced to three years' imprisonment in February by the State Security Court for lese-majesty under Article 195(1) of the Penal Code in connection with an interview he had given to the newspaper *al-Hiwar* (see *Amnesty International Report 1996*). The statements on which the charges were based did not advocate violence. Leith Shubeilat, head of the Engineers' Union and an Islamist leader, who had been arrested in December 1995 (see *Amnesty International Report 1996*) and sentenced to three years' imprisonment in March by the State Security Court on charges that included lese-majesty, was released in November when King Hussein bin Talal came personally to the prison and granted him an amnesty. Four other members of the LPJ, sentenced in previous years for distributing leaflets, remained held as prisoners of conscience (see *Amnesty International Report 1995*).

Prisoners of conscience included at least five journalists who were held in detention on remand for up to 10 days on charges such as lese-majesty or inciting sectarian or ethnic disorder. Hilmi Asmar, editor of the newspaper *al-Sabil*, was held for nine days in September before being released without charge after publishing a report which alleged that members of the internal security service had tortured detainees.

Other prisoners of conscience included members of various political opposition groups, including the Arab Socialist Ba'th Party and *Hashad*, the Jordan People's Democratic Party, arrested at the time of the violent anti-government protests in August and charged with inciting riots.

Hundreds of people arrested on political grounds were held incommunicado for up to 40 days. They included members of groups opposed to the peace process with Israel and more than 500 people accused of inciting or participating in the August bread riots. Walid Ahmad Taylakh, arrested in March, was held for 37 days in incommunicado detention in the General Intelligence Department (GID) detention centre, where he was allegedly tortured by methods including *falaqa* (beatings on the soles of the feet). 'Umar Abu Ragheb, a board member of the Arab Organization for Human Rights in Jordan, was held incommunicado in the GID headquarters in Amman and released in August. Many of those arrested were released without charge. Others were charged with offences including lese-majesty or destruction of property.

At least 120 people were brought to trial for political offences. They included journalists, most of whose trials ended in acquittals. Among them were Jihad al-Khazen, director of the newspaper *al-Hayat* in the United Kingdom, who was tried *in absentia*, and Salameh Ne'mat, a journalist on the newspaper. They were brought to trial in April before the Court of First Instance in Amman and acquitted on four charges, including slander, after writing an article stating that a number of journalists and officials were on the payroll of the Iraqi authorities.

Those brought before the State Security Court on charges involving political violence included seven members of an Islamist group known as the *Bay'a al-Imam* (Allegiance to the Imam) who were tried on charges including manufacturing explosives (see *Amnesty International Report 1996*). Six others, tried in the same case but released on bail, were charged with lese-majesty. At a session in June all retracted their confessions, stating that they had been subjected to physical and psychological torture during more than six months' pre-trial incommunicado detention in the GID headquarters in Amman. The judge agreed to hear evidence on alleged falsification of arrest dates to conceal their prolonged detention. In November, nine defendants were sentenced to between two years' and life imprisonment and four were acquitted. Salem Bakhit and Ahmad Khaled, accused of attacking a French diplomat in March 1995 (see *Amnesty International Report 1996*), were sentenced to life imprisonment with hard labour and 10 years' imprisonment respectively on charges which included "conspiring to carry out terrorist actions".

Reports of torture or ill-treatment continued. Most such reports concerned those held by the police, the police of the capital or the preventive security. However, six supporters of *Hamas* arrested in March and April alleged that they were tortured in the headquarters of the GID by being severely beaten, especially by *falaqa*, after arrest. Medical certificates of four of the detainees, who were released without charge in May and June, showed injuries consistent with their allegations. A complaint about the alleged torture was made to the military public prosecutor but no action was known to have been taken by the end of the year.

Dozens of those arrested in August after riots in Krak and other towns stated that they were beaten after arrest by police or preventive security in local police stations or in Swaqa Prison. One person, arrested in Tafileh, said that he was tortured by the preventive security police with electric shocks, beatings and suspensions in a painful position. He was brought before the military public prosecutor after 23 days' incommunicado detention. He stated that he made a complaint about his treatment, but was not informed about any action taken.

Yunus Abu Dawleh died in December, three hours after he had been arrested by the police in Jabal Hussein, Amman. His body reportedly showed signs of bruising on the shoulder and neck; however, the medical certificate stated that he died of "heart disease".

No investigation was carried out into the alleged extrajudicial execution of Mahmud Khalifeh in July 1995 (see *Amnesty International Report 1996*).

At least nine people were executed during the year. They included 'Uthman 'Ali Abu Lawi and Sabri 'Abdallah Abu Fawdeh, both convicted of raping minors. These were the first executions for rape, which had been made a capital offence under an amendment to the Penal Code in 1988. At least 21 people were sentenced to death including Muntasser Rajab Abu Zayd, who was allegedly beaten and deprived of sleep, together with his wife, who was not a suspect. His confession reportedly formed the basis of his conviction for murder. Death sentences on 18 prisoners were commuted, including the death sentences imposed in 1995 on eight prisoners known as the "Arab Afghan" group. They had been convicted of attempting to destabilize the Jordanian Government by carrying out armed attacks on cinemas. Death sentences imposed on the eight in 1994 had been overturned by the Court of Cassation in March 1995 and reimposed by the State Security Court in July 1995 (see *Amnesty International Reports 1995 and 1996*).

Asylum-seekers continued to be returned to countries where they were at risk of torture. They included Hassan Adam 'Ali, a Sudanese national and a political activist, who had lived in Jordan since 1993. He was arrested by Jordanian security officials in January and deported to Khartoum, Sudan, where he was detained for six weeks. A deserter from the Iraqi army deported to Jordan from the United Arab Emirates in June was deported the same month to Iraq where he was arrested and may have suffered torture or amputation of the ear as punishment.

In correspondence with the Jordanian Government, Amnesty International raised concerns about continuing executions and the expansion of the number of crimes punishable by the death penalty; the *refoulement* of asylum-seekers; and the detention of prisoners of conscience. The GID responded on specific questions concerning individual detainees and sent a response to the *Amnesty International Report 1996*.

KAZAKSTAN

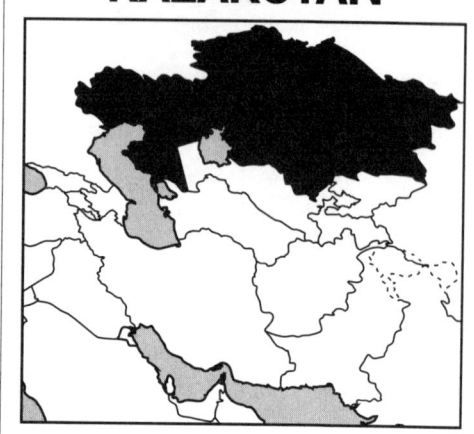

A Cossack leader imprisoned apparently for political reasons was released. Another Cossack activist whose detention appeared to be politically motivated was allegedly tortured. There were allegations of widespread torture and ill-treatment in police custody and in the penitentiary system. Prison conditions amounting to ill-treatment reportedly resulted in a number of deaths in custody. At least 50 people were sentenced to death and there were at least 12 executions.

A new bicameral parliament was inaugurated by President Nursultan Nazarbayev in January. In the same month, the President created, by decree, a Constitutional Council to replace the Constitutional Court which he had effectively disbanded in 1995.

Nikolai Gunkin, a Cossack leader who had been sentenced in late 1995 to a three-month prison term for "organizing an unsanctioned meeting", amid allegations that the prosecution was politically motivated (see *Amnesty International Report 1996*), was released in January at the end of his sentence.

In August, police in Almaty, the capital, arrested Nina Sidorova, a Cossack activist and associate of Nikolai Gunkin. She was charged with defamation of the judge at Nikolai Gunkin's trial and, in relation to incidents which occurred in 1995, hooliganism and assault of procuracy officials. There were allegations that the charges were brought for political reasons following Nina Sidorova's attempt on the day of her arrest to obtain legal registration for an organization promoting the interests of Kazakstan's Cossack minority. Nina Sidorova was detained for over a month, during which time she was allegedly severely beaten. A sufferer from acute claustrophobia, she was also ill-treated by being placed periodically in small, unventilated and unlit punishment cells. In September, Nina Sidorova's lawyer, Maria Larshina, was assaulted outside her home by an unknown man, in an incident reminiscent of the treatment of the wife of Nikolai Gunkin's lawyer in 1995 (see *Amnesty International Report 1996*). In December, Nina Sidorova was given a two-year prison sentence but was immediately amnestied and released.

Information was received about other cases of alleged torture and ill-treatment in police custody and in pre-trial detention. One such case concerned Valery Zippa, who allegedly had been severely beaten during interrogation by police in 1994, and as a result required surgery to remove his spleen. Information was also received about torture and ill-treatment in the penitentiary system, including allegations that guards at a prison in Arkalyk beat prisoners, who then mutilated themselves with knives in protest. These and other prisoners also complained of unwarranted confinement in punishment cells, sometimes in freezing temperatures or complete darkness.

Poor conditions amounting to ill-treatment in pre-trial detention and in penitentiaries were also reported. In April, officials publicly admitted that Kazakstan's prisons were overcrowded and disease-ridden. Prisoners suffering from tuberculosis were allegedly not segregated from the rest of the prison population, and it was even alleged that, as a form of punishment for misbehaviour, officers would deliberately expose prisoners to the risk of infection by placing them in cells containing prisoners seriously ill with tuberculosis. Deaths of prisoners from wasting conditions associated with starvation were also alleged. Information was received early in the year about harsh conditions in a prison for male juveniles near Almaty, where at least four inmates were known to have died in the latter part of 1995, apparently as a consequence of their treatment there.

In June, the authorities declared an amnesty for nearly 20,000 prisoners, about one quarter of the entire prison population, because of budget constraints, but in August it was reported that the number of prisoners to be released had been reduced to around 8,500, for undisclosed reasons.

The use of the death penalty remained extensive. At least 50 people were sentenced to death and at least 12 executions took place. Five death sentences were commuted during the year.

Amnesty International sought further information about the basis for the charges against Nina Sidorova. The organization called for an investigation into allegations that she had been ill-treated by police, and for an investigation into the assault on Maria Larshina. It also called on the authorities to investigate all allegations of torture and ill-treatment, and to take effective steps to end the problem of poor prison conditions amounting to ill-treatment. Amnesty International called for an investigation into the deaths in detention of male juvenile prisoners in Almaty. The organization continued to call for commutation of all death sentences and the complete abolition of the death penalty.

In response to a statement by Amnesty International in March deploring the very high number of death sentences and executions reported for 1995 (see *Amnesty International Report 1996*), officials publicly rejected the figure of 101 executions cited by the organization, claiming that the true number for 1995 was 63, but did not provide detailed information to support this.

In February and March, an Amnesty International delegate visited Kazakstan and held talks with government and law enforcement officials and members of the judiciary. In July, the organization published a report, *Kazakstan: Ill-treatment and the death penalty – a summary of concerns*.

KENYA

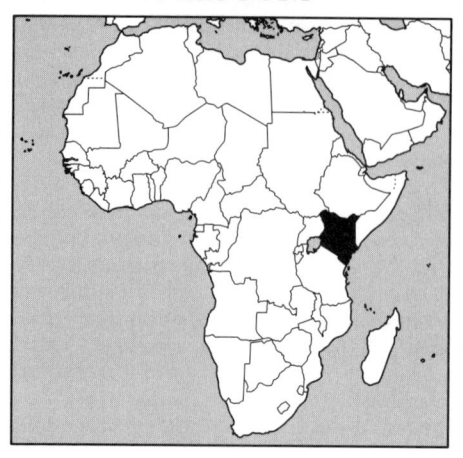

At least three prisoners of conscience were held throughout the year following an unfair trial; one of them was released on bail in December in order to receive medical treatment abroad. At least 50 more were detained for periods of several hours or days, including human rights activists, journalists, members of opposition parties, students and a priest. There were reports of torture, including rape, and ill-treatment of prisoners. At least five people reportedly died in custody as a result of torture. Sentences of caning continued to be imposed. Prison conditions were harsh, amounting to cruel, inhuman or degrading treatment, and scores of prisoners died during the year. The leader of a human rights organization was killed in suspicious circumstances. At least 63 people were sentenced to death and over 739 people were under sentence of death at the end of the year. There were no reports of executions. At least seven refugees were arbitrarily detained for nearly four weeks and over 900 were forcibly returned to Somalia.

There were sporadic outbreaks of inter-ethnic clashes in which at least 15 people were killed (see Amnesty International Reports 1993 to 1995). Allegations persisted that some of the violence was instigated or tolerated by the government. By-election campaigns were marred by violence.

In May, President Daniel arap Moi appointed a Standing Committee on Human Rights to investigate human rights violations within a limited mandate. The Committee's first report, submitted to the government in December, was not made public.

In February, the charge against Mbuthi Gathenji, a lawyer, of publishing material "likely to cause fear and alarm" was dropped. The charge related to witness statements taken by police from his office which implicated senior government officials and others in ethnic violence in Narok district in 1993 (see Amnesty International Report 1995).

In June, the ban on the Centre for Law and Research International was lifted following an appeal in the High Court (see Amnesty International Report 1996). In August and September, respectively, the premises of Fotoform Printers and those of a newspaper it prints, The People, were fire bombed. Fotoform had previously been attacked in 1993 (see Amnesty International Report 1994).

In December, the Commissioner of Police was dismissed following a public outcry at the shooting by police of three unarmed students during demonstrations at Egerton and Kenyatta universities.

Human rights and other non-governmental organizations, journalists and other government critics continued to be harassed by the authorities. Meetings organized by opposition politicians, church groups and women's organizations were disrupted by the police, sometimes violently. In February, a meeting of nearly 100 women organized by the League of Women Voters at Bondo Catholic Church was broken up by armed police who threatened them with violence if they did not leave.

Three prisoners of conscience remained in prison following an unfair trial. They were Koigi wa Wamwere, a human rights activist, journalist and former member of parliament, his brother Charles Kuria Wamwere, and G.G. Njuguna Ngengi, who were sentenced to four years' imprisonment and six strokes of the cane for robbery in October 1995. In February, they were moved from solitary confinement. In July, their application for bail pending appeal was dismissed. The appeal had not been heard by the end of the year and defence lawyers were still awaiting a transcript of the proceedings of the trial (see Amnesty International Reports 1994 to 1996). In October and November, the three men were taken to hospital on separate occasions for tests. They were chained to the bed for 24 hours a day and Koigi wa Wamwere was guarded by dozens of prison warders. Friends and relatives were initially prevented from visiting him, but after a protest by members of the human rights group Release Political Prisoners (RPP) his mother was allowed to see him for 15 minutes. On 13 December Koigi wa Wamwere was released on bail in order to receive medical treatment abroad.

At least 50 people were detained solely for their non-violent political activities. The majority were held for several hours or days before being released without charge, but at least 22 were held for two weeks before being released on bail. Their trial had not started by the end of the year. In March, Reverend Daniel Githu Ugunyu was arrested and beaten by police, apparently after being mistaken for a wanted criminal. In July, 21 members of the RPP, including three women, were detained for two weeks following an attempt to hold a three-day cultural event in memory of Karimi Nduthu, Secretary General of the RPP, who was murdered in suspicious circumstances in March. They were charged with holding an illegal meeting and possessing seditious documents and were released on bail. Their trial had not started by the end of the year. In September, the deputy mayor of Homa Bay and five others were detained for five hours for holding an illegal meeting.

At least six journalists were arrested during the year and several others were reportedly beaten by police and members of the youth wing of the ruling Kenya African National Union (KANU) party. In January, Evans Kanini, the *Daily Nation* correspondent in Eldoret, was arrested and held for three days in connection with an article he had written on torture by police. The article included his own experience of torture in November 1995. In February, he was convicted of creating a disturbance and sentenced to one year's probation. In April, he was attacked and threatened with death by over 20 members of the KANU youth wing. In March, John Wanjala, another *Daily Nation* journalist, was reportedly beaten with whips and kicked for an hour by police, and suffered injuries to his chest and legs. In May, Njehu Gatabaki, a journalist, publisher and opposition member of parliament, was arrested and held for nine days after he failed, because of ill health, to attend court on a sedition charge dating from May 1995 (see *Amnesty International Report 1996*). Shortly after his release, he spent two weeks in hospital suffering from severe hypertension. The case of Father Charles Kamori and three seminarians, charged with incitement and possession of a banned publication, *Inooro*, had not come to court by end of the year (see *Amnesty International Report 1996*).

Disturbances at universities over student loans and conditions resulted in arrests of students; dozens of students were reportedly beaten when police broke up meetings. In February, Suba Churchill Mechack, Chairman of the unregistered Kenya Universities Student Organization at Egerton University, was arrested and charged with trespassing on the university campus. He had been arrested on three occasions in 1995, reportedly tortured by the police and expelled from the university. Following the arrest of Suba Churchill Mechack and the suspension or expulsion of 11 others, students boycotted classes and over 200 police officers were drafted into the university campus. According to reports, student meetings were violently disrupted by the police. At least one female student at Egerton University was raped by the police and another, Doreen Kinoti, suffered serious back injuries after jumping out of a first-floor window of a student hall while attempting to escape.

In March, Josephine Nyawira Ngengi, a member of the RPP and a prisoner of conscience, was released after being found not guilty of robbery with violence. She had been held for nearly two years following the repeated adjournment of her trial (see *Amnesty International Reports 1995* and *1996*). In July, she was arrested again, detained for two weeks with other members of the RPP and charged with them (see above). Geoffrey Kuria Kariuki (see previous *Amnesty International Reports*) remained on bail throughout the year.

In May, Wang'ondu Kariuki, a prisoner of conscience, failed to have his case concerning the violation of his right to freedom of expression referred to a constitutional court. He appealed to the High Court against the decision. He had been charged with belonging to an illegal organization after being detained incommunicado for seven days and tortured (see *Amnesty International Report 1996*). Wang'ondu Kariuki remained on bail throughout the year. In June, Joseph Baraza Wekesa, aged 69, was released on appeal after his sentence was reduced to two years. He had been sentenced to six years' imprisonment in 1995 for membership of an illegal organization. He was one of at least 50 men arrested by police in Bungoma, Western Province, between late 1994 and mid-1995 and reportedly tortured at an unknown detention centre (see *Amnesty International Report 1996*).

Torture and ill-treatment of both men and women continued to be reported throughout Kenya. In May, 20 alleged criminals were reportedly beaten by police in Muranga district, Central Province and one, Noah Njuguna Ndunga, died as a result of his injuries. In November, Solomon Muruli, a student leader, was reportedly arbitrarily detained by police and tortured. He was held for six days before being left unconscious in a church compound in Kiambu district, Central Province. Sentences of caning – a cruel, inhuman and degrading punishment – continued to be imposed by the courts. In July, two men were sentenced to 10 years' imprisonment and 13 strokes of the cane for rape.

At least five people died in custody during the year, apparently as a result of torture. In May, Henry Mutua M'Aritho died, three days after his arrest by Administrative Policemen in Nyambene District. He was reportedly whipped, slapped, kicked and beaten on at least three separate occasions, and on one occasion his legs were burned. In July, Amodoi Achakar Anamilem died while in police custody in Lokichar, Turkana District. According to eye-witnesses, he was beaten in public, then at a disused building and also at the Lokichar Administration Police camp. He was beaten with his own stick and with gun butts, and received kicks and blows to all parts of his body. He had reportedly been arrested after being incorrectly identified as a robber when the police put pressure on the relatives of the real culprit. Following pressure from local human rights groups, the Attorney General ordered an investigation into the incident in August. However, at the end of the year the police officers allegedly responsible for Amodoi Achakar Anamilem's death were still on duty and no public inquiry had taken place.

Conditions were harsh in many prisons, amounting to cruel, inhuman or degrading treatment. There were reports that scores of prisoners died, the majority from infectious diseases resulting from severe overcrowding and shortages of food, clean water and basic medication. A government committee set up to look into reducing the number of custodial sentences had not reported by the end of the year. In October, the President pardoned 4,288 prisoners, but by the end of the year the prison population had increased by over eight thousand to nearly 41,000.

In March, Karimi Nduthu, Secretary General of the RPP, was killed in suspicious circumstances. According to eye-witnesses, the police investigating the incident searched the house, removing Karimi Nduthu's papers, computer, books and typewriter.

Over 70 alleged criminals were killed by police officers during the year. Human rights groups criticized excessive use of force by the police, and the government's failure to investigate killings by police.

Sixty-three people were sentenced to death during the year, including three men who were sentenced to death on appeal, two at the High Court and one at the Court of Appeal. A total of 739 people were on death row at the end of the year. No executions were reported.

In March, seven recognized refugees and several others were detained beyond the legal limit and threatened with *refoulement*. Almost all those arrested were Ethiopian Oromos and members or supporters of the Oromo Liberation Front. They were eventually released in April, following national and international appeals. In July, over 900 Somali refugees were forcibly returned to Somalia by the Kenyan army six days after seeking asylum in Kenya.

In March, the government sent Amnesty International a commentary on the organization's December 1995 report, *Kenya: Torture compounded by the denial of medical care*, which it accused of presenting only generalizations, of containing factual inaccuracies and of failing to acknowledge improvements in the protection of human rights in Kenya in recent years.

Amnesty International continued to appeal to the government to stop the harassment and arrests of human rights activists, journalists, refugees and others. In April, the organization urged that the killing of

Karimi Nduthu be investigated according to international standards, and sent a forensic pathologist to attend his autopsy. Amnesty International representatives visited Kenya twice – in April and in September – and met government officials, civil servants, members of the opposition parties, lawyers, doctors, religious and human rights groups to discuss ways of increasing human rights protection.

KOREA
(DEMOCRATIC PEOPLE'S REPUBLIC OF)

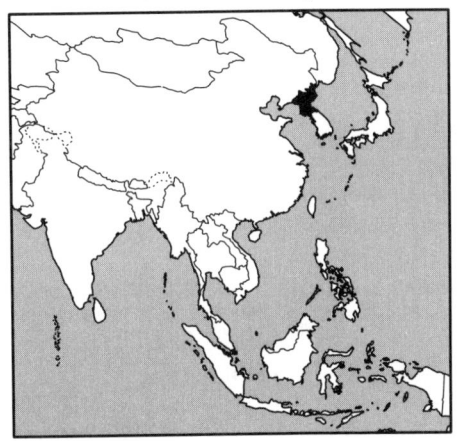

The fate of nationals of the Democratic People's Republic of Korea (North Korea) who had reportedly been detained or killed following their return to North Korea remained unclear. No executions were officially reported, but according to unofficial sources, executions took place.

The positions of President of the Democratic People's Republic of Korea and General Secretary of the ruling Workers' Party of Korea, vacant since the death of former President Kim Il Sung in July 1994, remained unfilled, but it was widely reported that Kim Il Sung's son, Kim Jong Il, had assumed effective leadership. The annual session of the legislature, the Supreme People's Assembly, was cancelled for the second year running. Personnel changes among second-ranking leaders suggested that some powers had shifted to younger officials, with long-serving senior leaders remaining titular holders of leadership posts.

Food shortages resulting from the floods of 1995 continued and heavy rains in July caused malnutrition and disease to spread. The shortages led to renewed international appeals by the authorities for aid from UN agencies and non-governmental organizations. Rations distributed through official channels were reportedly reduced further in the latter part of the year.

Independent monitoring of the human rights situation continued to be hampered by restrictions on visits and on access to impartial information.

North Korea's first periodic report to the UN Human Rights Committee on the implementation of the International Covenant on Civil and Political Rights had not been submitted by the end of the year. The report was almost 10 years overdue.

The fate of North Korean nationals who had reportedly been detained or killed following their return to North Korea remained unclear. Amnesty International received reports during the year that North Korean nationals – including asylum-seekers and forestry workers employed at work sites in Russia until the early 1990s – who did not wish to return to North Korea continued to be subjected to human rights violations and harassment by North Korean and Russian officials. Asylum-seekers and forestry workers who had escaped from work camps reportedly risked detention and forcible return to North Korea; some had allegedly been held in ankle shackles by North Korean officials pending their return. It was unclear whether under the amended Criminal Law of 1995 they still faced detention on their return to North Korea.

The government denied reports that Li Young Son (also referred to as Lee Yen Sen) (see *Amnesty International Report 1996* **Russia** entry), who had been serving a prison sentence in Russia, was imprisoned in September 1995 after being forcibly returned to North Korea before consideration of his claim for refugee status. At the time of his return, Li Young Son was believed to risk further imprisonment under the 1987 Criminal Law, which provided for imprisonment of those who "defected" to a foreign country. According to the authorities, the relevant article of the Criminal Law had been amended in 1995 to restrict punishment for acts such as "defection" to cases where they were committed "with a view to overthrowing the Republic". However, the text of the amended legislation was not made available to Amnesty International, despite repeated requests.

The whereabouts of possible prisoners of conscience Choi Gyong Ho, Choi Yen Dan and Lee Sung Nam, all reported to have been detained in previous years following forcible return to North Korea from Russia (see *Amnesty International Report 1996*), remained unknown.

There were allegations that a North Korean national had been extrajudicially executed in May by North Korean officials after being handed over to them by Russian police. Despite statements by a Russian official confirming the allegations, they were strongly denied by the North Korean authorities. The authorities did not deny that one of their nationals had been returned, but they did not name or give the current whereabouts of that person.

In April, Amnesty International received a photograph of Song Chang Gun (also known as Song Chang Keun), who previous reports suggested had been extrajudicially executed after being handed over to the North Korean authorities in Russia in 1995. The photograph was supposedly taken in North Korea after his return from the Russian Federation in July or August 1995. However, efforts by Amnesty International to contact Song Chang Gun in North Korea were unsuccessful.

Requests for further information about the circumstances surrounding the deaths of former North Korean resident in Japan, Cho Ho Pyong, and Japanese national Shibata Kozo remained unanswered (see *Amnesty International Reports 1995* and *1996*).

No executions were officially reported during the year, although people who had illegally left North Korea alleged that they had taken place.

During the year, Amnesty International sought information from the authorities on the use of "re-education" as a substitute for criminal punishment. According to the 1992 Criminal Procedure Law, amended in 1995, "social education" could be used to "reform" suspects, instead of criminal punishment. The form this "education" took remained unclear; it appeared to involve punishment without trial. Amnesty International also expressed concern about the amended Criminal Procedure Law, which appeared to allow for detention, possibly without trial, under unspecified other laws. The authorities failed to respond.

In February, Amnesty International published a report, *Refoulement of Lee Yen Sen: Fear for safety in North Korea*. In September, the organization published *Democratic People's Republic of Korea/Russian Federation: Pursuit, intimidation and abuse of North Korean refugees and workers*, highlighting reports of human rights violations suffered by North Korean nationals seeking asylum in Russia and expressing concern about the safety of those forcibly returned to North Korea. The report recommended that North Korean nationals in Russia be permitted to seek refugee status and be given adequate protection if their claim was deemed valid, and expressed Amnesty International's opposition to the use of ankle shackles as cruel, inhuman or degrading treatment or punishment. Amnesty International made public the comments received from the North Korean authorities on issues covered by these reports.

KOREA
(REPUBLIC OF)

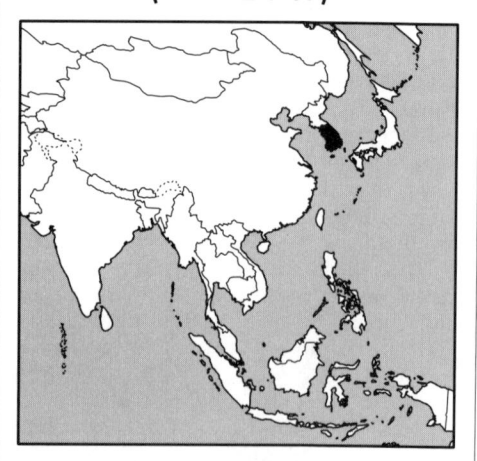

Over 450 people, including prisoners of conscience, were arrested under the National Security Law and at least 150 other political prisoners convicted in previous years remained held. Trade union leaders continued to face arrest under legislation restricting their rights to freedom of expression and association. There were reports of ill-treatment by police. Conditions in some prisons amounted to cruel, inhuman or degrading treatment. Some 50 prisoners remained under sentence of death at the end of year. No executions were reported.

A Commission on Industrial Relations Reform, established by President Kim Young-sam in May, made recommendations for the revision of labour legislation.

Labour and security legislation adopted in December by the National Assembly, without the knowledge of opposition legislators, led to mass protests and strike action at the end of the year. The labour legislation did not include expected key reforms relating to freedom of expression and association, including the immediate recognition of independent trade unions; the complete removal of the ban on "third party intervention" in labour disputes; and recognition of the right of teachers and public employees to form trade unions. An amendment to the Agency for National Security Planning (ANSP) Act strengthened the powers of the ANSP by restoring its right to investigate people detained under Articles 7 and 10 of the National Security Law.

After a violent confrontation between students and riot police in August, and the alleged "infiltration" of military personnel from the Democratic People's Republic of Korea (North Korea) into the Republic of Korea (South Korea) in September, the authorities announced a new offensive against "leftist" and "pro-North Korean" activities.

In August, former Presidents Chun Doo-hwan and Roh Tae-woo were sentenced to death and to 22 and a half years' imprisonment, respectively, on charges relating to a military coup in 1979 and the killings of civilians in Kwangju in May 1980 (see previous *Amnesty International Reports*). At an appeal in December, these sentences were reduced to life imprisonment and 17 years' imprisonment.

In November, the Constitutional Court ruled the death penalty to be constitutional. The Court's ruling was on a petition by Chong Sok-bom whose 1994 death sentence for murder had been commuted to life imprisonment.

Over 450 people, including political activists, teachers, students, singers, businessmen, members of religious groups and workers, were arrested under the National Security Law for alleged pro-North Korean activities. Many were prisoners of conscience. Most were arrested under Article 7 of the Law which provides for up to seven years' imprisonment for those who "praise" and support an "anti-state" organization. The Law specifies the Government of the Democratic People's Republic of Korea as an "anti-state" organization.

Prisoners of conscience arrested under Article 7 of the National Security Law included singer Lee Eun-jin and publisher Won Yong-ho who were arrested in February for producing and distributing a songbook alleged to "praise" and "benefit" North Korea. They were given suspended prison sentences and released in April. Other prisoners of conscience included six students belonging to the student organization 21st Century Group who were arrested in July for alleged pro-North Korean activities. The Group, comprising some 300 student members, had campaigned on a variety of issues including corruption, the environment and reunification of North Korea and South Korea, and had not used or advocated violence. The six prisoners were given suspended prison sentences and released in November.

Another prisoner of conscience, Lee Eun-soon, was arrested in July for printing the name of a North Korean university on T-shirts which she distributed to fellow students. She was given a suspended sentence and released in September. In October, Yun Sok-jin, a student, was arrested for posting a "dangerous" opinion on a computer bulletin board about the grounding of a North Korean submarine in South Korean waters. His trial, which opened in December, was continuing at the end of the year.

Those arrested under other provisions of the National Security Law included novelist Kim Ha-ki, who had made an unauthorized entry into North Korea in July while on a study trip to Yanji in the Chinese province of Jilin. He claimed that he had crossed the Tumen river while under the influence of alcohol and was held by the North Korean authorities for two weeks. Upon his return to South Korea in August, he was arrested and charged under the National Security Law for making an unauthorized visit to North Korea and leaking "state secrets". His trial had not concluded by the end of the year.

Buddhist human rights activist Jin Kwan was arrested in October under the National Security Law on charges relating to his religious and human rights activities. He was accused of having unauthorized contacts with North Korean Buddhists he had met in Canada and China, and of joining the *Pomminnyon*, Pan-National Alliance for Reunification of Korea. Nine other members of *Pomminnyon* were sentenced to up to one and a half years' imprisonment in May, including 74-year-old prisoner of conscience Chun Chang-il.

A small number of people were acquitted of charges under the National Security Law, including Ho In-hoe, a former politician, who was acquitted in November of failing to report a meeting with an alleged "spy" from North Korea.

At least 150 people, including prisoners of conscience, who had been convicted of national security offences in previous years, remained held. One was prisoner of conscience Kim Nak-jung, a 65-year-old political writer and activist, who was arrested in 1992 and sentenced to life imprisonment on charges of "espionage". He had met North Korean officials but there was no evidence that he had passed on "state secrets". Two other prisoners of conscience were Park Noh-hae and Baik Tae-ung, sentenced in the early 1990s to life and 12 years' imprisonment respectively for their activities as leaders of the *Sanomaeng*, Socialist Workers' League.

Trade unionists continued to face arrest under legislation which bans "third party intervention" in labour disputes. This legislation has been used to prevent trade union leaders who belong to the unrecognized trade union confederation *Minju Nochong*, Korean Confederation of Trade Unions (KCTU), from giving advice to member unions. KCTU President Kwon Young-kil, who was arrested in November 1995 and was a prisoner of conscience (see *Amnesty International Report 1996*), was released on bail in March. At least four other trade union leaders were arrested for "third party intervention" during the year, including KCTU First Vice-President Yang Kyu-hun, also a prisoner of conscience, who was arrested in February and later released on bail. Ten others were under investigation and faced possible arrest.

At least 20 political prisoners sentenced to long prison terms for national security offences during the 1970s and 1980s after trials which were believed to have fallen short of international fair trial standards were among those who remained in prison throughout the year. They were reported to have been held incommunicado for long periods, tortured and convicted largely on the basis of coerced confessions. For example, Yu Chong-sik, sentenced to life imprisonment for espionage, was held incommunicado for one month after his arrest in March 1975 and tortured. He was a prisoner of conscience.

Most political suspects were reported to have been deprived of sleep and threatened during interrogation. Police were responsible for widespread ill-treatment in August when more than 5,800 students were arrested at a violent demonstration at Yonsei University in Seoul, the capital. Some students who had no connection with the demonstration were detained and beaten in areas around the campus. Female students said that police had grabbed their breasts and shouted sexual insults. At Seoul police stations, detained students were forced to sit or kneel in the same position for hours. Some were reportedly beaten during interrogation and forced to write a "confession". Some injured students received no medical attention.

The conditions in which some political prisoners were held amounted to cruel, inhuman or degrading treatment. For example, 16 long-term political prisoners held in Block 15 of Taejon Prison were reportedly denied contacts with other prisoners and held in small, unheated cells despite freezing temperatures. Most were reported to be suffering from ill health but received little medical attention. They were among dozens of political prisoners under pressure to "convert" (to sign a statement renouncing communism). Prisoners who refuse to "convert" are subject to harsher regimes than other prisoners and are denied the possibility of release on parole.

Medical provision in prisons continued to be poor and some sick prisoners experienced difficulty in obtaining permission to visit a doctor outside the prison. They included Koh Ae-soon, who was in her 28th week of pregnancy when she was arrested on 4 December 1995 under the National Security Law. In spite of repeated requests, she was not examined by an obstetrician until 29 January 1996. She lost her baby through medical complications.

Some 50 prisoners convicted of murder remained under sentence of death throughout the year. No executions were reported.

Amnesty International called for the release of prisoners of conscience and for a review of the cases of political prisoners who had been unfairly tried. The organization urged the amendment of the National Security Law and labour legislation in accordance with international standards.

In October, Amnesty International submitted a report to the UN Committee against Torture entitled *Republic of Korea (South Korea): Summary of concerns on torture and ill-treatment*. The report's recommendations included calls for an independent inquiry into the ill-treatment of students in August and for a review of police training. The organization also called for a full and impartial investigation into human rights violations committed under past military governments.

KUWAIT

Over 150 people, including prisoners of conscience, continued to serve prison terms imposed after unfair trials since 1991. No information was available about scores of other political prisoners arrested in 1991 and accused of "collaboration" with Iraqi forces during the occupation of Kuwait. Four women prisoners of conscience were released in an amnesty. The fate and whereabouts of more than 70 detainees who "disappeared" in 1991 remained unknown. Five people were sentenced to death, one person was executed and 12 others remained under sentence of death at the end of the year.

In October, elections were held for the 50-seat National Assembly (parliament). However, political parties were banned and the electorate consisted of only 15 per cent of Kuwaiti citizens, since women, some naturalized Kuwaitis and members of the armed forces were excluded from voting.

In March, Kuwait acceded, with reservations, to the UN Convention against Torture and Other Cruel, Inhuman or Degrading Treatment or Punishment. In May, Kuwait acceded to the International Covenant on Civil and Political Rights and the International Covenant on Economic, Social and Cultural Rights, again with reservations.

In June, parliament rejected the first draft bill to establish an independent Kuwaiti Commission on Human Rights. After some amendments, the bill was reintroduced but had not been passed by the end of the year.

The government announced in June that over 100,000 stateless people, members of the *Bidun* community, who claim Kuwaiti nationality, were to have their status reviewed. The review had not been completed by the end of the year.

A Kuwaiti prisoner, one of eight women listed among prisoners of war or missing persons believed to be held in Iraq, was handed over to the International Committee of the Red Cross in May at the Iraq-Kuwait border. According to the Kuwaiti authorities, more than 600 prisoners were still missing since the withdrawal of Iraqi forces in February 1991 (see **Iraq** entry and previous *Amnesty International Reports*).

At the beginning of the year, three independent Islamist lawyers brought a lawsuit against Hussein Qambar 'Ali, a businessman, to declare him an apostate and strip him of his civil rights. Hussein Qambar 'Ali, representing himself, first appeared in an Islamic family court in March and confirmed that he had become a Christian but asked for his case to be sent to the Constitutional Court on the grounds that the Constitution allows for freedom of thought and belief. He was reported to have received death threats. Following a hearing in May, the Islamic court declared him an apostate and ordered him to pay the costs of the case. Hussein Qambar 'Ali appealed against the ruling on the grounds that the Islamic court had no jurisdiction in his case but left the country before the appeal was heard.

Over 150 political prisoners, including nine women, continued to serve prison terms in Kuwait Central Prison following their conviction on charges of "collaboration" with Iraqi forces during the occupation of Kuwait. At least 16 were prisoners of conscience. Fifty-three had been sentenced by the Martial Law Court in 1991 and the others by the State Security Court in 1992 and 1993 after trials which were unfair (see previous *Amnesty International Reports*). No information was available about scores of other political prisoners arrested in 1991 on suspicion of "collaboration" with Iraqi forces.

Four women prisoners of conscience, one of Iraqi and three of Jordanian nationality, were granted an amnesty by the Amir, al-Shaikh Jaber al-Ahmad al-Sabah. Two political prisoners, members of the *Bidun* community, were reported to have been transferred to a deportation centre in 1993 and 1994 following their release before completion of their prison sentences. One of them was believed to have been deported but it was not known to which country. No information was available on the whereabouts of the other prisoner.

Many of the hundreds of detainees at the Talha detention centre, set up in 1991 following the war with Iraq, remained held under administrative deportation orders which were reportedly rarely subject to any judicial review. Among those held were foreign nationals and stateless persons, some of whom may have served prison terms and continued to be held in indefinite detention after the expiry of their sentences. There were fears that the deportation of those for whom Kuwait was their own country could amount to forcible exile. Officials announced in November that plans to close down the Talha detention centre had begun in October and included the release of a "large number" of detainees.

The fate and whereabouts of more than 70 detainees who "disappeared" in custody in 1991 remained unknown (see previous *Amnesty International Reports*). They included Muhammad Asia, who reportedly "disappeared" after being arrested in 1991.

Two Kuwaiti men were sentenced to death in October and three others, in a separate case, in November. All had been convicted of murder. A Kuwaiti police officer, Badr 'Abd al-Karim Sultan al-Bashir, was executed in September. He had been convicted of possession of drugs and of premeditated murder. At least eight political prisoners remained under sentence of death. Four other people convicted by criminal courts in previous years were believed to be on death row at the end of the year.

In February, Amnesty International published a report, *Kuwait: Five years of impunity – human rights concerns since the withdrawal of Iraqi forces*, which highlighted the government's failure to address long-standing reports of the detention of prisoners of conscience, torture and ill-treatment, unresolved extrajudicial executions, "disappearances", and manifestly unfair trials. Other concerns documented in the report included the expulsion of people without due process, the resumption of executions and the widened scope of the death penalty.

In August, Amnesty International published a report, *Kuwait: Hussein Qambar 'Ali – death threats*. It included a statement issued in July by the Kuwaiti Embassy in the United Kingdom which said, among other things, that Kuwaiti law does not punish a person who converts from Islam to another faith and that, if necessary, the relevant authorities in the country would take appropriate measures to ensure Hussein Qambar 'Ali's safety.

In response to Amnesty International's concerns about the forcible deportation of members of the *Bidun* community, the Ministry of the Interior stated that there was no intention on the part of the authorities at present to deport any stateless persons "as long as they respect laws and regulations which secure the country's security".

KYRGYZSTAN

Three men detained on defamation charges were prisoners of conscience. There were allegations of ill-treatment by police and by militias operating under the authority of so-called elders' (*aksakal*) courts. At least two death sentences were passed and at least one execution took place.

A referendum in February approved constitutional changes proposed by President Askar Akayev which increased his powers. A new government appointed by the President took office in March.

In October, Kyrgyzstan acceded to the UN Convention and the Protocol relating to the Status of Refugees.

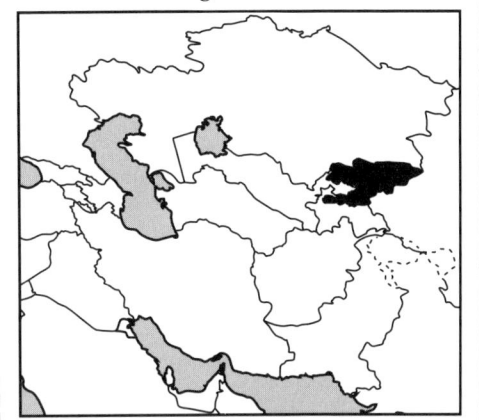

Prisoners of conscience Topchubek Turgunaliyev and Dzhumagazy Usupov, political activists who had been detained since late December 1995, stood trial in April on charges of "defaming" and "insulting" the President and "inflaming national discord or hatred". Both men were found guilty but received one-year suspended prison sentences and were released. Prisoner of conscience Rysbek Omurzakov, a journalist, was arrested in April and charged with "defamation" of the President. In July, he was found guilty and sentenced to two years' imprisonment, but in the same month an appeal hearing substituted a suspended sentence and he was released.

Dzhumagazy Usupov was among several people arrested in December in connection with the founding congress of a new opposition movement, For Deliverance from Poverty. All were released the same day except for Dzhumagazy Usupov, who was given an administrative punishment of 15 days' detention for "organizing an unsanctioned meeting". He was a prisoner of conscience. Topchubek Turgunaliyev also was arrested again in December, on an embezzlement charge, and was on trial at the end of the year. His supporters claimed that he was being prosecuted to punish him for his opposition political activities, including the recent foundation of the movement For Deliverance from Poverty. He was a possible prisoner of conscience.

Reports were received early in the year that militias operating under the authority of so-called elders' courts had detained people and ill-treated them, administering punishments which included flogging and stoning. The authorities appeared to ignore attempts to seek redress for such actions. The courts had been established by presidential decree in early 1995 and given responsibility for examining cases of administrative violations; property, family and other disputes; and minor crimes passed to them by state procurators.

Full statistics on the application of the death penalty were not available, but at least two death sentences were known to have been passed during the year. One of these, passed on Lyubov Sirotkina in January, was changed on appeal in March to 15 years' imprisonment. The other, passed on Nikolay Sokolov in April, was changed by judicial review to 15 years' imprisonment in December. At least one execution was known to have taken place.

Amnesty International called for the immediate and unconditional release of prisoners of conscience detained for defamation of the President. The organization argued that, while all who believed themselves to have been victims of defamation had a right to seek redress through the courts, it was widely recognized that the degree of restriction permitted to protect an individual's reputation should be more limited in the case of a public official than a private person. Public officials who considered themselves defamed should be able to seek redress through civil laws in order to protect their reputation, and criminal legislation should not be used in such a way as to stifle criticism of public officials, or to intimidate those who voiced legitimate concerns about the actions or practices of public officials. Amnesty International also assessed the charge against Topchubek Turgunaliyev and Dzhumagazy Usupov of "inflaming national discord or hatred" as having been without foundation. Amnesty International sought further information from the authorities about the basis for the prosecution of Topchubek Turgunaliyev on a charge of embezzlement.

Amnesty International called for investigations into all cases of alleged ill-treatment of criminal suspects. Regarding the alleged activities of militias attached to the *aksakal* courts, it called for an end to punishments such as stoning and flogging, as well as illegal detention and the ill-treatment of people so detained. The organization also noted that the *aksakal* courts did not satisfy the requirements of the International Covenant on Civil and Political Rights, to which Kyrgyzstan acceded in 1995.

Amnesty International continued to call for commutation of all death sentences and for total abolition of the death penalty.

In May, the organization published a report, *Kyrgyzstan: A tarnished human rights record*.

LAOS

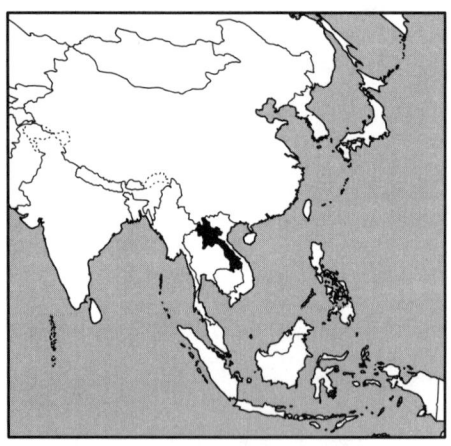

Three prisoners of conscience continued to be held. Three political prisoners continued to serve sentences of life imprisonment imposed in 1992 after an unfair trial.

The ruling Lao People's Revolutionary Party held its Sixth Congress in March. The National Assembly approved a reshuffle of President Nouhak Phoumsavan's government in April. Censorship of the news media, restrictions on freedom of expression and lack of official information continued to make it difficult to obtain information about human rights violations.

Three prisoners of conscience continued to be held in "Re-education" Camp 7 in a remote area of the northern province of Houa Phanh. Thongsouk Saysangkhi, Latsami Khamphoui and Feng Sakchittaphong had been sentenced to 14 years' imprisonment in 1992 after a grossly unfair trial. Although officially charged with "making preparations to stage a rebellion and for conducting propaganda against [the Lao Government], gathering groups of people to create disturbances and carry out slanderous charges against other people, and creating disorder in prison", they were believed to have been detained for peacefully criticizing the country's political and economic systems and for holding meetings advocating a multi-party system (see *Amnesty International Report 1993*). Conditions in Camp 7 were harsh and no medical facilities were provided. All three men were believed to be suffering from ill-health which required medical treatment.

Three political prisoners sentenced to life imprisonment after an unfair trial in 1992 continued to be held. They had been convicted of crimes committed in 1963 and 1975 while they held minor official positions. Pangtong Chokbengboun, Bounlu Nammathao and Sing Chanthakoummane had previously been detained for 17 years without charge or trial (see *Amnesty International Report 1993*). Early in 1996, all three men were transferred from their previous place of detention at Sop Pan camp in Houa Phanh province to "Re-education" Camp 7.

In November, Amnesty International published a report, *Lao People's Democratic Republic: Prisoners of conscience suffering in isolation*. This report called for the immediate and unconditional release of Thongsouk Saysangkhi, Latsami Khamphoui and Feng Sakchittaphong and urged that while they remained in prison they be treated in accordance with internationally recognized standards for the treatment of prisoners, particularly with regard to provision of medical treatment. The organization also continued to call for the fair trial, or release from detention or restriction, of other long-term political prisoners. By the end of the year, no responses had been received from the authorities.

LATVIA

Two men were executed and two were sentenced to death. Approximately 130 asylum-seekers remained in detention throughout most of the year.

In June, President Guntis Ulmanis was elected for a second term by the Latvian parliament (*Saeima*).

In January, Igor Strukov and Rolans Laceklis-Bertmanis were executed. Igor Strukov had been sentenced to death in November 1994 for robbery and the murder of two people. Rolans Laceklis-Bertmanis had been convicted in August 1995 of the murder of two policemen. These were the first executions to have been carried out since Latvia became a member of the Council of Europe and signed the European Convention for the Protection of Human Rights and Fundamental Freedoms (European Convention on Human Rights) in February 1995.

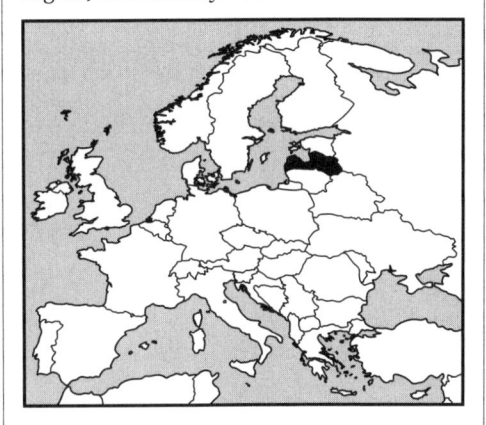

In June, the Parliamentary Assembly of the Council of Europe adopted Resolution 1097 (1996) in which it expressed its regret that Latvia had not kept its commitment to ratify Protocol No. 6 to the European Convention on Human Rights, which abolishes the death penalty in peacetime, within one year of its accession to the Council of Europe. The Assembly called upon Latvia "to honour [its] commitments regarding the introduction of a moratorium on executions and the abolition of capital punishment immediately". In a speech to the Assembly in September, President Ulmanis announced that he would grant all requests for clemency submitted to him, pending a decision by the *Saeima* on abolition of the death penalty. Two men were sentenced to death, including Vladimir Lesik who was convicted in November of murdering three people.

In December, most of the approximately 130 asylum-seekers detained throughout the year were allowed to enter Denmark, Finland, Norway or Sweden, where they were granted political asylum. The asylum-seekers were originally detained on a train on the Latvian/Russian border in March 1995 and later moved to a detention camp in Olaine near the capital, Riga (see *Amnesty International Report 1996*).

Throughout the year Amnesty International urged the authorities to impose an immediate moratorium on all death sentences and executions in Latvia and to ratify Protocol No. 6 to the European Convention on Human Rights. The organization also asked the authorities for information on the outcome of clemency appeals submitted by death-row prisoners. In August, Amnesty International was informed by the Minister for Foreign Affairs that four prisoners sentenced to death in previous years had had their sentences commuted to life imprisonment, three of them following appeals to President Ulmanis. The Minister also confirmed that a revised draft of the Criminal Code, providing for abolition of the death penalty, had been submitted to parliament for consideration.

In August, Amnesty International urged the authorities to take immediate steps to provide all asylum-seekers with the necessary protection against *refoulement* and to treat them fully in accordance with the relevant international standards for the protection of asylum-seekers, including standards providing that asylum-seekers should not normally be detained (see *Amnesty International Report 1996*). The organization also called upon the authorities to ratify the 1951 UN Convention relating to the Status of Refugees and its 1967 Protocol. In his letter to Amnesty International in the same month, the Minister for Foreign Affairs stated that people who had been detained for "illegal entry" into Latvia were "guaranteed non-*refoulement* to countries where they could face persecution". The Minister added that a working group had been established to draw up a draft law on refugees.

LEBANON

Scores of possible prisoners of conscience were arrested by the security forces. Most were briefly detained and released without charge. Several political prisoners

were tried and sentenced after trials, some aspects of which fell short of international standards. Allegations of torture and ill-treatment continued and one person died in custody. At least one person may have been extrajudicially executed. At least 10 people were sentenced to death and two others were executed. A militia allied to Israel continued to hold prisoners. Israeli forces unlawfully killed Lebanese civilians in southern Lebanon, including over a hundred in a single attack. The fate of thousands of people abducted by armed groups in previous years remained unknown.

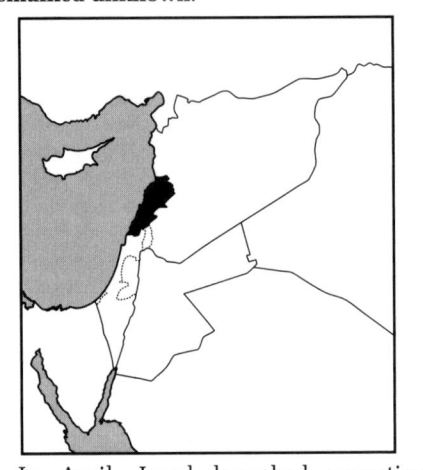

In April, Israel launched operation "Grapes of Wrath", which lasted 17 days and was directed against *Hizbullah*, Party of God, the main armed group fighting Israel and its allied militia, the South Lebanon Army (SLA) in and around Israel's self-declared "security zone". For the duration of the operation, Israel maintained a steady barrage of fire from its artillery, air and naval forces on southern Lebanon resulting in the displacement of more than 300,000 Lebanese from their homes. At least 154 Lebanese civilians were killed as a result of the Israeli operation, 102 of them when Israeli artillery shelled a UN compound in which they were sheltering. Throughout the operation, *Hizbullah* fired Katyusha rockets on populated areas of northern Israel on a daily basis, but no Israeli civilians were reported to have died. The operation ended after a new, written "understanding" was reached between the warring parties which included provisions for the protection of civilians and established a Monitoring Group consisting of the USA, France, Syria, Lebanon and Israel. The Group had met six times by the end of the year to look at complaints of breaches of the "understanding".

In March, the Lebanese Government ordered the army to take over responsibility for internal security for three months. The decision followed the announcement by the General Workers' Union of its intention to organize a strike and other protest actions to demand pay rises, the doubling of the minimum wage and a guarantee of rights and freedoms.

Parliamentary elections were held in August and September. For the first time Prime Minister Rafiq al-Hariri, who contested and won a seat in Beirut, formed a parliamentary bloc of his own. He was again appointed premier by President Elias al-Hrawi, in consultation with the new parliament, and a new government was formed in November. With the agreement of the Lebanese Government, Syrian forces remained deployed throughout most of the country.

In September, the Lebanese Government issued a new law regulating audiovisual media, which restricted broadcasting to six television and 12 radio stations. The remaining media companies were given until the end of November to submit new applications for licences or face liquidation, a deadline which was later extended. The new measures met opposition from various political and interest groups, who repeatedly organized protest actions demanding the repeal of the new law, which they believed would restrict freedom of expression.

Scores of possible prisoners of conscience were arrested by the security forces during the year. At least 76 people, mainly from Christian opposition groups, were arrested following an attack in December on a Syrian minibus in which the driver was killed and a passenger wounded. Those arrested included human rights defender Wa'el Kheir, Director of the Foundation for Human and Humanitarian Rights, and Pierre 'Atallah, an editor on *al-Nahar* newspaper, as well as a number of lawyers and other professionals. All those detained were released after questioning, the majority without charge. Two, including Pierre 'Atallah, were charged with distributing leaflets and making contact with Israel. None were charged for the attack on the Syrian minibus. Allegations of torture were made by some of the detainees. All those detained were possible prisoners of conscience.

About 25 members of the *al-mu'tamar al-sha'bi al-lubnani*, Lebanese Popular Congress (LPC), a Nasserite-oriented organization, were arrested throughout the year. In February, six LPC members were arrested for displaying placards criticizing government policies. They were tried on charges of disruption of public order and security and acquitted by the Criminal Court of Beirut. Five other LPC members were arrested in March for distributing the Congress newspaper *Sawt Beirut*, and released the same day without charge. In September, 11 LPC members were arrested for burning the US flag after the Friday sermon in front of al-Tariq al-Jadida mosque in Beirut. They were released the following day without charge. Another five LPC members arrested in October for burning the Israeli flag were detained for five days and released without charge. One of the five, Muhammad Sannu, a student, was allegedly beaten during his arrest.

Possible prisoners of conscience were also among members of the *al-mu'tamar al-watani al-lubnani*, Lebanese National Congress (LNC) – followers of former military leader General Michel 'Aoun – detained during parliamentary elections in August, mostly in connection with distribution of leaflets calling for a boycott of the elections. All were released without charge after brief periods of detention. They included Faris Anton, Michel Chukri, and Ziad Karam, reportedly arrested by military intelligence officers in Jubail and released after several hours of interrogation, and students Tareq Trabulsi, Khalil Harfuch and Camille Harfuch, who were allegedly arrested by unidentified armed men accompanied by a police officer and illegally detained for one night in Brummanah in the Metn district. A further nine LNC members were reportedly arrested in September by the Syrian intelligence forces in Lebanon, interrogated in Zahle and Chtourah and released the following day without charge. They were also possible prisoners of conscience.

Zafer al-Muqadam and Hani Chu'aib were arrested in February on suspicion of membership of the unauthorized pro-Iraqi wing of the Arab Socialist Ba'th party and transferred to Syria. Most of the 13 members of the pro-Iraqi wing of the party detained in 1994 and taken to Syria (see *Amnesty International Reports 1995* and *1996*) were released. Two of them, Rafiq Abu Younes and Hasan Gharib, remained in detention in Syria without charge or trial. At least 200 Lebanese detained in Syria in previous years also remained held at the end of the year. Although some received family visits, most were reportedly held in incommunicado detention (see **Syria** entry).

Several political prisoners were tried and sentenced after trials which in some aspects fell short of international fair trial standards. The trial of Samir Gea'gea', leader of the banned Lebanese Forces (LF), and seven other LF members for the bombing of a church in 1994 (see *Amnesty International Annual Reports 1995* and *1996*) resumed before the Justice Court and concluded in July. Samir Gea'gea' was acquitted of the charges relating to the church bombing, but sentenced to 10 years' imprisonment for "maintaining a militia in the guise of a political party" and "dealing with military weapons and explosives". Fu'ad Malek, his deputy, was sentenced on the same charges to three years' imprisonment, reduced immediately to one and a half years. Jirjis al-Khoury was sentenced to life imprisonment with hard labour. Antonios Elias Elias, Ruchdi Tawfiq Ra'd and Jean Yusuf Chahin, who were tried *in absentia*, were sentenced to death. Paul and Rafiq al-Fahal were acquitted for lack of evidence. Jirjis al-Khoury, who retracted his initial statements in 1995, alleging that they had been extracted under torture, maintained his retraction when the trial resumed. However, the court rejected the torture claim on the basis of a medical report and the testimony of the prison doctor, who stated that he had examined the defendant during the interrogation period. No independent judicial investigation appeared to have been ordered into this case.

Ahmad Hallaq, who had been tried *in absentia* in 1995 for the killing of three people, including two members of *Hizbullah*, in an explosion in December 1994 (see *Amnesty International Reports 1995* and *1996*), was apprehended in February by Lebanese security forces in Israel's occupied zone and retried. He was sentenced to death in July and executed in September (see below). Appeals against his sentence had been rejected. Ahmad Hallaq's co-defendant, Tawfiq Nasser, who had also been tried *in absentia*, returned to the country earlier and gave himself up. He was retried with Ahmad Hallaq and sentenced to 10 years' imprisonment. Hanan Yassin, Ahmad Hallaq's wife, who was serving a 15-year sentence imposed following the original trial, was awaiting a review of her case by the military court of appeal.

The trial of those charged with the assassination of Sheikh Nizar al-Halabi, leader of the *al-Ahbash* movement (see *Amnesty International Report 1996*), started in May and was still in progress at the end of the year. Twenty defendants, nine Palestinians and 11 Lebanese, were charged with the killing. Three of those charged, including the main defendant, Ahmad 'Abd al-Karim al-Sa'di, known as Abu Mahjan, a Palestinian and leader of *'Usbat al-Ansar*, an Islamic group, were being tried *in absentia*.

There were continuing allegations of torture and ill-treatment in custody. A number of defendants in the Sheikh al-Halabi assassination trial, including Muhammad Ahmad Isma'il, a Palestinian, Hani Subhi al-'Uthman and Tareq Isma'il, retracted statements made during the initial interrogation and before the investigating judge, alleging that they had been extracted under torture.

Torture and ill-treatment of non-political suspects were also reported. In February, a suspected drug-dealer, Munir Mtanios, died in custody, reportedly as a result of torture. It is not known whether any investigation was held. In February and March, the Parliamentary Human Rights Committee discussed reports of torture and urged the government to open an inquiry into allegations of torture and police brutality. The Justice Minister promised to investigate the allegations. In June, a criminal court in Zahle concluded that security force officials had tortured Elya Harb, held on drugs charges, causing him permanent paralysis, and instructed the State Prosecutor to initiate judicial proceedings against these officials.

At least one person may have been extrajudicially executed. In November, Farid Hanna Musalli, a suspect in a financial fraud case, was shot dead by police, who were reportedly trying to arrest him. Seven officers were arrested in connection with the killing and for entering the victim's home without a search warrant. Five were released immediately, but two, Eala Ra'ad and Jean 'Aqal, were remanded in custody. In December, Jean 'Aqal, the commanding officer, was released by the investigating judge in a military court.

At least 10 people were sentenced to death; most had been convicted of murder or spying for Israel. Two men were executed. In September, Ahmad Hallaq was executed by firing-squad in Rumieh prison, two months after his conviction for the December 1994 bombing (see above). All trial and appeals proceedings were completed, and presidential approval obtained in this two-month period. In October, Anas Dhibyan, sentenced to death in July, was executed by a firing-squad in Rumieh prison for the murder of his fiancée and a police officer. Those sentenced to death included Yusuf Ibrahim al-Hashim, sentenced in April *in absentia*; Hussam Suleiman and Muhammad 'Ali Mustafa, sentenced in May; and Ahmad al-Zamil, Chahin Aybu and Adib 'Abd Sabra, all Syrian nationals, also sentenced in May.

At least 130 prisoners, most of them suspected of membership of armed groups opposed to the Israeli presence in Lebanon, continued to be held by the SLA outside any legal framework in the Khiam detention centre in the "security zone". Visits by representatives of the International Committee of the Red Cross and by prisoners' families continued to be permitted (see *Amnesty International Report 1996*). About 82 prisoners were released during the year. Of these, 45 were released in July in an exchange of bodies and prisoners between *Hizbullah* on the one hand, and the SLA and Israel on the other. Among those who remained in Khiam at the end of the year were Suha Bechara, now the only woman prisoner following the exchange, Mahmud Ramadan, Ni'ma Bazzi, Lafi al-Masri and 'Ali Hijazi. 'Ali Hijazi's medical condition had deteriorated, reportedly as a result of ill-treatment and the absence of adequate medical care. At least 10 Lebanese were abducted in Lebanon and taken to Israel. Six remained in detention in Israel at the end of the year.

Israeli forces killed Lebanese civilians in clear breach of international law in southern Lebanon as a result of the "Grapes of Wrath" operation in April, during which more than 150 civilians died. In addition to the 102 civilians killed in the UN compound in Qana, which Amnesty International believed was deliberately attacked, six were killed when an Israeli helicopter fired rockets at an ambulance carrying 13 civilians fleeing the village of al-Mansuri. A further nine civilians were killed when Israeli warplanes demolished a house in Upper Nabatiyya (see **Israel and the Occupied Territories** entry).

The fate of thousands of people, including Palestinians, Lebanese, Syrians and other nationals abducted in Lebanon by armed groups since 1975 remained unclear. They included 'Adnan Hilwani, who went missing in 1982, and Christine and Richard Salim, who were abducted in 1985.

In an oral statement to the UN Commission on Human Rights in February, Amnesty International repeated its call for the release of Lebanese detainees believed to be held in the Khiam detention centre and in Israel, as well as the release of any Israeli soldiers and SLA members missing in Lebanon who were being held as hostages (see **Israel and the Occupied Territories** entry).

Amnesty International sent a delegation to Lebanon in May to investigate the killing of civilians by Israel in April. In July, the organization published a report, *Israel/Lebanon: Unlawful killings during operation "Grapes of Wrath"*, which called for an Israeli judicial inquiry into the killings and effective protection for all civilians.

In September, Amnesty International delegates met government officials in Lebanon to discuss human rights concerns and submitted a memorandum relating to arbitrary detention, torture, unfair trial and the death penalty. No response had been received from the government by the end of the year. In December, Amnesty International wrote to the authorities requesting information about the progress of the investigation into the killing of Farid Hanna Musalli. Throughout the year Amnesty International urged the authorities to commute all death sentences.

LESOTHO

At least five construction workers were shot dead and dozens of others wounded when police opened fire to disperse them. There were reports of ill-treatment and torture. Four people were sentenced to death.

In January, King Moshoeshoe II died in a motor accident and was succeeded by his son, King Letsie III.

Tensions within the ruling Basotholand Congress Party, said to revolve around the succession to Prime Minister Ntsu Mokhehle, hampered the effective functioning of parliament. In May, four cabinet ministers were dismissed and two others resigned. Journalists critical of the government were harassed.

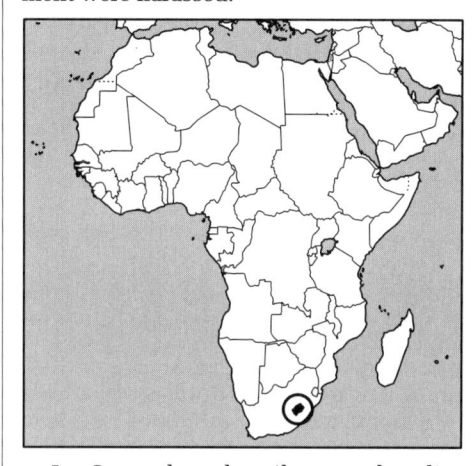

In September, heavily armed police stormed a construction workers' compound at Butha-Buthe in the north of the country, shooting dead at least five workers and injuring dozens of others. The shootings occurred when, following a prolonged labour dispute at the Lesotho Highlands Water Project Butha-Buthe worksite, dismissed workers were called to the compound to receive their final pay. Before they had been paid, armed police ordered them to disperse. Police then stormed the compound firing tear-gas and automatic weapons at the workers. According to eye-witnesses, foreign employees joined the police in shooting at the workers. Police also shot and wounded workers trying to assist the injured. Worksite security personnel assisting the police used automatic gunfire to halt an ambulance which was attempting to pick up injured workers. The police arrested and assaulted the ambulance driver and three other people. They were released without charge after several days, but were required to report regularly to the police.

The police claimed workers had fired on them, but presented no corroborative evidence. Independent post-mortem examinations on three of the workers killed indicated that the men died from single shots fired from high-velocity military-style weapons. The use of such weapons in the context of a labour dispute indicated that the police used lethal force without justification, suggesting that the killings may have been extrajudicial executions.

Local non-governmental organizations, human rights workers, victims' relatives, and Amnesty International expressed concerns about the adequacy and impartiality of an internal inquiry into the shootings announced by the government in September. The inquiry body consisted of an official from the Ministry of Home Affairs, which is responsible for the police force, and a British police officer on secondment to Lesotho. In November, it issued an interim report which endorsed the police decision to clear the workers' compound, but found that police equipment and training were inadequate to achieve this with minimum possible force.

After the shootings, hundreds of workers fled into the countryside or sought refuge at a nearby Roman Catholic mission. Workers' families, local residents and human rights workers investigating the incident were reportedly harassed by police in the ensuing days.

There were reports that suspects in criminal investigations were routinely tortured and ill-treated in police custody. In September, four Butha-Buthe workers were arrested, ostensibly for theft, held for one week at Ha Lejone police station, and tortured. The police forced them to lie on the floor, tied their hands and feet tightly behind their backs, nearly suffocated them by pulling plastic bags over their faces and crushed their backs with heavy objects. Two of the workers reported that they lost consciousness. Charges against them, although not formally withdrawn, appeared to have been dropped by the end of the year.

In October, it was reported that Matlaselo Maramane Konyana died at Roma police station in December 1995, hours after his arrest in connection with a criminal investigation. There had been no inquest into his death by the end of the year, nor into that of Thabo Lefosa in June 1995 (see *Amnesty International Report 1996*).

Three men were sentenced to death after being convicted in May of the 1991 murder of a bank manager during a labour dispute between the bank and its employees, represented by the Lesotho Union of Bank Employees (LUBE). Two, who were former LUBE officials (see *Amnesty International Report 1995*), were not present when the victim was killed. Their conviction rested on the finding that they conspired with others to commit the murder. The evidence against them came largely from an alleged co-conspirator, who was granted immunity from prosecution. An appeal against conviction and sentence was lodged. A fourth person was sentenced to death in November. No executions were reported.

Amnesty International received no substantive response from the government regarding concerns raised during 1995 about police accountability and use of lethal force. After the shooting of construction workers by the police, the organization appealed to the authorities to protect workers, their families, and human rights workers attempting to assist them, and to establish an impartial, independent and public commission of inquiry. In October, the organization sent a forensic pathologist to observe post-mortem examinations on three of the workers killed, and an Amnesty International delegate took testimony from eye-witnesses to the shooting of workers at Butha-Buthe.

LIBERIA

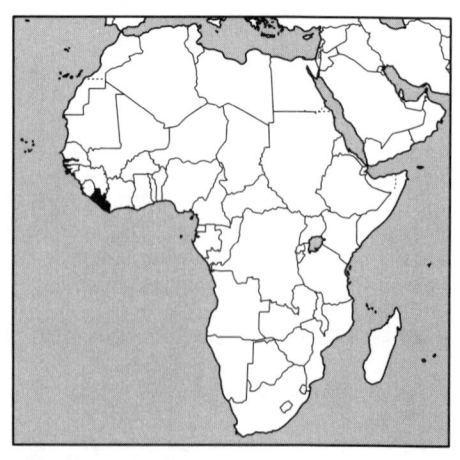

All parties to the continuing conflict committed gross human rights abuses, including arbitrary detention, torture and ill-treatment, hostage-taking and deliberate and arbitrary killings of civilians.

Some armed groups punished their members for attacking civilians: at least one combatant was found guilty by a court-martial and executed. Some prisoners of conscience were arrested outside the context of the armed conflict.

On 3 September a civilian Chairperson of the Liberian National Transitional Government, Ruth Perry, was sworn in. She took office after the foreign ministers of the Economic Community of West African States (ECOWAS) met to oversee the transition to an elected government, in accordance with the terms of the 1995 Abuja peace agreement (see *Amnesty International Report 1996*). The ECOWAS meeting also agreed a revised timetable for the Abuja agreement, envisaging its full implementation by June 1997, and called for an increase in the number of ECOWAS Cease-fire Monitoring Group (ECOMOG) troops to monitor the cease-fire and to oversee the disarming of combatants in preparation for elections in May 1997. In November, ECOMOG began the disarmament process, but by the end of the year few weapons had been handed over. Of the estimated 60,000 combatants only about 5,000 had handed in weapons.

The UN Security Council renewed the mandate of the UN Observer Mission in Liberia (UNOMIL), sent to Liberia in 1993 to monitor an earlier peace agreement and coordinate with ECOMOG. The Security Council stressed the human rights aspect of UNOMIL's mandate.

The fighting, which had remained sporadic in rural areas, spread to the capital, Monrovia, in April, when police believed to be allied to the National Patriotic Front of Liberia (NPFL) attempted to arrest Roosevelt Johnson, leader of the rival United Liberation Movement of Liberia for Democracy-Johnson branch (ULIMO-J). The initial protagonists were the NPFL and ULIMO-J, but all the other armed groups were later involved in the fighting. The national army, the Armed Forces of Liberia (AFL), the Liberian Peace Council (LPC) and ULIMO-J fought together against the NPFL and its former rival, the ULIMO-Kromah branch (ULIMO-K).

The fighting centred on the Barclay Training Centre military barracks in central Monrovia. Rival armed groups controlled different zones of Monrovia and many civilians fled Liberia or sought refuge in the US Embassy compound and at the ECOMOG base. A cease-fire in Monrovia was re-established in May and appeared to be holding, but fighting involving the two factions of ULIMO, the NPFL and the LPC continued in various parts of the country, in particular in Grand Gedeth, Tuzona and Zwedru. In June, a new armed group, the Congo Defence Force, believed to be close to ULIMO-K, engaged in fighting against ULIMO-J in the area around Tubmanburg.

During the first week of fighting in Monrovia, Charles Julue and six other officers serving prison sentences for treason (see *Amnesty International Reports 1995* and *1996*) were freed when the AFL and ULIMO-J stormed the prison.

In October, there was an attempt on the life of Charles Taylor, the NPFL leader. An investigation by the Liberian Ministry of Justice, UNOMIL and ECOMOG was begun into the incident.

All parties to the conflict committed gross human rights abuses. During the fighting in Monrovia in April and May, the mutilated bodies of those killed were openly displayed. Elsewhere, fighters from all the warring factions tortured and deliberately killed unarmed civilians suspected of opposing them, as they seized territory or raided another group's territory. All armed groups were responsible for deliberate and arbitrary killings of civilians, although in many cases it was not possible to establish which group was responsible.

All armed groups detained non-combatants whom they suspected of being supporters of rival factions. Peace-keeping troops who were detained, as well as civilians, were ill-treated. In January, in the area around Tubmanburg, ULIMO-J detained 130 ECOMOG troops who had been engaged in clearing mines and held them for 10 days as a shield against attacks. During the fighting in Monrovia, members of ECOMOG and other foreign nationals were held at the Barclay Training Centre military barracks by Krahn groups loyal to Roosevelt Johnson. In February, eight aid workers were held for three days by the LPC in southeastern Liberia. In July, aid workers reported that ULIMO-K was restricting the movement of civilians in a displaced persons' camp in Suehn and starving the inhabitants to cause food supplies to be diverted to their troops. ULIMO-K released some 60 starving children within a few days, but did not permit the evacuation of other inhabitants for a further two weeks.

In January, the bodies of five civilians were exhumed in Tubmanburg, together with those of nine ECOMOG soldiers, allegedly killed by ULIMO-J. One of the victims had been decapitated and, according to a pathologist, another had apparently been tied up and then shot. Witnesses reported that there were more than 50 other fresh graves, and that residential areas of the town had been devastated by shelling.

Also in January, there were reports that members of the LPC were killing, raping and harassing members of the Grebo ethnic group in southeast Liberia. In March, at least four civilians were reportedly killed when LPC combatants in Buchanan opened fire on them after running over a pedestrian with their vehicle.

In April and May, during the fighting in Monrovia, widespread killings and mutilations of civilians were reported. The body of Benson Wyen, former Managing Director of the Forestry Development Agency, was found near the police academy in Paynesville. He was reportedly killed by the NPFL. Fighters loyal to the NPFL displayed the head of a ULIMO-J fighter who had been shot and then decapitated. In May, five bodies were found in Benson Street, Monrovia. The victims reportedly had their ears cut off or their throats cut before being shot, following fighting between ULIMO-J and the NPFL.

In late September, dozens of civilians were killed after clashes between ULIMO-J and ULIMO-K. At least 21 civilians were killed in Sinje, Cape Mount County, reportedly by ULIMO-K. One of those killed was a baby girl, whose skull had been fractured.

Both the LPC and NPFL were reported to have tortured and in some cases summarily executed their members for attacking civilians. In February, Lieutenant Prince Musa of the NPFL was killed a few minutes after being found guilty by a court-martial of killing a civilian who refused to hand over money. In March, NPFL officials shot two men in the legs after they were found threatening civilians. An LPC official publicly stated that LPC fighters responsible for the killing of three civilians in Buchanan would be executed. In May, Alhaji Kromah, leader of ULIMO-K, publicly stated that he would summarily execute any of his men who harassed civilians.

There were some arrests of prisoners of conscience outside the context of the armed conflict. For example, in March, Bishop Ronald Diggs was arrested and charged with hindering law enforcement when the Inter-faith Mediation Committee of which he was chairperson proposed that a national commission of inquiry be set up to investigate alleged human rights abuses carried out by Roosevelt Johnson and others. The Committee had intervened to mediate in the crisis surrounding the Council of State's attempts to arrest Roosevelt Johnson. Bishop Diggs was released on bail to face trial the day before fighting broke out in Monrovia.

In April, Amnesty International appealed to all parties in the conflict and to the international community to take immediate action to protect civilians. The organization called on all protagonists to release hostages, cease attacks on civilians and allow civilians to leave areas of fighting. In August, Amnesty International urged ECOWAS to include respect for human rights in any political solution, and in particular to set up a panel of experts to investigate human rights abuses.

LIBYA

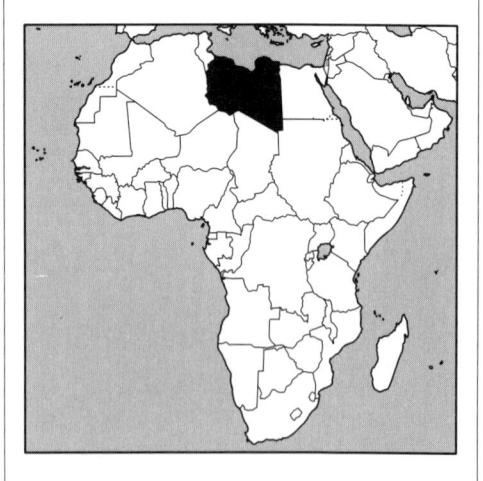

Five prisoners of conscience held since 1973 continued to serve life sentences. Hundreds of political prisoners, including possible prisoners of conscience, who were arrested in previous years continued to be held without charge or trial. Scores of suspected Islamist activists, including possible prisoners of conscience, were arrested during the year. Torture and

ill-treatment in prisons and detention centres continued to be reported. Scores of political prisoners and detainees were shot dead by special security forces during a prison mutiny. A possible prisoner of conscience "disappeared". Two opposition activists living abroad were killed in circumstances suggesting they were extrajudicially executed. A new law increasing the scope of the death penalty was introduced. Thirty-one death sentences were reportedly commuted to life imprisonment.

The UN sanctions on Libya (see previous *Amnesty International Reports*), imposed in 1992 in connection with the 1988 bombing of a US passenger airliner, remained in force.

A new law came into effect in July widening the scope of the death penalty to include "speculation in food, clothes or housing during a state of war or blockade" and "crimes relating to drugs, alcohol and speculation in foreign currency."

Around 250 Palestinian refugees, among thousands of those expelled by Libya last year (see *Amnesty International Report 1996*), remained in an open-air camp in no-man's land between the Libyan and Egyptian borders.

Sporadic violent clashes continued between the security forces and members of Islamist armed groups, particularly in northeastern Libya.

Five prisoners of conscience, arrested in 1973 and convicted of membership of the prohibited Islamic Liberation Party, continued to serve life sentences in Abu-Salim Prison in Tripoli (see previous *Amnesty International Reports*).

Hundreds of political prisoners arrested in previous years, including possible prisoners of conscience, remained held without charge or trial (see previous *Amnesty International Reports*). They included members or supporters of banned Islamist groups. Jum'a 'Ateyqa, a lawyer, remained in administrative detention at Abu-Salim Prison. He is a diabetic and was reported to be suffering from unspecified liver problems. He had been arrested in 1989 in connection with the murder of a Libyan diplomat in Rome, Italy, in January 1985, but was acquitted by a criminal court in Tripoli in 1990. Jum'a 'Ateyqa had been living in exile until 1988, when he returned to Libya following a general amnesty issued by Colonel Mu'ammar Gaddafi, the Head of State.

Nurya Ahmad al-Firjani, a possible prisoner of conscience, remained held without charge or trial. She had been arrested in June 1995 after her husband, allegedly a member of an armed Islamist group, was killed during a gun battle with security forces in al-Qwarsha near Benghazi. Her daughter, 'Ayesha, who was six months old at the time of arrest, was reported to be with her in Abu-Salim Prison.

Scores of suspected Islamist activists were arrested during 1996, following clashes between the security forces and armed Islamist groups. Thuraya Mohammad al-Briki, a possible prisoner of conscience, was arrested in March after the security forces stormed her house in search of her husband, whom they believed to be an Islamist activist. She was reported to have been tortured. She was released uncharged after a few months.

There were continued reports of ill-treatment in prisons and detention centres. Gasmalla 'Osman Hamad Sharah, a Sudanese national, died in detention in al-Kufra camp, apparently as a result of lack of medical care. He was among hundreds of Sudanese and other African workers in Libya arrested in their homes and workplaces in June and July and taken to Al-'Ataba Prison in Tripoli and al-Kufra Camp, near the Sudanese border. Gasmalla Sharah had been in ill health and was reportedly receiving treatment in Tripoli Central Hospital at the time of his arrest.

Scores of political prisoners and detainees were killed in Abu Salim Prison in Tripoli during a one-week mutiny which took place at the beginning of July. The mutiny was said to have been caused by the appalling conditions in the prison, including lack of medical care, inadequate hygiene, overcrowded cells and a poor diet. A number of guards were allegedly taken hostage by the prisoners, who were demanding an improvement in prison conditions. According to reports, special security forces stormed the prison, shooting and killing scores of prisoners and a number of hostages. No investigation was known to have been carried out into the incident by the end of the year.

A Palestinian, a possible prisoner of conscience, "disappeared" following his arrest by the security forces. Aymam Salim Mohammad Dababish was arrested in September in Tubruq on suspicion of having connections with a Libyan Islamist opposition group. At the end of the year his whereabouts remained unknown. Ibrahim Mohammad Ibrahim Jad, who "disappeared" in the same month from the Palestinian refugee camp near Salloum, on the border between Libya and Egypt, was released by the security forces in November and returned to the camp.

The fate of Mansur Kikhiya, a prominent Libyan opposition leader and human rights activist who "disappeared" in Egypt in December 1993 (see previous *Amnesty International Reports*), and of Jaballah Hamed Matar and 'Izzat Youssef al-Maqrif (see *Amnesty International Report 1996*), who also "disappeared" in Cairo in March 1990, remained unknown at the end of the year. Information came to light during the year about 'Abdullah Mohammad Mas'ud al-Zubaidi, an alleged member of the Islamic Liberation Party who "disappeared" in 1982, and about Kadhim Mutasher Malih, an Iraqi national who "disappeared" in Libya in October 1993. Both were believed to have been arrested, but their subsequent fate remained unknown.

Two opposition activists living abroad were killed in circumstances suggesting they were extrajudicially executed. Mohammad ben Ghali was shot dead in Los Angeles, USA, in February. 'Amer Hisham 'Ali Mohammad was found stabbed to death in Sliema, Malta, in August. Reports suggested that individuals acting on behalf of the Libyan Government were responsible for their deaths.

Twelve of those arrested following the alleged October 1993 army rebellion in Misrata and Bani Walid (see previous *Amnesty International Reports*) were reportedly sentenced to death in a military court following a summary retrial at the end of December 1995. One of them, Captain Salam Deynun al-Waa'ir, was tried *in absentia*. The retrial had allegedly been ordered by the authorities on the grounds that the initial sentences – which ranged from five years to life imprisonment – were too lenient. The executions had reportedly not been carried out by the end of the year.

There were reports that 31 death sentences had been commuted to life imprisonment in August to mark the 28th anniversary of the 1 September revolution.

Amnesty International continued to appeal for the immediate and unconditional release of prisoners of conscience and for the fair trial, or release, of all other political prisoners. The organization also called for immediate, thorough and impartial investigations into the circumstances surrounding the killings at Abu Salim Prison, the death in custody of Gasmalla 'Osman Hamad Sharah, and the possible extrajudicial executions of Libyan opposition activists based abroad. Amnesty International welcomed the decision to commute 31 death sentences and urged Colonel Gaddafi to commute all remaining death sentences. The organization received no response to its communications.

LITHUANIA

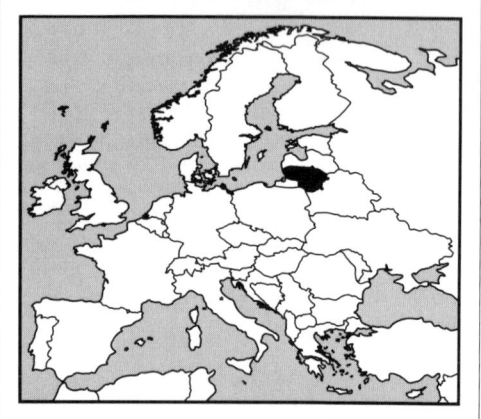

At least nine prisoners were believed to be under sentence of death at the end of the year.

Following elections in October and November, Gediminas Vagnorius was confirmed by Parliament as Prime Minister.

In February, Lithuania acceded to the UN Convention against Torture and Other Cruel, Inhuman or Degrading Treatment or Punishment.

In June, the Parliamentary Assembly of the Council of Europe adopted Resolution 1097 (1996) in which it urged Lithuania "to institute a moratorium on executions without delay". In July, President Algirdas Brazauskas signed a decree effectively halting all executions pending discussion of a new criminal code by the *Seimas* (parliament). Nine prisoners were reported to be under sentence of death at the time the decree was announced.

Throughout the year Amnesty International appealed to the authorities for commutation of all pending death sentences.

The organization also urged the authorities to ratify Protocol No. 6 to the European Convention for the Protection of Human Rights and Fundamental Freedoms, which abolishes the death penalty in peacetime. In its letters to the authorities Amnesty International also expressed regret at the execution of Aleksandras Gudkovas, which it had learned about in December 1995, and asked for information regarding the exact date and place of execution, who was present and whether and how the execution was officially announced or reported. No response had been received by the end of the year.

MACAO

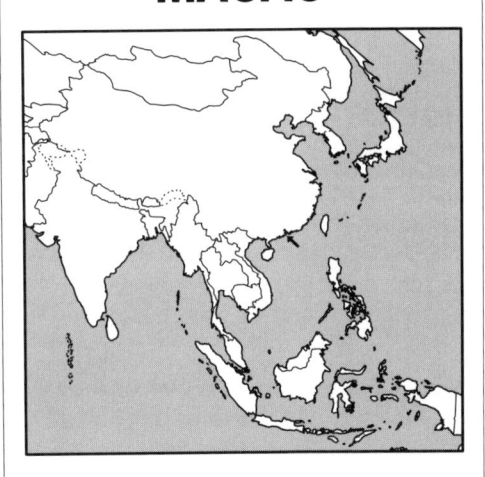

Uncertainty grew over the implementation of human rights safeguards after Macao returns to Chinese administration in 1999.

The Basic Law of the Macao Special Administrative Region, which was adopted by China's National People's Congress in 1993 and will form the constitutional framework of Macao after it returns to Chinese administration on 20 December 1999, lacked some fundamental safeguards for human rights (see *Amnesty International Report 1995*). In March, the Sino-Portuguese Joint Liaison Group, which deals with issues surrounding the transfer of Macao to Chinese administration, said that it had agreed principles for the application to Macao of international human rights treaties ratified by Portugal and China, such as the UN Convention against Torture and Other Cruel, Inhuman or Degrading Treatment or Punishment (Convention against Torture), the Convention on the Elimination of All Forms of Discrimination against Women, and the Convention on the Rights of the Child. However, it was unclear how some of the differences in the way China and Portugal recognized the competence of the UN Committee against Torture could be reconciled. In particular, while Portugal has made a declaration which allows citizens to complain directly to the Committee against Torture if they consider their rights under the Convention against Torture to have been violated, China has not, therefore denying its citizens this right. The Sino-Portuguese Joint Liaison Group had reached no conclusion on the continued implementation in Macao of the International Covenant on Civil and Political Rights (ICCPR), which applies to Macao through Portugal's accession, and which is due to remain in force after 1999. As China is not a party to the ICCPR, the procedure for reporting to the UN Human Rights Committee on the implementation of the ICCPR remained unclear.

The death penalty, life imprisonment and imprisonment of indefinite duration were banned under Article 39 of the new Criminal Law, which came into force in January. The prohibition of the death penalty enshrined in law a long-standing practice, as no execution has taken place in Macao for over a century. The Joint Liaison Group, which examined the text before it was adopted, publicly supported it, suggesting that the death penalty would not be restored after 1999. However, no formal guarantee to that effect was given by China.

There was continuing confusion about the legal rights of Macao residents wanted in China in connection with crimes committed there, which may carry the death penalty. However, claims that Macao residents suspected of crimes punishable by death under Chinese law had been handed over to law enforcement officials in China without a formal judicial process had not been confirmed by the end of the year.

In December, an Amnesty International delegation met the President of Portugal and called on the Portuguese Government to seek further assurances that the death penalty would not be reinstated in Macao after 1999 and that arrangements would be agreed with the Chinese authorities for reporting to the relevant UN bodies on the implementation after 1999 of the ICCPR and other international human rights instruments. Amnesty International also urged the Portuguese authorities to ensure that Macao residents were not transferred to Chinese jurisdiction if accused of crimes which carry the death penalty under Chinese law.

MALAWI

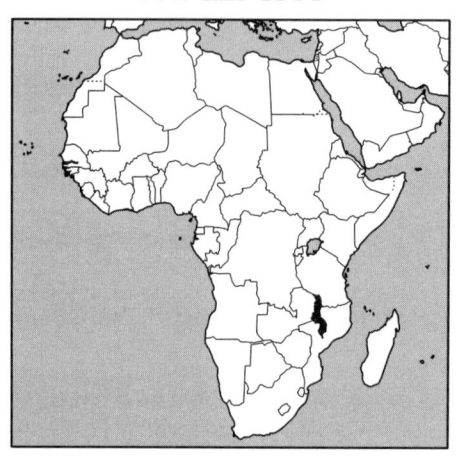

Seventeen prisoners suffocated to death in one night in overcrowded jail cells. Ten prisoners remained under sentence of death.

In June, the Alliance for Democracy (AFORD) party pulled out of the United Democratic Front-led government and AFORD leader Chakufwa Chihana resigned as Second Vice-President.

Also in June, Malawi acceded to the (First) Optional Protocol to the International Covenant on Civil and Political Rights and to the UN Convention against Torture and Other Cruel, Inhuman or Degrading Treatment or Punishment.

In September, police arrested Malawi Congress Party opposition leader John Tembo on charges of plotting to kill three cabinet ministers in 1995. Cecilia Kadzamira also faced charges of plotting the murders.

Seventeen prisoners died of suffocation in January when police held more than 70 suspects overnight in two jail cells. In September, the government appointed a commission of inquiry which investigated the deaths and made a series of recommendations.

Ten people remained under sentence of death in Zomba Central prison, awaiting appeals in the High Court.

In June and again in November, Amnesty International met Ombudsman James Chirwa to discuss his office's role in investigating human rights.

In October, Amnesty International appealed to the authorities to abolish the death penalty.

MALAYSIA

Fourteen possible prisoners of conscience were detained without trial under the Internal Security Act (ISA). An opposition member of parliament went on trial charged with sedition and publishing "false news". The head of a women's non-governmental organization faced imprisonment for publishing a report on ill-treatment in camps for detained migrant workers. It was reported that 71 detainees had died in migrant worker detention camps since 1992. Caning continued to be inflicted for a range of crimes. At least six people were sentenced to death and at least three were executed.

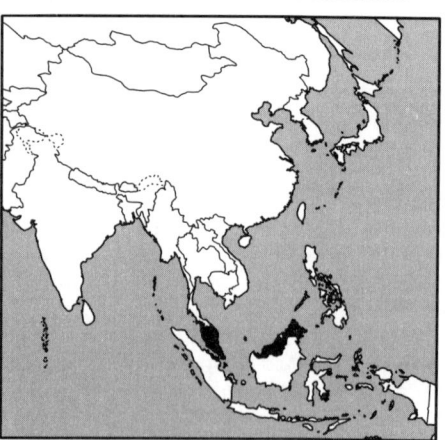

In February, the government of Prime Minister Mahathir Mohamad pledged to amend the ISA, which allows the Home Minister to impose a renewable detention order of up to two years without charge or trial on anyone suspected of threatening the national security or economic life of Malaysia. The amendments would specify, for the first time, the offences covered by the ISA (espionage, incitement to race and religious hatred, economic sabotage and falsifying identification and travel documents), and would allow the Home Minister discretion in setting the length of detention orders. These amendments had not been implemented by the end of the year.

In April, the government announced plans to provide for mandatory jail sentences and caning under the Passport Bill. In June, officials proposed the caning of inmates who run away from drug rehabilitation centres more than twice and in November the government proposed amendments to the Immigration Act to provide mandatory caning for illegal immigrants who re-enter the country after deportation (see *Amnesty International Report 1995*).

Fourteen former members of the banned *Al Arqam* Islamic sect were ordered to be detained without trial for two years under the ISA. They were possible prisoners of conscience. They were among 18 former members of *Al Arqam* arrested between May and June and accused of attempting to revive the sect. Four of those arrested were released but reportedly placed under a restriction order limiting their freedom of expression and of movement. In December, the government threatened to use the ISA to arrest members of local non-governmental organizations seeking to hold a forum on alleged abuses of police powers. The organizers suspended the forum.

Six former members of the Communist Party of Malaya detained under the ISA in 1989 were reportedly released (see *Amnesty International Report 1995*).

In November, police arrested 106 people attending an international conference on East Timor. The peaceful meeting was forcibly disrupted by members of the youth wing of the United Malays National Organisation and other members of the *Barisan Nasional*, National Front, ruling coalition. Forty-eight foreign participants were deported and the remaining detainees were released in stages, ending with the release, on the orders of the High Court, of 10 detainees still held five days after the arrests. No charges had been brought against the conference participants by the end of the year.

In January, Lim Guan Eng, deputy leader of the opposition Democratic Action Party, went on trial charged under the Sedition Act with "prompting disaffection with the administration of justice" and under the Printing Presses and Publication Act with publishing "false news" (see *Amnesty International Report 1996*). His trial was adjourned in March pending a judicial ruling on the standard of proof required in all criminal cases. In July, the Federal Court ruled that a judge must be satisfied that the prosecution had proved its case "beyond a reasonable doubt" before calling on the accused to make his defence, rather than the previous requirement of *prima facie* standard of evidence. When Lim Guan Eng's trial resumed in October the judge ruled that the prosecution had in fact proved "beyond reasonable doubt" that the defence had a case to answer on both charges. In December, the government introduced a bill amending the Criminal Procedures Code to restore the *prima facie* standard of evidence requirement. The trial had not concluded by the end of the year. If convicted, Lim Guan Eng faces imprisonment and disqualification from parliament.

In June, Irene Fernandez, director of the non-governmental organization *Tenaganita* (Women's Force), went on trial charged under the Printing Presses and Publication Act with maliciously publishing "false news" in a 1995 report on conditions in camps for detained migrant workers (see *Amnesty International Report 1996*). *Tenaganita*'s report detailed a pattern of abuses in the camps, including ill-treatment and sexual abuse, denial of medical care and deaths caused by malnutrition and treatable illnesses. If convicted, Irene Fernandez faces up to three years' imprisonment or a fine, or both. The trial continued at the end of the year.

In April, the Ministry of Home Affairs stated that 71 detainees had died in migrant worker detention camps since 1992 but claimed that these deaths were due to the detainees' poor state of health when apprehended. A government visitors' panel set up in September 1995 to examine conditions in the camps did not have the authority to investigate past deaths and had not made public its findings by the end of the year.

Caning, a form of cruel, inhuman or degrading treatment, was imposed as an additional punishment to imprisonment throughout the year. In February, Yusof Rahim was jailed for six and a half years and received 10 strokes of the cane for possession of cannabis.

During the year at least six people were sentenced to death and at least three executed. Most had been convicted of drug-trafficking offences, for which the death sentence is mandatory. Mustaffa Kamal Abdul Aziz and Mohd Radi Abdul Majid were executed in January after being convicted in 1991 of drug-trafficking.

In January, Amnesty International urged the government to drop the charges against Lim Guan Eng and to allow him to peacefully express his political opinion and represent his constituents' views without fear of imprisonment. In May, Amnesty International expressed concern that Irene Fernandez had been charged in connection with her peaceful human rights activities and called for charges against her to be withdrawn. The organization repeated its call for a full public inquiry into poor conditions and past deaths in migrant worker detention camps. In August, the organization urged that former *Al Arqam* members detained without trial be charged with a recognizably criminal offence or else released. In November, the organization called for the immediate release of those detained for peacefully participating in the international conference on East Timor. In December, the organization called on the government to lift threats to use the ISA to prevent a forum being held on alleged abuses of police powers. Throughout the year Amnesty International appealed to the authorities to end the punishment of caning and to commute all death sentences.

MALDIVES

Over a dozen political prisoners, among them prisoners of conscience, were detained for expressing views critical of government policies. Many of them were held without charge or trial. At least one prisoner of conscience was sentenced to imprisonment after an unfair trial.

The government of President Moumoon Abdul Gayoom maintained tight restrictions on freedom of expression.

Intellectuals were imprisoned for peacefully criticizing the government. In April, Mohammed Nasheed, a freelance journalist, was sentenced to two years' imprisonment by a court in Malé, apparently for making comments about the 1994 general elections and the 1993 presidential elections in an article which was published in a magazine in the Philippines. He was denied the right to be represented in court by his lawyer. After three months in Gaamadhoo Prison, he was transferred to house arrest in Malé with no access to visitors or telephone calls. On appeal, the High Court reduced his sentence to six months' imprisonment – about nine days short of the period he had spent in prison and under house arrest. The government did not, however, take into account his period under house arrest and sent him to Gaamadhoo Prison for a further three months. He was released in December on completion of his sentence. He was a prisoner of conscience.

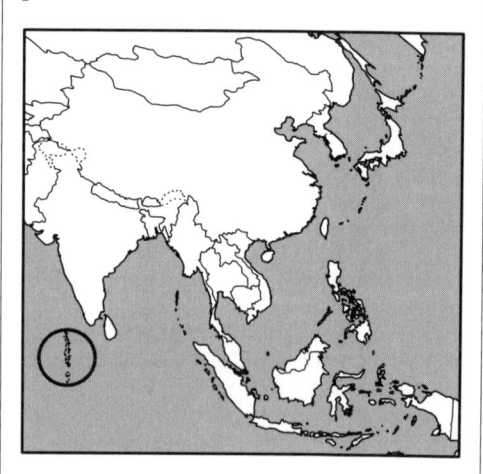

Another prisoner of conscience held under house arrest was Ilyas Ibrahim, President Gayoom's brother-in-law, who had sought to run as a presidential candidate in August 1993 and was subsequently charged with unconstitutional behaviour. He fled the country, but was sentenced to 15 years' imprisonment *in absentia*. Amid reports of assurances from the authorities that he would not be detained, he returned in March and was placed under house arrest.

Prisoners of conscience were believed to be among a group of more than 10 people arrested on Fuvahmulaku Island in January and February, apparently in connection with a reportedly peaceful demonstration about a rise in electricity prices. Among those arrested were Mohamed Didi, Hussain Shareef, Hussain Shakir and Ahmed Saeed. Most of them were believed to be detained without charge or trial at the end of the year.

In May, Amnesty International issued a report, *Republic of Maldives: Continued detention of prisoner of conscience,* urging the government to release Mohammed Nasheed immediately and unconditionally. In November, Amnesty International reiterated its call for the release of several prisoners of conscience and a fair trial for about a dozen other political prisoners. In December, the organization learned that the banishing order on Mohamed Saleem (see *Amnesty International Report 1996*), who was serving five and a half years' banishment on Nilandhoo island, had been lifted. No further details were available.

MALI

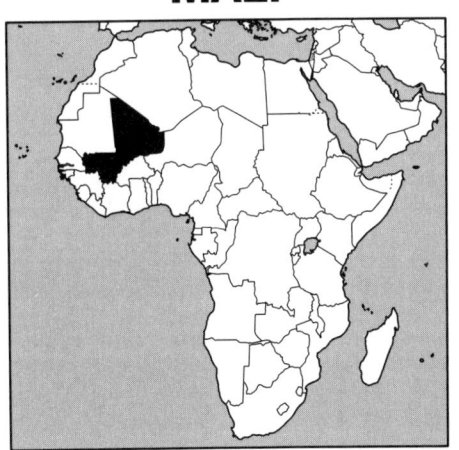

Scores of people, including students and retired workers, were detained briefly following a strike and a peace march. Five retired workers remained in detention. Some of those detained appeared to be prisoners of conscience. Six people were sentenced to death. A former President of Mali and five other prisoners remained under sentence of death. No executions were reported.

In March, a ceremony known as the Torch of Peace, presided over by President Alpha Oumar Konaré and the President of Ghana, Jerry John Rawlings, Chairman of the Economic Community of West African States, took place in Timbuktu, in the northern part of the country. The ceremony symbolized the end of the rebellion led by armed opposition groups in the north of Mali; they promised to disband and pledged never to take up arms against the state again. In October, more than a thousand former armed opposition group members were integrated into the army.

Mady Diallo, a minister in the government of former head of state Moussa Traoré, and seven soldiers were arrested in October and charged with "inciting an attack on the legitimate Malian Government with the aim of overthrowing it by force, and with complicity in a conspiracy against the internal security of the state, by donations, promises and supplies of means".

In January, at least 40 students, including Operi Berthé, Secretary General of the *Association des élèves et étudiants du Mali* (AEEM), Association of Malian students, and Koré Toumou Téhéra, Nohoum Togo and Alassane Touré, all AEEM members, were arrested and charged with "causing offence to rightful authority, violation and assaults and for undermining the freedom of work". All were released provisionally after two weeks. The students were arrested after they launched a strike for payment of scholarships and for better conditions of study.

In August, Youssouf Traoré, an opposition party member in the National Assembly, was arrested in San, in the south of Mali, after repeatedly criticizing the local administration of corruption. He was later charged with defamation and insulting a civil servant in the course of his duties. Youssouf Traoré was released provisionally after three months.

In September, more than 30 members of the *Association des travailleurs volontaires partant à la retraite,* Association of Voluntarily Retired Workers, including 23 women, were arrested after police broke up a peace march in protest at what they said was the authorities' failure to keep their promises. They were charged with participating in an armed gathering and damaging state property. Twenty-five of them were provisionally released after being held for between three and 10 days, but five were still detained at the end of the year. Some of the five were believed to be possible prisoners of conscience.

In June, six people were sentenced to death by the *Cour d'Assises,* Court of Assizes, in Ségou. Diango Sissoko, Daouda Traoré and Karim Koné were convicted on charges of theft of public property and armed robbery; the others were convicted of arson, aggravated theft and possession of drugs. Former President Moussa Traoré and Boubacar Dembelé, former head of the National Tobacco and Match Company, as well as three other former government officials, remained under sentence of death (see *Amnesty International Report 1996*). There were no reports of executions. In March, President Konaré made a statement in which he mentioned that he opposed the death penalty.

MAURITANIA

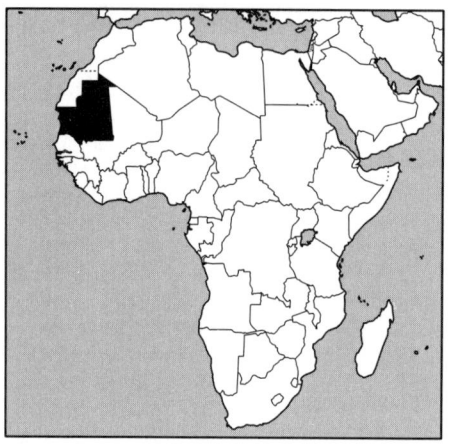

Fifty-two political prisoners held for over a year were acquitted on appeal and released. There were still no investigations into past human rights violations.

In October, the first ever multi-party elections were held. The majority of seats were won by President Maaouiya Ould Sid Ahmed Taya's ruling Democratic Republican Party. The main black Mauritanian opposition party, *Action pour le changement*, Action for Change, won one seat and six independent candidates also won seats in the 79-member Legislative Assembly. The opposition political parties made allegations of electoral irregularities.

According to the estimate of the UN High Commissioner for Refugees (UNHCR) in June 1995, more than 66,000 Mauritanians remained in refugee camps in Senegal and Mali. More than 50,000 black Mauritanians had been expelled by the government in 1989 following intercommunal violence, and many thousands more had fled to escape human rights violations. Plans to voluntarily repatriate 10,000 of the refugees from Senegal and Mali were halted in June, apparently when the Mauritanian authorities refused to agree with the UNHCR on a date for the repatriations. However, in December, the UNHCR estimated that over 30,000 refugees had returned to Mauritania.

Press freedom continued to be limited. All newspapers had to pass the scrutiny of a censor commission before being given permission to circulate by the Ministry of the Interior. In April, an opposition newspaper, *Mauritanie Nouvelles*, was banned by the Ministry of the Interior for three months on the grounds that recent editions had been subversive and damaging to the country's interests. Shortly after the ban was lifted, the French and Arabic versions of one edition were again seized; no reason was given.

In January, the appeal court in the capital, Nouakchott, acquitted 52 political prisoners arrested in October 1995 (see *Amnesty International Report 1996*). They were all believed to be current or former members of the Mauritanian branch of the Arab Socialist *Ba'th* Party, whose headquarters are in Iraq, and members of *At-tali'à*, a political party formed following a spilt within the *Ba'th* party. The appeal had been lodged both by the defence lawyers, who felt they had had inadequate opportunity to deliver their defence, and by the Public Prosecutor, who felt the sentences handed down had been too lenient. In December 1995, 29 of the accused had been acquitted, 13 had received suspended prison sentences and 10 had been sentenced to prison terms of between six months and one year.

The government continued to prevent investigations into past human rights violations, including the suspected extrajudicial executions of over 500 black Mauritanians held in military custody between 1990 and 1991.

MEXICO

Scores of prisoners of conscience were detained, and scores of human rights defenders threatened and attacked. Torture by law enforcement officers and the army was widespread. At least three people died as a result of torture. Prison conditions amounting to cruel, inhuman or degrading treatment were reported. At least

20 people "disappeared" and the whereabouts of hundreds who "disappeared" in previous years remained unknown. Scores of people were extrajudicially executed. Those responsible for human rights violations continued to benefit from impunity.

In March, the government established the *Consejo Nacional de Seguridad Pública*, National Public Security Council, which incorporated the army and the navy into law enforcement operations. Human rights violations, including torture, by members of the military increased.

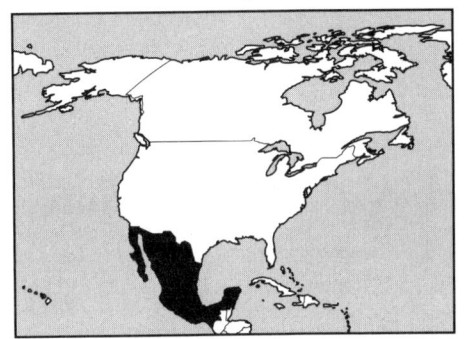

Peace talks between the government and the *Ejército Zapatista de Liberación Nacional* (EZLN), Zapatista National Liberation Army – an armed opposition group – stalled in September, following EZLN allegations about the authorities' failure to implement previous agreements on indigenous people's rights (see *Amnesty International Report 1996*). In June, the *Ejército Popular Revolucionario* (EPR), Popular Revolutionary Army, another armed opposition group, launched attacks against military targets, resulting in dozens of deaths. The government launched army operations in several states, especially in Guerrero, Oaxaca and Veracruz, during which widespread human rights violations were reported.

In December, the Attorney General's Office established a unit to investigate the growing number of threats and attacks against human rights defenders and prosecute those responsible.

In July, a delegation from the Inter-American Commission on Human Rights visited Mexico for the first time and investigated reports of human rights violations in the states of Chiapas and Guerrero.

Scores of prisoners of conscience were arrested and dozens continued to be imprisoned for their peaceful political or civil rights activities. In January, José Carrillo Conde and Gerardo Demesa Padilla, leaders of the *Comité de Unidad de Tepoztlán* (CUT), Committee of Unity of Tepoztlán, a civil rights organization, were imprisoned on charges related to their opposition to a local development project in Morelos State. José Carrillo Conde was released in October, together with Fortino Mendoza, another CUT activist arrested in December 1995, but Gerardo Demesa Padilla remained in prison at the end of the year. Hilario Mesino Acosta, a leader of the *Organización Campesina de la Sierra del Sur* (OCSS), Southern Sierra Peasants' Organization, in Guerrero State, was arrested in Mexico City in July on charges of participating in violent activities; the charges were believed to be politically motivated. He was tortured and threatened with the "disappearance" of his daughters, Rocío and Norma Mesino, who had received previous death threats after lodging complaints about the massacre of 17 peasants in Guerrero State in 1995 (see below).

Scores of prisoners of conscience were imprisoned on politically motivated charges and denied the right to fair and prompt trail. In July, Cecilia Elizalde Mora, aged 69, and Maximina Escobar Sánchez, aged 70, both Nahuatl Indian peasants, were arrested at an army roadblock in San Felipe Neri, Morelos State. They were reportedly held incommunicado for several hours, denied legal assistance, and charged with drug-trafficking, solely on the basis of the soldiers' statements. They remained in prison awaiting trial at the end of the year.

Seven members of the *Sindicato de Trabajadores Petroleros de la República Mexicana*, the Mexican oil workers' union, including 75-year-old Joaquín Hernández Galicia (known as "La Quina") who was imprisoned in 1989, remained in prison at the end of the year. Brigadier General José Francisco Gallardo, detained in 1993 for calling for the establishment of a human rights Ombudsman for the armed forces, remained in the *Campo Militar Número Uno*, a military prison in Mexico City. In June, his son, Marco Vinicio Gallardo Enríquez, who campaigned for his father's release, survived an attack by unidentified individuals in Mexico City.

Eight shoe-factory workers, including a 16-year-old and four women, imprisoned in 1995 on charges of belonging to the

EZLN, were released in November (see *Amnesty International Report 1996*).

Scores of human rights defenders received death threats, and some were attacked, abducted and tortured. The authorities failed to bring those responsible to justice. Among those repeatedly threatened with death were members of the church-based organization *Centro de Derechos Humanos Miguel Agustín Pro Juárez*, A.C. (PRODH), Miguel Agustín Pro Juárez Human Rights Centre, in Mexico City. They included Pilar Noriega, Digna Ochoa, Enrique Flota, Víctor Brenes, José Lavanderos and David Fernández, a Jesuit priest; and Araceli Muñoz, a member of *Acción Cristiana para la Abolición de la Tortura*, Christian Action for the Abolition of Torture, in Mexico City.

Civil rights activists and politicians also received death threats. For example, in July, Leticia Moctezuma Vargas received death threats for her community activism in Tepoztlán, Morelos State (see above). Her 11- and 13-year-old daughters were also threatened. Graco Ramírez Abreu, state congressman for the opposition *Partido de la Revolución Democrática* (PRD), Democratic Revolutionary Party, in Morelos, received death threats in October for campaigning against human rights violations by the police.

Dozens of journalists were targeted for reporting on politically sensitive issues, including human rights violations. In January, José Barrón Rosales, a Nahuatl Indian journalist in Veracruz, survived an armed attack. He had received death threats for his work campaigning for Indian rights. In September, the Guerrero State Attorney's Office published a list of 27 journalists whom it accused of having links with the EPR. Some of those listed later received anonymous death threats. In October, Filiberto Lastra and Martín Enríquez, reporters for *Radio Xeva* in Villahermosa, Tabasco State, survived an attack by three men, including an official of the *Dirección de Seguridad Pública*, Department of Public Security, who had threatened them with death for criticizing the State Governor.

Hundreds of detainees, including children, human rights defenders, journalists and members of ethnic minorities, were tortured by the security forces, including the army and paramilitary groups. At least three people, including a minor, died as a result of torture. The courts continued to admit as evidence confessions extracted under torture. Methods of torture included beatings, near-asphyxiation with plastic bags and with water, forcing peppered water into the nose and electric shocks. Proper medical treatment for the victims was unavailable in detention. Impunity for the perpetrators prevailed.

In June, 25 members of the Amuzgo Indian community of Coachapa, Guerrero State, suspected of theft, were subjected to beatings, prolonged hanging by the wrists and semi-asphyxiation by state police to extract a confession. Among them was 16-year-old Alfredo Ramírez Santiago, who was hanged by the neck from a tree and beaten on the head and body. In June, journalist Oswald Alonso was abducted from his home in Cuernavaca, Morelos State, by three men believed to be members of the security forces. He was tortured and threatened with death for criticizing the state police before being released the following day.

Manuel Ramírez Santiago and Fermín Oseguera Santiago, respectively chairpersons of the *Comité de Defensa de los Derechos del Pueblo*, People's Rights Defence Committee, and the *Unión de Tablajeros* A.C., the woodworkers' union, were abducted in October in Tlaxiaco, Oaxaca State, by members of the security forces and interrogated under torture, including beatings and burning with cigarettes. Both were released without charge in November. In November, Javier López Montoya, administrator of the *Coordinación de Organismos No Gubernamentales por la Paz* (CONPAZ), Coalition of Non-governmental Organizations for Peace, his wife and two children, were abducted in San Cristóbal de las Casas, Chiapas State, by unidentified individuals believed to be members of the security forces. They remained in secret detention for two days during which Javier López Montoya was interrogated about CONPAZ' activities. His interrogators beat him and threatened him and his family with death.

Scores of peasant activists in Guerrero and Oaxaca States were tortured to confess to having links with the EPR. Eight people arrested in July in Guerrero State were subjected to beatings, electric shocks, semi-asphyxiation and prolonged hanging by the wrists for up to seven days by members of the army and state police. They were charged with having links with the EPR on the basis of statements extracted under torture and remained in prison awaiting trial at the end of the year.

On 8 July, Pedro Valoy Alvarado and 17-year-old Marcelino Zapoteco Acatitlán, members of the *Organización de Pueblos y Colonias de Guerrero*, a peasant organization, were arrested by the state police in Chilpancingo, Guerrero State, and tortured in a local police station to confess to burglary. Pedro Valoy Alvarado was released on 10 July, but Marcelino Zapoteco Acatitlán, a Zapotec Indian, remained in detention with serious injuries, from which he died on 15 September. On 12 October, Valentín Carrillo Saldaña, a Tepehuan Indian peasant, was arrested by soldiers near his community of San Juan Nepomuceno in Chihuahua State. Witnesses saw him being beaten and carried away. His body, bearing signs of torture, was discovered on 17 October. This was the only known case in which reports of torture resulted in the arrest of the alleged perpetrators. Those believed to be responsible for his death were awaiting trial at the end of the year.

Prison conditions amounting to cruel, inhuman or degrading treatment continued to be reported in many prisons. In October, scores of inmates of the Barrientos prison in Mexico City rioted, demanding better conditions and an end to torture by prison guards. At least 30 were seriously beaten by the police. The authorities later acknowledged that police had used excessive force and promised to improve conditions. However, those responsible were not brought to justice and prison conditions had not improved by the end of the year.

At least 20 people "disappeared". Students Juan Emerio, Jorge Cabada and 17-year-old Abrahám Hernández were detained in June by members of the municipal police in Culiacán, Sinaloa State. Their whereabouts remained unknown at the end of the year. In September, Rómulo Rico Urrea "disappeared" after his arrest by members of the security forces in Culiacán, Sinaloa State. His detention was initially acknowledged but later denied by the authorities. Gregorio Alfonso Alvarado López, a teacher and trade union and Indian rights activist who had received death threats, "disappeared" on 26 September in his home town of Chilpancingo, Guerrero State. The state authorities later told his relatives that he had been abducted by a paramilitary group, but failed to disclose his whereabouts. The whereabouts of Cuauhtémoc Ornelas Campos (see *Amnesty International Report 1996*) and Gilberto Romero Vásquez, who "disappeared" in 1995, remained unknown. No progress was reported in the investigations into the "disappearance" of hundreds of political activists in previous years, including those of at least 14 peasants who "disappeared" in Chiapas State in January 1994. The whereabouts of political activist José Ramón García, who "disappeared" in 1988, also remained unknown (see *Amnesty International Report 1996*).

Scores of people, including political activists, were extrajudicially executed by members of the security forces and paramilitary groups. Most perpetrators benefited from impunity. In January, Gildardo Dorantes Muñoz, a member of the OCSS and the PRD, was murdered in Mexcaltepec, Guerrero State, by local officials who had previously threatened him for his political activities. In February, nine peasants from El Paraíso, Guerrero State, were killed by the state police. They had reportedly discovered evidence of local police involvement in kidnappings. In April, Marcos Olmedo Gutiérrez, a CUT activist, was extrajudicially executed by members of the Morelos state police. He had been wounded and arrested during a peaceful demonstration which was attacked by police. In September, Manuel Martínez de la Torre, a peasant activist, was detained, hooded and shot twice in the head, outside his home in Venustiano Carranza, Chiapas State, by members of the *Alianza San Bartolomé de los Llanos*, a paramilitary group with close links with local government officials. In November, three peasant activists were killed in Laja Tendida, Chiapas State, when soldiers and state police shot into a peaceful demonstration. Soldiers responsible for extrajudicial executions reported in January 1994 in Morelia and Ocosingo, Chiapas State, continued to benefit from impunity (see *Amnesty International Report 1995*). Human rights defenders working on these cases, including lawyers from the PRODH, received death threats (see above).

On 4 March, President Ernesto Zedillo ordered a Supreme Court investigation into the 1995 massacre of 17 peasants in

Aguas Blancas, Guerrero State (see *Amnesty International Report 1996*), and on 12 March Rubén Figueroa Alcócer, the State Governor, resigned. In April, the Supreme Court announced its findings, which included evidence of the involvement of senior state officials in the massacre. However, the former governor and other senior officials were not brought to justice.

At least one person was deliberately and arbitrarily killed by an armed opposition group. In August, Alberto Zamudio Estrada, a municipal police officer in Papalotla, Mexico State, was shot dead at close range by members of the EPR.

During the year, Amnesty International repeatedly urged the authorities to release prisoners of conscience, to end the impunity enjoyed by perpetrators of human rights violations and to bring an end to the practices of torture, "disappearance" and extrajudicial executions.

Amnesty International delegates visited the country in June, and again in November and December, to investigate reports of human rights violations. In March, the organization published a report, *Overcoming fear: Human rights violations against women in Mexico*. In December, it published *Human rights defenders on the front line*, expressing growing concern about the threats and attacks suffered by human rights defenders in central America and Mexico.

MOLDOVA

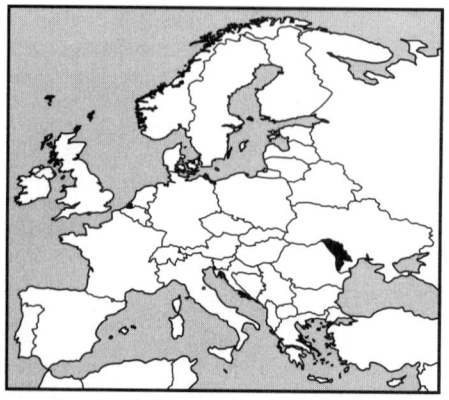

Death sentences on 19 prisoners awaiting execution were commuted to life imprisonment. An official of the self-proclaimed Dnestr Moldavian Republic (DMR) was found guilty of causing a death in custody; torture and ill-treatment by law enforcement officials continued to be reported.

Presidential elections in November were won by the chairman of the parliament, Petru Lucinschi.

Negotiations continued on the status of the DMR but a draft memorandum had not been signed by the end of the year.

A new court system was introduced in August to provide greater independence of the courts from the government and the procuracy.

In February, death sentences on 19 prisoners awaiting execution were commuted to life imprisonment by presidential decree. This followed a parliamentary vote at the end of 1995 to remove the death penalty from Moldova's Penal Code (see *Amnesty International Report 1996*).

In May, Moldova signed Protocol No. 6 to the European Convention for the Protection of Human Rights and Fundamental Freedoms, thus fulfilling a great part of its commitment to the Council of Europe to abolish the death penalty (see *Amnesty International Report 1996*). Moldova also signed the European Convention for the Prevention of Torture and Inhuman or Degrading Treatment or Punishment.

A DMR official was found guilty of ill-treatment resulting in the death of a detainee. Four officials from the Rybnitsa City Department of Internal Affairs had reportedly been detained and charged in connection with the death in custody in 1995 of Aleksandr Kalashnikov (see *Amnesty International Report 1996*), but three were released under a special amnesty covering people who had fought on the side of the DMR. The fourth, Vladimir Luchinets, confessed to killing Aleksandr Kalashnikov, but later claimed he only agreed to do so when a superior officer promised that he too would benefit from the amnesty. Vladimir Luchinets was reportedly tried before the Supreme Court of the DMR in August and found guilty of "misconduct and exceeding his powers" and "the use of torture and physical violence, which resulted in the death of a person". He was sentenced to eight years' imprisonment.

Further allegations of torture and ill-treatment by DMR law enforcement officers emerged during Vladimir Luchinets' trial. A number of witnesses reportedly testified that they had been tortured and ill-treated in an attempt to force confessions while detained at the Rybnitsa City Department of Internal Affairs on suspicion of the same offence as Aleksandr Kalashnikov. Among the alleged victims were G. Kachurovsky, S. Boynovich and A. Marchenko.

It was reported in September that Andrei Ivanţoc and Alexandru Leşco, two of the "Tiraspol Six" (see *Amnesty International Report 1994*), were seriously ill and had not been provided with adequate medical assistance. They had been sentenced in 1993 for crimes against the DMR after a trial which seemed to fall short of international standards.

Amnesty International welcomed the abolition of the death penalty in Moldova. It urged the DMR authorities to investigate all allegations of torture and ill-treatment in detention by law enforcement officials and expressed concern about irregularities in investigations. In a reply received in November, the Minister of the Interior of the DMR, I. Fuchedzi, stated that appropriate measures had been taken to address the violations by law enforcement officers raised by the organization, including disciplinary actions and dismissals. Amnesty International continued to call for a review of the case of the "Tiraspol Six", asking for those still detained to receive appropriate medical treatment.

MONGOLIA

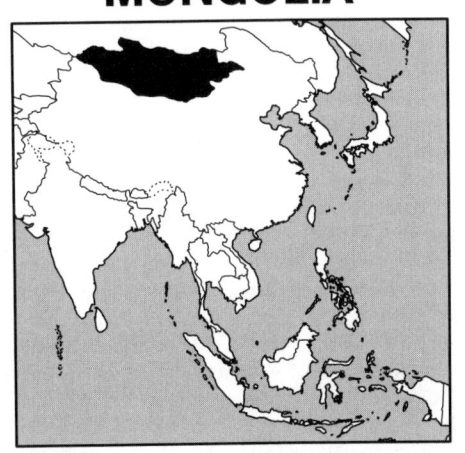

Prisoners in corrective labour institutions died from starvation. At least five death sentences were passed and at least two executions were carried out.

In elections in June to the Great Hural (parliament), the Mongolian People's Revolutionary party, which had held power for the previous 75 years, was defeated by the Mongolian Democratic Union coalition, in which the senior partners were the National Democratic Party (NDP) and the Social Democratic Party (SDP). President Puntsalmaagiyn Ochirbat appointed Mendsayhany Enhsaihan of the NDP as Prime Minister, and SDP leader Radnaasurenbereliyn Gonchigdorj became Chairman (speaker) of the Great Hural.

Reports continued to be received that inmates of corrective labour institutions were dying from starvation or from illnesses possibly caused or exacerbated by starvation (see *Amnesty International Report 1996*). As part of official moves to tackle the problem, the Minister of Justice stated in December that new legislation taking effect at the end of the year would end the requirement that prisoners should work for food, clothing and other provisions, the cost of which would henceforth be covered solely by the state.

In October, in response to a request for clarification from the country's senior Buddhist abbot, the government confirmed that Buddhist monks were not exempt from performing compulsory military service. A 1992 law on military service required all men aged between 18 and 26 to perform military service for one year, and made no provision for a civilian alternative service for those who declared a conscientious objection.

The death penalty remained in force. No official statistics were made available, but at least five people were sentenced to death and at least two executions were carried out. The true figures were almost certainly higher.

In a written response received in March to Amnesty International's 1995 report, *Mongolia: Prison inmates starve to death* (see *Amnesty International Report 1996*), a senior official of the State Police Department rejected allegations that deliberate starvation was used to force confessions from people in pre-trial detention.

Amnesty International continued to call for improvements in the prison system to end deaths by starvation. The organization urged the introduction of a civilian alternative to compulsory military service. It continued to call for abolition of the death penalty.

MOROCCO AND WESTERN SAHARA

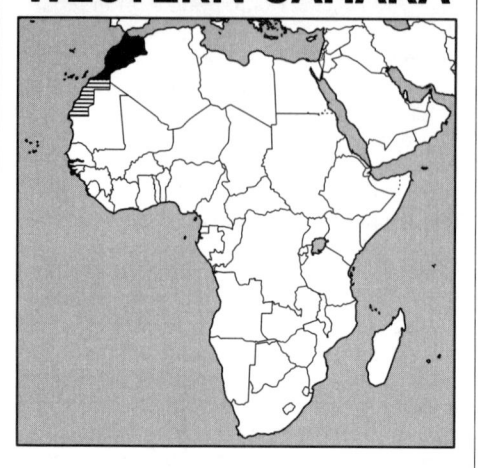

Over 50 political prisoners and prisoners of conscience continued to serve long sentences imposed after unfair trials in previous years. Fifteen political opposition activists were detained for several hours for the non-violent expression of their beliefs. Six Sahrawi prisoners of conscience serving long prison terms were pardoned and released. Torture and ill-treatment continued, particularly of individuals charged with smuggling and drug-trafficking offences. At least eight people died in custody. Hundreds of Sahrawis and Moroccans who "disappeared" in previous years remained unaccounted for. A former prisoner of conscience forcibly exiled in 1991 remained unable to return to Morocco. At least 40 prisoners were reported to remain on death row. No executions were carried out.

In September, a referendum approved constitutional reforms proposing the division of the single-chamber *Chambre des représentants* (Chamber of Representatives) into two chambers by creating a new upper house, the *Chambre des conseillers* (Chamber of Counsellors). King Hassan II retained the right to dissolve both chambers.

The UN-sponsored referendum on the future of Western Sahara, originally scheduled for 1992, but postponed several times, was again postponed – this time indefinitely. In May, the UN Security Council voted to suspend voter registration in the territory until both parties could resolve a dispute over voter identification procedures. UN observers remained in place but its contingent of civilian police (CIVPOL) was reduced from 91 to nine officers.

More than 50 political prisoners and prisoners of conscience, imprisoned after unfair trials in previous years, continued to be detained. They included 'Abdelkader Cheddoudi, sentenced in July 1995 to three years' imprisonment on charges of insulting the King (see *Amnesty International Report 1996*), whose sentence was reduced on appeal in July to 18 months. He was released in December on expiry of his sentence. Ahmed Haou, 'Abdelkader Sfiri, Mustapha Marjaoui and Youssef Cherkaoui-Rbati, arrested in 1983 with other supporters and sympathizers of unauthorized Islamist groups and accused of putting up anti-monarchist posters, distributing leaflets and participating in demonstrations, continued to serve life sentences (see *Amnesty International Reports 1995* and *1996*).

Non-violent protests against the referendum on constitutional reforms resulted in the short-term detention of a number of opposition party members. In September, five members of the opposition *Parti d'avant-garde socialiste et démocratique*, Socialist and Democratic Avant-garde Party, were arrested in Mohammedia for distributing leaflets calling for a boycott of the referendum. Two days later, 10 alleged members of the opposition *Organisation d'action démocratique populaire*, Organization of Popular Democratic Action, were arrested in Rabat, the capital, and Oujda for campaigning for a boycott of the referendum. All were released the same day.

Kelthoum Ahmed Labid El-Ouanat and five youths, all Sahrawi prisoners of conscience who had been sentenced in July 1993 to 20 years' imprisonment by the Moroccan Military Court, were released by royal pardon in May. Eight others, who had been arrested in May 1995 on charges of threatening the external security and territorial integrity of Morocco and sentenced in June 1995 to between 15 and 20 years' imprisonment (reduced to one year by royal pardon in July 1995), were released in August. They had continued to be detained for three months beyond the expiry of their sentences.

Prisoner of conscience 'Abdessalem Yassine, the spiritual leader of the banned

Islamist association *al-'Adl wa'l-Ihsan* (Justice and Charity), remained under administratively imposed house arrest, over six years after its imposition. His house arrest was lifted in December 1995 but reinstated within days by the Interior Ministry.

In January, eight people, including four Algerian nationals, were sentenced to up to 14 years' imprisonment by the Military Court in Rabat. They had been arrested in September and October 1995 on charges of smuggling arms to Algeria (see *Amnesty International Report 1996*). Trial proceedings fell short of internationally recognized standards for fair trial. Defendants and their lawyers alleged in court that the defendants' confessions had been extracted under torture but the Court failed to investigate these claims. The eight were awaiting a review of their case by the Supreme Court at the end of the year.

Reports of torture and ill-treatment continued to be received, particularly in cases of individuals arrested on charges of drug-trafficking and smuggling. For example, 'Abdelaziz Al-Yakhloufi, arrested in December 1995, was allegedly subjected to torture including suspension in contorted positions, sexual abuse and being forced to sit on a bottle. The Interior Ministry rejected these allegations, but no investigations were known to have been carried out. The authorities also failed to investigate complaints made in previous years of torture and ill-treatment of detainees during incommunicado detention, sometimes illegally prolonged for weeks, and the use as evidence of confessions allegedly extracted under torture (see previous *Amnesty International Reports*).

At least eight detainees died in custody, allegedly as a result of beatings and ill-treatment. In most cases, requests by relatives, lawyers and human rights organizations for independent investigations were disregarded by the authorities. However, in the case of Houssein Al-Mernissi, who died in Safi police station in July, an investigation was ordered and was being carried out at the end of the year.

An investigation was ordered into the death of Semmane Bouchta, who died in Khouribga police station in August 1994. However, the two policemen accused of having beaten Semmane Bouchta to death were acquitted in October amid allegations that witnesses against the defendants had been subjected to pressure. No other investigations were known to have been carried out into deaths in custody which occurred in previous years (see previous *Amnesty International Reports*).

Scores of demonstrators were reportedly injured in clashes with police. In March, a non-violent sit-in by university lecturers and school teachers outside the Ministry of Education in Rabat was violently broken up by police. In May and October, police reportedly used excessive force to break up non-violent demonstrations organized by the *Association des chômeurs diplômés*, Association of Unemployed Graduates. Scores of demonstrators were reported to have sustained injuries, including broken limbs.

Hundreds of Sahrawis and Moroccans who "disappeared" after arrest in previous years remained unaccounted for (see previous *Amnesty International Reports*). They included 'Abdelhaq Rouissi, a trade unionist who "disappeared" in 1964; 'Abdallah Cherrouk, a student who "disappeared" in 1981; and Mohamed-Salem Bueh-Barca and Tebker Ment Sidi-Mohamed Ould Khattari who "disappeared" in Laayoune in 1976.

No steps were taken to investigate the "disappearance" of hundreds of Sahrawis and Moroccans who were released in 1991 after up to 18 years in secret detention and the deaths of scores of others or to bring to justice those responsible. Neither those released in 1991 nor the families of those who died in secret detention received any compensation. Gleimina Ment Tayeb Yazidi, a former "disappeared" who had been released from the secret detention centre in Qal'at M'Gouna in 1991 and who had been rearrested in November 1995 in Laayoune, was believed to have been released at the beginning of the year.

Christine Daure-Serfaty, President of the *Observatoire international des prisons*, International Prisons Watch, was arrested by police in July at a public ceremony organized by the opposition political party *Union socialiste des forces populaires*, Socialist Union of Popular Forces, in Casablanca. She is the wife of Abraham Serfaty, a former prisoner of conscience who was forcibly expelled to France on his release in 1991 and who remained unable to return to Morocco. She was detained for one night in Casablanca police station and sent back to France the following day without explanation.

In December, the Supreme Court in Rabat upheld the sentences on Stéphane Ait Iddir, Radouane Hamadi and Hamal Marzoug, who were sentenced to death in January 1995 for allegedly having carried out armed attacks on behalf of armed opposition groups, including the armed attack on a hotel in Marrakech in August 1994 (see *Amnesty International Report 1996*). The Supreme Court only rules on procedural matters and does not re-examine the facts of a case. At least 40 people were reported to remain on death row at the end of the year. No executions were carried out.

Amnesty International wrote to the authorities requesting information about cases of allegations of torture and ill-treatment and deaths in custody, and calling for independent investigations to be carried out. The organization also called on the authorities to release all prisoners of conscience. No response was received. A list of the names of "disappeared" Sahrawis was sent to the government's human rights body, the *Conseil consultatif des droits de l'homme*, Consultative Council for Human Rights, and information was sought on the fate and whereabouts of the "disappeared", but no reply was received.

In April, Amnesty International issued a report, *Morocco/Western Sahara: Human rights violations in Western Sahara*. The report detailed human rights violations committed by Moroccan security forces in Western Sahara despite the presence, since 1991, of observers of the UN Mission for the Referendum in Western Sahara. In the report Amnesty International called on the UN to ensure respect of human rights safeguards included in the Implementation Plan and full deployment of CIVPOL. The report also detailed Amnesty International's concerns about past abuses committed in the Sahrawi refugee camps administered by the *Frente Popular para la Liberación de Saguia el-Hamra y Rio de Oro*, Popular Front for the Liberation of Saguia el-Hamra and Rio de Oro (known as the Polisario Front), in southern Algeria.

MOZAMBIQUE

Criminal suspects were tortured and ill-treated, and one man died as a result of torture. One person reportedly "disappeared" in police custody. Little progress was made in bringing those responsible for human rights violations to justice.

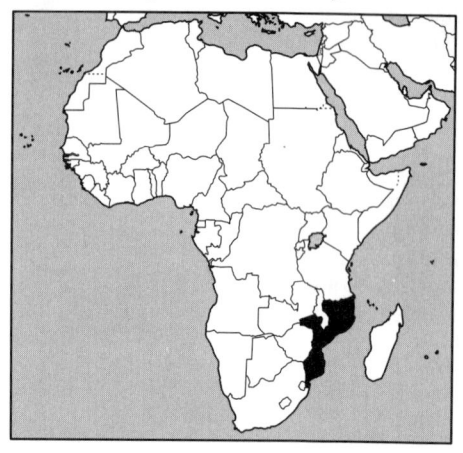

In areas formerly occupied by the *Resistência Nacional Moçambicana* (RENAMO), Mozambique National Resistance, and where the government of President Joaquim Chissano had not fully extended its authority, armed groups continued to commit crimes including looting, murder and rape. One such group, known as *Chimwenje* (Torch), was said to be connected with a Zimbabwean opposition politician and to comprise both Zimbabwean and Mozambican nationals, including former RENAMO soldiers. Government sources reported that RENAMO groups still controlled areas around their former military bases, where they continued to detain some people taken prisoner during the war.

In early August, seven alleged *Chimwenje* members, including two Zimbabwean nationals, were convicted of armed rebellion and sentenced to between two and 16 years' imprisonment. They had been arrested in late 1995 in connection with an attack on a police post in Dombe, Manica province (see *Amnesty International Report 1996*).

There was a sharp increase in the already high levels of violent crime, and the Attorney General expressed concern that some criminals were operating under the protection of influential people. The 1992 peace process entailed a requirement that the police would be restructured and retrained with the assistance of the international community, but little progress was made. Amid public concern about the crime rate, the Minister of the Interior was replaced in November.

Reports of the torture and ill-treatment of criminal suspects indicated that the practice was widespread. The most detailed reports came from the capital, Maputo, where journalists and the *Liga Moçambicana dos Direitos Humanos* (LMDH), Mozambique Human Rights League, were able to make inquiries.

In May, university students striking for improved study conditions were subjected to beatings by members of the Rapid Intervention Police. Police arrested four students, beat them and then released them without charge. One of them, a disabled man, sustained injuries to his arms, back and head as the result of the beatings and was taken to hospital. Another student was stopped in his car and beaten. No investigation was known to have taken place into the incidents.

Franque Luís Tchembene, a driver, died in June as a result of torture after being arrested and accused of stealing a vehicle from his employer. He was reportedly taken to the Seventh Police Station in Maputo, beaten severely for several hours and shot at while immersed in a pool containing dirty water. The bullets did not penetrate his body. Representatives of the LMDH visited the police station and insisted that Franque Luís Tchembene be taken to hospital. He died a few days later. The Minister of the Interior reportedly failed to respond to a request from the parliamentary human rights commission for information about the incident. A criminal investigation into the allegations of torture continued at the end of the year.

According to reports, 19-year-old triplets who had been arrested in November 1995 in connection with a complaint made against one of them by an employer were tortured. They were taken to a police station in Matola, a Maputo suburb, where José Zacarias Moçambique was handcuffed and given 18 lashes with a whip, and his sisters, Ana and Leonor Zacarias Moçambique, were beaten and forced to have sexual relations with male prisoners in the presence of a policeman. They were held for about three weeks before being released without charge. Following the intervention of the LMDH, the Maputo provincial police commander initiated a criminal investigation, but the results had not been published by the end of the year.

Further information was received about the case of a police chief accused of illegally detaining and beating two RENAMO members of parliament in 1995 (see *Amnesty International Report 1996*). He was tried by the Tete Provincial Court in November 1995 and convicted of illegal detention, but acquitted of the charge of beating the two men. He was sentenced to nine months' imprisonment and a fine, and ordered to pay an indemnity to the plaintiffs.

Abdul Mota reportedly "disappeared" in police custody in June. According to reports, members of a special police battalion set up to fight vehicle theft had detained him and other young men in May and impounded four cars they were driving. The police took the men to the battalion's base in Moamba, near the South African border, questioned them about a stolen vehicle, and then released them, saying they could have their cars back when it was returned. Three of the cars were subsequently given back by the police, but when questioned by Abdul Mota's family about the fourth car, the police could not account for it. Abdul Mota was reportedly last seen getting into a vehicle with a member of the special battalion, who subsequently denied any involvement in the "disappearance".

Amnesty International wrote to the police authorities in January and November to express concern about reports of torture. It received no response.

MYANMAR

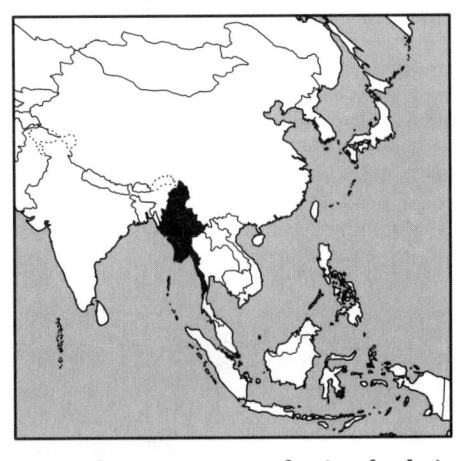

More than 1,000 people involved in opposition political activities, including 68 prisoners of conscience and hundreds of possible prisoners of conscience, remained in prison throughout the year. Almost 2,000 people were arrested for political reasons, including at least 23 prisoners of conscience. Although most were released, 45 were sentenced to long terms of imprisonment after unfair trials and 175 were still detained without charge or trial at the end of the year. Political prisoners were ill-treated and held in conditions that amounted to cruel, inhuman or degrading treatment. Members of ethnic minorities continued to suffer human rights violations, including extrajudicial executions and ill-treatment during forced labour and portering, and forcible relocations. Seven people were sentenced to death.

The State Law and Order Restoration Council (SLORC), Myanmar's military government chaired by General Than Shwe, continued to rule by decree in the absence of a constitution. Martial law decrees severely restricting the rights to freedom of expression and assembly remained in force throughout the year. In June, the SLORC issued Law No. 5/96, which allows for up to 20 years' imprisonment of anyone who expresses their political opposition views publicly.

The National Convention, convened by the SLORC in 1993 to agree principles for a new constitution, met intermittently during the first three months of the year, despite the withdrawal in November 1995 of the National League for Democracy (NLD), the opposition party led by Daw Aung San Suu Kyi. In March, the Convention approved guidelines for the composition of the executive, judicial, and legislative branches of the government, including a legislature in which the military would hold 25 per cent of the seats. The Convention was adjourned on 31 March and had not reconvened by the end of the year. The NLD appealed to the SLORC to enter into discussions, but there had been no dialogue by the end of the year.

Cease-fire talks continued between the armed opposition group, the Karen National Union (KNU), and the SLORC, but by the end of the year no agreement had been reached. In January, the SLORC agreed a cease-fire with the Shan *Muang Tai* Army (MTA), led by Khun Sa. Following the cease-fire, thousands of MTA troops surrendered to the SLORC; however, some MTA forces along with other Shan nationalist armed opposition groups retained their weapons. Sporadic fighting between the Karenni National Progressive Party (KNPP) and the government continued throughout the year.

The cease-fire between the SLORC and the New Mon State Party (NMSP) continued. Forcible repatriation, without international monitoring, of 10,000 Mon refugees living in Thai camps began in December 1995 and was completed by June (see **Thailand** entry). However, repatriated refugees remained in NMSP-controlled areas, reportedly because they feared returning to their villages. In April and May, more than 1,000 Mon villagers reportedly fleeing human rights violations in SLORC-controlled territory, including forced labour on the Ye-Dawei railway, moved into camps in NMSP areas.

More than 26,000 Burmese Muslim refugees remained in camps in Bangladesh, awaiting repatriation under a 1993 Memorandum of Understanding signed by the SLORC and the UN High Commissioner for Refugees (UNHCR) (see *Amnesty International Reports 1994* and *1995*). Although UNHCR maintained a presence both in camps in Bangladesh and in Rakhine State, to which some 200,000 refugees had already been repatriated, reports of human rights violations against Burmese Muslims, including ill-treatment during forced labour, continued.

In February, the UN Special Rapporteur on Myanmar submitted an extensive report to the UN Commission on Human Rights. In April, the Commission adopted by consensus a resolution extending the Special Rapporteur's mandate for another year and expressing grave concern at the extremely serious human rights situation in Myanmar. In May, Yozo Yokota resigned as Special Rapporteur, to be replaced in June by Rajsoomer Lallah. The new Special Rapporteur and officials in the UN Secretary General's office were repeatedly denied access to the country by the SLORC. In December, the UN General Assembly adopted by consensus a resolution expressing grave concern at continued human rights violations in Myanmar.

In response to the deteriorating human rights situation, the European Parliament adopted several resolutions, and the European Union agreed a Common Position, calling on the SLORC to, among other things, immediately and unconditionally release all political prisoners. In December, the European Commission recommended to the Council of Ministers of the European Union the suspension of preferential tariffs to Myanmar under the Generalized System of Preferences.

In July, the Association of South East Asian Nations (ASEAN) granted Myanmar Observer Status as a preliminary step towards full ASEAN membership.

More than 1,000 political prisoners arrested in previous years, including 68 prisoners of conscience and hundreds of possible prisoners of conscience, remained in detention. Almost 2,000 people were arrested for political reasons during the year, among them at least 23 prisoners of conscience. Although most were released, at least 175 were still detained without charge or trial at the end of the year. No political prisoners arrested in previous years were released. Prisoners of conscience U Thu Wai and U Htwe Myint remained imprisoned, but Tun Shwe died of cancer in May (see *Amnesty International Report 1996*). In May, the SLORC arrested more than 300 political activists after the NLD called a party conference. U Aye Win, Daw Aung San Suu Kyi's assistant, was arrested in May and was still held under the administrative detention provisions of the 1975 State Protection Law at the end of the year. He was a prisoner of conscience.

In August, 35 political activists who had been detained since May were sentenced to long terms of imprisonment after unfair trials. U Kan Shein, a rice farmer, was one of five prisoners of conscience sentenced for their involvement in producing a videotape documenting a poor rice harvest. The authorities claimed that the five had sent false information to Daw Aung San Suu Kyi in the hope that it would be passed to the UN Commission on Human Rights. According to unofficial sources, a group of villagers, including U Kan Shein, had made the videotape in order to appeal to the authorities for increased agricultural assistance. Their trial was reportedly held *in camera* in three sessions at Insein Prison. In a separate trial, prisoner of conscience Maung San Hlaing, also known as Eva, Daw Aung San Suu Kyi's bodyguard and a former political prisoner, was sentenced to seven years' imprisonment. He had provided testimony on video to foreign journalists in April about the torture of political prisoners.

In September, hundreds of members of parliament-elect and other NLD supporters seeking to attend a party congress were briefly detained. The authorities claimed that 573 people were arrested; the opposition put the number of arrests at 800.

Senior NLD leaders Dr Aung Khin Sint, U Win Htein and U Kyi Maung were rearrested during the year (see *Amnesty International Report 1996*). In August, U Win Htein was sentenced to 14 years' imprisonment in two separate trials, and in September Dr Aung Khin Sint was reportedly sentenced to 20 years' imprisonment. Both were prisoners of conscience. U Kyi Maung, aged 78, was released without charge after being detained for five days in October. The authorities had accused him of involvement in student protests in Yangon against alleged beatings of three students arrested by Insein township police. Unofficial sources stated that U Kyi Maung had merely listened to students' grievances.

In November, security forces failed to intervene when 200 men armed with sticks and bricks attacked a motorcade of NLD leaders in Yangon, slightly injuring NLD Vice-Chairman, former General U Tin U. The attack was widely believed to have been orchestrated by the SLORC.

In December, two large student demonstrations protesting against the poor quality of education and calling for democracy and human rights took place in Yangon and, on a smaller scale, in other parts of the country. There were reports that the security forces beat demonstrators and journalists with batons. The SLORC stated that the NLD and the largely defunct Burma Communist Party (BCP) instigated the student unrest; 13 NLD youth members and 34 BCP members were detained for their involvement. According to official figures, 859 people were arrested. The authorities claimed that all of them were released, but at least 96 people remained in detention at the end of the year.

Reports of ill-treatment of prisoners of conscience and political prisoners in both prisons and labour camps continued throughout the year. Prisoners of conscience U Pa Pa Lay and U Lu Zaw, two comedians sentenced to seven years' imprisonment in March for satirizing the SLORC, were transferred to a labour camp for several months and forced to work under extremely harsh conditions while shackled. Both men were reported to be in poor health after their transfer to Mandalay prison. Prolonged sleep deprivation was reportedly used during interrogation. In June, prisoner of conscience James Leander Nichols, a Myanmar national of European and Burmese descent, who suffered from a heart condition, died after having reportedly been deprived of sleep for four nights. A close friend of Daw Aung San Suu Kyi, he had been sentenced to three years' imprisonment in May under Section 6(1) of the 1933 Burma Wireless Act for operating unregistered telephone and facsimile lines from his home.

Prison conditions for political prisoners were harsh, often amounting to cruel, inhuman or degrading treatment. Prisoners suffered from lack of medical care and an inadequate diet. From January to April, a group of 29 political prisoners, including prisoner of conscience U Win Tin, were reportedly held incommunicado in dog kennels in Insein Prison. In March, 21 of them were sentenced to additional terms of imprisonment for attempting to pass on information about poor prison conditions to the UN Special Rapporteur on Myanmar. In August, U Hla Than, an NLD member of parliament-elect who was part of the group, died of tuberculosis associated with AIDS, which opposition sources claim he may have contracted while in prison. Hypodermic needles are reportedly re-used without sterilization by medical personnel in Myanmar's prisons.

Human rights violations against ethnic minorities continued throughout the year. Soldiers routinely seized them for forced labour on infrastructural projects such as roads and railways in harsh conditions which often amounted to cruel, inhuman or degrading treatment. In May, the SLORC stated that soldiers rather than civilians would be used for railway construction, but it was not clear to what degree this policy was being implemented. From January, some 20,000 members of the Chin ethnic minority were reportedly forced to work on the construction of a road from Sagaing Division to Haka, capital of Chin State, in western Myanmar. Members of the Rohingya ethnic minority and other residents of Rakhine State were reportedly forced to work in prawn farms, army camps and brick-making projects for the military. As a result, at least 5,000 Rohingyas fled to Bangladesh during the year.

In an apparent effort to break civilian support for Shan armed opposition groups, the SLORC forcibly relocated at least 100,000 members of ethnic minorities in Shan State, reportedly threatening to shoot those who refused to leave their homes. As a result, at least 20,000 Shan civilians had fled to Thailand by the end of the year.

In mid-1996, the SLORC forcibly relocated some 30,000 members of ethnic minorities in Kayah State, reportedly subjecting many to forced labour. Villagers received written orders stating that if they did not leave their villages they would be "regarded as enemies". In June, Sein Tun, a farmer from Ywa Thit, was reportedly shot dead by government troops in an apparent extrajudicial execution as he returned from his farm after curfew. At least 5,000 displaced people subsequently sought refuge in Thailand.

Widespread human rights violations, including forcible relocations, extrajudicial killings, and ill-treatment during portering, continued to be reported in Kayin State.

Seven people were sentenced to death during 1996 for drugs offences. No executions were reported.

The Democratic Kayin Buddhist Army, a Kayin armed opposition group, continued its attacks against Kayin refugees in camps in Thailand (see **Thailand** entry). At least three Kayin refugees were killed and several injured.

In April and August, Amnesty International published reports on human rights violations against the Mon, Karen and Shan ethnic minorities. In July, the organization published *Myanmar: Renewed repression*, and in September, *Myanmar: Update on political arrests and trials*. Both reports highlighted the SLORC's repression of the NLD since the release of Daw Aung San Suu Kyi. In September, Amnesty International launched a campaign to draw attention to the increase in human rights violations in Myanmar. In November, an Amnesty International delegation met the Myanmar Ambassador accredited to the United Kingdom. Throughout the year Amnesty International continued to call for the release of prisoners of conscience.

NEPAL

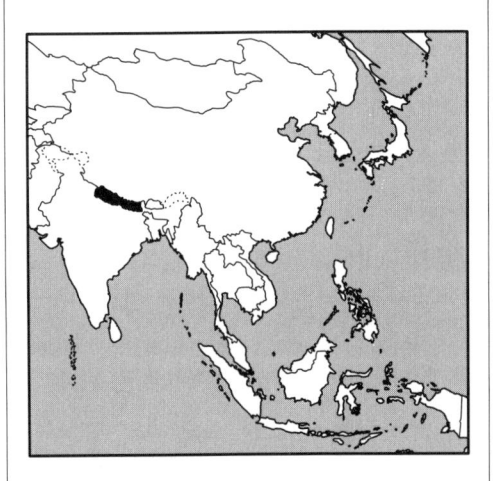

Nineteen prisoners of conscience, including members of Amnesty International, were detained for several days. More than 1,350 people, including possible prisoners of conscience, were detained on suspicion of being members or sympathizers of an armed opposition group; 600 of them were in detention awaiting trial at the end of the year. There were widespread reports of torture and ill-treatment by police, in at least five cases resulting in death. At least 50 people were killed by police in disputed circumstances. An armed opposition group was responsible for serious human rights abuses, including deliberate and arbitrary killings.

In February, the Communist Party of Nepal (CPN) (Maoist) and its political wing, the *Samyukta Jana Morcha* (SJM) *(Bhattarai)*, United People's Front, declared a "people's war" after the government failed to meet 40 demands they had submitted to Prime Minister Sher Bahadur Deuba. The demands included the abolition of royal privileges, the promulgation of a republican constitution and the abrogation of several treaties with India. In the following months, there were reports of CPN attacks on police stations, banks, offices of Village Development Committees, and against local landlords and politicians, particularly in the Mid-Western Region.

The UN High Commissioner for Human Rights visited the country in February and held talks with officials about human rights protection. In August, a law came into force providing for compensation of victims of torture. In October, legislation was passed to set up a National Human Rights Commission, but its members had not been appointed by the end of the year.

Nineteen prisoners of conscience were detained for several days. On 17 March, three members of Amnesty International were arrested by police in Kathmandu while collecting signatures and distributing materials about the organization's human rights concerns in China. The following day more than 100 others, including members of Amnesty International and Tibetans, were detained in Kathmandu at the start of a peaceful demonstration against human rights violations in China. Most were released the same day. Five Amnesty International members were held without charge until 21 March and 14 Tibetans until 24 March.

Twenty-nine blind people were arrested in July, during peaceful demonstrations demanding improvements in the national policy for disabled people, and held for several hours. Binod Rai, a board member of the Nepal Blind Association, was tortured for two hours while detained at Mahendra Police Club. He was reportedly kicked in the face and chest and beaten with *lathis* (canes).

Scores of possible prisoners of conscience were detained on suspicion of being members or sympathizers of the CPN (Maoist) or SJM. They included people holding office in the local administration, teachers, journalists and human rights activists based in the Mid-Western Region. Rajendra Dhakal, a human rights activist, lawyer and volunteer worker for the Forum for the Protection of Human Rights, a national human rights organization, was arrested in Gorkha in late February. The court ordered his release but the police re-arrested him at least five times. There were also reports of arrests of relatives, including children, of suspected Maoist activists. By the end of November, 1,358 people had been arrested. Approximately 600 remained in detention awaiting trial at the end of the year.

Reports of torture and ill-treatment by police were widespread. Many of those arrested in the context of the "people's war" complained of torture, including rape, and other cruel, inhuman or degrading treatment by police. They particularly complained of *falanga* (beatings on the soles of the feet) and *belana* (rolling a weighted bamboo cane over the thighs of the prisoner). In Khubinde, Sindhupalchok district, several children were reportedly beaten during interrogation by police in February after they had chased away a police officer who had come to arrest a teacher. The police officer had drowned when he ran into a river. The head teacher, Dil Prasad Sapkota, was allegedly beaten while being hung upside down. In February, Jhakku Prasad Subedi, Chairman of the District Development Committee of Rolpa, had difficulty walking for several days after police officers kneed him repeatedly on his thighs while he was in their custody.

Several women complained of sexual abuse and rape in police custody. Three young women, including a 14-year-old, were reportedly ordered to strip naked and then raped by police in Leka, Rukum district, in February. No independent investigations took place into these incidents.

There were at least five cases of deaths in police custody reportedly as a result of torture. In one such case, Deepak Parajuli, a tailor from Tusal, Kathmandu, died, allegedly as a result of beatings, at Hanumandhoka police station between 5 and 18 September. His relatives were allegedly forced by police officers to sign a document saying that Deepak Parajuli was a drug addict.

At least 50 people were killed by police in disputed circumstances. Several of these incidents involved Maoist activists who were, according to the authorities, killed in armed confrontations with the police. Evidence suggested that they may have been extrajudicially executed.

At least 13 civilians were reported to have been killed by armed Maoist activists. The victims included members of mainstream political parties, former members of the SJM and suspected informants. Members of the CPN (Maoist) were also responsible for attacks on civilians, using weapons including hammers, *khukuris* (traditional Nepali curved knives) and other tools, which often resulted in severe injuries.

In August and late November to early December, Amnesty International delegates visited Nepal to discuss with government officials the organization's concerns about arbitrary arrest and detention, torture and extrajudicial executions in the context of the "people's war". In November, the delegates visited Rukum and Sindhuli districts.

Amnesty International appealed for the release of prisoners of conscience arrested in connection with the organization's campaign against human rights violations in China. It also called for investigations into reports of torture, deaths in custody and alleged extrajudicial executions, and for those found responsible to be brought to justice.

NICARAGUA

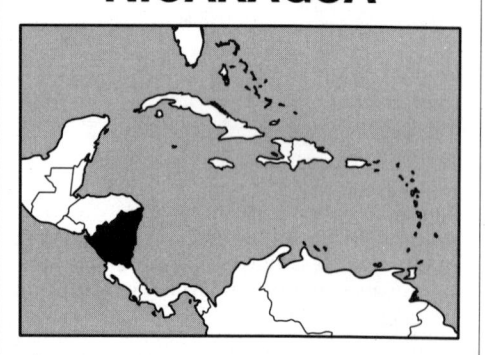

The Inter-American Court of Human Rights held hearings in the case of Jean Paul Genie Lacayo, allegedly killed by members of the military in 1990. Prison conditions frequently amounted to cruel, inhuman or degrading treatment. At least 30 people were killed in circumstances suggesting that they may have been victims of deliberate and arbitrary killings by armed political groups.

General elections were held in October. Arnoldo Alemán, the *Alianza Liberal* (Liberal Alliance) candidate, was elected President in the first round of voting.

In January, the creation of the office of the *Procuraduría para la Defensa de los Derechos Humanos* (Human Rights Procurator) was reported in the official newspaper, the *Gazette*. In December, Miriam Argüello, a former member of parliament, was elected as Procurator and Carlos Gallo as Deputy Procurator.

There were reports of renewed violence and abuses in the area most afflicted by conflict in the 1980s, a stretch of land in the middle of the country.

In September, the Inter-American Court of Human Rights held hearings in the case of 17-year-old Jean Paul Genie Lacayo, who was allegedly killed by escorts of

General Humberto Ortega, the then head of the army, in 1990 (see *Amnesty International Reports 1993* to *1996*). The Inter-American Commission on Human Rights (IACHR) called six witnesses to give testimony, and oral statements were heard from both the IACHR and the Government of Nicaragua. Two key witnesses – retired General Humberto Ortega and General Joaquín Cuadra – did not attend the session, despite having been summoned. The IACHR requested that they be summoned again. The Court heard statements on the existing evidence and decided that, if necessary, additional hearings could take place if the absent witnesses appeared before the Court at a later date. In its statement, the IACHR requested, *inter alia*, that the Court find that Nicaragua had violated Jean Paul Genie Lacayo's right to life, and that the Nicaraguan Government should pay compensation and continue to investigate the case until those responsible for his death were brought to justice. The government's representative questioned the Court's jurisdiction in the case on the basis that domestic remedies had not been exhausted, and argued that due process had been respected. The decision of the Court had not been given by the end of the year.

Conditions in prisons and police cells frequently amounted to cruel and degrading treatment. There was severe overcrowding; some institutions held three times the number of prisoners they had been designed for. Prisoners slept on the floor without bedding, sanitary facilities or drinking water. There was no budgetary provision for health care, and contagious diseases spread quickly among the prison population. Conditions fell short of international standards, including the UN Standard Minimum Rules for the Treatment of Prisoners.

Armed opposition groups of *recontras* – former members of the Nicaraguan Resistance or *contra* forces who fought against the former Sandinista government – were believed to be responsible for the murder of at least 30 people, and the kidnapping and torture, including rape, of peasants, women, children and sympathizers of groups across the political spectrum. For example, in January it was reported that members of an armed group tied up three women and seven children inside their hut in El Guayabo, Waslala, Department of Matagalpa, and set fire to it, killing them all. According to reports, the women had refused to reveal the whereabouts of their older sons, as they feared the group would kill them for refusing to join it. The women's husbands had also been killed by the same group.

Leaders and members of popular organizations were also targeted. In August, Amado Leiva Flores, President of the *Cooperativa Agrícola Emir Cabezas Lacayo*, Peasants' Cooperative Emir Cabezas Lacayo, and José Granados Cruz, a member of the cooperative, were shot dead in Zinica, Waslala. The perpetrators, according to witnesses, were members of the Pablo Negro band, a group of *recontras*.

There was no reply during the year to Amnesty International's December 1995 letter to President Violetta Barrios de Chamorro seeking information about incidents in Portezuelo and Rubenia (Managua) in which two demonstrators were killed and several detained and beaten, and expressing concern about reported inadequacies in the investigation into the killing of 13 people in La Marañosa (see *Amnesty International Report 1996*).

An Amnesty International observer attended the Inter-American Court on Human Rights hearing of the case of Jean Paul Genie Lacayo in September.

NIGER

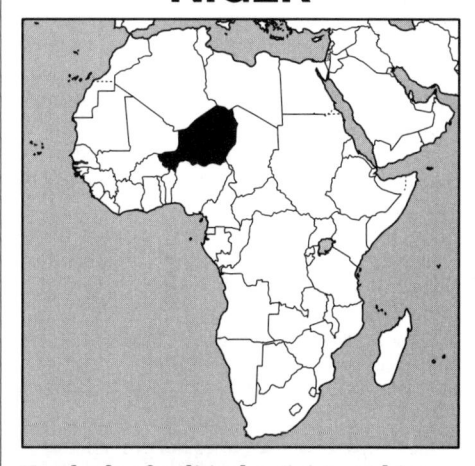

Hundreds of political activists and journalists were held, often incommunicado, for periods of up to three months. Most of them were prisoners of conscience. Many of those detained were ill-treated or tortured by members of the security forces.

In January, a military coup led by Colonel Ibrahim Baré Maïnassara overthrew the government, ousting Niger's first democratically elected President, Mahmane Ousmane, and putting an end to the multi-party political system set up in 1990. The coup leaders, who claimed that they were taking power in order to end a period of chaotic political deadlock, declared a state of emergency. The 1992 Constitution was suspended, parliament was dissolved and political parties were banned. Public demonstrations and all forms of political activity were prohibited.

In May, a new Constitution was adopted, the state of emergency was lifted and presidential elections were called for July. The elections saw a new wave of political repression and widespread arrests. Gross irregularities occurred – including the suspension of the *Commission nationale électorale indépendante*, National Independent Electoral Commission. Despite international and national condemnation of electoral irregularities, Ibrahim Barré Maïnassara was pronounced the winner. In November, legislative elections, which were boycotted by the main opposition parties, took place without violent incidents and resulted in a landslide victory for the President's supporters.

Hundreds of political activists, most of them prisoners of conscience, were detained for short periods and then released. All these arrests took place without a warrant, and people were detained, often incommunicado and in secret, well beyond the time (48 hours, renewable once) during which a prisoner can legally be held without charge. All were released without charge and none had been charged or brought before a court by the end of the year.

Those arrested included former members of government. After the military coup in January, the then President, Mahmane Ousmane, the Prime Minister, Hama Amadou, and the President of the National Assembly, Mohamadou Issoufou, were placed under house arrest for almost three months. None had advocated violence. They were prisoners of conscience.

In July, following the presidential elections, the four opposition candidates were placed under house arrest for two weeks. They had called for peaceful protests against the election results. They were also prisoners of conscience.

Opposition supporters in the capital, Niamey, and the second city, Zinder, were also detained. At least 40 people who were arrested in Niamey on 11 July, following a peaceful demonstration which was violently dispersed by the security forces, were prisoners of conscience. They were taken to Ekrafane, a military camp 300 kilometres north of Niamey, and held there for over a week. During this time they were tortured and ill-treated. Some had their heads shaved, others were beaten and some, including former government minister Massaoudou Hassoumi, were subjected to mock executions. Some of the 90 people arrested on the same day following a violent demonstration by opposition supporters were also reportedly subjected to beatings and mock executions. They were also alleged to have been forced to strip and simulate sexual acts.

Journalists who denounced human rights violations or opposed the new military government were targeted. In February, Moulaye Abdoulaye, editor of the daily newspaper *Le Soleil*, was arrested by soldiers in Niamey. He was taken out of town, beaten and then released. On 7 July – the first day of the election – police raided the offices of a private radio station, *Radio Anfani*, detaining one journalist, Souleymane Issa Maïga, for several hours and suspending radio transmission for three weeks. Some journalists who were briefly arrested had their heads shaved, including Maman Abou, editor of the weekly newspaper *Le Républicain* and president of an association of independent newspaper editors. Two Niger nationals working for international press agencies were publicly threatened by the Minister of the Interior, Idi Ango Omar. None of the journalists had used or advocated violence, and those detained were prisoners of conscience.

In October Amnesty International published a report, *Niger: A major step backwards*, in which it expressed concern at the bypassing – by members of the police and the armed forces – of legal provisions governing procedures for arrest and at the pattern of detention, torture, ill-treatment and intimidation of journalists and supporters of opposition parties. The organization called on the President to make restoring respect for human rights an absolute priority and urged that all allegations of human rights violations be

NIGERIA

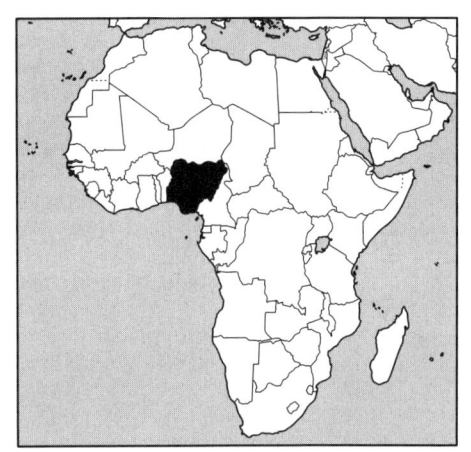

Prisoners of conscience and possible prisoners of conscience remained imprisoned throughout the year. Many were detained without charge or trial and some had been convicted in unfair political trials. Prisoners were subjected to cruel, inhuman or degrading treatment, including harsh conditions of imprisonment. There was at least one killing which appeared to be an extrajudicial execution. At least 12 prisoners were sentenced to death and 14 were executed.

Under the military government's timetable for a return to civilian rule by October 1998, local government elections on a non-party basis were held in March. In September, five political parties were registered but the main pro-democracy opposition was effectively excluded. Further local government elections, due to be contested by the registered parties in December, were postponed until 1997. Repressive military decrees which overturn the rule of law and allow the arbitrary detention of prisoners of conscience remained in force.

In March and April, the UN Secretary-General sent a mission to Nigeria to investigate the unfair political trials which resulted in the execution for murder of Ken Saro-Wiwa and eight other members of the Ogoni ethnic group in November 1995 (see *Amnesty International Report 1996*). It recommended fundamental reforms to bring the Civil Disturbances Special Tribunal, the special court which had conducted the trials, into line with international standards for fair trial. However, the government's subsequent measures left intact its control of the tribunal, including the direct appointment of its members, a right of appeal only to another government-appointed special tribunal, and government confirmation of convictions and sentences. In June, the government appointed a National Human Rights Commission which had power only to make recommendations to the Head of State. A detention review panel was appointed in October but it was not an independent, judicial body. It was headed by senior security officials and its reviews were conducted in secret.

The African Commission on Human and Peoples' Rights, which had decided in December 1995 to send a mission, was unable to reach agreement with the authorities on dates.

In March, the UN Human Rights Commission requested its Special Rapporteurs on extrajudicial, summary or arbitrary executions and on the independence of judges and lawyers, to conduct investigations in Nigeria, but they had been unable to obtain access to the country by the end of the year. In July, the UN Human Rights Committee criticized the Nigerian Government for a wide range of human rights violations and urged it to repeal military decrees which suspend fundamental rights. In October, the UN General Assembly adopted a resolution expressing concern about continued human rights abuses and calling on the Nigerian Government to cooperate with the international community and abide by its international treaty commitments to uphold human rights. In November, the Commonwealth Ministerial Action Group, set up after the Ogoni executions, visited Nigeria briefly for government talks after being denied access to conduct a fact-finding mission earlier in the year. The mission was not allowed to meet political prisoners.

There were several deaths and scores were arrested following religious conflict in northern Nigeria. In August, three people were killed in clashes between rival muslim groups, and in September at least two died in unrest between Christians and Muslims in Kafanchan. At least seven more died when police tried to disperse protests over the arrests of Ibrahim El-Zakzaky, a Muslim Shi'ite leader, and about 20 supporters. The police accused Ibrahim El-Zakzaky of inciting unrest, but he was still detained without charge or trial and incommunicado in Port Harcourt, southeast Nigeria, at the end of the year. More than 100 Shi'ite demonstrators arrested in September were charged with offences ranging from illegal assembly to murder, but had not been brought to trial by the end of the year. Some were reportedly arrested for non-violent protests.

The government blamed pro-democracy activists for a number of bomb attacks throughout the year in which several people were killed. It accused the National Democratic Coalition (NADECO), led by former government officials and political leaders, and the National Council for the Liberation of Nigeria, an exile group led by Nobel laureate Wole Soyinka, of responsibility for some of the attacks.

Key human rights defenders remained imprisoned throughout the year. Moshood Abiola, winner of the 1993 presidential elections, had been imprisoned since June 1994, ostensibly awaiting trial for treason but denied access to his family, lawyers and doctor. Others continued to be held without charge or trial, usually incommunicado. Frank Kokori, former Secretary General of the National Union of Petroleum and Natural Gas Workers, was still held in incommunicado detention nearly two and a half years after a major oil workers' strike in mid-1994.

In January, the Internal Security Task Force, the joint military/mobile police force which has occupied Ogoniland since April 1994, detained at least 20 and possibly as many as 100 supporters of the Movement for the Survival of the Ogoni People who were commemorating Ogoni Day. Before and during the UN mission in March and April, defenders of human rights in Ogoniland were detained without charge or trial, apparently to prevent them from speaking to the delegation. Those detained included Anyakwee Nsirimovu, head of the Institute of Human Rights and Humanitarian Law in Port Harcourt. In June, Nnimmo Bassey, an environmental rights campaigner, was arrested and detained without charge or trial for a few weeks, apparently to stop him attending an international meeting of environmentalists. The authorities denied reports of further arrests in August before a proposed visit by Commonwealth Ministers.

At least 19 Ogoni possible prisoners of conscience remained held in harsh prison conditions throughout the year. Most were detained in mid-1994 and were allegedly ill-treated after their arrest. They faced trial by the Civil Disturbances Special Tribunal on identical murder charges to those which were used to execute the nine Ogoni in 1995. In July, some were allowed a supervised meeting with their lawyer and were brought before a magistrates' court to be remanded in custody. In August, two of their defence lawyers were arrested in court and charged with obstructing the police when photographs were taken of the prisoners in court. In December, the High Court in Port Harcourt rejected an application for the prisoners' release on the grounds that the evidence of their torture and ill-treatment was hearsay. There was still no independent inquiry into the death in detention of one of the group, Clement Tusima, in 1995.

There were reports of at least 20 further detentions in Ogoniland in the period leading up to the first anniversary of the November 1995 executions, and the authorities announced that security operations had successfully prevented public commemorations. In December, the authorities detained a number of pro-democracy leaders, including two leading members of NADECO, 63-year-old lawyer Chief Olabiyi Durojaiye and former government minister Dr Olu Falae, and Dr Frederick Fasheun, a medical practitioner and Acting Chairman of the Campaign for Democracy. They were still detained incommunicado without charge or trial at the end of the year. Ayodele Anselm Akele, Chairman of the Campaign for Independent Unions, was also detained for a few days twice in December and questioned about trade union and political activities, and the bombings, before being released without charge.

Most of those convicted of treason and related offences in grossly unfair trials by Special Military Tribunal in 1995 were still imprisoned at the end of the year. Many were held in harsh conditions in prisons far from their homes. Many suffered ill health caused by malnutrition and inadequate medical care. They included several prisoners of conscience, notably retired General Olusegun Obasanjo, a former head of state, and his deputy, retired Major-General Shehu Musa Yar'Adua, imprisoned for 15 years and life respectively because of their public advocacy of political rights and a swift return to civilian government. Leading human rights activist Dr Beko Ransome-Kuti, Chairman of the Campaign for Democracy, and Shehu Sanni, his deputy, both serving 15-year sentences, remained in harsh conditions in prisons hundreds of miles from their homes.

A number of political detainees were freed during the year. Most had been detained incommunicado without charge or trial, some for more than 18 months, and they were released without explanation. In June, during its first meeting with Commonwealth Ministers, the government announced the release of seven political detainees, although it later emerged that some had been released several months earlier and others were not actually released until October. Abdul Oroh, Executive Director of the Civil Liberties Organisation, and Dr Olatunji Abayomi, head of Human Rights Africa, were among those released in June, having been detained without charge or trial since August 1995.

In July, 11 former soldiers imprisoned since a coup attempt in April 1990 were released. Most had been convicted after being tried three times by Special Military Tribunal in secret and grossly unfair trials in 1990; others were reportedly redetained after acquittal by the same tribunal.

In November, three human rights defenders who had been detained incommunicado without charge or trial for nearly a year were released on the occasion of the Commonwealth Ministers' visit to Nigeria. Veteran civil rights campaigner Chief Gani Fawehinmi had been held from January to November. Chief Fawehinmi had been a member of the team of defence lawyers who withdrew from the Ogoni trials in protest at government interference, and had challenged the legality of the November 1995 Ogoni executions and the constitutionality of the Civil Disturbances Special Tribunal which passed the death sentences. The courts repeatedly adjourned hearings on these legal actions throughout the year. Also released were Femi Falana, another of the defence lawyers in the Ogoni trial, and Femi Aborisade, a labour activist and leading member of the National Conscience Party.

Prison conditions remained harsh and life-threatening for most prisoners. Gani Fawehinmi required emergency hospital treatment for pneumonia on five occasions as a result of the conditions in which he was held for 11 months.

No independent or judicial inquiry was carried out into allegations that the security forces had shot dead at least two boys who were demonstrating support for Ogoni Day and wounded several others. In June, Alhaja Kudirat Abiola, senior wife of Moshood Abiola, was killed in what appeared to be an extrajudicial execution by government agents. She had remained outspoken in support of her husband despite having been denied access to him since 1994, being arrested and prosecuted for publishing allegedly subversive material, and receiving death threats. Suspicions about government involvement were not allayed when it failed to set up an independent inquiry into her killing and arrested more than 20 members of the Abiola family and four leading NADECO members, holding them in harsh conditions before releasing them uncharged after several weeks. Former Senator Abraham Adesanya, a 74-year-old lawyer, and two other NADECO elders were detained as prisoners of conscience for four months without charge or trial in defiance of court orders.

There was a sharp reduction in the number of executions, which had totalled more than 200 in 1994 and 1995. At least 12 prisoners were sentenced to death and 14 were executed following convictions by Robbery and Firearms Tribunals, special courts which allow no right of judicial appeal. Executions were carried out in public by firing-squad. In January, an Assistant Commissioner of Police, a police sergeant and three others convicted of involvement in armed robberies were executed before a crowd of more than 2,000 near Birnin Kebbi, northern Nigeria.

Following the November 1995 executions and renewed repression in January 1996 in Ogoniland, Ogoni refugees fled to neighbouring Benin until the Nigerian Government increased security at the border. The Government of Benin gave asylum to about a thousand, who included relatives of the nine executed men.

Throughout the year, Amnesty International appealed for the release of prisoners of conscience, for the fair trial and humane treatment of all political prisoners, for an end to the death penalty and for an investigation into the killing of Kudirat Abiola. In November, the organization launched a worldwide campaign, publishing reports which documented the attack on human rights defenders and advocated a 10-point program for human rights reform in Nigeria.

In May and November, Amnesty International personnel visited Nigeria for research and membership development. Requests for visas for four other visits by Amnesty International staff to undertake research, membership development and to hold talks with the government were denied. During the November visit, an Amnesty International staff member and two local Amnesty International officers were questioned for 12 hours after being detained while on their way to a meeting with foreign diplomats. The staff member was deported, and for several days in a row the two others had to spend the day at a police station.

PAKISTAN

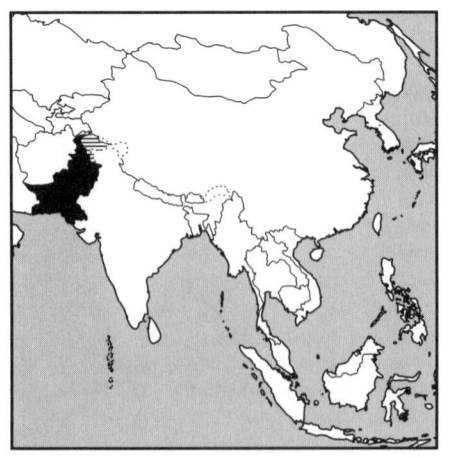

Dozens of prisoners of conscience were held; many opponents of the government charged with criminal offences may also have been prisoners of conscience. Torture remained widespread, reportedly leading to at least 70 deaths. At least four people "disappeared". Over a hundred people were killed, many of whom may have been victims of extrajudicial executions. At least 35 people were sentenced to death; one person was executed. Armed opposition groups committed human rights abuses, including deliberate and arbitrary killings.

In March, the Supreme Court curbed the authority of the government to appoint judges of the higher judiciary without consulting the relevant chief justices. Judicial appointments made earlier without consultation or by non-permanent chief justices became void.

In November, President Farooq Leghari dismissed the government of Prime Minister Benazir Bhutto and dissolved the National Assembly on the grounds that a "sustained assault" on the judiciary, "corruption, nepotism and violations of rules", and widespread human rights violations including extrajudicial executions, had prevented the orderly functioning of the government. All provincial assemblies were subsequently also dissolved. Caretaker Prime Minister Meraj Khalid promised to ensure fair elections in February 1997.

In Azad Jammu and Kashmir, the local Pakistan People's Party (PPP) won a majority in assembly elections in July. Thirty-six Kashmir National Alliance candidates who opposed accession of the region to Pakistan had been disqualified.

The governmental Human Rights Cell was upgraded to a ministry in July. A tribunal was set up by presidential ordinance in March to investigate and redress violations of the rights of disadvantaged groups, including women, children and minorities.

In March, Pakistan acceded to the UN Convention on the Elimination of All Forms of Discrimination against Women, with a reservation stating that accession was "subject to the provisions of the Constitution". A committee reviewing laws disadvantaging women had not submitted recommendations by the end of the year.

In April, the punishment of flogging was abolished, except when imposed as a mandatory punishment under Islamic provisions of the penal code. Flogging continued to be judicially imposed for drug offences but was apparently not carried out.

Some legal reforms were initiated but not concluded by the end of the year. The Juvenile Offenders Bill, which banned the death penalty as well as flogging, judicial amputations and fettering of anyone below the age of 16, remained pending in the

Senate. Its provisions fell considerably short of Pakistan's obligations under the UN Convention on the Rights of the Child. In June, the federal cabinet approved the abolition of the death penalty for women provided the penalty had not been imposed as a mandatory punishment under Islamic provisions of the penal code. The bill lapsed when the National Assembly was dissolved.

The government appealed against some court judgments likely to contribute to human rights protection, including the Punjab High Court's abolition of the Special Courts for the Suppression of Terrorist Activities. A Sindh government appeal against the Sindh High Court's ban on fettering prisoners was dismissed by the Supreme Court in April, but later readmitted.

In June, the Peshawar High Court held that public executions were incompatible with the constitutionally guaranteed dignity of human beings.

Some 120 members of the Ahmadiyya community were charged with religious offences. The charges included blasphemy, which carries the mandatory death penalty. At the end of the year, 2,589 Ahmadis had such charges pending against them.

Ahmadis charged with blasphemy were often denied bail. Riaz Ahmed Chowdhury, from Mianwali in Punjab, and his son and two nephews, had been detained without trial since their arrest for alleged blasphemy in November 1993. Their bail applications, which had been rejected by the sessions court and the Lahore High Court, had been pending in the Supreme Court since 1994.

Ayub Masih, a Christian from Arifwala, Punjab Province, was arrested in October on charges of blasphemy after quarrelling with a Muslim neighbour.

Dozens of political activists were held incommunicado and in unacknowledged places of detention. Dr Rahim Solangi and Punhal Sario of the Sindh Taraqqi Passand Party were arrested on criminal charges in late June in Hyderabad, Sindh Province. After their remand lapsed, their whereabouts became unknown. Acting on a *habeas corpus* petition, a high court bailiff found them on 28 August in private police quarters in Tando Allayar, along with 23 other detainees. Their detention had not been recorded. Police claimed that they had been arrested the previous day. Before they could be released, they were transferred to Jamshoro police station on a "blind" First Information Report (a criminal complaint which does not name any suspect). They were later remanded on a series of "blind" First Information Reports to other police stations in Sindh, and in October were again remanded to Hyderabad Central Jail. No action was taken against those responsible for their arbitrary and unacknowledged detention witnessed by high court staff.

Criminal charges, intended to punish or intimidate, were arbitrarily brought against political opponents and journalists who exposed human rights violations. M.H. Khan of the daily newspaper *Dawn* reported that prisoners in Hyderabad Central Jail were unlawfully held in iron bar fetters. The authorities first denied the allegations, then filed charges of "forgery and cheating" against the journalist. Following an inquiry, the jail superintendent was suspended, but charges against M.H. Khan were not withdrawn. Sedition charges against journalist Zafaryab Ahmed (see *Amnesty International Report 1996*) were also still pending.

Torture, including rape, in police and paramilitary custody was widespread and systematic, leading to at least 70 deaths. In April, Huzur Bux was detained along with four other men in Dajal, Rajanpur district, on charges of criminal abetment. Police stripped him naked, pierced a metal ring through his nose and dragged him through the streets. Huzur Bux was released after 10 days following the intervention of influential local people. A police officer told a human rights investigator examining the case that he would have staged an "encounter" killing (a killing in a supposed gun-battle with police) if he had expected intervention. No official investigation was known to have taken place.

Niaz Jatoi, a labourer, was arrested on 12 February by police in Tando Allayar, Sindh Province. When his family was unable to raise the bribe demanded by police for his release, he was transferred to the Criminal Investigation Agency centre in Hyderabad where his brother saw him. Niaz Jatoi died there on 29 February. Police claimed that he was a "bandit" killed in a shoot-out with police and that he had never been arrested. No investigation took place into the death.

Retired government servant Zameer Ansari, his wife and two children "disappeared" from their home in Islamabad in May. They were allegedly arrested by an intelligence agency.

Over one hundred people were killed, many of whom may have been victims of extrajudicial executions. Most were claimed by the authorities to be the result of deaths in "encounters" with police. In June, police opened fire on a demonstration by members of *Jamaat-i-Islami*, Society of Islam, in Rawalpindi, apparently deliberately killing three demonstrators. An inquiry was set up but its results were not made public. In March, Mohammad Naeem, a member of the Mohajir Qaumi Movement, Refugees National Movement, and his associate, Amjad Beg, were shot dead by paramilitary Rangers in Amjad Beg's house in Karachi. The Rangers claimed they had fired in self-defence, but members of the Beg family who were present at the time said that Mohammad Naeem had hidden behind a cabinet and was shot dead at point-blank range, and that Amjad Beg was arrested and then shot dead outside the house. The federal cabinet reportedly expressed its "satisfaction" with the death of the two men.

Mir Murtaza Bhutto, leader of the opposition Pakistan People's Party (Shaheed Bhutto) and brother of Benazir Bhutto, and seven associates were apparently extrajudicially executed by police in Karachi in September. Police stated that they had fired in self-defence but Murtaza Bhutto and Ashiq Jatoi were reportedly unarmed when shot dead in their car. Two police officers were slightly injured and one of the injuries was later found to be self-inflicted. A judicial inquiry under a Supreme Court judge began investigating the deaths, but it had not concluded by the end of the year.

The perpetrators of human rights violations enjoyed a high degree of impunity. In August, Minister for Human Rights Iqbal Haider said that 136 alleged extrajudicial killings in Karachi were under investigation and that some 500 Karachi police officers had been dismissed and a few had been prosecuted for "misconduct". However, criminal charges were rarely brought and no law enforcement personnel were known to have been convicted. Inquiries rarely concluded, or if they did, their findings were not made public.

More than 35 people were sentenced to death for murder. Seven of these sentences were passed by Special Courts for the Suppression of Terrorist Activities, whose procedures did not meet international standards for fair trial.

At least one man was executed. Arshad Jamil, sentenced to death by court-martial in 1992 for the killing of nine villagers in Tando Bahawal (see *Amnesty International report 1993*), was hanged in October after his appeal to the Supreme Court failed.

Two Sh'ia Afghan refugees, Qambar Ali and Barat Ali, sentenced to death for blasphemy in January 1995 in Peshawar for commissioning the printing of pictures of Prophet Mohammed, were acquitted on appeal in May and released. They remained in hiding after receiving death threats from Islamists who regarded them as blasphemers.

Dozens of people were deliberately and arbitrarily killed by armed opposition groups on account of their ethnic or religious identity. Armed Shi'a and Sunni groups shot dead several dozen members of each other's community.

In February, Amnesty International issued a report, *Pakistan: Human rights crisis in Karachi*, which documented hundreds of cases of arbitrary detention, torture, deaths in custody, extrajudicial executions and "disappearances" reportedly carried out by law enforcement personnel in Karachi, as well as reports of torture, hostage-taking and killings by armed opposition groups.

In May, an Amnesty International delegation visited Pakistan for discussions on a wide range of concerns; the delegation expressed its dismay at the lack of political will to tackle key problems such as impunity. By the time of the government's dismissal, Amnesty International had received no response to the 127 cases of deaths in custody and possible extrajudicial executions which it had raised with the authorities.

In September, Amnesty International issued a report, *Pakistan: The death penalty*, appealing for the abolition of the death penalty and commutation of all death sentences. In a report published in October, *Pakistan: Journalists harassed for exposing abuses*, Amnesty International documented the harassment of journalists uncovering human rights abuses.

Following the dismissal of the government of Benazir Bhutto, Amnesty International urged the interim government to act on the President's acknowledgment of massive human rights violations and to tackle the problem of impunity.

PALESTINIAN AUTHORITY
(AREAS UNDER THE JURISDICTION OF THE)

At least 1,200 people were arrested on security grounds; most were released without charge after having been held for up to 11 months. They included prisoners of conscience and possible prisoners of conscience. At least 20 received grossly unfair trials before State Security Courts. Torture of detainees was widespread. Four people died in detention, including three who died after torture. At least 10 people were killed by members of the Palestinian security services, some in circumstances suggesting extrajudicial executions or other unlawful killings. Eleven people were sentenced to death; two death sentences were later commuted.

Elections for the President of the Palestinian Authority and for the Legislative Council took place in January. Yasser Arafat was overwhelmingly elected President while the *Fatah* Party won the majority of seats in the Council. The Legislative Council passed a first reading of a Basic Law which declared the Palestinian Authority's respect for UN human rights standards, but the executive authority had not completed its consideration of the law by the end of the year. The implementation of the next stage of the 1995 Oslo II accord which was to involve Israeli withdrawal was delayed after suicide bombings in February and March and the election in May of a new Israeli Government under Binyamin Netanyahu.

The Palestinian Authority's security forces arrested more than 1,200 people on security grounds, including prisoners of conscience and possible prisoners of conscience. Those detained included over 900 people arrested after the suicide bombings in Israel in February and March by Palestinian groups opposed to the peace process with Israel which resulted in 63 deaths (see **Israel and the Occupied Territories** entry). Detainees were rarely charged with any offence or brought before a judge within the legal limits laid down by Palestinian law. In August, the High Court of Justice in Ramallah ruled that the detention of 10 Birzeit University students, held since March without charge or trial, was illegal. However, the students were not released after the ruling and two remained in detention at the end of the year. The President of the High Court was retired soon after the judgment.

Among the prisoners of conscience arrested during the year were human rights activists. Bassem Eid, a fieldworker for the Israeli human rights organization *B'Tselem*, was detained in Ramallah for 24 hours in January. Dr Iyad al-Sarraj, Commissioner-General of the Palestinian Independent Commission for Citizens' Rights, an independent human rights monitoring body set up by President Arafat in 1993, was detained for making statements critical of the Palestinian Authority. He was held in Gaza Central Prison for eight days in May and rearrested in June and charged with possession of drugs. He was beaten after arrest and, after smuggling out a note concerning the beating, charged with assaulting the police. The drugs charge was rejected by a magistrates' court, but the State Security Court remanded him in custody; he was released after 16 days. Muhammad Dahman, Director of *al-Damir* (Conscience), a human rights organization, was detained for 15 days in August, charged with incitement by spreading false information after the organization issued a communique suggesting that a detainee had died as a result of torture. Muhammad Dahman appeared before the

State Security Court before being released without trial. It remained unclear whether charges against Dr Iyad al-Sarraj and Muhammad Dahman had been dropped.

At least 20 political detainees received unfair trials before the State Security Court. The Court was presided over by military judges; prosecutors and defence lawyers were normally state-appointed lawyers who worked for the security services; trials were often summary; and there was no right of appeal.

Torture of detainees was widespread. Methods of torture included burning with electric elements, beatings, suspension from the ceiling, dropping molten plastic on the body, cigarette burns and sleep deprivation. Three detainees died in custody after torture. In July, Mahmud Jumayel died in Jneid Prison in Nablus. He had been whipped with cables while suspended upside-down, by the naval police (*bahriyya*). He had been arrested in December 1995 and detained in Jericho before being transferred to Jneid Prison in July. The executive authority and the Legislative Council set up inquiries into his death and made a number of recommendations, including provision for tighter control of the security forces. Three members of the naval police were charged with causing unintentional death and sentenced to up to 15 years' imprisonment after a summary trial before the State Security Court in Jericho. The trial was unfair; defendants had a state-appointed military lawyer who offered no defence, no witnesses were called and no information was given as to who had ordered the torture.

No findings of any of the other inquiries announced by the Palestinian Authority were made public, including the inquiry announced into the death in detention of Azzam Muslah (see *Amnesty International Report 1996*). Three members of the security services were said to have been sentenced to up to seven years' imprisonment for their part in his death, but no information about their trial was available.

At least 10 people died as a result of possible extrajudicial executions or other unlawful killings by Palestinian Authority security forces during the year. Two Islamic *Jihad* activists, 'Ayman al-Razayna and 'Amar al-A'raj, were killed in their home in Gaza in February when members of the Palestinian Authority's security forces entered the house. There was no evidence to suggest that they had resisted arrest. An inquiry was ordered into the killings but no report had been made public by the end of the year. Others were killed during a demonstration as a result of the accidental discharge of a weapon and in cross-fire between rival branches of the security forces.

Eleven people were sentenced to death in Gaza on charges of murder. Two death sentences were commuted. Those sentenced to death included three members of the special forces convicted of carrying out a revenge killing in October. They were tried before the State Security Court, reportedly without access to defence lawyers. There were no executions.

Amnesty International delegates met President Arafat and raised the organization's concerns about impunity for the perpetrators of human rights abuses, including torture, and stressed the need to guarantee freedom of association and expression for human rights organizations. President Arafat stated that no one, including the security forces, should be above the law. In a press conference in Oslo in November, President Arafat stated that he was committed to ending torture.

Throughout the year, Amnesty International called for the commutation of death sentences and raised concerns about torture and prolonged political detention without trial. Responses on specific cases of reported torture were received from the authorities and security and local officials.

Amnesty International published a report, *Palestinian Authority: Death in custody of Mahmud Jumayel*, in September and in December it published *Palestinian Authority: Prolonged political detention, torture and unfair trials*.

PANAMA

Numerous cases of ill-treatment of prisoners and criminal suspects, and possible excessive use of force by the police were reported. An amnesty law was discussed in Congress. Eighty-eight Colombian refugees, who fled to Panama to escape political violence, were repatriated.

In February, the Panamanian Government ratified the Inter-American Convention on the Forced Disappearance of Persons.

There were reports of ill-treatment of inmates in the overcrowded prison of La Modelo in Panama City, which although designed to house some 200 prisoners allegedly holds more than 2,000 people, most of them in preventive detention. Following a riot in the prison in July, in which two inmates died, scores of prisoners were ill-treated. Naked inmates were reportedly lined up in the prison courtyard by police officers and prison guards and severely beaten. The prison director and 12 members of the security forces were suspended from their duties. President Ernesto Pérez Balladares ordered an investigation into the beatings and an Interior Ministry spokesperson said that La Modelo prison would be closed. The prison was demolished in November, but the official investigation was not known to have been completed by the end of the year.

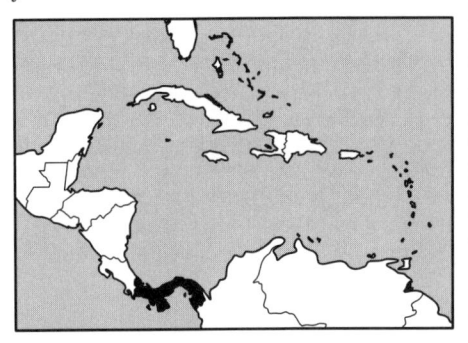

There were reports of ill-treatment and excessive use of force by police officers when detaining people suspected of criminal offences. In January, Julio Aznal Henríquez Meléndez, aged 17, was reportedly shot in both legs by a police officer who detained him for questioning about alleged criminal activities in Valle San Isidro, district of San Miguelito. According to a Public Ministry medical certificate issued in May, Julio Aznal Henríquez' injuries were life-threatening.

In April, during a search for "delinquents", several police officers broke into Leonora Beard's house, without a judicial order. They beat her two sisters, Yolanda and Sandra Beard, when they asked to see a judicial order and attempted to telephone the police. Sandra Beard sustained injuries to her arm which required prolonged medical treatment.

Little progress was made in the investigations into the death of four people in August 1995 during widespread protests against government policies (see *Amnesty International Report 1996*).

In March, an *ad hoc* parliamentary commission was created to draft a new amnesty law and draw up a list of all those who would benefit from it. The commission was due to submit its report in June, but by the end of the year Congress had not finished discussing the drafts.

If passed, the amnesty law will be the third such measure in two years. In September 1994, 222 former officials and military supporters were granted pardons, and in September 1995, 130 people were granted pardons (see *Amnesty International Reports 1995* and *1996*).

The repatriation of 88 Colombian refugees, who fled to Panama in November to escape political violence in Colombia, raised fears for their safety and that of more than 200 other refugees facing deportation by the Panamanian authorities. According to reports, on arrival in Panama the refugees set up improvised camps in the province of Darien, but as soon as the Panamanian authorities became aware of their presence they organized their return to Colombia in collaboration with the Colombian Air Force, which provided an aircraft and returned the first group on 23 November.

In February, Amnesty International wrote to President Pérez Balladares, calling for impartial investigations into human rights violations committed in the period covered by the amnesty law – provisionally approved by Congress in December 1995 – and urging that those responsible be brought to justice and compensation awarded to the victims. The law provides for the closure, one week after it comes into force, of all current judicial proceedings against alleged perpetrators of human rights violations. In March, the President responded to Amnesty International, stating his "intention to veto the proposed law if it is not changed". He also stated that "under no circumstances will common crimes such as ... torture and homicide be included".

Amnesty International expressed concern about the repatriation of Colombian refugees and called on the Panamanian Government to fulfil its obligations under international human rights law not to deport anyone to a country where they are at risk of serious human rights violations.

PAPUA NEW GUINEA

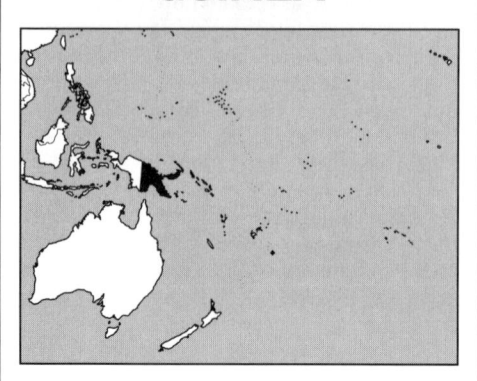

Several people were briefly detained without charge on suspicion of having links with armed secessionists. Torture and ill-treatment by members of the security forces continued to be reported and resulted in the death of at least one person. "Disappearances" continued to be reported and dozens of people were believed to have been extrajudicially executed on the island of Bougainville. In other parts of the country several people were killed by police in suspicious circumstances. A prisoner sentenced to death for murder in 1995 was acquitted by the Supreme Court. An armed secessionist group committed human rights abuses, including hostage-taking and deliberate and arbitrary killings.

In March, fighting resumed in the eight-year conflict between the secessionist Bougainville Revolutionary Army (BRA) – an armed opposition group – and the Papua New Guinea Defence Force (PNGDF) and government-backed paramilitary Resistance Forces. Government forces launched a major military offensive in June. In November, Gerard Sinato was elected as the new Premier of the Bougainville Transitional Government, following the assassination of his predecessor, Theodore Miriung. An amnesty, which could offer impunity to those responsible for human rights violations, remained in force for crimes committed by members of the security forces and the BRA between 1 October 1988 and 1 July 1995.

Legislation establishing a National Human Rights Commission was expected to be introduced to parliament in 1997.

In February, the UN Special Rapporteur on extrajudicial, summary or arbitrary executions, who visited Papua New Guinea in October 1995, reported that human rights violations by the security forces continued on Bougainville, that violations of human rights by all parties to the conflict were not adequately investigated and hardly any alleged perpetrators had been brought to justice.

There continued to be restrictions on access to Bougainville for domestic and international human rights monitors.

Several people were detained without charge or trial by members of the security forces on Bougainville and the neighbouring island of Buka, most on suspicion of having links with pro-independence individuals or the BRA. In May, Sam Tulo was arrested on Buka by members of the Resistance Forces and taken to a plantation, where he was questioned by a senior PNGDF officer about complaints he was alleged to have made about the PNGDF. James Togel was detained overnight on Buka in May for allegedly attempting to contact a pro-independence church leader. Both men were released without charge. In June, a couple and their child were arrested without warrants by the security forces, after the woman's brother – a BRA leader – was alleged to have taken captive a soldier and a Catholic priest. The PNGDF reportedly offered to release the woman and her family if the BRA released the soldier. The couple and their child were released without charge after several days in military custody.

There were further reports of torture and ill-treatment in police and military custody on Bougainville and in other parts of the country. In June, two youths were beaten and kicked by members of the PNGDF after being arrested for breaking a curfew in North Buka. One was beaten unconscious and both were reported to have suffered swollen jaws. Throughout the country, dozens of people were subjected to ill-treatment and torture, including beatings, in police custody, in some cases resulting in serious injury or death. In June, William Tanka, Michael Peterson and Steve Pokua were beaten by police after they were detained in connection with an alleged driving offence in the capital, Port Moresby. William Tanka was reportedly hit in the face and head with a set of handcuffs. As a result of the beating, he had multiple bruising and swelling on his face and bleeding in one ear. In May, Paul Opa Were died, allegedly after being severely beaten by police and falling from an open police truck in Minj, Western Highlands. An eye-witness claimed that Paul Opa Were, who had been arrested on suspicion of involvement in building an illegal roadblock, fell from the truck while being kicked, punched and hit with rifle butts.

At least three people "disappeared" on Bougainville. In April, Peter Ugua "disappeared" after being arrested by members of the PNGDF and the Resistance Forces at a house on Sohano Island, near Buka. He had been arrested on suspicion of having links with the BRA because he had been admitted to hospital with gunshot wounds. Two weeks before his "disappearance", Peter Ugua had been arrested and held incommunicado for six days in military custody in Buka before being released without charge.

Dozens of extrajudicial executions were reportedly carried out on Bougainville by the PNGDF and the Resistance Forces. In February, James Lakana was believed to have been shot by the Resistance Forces in Monoitu, South Bougainville. In June, eight former members of the BRA were believed to have been killed by the PNGDF and the Resistance Forces in Sipai, West Bougainville. The eight, including Hubert Oparive, had left the BRA two years earlier and joined the Resistance Forces. They were reported to have been shot by the security forces on suspicion of having attempted to contact the BRA. The military announced an internal inquiry into the incident, but the outcome was not known by the end of the year. In October, Theodore Miriung, then Premier of the Bougainville Transitional Government, was killed in southwestern Bougainville. The government initiated an independent coroner's inquiry into his death in November, which found that he had been killed by members of the Resistance Forces and the PNGDF. By the end of the year, no member of the security forces was known to have been questioned, suspended or charged in relation to Theodore Miriung's death.

No members of the PNGDF or the Resistance Forces were known to have been brought to justice for their role in other human rights violations on Bougainville, despite an admission by Prime Minister Sir Julius Chan in August that members of the PNGDF had committed human rights violations. There was no information about an inquiry, announced by the PNGDF in February 1995, into the December 1994 deaths of Shane Seeto, Damien Ona, Apiato Bobonung and Robert (see *Amnesty International Report 1996*).

Several people were shot by police in suspicious circumstances in other parts of the country; at least one person died. In July, Mathew Fugo was shot dead by police in Port Moresby during a search for a man allegedly threatening people with a pistol. The police confronted Mathew Fugo by a roadside and asked him to approach them; as he did so they reportedly opened fire. He did not appear to have been threatening the police with a weapon at the time he was shot. An inquiry was announced into the shooting. The outcome was not known at the end of the year.

While investigations appeared to have been initiated into some cases of human rights violations by members of the police, many remained unresolved. In April, two policemen were jailed for four years for abducting and raping a teenage girl in Port Moresby in December 1994. There was no information about the progress of the inquiry into the death of Simi Kugame, who had been shot dead by police as he was running from a demonstration in Kundiawa, Chimbu Province, in July 1995. There was also no information about an inquiry into the death of Robin Robuna, who had been shot by police after he was arrested on suspicion of car theft in Goroka, Eastern Highlands Province, in May 1995. Robin Robuna was beaten and kicked by police and then shot in the thigh at close range as he was ordered to get into a police vehicle. He died from loss of blood.

In April, the Supreme Court acquitted Charles Ombusu of wilful murder, for which he had been sentenced to death in 1995 (see *Amnesty International Report 1996*). No one was sentenced to death and there were no executions during the year.

On Bougainville, the BRA carried out human rights abuses, including hostage-taking and deliberate and arbitrary killings. In September, five members of the security forces were taken hostage by the BRA after a clash with the PNGDF. The BRA leader, General Sam Kauona, threatened to kill the five men if his organization's demands for a withdrawal of the PNGDF from

Bougainville and steps towards independence for the island were not met. By the end of the year, the five were still alive in BRA custody. Another three soldiers were taken hostage in northern Bougainville in October and were believed to have been killed shortly after by the BRA. In May, at least two civilians living in the Asitoki government-run Care Centre in Tohei were killed by the BRA as they went to collect food from their gardens.

In June, Amnesty International delegates visited Port Moresby, Buka, Chimbu Province and the Western Highlands Province. The delegation was prevented by the government and the PNGDF from travelling from Buka to Bougainville to monitor human rights. The delegation met representatives of the government and the PNGDF.

In February, Amnesty International issued a report, *Papua New Guinea: The death penalty – not the solution*. In October, the organization called on the authorities to ensure that there was a full and impartial inquiry into the killing of Theodore Miriung.

In September, Amnesty International called on the BRA to remove the threat of execution from five soldiers being held hostage on Bougainville.

PARAGUAY

Grave human rights violations in the context of land conflicts increased during the year. At least three landless peasant activists were shot dead by gunmen acting with the support or acquiescence of local authorities and police. The authorities took no action to prevent the killings or bring those responsible to justice. There were reports of threats, arbitrary arrest and torture by police. Prosecutions for past human rights violations continued.

A serious political crisis was triggered in April when General Lino Oviedo defied President Juan Carlos Wasmosy's order to relinquish his post as head of the army and attempted a coup. After several days of widespread demonstrations against the army rebellion, General Oviedo resigned his post, and in June he was arrested and charged with "insurrection and insubordination", an offence punishable by up to 15 years' imprisonment. He was released on appeal in August.

In September, Congress overturned a presidential veto and passed a law entitling victims of human rights violations during the government of General Alfredo Stroessner (1954 to 1989) to compensation.

In November, Paraguay ratified the Inter-American Convention on the Forced Disappearance of Persons.

An amendment to the military service law, which would allow conscientious objectors to opt for civilian service, was passed by the lower chamber of Congress in December. The bill was before the Senate at the end of the year.

Human rights violations during land disputes escalated as landless peasant farmers continued to occupy large tracts of under-developed property claimed by foreign nationals and local and national authorities (see *Amnesty International Report 1996*). Police and armed civilians operating with their support or acquiescence were responsible for the abuses. Violent expulsions, some without judicial order, were common and hundreds were detained, usually for brief periods; some were ill-treated or tortured. In March, police arrested peasant leader Francisco Ayala without a warrant, as he addressed a meeting near Tuna, Caazapá Department. He was shot in both legs as he allegedly resisted arrest. He was released after 40 days' detention when charges against him were dropped.

In July, peasant leader Arsenio Vázquez was shot dead by gunmen in Santa Carmen, Caaguazú Department. Mariano Díaz, wounded in the attack, died 10 days later. The *Federación Nacional Campesina*, National Peasant Federation, presented a formal complaint against a retired army general who they alleged had hired the gunmen.

In November, José Martínez, a member of the *Organización de Lucha por la Tierra*, Fight for Land Organization, was shot dead by gunmen on his farm in Cleto Romero, Cordillera Department. He had received death threats from gunmen hired by the owner of land which he and other peasant farmers were occupying. At least five other members of the landless peasant movement have been killed by gunmen in this area in the past two years. Although investigations were opened, the security forces made no effort to capture the gunmen responsible or their employers.

Several land activists and criminal suspects reported having been tortured by police. In July, two peasant farmers arrested in connection with a murder case in Guairá Department said they had been tortured by police, including by near suffocation with plastic bags and being repeatedly beaten around the head. Although police medical reports failed to find evidence of torture, a parliamentary commission found the detainees' injuries to be consistent with torture. A delegation of the Senate human rights commission, who visited a group of 50 landless peasants held in Coronel Oviedo police station, concluded that at least three had been tortured.

Ill-treatment of army conscripts, some as young as 15, was widespread. In the past seven years, 37 conscripts have died in military barracks, reportedly as a result of ill-treatment.

Investigations into past human rights violations continued. In May, the Appeals Court confirmed a 25-year prison sentence on Pastor Coronel, the former head of the Police Investigations Department (DIP-C), and on several other DIP-C officials convicted of torturing and murdering teacher Mario Raúl Schaerer Prono in 1976. Other sentences passed on these DIP-C officials were confirmed by the Appeals Court during the year (see previous Amnesty International Reports).

Paraguayan judicial officials cooperated in the investigation of the "disappearance" of Argentine nationals arrested in Paraguay in 1977 (see **Argentina** entry). In July, the Supreme Court released files to the Argentine authorities on the arrest and subsequent "disappearance" of three detainees who had been handed over to members of the Argentine security forces.

In November, Amnesty International expressed concern to the government about the killings of José Martínez and other peasant leaders and the authorities' failure to take measures to capture and bring to justice those responsible for these and other human rights violations.

PERU

Some 640 prisoners of conscience and possible prisoners of conscience remained in prison. Thousands of prisoners accused of terrorism-related offences experienced delays in being brought to trial or were serving sentences under procedures which fell short of international fair trial standards. Numerous cases of torture and death under torture were reported. Three detainees allegedly "disappeared". Two men were killed in circumstances suggesting they may have been extrajudicially executed. Thousands of past cases of human rights violations remained unclarified. The armed opposition continued to commit human rights abuses, including the deliberate and arbitrary killing of civilians and the taking of hostages.

The number of reported attacks by armed units attached to the clandestine *Partido Comunista del Perú (Sendero Luminoso)* (PCP), Communist Party of Peru (Shining Path), and the *Movimiento Revolucionario Túpac Amaru* (MRTA), Túpac Amaru Revolutionary Movement, continued to decline. President Alberto Fujimori claimed in July that "the pacification [of Peru] is being firmly consolidated". However, the government's pacification policy was questioned by several sectors of

Peruvian society, particularly in the face of continuing attacks by the PCP and the taking of several hundred hostages by the MRTA at a Japanese Embassy function in December (see below).

Significant areas of the country, including in and around Lima, the capital, remained under a state of emergency. The authorities claimed the activities of the armed opposition justified the periodic renewing of emergency legislation. However, members of the parliamentary opposition and independent human rights organizations stated that maintaining emergency powers in some rural areas was not consistent with official claims that the armed opposition no longer had an effective presence in those areas.

In April and June, respectively, the Ombudsman's Office and the Constitutional Tribunal, institutions relevant to the protection of human rights, came into operation (see *Amnesty International Report 1996*). In July, the Council for the Coordination of the Judiciary, charged with comprehensively reforming the judicial system, was established.

In March, Congress made a further amendment to the anti-terrorism laws by making provision for released defendants whose High Court acquittal was subsequently overturned by the Supreme Court of Justice, to remain free pending their new trial. In October, provisions in the anti-terrorism legislation allowing for the identity of judges to remain secret were extended by Congress for a further 12 months (see *Amnesty International Report 1996*).

In August, the government approved a law bringing into effect an *Ad-hoc* Commission, presided over by the Ombudsman, charged with proposing to the President of the Republic that he pardon or show mercy to prisoners unjustly accused of crimes of terrorism. The Commission was set up for six months but can be extended for a further six months. Dr Carlos Hermoza Moya, Minister of Justice and member of the Commission, publicly stated that there were some 400 prisoners whose cases merited review by the Commission. By the end of the year, 110 such prisoners had been released.

In September, the UN Special Rapporteur on the independence of judges and lawyers visited Peru. At the end of his visit the Special Rapporteur publicly called for an end to the system of secret judges and the trial of civilians by military tribunals.

In July, the UN Human Rights Committee issued a series of observations and recommendations, following partial consideration of the third periodic report submitted to the Committee by the Government of Peru in compliance with the International Covenant on Civil and Political Rights. The Committee stated that "many of the [counter-insurgency] measures adopted by the Government frustrated implementation of the rights protected under the Covenant." The Committee recommended, *inter alia*, that the government implement prompt measures to release and compensate prisoners falsely accused of terrorism-related offences and judicially review their sentences; ensure that all trials be conducted with full respect for the safeguards of the accused; strictly limit incommunicado detention; and repeal the amnesty laws (see *Amnesty International Report 1996*). In November, the Committee concluded its consideration of Peru's report. The Committee took note of the measures adopted to pardon prisoners convicted of crimes of terrorism. However, the Committee stated that pardoning convicted prisoners did not offer them full reparation and reiterated its call for the establishment of an effective review mechanism for those pardoned. The Committee also deplored the government's disregard for its other recommendations made in July and reiterated the need for their adoption.

Thirty-five prisoners of conscience and at least 600 possible prisoners of conscience remained in prison at the end of the year. Prisoners of conscience Carlos Florentino Molero Coca and Marco Antonio Ambrosio Concha, university students, had been arrested in April 1992 in Lima and jointly charged with crimes of terrorism. Both claim to have been tortured during interrogation by the police. Although the judge examining their cases concluded there was insufficient evidence linking them to the crimes, they were convicted and sentenced by a High Court to 12 and 10 years' imprisonment respectively.

Ninety-eight prisoners of conscience and at least 700 possible prisoners of conscience have been released since 1992. Among prisoners of conscience released in 1996 were Michael Soto Rodríguez,

Pelagia Salcedo Pizarro, her husband Juan Carlos Chuchón Zea, Eugenio Bazán Ventura and César Augusto Sosa Silupú (see *Amnesty International Reports 1993, 1995* and *1996*). Also released was prisoner of conscience Julio Ismael Loa Albornoz, a practising Buddhist who had been sentenced in 1994 to 15 years for the crime of treason. The military judge who examined his case stated that, in view of there being an element of doubt as to Julio Ismael Loa Albornoz having committed the offence, "it [was] preferable to impose a punishment immediately". In August, more than three years after he was detained, Julio Ismael Loa Albornoz was acquitted by the Supreme Council of Military Justice.

Rodolfo Robles Espinoza, a retired army general and active human rights defender who in 1993 publicly accused the *Grupo Colina*, a military "death squad", of murdering nine students and a professor from La Cantuta University (see *Amnesty International Reports 1993* to *1996*), was arrested on 26 November. Amnesty International declared General Robles a prisoner of conscience and publicly called for his immediate and unconditional release. General Robles was charged with "insulting the Armed Forces" and other military offences, following public declarations in which he claimed that the *Grupo Colina* was responsible for detonating a bomb at a television station in the city of Puno in November. General Robles was released on 7 December under an amnesty law passed by Congress two days earlier.

Thousands of prisoners accused of terrorism-related offences awaited trial or were serving sentences under procedures which failed to guarantee international fair trial standards (see *Amnesty International Reports 1993* to *1996*). For example, these prisoners were subject to procedures which denied them a public trial, concealed the identity of judges and prosecutors, referred civilians charged with treason to military courts, and prohibited defence lawyers from cross-examining members of the security forces involved in their arrest and interrogation.

Amnesty International continued to receive numerous reports of torture and death under torture. For example, on 23 August soldiers reportedly ransacked the shop of Juana Ibarra Aguirre in the town of Monzón, Huánuco department, following an earlier unsuccessful search for a firearm said to have been left behind on the premises by a soldier. Six days later Juana Ibarra and her five-year-old daughter were detained when she went to the local military base to request that her merchandise be returned, and to clarify the situation concerning the weapon. Both were held incommunicado at the base until 11 September when they were released. Juana Ibarra was not charged. She subsequently filed a complaint before the Public Ministry in the judicial district of Huánuco-Pasco. She claimed that she was raped, beaten and had water, salt and detergent forced up her nose.

In July, the Huánuco Criminal Court found two police officers responsible for the death in custody of Jhoel Huamán García, a student suspected of assault and robbery who was last seen alive in a police precinct in the town of Pasco, department of Junín, in May 1995. An autopsy revealed that Jhoel Huamán died as a result of multiple blows to his body with a blunt instrument. The officers were sentenced to five and six years' imprisonment respectively. An appeal against the convictions had not been heard by the end of year.

Three detainees allegedly "disappeared" following detention by members of the army. One of them, María Cárdenas Espinoza, a cook, was detained with two brothers by a military patrol on 27 May, in the hamlet of Chinchavito, district of Chinchao, department of Huánuco. The two brothers were subsequently transferred to a military base in the city of Tingo María, but at the end of the year the whereabouts of María Cárdenas Espinoza remained unknown. A complaint about her "disappearance" was filed before a representative of the Public Ministry. By the end of the year her whereabouts remained unknown.

Two men were killed, in separate incidents, in circumstances suggesting they may have been extrajudicially executed. Nicolás Carrión Escobedo, aged 73, was detained on 23 August by soldiers and taken to a military base in Sarín from his home in the hamlet of Uruspampa, province of Sánchez Carrión, La Libertad department. Hours later he was found dead. An autopsy revealed that he had been stabbed in the back of the head.

Thousands of complaints of torture, "disappearance", extrajudicial execution and death threats remained unclarified.

These included the vast majority of cases filed since May 1980 and closed by the passing of amnesty laws in June 1995 (see *Amnesty International Reports 1981* to *1996*). A congressional bill to repeal the amnesty laws and create a Truth Commission, submitted in 1995, was never debated (see *Amnesty International Report 1996*).

Hundreds of people were victims of human rights abuses by the armed opposition. The victims included civilians deliberately and arbitrarily killed by the PCP and hostages held by the MRTA. In March, community leader Pascuala Rosado Cornejo was shot dead by PCP members in Huaycán, a shanty town on the outskirts of Lima. She had been actively opposing PCP activities in her community for over 10 years. In July, members of the PCP were reported to have claimed responsibility for the killing of community leader Epifanio Santamaría Rodríguez in the shanty town of San Martín de Porres, also on the outskirts of Lima.

On 17 December a heavily armed MRTA unit broke into a function organized by the Ambassador of Japan at his residence in Lima, taking some 700 men and women hostage, including scores of Peruvian government officials, foreign ambassadors and diplomats, and Peruvian and Japanese businessmen. The hostage-takers, who included among their demands the release of imprisoned MRTA members, initially threatened to kill their captives. Amnesty International condemned the hostage-taking, expressed concern for the hostages' safety and publicly called on the MRTA and the Peruvian authorities to bring about a solution designed to ensure their prompt release. By the end of the year at least 600 hostages had been released and 81 remained captive.

In May, an Amnesty International delegation visited Peru and held talks with government and military authorities. The delegation expressed concern about prisoners of conscience falsely accused of crimes of terrorism and called for their immediate and unconditional release. The delegation also expressed concern that prisoners accused of terrorism-related offences were not guaranteed a fair trial. In response, several government officials acknowledged that prisoners unjustly accused of terrorism remained in detention, and indicated that steps would soon be taken to have their cases reviewed. However, the President of the Supreme Council of Military Justice told the delegation that not one of at least 1,200 civilians tried by military courts since 1992 had been unjustly convicted of treason. The authorities also informed the delegation that provisions in the anti-terrorism laws, including the use of secret judges and military tribunals, were justified by the serious threat posed to the state by the armed opposition, but added that the laws would be reformed as the country became increasingly "pacified".

Also in May, Amnesty International published a report, *Peru: Prisoners of conscience*, calling for the release of prisoners unjustly accused of terrorism and for internationally recognized fair trial guarantees to be respected.

In June, the organization published a second report, *Peru: Human rights in a time of impunity*, urging the authorities to repeal the 1995 amnesty laws, to reopen judicial investigations into thousands of unresolved cases of human rights violations, and to bring to justice those responsible.

In both publications, and through the Peruvian press, Amnesty International condemned human rights abuses by the PCP and MRTA and called on both organizations to fully abide by internationally recognized humanitarian standards.

In July and October, the UN Human Rights Committee was informed by Amnesty International of its human rights concerns in Peru. The Committee addressed many of these concerns in its recommendations to the Government of Peru.

Amnesty International made a submission in August to the UN Sub-Commission on Prevention of Discrimination and Protection of Minorities concerning Peru's amnesty laws. Although the Chairman of the Sub-Commission had previously indicated that it would address the issue in August (see *Amnesty International Report 1996*), it failed to do so.

PHILIPPINES

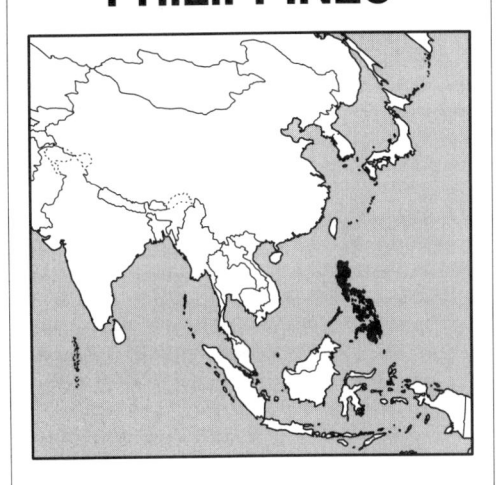

More than 175 political prisoners, including possible prisoners of conscience, remained in detention. People arrested for alleged involvement in violent political activity and ordinary criminal suspects continued to be tortured and ill-treated during interrogation. At least seven people were reported to have "disappeared", although most of them were later found to be held in official custody. At least 127 people were sentenced to death; no executions were carried out. Armed opposition groups committed human rights abuses, including deliberate and arbitrary killings and hostage-taking.

The government of President Fidel Ramos signed a peace settlement with the Muslim secessionist Moro National Liberation Front (MNLF) in September, ending 24 years of MNLF-led rebellion in the southern region of Mindanao. An interim regional administrative council and assembly, including representatives of the MNLF, was created pending a referendum in 1999 on the shape of a proposed autonomous region in Mindanao. However, despite attempts to extend peace negotiations to the Moro Islamic Liberation Front (MILF), military operations continued against the MILF and other Muslim armed groups in the region.

Counter-insurgency operations against communist rebels and their supporters continued to decline. Formal peace talks with the National Democratic Front, representing the Communist Party of the Philippines (CPP) and its armed wing, the New People's Army (NPA), resumed in June but were suspended by the NDF in November.

Public confidence in the judiciary was weakened by apparent failures to deliver justice and by accusations of corruption among its officers. Protracted delays in the prosecution of those responsible for contemporary human rights violations, and the continued failure to prosecute many of those believed to be responsible for human rights violations under former Presidents Ferdinand Marcos and Corazon Aquino, served to maintain the impression that some government and security personnel, especially those with influence or wealth, enjoyed impunity. The reputation of the Office of the Ombudsman, responsible for investigating complaints against government personnel, was damaged by controversy surrounding its investigation of 98 police officers, including four police generals, allegedly involved in the extrajudicial execution while in police custody of 11 suspected members of a bank-robbery gang in Manila in May 1995 (see *Amnesty International Report 1996*). The Ombudsman initially exonerated all 98 officers, but then indicted 27 officers, with only one general among the principal accused. The Ombudsman later downgraded charges against the general; no convictions had been reached by the end of the year. In early 1996, the Ombudsman, despite witness statements and supporting medical evidence, dismissed charges of attempted murder against four police officers of the National Bureau of Investigation who were alleged to have arbitrarily detained, beaten and threatened to kill university student Stephen Guerrero after he had intervened in a traffic dispute involving one of the officers outside the Bureau headquarters in Manila in March 1995.

More than 175 political prisoners, including possible prisoners of conscience, remained in detention at the end of the year. Most of the political detainees were held on criminal charges, particularly illegal possession of firearms, robbery and murder, which allegedly occurred within the context of the CPP-NPA insurgency. Most had not been convicted by the end of the year. In January, 22 political prisoners were released on the recommendation of the Presidential Committee for the Grant of Bail, Release or Pardon. In November, over 130 political prisoners began a protest fast calling for the Committee and the

National Amnesty Commission to act on pending applications and recommendations for release and amnesty.

Torture and ill-treatment of people detained for alleged involvement in violent political activity and of criminal suspects, continued to be reported. Following attacks in December 1995 by the communist armed group the "Alex Boncayao Brigade" (ABB) on three Chinese-Filipino businessmen accused by the ABB of labour abuses, police and military intelligence personnel detained more than 15 suspects, mainly in Manila and in surrounding provinces. Some of the detainees, who were reportedly arrested without warrants and denied access to legal counsel, were held in unacknowledged detention for periods ranging from several days to over two weeks. Some were reported to have been subjected to torture, including beatings and having their toes crushed with weighted tables, to extract confessions. In June, six men arrested on suspicion of involvement in the killing of a former military intelligence colonel in Manila were allegedly subjected to electric shocks and beatings to extract confessions.

Criminal suspects were reportedly tortured and ill-treated, particularly while held in police cells during the initial interrogation period before formal charges were laid. Throughout the year, there were allegations that police in Manila beat and harassed suspected squatters during forced evictions in poor residential areas designated for demolition and clearance.

Overall levels of human rights violations occurring within the context of counter-insurgency operations continued to decrease. Nevertheless, at least seven "disappearances" were reported. Four of the victims were suspected ABB members who, after periods of unacknowledged detention ranging from several days to over two weeks, were found to be held in official custody. However, the fate and whereabouts of alleged ABB member Jose De Guzman and of NPA member Aldrin Suyat, who "disappeared" in January and May respectively, remained unknown at the end of the year. In October, Domingo Banaag, a farmers' association leader in Cavite province, "disappeared" after confrontations with the private security guards of a local development company involved in a land dispute with the farmers' association. It was alleged that local police and district officials had connived with the private security guards in Domingo Banaag's "disappearance". His whereabouts remained unknown at the end of the year.

The number of extrajudicial executions, mainly insurgency-related, declined but cases continued to be reported. The Philippine National Police, followed by the Armed Forces of the Philippines or their militia units, were reported to be the main perpetrators. In February, human rights lawyer and journalist Ferdinand Reyes was shot dead in his office in Dipolog, Mindanao, by an unidentified man. Unconfirmed reports stated that his killer may have been a member of the armed forces. In August, Rejenaldo Gambutan was reported by witnesses to have been arrested in Misamis Oriental, Mindanao, by military units conducting operations against suspected NPA rebels. In September, a writ of *habeas corpus* was filed in the regional trial court, but in October a body believed to be that of Rejenaldo Gambutan was discovered in a shallow grave.

Despite peace negotiations with the MNLF, military operations continued in Mindanao against units of the MILF and the *Abu Sayyaf* Muslim armed group and their suspected supporters. Such operations, at times in response to Muslim rebel attacks, included indiscriminate shelling and bombing of civilian areas. Scores of civilians were reportedly killed or injured. Muslim, Christian and indigenous communities, including those living in development project zones allegedly affected by NPA activity, were displaced.

At least 127 death sentences were passed, but only one sentence, that against house painter Leo Pilo Echegary who was convicted of raping his step-daughter, was confirmed by the Supreme Court. Since the death penalty was restored in December 1993, at least 240 people have been sentenced to death for a range of crimes, including murder, rape and drug-trafficking. No executions have been carried out. In March, President Ramos signed a law providing for execution by lethal injection.

Armed opposition groups were responsible for human rights abuses. Members of Muslim armed groups in Mindanao, including the MILF, *Abu Sayyaf* and renegade MNLF units, continued to take civilians hostage and to carry out deliberate and arbitrary killings.

In February, Amnesty International called on the government to launch an impartial public inquiry into allegations that military or other government personnel may have been involved in the killing of Ferdinand Reyes. In March and October respectively, the organization called for renewed investigations into the "disappearances" of Noel Campilan (see *Amnesty International Report 1996*) and Domingo Banaag. In November, Amnesty International published a report, *Philippines: Not forgotten – the fate of the "disappeared"*, which called on the government to resolve the cases of over 1,600 people who had "disappeared" since the early 1970s and to address the issue of impunity. Throughout the year, Amnesty International called for all death sentences to be commuted and, in March, it appealed to President Ramos not to sign the law providing for execution by lethal injection.

PORTUGAL

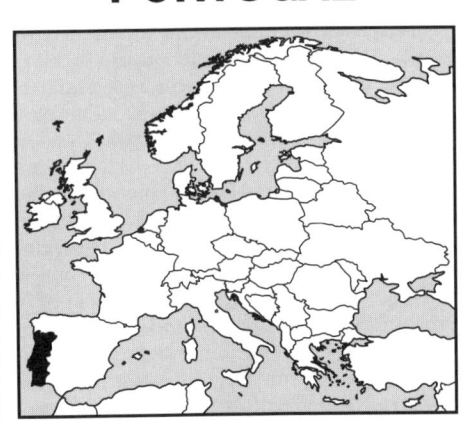

There were further allegations of torture and ill-treatment by law enforcement officers and several deaths in custody were reported. Judicial inquiries into such allegations, whether by military or civilian courts, were slow. The trials of several law enforcement officers accused of ill-treatment were held during the year.

In January, Jorge Sampaio, the former Mayor of Lisbon, was elected President, succeeding a fellow Socialist Party member, Mario Soares, who stood down after serving the maximum permitted period.

In February, the government appointed the first Inspector General of a new institution which could play a major role in promoting respect for human rights. The General Inspectorate of Internal Administration (IGAI) was created under Decree Law 227/95 of 11 September 1995, modified by Decree Law 154/96 of 31 August 1996. It is especially charged with the supervision of the activities of law enforcement forces "in order to defend the rights of citizens and to achieve a better and quicker implementation of disciplinary justice in situations of major social importance". IGAI is part of the Ministry of the Interior and its mandate covers all the Ministry's law enforcement agencies, notably the Public Security Police (PSP) and the paramilitary Republican National Guard (GNR), but not the Judiciary Police which is responsible to the Ministry of Justice.

The findings of the 1995 visit of inspection by the European Committee for the Prevention of Torture and Inhuman or Degrading Treatment or Punishment and the reply of the Portuguese Government were published in November. The Committee's report concluded: "A significant proportion of the persons interviewed alleged that they had been ill-treated while in police custody". It further found that almost none of the core recommendations on safeguards against ill-treatment made following its visit of inspection in 1992 had been implemented and did not feel able to modify its earlier statement that the "... ill-treatment of persons in police custody was a relatively common phenomenon".

There were further allegations of physical and verbal abuse by law enforcement officers. The most common complaints were of kicking, punching and beatings with truncheons. People across the entire spectrum of Portuguese society, including a high proportion of people of non-European ethnic origin, complained of such treatment. There were also reports of an illegal shooting and of the killing of a detainee.

In May, the Ombudsman, Dr José Menéres Pimentel, publicly recognized that a worrying proportion of the complaints he had received alleged police violence.

In February, four workers were injured, one seriously, when PSP officers used batons to evict workers occupying a factory facing closure in Santo Tirso. An inquiry by the Ombudsman concluded that some officers had exceeded the rules and, for revenge, had assaulted citizens with batons. The Minister of the Interior questioned the use of batons against the workers, who, in his view, were isolated and not aggressive, but decided that it would be unwarranted to punish the individual officers because they had not received adequate training.

António Guerreiro, a magistrate in the Criminal Investigation Department (DIAP) of the Public Prosecutor's office, brought a judicial complaint against four GNR officers. In December 1995, he was stopped by the officers while driving into the town of Cascais. He claimed they punched and kicked him, before searching and handcuffing him. He stated that he was a magistrate and asked to contact a colleague. This was refused. One officer insulted him and suggested that he must be involved in drug dealing to be driving a car such as his. He was taken to the GNR post and threatened before being taken to hospital. He was later charged with refusing to present identity documents on demand and insulting an officer. The duty magistrate released him and an investigation was opened.

In April, Francisco Monteiro, a black African, was shot in the stomach by a man in plain clothes. Eye-witnesses reportedly claimed that he was standing in the doorway of a bar when two men got out of a car and assaulted him. One of them then shot him. They maintained that the two assailants were off-duty PSP officers and it was confirmed that the car at the scene belonged to a PSP officer. The commanding officer of the PSP was reported as saying that the incident occurred "during an argument between the victim and a white man". Both DIAP and the Ombudsman opened inquiries.

During the year, Amnesty International received several reports of killings or deaths in police custody. In May, Carlos Rosa was killed while in custody in the GNR post in Sacavém. A GNR sergeant confessed to the killing, claiming that he had accidentally shot him in the head during an interrogation and, in panic, cut off his head to prevent identification. Two weeks later the body was found in a ditch and the head buried in a field. Following an inconclusive first autopsy, a second examination concluded that the death was caused by shooting at close range followed by decapitation. A judicial inquiry was opened and the court committed the sergeant to preventive detention. In December, he was charged with aggravated homicide. Six other soldiers from Sacavém were allowed to remain at liberty.

In January, the civilian court in Almada acquitted six GNR soldiers charged with assaulting a local butcher, Paulo Portugal, in 1991 (see *Amnesty International Reports 1993* and *1996*). Allegations by the GNR officers that Paulo Portugal had assaulted them were found to be groundless and he was acquitted. Criminal proceedings against Paulo Portugal for insulting behaviour and refusal to obey orders were closed after an amnesty.

In September, the trial in Vila Real of Joaquim Teixeira, a computer specialist, for assault of a PSP officer, was adjourned until December. At the request of the defence, the judge again postponed the opening of his trial pending the decision of the Appeal Court on the case brought by Joaquím Teixeira against the PSP officer. The judge agreed that the two cases should be tried together. Until December, the allegations had been the subject of two parallel investigations. Joaquim Teixeira alleged that he and a friend had been assaulted by the PSP officer in 1995 (see *Amnesty International Report 1996*). The PSP claimed that Joaquim Teixeira had assaulted the officers. The prosecutor in the trial was replaced after it was discovered that he had not asked the local hospital for the medical certificate which recorded the injuries inflicted on Joaquim Teixeira while he was in police custody.

Amnesty International urged the authorities to ensure full and prompt investigations into all allegations of torture and ill-treatment. It requested information on the progress of judicial and administrative inquiries into such allegations. In 1996, it noted a welcome increase in the information supplied to the organization by the authorities, in particular by the newly created office of the IGAI, and by the Ombudsman.

In December, Amnesty International delegates visited Portugal and held talks with the President of the Republic and senior government ministers. The delegates discussed means of increasing access to the judicial system for victims of physical assault by law enforcement officers, improving safeguards for detainees and the urgent need for substantial improvements in the training of officers. The government gave encouraging assurances of legislative and administrative reforms to take place in 1997. The delegates stressed that these assurances only constituted the beginning of an urgently required reform program to fight human rights violations in Portugal.

QATAR

Scores of political arrests took place and approximately 12 people remained in detention without charge or trial at the end of the year. There were reports that some detainees were tortured or ill-treated.

Scores of people were arrested in February following a reported attempt to overthrow the government headed by the Amir, al-Shaikh Hamad Ibn Khalifa Al Thani, who had deposed his father in a bloodless coup in June 1995. All those arrested were held incommunicado. However, most were released after a short period in detention.

The government acknowledged the continued detention of a group of people but did not make public their names or personal details. Most were believed to be army officers loyal to the deposed Amir. According to reports, the detainees included Brigadier Bakhit Marzug, Lieutenant-Colonel 'Abd al-Hadi Rashid al-Sihabi and Lieutenant-Colonel Rashid 'Ali. They and other detainees were allegedly tortured or ill-treated in custody.

Amnesty International sought assurances from the government that the detainees' right to prompt and fair trials and the right to be treated humanely were being respected, and called for the immediate and unconditional release of anyone held solely for the non-violent expression of their beliefs. In response, the government said that they would be given a fair trial in accordance with international standards and denied all allegations of torture or ill-treatment of any detainees.

Amnesty International asked for further information about the detainees, including the details of any charges brought against them.

ROMANIA

At least one prisoner of conscience was held. There were reports of torture and ill-treatment which resulted in at least one death. Shootings by police officers in disputed circumstances resulted in at least two deaths. Many of the victims of human rights violations were Roma. An asylum-seeker, who had been a prisoner of conscience, was returned to Syria, where he was immediately arrested and allegedly tortured.

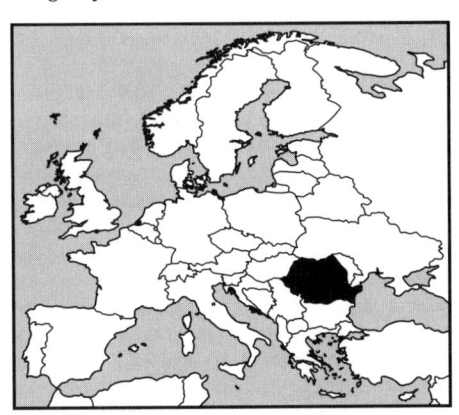

In November, Emil Constantinescu was elected President. A new government formed by the Democratic Convention, the Social Democratic Union and the Hungarian Democratic Union of Romania was appointed following parliamentary elections.

In April, Law No. 15/1996 regulating the status of refugees was promulgated. It imposes a 10-day limit on applications for asylum and denies asylum to anyone who has violated any of Romania's laws or who does not have "correct and civilized conduct".

In May, parliament adopted Law No. 46/1996 providing for an alternative military service for those who refuse to perform armed military service on religious grounds. The alternative service was proposed to be twice the length of ordinary military service. A government decision on the implementation of the Law had not been adopted by the end of the year.

In October, parliament adopted amendments to the Penal Code. Article 200, paragraph 1, criminalizes homosexual relations between consenting adults "if the act was committed in public or has produced public scandal". The newly adopted paragraph 5 of the same law makes "enticing or seducing a person to practise same-sex acts, as well as forming propaganda associations, or engaging in other forms of proselytizing with the same aim" punishable with one to five years' imprisonment. These provisions would permit the continued imprisonment of adults solely for engaging in consensual homosexual relations in private, and could also lead to imprisonment of individuals solely for exercising their rights to freedom of expression and freedom of peaceful assembly and association. Several other amendments to the Penal Code, concerning dissemination of false news, defamation of the state or nation, "offences against the authorities" and "outrage", also imposed excessive restrictions on the right to freedom of expression.

At least one person was in prison solely because of his homosexuality; he was considered to be a prisoner of conscience. According to information supplied by the General Directorate of Penitentiaries, a prisoner in Poarta Albă penitentiary convicted under Article 200, paragraph 1, of the Penal Code, "for repeatedly engaging in sexual relations with another man" began a two-year sentence in November 1995.

In October, a municipal court in Bucharest sentenced journalists Sorin Roşca Stănescu and Tana Ardeleanu to 12 and 14 months' imprisonment respectively, under Article 238, paragraph 1, of the Penal Code, concerning "offences against the authorities", for defaming a state official. In May 1995 they had published an article entitled "A Murderer Leads Romania" in *Ziua*, a daily newspaper, as well as several articles claiming that the President of Romania was "a KGB agent". They were free at the end of the year pending appeal. If they were imprisoned, Amnesty International would consider them to be prisoners of conscience.

There were reports of torture and ill-treatment, which in at least one case resulted in death. In January, Ion Axente was reportedly beaten by a police officer outside a bar in Piscu, Galaţi county. After he fell to the ground the police officer allegedly sprayed a paralysing gas into his face and kicked him in the head. Ion Axente was later found, semi-conscious, in the courtyard of his house. He went into a coma that evening and was taken to hospital, where he died in June without regaining consciousness.

In June, two women were ill-treated when around 70 police officers in Bucharest, the capital, raided a yoga class and checked the identification documents of all people present. Carmen Efta and Camelia Rosu were standing next to a man who was videotaping the police action. A police officer who tried to take away the camera reportedly hit Carmen Efta, while another officer slapped Camelia Rosu in the face. According to medical certificates Camelia Rosu suffered bruising to the right temple, forehead and cheekbone and bruising and lacerations on her upper arms and left hand. Carmen Efta sustained bruising to the left cheekbone, left knee and left hand.

Many of the victims of human rights violations were Roma. In July, police officers in Târgu-Mureş reportedly ill-treated three Roma minors, Gheorghe Notar Jr, Ioan Őtvős and Rupi Stoica. One officer allegedly hit 17-year-old Gheorghe Notar Jr on the neck with a truncheon causing him to fall down several steps in the apartment block where he was apprehended. He was then taken to the police station together with 15-year-old Ioan Őtvős and 16-year-old Rupi Stoica, who had been detained earlier. In the police car the three youths were reportedly slapped and beaten by two police officers. At the police station Gheorghe Notar Jr was hit on the back. He fell and briefly lost consciousness. The beating of the three youths continued intermittently during their interrogation in the police changing room. They were then held in custody for five days in the Centre for the Protection of Minors, solely on the basis of a police statement and with no possibility of a judicial review of the decision to detain them. During this period they were taken back to the police station and interrogated on several occasions by police officers without the presence of a lawyer or their parents.

In June, police officers in a suburb of Bucharest failed adequately to protect Roma and their property from racist violence, despite receiving prior warning that an attack on the Roma community was being prepared. The police chief and between 10 and 15 officers came to the neighbourhood when a large group of people started to break windows and doors of Roma houses, forcing the Roma to abandon their homes. One house was set on fire. The local police reportedly took no steps to prevent the violence or protect the victims. Order was only re-established following the intervention of a police unit from the centre of the capital.

There were shootings by police officers in disputed circumstances, resulting in at least two deaths. In May, two police officers in Bucharest, who were pursuing a deserter, shot and killed Marius Cristian Palcu, an unarmed soldier. A police officer was charged with his murder. The same month in Măruntei, Olt county, Mircea-Muresul Mosor, a Rom, was shot in the back and killed by a police officer who, together with three other officers, had pursued him after he failed to stop his horse-drawn carriage.

In June, a police officer in Mangalia reportedly shot six times at Isai Iaşar, whom he suspected of pick-pocketing. One of the bullets hit 13-year-old Ionuţ Vlase in the head while he was playing with other children in front of his apartment block. The police officer then reportedly left the scene of the shooting without assisting the injured boy, who was later taken to Constanţa county hospital by his parents.

Decisions were reached by the prosecuting authorities on a number of cases of alleged ill-treatment and shootings by police in previous years. However, neither the victims nor their families appeared to have received compensation. A police officer who had reportedly tortured Robert Radu was indicted in November 1995 for illegal arrest and abusive investigation, and three police officers and a civil guard were indicted in July for abusive conduct against Viorel Constantin (see *Amnesty International Report 1996*). An investigation into the death in suspicious circumstances of Alfred Pană (see *Amnesty International Report 1996*) established that he had been "subjected to violence during questioning", but the prosecution of the police officer "responsible for abusive conduct" was suspended following the officer's death in a traffic accident.

Investigations into the shootings of Nicolae Sebastian Balint and Marcel Ghinea (see *Amnesty International Report 1996*) were suspended following prosecutors' decisions that in both cases police officers had acted in accordance with Law No. 26/1994 which "permits the use of firearms to apprehend suspects caught in the criminal act who try to run away and do not obey the order to stay in place".

In March, an asylum-seeker who had been a prisoner of conscience between 1987 and 1994 was sent back to Syria, where he was immediately arrested and allegedly tortured.

Amnesty International urged members of parliament throughout the year to ensure that the revised Penal Code was consistent with Romania's legal obligations under international human rights treaties. In March, Amnesty International urged the authorities to clarify the fate and whereabouts of the Syrian asylum-seeker following his *refoulement*. The organization called on the authorities to initiate investigations into reports of ill-treatment and incidents of police shootings in disputed circumstances. In June, Amnesty International urged the General Prosecutor to investigate allegations that police officers failed adequately to protect Roma from racist violence in Bucharest. In October, the organization urged the government to revise Law No. 3/1970 which allows for the detention of minors for up to 30 days solely on the basis of police statements. Also in October, Amnesty International informed President Ion Iliescu that if imprisoned, the two journalists would be considered prisoners of conscience. In November, the organization called for the release of the man imprisoned solely because of his homosexuality. Following presidential and parliamentary elections Amnesty International published an open letter to the new authorities summarizing the organization's major concerns.

The authorities provided some information about investigations into reports of torture and ill-treatment in previous years, and about people imprisoned under Article 200, paragraph 1, of the Penal Code.

RUSSIAN FEDERATION

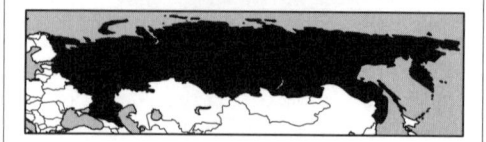

Conscientious objectors continued to be imprisoned. Two other prisoners of conscience were held. There were numerous allegations of torture and ill-treatment in detention. Prisoners awaiting trial were held in conditions which amounted to cruel, inhuman, or degrading treatment, sometimes resulting in deaths. Human rights violations by government forces took place in the context of the conflict in the Chechen Republic, including indiscriminate killings of civilians, detention without trial, torture and ill-treatment, and extrajudicial executions. At least 140 people were reported to have been judicially executed despite a promise to institute a moratorium. Between 500 and 600 prisoners were believed to be held on death row. Reports of inadequate legal protection for refugees and asylum-seekers continued. Human rights abuses by Chechen armed opposition groups were reported, including deliberate and arbitrary killings, torture and ill-treatment of prisoners and hostage-taking.

In January, Sergey Kovalyov resigned as Chairman of the Presidential Commission on Human Rights, followed by most other members of the Commission. In February, the Commission released its report on human rights in the Russian Federation for 1994 and 1995, which criticized government policies and practices. Later that month, the Russian Federation became a member of the Council of Europe and signed the European Convention for the Protection of Human Rights and Fundamental Freedoms. In May, a new Criminal Code was adopted by parliament, effective from January 1997.

In November, the UN Committee against Torture examined the second periodic report of the Russian Federation on implementation of the provisions of the Convention against Torture and Other Cruel, Inhuman or Degrading Treatment or Punishment. The Committee expressed concerns about allegations of systematic and widespread torture and ill-treatment in Russia, including violations during the conflict in the Chechen Republic, and made extensive recommendations to remedy these violations.

In July, President Boris Yeltsin won a majority of votes in the second round of the presidential elections. In August, a peace agreement ended the hostilities in the armed conflict in the Chechen Republic.

There was still no law on a civilian alternative to military service, which placed all conscientious objectors under the threat of imprisonment.

In December 1995, Vadim Hesse submitted his appeal to perform alternative civilian service to the Military Recruitment Office of Noginsk district, Moscow Region. He was arrested in January 1996 and charged with "evading the regular draft to active military service" under Article 80 of the Criminal Code of the Russian Federation. He was released from detention in March. Vadim Hesse was subsequently acquitted by Noginsk City Court in May, and by Moscow Regional Court in June.

In February, Aleksandr Nikitin, a retired Russian naval officer who had worked on a report on the dangers of nuclear waste in the Northern Fleet for the Norwegian non-governmental group the Bellona Foundation, was arrested by the Federal Security Services in St Petersburg. He was charged with treason for revealing state secrets, despite the fact that all the information he used had been taken from public sources. Aleksandr Nikitin faced a possible death sentence if convicted. In December, he was released from detention and awaiting trial. He was a prisoner of conscience.

Yury Shadrin, a human rights advocate and public defender, was arrested in November in the Siberian city of Omsk on the orders of the Regional Procurator. He was charged with violating "the rules of traffic safety and operation of transport vehicles", making "a threat of physical force to person or property" and "defamation of judges and people's assessors in the process of their judicial activities". Yury Shadrin declared a hunger-strike to protest against his arrest and against the charges on which he was held. In December, he was released pending trial – allegedly on the personal initiative of Anatoly Chubais, head of the Presidential Administration – but was not allowed to leave Omsk. Yury Shadrin appeared to have been arrested solely for his human rights activities as a public defender and for the peaceful expression of his conscientiously held beliefs. He was a prisoner of conscience.

There were numerous allegations of torture and ill-treatment in detention, both in criminal cases and in the context of the conflict in the Chechen Republic; most did not appear to receive prompt and impartial investigation. Ethnic minorities were particularly vulnerable. Sultan Kurbanov, a Chechen resident in Moscow, was arrested in January by two policemen who came to his apartment claiming he was wanted for questioning at police headquarters and would be released after two hours. Instead he was driven to a warehouse depot in the Kuntsevsky district of Moscow and beaten with truncheons and sticks by about 10 police officers who emerged from a bus parked nearby. He said he was hit repeatedly, including on his legs, head and face, by what he described as metal implements. Later that evening, a woman found Sultan Kurbanov lying "wounded and half dead" in a street in Kuntsevsky district. The local police refused to help her but they allowed her to telephone his family. He was then taken to Moscow City Hospital No. 1 by a relative, who claimed he overheard nurses saying there had been a directive from the head of the hospital that no one of Chechen origin was to receive medical treatment. The relative told them that Sultan Kurbanov was an Ossetian, and he received treatment.

The conditions in pre-trial prisons continued to amount to cruel, inhuman or degrading treatment. In October, it was reported that 280 people died in pre-trial detention centres in Moscow during the first nine months of the year.

Human rights violations carried out by government forces in the context of the armed conflict in the Chechen Republic included indiscriminate killings, detention without trial, torture and ill-treatment, and extrajudicial executions.

In early March, Russian forces bombarded the town of Sernovodsk, without any apparent concern for the safety of the trapped civilian population, after claiming that armed Chechen groups had set up in the town. Between 10,000 and 16,000 people were believed to have fled Sernovodsk at this time, but some 7,000 civilians remained. Many of those who stayed in the town were people displaced by the conflict from elsewhere in the Chechen Republic. Hundreds were killed and injured by the Russian federal forces. During the attack, representatives of the International Committee of the Red Cross were denied access to the town. Russian troops who entered Sernovodsk were also reported to have carried out extrajudicial executions. One eye-witness stated that a young woman was arrested in the street by several soldiers and taken to a nearby house. Her dead body was later found there. Indiscriminate attacks by the Russian federal forces were also carried out in March, April and August against civilians in the Chechen villages of Samashki, Shali, Komsomolskoye and the capital, Grozny.

There were numerous reports of torture and ill-treatment of civilians in the so-called "filtration points", detention camps set up by the Russian army during the conflict in the Chechen Republic. None of these reports was known to have been promptly or impartially investigated. In March, during the Russian military attack on Sernovodsk, men between the ages of 16 and 55 were moved to "filtration points". All the men were believed to have been freed when the camps were closed down.

The Russian Federation made a formal commitment to suspend all executions, pending the full abolition of the death penalty within three years, when it acceded to the Council of Europe in February. Nevertheless, executions in Russia continued and no effective steps were taken to impose the moratorium on executions. In November, Anatoly Pristavkin, Chairman of the Presidential Clemency Commission, reported that 140 executions had been carried out during the year, 103 of them after Russia joined the Council of Europe. In September, Valery Borschev, a member of parliament and representative of the Chamber of Human Rights under the President, referred to a study carried out in Russia which claimed that judicial errors had been made in 30 per cent of death penalty cases.

An estimated 500 to 600 prisoners remained on death row. A draft law on the moratorium on executions, prepared by two Duma deputies, was under discussion at the end of the year.

Reports indicated that legal provisions for refugees and asylum-seekers were inadequate. In March, Elgudzha Khutayevich Meskhia, an opponent of the Georgian Government, sought political asylum in Russia. He was arrested at the request of the Georgian Government and forcibly repatriated to Georgia, where he was at risk of torture and ill-treatment. In April, Rahim Qaziyev, the former Minister of Defence of Azerbaijan, was forcibly returned to that country, where he faced ill-treatment and the death penalty. In November, reports claimed that he was being kept in detention in Azerbaijan and had not been able to see his lawyers since August. His family had been allowed to see him only once since his return.

Forces loyal to Chechen President Dzhokhar Dudayev, who was reportedly killed in April by the Russian army, were responsible for human rights abuses, including torture and ill-treatment, hostage-taking and deliberate and arbitrary killings. In January, an armed group of Chechens calling itself "Lone Wolf" entered the southern Russian town of Kizlyar in Dagestan and took over the central hospital and adjoining maternity home. Civilians from apartment blocks surrounding the medical complex were forced into the hospital. The group's leader, Salman Raduyev, said the hostages would be shot if Russian troops did not withdraw from the Chechen Republic. At the same time, hostages were taken by armed Chechens at an electrical plant near Grozny. The hostages from Kizlyar were taken to the village of Pervomaiskoye. The Russian army launched heavy artillery and Grad-rocket attacks on the village in an apparently indiscriminate attack, without regard for the lives of the civilians in the village or the hostages themselves. The Russian army reportedly secured the freedom of 82 hostages from Pervomaiskoye; the remaining hostages were later freed by their Chechen captors.

In an open letter to the presidential candidates during the June presidential elections, Amnesty International urged the future president to consider as a first priority the improvement of the country's human rights situation.

Amnesty International urged the government to release any conscientious objectors held as prisoners of conscience, and to introduce a civilian alternative to military service for conscientious objectors. The organization called for the immediate and unconditional release of Aleksandr Nikitin and Yury Shadrin.

In a report published in October, *Russian Federation: Comments on the Second Periodic Report submitted to the United Nations Committee against Torture*, the organization urged the authorities to initiate thorough and impartial investigations into all allegations of torture and ill-treatment in detention, to make the results public, and to bring those responsible to justice.

Amnesty International urged the Russian authorities to hold a comprehensive and impartial investigation into the deliberate and indiscriminate killings of civilians during the conflict in the Chechen Republic and to take steps to protect non-combatants in accordance with international humanitarian law.

During the year, Amnesty International continued to urge the Russian President to commute all death sentences and to introduce a moratorium on executions. It also called on the authorities to ensure that no asylum-seekers were returned to countries where they could face human rights violations, and to take steps to ensure effective protection of refugees and asylum-seekers.

Amnesty International urged the command of the Chechen forces to ensure that all detainees were treated humanely. It condemned hostage-taking by the Chechen forces as unacceptable in any circumstances and called for the release of all hostages.

RWANDA

Critics of the government, including human rights activists and journalists, were subjected to human rights violations including arbitrary arrest, ill-treatment and attempted extrajudicial execution. Tens of thousands of people were arrested in connection with the 1994 genocide, many arbitrarily; more than 92,000 were held without trial at the end of the year. Some were ill-treated in detention, and most were held in extremely harsh conditions, with scores dying as a result. The first trials of those accused of participation in the genocide did not conform to international standards of fairness. There were

reports of "disappearances". The army extrajudicially executed hundreds of civilians. The government forcibly expelled nearly 400 refugees to Burundi. Armed opposition groups committed grave human rights abuses, including deliberate and arbitrary killings.

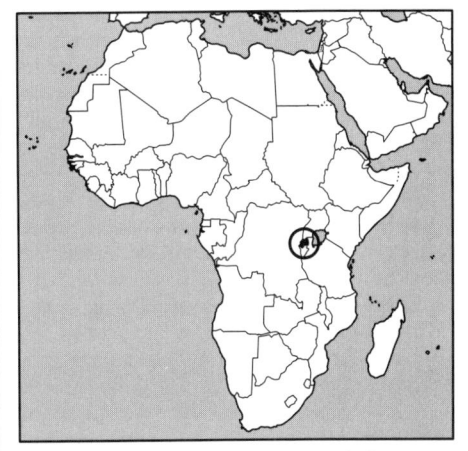

In the first three-quarters of the year, conflict increased between armed groups, based primarily in Zaire, and government forces, the Rwandese Patriotic Army (RPA). The armed groups were believed to be composed of former Rwandese government forces and *interahamwe* militia responsible for the 1994 genocide. They operated in and around the refugee camps in Zaire, Tanzania and Burundi, where more than two million, mostly Hutu, refugees had fled when the Tutsi-dominated Rwandese Patriotic Front took power in July 1994. The armed groups continued to intimidate the refugee population and attempted to prevent them from returning to Rwanda.

In September, fighting broke out in Zaire between Tutsi-led Zairian armed groups, apparently supported by the Rwandese Government, and Zairian government soldiers acting in conjunction with the former Rwandese government forces and militia. More than one million Rwandese refugees were deprived of all humanitarian aid by the fighting. The international community proposed a multinational military intervention force but it was not deployed. Between 15 and 19 November, some 500,000 refugees returned to Rwanda for fear of being killed in Zaire. Around 200,000 more crossed over into Rwanda in the following weeks.

Several hundred thousand Rwandese refugees remained in eastern Zaire, without assistance or protection, where they suffered grave abuses by Zairian soldiers and Zairian and Rwandese armed groups.

In December, most of the estimated 540,000 Rwandese refugees in Tanzania were also forced to return to Rwanda, following a joint statement issued by the Tanzanian Government and the UN High Commissioner for Refugees that all Rwandese refugees were expected to leave by 31 December. The statement made no mention of any options for those who continued to fear human rights violations in Rwanda. There were reports of ill-treatment of refugees by Tanzanian security forces during the mass forced repatriation.

In July and August, around 75,000 Rwandese refugees in Burundi had also been forced back to Rwanda; several had previously been subjected to human rights violations by the Burundian security forces.

By the end of the year, several thousand returnees from Zaire, Tanzania and Burundi had been arrested in Rwanda on accusations of genocide. There were also reports of killings and "disappearances" of returnees. Many returnees experienced difficulties in recovering land and property which had been occupied by others during their exile.

Members of human rights organizations, journalists and judicial officials who spoke out about human rights violations by government forces were subjected to intimidation, threats, arrests and other forms of harassment. Célestin Kayibanda, prosecutor of Butare, was arrested in May and accused of genocide and murder. Shortly before his arrest he had denounced interference in the judiciary by political and military officials. Fidèle Makombe, prosecutor of Kibuye, was beaten by RPA soldiers in May after protesting at interference by local authorities in the functioning of the judiciary and refusing to order arrests and imprisonment in the absence of sufficient evidence.

Amiel Nkuriza, Director of the independent weekly newspaper *Intego*, was abducted in August by four men, one in military uniform and three in civilian clothes, in the centre of Kigali. He was held for one week and reportedly beaten and interrogated about articles in *Intego*, including one about his previous arrest in June. A soldier warned him that his life would be at risk if he wrote any further "subversive" articles. Appolos Hakizimana, a journalist on *Intego*, was arrested in July in Kigali, beaten by soldiers and detained for nearly three weeks.

By the end of the year, more than 92,000 people were detained, many of them without charge and all without trial. Most were accused of participation in the genocide, but many were arrested on the basis of one person's denunciation or unsubstantiated evidence. The number of arrests rose to more than 4,000 a month in August and increased when refugees returned from neighbouring countries. Around 7,000 people were arrested in December.

There were many arbitrary arrests. In November, a priest, Abbé Jean-François Kayiranga, was arrested in Kibuye on the basis of an unspecified accusation that he had participated in the genocide. Independent sources stated that Abbé Kayiranga was the only priest in his area who did not leave the country in 1994 and was commended by survivors of the genocide for his role in saving several people from the massacres.

Some people were arrested because of the alleged role of their relatives during the genocide. Sylvère Kanani, a mechanic, was arrested in September, apparently because of the alleged actions of his father and brothers in 1994. He had been arrested twice in 1995, but released for lack of evidence. Soldiers sent to arrest him reportedly beat his nephew, François Iyakaremye, so severely that he died of his injuries. Sylvère Kanani was released at the end of November; he had been beaten and received death threats in detention.

Ill-treatment of detainees was common immediately after arrest and in communal detention centres. Most prisoners were held in overcrowded conditions amounting to cruel, inhuman and degrading treatment. These conditions led to scores of deaths. Twenty-two detainees died at the communal detention centre at Kivumu, in Kibuye, in May. The authorities claimed that the deaths were caused by fighting among the detainees, but the detainees apparently died as a result of lack of air and extreme heat in the grossly overcrowded cells. Prison guards had refused to open the cell doors, although they heard detainees screaming for air and water. Sixteen detainees died in similar circumstances in an extremely overcrowded cell with little ventilation at Gitesi, in Kibuye, in late October.

Progress was made in rebuilding the judicial system and many new judicial officials were appointed. However, most of them, including judges and magistrates, had only received up to six months' training. By the end of the year there were still only 16 defence lawyers. At the end of August, a new law was adopted on the organization of prosecutions for offences constituting the crime of genocide or crimes against humanity.

The first trials of those accused of participation in the genocide took place in December. On 27 December, Deogratias Bizimana and Egide Gatanazi were tried in Kibungo on charges of genocide and crimes against humanity. They had no access to a defence lawyer before or during their trial, were given only one day to study their case file and were not given the opportunity to summon witnesses for their defence or to cross-examine prosecution witnesses. They and thousands of others accused of these crimes were likely to face the death penalty.

Half of the 22 suspects indicted by the International Criminal Tribunal for Rwanda were in custody. Promises were made to the Tribunal that other suspects held by governments would be transferred to its custody. The first proceedings commenced in May.

The first half of the year was marked by a sharp escalation in killings by members of the RPA and by armed opposition groups. More than 1,000 people are estimated to have been killed during the year.

Several hundred people were shot dead by the RPA during "cordon and search" operations, mostly in the western regions. In April, eight civilians (three men, four women and one infant) were killed in Gisovu, Kibuye, after an RPA soldier was shot dead by an unknown assailant. According to the authorities, the victims died in a shoot-out between RPA soldiers and *interahamwe*, but witnesses stated that they were shot by soldiers who fired into a fleeing crowd.

In July, an estimated 170 people – most of them civilians – were killed in Gisenyi and Ruhengeri, during RPA searches for insurgents. One man said that his four sons, the youngest only 10 years old, had all been killed. Many of the victims were reportedly shot while trying to flee.

RPA soldiers extrajudicially executed a number of local officials. In July, 18 local officials and their relatives and colleagues were assassinated in Rural Kigali: Vincent Munyandamutsa, mayor of Rushashi; Laurent Bwanacyeye, director of Rwankuba secondary school; and Floribert Habinshuti, assistant prosecutor in Rushashi. All the victims, except Vincent Munyandamutsa, were killed on their way back from an ordination ceremony. They were travelling in two separate cars when they were ambushed and shot dead. Independent local witnesses believed they were killed by soldiers. Vincent Munyandamutsa was stabbed to death as he returned home from a meeting. Witnesses reported that soldiers prevented them from intervening. Vincent Munyandamutsa had opposed human rights violations under the previous government, as well as under the current government.

A pattern of killings of detainees by the security forces emerged during the year. Most occurred while detainees were held in communal detention centres before being transferred to central prisons. The single largest incident occurred in May, when at least 46 detainees were killed in an attack on the communal detention centre at Bugarama, Cyangugu. The detainees died from injuries caused by gunshots and grenades. The authorities blamed the killings on armed groups, who they said were trying to free the detainees. However, according to other reports, some of the detainees were shot by guards and others died when guards threw grenades in through cell windows. UN human rights observers and local human rights organizations reported that the detention centre building showed no sign of an attack from outside.

Three RPA soldiers remained under sentence of death (see Amnesty International Report 1996). No executions were reported.

In late September, RPA soldiers forcibly expelled nearly 400 refugees to Burundi's northwestern province of Cibitoke, an area characterized by a high level of killings by the Burundian security forces and armed opposition groups.

Armed opposition groups continued to carry out deliberate and arbitrary killings of unarmed civilians, including children and infants, often in the context of cross-border incursions. Many of the victims were described as "genocide survivors" or "witnesses" – Tutsi who stayed in Rwanda during the genocide and were likely to have witnessed killings by the Hutu-dominated former army and militia during that period.

In June, at least 13 civilians, including children, and one RPA soldier were killed in Kibuye. They included Séraphine Uwampinka and Callixte Kabandana. Survivors of the attack said that they recognized the voices of some of the assailants and identified them as their neighbours before the genocide.

Also in June, 28 people, including several children, were killed and six injured in Gisenyi. Those who died were thought to have included Tutsi survivors of the 1994 genocide as well as Tutsi refugees who had lived in Zaire for several decades and had recently returned to Rwanda. The victims included Mukarusagara and her one-year-old baby.

Throughout the year, Amnesty International appealed to the Rwandese authorities to ensure respect for human rights. In February, the organization published a report, *Rwanda and Burundi: The return home – rumours and realities*, which described the situation of the refugees from Rwanda and Burundi and the risks facing them if they were to return home. In April, Amnesty International sent an open letter to President Pasteur Bizimungu urging him to make human rights a priority, and appealing to the international community for help in reconstructing the judiciary and other institutions. In August, Amnesty International published *Rwanda: Alarming resurgence of killings*. When the crisis in eastern Zaire erupted in September, Amnesty International appealed to African heads of state to take measures to protect human rights in Rwanda and other countries in the region. Amnesty International also called for effective action to stop further arms supplies to the region. Amnesty International delegates visited Rwanda in May and November.

SAUDI ARABIA

Hundreds of people, including possible prisoners of conscience, were detained on political grounds. They included over 200 people arrested in previous years. More than a dozen political prisoners were

reportedly convicted after unfair trials, four of them being sentenced to death and executed. Reports of torture and ill-treatment of detainees continued, and the judicial punishment of flogging was frequently imposed. At least 69 people, including one woman, were executed and at least three prisoners were on death row at the end of the year. Up to 20 possible asylum-seekers were forcibly returned to Egypt.

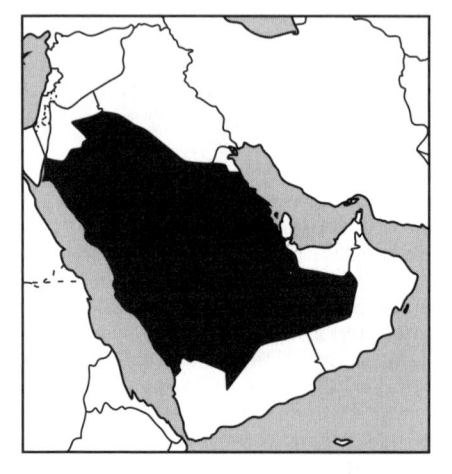

The government of King Fahd bin 'Abdul-'Aziz maintained its ban on political parties and trade unions. Press censorship continued to be strictly enforced. Information on human rights remained severely limited owing to restrictions on access to the country for international organizations, and lack of communication on these matters by the government.

Hundreds of people, including possible prisoners of conscience, were detained during mass arrests, particularly following the bombings of the Saudi Arabian National Guard training centre in Riyadh, the capital, in November 1995 and of the US military complex at al-Khobar in June 1996, which together resulted in 26 deaths. All were denied access to lawyers and many were not allowed family visits for weeks or months after arrest.

Hundreds of people were arrested and detained without charge or trial during the first half of the year in the wake of the bombing of the National Guard's training centre in Riyadh. Those arrested included the so-called Arab Afghan veterans, who had returned to Saudi Arabia after taking part in the armed conflicts in Afghanistan and Bosnia; foreign Arab nationals living in Saudi Arabia; and about a dozen Saudi Arabian nationals who had been forcibly returned from Pakistan and Yemen. Four of those arrested were summarily executed in connection with the bombing (see below). The others were not known to have been charged with any recognizably criminal offence, and were believed to be detained on suspicion of membership of illegal organizations with political and religious links with the armed conflicts in Afghanistan and Bosnia. Most of them were reportedly held by the al-Mabahith al-'Amma, General Intelligence, in al-Ruwais Prison in Jeddah.

Shi'a Muslim critics or opponents of the government were targeted for arrest throughout the year, particularly after the bombing in June of the US military complex in al-Khobar. The authorities reportedly suspected that the attack had been planned by a foreign force with links with the Shi'a community in the Eastern Province. Over 100 people, including more than a dozen leading Shi'a clerics, were arrested in the Eastern Province. Among them was Hojatoleslam Sheikh Habib 'Abd al-'Ali Hamada, from al-Qatif, who was arrested in March but later released. He was rearrested in August, together with other clerics, including Sheikh Ja'far 'Ali al-Mubarak, who had been repeatedly arrested and detained in previous years because of his criticism of government policies (see Amnesty International Report 1996), and Shakir Hajlis, who had been detained and subsequently released in March 1995. Three others arrested with Shakir Hajlis in 1995 – Zuhair Hajlis, Ridha al-Huri and Mahdi Hazam – were believed to have been released after short periods in detention (see Amnesty International Report 1996). It was not known if any of the detainees were charged in connection with the June 1996 bombing, but most were believed to be detained because of their criticism of government policies, and may have been prisoners of conscience.

Scores of suspected Sunni Islamist critics of the government were arrested in various parts of the country and most of them reportedly remained in detention at the end of the year. In August, four relatives of Mohammad al-Mas'ari, a government opponent living in exile, were arrested in Riyadh, including his son, Anmar al-Mas'ari, who had been arrested in 1994 (see *Amnesty International Report 1995*). The precise reasons for the arrests were not known. If they were detained because of their kinship with Muhammad al-Mas'ari, they would be considered prisoners of conscience.

More than 200 people arrested on political or religious grounds in previous years continued to be detained without trial. They included Donato Lama, a Philippine national who was reportedly arrested in October 1995 on suspicion of preaching Christianity and detained in al-Malaz Prison in Riyadh. However, the majority of those still in detention were Sunni Islamist critics or opponents of the government. Among them were Sheikh Salman bin Fahd al-'Awda and Sheikh Safr 'Abd al-Rahman al-Hawali, held since 1994, and Dr Nasser-'Umr, who was arrested in March 1995 (see *Amnesty International Report 1996*). Most were held in al-Hair Prison near Riyadh.

Dozens of so-called Arab Afghan veterans, who were arrested immediately after the bombing in Riyadh in November 1995, were also believed to be still held. It was not known whether Sheikh 'Abdul-Rahman bin Muhammad al-Dakhil, arrested in July 1995, remained in detention (see *Amnesty International report 1996*).

Muhammad al-Fasi, a businessman, whose detention in Saudi Arabia after his forcible return from Jordan in October 1991 was never acknowledged by the government, was released in May.

More than a dozen political prisoners were convicted after unfair trials. They included possible prisoners of conscience such as 'Uthman Bakhash, a Lebanese national, who was arrested in March 1995 in Riyadh and, with several others, charged with membership of an illegal organization, the *Hizb al-Tahrir al-'Islami*, Islamic Liberation Party. All were tried in April or May by the Grand Shari'a Court in al-Taif, following summary proceedings in which they were not allowed access to defence lawyers. Seven were convicted and sentenced to prison terms ranging from eight to 30 months. 'Uthman Bakhash received a 30-month sentence. The eighth defendant, Muhammad al-Ja'bari, was acquitted but not released until October. Four other political prisoners were sentenced to death and executed. They had been detained during the wave of arrests at the beginning of the year targeting the so-called Arab Afghan veterans (see above). In April, the four gave televised "confessions" in which they admitted having carried out the bombing of the National Guard training centre in Riyadh. Forty days later they were beheaded. Throughout their detention, the four had had no access to defence lawyers and their trial was held *in camera*. Their confessions, believed to have been the main evidence on which they were convicted, may have been obtained as a result of torture or ill-treatment. The remaining political prisoners convicted during the year were reportedly sentenced to prison terms for activities such as distributing leaflets of opposition organizations.

There were frequent allegations of torture and ill-treatment of political and criminal detainees. Methods included beatings, the use of shackles and threats of sexual assault. 'Uthman Bakhash (see above) was reportedly severely beaten while handcuffed and shackled with his arms and legs tied together behind his back. He was also reported to have been kept in solitary confinement in an underground cell for over a year. Hojatoleslam Ehsani, an Iranian clergyman who was detained while on pilgrimage to Mecca, stated after his release that he had been beaten with sticks. A former detainee released during the year stated that during his detention by *al-Mabahith al-'Amma* in al-Ruwais Prison, he had been threatened with sexual assault and beaten while shackled and handcuffed.

At least 27 individuals were sentenced to flogging, ranging from 120 to 200 lashes. They included two secondary-school students convicted of assaulting a teacher and 24 Philippine nationals, possible prisoners of conscience, who were reportedly sentenced for homosexual behaviour. All the sentences were believed to have been carried out by the end of the year. However, it was not known whether the sentence of 4,000 lashes passed on Mohammad 'Ali al-Sayyid, an Egyptian national, had been completed by the end of the year (see *Amnesty International Report 1996*).

At least 69 people were executed, including a woman. All but four (see above) had been convicted on charges which included murder, rape, drug-trafficking, robbery and witchcraft.

At least three people sentenced in previous years, two Philippine nationals and one Kuwaiti national, were reported to be on death row at the end of the year. They included Sarah Dematera, a Philippine domestic worker convicted of the murder of her employer in 1992. Her execution was suspended until the victim's oldest child reaches the age of 18 and decides whether to accept blood money instead of her execution. New information came to light that 'Abd al-'Aziz Muhammad Isse, a Somali national previously reported to be on death row, was serving a five-year prison term (see *Amnesty International Report 1996*). No further information was available concerning the change in his sentence.

Up to 20 Egyptian nationals, possible asylum-seekers living in Saudi Arabia, were forcibly handed over to the Egyptian authorities. Most of them were sought by the Egyptian Government, possibly solely for their non-violent political activity. They were detained on arrival in Egypt, where they were at risk of torture. They were not known to have been offered any access to asylum procedures in Saudi Arabia. They included Nasr Abd al-Salem, a university lecturer.

Amnesty International requested clarification of the reasons for the arrest and detention of political detainees, and sought assurances that they were being treated humanely and given access to relatives, lawyers and medical care. The organization appealed for the immediate and unconditional release of all political detainees not charged with a recognizably criminal offence, and for those charged to be given a fair trial in accordance with international standards. Amnesty International also called for reports of torture to be investigated and anyone found responsible to be brought to justice, and for the commutation of all death sentences.

Following Amnesty International's statements on the summary execution of the four prisoners after an unfair trial, the Saudi Arabian Ambassador to the United Kingdom stated publicly, "it is regrettable that Amnesty International should compromise its credibility by expressing anger and outrage at the punishment of criminals who were found guilty of terrorism and sentenced in accordance with the law of Saudi Arabia after full due process", but failed to explain why the case was shrouded in secrecy. The government did not respond to any of Amnesty International's communications.

In April, Amnesty International updated its previous submissions for UN review under a procedure established by Economic and Social Council Resolutions 728F/1503, for confidential consideration of communications about human rights violations in Saudi Arabia.

SENEGAL

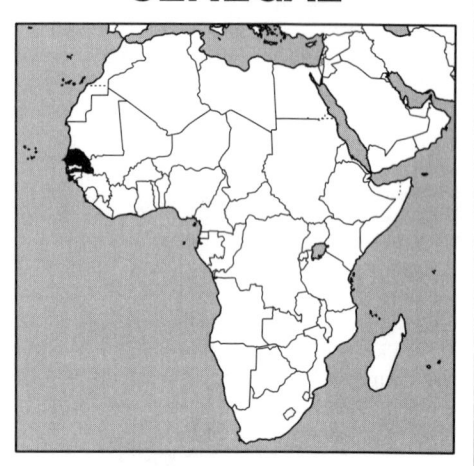

More than 120 alleged supporters of an armed separatist organization, including many possible prisoners of conscience, arrested in connection with political unrest in the Casamance region, remained detained without trial. At least one criminal suspect was reportedly tortured. Members of armed opposition groups in Casamance committed human rights abuses, including beatings and deliberate and arbitrary killings of civilians.

Tension in Casamance between government forces and armed separatists belonging to the *Mouvement des forces démocratiques de Casamance* (MFDC), Democratic Forces of Casamance Movement, subsided after an appeal for peace made by MFDC Secretary General, Father Diamacoune Senghor in December 1995. Preliminary peace talks between the government of President Abdou Diouf and the MFDC began in January. The talks were mediated by the National Commission for Peace in Casamance. However, substantive negotiations between the authorities and the MFDC, due to start in April, were postponed indefinitely. The negotiations stalled on two issues: the location of the peace talks and the refusal of the government to allow Father Diamacoune to travel to France to meet the external wing of the MFDC.

In May, the UN Committee against Torture, which examined Senegal's second periodic report, made recommendations which included the introduction of national legislation to make torture a specific offence and to establish a blanket prohibition of torture. This legal reform was adopted by the Senegalese National Assembly in August.

Despite the relaxation of tension on the ground, more than 120 suspected MFDC sympathizers, including many possible prisoners of conscience, remained in detention without trial throughout the year. Many of the detainees were beaten at the time of arrest. They had been arrested from April 1995 onwards during a series of mass arrests by the army which followed the abduction of four French tourists. The latter remain unaccounted for (see Amnesty International Report 1996).

Fifty-six people, mostly minors and sick people, arrested during these round-ups were provisionally released in December. However, more than 80 remained detained without trial in Dakar, the capital, and about 45 in Ziguinchor, the Casamance regional capital, at the end of the year. Although the detainees were charged with threatening state security, they were reportedly arrested because they were carrying MFDC membership cards. Such cards are often forced upon farmers by the MFDC. By the end of the year, a preliminary investigation to establish cases for trial had been officially initiated, but there were fears that the detainees were being held indefinitely without trial until a new agreement could be reached with the MFDC.

In January, Daouda Dhiédhiou, an MFDC field officer in charge of liaison between the leadership and the military wing, was arrested in Ziguinchor. He remained in detention without charge or trial at Ziguinchor prison at the end of the year.

No members of the security forces accused of torture or ill-treatment of ordinary criminal prisoners were brought to trial during the year. In April, Mohamed Hussein, a Mauritanian watchman, was reportedly tortured in a police station in Dakar. He was accused of shooting people he thought were armed robbers, an accusation he denied. In order to extract a confession, the police officers reportedly poured inflammable liquid on Mohamed Hussein's buttocks and set it alight. Two police officers were later charged with "involuntary blows and wounds"; they had not been brought to trial by the end of the year.

Seven police officers and gendarmes charged in 1995 with acts of torture were provisionally released after several months of detention and none had been brought to trial by the end of the year. The gendarmes were charged with torturing Babacar Thior, a criminal suspect, whose body was doused with inflammable liquid and set alight, causing first- and second-degree burns. Five other police officers were charged with torturing Marème Ndiaye, also a criminal suspect, who reportedly had inflammable liquid poured onto her genitals (see Amnesty International Report 1996).

The MFDC was responsible for human rights abuses, including deliberate and arbitrary killings of civilians on the basis of their ethnic origin or because they were suspected of assisting government forces. Villagers were beaten by MFDC members in an attempt to prevent them from harvesting crops. Armed men claiming to belong to the MFDC killed two brothers, Etienne and Paul Mendy, in July at Niaguis village, apparently because they were suspected of helping the Senegalese army.

In February, Amnesty International published a report, *Senegal: Widespread use of torture persists with impunity while human rights abuses also continue in Casamance*, calling on the authorities to open inquiries into allegations of torture and to bring those responsible to trial. The organization also asked for the immediate and unconditional release of anyone detained in the context of the conflict in Casamance unless they were charged with a recognizably criminal offence. Following Amnesty International's report, the government promised also to create a *guichet* (office) for human rights which would deal with complaints of human rights violations. This office was not functioning by the end of the year.

SIERRA LEONE

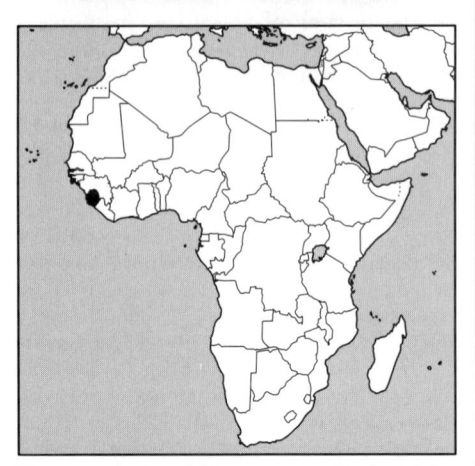

Government soldiers committed widespread human rights violations, including torture and extrajudicial executions. Over 100 political detainees held without charge or trial, including prisoners of conscience, were released. Several journalists were detained for brief periods. The trial of nine soldiers charged with conspiring to overthrow the government in September had not concluded by the end of the year. They were reported to have been tortured and ill-treated; one died in custody. A soldier was sentenced to death by military court. By the end of the year some 60 people were under sentence of death. There were no executions. Armed opponents of the government were also responsible for deliberate and arbitrary killings and torture.

In January, Captain Valentine Strasser, Chairman of the National Provisional Ruling Council (NPRC), which came to power in a military coup in 1992, was overthrown by his second-in-command, Brigadier Julius Maada Bio. Despite arguments that elections for a civilian government scheduled for February be postponed because of continued armed conflict between government forces and the armed opposition Revolutionary United Front (RUF), a national consultative conference overwhelmingly decided that elections should proceed. A civilian government headed by President Ahmad Tejan Kabbah took office in March. The first talks between government representatives and the RUF since the conflict began in 1991 took place in February and peace negotiations continued with the new government. A cease-fire came into effect in March, but confrontations between government soldiers, local hunters (kamajors) acting as a civil defence force and rebel forces continued. Negotiations were held in Côte d'Ivoire, under the auspices of the Ivorian Government, and included UN, Organization of African Unity and Commonwealth delegations. Although significant progress towards a settlement had been made by May, disagreement remained on disarmament and withdrawal of foreign troops, including mercenaries of a South African company, Executive Outcomes. However, a peace agreement, which contained important human rights provisions, was signed on 30 November. It provided for an immediate cessation of hostilities and an international monitoring group to monitor the implementation of the agreement, including the cease-fire, disarmament and demobilization.

Some of the worst atrocities of the conflict occurred in the period before the elections. In an apparently deliberate strategy by both government and RUF forces to prevent elections, civilians were mutilated: limbs were cut off and slogans denouncing the elections were carved into victims' backs and chests. Despite the cease-fire declared in March, civilians continued to be tortured and killed. Establishing responsibility for human rights abuses remained difficult; there was often little or no distinction in the appearance and behaviour of soldiers and rebels. For example, the identity of those responsible for an attack on Foindu, Kenema District, in late August, during which dozens of civilians were killed, remained unclear. Hundreds of thousands of people remained internally displaced or were refugees in neighbouring Guinea and Liberia, although following the peace agreement in November, large numbers of displaced people began to return to their villages. However, during December reports continued to be received of attacks on civilians by armed groups in Tonkolili District, Northern Province, and Moyamba District, Southern Province.

There was no attempt to investigate human rights abuses in the conflict or to bring those responsible to justice. Shortly before ceding power, the NPRC passed The Indemnity and Transition Decree, 1996, (NPRC Decree No. 6) which provided immunity from prosecution for acts committed by members of the NPRC, the armed forces and those acting under their authority since 1992. In June, President Tejan Kabbah promised an amnesty for RUF forces and the peace agreement contained guarantees that no action would be taken against any individual for activities in pursuit of the RUF's aims. A National Unity and Reconciliation Commission was inaugurated in July to investigate abuses against civilians by the NPRC. However, its mandate did not include investigation of or compensation for human rights abuses committed by either government soldiers or RUF forces during the conflict.

Legislation allowing indefinite detention without charge or trial was revoked by NPRC Decree No. 6 and in July the Constitutional Reinstatement Provisions Act, 1996, reinstated parts of the 1991 Constitution suspended by the NPRC.

In August, the government acceded to the International Covenant on Civil and Political Rights and its (First) Optional Protocol and to the International Covenant on Economic, Social and Cultural Rights.

Government soldiers were responsible for widespread human rights violations, including torture, mutilation and extrajudicial executions. They were implicated in attacks, officially attributed to RUF forces, in the months preceding the elections in the area around Mano, Taiama and Njala in Moyamba District. Dozens of civilians were killed in these attacks; survivors suffered gunshot wounds, deliberate amputation of limbs, lacerations from machetes and stabbing by bayonets. In Taiama, a five-year-old boy suffered extensive burns after men in army uniforms set alight plastic placed over him; his mother was killed. Government soldiers attacked unarmed civilians during elections in the towns of Bo and Kenema. On the first day of elections, about 20 civilians were killed in Bo; some 10 soldiers were subsequently captured, mutilated and killed in reprisal by civilians.

Many political detainees held at the Central Prison, Pademba Road, Freetown, suspected of involvement in rebel activities, had been tortured and ill-treated while in military custody; they had scars from having their arms tied tightly behind their backs for long periods, beatings and stabbing with bayonets. Several soldiers held in the Pademba Road prison for criminal or military offences had been similarly ill-treated while in military custody.

Civilians were also tortured and ill-treated by government soldiers in circumstances unrelated to the conflict. Paul Kamara, editor of *For di People* newspaper and Chairman of a non-governmental human rights organization, the National League for Human Rights and Democracy, who had accepted a ministerial post in the NPRC under Brigadier Maada Bio, was seriously injured on the first day of elections. He was shot by uniformed soldiers shortly after a curfew was imposed. Although military officials said there would be an official inquiry, no investigation took place. Also in February, 12 elderly people, including two women, were rounded up by soldiers in a village near Tikonko, Bo District, following the killing of a soldier who had attempted to steal palm oil. They were beaten when arrested and later at a military barracks. Two sustained fractures; three others suffered burns. They were subsequently transferred to police custody where all but one was released without charge.

After return to civilian rule, efforts were made to improve military discipline and bring to justice soldiers responsible for human rights violations.

RUF forces were responsible for gross human rights abuses, including torture and deliberate and arbitrary killings. In March, the RUF leader, Foday Sankoh, while in Côte d'Ivoire, publicly admitted that the RUF had committed atrocities. Civilians were deliberately and arbitrarily killed, tortured and ill-treated in the weeks before elections, but these abuses also continued after the elections. In March, RUF forces opened fire on a group of women from Kenema in the village of Boaboabu. The number of deaths was unclear, but six women were subsequently admitted to hospital with serious gunshot wounds. During attacks by RUF forces on villages in Bo District in May, civilians were beaten, stabbed or cut with machetes. In Sumbuya, for example, several civilians suffered gunshot wounds and many others, including children, were abducted; one was shot in the arm when he refused to accompany rebel forces. Up to 100 civilians were reported to have been killed at Bendu, Pujehun District, in May following an offensive by *kamajors* in an attempt to free people captured by RUF forces. While some were caught in cross-fire, others were rounded up and forced into a house which was subsequently set alight. Most victims were described as aged over 50, while younger people were abducted. In October, dozens of civilians died in RUF attacks in Tonkolili District. At Massanga, about 35 people, including six hospital patients, were killed and 12 wounded; other patients and hospital staff were abducted. In December, shortly after the peace agreement was signed, about 15 civilians were reportedly killed by RUF forces in Tonkolili District; about 60 others were abducted, some of whom were released shortly afterwards.

The fate of civilians abducted by RUF forces remained unknown until their escape or release. Some were killed when they attempted to hide or escape; others were beaten and tied. Girls and women were raped. Many captured civilians were severely malnourished; some died as a result. However, several thousand captured civilians, including many women and children, were freed during the year, often after offensives by *kamajors*. Some had been held for several years. Over 500 people released in Bo District in October were suffering from severe malnutrition. Reports referred to a 75-year-old woman with a scar on her head where she had been hit for failing to work after collapsing from hunger.

Over 100 political detainees, including prisoners of conscience, were released during the year. Most had been held for suspected involvement in rebel activities. In April, President Tejan Kabbah announced the release of 67 detainees, and also the release from house arrest of three members of the government of former President Joseph Saidu Momoh, overthrown by the NPRC in 1992 (see *Amnesty International Reports 1995* and *1996*). Some 30 other detainees were released in August, including Victor Alimamy Kanu, held since 1994 apparently because of his family association with a member of President Momoh's government. Also released were seven soldiers detained without charge or trial since October 1995 in connection with an alleged coup attempt (see *Amnesty International Report 1996*); four others had been released in February.

Following these releases, about 10 political detainees remained held. They included four alleged members of the RUF, including a woman, arrested in Guinea in November 1995 (see *Amnesty International Report 1996*). They were transferred from military custody to the Criminal Investigation Department in Freetown in April but were not charged or tried. All those accused of involvement in rebel activities who remained in detention were believed to have been released following the peace agreement in November.

Several journalists were detained following newspaper articles critical of President Tejan Kabbah's government. They included Philip Neville and Ibrahim Karim-Sei of the *Standard Times*, detained for three days without charge in May. Edison Yongai, editor of *The Point*, was detained for five days in July before being charged with seditious libel, exceeding the legal limit of 72 hours before either being charged or released. He was released on bail and the charges were later dropped. In October, Sheka Tarawallie, editor of *The Torchlight*, was arraigned before parliament and imprisoned for one month in the Pademba Road prison for contempt of parliament under Section 95 of the Constitution.

Six soldiers were arrested in early September, accused of conspiring to overthrow the government; others were subsequently arrested. There were allegations that they had been tortured and ill-treated. At the end of October, Staff Sergeant Lamin Kamara died during interrogation by the security forces, including Nigerian security officials assisting investigations. The authorities claimed that he had died while attempting to escape by jumping from a window. In December, nine soldiers were charged with conspiring to overthrow the government; their trial was adjourned until January 1997. In mid-December, six soldiers and five civilians were arrested. Speculation that the arrests were linked with a further conspiracy to overthrow the government was dismissed by the authorities, but the reasons for the arrests remained unclear. Most of the civilians were subsequently released, but the soldiers remained held without charge at the end of the year.

A soldier was convicted of murder and sentenced to death by a military court in Kenema in August. Some 60 people were under sentence of death at the end of the year, including soldiers convicted by military courts allowing no right of appeal to a higher jurisdiction. The death sentence imposed on Lieutenant-Colonel Chernor Deen in January 1995 (see *Amnesty International Report 1996*) was commuted by the NPRC to life imprisonment. No executions were carried out.

Although several thousand Liberian refugees had previously been allowed to enter Sierra Leone, in May about 40 Liberians, mostly women and children, were refused entry to seek asylum, placing them at risk of forcible return to Liberia's capital, Monrovia, where they faced serious human rights abuses as violence escalated in Liberia's internal armed conflict.

Amnesty International delegates visited Sierra Leone in April to meet members of the government. They also discussed Amnesty International's concerns with other individuals and organizations in Freetown and Southern and Eastern Provinces. The organization called for strong human rights guarantees to be included in a political settlement to the conflict and also for investigations into human rights abuses in order to bring those responsible to justice. Amnesty International repeatedly called on the RUF leadership to take effective measures to end human rights abuses by its forces.

In September, the organization published a report, *Sierra Leone: Towards a future founded on human rights*, which detailed human rights abuses by both government soldiers and the RUF and made recommendations to the government, the RUF and the international community. In particular, it called for human rights monitoring during negotiation and implementation of the peace agreement. Amnesty International called for the release of political detainees unless they were to be charged and fairly tried.

In May, Amnesty International urged the government not to forcibly return those fleeing the Liberian conflict.

In November the organization sought clarification concerning the circumstances of the death in custody of a soldier alleged to have died while trying to escape and the continued detention of others arrested for allegedly conspiring to overthrow the government.

SINGAPORE

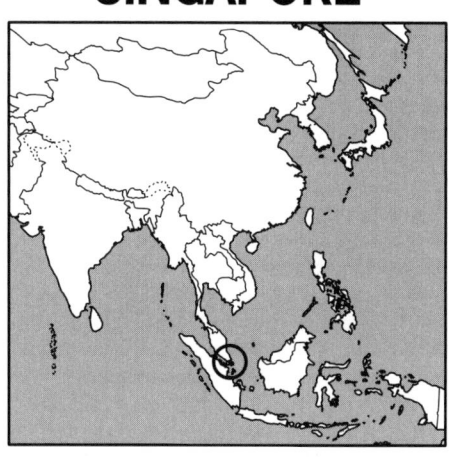

At least 34 prisoners of conscience were held throughout the year for their conscientious objection to military service. A further 47 people were imprisoned for peacefully exercising their right to freedom of expression. One former prisoner of conscience continued to be subject to government orders restricting his freedom of expression and association. Criminal offenders continued to be sentenced to caning. At least 38 people were executed and at least 19 death sentences were passed.

At least 34 conscientious objectors to military service were imprisoned during the year. All were members of the Jehovah's Witnesses' religious group, which has been banned in Singapore since 1972. All refused to perform military service on religious grounds; they were prisoners of conscience. They included Edgar Chua, who was sentenced in October to 15 months' imprisonment. Young men who refuse to comply with military orders are court-martialled and sentenced to an initial 12 or 15 months' detention in military barracks. A second refusal to comply results in a further two years' imprisonment. There is no alternative civilian service for conscientious objectors to military service in Singapore.

Trials of other Jehovah's Witnesses (see *Amnesty International Report 1996*) took place during the year. Between November 1995 and July 1996, more than 60 Jehovah's Witnesses were convicted of membership of an illegal society or possession of banned literature. All were fined but most were imprisoned for up to four weeks after refusing to pay the fines on conscientious grounds. All were prisoners of conscience. They included Yu Nguk Ding, a 72-year-old woman, who was sentenced to one week's imprisonment in July under the Undesirable Publications Act.

Government restriction orders against Chia Thye Poh, a former prisoner of conscience, were partially amended but continued to curtail his freedom of association and expression.

In March, three prison officers were sentenced to between six and 10 years' imprisonment and to strokes of the cane for causing the death of a prisoner at Queenstown Remand Prison in July 1995. The court found that they had beaten Ghazali Abdul Manaf so severely that he sustained more than 120 injuries.

Caning, which constitutes a cruel, inhuman and degrading form of punishment, remained mandatory for some 30 crimes, including attempted murder, rape, armed robbery, drug-trafficking, illegal immigration and vandalism. It remained an optional penalty for a number of other crimes, including extortion, kidnapping and causing grievous injury. In August, Lim Chee Wei, aged 16, was sentenced to six strokes of the cane in addition to a prison sentence for rape.

At least 38 executions by hanging were reported to have been carried out, the majority for drug-related offences. Despite the lack of official information, there were reliable indications that the real figure was much higher. In March, five Thai migrant workers convicted of murder were executed despite appeals for clemency by Thai non-governmental organizations and Thai government officials. In September, two Malaysian nationals, Zulkifli Awang Kechik and Pauzi Abdul Kadir, sentenced to death in February for trafficking in cannabis, were executed.

At least 19 people were sentenced to death, of whom 15 were convicted of drug-trafficking, three of murder and one of discharging a firearm during an armed robbery.

Amnesty International urged the government of Prime Minister Goh Chok Tong to release all prisoners of conscience and to lift the restrictions on Chia Thye Poh. The organization also urged the authorities to end the punishment of caning and to commute all death sentences.

SLOVAKIA

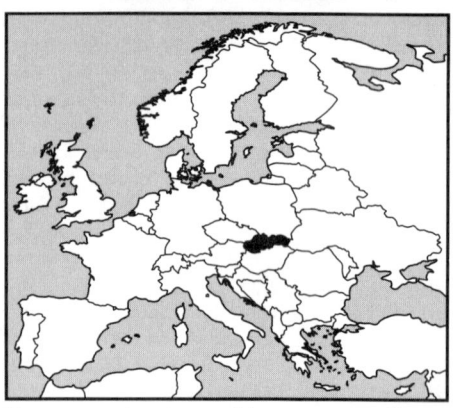

Two conscientious objectors to military service were imprisoned. They were prisoners of conscience.

In October, the National Council (parliament) rejected a draft law which would have amended the Penal Code to create new criminal offences based on broad and ambiguous definitions of "subversive conduct" and "defamation of the state". President Mihál Kováč had refused to sign this law into force following the first vote in the National Council in March. A new draft law defining "subversive conduct" in similar terms, which was adopted by the National Council in December, was also rejected by the President.

In April, Bratislava District Military Court sentenced Erik Kratmüller, a conscientious objector to military service, to 18 months' imprisonment for evading military service, on the basis that he had not applied for civilian service within the legal time limit. The Law on Civilian Service states that conscientious objectors must submit declarations refusing military service within 30 days of being declared fit to serve in the armed forces. Erik Kratmüller was imprisoned in June. In July, Trenčin Superior Military Court sentenced Martin Badin, another conscientious objector, to 12 months' imprisonment on the same charge. He was imprisoned in August. At the end of the year, at least three other conscientious objectors were being prosecuted on the same charge.

In October and December, Amnesty International called on the members of the National Council to reject the draft law amending the Penal Code as the enforcement of some provisions would violate the right to freedom of expression and the right to freedom of association. Also in October, Amnesty International called for the release of Erik Kratmüller and a revision of the Law on Civilian Service to bring it in line with internationally recognized principles, in particular that there should be no time limit within which conscientious objectors must submit applications for alternative service. In December, Amnesty International called for the release of Martin Badin.

SOMALIA

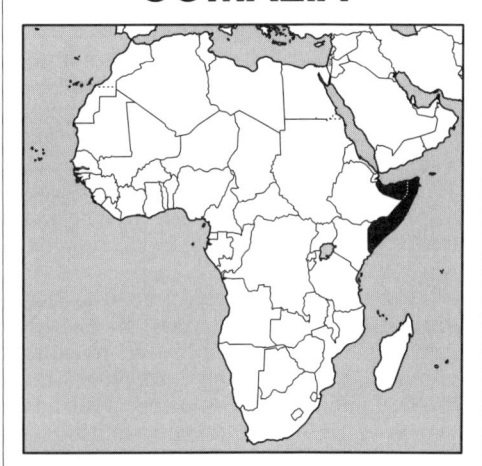

Unarmed civilians, including women and children, were among the victims of human rights abuses carried out by warring militias of clan-based factions. Hundreds of deliberate and arbitrary killings, scores of politically motivated detentions, hostage-taking, torture, including rape, and ill-treatment were reported. Prisoners of conscience were detained. Islamic courts imposed several sentences of amputation and flogging. Several people were executed after being condemned to death by Islamic and other courts.

A year after the UN withdrawal (see *Amnesty International Report 1996*), there was still no central or recognized government in the former Somali Republic. The UN Security Council appealed for peace between the rival factions, and urged them to work to establish a broad-based national government. It condemned abuses against humanitarian organizations, whose staff had been kidnapped and property looted.

The UN Commission on Human Rights expressed deep concern at reports of arbitrary and summary executions, torture and other cruel, inhuman or degrading treatment or punishment, violence against women and children and attacks on humanitarian personnel. Noting the difficulties of the UN Independent Expert on Somalia in fulfilling his mandate, the Commission appealed for resources for an advisory service for the promotion and protection of human rights.

Despite the threat of famine and disease, aid operations were obstructed by the continued closure due to faction fighting of Mogadishu's port and airport. At the end of the year more than one and a half million Somalis who had fled the conflict remained outside the country, and half a million were internally displaced.

Hundreds of people, including unarmed civilians, were casualties of the faction fighting which continued to break out in certain areas – particularly Mogadishu and the surrounding regions, and Kismayu in the southwest – between forces linked to General Mohamed Farah Aideed and Ali Mahdi's Somali Salvation Alliance (SSA). Both leaders claimed overall governmental authority, but failed to obtain international recognition. In August, General Aideed died of battle wounds and his son, Hussein Mohamed Aideed, was chosen to succeed him. Despite peace talks in October brokered by the Kenyan Government, fighting in Mogadishu escalated towards the end of the year between Hussein Aideed's forces in the south of the city and the militias of Ali Mahdi, in the north, and his SSA allies, including Osman Ali Atto. Peace talks continued in Ethiopia in December, although Hussein Aideed refused to participate. There was intermittent fighting throughout the year in the Bay and Bakol regions in the southwest, and especially around the towns of Baidoa and Hoddur, between General Aideed's (and later Hussein Aideed's) forces and the Rahenweyn Resistance Army (RRA). The towns of Merca and Kismayu further south also experienced outbreaks of faction fighting in the first half of the year. The northeastern regions were relatively peaceful.

In the southwestern Gedo region, in August, September and December, Ethiopian government troops crossed the border and attacked Islamist *Al-Itihad* militias allegedly responsible for hotel bombings in Ethiopia and an assassination attempt against an Ethiopian government minister. There were reports that unarmed Somali civilians were deliberately killed, as well as Islamist fighters.

There was clan-based faction fighting, but on a much smaller scale, in parts of the self-declared Somaliland Republic in the northwest, where relative stability and economic recovery were beginning to be seen. After fighting in the middle of the year around the central town of Burao, peace was agreed between forces supporting the interim administration of Mohamed Ibrahim Egal and militias of the Garhajis sub-clans. A national conference of Somaliland clans began at the end of the year as a step towards elections.

There was no consistent, effective or fair criminal justice system. Most governmental institutions had been destroyed in the civil war since 1991. Attempts to maintain public order were based on various local combinations of traditional clan dispute-settlement mechanisms, new and weak regional administration structures, faction militias (some of which abused human rights with impunity), and Islamic courts. In north Mogadishu, the controlling Islamic court system had its own militias and prison and applied an unwritten version of Islamic law. In addition to prison sentences, it handed down penalties of death, and the cruel, inhuman or degrading punishments of amputation and flogging. International standards for fair trial were not respected. There were similar Islamic courts in some other regions, particularly Gedo region.

Hundreds of unarmed civilians, including women and children, were deliberately and arbitrarily killed by members of the warring factions. Individual incidents were difficult to verify, and responsibility was often hard to ascertain. In March, a prominent peace activist, Mohamud Ali Ahmed (known as "Elman"), was murdered by gunmen in south Mogadishu in an execution-style killing. There were reports of many deliberate killings of unarmed civilians from opposing clans by faction militias operating with impunity. Fifteen unarmed people, for example, were shot dead by unidentified faction gunmen in south Mogadishu in October. More than 300 civilian casualties were reported during one week's faction fighting in mid-December in Mogadishu, many of them killed in the deliberate bombardment of opposing clan areas.

In places where courts and prisons existed, some people were imprisoned for peacefully expressing their opinions. Around 30 folk musicians were arrested by Islamic court militias after a concert in north Mogadishu in January, swiftly tried and convicted on a charge of violating Islam in their concert performance, which they denied, and flogged. In Baidoa, scores of people were detained for expressing opposition to General Aideed's rule there; some were captured RRA fighters, but others appeared to be prisoners of conscience. There were reports that political opponents of the controlling clan-based factions had been detained in the towns of Merca and Kismayu.

In November, 20 people were arrested after a peaceful demonstration in Hargeisa against the Egal administration. They were sentenced to one year's imprisonment after an unfair trial. One of them, Mohamed Haji Mohamud (known as "Omar Hashi"), was released in December. They were prisoners of conscience.

Over 20 political prisoners held in Baidoa since it was captured by General Aideed in late 1995 remained in detention without charge or trial during the year. They included members of the former regional administration who were prisoners of conscience. There were unconfirmed reports that they were among 30 prisoners in Baidoa released by Hussein Aideed in December.

Justin Fraser, an Australian commercial pilot who made an emergency landing in Bay region, was detained in May by General Aideed's militia, summarily sentenced by a court in Baidoa to 25 years' imprisonment and a US$500,000 fine for illegal entry. These excessive penalties seemed to be related to General Aideed's demand for recognition as the government authority throughout Somalia. However, Justin Fraser was released in October. Kidnap gangs detained hostages to make ransom demands – often containing political elements – on international humanitarian agencies, clans and business companies. Hilal Mohamed Aden, a Kenya-based Somali employee of the Swedish Life and Peace Institute, was kidnapped in August in north Mogadishu and held for three months for a ransom payment. Three members of the Marehan clan detained in the central Galgudud region in March by Abgal sub-clan gunmen were still held at the end of the year under threat of death if the Marehan clan did not pay compensation for Abgal members killed in October 1995 by Marehan clan members.

In Somaliland, in February, the High Court in Hargeisa convicted five political opponents of the administration of Mohamed Ibrahim Egal on charges of treason and armed rebellion. Their trial *in absentia* began in mid-1995 (see *Amnesty International Report 1996*). Three were sentenced to death and two to life imprisonment; the latter included Jama Mohamed Ghalib, a former member of the Somaliland parliament who had joined General Aideed's faction in south Mogadishu. Scores of rebel Garhajis fighters detained in Somaliland since 1995 without charge or trial were released in the mid-1996 and more than 600 others captured during the year were released in November, as a result of clan reconciliation talks, but some were still reportedly held in Hargeisa prison at the end of the year.

Conditions of detention were generally harsh. In October, dozens of remanded and convicted criminal prisoners held by the Islamic court in north Mogadishu were released after refusing all food, in protest at virtual starvation.

Cases of torture, including rape, were reported in armed conflict situations, but were difficult to document and verify.

Islamic courts reportedly imposed cruel, inhuman or degrading punishments, including at least a dozen amputations and many floggings, which were carried out immediately.

In March, the north Mogadishu Islamic court sentenced Mohamed Ali Arran to death for raping a girl. He was executed by stoning in the nearby town of Jowhar. Several other executions were also reportedly ordered by Islamic and clan courts in other areas.

In August, three Ethiopian government opponents, Abdullahi Haliye, Abdullah Qaji and Ahmed Mohamed, members of the Ogaden National Liberation Front, were arrested in Hargeisa. After three months in detention, they were handed over to the Ethiopian security forces, detained and allegedly tortured in Ethiopia (see **Ethiopia** entry).

Amnesty International renewed its appeals to all Somali political groups to end human rights abuses, and in particular to protect women and children from abuses during armed conflict. The organization urged them to take steps to re-establish the rule of law in conformity with international standards of justice.

Amnesty International appealed to the Somaliland authorities not to return to Ethiopia the three Ethiopians detained in August, and to release the prisoners of conscience imprisoned in November.

SOUTH AFRICA

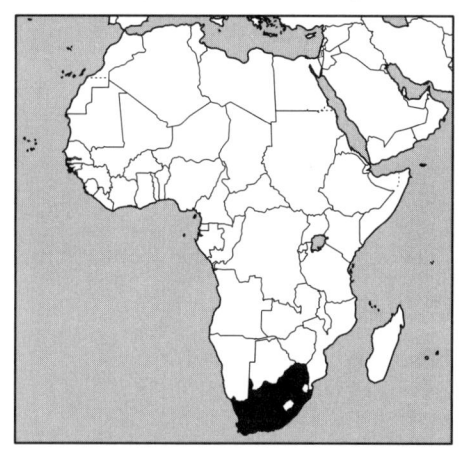

At least 500 people were killed in continuing political violence in KwaZulu Natal; some appeared to have been extrajudicially executed. Reports of torture and ill-treatment in police custody continued. Four people were killed by right-wing opponents of the government. Further evidence emerged, through court proceedings and Truth and Reconciliation Commission hearings, of official involvement in human rights violations under the former government.

The process of democratizing South Africa's political structures was completed when local government elections were held in the provinces of KwaZulu Natal and the Western Cape.

In December, President Nelson Mandela signed the final Constitution into law. The Constitution maintains the Interim Constitution's guarantees of certain "fundamental human rights" (see *Amnesty International Report 1995*), including the unqualified right to life. The Inkatha Freedom Party (IFP) continued to boycott the national constitution-writing process. In

September, the Constitutional Court rejected a draft provincial constitution which had been adopted by the IFP-controlled KwaZulu Natal Legislature in March. The Court ruled that its provisions ascribed powers to the provincial legislature and executive beyond those allowed by the Interim Constitution and were an attempt to usurp the powers of the national government.

The Constitutional Court issued further rulings affecting human rights. In July, the Court ruled in a case brought by the Azanian People's Organization and the families of several prominent victims of human rights violations, challenging the constitutionality of the amnesty provisions of the 1995 Promotion of National Unity and Reconciliation Act 34 ("Truth and Reconciliation Act"). The Court ruled that the Interim Constitution authorized a limitation on the right to obtain redress through the courts and allowed for amnesties in respect of both criminal and civil liabilities.

In January, South Africa acceded to the 1951 UN Convention relating to the Status of Refugees and its 1967 Protocol. In July, it ratified the African Charter on Human and Peoples' Rights.

The statutory Human Rights Commission (see *Amnesty International Report 1995*) came into operation in March. It undertook a number of investigations, including into complaints of torture of street children by police, and held hearings on abuses and violence in prisons.

The statutory Independent Complaints Directorate, responsible for investigating complaints against the police, began to function late in the year. President Mandela made the final appointments to the Gender Equality Commission, the last of the statutory bodies provided for under the Constitution to monitor and protect human rights.

The judicial commission of inquiry into illegal arms dealing, led by Judge Edwin Cameron, issued a second report, calling for comprehensive measures to regulate the country's arms trade and for greater accountability to the national parliament (see *Amnesty International Report 1996*).

In April, the Truth and Reconciliation Commission, chaired by Archbishop Desmond Tutu, began public hearings into past human rights violations. By the end of the year the Commission's Amnesty Committee had received more than 4,000 applications from individuals disclosing offences for which they requested amnesty.

In December, President Mandela extended the cut-off date for offences for which amnesty may be granted to 10 May 1994. The decision was apparently made to include white right-wing parties in the reconciliation process. Also in December, political leaders from KwaZulu Natal began discussions with the President on the possibility of a blanket amnesty covering the province for the period after 10 May 1994.

Political violence remained at a high level in the province of KwaZulu Natal, particularly in the four months before local government elections. The non-governmental Human Rights Committee documented 491 deaths, a number regarded as a conservative estimate of the total. The death toll declined after the June elections, but rose again in December, when 41 people were killed, including five in an execution-style killing in the African National Congress (ANC) stronghold of Tintown, Inchanga.

A number of political and investigative initiatives helped lower the death toll for the year in comparison with previous years. These included the creation of additional police investigation units; the arrest of some suspects linked to multiple murders, such as the massacre of 19 people in Shoba Shobane on 25 December 1995 (see *Amnesty International Report 1996*); and reinforcements of soldiers and police sent to the province during the elections.

Before the June elections, candidates for the different political parties were targets of attack. In April, Abraham Faniswayo Dubazane, IFP candidate for Wembezi, was shot and killed outside the IFP's Estcourt offices by an alleged ANC gunman. In June, Thulani Gumede, the ANC candidate for the Shakaville ward of Lindelani Extension, was assaulted while putting up posters in the area. ANC supporters who had earlier fled their Lindelani homes were prevented from voting, allegedly by armed IFP supporters. Police at the polling station failed to intervene to protect them.

Groups of armed men and known killers continued to operate with impunity throughout the year. In October, Joseph Myeni was abducted with his brother S'bonelo from their home in northern

KwaZulu Natal. S'bonelo escaped and went to the local police station in KwaMsane to request help. The police took no steps to record the incident, take statements from witnesses or alert other police stations about the missing man. About 10 days later, the family found Joseph Myeni's body in the police mortuary in Empangeni. In November, an IFP member was charged in connection with Joseph Myeni's murder and his brother's abduction. The suspect was already on bail awaiting trial in connection with three political killings in August 1995.

Extrajudicial executions by the security forces continued to be reported. In August, Thulani Nzuza was shot dead in his bed, after about 20 police officers had forced their way into the family's Durban home. In May, during an election rally in Wembezi, Shulani Ndungwe, an IFP Youth Brigade official, was shot and killed by high-velocity rifle fire. An investigation was ordered into allegations that he was killed by members of the military or police.

In July, 16 rail commuters were killed and 80 others injured when security guards at Tembisa Station, near Johannesburg, used electro-shock batons against the commuters. The security guards, who were checking tickets, prodded commuters with the batons, causing some of them to collapse from pain or momentary paralysis. In the ensuing panic, dozens of people were trampled, crushed or suffocated. The report of the preliminary inquiry into the incident condemned the excessive force employed by the security guards and recommended the banning of electro-shock batons, improved regulation of the security guard industry, and further investigations leading to possible criminal proceedings against officials and others responsible for the deaths and injuries.

There were frequent reports of torture and ill-treatment by specialized police units, primarily of criminal suspects but also of marginalized groups, including street children. Torture equipment was seized, under court order, from a number of police stations, including, in November, from the Middelburg Murder and Robbery Unit. Members of the Cape Town Traffic Department "Vagrancy Squad" allegedly assaulted homeless people, including subjecting them to electric shocks. Recommendations for action to be taken against those implicated, made following a City Council inquiry, were not acted upon by the police authorities.

Victims were sometimes tortured in informal locations. In August, Rajie Chetty was taken in her night clothes from her home near Durban by a group of policemen investigating a robbery. While being driven around in the police vehicle, she was allegedly subjected to near suffocation, had a gun pointed at her head, and was sexually assaulted and verbally abused, before being returned to her home.

There were numerous complaints against the Brixton Murder and Robbery Unit (see *Amnesty International Report 1996*). In September, Mandla Michael Ntsibande was tortured with electric shocks, while held in a toilet cubicle at the Unit's offices. Medical examinations corroborated his allegations.

The end of the year saw an upsurge in violent attacks by white right-wing opponents of the government. In December, four people died in a bomb attack in the Western Cape town of Worcester.

During trials and Truth and Reconciliation Commission hearings, significant evidence emerged of official involvement in assassinations, torture and other crimes against government opponents under the former *apartheid* government. In October, the Durban Supreme Court acquitted the former Defence Minister, General Magnus Malan, and 19 other defendants, of charges of murder and conspiracy to murder in connection with the 1987 massacre of 13 people in KwaMakhutha township. However, the Court found that the killings were carried out by IFP members trained secretly by the South African Defence Force (SADF) in 1986 (see *Amnesty International Report 1996*). The Court also found that the perpetrators acted under the direction of two officers of the SADF's Directorate of Special Tasks (the officers appeared in the trial as prosecution witnesses), and that the murder weapons had been procured from the SADF.

In October, the Pretoria Supreme Court sentenced Colonel Eugene de Kock, former commander of the security police counter-insurgency unit at Vlakplaas, to 212 years' imprisonment and two life sentences after finding him guilty of 89 charges (see *Amnesty International Report 1996*). Among other crimes, he was convicted of the murder of five alleged Pan Africanist Congress members in 1992; of conspiracy to murder former Vlakplaas commander Captain Dirk Coetzee, who had made public the unit's involvement in assassinations; of the culpable homicide of human rights lawyer Bheki Mlangeni in 1991, who died in an explosion intended to kill Captain Dirk Coetzee; and of conspiring to murder Japie Maponya, who "disappeared" in 1985. The defendant was also convicted of nine counts of illegal possession of arms and ammunition, after the Court found that he had taken "truck loads" of arms to Natal. In his evidence in mitigation, Eugene de Kock stated that the arms had been handed over to KwaZulu "homeland" and IFP officials. He also implicated named members of the former government in operations carried out by the Vlakplaas unit in South Africa and in neighbouring countries.

In November, following renewed investigations in light of the evidence which emerged during Eugene de Kock's trial, four former security policemen were charged with the murder of Johannes Sweet Sambo, who died in police custody in Komatipoort in 1991.

Towards the end of the year, a number of former senior police officers testified to the Truth and Reconciliation Commission, naming senior political figures whom they alleged were involved in, or fully aware of, assassinations and other crimes against anti-*apartheid* activists. In October, five former members of the Northern Transvaal Security Branch, two of whom had already been charged with 27 offences including murder, gave evidence on the activities of a previously unknown organization, TREWITS, involving members of the security forces and intelligence services, which planned assassinations in and outside South Africa during the 1980s. Among the deaths attributed to TREWITS were those of Dr Fabian Ribeiro and Florence Ribeiro, shot dead in 1986.

In other evidence heard by the Truth and Reconciliation Commission's Amnesty Committee, former police officer Brian Mitchell, imprisoned in 1992 for his involvement in the 1988 Trust Feed massacre of 11 people, gave evidence of police involvement in attacks against supporters of the ANC and the allied United Democratic Front (UDF) in Natal in the 1980s. During a special public hearing in November on the Natal Midlands "Seven-Day War", another former police officer serving a prison sentence for murder told the Commission that, during his posting in the Pietermaritzburg area between 1988 and 1991, he had participated in assaulting and torturing as many as 1,000 people, and taken part in attacks with the IFP against UDF-supporting communities.

In February, Amnesty International submitted a memorandum about the death penalty to members of the Cabinet and the National Parliament and urged them to retain an abolitionist position in the final constitution.

In March, an Amnesty International delegate attended the initial proceedings in the trial of General Magnus Malan and 19 others, and inquired into the progress of investigations into political killings in KwaZulu Natal. Before the local government elections, Amnesty International appealed to the authorities to ensure that proper investigations were held into human rights violations in the province and to end the climate of impunity.

In June, an Amnesty International delegate visited South Africa to continue these inquiries, to investigate allegations of police torture, to meet staff of the Truth and Reconciliation Commission and also members of non-governmental organizations and victim-support groups concerned with the Commission's work. In November, Amnesty International's Secretary General and several other delegates visited South Africa to publicize with local organizations human rights violations in Nigeria. The delegation held meetings with several government ministers and officials to discuss South Africa's policies on Nigeria and on the arms trade with Rwanda and other central African countries.

In August, Amnesty International made a submission to the Tembisa inquiry, recommending a temporary ban on the export of electro-shock devices and their use by members of the security forces, pending a full investigation into their effects and an investigation into the training and regulation of the security guard industry.

SPAIN

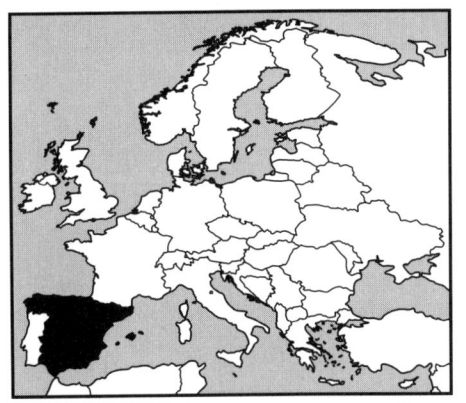

Judicial inquiries continued into allegations of a clandestine "dirty war" in the 1980s against the armed Basque group *Euskadi Ta Askatasuna* (ETA), Basque Homeland and Liberty. Two prisoners of conscience served prison terms during the year. There were further allegations of ill-treatment by law enforcement officers. Officers charged with torture and ill-treatment were tried. More than 100 Africans, including asylum-seekers, were expelled to countries where some suffered human rights violations. ETA continued to commit human rights abuses, including deliberate and arbitrary killings and hostage-taking.

The Popular Party won a narrow victory in the March general elections. In May, José María Aznar was invested as leader of the government, replacing Felipe González of the Socialist Party.

A new penal code came into force in May. In November, Congress voted to discuss a proposal to reform the law on conscientious objection to military service. The text included a proposal to allow conscripts to claim conscientious objector status after entering the armed forces. However, the major political parties indicated that they would be introducing important amendments.

In March, the European Committee for the Prevention of Torture and Inhuman or Degrading Treatment or Punishment published reports on its three visits to Spain between 1991 and 1994 and the government's reply. The Committee expressed concern over the continuing ill-treatment of detainees. It remarked that the use of torture and severe ill-treatment was not commonplace, but noted complaints of such treatment, particularly of those held incommunicado under "anti-terrorism" legislation.

In March, the UN Human Rights Committee considered Spain's Fourth Periodic Report on its implementation of the International Covenant on Civil and Political Rights (ICCPR). The Committee highlighted its concern that it had received "numerous reports ... of ill-treatment and even torture inflicted on persons suspected of acts of terrorism by members of the security forces"; that investigations into such allegations were "not always systematically carried out by the public authorities"; and that members of the security forces found guilty of torture or ill-treatment and sentenced to imprisonment were "often pardoned or released early, or simply do not serve the sentence". The Committee emphasized that certain provisions of the legislation were not in conformity with the ICCPR and recommended that legislation preventing detainees from choosing their own lawyer be rescinded and incommunicado detention be abandoned. The Committee stated that it was "greatly concerned" that individuals had no right to claim conscientious objector status after entering the armed forces and urged that legislation be introduced respecting that right.

Judicial investigations continued into acts of kidnapping, torture and murder during a "dirty war" between 1983 and 1987 against supposed ETA members carried out by a clandestine organization in which senior government officials were apparently involved, the so-called *Grupos Antiterroristas de Liberación* (GAL), Anti-Terrorist Liberation Groups (see *Amnesty International Report 1996*). Numerous senior officials, including a former minister of the interior, a former secretary of state for security and a general formerly commanding the Civil Guard were indicted on charges related to GAL.

Judicial inquiries continued into the kidnapping, torture and murder of two ETA members, José Antonio Lasa and José Ignacio Zabala, by GAL. The courts also investigated other cases, including the kidnapping of Segundo Marey and the killing of a presumed ETA member, Ramón Oñederra, in the 1980s. In November, a former intelligence officer and witness in the Lasa and Zabala inquiry was abducted after giving evidence to the investigating judge, reportedly implicating Civil Guard members. He claimed that armed men took him to a beach near Cadiz and severely beat him, burned him with cigarettes and sodomized him with a blunt instrument. A copy of the judge's order requesting that he be given protection was forced into his mouth. Medical reports recorded 22 cigarette burns and anal injuries.

Two conscientious objectors, José Antonio Escalada and Manuel Blázquez Solís, imprisoned in December 1995 for desertion from the armed forces, were conditionally released in April and May respectively. Both were prisoners of conscience (see *Amnesty International Report 1996*).

Allegations of ill-treatment by law enforcement officers continued to be received. In January, an inquiry opened into the allegations of ill-treatment by municipal police of Sallam Essabah, a Moroccan national, near Alicante. He claimed that two officers stopped him in December 1995, beat him and left him naked and unconscious. He received medical treatment for multiple injuries to the stomach, chest and lumbar region.

Law enforcement officers charged with torture and ill-treatment were tried. Fourteen Civil Guards stationed in Colmenar Viejo were charged in February with torture. They had arrested three young men in October 1994 who claimed they were systematically threatened, punched, slapped and kicked while naked and handcuffed.

In November, two Civil Guards in Barcelona were acquitted of the torture and murder of Jorge Xurigué who had been arrested with another man in August 1994 during an attempted robbery. Jorge Xurigué died of a cerebral haemorrhage following a blow to the temple. The court found that the officers kicked and beat them while they were lying on the ground, but did not accept as proved that the cause of the fatal lesion was a kick from one of the officers, and could not identify with certainty which of the two arresting officers was responsible for the injuries to each of the prisoners.

In June, 103 people, including asylum-seekers, from various African countries, were expelled in military aircraft from Melilla and Malaga. Some were given water containing sedatives during the flight and there were reports that some were beaten by police officers. Fifty of them, including asylum-seekers, were deposited in Guinea-Bissau where they were detained and beaten. In September, one was shot dead and others were injured by police during a violent demonstration (see **Guinea-Bissau** entry).

ETA continued to commit human rights abuses, including attacks on security forces and civilians in which five people were killed. There were bombing campaigns in many regions. In February, Francisco Tomás y Valiente, a former Constitutional Court President, and Fernando Múgica, a lawyer and brother of a former minister of justice, were murdered. At the end of the year ETA held two hostages: José Antonio Ortega Lara, a prison officer abducted in January, and Cosme Delclaux Zubiria, a lawyer and businessman kidnapped in November. In April, ETA freed José María Aldaya after 11 months in captivity.

In March, Amnesty International published a report, *Spain: Comments by Amnesty International on the government's Fourth Periodic Report to the Human Rights Committee*, containing details of violations of the rights set out in the ICCPR.

Amnesty International expressed concern at the failure to protect witnesses in the GAL investigation and urged the government to guard important witnesses.

Amnesty International appealed for the release of Manuel Blázquez Solís and José Antonio Escalada and called for legislation to provide for conscientious objection developed after joining the armed forces. The organization urged the authorities to ensure that all allegations of ill-treatment were thoroughly and impartially investigated and that those responsible were brought to justice.

Amnesty International called on the Governments of Spain and Guinea-Bissau to respect their treaty obligations on non-*refoulement* of persons to countries where they might suffer serious human rights violations and called for a full inquiry into the allegations of ill-treatment.

Amnesty International repeatedly condemned abuses by armed opposition groups, such as deliberate and arbitrary killings and hostage-taking, as a contravention of international humanitarian standards. The organization publicly called on ETA to release the hostages immediately and without conditions.

SRI LANKA

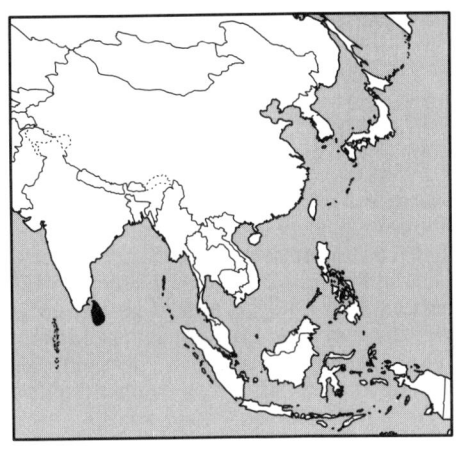

Thousands of Tamil people were arrested, including scores of possible prisoners of conscience. Around 1,600 people were detained without charge or trial, 600 of them for more than a year. Torture and ill-treatment were widespread, particularly in military custody. Several people died in custody, some as a result of torture. At least 220 Tamil civilians were reported to have "disappeared" and an estimated 50 others were extrajudicially executed. The Liberation Tigers of Tamil Eelam (LTTE), an armed opposition group, was responsible for numerous human rights abuses, including deliberate and arbitrary killings of Sinhalese and Muslim civilians.

Armed conflict between the LTTE and the government continued. Large-scale military operations, particularly in the north, resulted in heavy loss of life on both sides. Tens of thousands of civilians were displaced. In May, the security forces took control of most of the Jaffna peninsula; control of much of the countryside in the east was disputed.

Access to the north was severely restricted throughout the year. As a result, independent information about alleged human rights violations in the area was limited.

The state of emergency, which had been in force in the north and east and other designated areas, was extended to the whole of the country in April. At the same time, censorship was imposed prohibiting publication of news relating to operations carried out by the security forces, procurement of arms, deployment of troops or military equipment and the official conduct or performance of members of the security forces. The censorship order was lifted in October.

In July, legislation was passed to set up a National Human Rights Commission (NHRC), but its members had not been appointed by the end of the year.

In September, the government announced that Sri Lanka would ratify the (First) Optional Protocol to the International Covenant on Civil and Political Rights.

One of the three commissions of inquiry established in late 1994 to look into human rights violations, in particular the thousands of "disappearances" that had occurred after 1 January 1988 (see *Amnesty International Reports 1995* and *1996*), finished hearing evidence at the end of the year. The report of the Presidential Commission of Inquiry into Involuntary Removal of Persons (see *Amnesty International Report 1995*) was not made public.

Thousands of Tamil people, including scores of possible prisoners of conscience, were arrested during security operations in all parts of the country. Around 1,600 people were detained without charge or trial under the Prevention of Terrorism Act or Emergency Regulations, 600 of them for over a year. Safeguards to protect the welfare of detainees introduced in 1995 (see *Amnesty International Report 1996*) were not fully adhered to. Some prisoners were held in unauthorized places of detention for several weeks. In one such case reported in July, a young man was held incommunicado for more than a month at Plantain Point army camp, Trincomalee. He claimed he was held blindfolded and with his arms and legs tied. His relatives and the Human Rights Task Force (HRTF) were not informed of his arrest nor was he allowed to communicate with his relatives (see *Amnesty International Reports 1995* and *1996*).

Torture and ill-treatment were widespread, particularly in military custody in the north and east. The methods used included applying electric shocks to sensitive parts of the body; hanging prisoners upside down or by their thumbs; beatings on the soles of the feet; pulling a bag filled with petrol or chillies over the prisoner's head; and repeatedly submerging the prisoner in water.

Several people were killed in custody, some as a result of torture. Kandiah Vairamuthu was reportedly killed in detention shortly after his arrest and buried within the compound of the People's Liberation Organization of Tamil Eelam (PLOTE), an armed group working with the security forces, in Chenkalady. In late July, two badly burned bodies were found in Galgamuwa, Nikaweratiya. Although neither was officially identified, one was believed to be Selliah Subramaniam, a businessman, who had been rearrested by members of the Counter-Subversive Unit of the Vavuniya police when he went to collect his possessions on his release by the order of the Supreme Court. He had been detained for nearly four months without charge or trial. The identity of the other person was not known.

At least 220 people "disappeared" after being arrested by members of the security forces in the north and east. After April, "disappearances" were increasingly reported in the Jaffna peninsula. Among the victims was 18-year-old Krishanthy Kumarasamy from Kaithady who was taken into custody at an army check-point between Chundikkuli and Kaithady on 7 September, while returning home after sitting an examination paper. Her mother, Rasammah Kumarasamy, her 16-year-old brother Pranaban Kumarasamy, and a friend, Kirupakaran Sithamparam, also "disappeared" after they were taken into custody at the army check-point when making inquiries about Krishanthy Kumarasamy. Their bodies were found in shallow graves in mid-October. Nine members of the security forces were arrested on suspicion of being responsible for the killings and of an attempted cover-up.

Tamil armed groups working with the security forces were also responsible for human rights violations, including "disappearances". Nagalingam Rishikeshamoorthy was seen being arrested by an armed member of the Tamil Eelam Liberation Organization in Chenkalady in January. His whereabouts remained unknown at the end of the year.

An estimated 50 civilians were extrajudicially executed. Twenty-four of them, including 13 women and seven children below the age of 12, were killed on 11 February in Kumarapuram, Trincomalee district, by soldiers from the 58th Mile Post and Dehiwatte army camps, accompanied by Home Guards from Dehiwatte. The killings were apparently in reprisal for the killing of two soldiers by the LTTE earlier that day.

In late January, the trial began of eight army personnel and a school principal charged in connection with the "disappearance" of a group of young people in Embilipitiya between late 1989 and early 1990 (see *Amnesty International Reports 1995* and *1996*). It had not concluded by the end of the year. There was little progress in inquiries into other past human rights violations, including the inquiries into the deaths of people whose bodies were found during exhumations of a dozen clandestine graves in 1994.

Although investigations were initiated into several recent incidents of human rights violations, including the "disappearance", torture and killing of at least 31 people in Colombo, the capital, in mid-1995 (see *Amnesty International Report 1996*), and the extrajudicial executions in Kumarapuram (see above), the alleged perpetrators had not been brought to trial.

The LTTE was responsible for grave human rights abuses, including deliberate and arbitrary killings of Sinhalese and Muslim civilians, summary executions of Tamil people considered to be "traitors", and torture and ill-treatment of prisoners and of children who were sometimes forced to join the armed group. In late January, more than 90 civilians were killed when a lorry containing explosives was driven into the entrance of the Central Bank in central Colombo. Two Muslim and nine Sinhalese civilians were killed in mid-September when LTTE members attacked a bus in Arantalawa, Amparai district. In Jaffna district, several people were executed by members of the LTTE on suspicion of collaborating with the security forces. In early July, Thambu Ramalingam, a local administrator, was executed in the street in Ariyalai. It was widely believed that the reason for his execution was that he had raised the Jaffna district council flag during a ceremony held by the security forces when they took control of Jaffna town in December 1995. The fate of several prisoners of conscience and Tamil and Muslim prisoners held for several years remained unclarified.

In August, Amnesty International published a report, *Sri Lanka: Wavering commitment to human rights*. While acknowledging several steps taken by the government for the protection of human rights, the organization expressed concern at continuing grave human rights violations and at the government's failure, despite its stated commitment, to bring perpetrators of human rights violations to justice. Throughout the year, Amnesty International called for full and impartial investigations into reports of "disappearances" and extrajudicial executions. The organization also submitted recommendations to strengthen the law establishing the NHRC, some of which were incorporated into the final legislation.

Amnesty International appealed to the LTTE to call an immediate halt to the deliberate killing of civilians and other grave abuses by its members and to make a clear public commitment to upholding human rights. In June, a memorandum was handed over to representatives of the LTTE abroad, appealing for the release of 24 prisoners of conscience, for information about 42 prisoners whose fate or whereabouts were unaccounted for, and for investigations to establish those responsible for 13 incidents since May 1990 in which a total of 674 civilians had been deliberately and arbitrarily killed. No response from the LTTE had been received by the end of the year.

SUDAN

Hundreds of suspected government opponents, including prisoners of conscience, were detained without charge or trial for periods ranging from a few days to several months. Over 70 political prisoners were charged with waging war against the state; 31 were tried *in camera* at an unfair military trial. Torture was widespread. Courts imposed the judicial punishments of flogging and amputation. Scores of children were abducted by paramilitary forces; the fate of hundreds of children abducted in previous years remained unknown. Hundreds of people were extrajudicially executed and indiscriminately killed in the war zones. At least 18 men were sentenced to death; two men who "disappeared" in 1992 were reportedly executed. Armed opposition groups committed human rights abuses, including the holding of prisoners of conscience and deliberate and arbitrary killings.

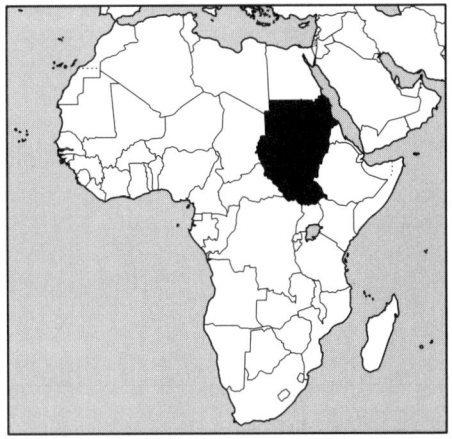

Sudanese from virtually all sectors of society, from northern Sudan, the war-torn south and the Nuba mountains, suffered human rights violations as the authorities continued to suppress political opposition. Presidential and parliamentary elections were held in March, with independent political activity, including political parties, banned under the continuing state of emergency. Omar Hassan Ahmad al-Bashir was re-elected President.

Anti-government demonstrations took place in several towns. In September, riots in Omdurman and Khartoum, the capital, in which at least three people were killed, followed changes in the price of flour and a strike by bakers.

Armed forces of the opposition National Democratic Alliance (NDA), an umbrella grouping of banned political parties, began military activity close to the Eritrean border. In the south and the Nuba Mountains war continued between the government and the armed opposition Sudan People's Liberation Army (SPLA), led by John Garang de Mabior. In April, the government concluded a peace agreement with a faction of the divided armed opposition South Sudan Independence Army (SSIA) led by Riek Machar Teny-Dhurgon. An armed group led by Kerubino Kuanyin Bol, which operated as a government militia in northern Bahr al-Ghazal, also signed the agreement with the authorities.

Serious human rights abuses were committed by all sides in continuing fighting.

Millions of people remained internally displaced – 1.8 million around the capital alone – and hundreds of thousands were refugees in neighbouring countries. The government extended its program of creating and supporting proxy militia groups to Ugandan armed opposition movements which were responsible for gross human rights abuses in Uganda (see **Uganda** entry).

In May, following repeated reports of the forcible abduction of children by the paramilitary Popular Defence Force (PDF) in the war zones of the south and west, the government announced the creation of a committee to investigate allegations of enforced or involuntary "disappearances" and of slavery. The committee had not issued a report by the end of the year.

In April, the UN Commission on Human Rights condemned the human rights situation in Sudan and recommended the placement of human rights field officers to monitor the human rights situation. The UN took no steps towards creating such monitors. In the same month, the government agreed to renew cooperation with the UN Special Rapporteur on Sudan, who had been denied access to the country since 1994. In August, the Special Rapporteur visited Khartoum. His interim report to the UN General Assembly in October concluded that the human rights situation had deteriorated since April 1996. In September, the UN Special Rapporteur on religious intolerance visited Sudan.

Hundreds of suspected government opponents were arrested and detained without charge or trial for periods ranging from a few days to several months. They included southern Sudanese, students, trade unionists, members of banned political parties and people suspected of having links with the NDA in Eritrea. The majority of prisoners arrested in the capital and held for more than a few days were detained in a section of Kober Prison run by the security services. Secret detention centres notorious for torture, known as "ghost houses", remained in use. On release many prisoners had to report daily to security offices where they were forced to wait until sunset.

Prisoners of conscience held at the start of the year included students, left-wing political activists and southern Sudanese detained in 1995. For example, 19 students detained days before the anti-government protest in September 1995 were released in January, but three men arrested with them, among them Adlan Ahmad Abdel Aziz, a supporter of the banned Sudan Communist Party (SCP), remained in detention until April and May.

In June, dozens of trade unionists and other activists were arrested in towns and cities in northern Sudan, after supporters of the NDA delivered a petition to the President calling on the government to step down. Eight men arrested in Wad Medani were held for three weeks after a similar petition was delivered to the Regional Governor of Central State. The clampdown continued into July with further detentions in Khartoum, New Halfa and Dongola. The majority of detainees were released shortly before the arrival of the UN Special Rapporteur on Sudan in August, but many, for example Ismail al-Azhari, a supporter of the SCP, were rearrested in early September after rioting in the capital.

Over 200 men were detained on suspicion of treason-related offences; 72 were subsequently charged, many after several months in detention in "ghost houses" and Kober Prison. For example, at least 28 civilians were arrested in January on suspicion of recruiting for the armed forces of the NDA. Nine were released, but in May, 19 were charged with waging war against the state. Released on bail, they were almost immediately rearrested.

In August, the military trial of Colonel Awad al-Karim Omar Ibrahim al-Naqar and 30 others, including 10 civilians, arrested in March and April, opened days after the men had been charged with waging war against the state. Over 120 soldiers and civilians had been initially detained in March but the majority were released within two weeks. The trial, which took place *in camera* and did not afford the accused rights to full defence representation, was still in progress at the end of the year.

Brigadier Mohamed Ahmad al-Rayah, who had been convicted at an unfair military trial in October 1991, was released in February. He had refused an offer of release in August 1995 made on condition that he withdraw a complaint that he had been tortured and raped in custody (see *Amnesty International Report 1992*).

Torture of suspected government opponents remained widespread; prisoners held in security offices and "ghost houses" on suspicion of plotting against the government or having information about opposition activities were particularly at risk. Methods used included beatings and forcing detainees to do physical exercises or to stand for long periods in the sun. In January, Abdallah Ali Adam and eight other men were badly beaten with rubber hosepipes and batons after their arrest in Kassala, close to the Eritrean border. Taj al-Sir Mekki Abu Zeid and others detained in Khartoum in the same month were beaten, tied and suspended from the wall, doused in cold water and locked in a deep freeze in order to extract confessions.

Amputations and floggings were imposed as judicial punishments. In May, 10 men convicted of *hiraba* (armed robbery) were sentenced to amputation of the right hand and left foot by a court in Darfur. In June, the Director of Prisons announced that there were 100 prisoners in Kober Prison awaiting the implementation of their sentences of limb amputation. In Khartoum 35 people, most of them school and university students, received 20 lashes in September immediately after they were convicted of instigating violent demonstrations after an unfair trial before a Public Order Court.

PDF paramilitary forces and other militias forcibly abducted scores of children in operations in the war zones which further displaced tens of thousands of civilians. In March, over 70 children were abducted in raids by PDF troops near Abyei. Some were reportedly freed but the majority remained unaccounted for. Dozens of children were abducted by PDF troops escorting a supply train in April. Hundreds of children abducted in Bahr al-Ghazal and the Nuba Mountains by the PDF and other militias in previous years remained missing, with many reported to be held in domestic slavery.

The fate of hundreds of prisoners who "disappeared" in previous years remained unknown; the commission of inquiry into events in Juba in 1992 when over 200 people "disappeared" again failed to produce a report (see *Amnesty International Report 1995*).

Hundreds of people were extrajudicially executed during raids by the PDF and other militias. PDF troops escorting a train were responsible for dozens of killings in villages west of Ariath in February; 13 civilians were extrajudicially executed in Marol Deng and others at Majok Kuom.

Over 60 people were extrajudicially executed by the PDF in March in villages around Abyei and along the Bahr al-Arab. The village of Mabior, made up of internally displaced people returned from Khartoum, was destroyed.

Government aircraft carried out indiscriminate and deliberate attacks on civilian targets throughout the year. In August, helicopter gunships killed five people in a rocket and machine-gun attack on civilians at Kotobi in Western Equatoria.

At least 18 men were sentenced to death after convictions for armed robbery; three of them were sentenced to be hanged and their bodies crucified. There were reports that two men among those who "disappeared" in Juba (see above) were executed at a military jail in Kerrari in February.

Armed opposition groups were responsible for serious human rights abuses, including holding prisoners of conscience, torture, abducting children and deliberate and arbitrary killings. In April, SPLA soldiers detained and tortured community elders in Huma near Ikotos. Although the elders were quickly released, there was reportedly no further action by the SPLA leadership. In August, six Roman Catholic nuns and priests were detained for 11 days by an SPLA commander at Mapurdit after they opposed his efforts to conscript schoolchildren.

SSIA forces were responsible for scores of deliberate and arbitrary killings in attacks on settlements of people from the Dinka ethnic group in territory controlled by the SPLA. In March, over 50 men, women and children were killed in attacks on cattle camps in Abuong; nine girls and a boy were abducted. Three children were among nine people hacked to death in an attack on Adior in the same month. Civilians were targeted in attacks on cattle camps and villages at Langkap and Akop in April. Eleven people were killed at Akop and at least 19 abducted.

Amnesty International urged both government and armed opposition groups to end human rights abuses. The organization called on the government to end detention without charge or trial and torture; to prevent extrajudicial executions and abductions; and to clarify the fate and whereabouts of children abducted and believed to be held in domestic slavery. It called on the SPLA and SSIA to take steps to end deliberate and arbitrary killings.

In April, Amnesty International wrote to the Minister of Justice welcoming the government's decision to renew cooperation with the UN Special Rapporteur. In May, the organization published a report, *Sudan: Progress or public relations?*, which described human rights developments since the launch of its international campaign against human rights violations in Sudan in January 1995, and renewed its call for the deployment of human rights monitors.

In March, as part of a response to the UN Special Rapporteur on Sudan's report to the UN Commission on Human Rights, the government accused Amnesty International of being "politically motivated against Islam". In July, the Minister of Foreign Affairs denied that the authorities were complicit in the abduction of children for the purposes of slavery. Also in July, the organization received a letter from the Minister of Justice which rejected the deployment of human rights monitors but said that the government was committed to dialogue on human rights concerns. In July and again in August, Amnesty International wrote to the government proposing to meet relevant officials in Sudan. The authorities did not respond to the letters.

In April, an Amnesty International delegation visited southern Sudan to attend a conference on civil society and civil authority and to meet senior officials. While accepting that human rights abuses had taken place in the past, the officials denied that SPLA forces had been responsible for specific incidents raised by the organization. In May, Amnesty International wrote to the leaders of both the SPLA and the SSIA calling on them to investigate deliberate and arbitrary killings.

Amnesty International included reference to its concerns in Sudan in an oral statement to the African Commission on Human and People's Rights of the Organization of African Unity in March.

SURINAME

The authorities announced that an investigation would take place into the extrajudicial execution of 15 people allegedly carried out by the army in 1982. There were fears for the safety of relatives of the victims and human rights activists who received death threats after the investigation was requested.

In September, Jules Wijdenbosch of the *Nationale Democratische Partij* (NDP), National Democratic Party, replaced Ronald Venetiaan as President after being elected by members of the National Assembly and regional and district councils, in accordance with the Constitution. There was concern about the commitment of the new government to ensuring respect for human rights because of allegations that Desi Bouterse, the founder and leader of the NDP, had been responsible for human rights violations. Desi Bouterse ruled Suriname as head of the army between 1980 and 1988 and again between 1990 and 1991, in both cases as a result of a coup, during which time the army allegedly carried out detention without charge or trial, torture and extrajudicial executions.

In December 1995, the National Assembly had passed a resolution calling on the government to carry out an investigation into the extrajudicial execution of 15 people in December 1982 (see *Amnesty International Reports 1983* and *1984*) and other human rights violations alleged to have been carried out by the army under the command of Desi Bouterse. In January, the then President, Ronald Venetiaan, publicly stated that his government would launch such an investigation. By the time of the parliamentary elections in May the inquiry had not been initiated, and by December no action had been taken by the new government to implement the resolution.

In the first half of the year, relatives of the 15 victims and human rights activists reportedly received anonymous death threats. Some were provided with police protection. In April, the home of Henri Behr, President of the group of relatives of the victims, was fire-bombed.

In March, Amnesty International sought information regarding the terms of reference of the inquiry into the 1982 extrajudicial executions. In April, the organization requested that the authorities investigate the fire-bomb attack on the home of Henri Behr. Later that month an Amnesty International delegation visited Suriname to monitor the progress of the inquiry into the 1982 killings. Meetings were held with government officials, relatives of the victims and human rights organizations. Following the visit, the organization wrote to President Venetiaan expressing concern at the continued delay in instituting the inquiry and asking whether an investigation had been carried out into the fire-bomb attack. In October, the same letter was sent to President Wijdenbosch. No reply had been received by the end of the year.

SWAZILAND

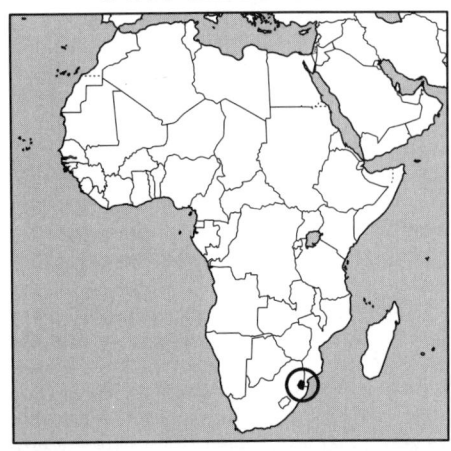

Dozens of prisoners of conscience were detained for short periods. There were allegations of torture and ill-treatment of detainees in police custody. A 15-year-old girl was killed and dozens of others injured when police shot at unarmed demonstrators. Three people remained under sentence of death. There were no executions.

Political activity continued to be banned and the rights of freedom of assembly and expression restricted, despite frequent public protests by organizations, including the Swaziland Federation of Trade Unions (SFTU) and the opposition Swaziland Democratic Alliance, a week-long national strike in January and some moves by King Mswati III and his advisers towards establishing a constitutional reform process.

In July, the King established a 30-person Constitutional Review Commission to draw up a new Constitution within two years. Swaziland's Constitution was suspended in 1973 when the current state of emergency was imposed. The Commission was given powers to fine and imprison for up to five years those who "belittle" or "insult" the Commission. Opposition group members appointed to the Commission threatened to withdraw in protest at the restricted nature of public participation in the process.

The Prime Minister, Prince Mbilini, was dismissed in the first half of the year and replaced by the former Finance Minister, Sibusiso Barnabas Dlamini.

Dozens of trade unionists, political activists, students and street vendors were detained for short periods for alleged participation in illegal strikes, demonstrations and meetings. Most were released without charge, but some were charged with public order offences. Many were prisoners of conscience. In one case, during the national strike in January, the police detained for four days Richard Nxumalo, Jan Sithole and Jabulani Nxumalo, the SFTU President, Secretary General and Assistant Secretary General, respectively, actively concealing their whereabouts and misleading their lawyers. The Director of Public Prosecutions and a local magistrate connived with the police in holding a secret remand hearing, during which the detainees were denied bail. However, on 25 January, the detainees' lawyers secured a High Court ruling declaring the detentions illegal and ordering the men's release. Shortly after, the government removed the presiding judge from his position as Acting Chief Justice. The trade unionists were later rearrested and appeared in court in March, charged with offences under the Industrial Relations Amendment Act, which had been promulgated by the government on the eve of the national strike.

Despite evidence that the law was invalid, the three men, who had been released on bail, were still facing the charges at the end of the year.

Detainees were reportedly tortured and ill-treated by police. In one case, on 5 October, police allegedly tear-gassed, shot at, kicked and beat with batons and fists 18 regional executive members of the Swaziland Association of Students – none of them more than 18 years old – detained when they attempted to deliver a petition to the Big Bend police station concerning the detention without charge or trial of fellow students. All were released without charge 24 hours later. A number of the students were later rearrested and detained for up to four days at Lobamba police station, where they were further assaulted and tortured. Although most were again released without charge, at least one student had been charged, but not brought to trial, by the end of the year.

Police used tear-gas, batons, *sjamboks* (whips) and live ammunition to disperse unarmed demonstrators, striking workers and participants in banned political gatherings, some of whom required hospitalization for gunshot and other injuries. In January, during a police operation to suppress the national strike, police shot and killed a 15-year-old girl. In August, police reportedly shot at and beat participants at a People's United Democratic Movement rally after they had complied with the police order to disperse. The authorities ordered only internal police inquiries into these incidents.

Criminal suspects were also subjected to torture. In several criminal cases, magistrates ordered that the accused be taken from court to hospital to be treated for injuries inflicted by the police. In one case, the presiding High Court judge expressed concern that the police appeared to routinely rely on torture as a means of investigating criminal cases.

Three people remained under sentence of death with appeals pending at the end of the year. In April, the Appeal Court had ordered the retrial of one of them because of irregularities in his trial. He was retried in the High Court on the same charges and again sentenced to death in October. There were no executions.

Amnesty International appealed to the government to release all prisoners of conscience. The organization expressed concern about the pattern of detention, ill-treatment and harassment of government opponents and called for the rights of freedom of expression and association to be fully respected.

SWITZERLAND

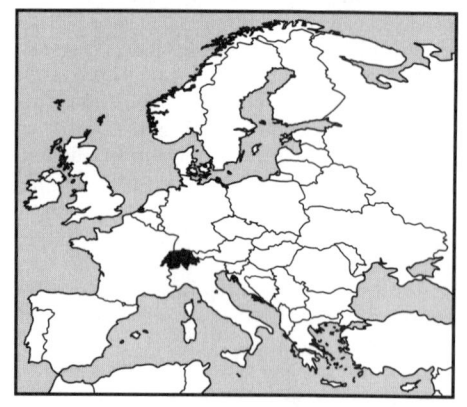

There were new allegations of ill-treatment of detainees by police officers.

In February, the European Committee for the Prevention of Torture, established under the European Convention for the Prevention of Torture and Inhuman or Degrading Treatment or Punishment, carried out its second periodic visit to follow up the criticisms and recommendations it made after its 1991 visit (see *Amnesty International Report 1994*) and to examine the treatment of people held in various places of detention in the cantons of Bern, Geneva, Ticino, Valais, Vaud and Zurich. The government indicated that it would allow publication of the European Committee's report on its visit, together with its own response, in March 1997.

In October, the UN Human Rights Committee considered Switzerland's initial report on its implementation of the International Covenant on Civil and Political Rights. The Committee expressed concern about several specific issues, including "numerous" allegations of ill-treatment, particularly of foreign nationals, at the time of arrest and during initial police custody; unsatisfactory investigations into complaints of ill-treatment; and failure to impose appropriate penalties on those responsible for such treatment.

The Committee recommended that Switzerland intensify discussions aimed at harmonizing the 26 cantonal codes of penal procedure, particularly concerning the provision of fundamental guarantees for detainees. The Committee stressed the need for all cantons to introduce a legal right for criminal suspects to have access to a lawyer and relatives from the moment of arrest and to be examined by an independent doctor upon arrest, after questioning and before appearing before a magistrate or being released. It also recommended that independent, publicly accountable, mechanisms be established in all cantons, to examine complaints of police ill-treatment.

Legislation providing, for the first time, a genuine civilian alternative to compulsory military service came into force in October. The service, one and a half times the length of ordinary military service, was available to conscripts able to demonstrate to the satisfaction of a civilian commission their inability to reconcile military service with their conscience.

Until October, refusal of military service remained a criminal offence, punishable by sentences of imprisonment or of work in the public interest. However, reports of prison sentences being imposed on, or served by, conscientious objectors were rare, as criminal proceedings already under way against such conscripts could be suspended to give them an opportunity to apply for civilian service and, pending its introduction, deferments were available to those ordered to report for military service during the year.

Allegations of police ill-treatment often concerned foreign nationals. An investigation was opened into a formal complaint lodged in January by A.S., an asylum-seeker from the Kosovo province of Yugoslavia. He alleged that five police officers slapped, kicked and punched him and banged his head against a desk in a Lugano police station after his arrest for theft in December 1995. He said he was denied medical treatment during his 30-hour detention but within an hour of his release he was examined at a local hospital, where doctors recorded heavy bruising to one leg, bruising and swelling to his right arm, extensive injuries to his right eye and blood in his urine. He claimed that, after questioning him, police officers ordered him to sign two documents written in Italian. He said he initially refused because he did not understand the language, but signed the first after being slapped across the face and the second after being told it would permit his release. However, the second document apparently informed the Federal Office for Refugees that he was withdrawing his asylum application.

There was confirmation that the Ticino Procurator General had opened an investigation into the complaint of police ill-treatment lodged by Ali Doymaz and Abuzer Tastan in June 1995 (see *Amnesty International Report 1996*). The investigation was still open at the end of the year; the men had not been questioned about their allegations.

There appeared to be delays in several judicial proceedings relating to alleged police ill-treatment. There was an interval of two and a half years between a complaint lodged by M.F., an Iranian political refugee, in December 1993, and the trial in June of three Zurich municipal police officers accused of abusing their authority and causing him bodily harm during a drugs search. The man required hospital treatment after being released without charge. A judge attached to Zurich District Court concluded that one or more of the police officers had used unwarranted and excessive force by kicking the man, but acquitted all three on the grounds that it had been impossible to establish which officer(s) had kicked him.

In a definitive sentence issued in March, the Zurich High Court concluded that all the injuries sustained by Hassan L. in February 1995 (see *Amnesty International Report 1996*) could be attributed to a violent struggle with police at the time of his arrest in the street and to a fall in his police cell, resulting from his drunken and poor physical state. The Court was unable to exclude entirely the possibility that he might have been ill-treated inside the police station but found no reliable evidence to support his allegations and convict any police officer.

In April, Geneva's cantonal parliament approved legislative reforms which would strengthen existing safeguards against ill-treatment for detainees in police custody and serve to protect police officers from unfounded allegations of ill-treatment. They were expected to be put to a cantonal referendum in 1997. New allegations of ill-treatment by Geneva police were reported during the year. Marc Guerrero was chased and arrested by Geneva police in February, after carrying out a bag-snatch. In March, he lodged a formal complaint with the Chief of Police and the Procurator General claiming that, after he had surrendered to the police, a police dog had been deliberately set on him, causing serious injuries to his left leg and shoulder, the latter requiring a surgical operation, and that police officers had ill-treated him, one hitting his head with a gun. He claimed they also deliberately deprived him of medical treatment for several hours, although they had been informed he was a diabetic, and a doctor, called in at his request after he had been in custody for over an hour, had recommended his urgent hospitalization. His complaint was accompanied by a medical certificate, issued by the cantonal hospital to which he was eventually transferred, stating that his injuries were consistent with his allegations of being struck with a gun and attacked by a dog.

In October, the Chief of Police stated that a judicial investigation was under way and commented that the accused officers strongly contested the allegations and that there was nothing "a priori to indicate that the use of the police dog contravened the principle of proportionality".

Amnesty International welcomed the availability of a genuine civilian alternative to compulsory military service and monitored its implementation. The organization expressed concern about allegations of ill-treatment and sought information on the progress and outcome of relevant investigations. In October, the government told the UN Human Rights Committee that concerns about allegations of police ill-treatment raised by the European Committee for the Prevention of Torture and by non-governmental organizations, including Amnesty International, would be addressed in its response to the European Committee's report.

SYRIA

Scores of people, including possible prisoners of conscience, were arrested on political grounds during the year. Hundreds of political prisoners arrested in previous years, including prisoners of conscience, remained held; some of them were serving prison sentences and others were detained without charge or trial. At least three political prisoners continued to be held after their sentences expired. The health of long-term prisoners of conscience gave cause for concern. The fate and whereabouts of scores of prisoners who "disappeared" in previous years remained unknown. At least seven executions took place.

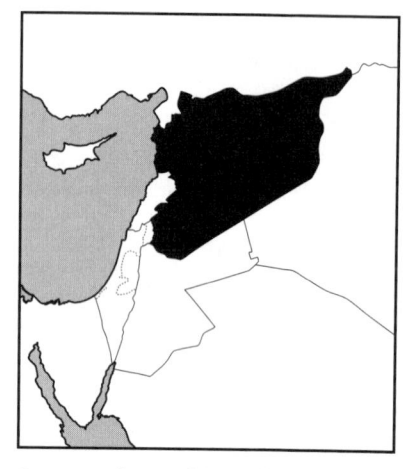

Scores of people, including possible prisoners of conscience, were arrested during the year on suspicion of involvement in unauthorized political organizations or activities. Thirteen Syrian Kurds were arrested by the security forces in February and March, apparently after they celebrated the traditional *Nawruz* (Kurdish New Year Festival) in the province of Aleppo. They were reportedly still detained in al-Musalamiya prison in Aleppo at the end of the year.

Hundreds of political prisoners, including prisoners of conscience, remained held. Some were detained without charge or trial; others were serving prison sentences, mainly imposed after unfair trials. Among them were at least 160 prisoners of conscience accused of having links with the *Hizb al-'Amal al-Shuyu'i*, Party for Communist Action (PCA). They included 'Abbas 'Abbas, arrested in January 1982 and sentenced to 15 years' imprisonment in 1994, and Khadija Dib, arrested in 1992 and not known to have been brought to trial. About a dozen prisoners continued to serve sentences for alleged links with the *al-Hizb al-Shuyu'i al-Maktab al-Siyassi*, Communist Party-Political Bureau (CPPB). Riad al-Turk, a leading member of the CPPB who was arrested in 1980, remained in incommunicado detention without charge or trial (see *Amnesty International Report 1996*). He received one visit from his family during the year, the third during his 16-year period of detention. About 29 prisoners of conscience detained in connection with the PCA, CPPB and the Ba'th Party were reported to have been transferred to Tadmur military prison, where conditions are known to be particularly harsh, after refusing to sign a statement dissociating themselves from all past political activities. Among them were Mustafa al-Hussain, 'Umar al-Hayek, Ratib Sha'bu and Mazin Shamsin.

Ten prisoners of conscience sentenced in March 1992 to between five and 10 years' imprisonment in connection with the unauthorized Committees for the Defence of Democratic Freedoms and Human Rights in Syria, remained held. They included Aktham Nu'aysa, a lawyer, and Nizar Nayyuf, a sociologist (see *Amnesty International Reports 1995* and *1996*).

Jalal al-Din Mustafa Mirhij, a former army officer who had been detained for more than 10 years beyond the expiry of his sentence, was released in January. Twenty-three prisoners of conscience who were held on suspicion of having links with the PCA were released during the year, most on completion of their prison terms.

In previous years, long-term political detainees, including prisoners of conscience, were brought to trial before the Supreme State Security Court (SSSC), whose procedures fall far short of international fair trial standards (see previous *Amnesty International Reports*). Many were sentenced to prison terms, while dozens were acquitted or had the charges against them dropped. It was not known whether any such trials were conducted during 1996.

Hundreds of political prisoners arrested on suspicion of having links with the unauthorized *al-Ikhwan al-Muslimun*, Muslim Brotherhood (see *Amnesty International Report 1996*), remained held in various prisons. Most had been held in incommunicado detention since the late 1970s and early 1980s, and their whereabouts were unknown (see previous *Amnesty International Reports*). They included Baha al-Din Aswad, a secondary-school student from Aleppo who was arrested in 1979, and two of his brothers, Muhammad and Dia al-Din Aswad, who were arrested in 1981.

Dozens of doctors and engineers remained held. They were among the many professionals who had been arrested in 1980 following a one-day general strike led by members of the Medical, Bar and Engineers associations (see previous *Amnesty International Reports*).

Scores of Palestinians arrested on political grounds in previous years in Lebanon and Syria remained in detention (see previous *Amnesty International Reports*). Most were held incommunicado and their whereabouts remained unknown. About 21 Palestinians arrested in connection with Palestinian political movements and held since 1985 and 1987 were released during the year.

At least 200 Lebanese nationals remained held in Syrian prisons. Most were arrested in Lebanon during the Lebanese civil war (1975 to 1990) and transferred to Syria, while others were arrested and taken to Syria after 1990. Most were believed to be detained without charge or trial and the whereabouts of many of them were unknown (see **Lebanon** entry).

Sixteen Syrian Kurds arrested in previous years remained held in 'Adra, Sadnaya and Far' Falastin. They included Muhammad Husayn Omri, a possible prisoner of conscience, who was arrested in May 1995 at Qmishli in northern Syria and was reportedly held without charge or trial.

At least three political prisoners remained in detention despite having completed their prison sentences (which are calculated from the date of arrest). They included Khalil Brayez (see *Amnesty International Report 1996*), a former army officer and writer in his sixties held for 26 years – 11 years beyond the expiry of a 15-year sentence imposed in 1970.

Most of the political detainees held for alleged links with the *Hizb al-Ba'th al-Dimuqrati al-Ishtiraki al-'Arabi*, Arab Socialist Democratic Ba'th Party, were serving prison terms averaging 15 years imposed by the SSSC in 1994. They included 'Ali Dib, who was arrested in 1982 and sentenced to 15 years' imprisonment in 1994.

Reports about the medical condition of long-term prisoners of conscience continued to give cause for concern. Of the 29 prisoners of conscience transferred to Tadmur prison, at least six were in ill health. Information came to light that Karim al-Hajj Hussain, a prisoner of conscience, had died one day after his release – four months after his sentence expired – in December 1995. He had suffered from tuberculosis and meningitis while in prison; it was not known whether he received adequate medical treatment. Karim al-Hajj Hussain was arrested in 1987 on suspicion of having links with the PCA and was held without charge or trial until 1994, when he was sentenced to eight years' imprisonment. There were reports that a further 20 prisoners of conscience were in ill-health, and that eight of them were in urgent need of medical attention. They included Faraj Birqdar, a prisoner of conscience and a poet, who was arrested in 1987 and sentenced to 15 years' imprisonment in 1993.

Scores of political prisoners arrested in previous years remained unaccounted for and it was feared that they had "disappeared". They included Mustafa Abu Qaws, a university student, who was arrested in October 1983 at his home in Aleppo. His family saw him two weeks after his arrest, but his subsequent fate and whereabouts remained unknown.

Two Sudanese asylum-seekers, Anthony Zakaria Laki and Samuel Lado Zakaria, were returned to Sudan in August after spending about two months in al-Yarmuk migration prison. They were allegedly ill-treated. They had been expelled from Hungary to Syria in June. No information was available about their fate after they were sent back to Sudan.

At least seven people were executed by hanging in a public square in the town of Yabrud, north of Damascus, in March. The seven had reportedly been convicted of murder and robbery committed in February.

Amnesty International continued to appeal for the immediate and unconditional release of prisoners of conscience and for all political prisoners to receive fair and prompt trials, or be released. The organization urged the authorities to initiate impartial investigations into torture allegations made in previous years and to end the use of the death penalty. It also urged the authorities to ensure that all asylum-seekers were given access to fair refugee procedures in accordance with international human rights standards. The government responded to some of Amnesty International's queries, but no measures were taken to address the organization's outstanding concerns.

In April, Amnesty International submitted information about its concerns in Syria for UN review under a procedure established by Economic and Social Council Resolutions 728F/1503, for confidential consideration of communications about human rights violations.

TAIWAN

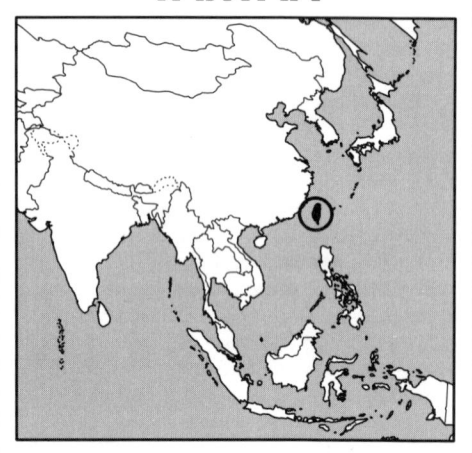

An aboriginal activist faced imprisonment as a prisoner of conscience. Fifteen people were sentenced to death and 21 were executed. There was growing evidence that three prisoners under sentence of death were innocent and had confessed under torture.

The first presidential election by universal suffrage took place in March, and was won by the incumbent, President Lee Teng-hui. Tension across the Taiwan Strait grew in the weeks before the election, as armed forces of the People's Republic of China carried out military exercises. These were apparently aimed in part at dissuading voters and politicians in Taiwan from advocating independence and the government from seeking further international recognition.

The new cabinet which was formed in June stated that it would work to eradicate corruption. Minister of Justice Liao Cheng-hao said that judicial reform would be a priority.

In July, the government announced that it would set up commissions to consider legal reforms on aboriginal issues and immigration. It also announced that a law on judges would be drafted, forbidding judges from joining political parties. No draft of the law had been made public by the end of the year.

Iciang Parod, a prisoner of conscience and member of the Amei, one of the aboriginal ethnic groups, was released in May after serving seven months of a one-year prison sentence for allegedly organizing an illegal demonstration (see *Amnesty International Report 1996*). Yukan Nafu, a member of the Taiya ethnic group, was facing imprisonment on similar charges, but his sentence was still under appeal by the end of the year. If imprisoned, he would be a prisoner of conscience.

In January, the Control Yuan, an independent body investigating complaints against officials, published a report highlighting the military authorities' failure to prevent the killing of army conscript Yeh Tzu-hsien in September 1995 (see *Amnesty International Report 1996*). It also criticized the authorities for classifying Yeh Tzu-hsien's death as suicide, despite evidence that he had been killed when hit by a military vehicle and that his body was dumped at a construction site in the capital, Taipei. Despite the Control Yuan's findings, no military officers had been brought to justice by the end of the year.

In February, nine prison guards and one prisoner reportedly received prison sentences of between eight and 12 years in connection with the death of Chu Jui-jen, an inmate of the Chiayi Detention Centre, who died in September 1995 (see *Amnesty International Report 1996*). Tu Cheng-ja, a senior supervisor at the detention centre, was reportedly sentenced to 12 years' imprisonment for ordering other officers and an inmate to beat Chu Ju-jen.

Fifteen people were sentenced to death, and 21 were executed. Among those sentenced to death in previous years, Su Chien-ho, Liu Ping-lang and Chuang Lin-hsiung remained imprisoned under sentence of death for a 1991 double murder, despite strong indications that they were innocent. In September, Wang Wen-chung, brother of another co-defendant in the case who was convicted and executed several years ago, stated that he had been tortured by police into incriminating the three men, as well as himself. Wang Wen-chung had been convicted in 1991 of being an accomplice in the case, and served a 32-month sentence. He said police officers used a lighter to burn his chin and threatened to arrest his mother, until he agreed to sign a confession which incriminated himself as well as the three above-named men. The police also refused him access to a lawyer. He said that, after signing his confession, he had been taken to another room in the same police station, where he saw Su Chien-ho tied to a chair while a police officer hit the soles of his feet with a wooden pole. Wang also said he saw Liu Ping-lang being held down in another chair as police used a cattle prod to apply electric shocks to his genitals, while Chuang Lin-hsiung was being beaten on the head.

Despite this testimony, and findings by the Control Yuan, which confirmed the allegations of police ill-treatment made by Su Chien-ho and his co-defendants, calls for a retrial by lawyers, members of the Legislative Yuan (parliament) and many non-governmental organizations remained unanswered by the end of the year.

In June, an Amnesty International representative visited Taiwan and met relatives of Su Chien-ho and his co-defendants. In May, Amnesty International had publicly called on the Taiwanese authorities to commute their death sentences, as a first step towards a full review of their case.

TAJIKISTAN

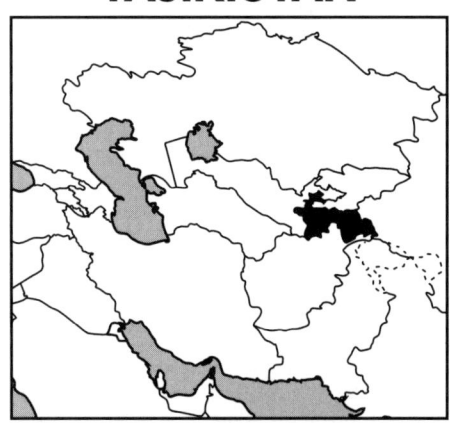

Two opposition activists accused of anti-government propaganda were detained by security officials for several days. A former opposition leader was detained for several hours in Russia at the request of the Tajik authorities in connection with his former political activities. Members of a UN military observer mission were tortured by government troops. Appalling

prison conditions amounted to ill-treatment; there were reports of deaths of prisoners from starvation and untreated disease. There was evidence of limited progress in ending impunity for former pro-government warlords responsible for past human rights violations. The death penalty remained in force for 41 offences, and at least nine people were sentenced to death. Opposition armed forces deliberately and arbitrarily killed captured government soldiers and civilians and took hostages.

A summit meeting in December between President Imomali Rakhmonov and Sayed Abdullo Nuri, leader of the United Tajik Opposition (UTO), made limited progress but failed to produce an agreement on a power-sharing formula to end Tajikistan's armed conflict. A cease-fire technically remained in force throughout the year, but was persistently violated in central Tajikistan, where UTO forces made significant gains from May onwards, occupying a number of major towns.

The government faced uprisings in other areas of the country. In January, two former commanders of the People's Front paramilitary group (see *Amnesty International Report 1994*), Ibod Boymatov and Mahmud Khudoyberdiyev, seized control of, respectively, the towns of Tursunzade and Kurgan-Tyube, in pursuit of demands which included the resignation of the government. The crisis was diffused in February after concessions by the government which included the dismissal of officials and an amnesty for participants in fighting between rival army units in Kurgan-Tyube in 1995 (see *Amnesty International Report 1996*). There was further unrest in Tursunzade in August, including clashes between rival armed groups. In May, there were mass demonstrations and rioting in towns in the northern Leninabad region which resulted in the dismissal of local officials.

In April, two local activists of the outlawed Democratic Party, Azimdzhon Abdurakhmonov and Dzhumaboy Vakhobov, were detained in the town of Ura-Tyube, reportedly by officers of the Ministry of Security, apparently on suspicion of making "anti-government propaganda". They were released without charge after around 10 days. In July, Davlat Khudonazarov, an exiled former opposition leader, was briefly detained in Moscow, Russia, by police who found him listed as wanted in Tajikistan on criminal charges connected with his opposition activities. He spent some nine hours in custody before the authorities in Tajikistan stated that he was no longer being sought on criminal charges.

In two separate incidents in December, members of the UN Mission of Observers in Tajikistan (UNMOT) were assaulted and subjected to mock executions by Tajik government soldiers. In the first incident, an Austrian army captain, a lieutenant from Bangladesh and their translator were intercepted near the town of Garm, close to the front line, by government soldiers who demanded that the UNMOT observers escort them to territory held by UTO forces, where government troops were allegedly being held captive. According to a UNMOT statement, when the UNMOT personnel refused they were beaten with weapons, kicked and punched, lined up in a row to be shot, and attempts were made to push one member of the UNMOT team off a mountain ledge. The UNMOT personnel were later allowed to leave in the direction of UTO-held territory under threat of death if they did not return with the captive soldiers, and were eventually escorted to a UNMOT outpost in Garm by UTO fighters.

In the second incident, less than two weeks later, two teams of UNMOT observers were stopped at a military check-point at Saripul, near Garm, and ordered to leave their vehicles and line up. The troops, reportedly acting on the orders of their commander, then fired machine-gun rounds over their captives' heads. The UNMOT teams escaped, reportedly when the appearance of another car distracted the soldiers' attention.

Information was received about appalling prison conditions amounting to ill-treatment. In August, the official press and other sources reported that deaths in prison had risen from 120 in 1994 to more than 400 in 1995, and to 509 during the first half of 1996, mainly because of starvation and disease. Tajikistan's parliament had reportedly responded by adopting a resolution on improving prison conditions.

The authorities made limited progress in resolving cases of "disappearance" and possible extrajudicial execution. There were inconsistencies in the official attitude towards former pro-government paramilitaries involved in violent crime. In

August, the Supreme Court sentenced to death two former members of the pro-government paramilitary People's Front for the murder, in March 1995, of Zayniddin Mukhiddinov, a member of parliament. However, in June an official from the President's office, confirming that a criminal investigation remained open into the death in 1992 of Muso Isoyev, a victim of extrajudicial execution, stated that the suspects in the case were believed to have left the country. The amnesty, announced in February, for participants in clashes between rival army units in 1995, gave rise to concern about continuing impunity for former pro-government paramilitaries, as did the political rehabilitation of warlord Ibod Boymatov. Ibod Boymatov left Tajikistan in 1994 after reportedly attempting to kill a factory manager, but was given a government post and parliamentary seat following the January 1996 events in Tursunzade. However, in December Ibod Boymatov's parliamentary mandate was terminated and President Rakhmonov announced that he was to face criminal prosecution.

The death penalty remained in force for 27 peacetime and 14 wartime offences. At least nine death sentences were passed; no executions were reported. In November, the authorities disclosed that five prisoners who had been sentenced to death in 1994 were still on death row.

Reports received during the year indicated that UTO armed forces operating in central Tajikistan had deliberately and arbitrarily killed civilians and captive government soldiers. For example, in February, 21 captive government soldiers and civilian drivers were killed by UTO forces who intercepted a convoy carrying food supplies to government troops. Survivors of the incident reported that after the commander of the convoy had been persuaded to disarm, he and others were led away and shot dead. Incidents were also reported in which UTO armed forces took government troops and police officers hostage. For example, in August it was reported that the UTO was holding hostage four police officers captured in the southern district of Yavan and offering to exchange them for imprisoned opposition members. The exchange subsequently went ahead. In October, the UTO demanded the removal of government roadblocks and the release of imprisoned opposition members as conditions for the release of 37 police officers captured in Komsomolabad. All of these hostages had been released by early November.

Amnesty International expressed concern to the authorities about the detention of people in connection with their involvement in the political opposition. It raised with the Russian police the arrest of Davlat Khudonazarov. The organization condemned the torture of UNMOT personnel by government troops. It sought information from the authorities about the steps being taken to end appalling prison conditions amounting to ill-treatment.

Amnesty International continued to call for investigations into all alleged "disappearances" and extrajudicial executions, and for an end to impunity for those responsible. The organization called for commutation of all pending death sentences and continued to urge complete abolition of the death penalty.

Amnesty International condemned deliberate and arbitrary killings and hostage-taking by armed opposition forces, and called on the UTO leadership to adhere to minimum standards of humane behaviour as set out in the Geneva Conventions.

TANZANIA

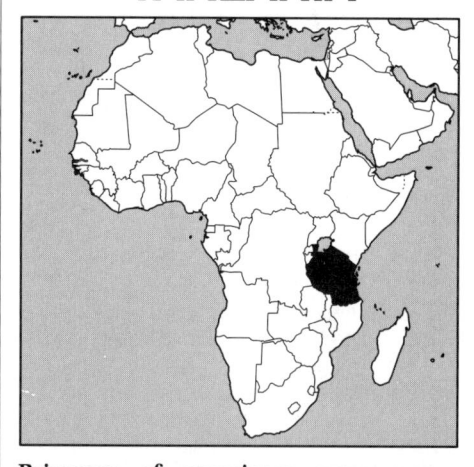

Prisoners of conscience were among scores of government opponents arrested and briefly detained on the islands of Zanzibar and Pemba. Many were held without charge or trial; others faced criminal charges and were denied bail. Scores of political prisoners were tortured and ill-treated on the islands. Prison conditions were poor and at least nine prisoners were reported to have died. Courts imposed sentences of caning. More than 50 possible extrajudicial executions took place on the mainland. Over 500,000 Rwandese refugees were forced to return to Rwanda.

Political tension remained high on the islands of Zanzibar and Pemba where political opponents accused the ruling *Chama Cha Mapinduzi*, Party of the Revolution, led on the islands by Salmin Amour, of using intimidation and ballot rigging to win the October 1995 presidential and parliamentary elections. The authorities were responsible, both before and after local elections in March 1996, for further harassment, sometimes violent, of supporters of the main opposition party, the Civic United Front (CUF), which boycotted the elections on Zanzibar but won large majorities on Pemba. The CUF was repeatedly denied permits to hold meetings and rallies. After the elections hundreds of Pemba islanders working on Zanzibar, many of them government employees, were dismissed and their houses demolished. Others were expelled from the island. Newspapers which carried reports critical of the government were banned or threatened with closure.

In the northwest of the country, the mainland was host to over 700,000 refugees from Rwanda, Burundi and Zaire for most of the year. Although the border remained officially closed, tens of thousands continued to arrive; 40,000 refugees from Rwanda and Burundi were admitted during the first half of the year and tens of thousands more crossed Lake Tanganyika from Zaire in November and December. In December, in a statement endorsed by the UN High Commissioner for Refugees (UNHCR), the government announced that all Rwandese refugees were expected to leave the country by the end of the year.

CUF supporters were among scores of government opponents arrested during the year on Zanzibar and Pemba. Many were prisoners of conscience and were detained without charge or trial beyond the 48 hours allowed by Zanzibar law. In February, CUF member of parliament Mussa Haji Kombo was held without charge or trial for over two weeks after he held a public meeting for which the authorities had refused permission. Suleiman Seif Hamad, a member of the CUF's national executive, and Mtumwa Khatib were detained without charge or trial for two weeks in March after violent clashes between villagers and the police in Shengejuu, on Pemba.

Criminal charges such as sedition, vagrancy, and involvement in acts of violence, often accompanied by the denial of bail for periods of two weeks or more, were also used as a method of intimidating government critics and opponents. In one such case in January, the editor and publisher of the Swahili newspaper *Majira* were charged with sedition. The charges were dropped in February but the newspaper remained banned and at least one journalist working for *Majira* was prohibited from exercising his profession. In April, charges of stealing firearms, brought against CUF member of parliament Salim Yusuf Mohamed after he had spent nearly two weeks in detention following the Shengejuu clashes in March, were ruled unconstitutional by the Zanzibar High Court. The authorities held him for a further 10 days.

Scores of suspected government opponents were tortured and ill-treated by police and Anti-Smuggling Unit (ASU) personnel on Zanzibar and Pemba; on the mainland, criminal suspects were regularly beaten. On Zanzibar, beatings and other ill-treatment and torture were inflicted, including shaving prisoners' heads with broken glass, spraying prisoners with motor oil and forcing them to eat faeces. In March, members of the ASU on Pemba forced Osman Hamad Osman to eat faeces and then beat him unconscious before dumping him in Mgogoni. In May, six men were beaten by police officers who suspected them of holding a political meeting in Pujini, on Pemba.

Overcrowding and poor conditions were reported in prisons throughout the country. Nine prisoners in Keko remand prison were reported to have died between December 1995 and February 1996 as a result of neglect and beatings. Built to house 340 prisoners, Keko remand prison held nearly 1,300 prisoners in April.

Sentences of caning, a cruel, inhuman or degrading punishment, were imposed, often for sexual offences against children. In March, a man was sentenced to 12 strokes of the cane and 34 years' imprisonment for defiling and sodomizing a child.

In August, over 50 gold-miners were killed in what may have been extrajudicial executions during evictions from disputed land in an operation involving the police, regional authorities in Shinyanga and a Canadian mining company. The men were buried alive when the Canadian company, guarded by police, bulldozed small-scale mines in Bulyanhulu, despite on-the-spot appeals from distraught villagers, in advance of the company taking possession of the land for industrial mining. The bulldozing was authorized by the regional authorities 12 hours after a court order halting evictions pending further investigations was announced over the radio. The bodies had not been recovered by the end of the year and criminal investigations appeared to have been discontinued.

Throughout the year, the government maintained a hard line on refugees from Rwanda and Burundi, forcibly returning, and refusing admission to, hundreds of thousands of people. In May and June, Tanzanian officials enforced the officially closed borders with Rwanda and Burundi more strictly, turning back over 7,000 refugees from Burundi. The refugees were mainly Rwandese Hutu fleeing assaults by the Burundi military. In May, the UN stated that an unknown number of refugees who had attempted to cross the border had been killed on return to Burundi.

The Tanzanian authorities declared their intention of expelling refugees who posed a threat to security. In January, police reportedly arrested 60 refugees from Burundi and Zaire as part of a crackdown on unregistered immigrants: 32 were handed over to the UN; the fate of the others was unknown. In August, seven Rwandese refugees, members of *Rassemblement pour le retour des réfugiés et de la démocratie au Rwanda*, Rally for the Return of Refugees and Democracy in Rwanda, a banned organization in Tanzania, were arrested because of their political activities. They were forcibly returned to Rwanda, where they were reported to have been detained.

In early December, the government issued a written statement, endorsed and co-signed by the UNHCR, which announced that all Rwandese refugees were expected to leave the country by 31 December. Refugees who feared for their safety if they returned to Rwanda were not informed of any mechanism whereby they could remain in Tanzania, or that they had any other option but to leave. Tens of thousands of refugees who fled the camps and attempted to escape into the interior of the country were intercepted by the army and police and redirected to the border. There were reports that excessive force and rape were used as means of coercion. By the end of the year, approximately 500,000 refugees had returned to Rwanda and 50,000 Rwandans remained in Tanzania.

In February, Amnesty International wrote to the government of President Benjamin Mkapa calling on the authorities to abide by their international obligations not to forcibly return to Rwanda and Burundi refugees who might be at risk of human rights violations on return. In October, the organization protested to the authorities at the arrest and forcible return to Rwanda of seven Rwandese refugees. In December, Amnesty International strongly criticized the decision to impose a 31-December deadline for the return of Rwandese refugees, and appealed to the authorities to ensure protection for refugees who have a well-founded fear of human rights violations.

THAILAND

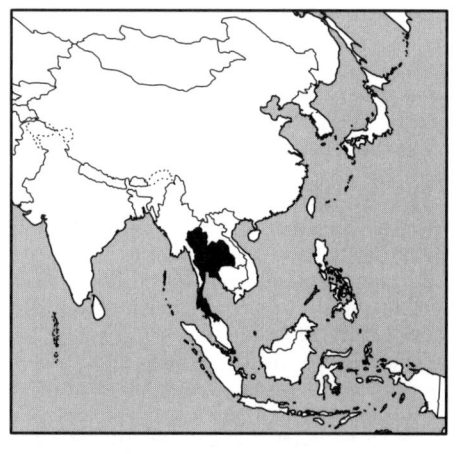

Six suspected drug traffickers were reportedly extrajudicially executed by police. One execution was carried out, the first in nine years. Ten death sentences were believed to have been imposed and some 100 people were believed to remain under sentence of death at the end of the year. Ten thousand Mon refugees living in Thai camps were forcibly repatriated to Myanmar. Burmese asylum-seekers continued to be arrested for "illegal immigration" and detained in harsh conditions.

In September, amid widespread allegations of corruption and economic mismanagement in the six-party coalition government, Banharn Silpa-archa resigned as Prime Minister and called elections for 17 November. The New Aspiration Party (NAP), won 125 parliamentary seats and its leader, Chaowalit Yongchaiyudh, formed a six-party coalition government.

In October, Thailand acceded to the International Covenant on Civil and Political Rights.

In February, the Deputy Director General of the Corrections Department announced that leg-irons would no longer be used in the maximum security Bang Kwang Prison in Nonthaburi. In March, after the publication of the US Government's annual human rights report on Thailand, the government publicly acknowledged that police brutality existed and stated that police officers found guilty of torturing or executing suspected criminals should be dismissed.

Also in March, two staff members of Amnesty International were detained for almost two hours by police in Bangkok in connection with their participation in a press conference on the organization's human rights concerns in China.

In November, six suspected drug traffickers were shot dead in Suphan Buri province after they had given themselves up to the police. The police claimed to have fired in self-defence when attacked by the suspects, whose handcuffs had been removed so that they could indicate where weapons were hidden. After protests by human rights organizations and the victims' relatives, the Attorney General's office opened an investigation into the shootings.

Some 120 people under sentence of death had their sentences commuted to life imprisonment in June, under a royal pardon to mark the 50th anniversary of the reign of His Majesty King Bhumibol Adulyadej. The Royal Pardon did not include people convicted of drugs offences. Over a thousand people held for "illegal immigration", including some 750 Myanmar nationals, were released under the Royal Pardon, as was Surachai Sae Dan, a member of the Communist Party of Thailand, who had been convicted of murder and robbery in 1986.

In January, Prommas Leamsai, who had been convicted in the 1980s of murdering a policeman, was executed by firing-squad, the first execution to take place in nine years. Ten death sentences were believed to have been imposed during the year, and at the end of the year some 100 people were believed to be under sentence of death.

Some 10,000 Mon refugees who had been living in Thai camps were forcibly repatriated to Myanmar between December 1995 and May 1996. No international monitors were present.

Twenty-two Burmese asylum-seekers were arrested in May after a demonstration in front of the Myanmar Embassy. Most had been released by the end of the year.

Immigration officials and police continued to detain asylum-seekers and refugees from Myanmar and other countries in harsh conditions, including severe overcrowding and inadequate access to medical care. Detained asylum-seekers were not given an opportunity to challenge the legality of their detention as required by international standards. Burmese asylum-seekers convicted of "illegal immigration" were fined and imprisoned in immigration detention centres before being taken to the border between Thailand and Myanmar.

At least 5,000 Karen people and 20,000 Shan people from Myanmar fled to Thailand to escape forcible relocation by the Myanmar armed forces. The Democratic Kayin Buddhist Army, a breakaway Karen faction allied to the Myanmar armed forces, attacked Karen camps inside the Thai border, killing at least one Thai civilian (see **Myanmar** entry). In August, Thai Forestry officials shot dead three Karen refugees from Myanmar near Mae La refugee camp, although the circumstances remain unclear.

In January, Amnesty International condemned the execution of Prommas Leamsai. In the same month, the organization published a report, *Thailand: Two Burmese asylum-seekers still detained* (see *Amnesty International Report 1996*). In September, the organization met a Thai Government delegation in London to discuss the protection of human rights in Thailand. In October and November, Amnesty International appealed to the authorities not to forcibly return asylum-seekers to Myanmar, where they faced serious human rights violations.

TOGO

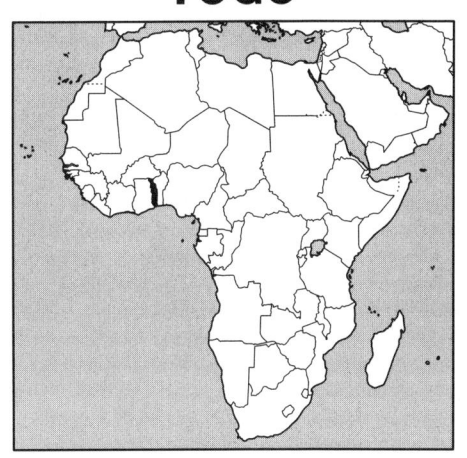

Members of opposition parties, and suspected government opponents, including prisoners of conscience and possible prisoners of conscience, were detained, mainly for short periods. Most were released without charge or trial, but two remained in detention at the end of the year. An army officer detained on his return from exile and two officers who returned in 1995 remained in detention without trial. An army officer and a German diplomat appeared to have been extrajudicially executed.

Following the August legislative by-elections, President Eyadema's *Rassemblement du peuple togolais*, Rally of the Togolese People, won the majority of seats in the Legislative Assembly. Edem Kodjo of the *Union togolaise pour la démocratie* (UTD), Togolese Union for Democracy, was replaced as Prime Minister by Kwassi Klutsé.

In April and June, at least five people closely linked with the UTD were arrested and held for 48 hours before being released without charge. The five, all prisoners of conscience, included David Oladakoun, Seth Glé and Octave Nicoué Broohm, special adviser to Prime Minister Edem Kodjo.

In May, three relatives of Komlavi Yebesse, whose photograph was published after he was tortured and shot dead in April, were arrested for giving photographs of the victim to *La Tribune des Démocrates*, an independent newspaper. Two of them were released after several hours, but one remained in detention for more than three days before being released without charge.

In June, Eric Lawson, Director of *La Tribune des Démocrates*, was sentenced *in absentia* to five years' imprisonment. The court suspended the newspaper for six months and imposed a large fine. The director was accused of incitement to hatred, and false reporting for publishing an article describing the circumstances of Komlavi Yebesse's death.

Alfred Adomayakpor, former Director of the national police and military adviser to Edem Kodjo, was arrested in July and detained for more than three months for allegedly producing a pamphlet calling on the army to rebel. He was released without charge in September.

Also in July, Claude Gumedzoe, a jeweller, and Sergeant Augustin Ihou of the Togolese Armed Forces, were arrested by members of the gendarmerie because of their links with Dr David Ihou, a former Minister of Health living in exile in Benin. The exact charges against them were not known, but the Togolese authorities accused Claude Gumedzoe of possessing a firearm. At the end of the year, they remained in detention.

In March, Folly Dagnon Koffi, a soldier who had fled to Ghana in 1993, was arrested on his return to Togo. He remained in detention at the end of the year, along with Adjété Ako and Djekpo Jolevi, army officers who had been arrested following their return from Benin in 1995 (see *Amnesty International Report 1996*). By the end of the year no charges had been brought against any of the men.

There were two killings by the armed forces in circumstances suggesting possible extrajudicial executions. In January, Captain Azote, an army officer, was shot dead in Lomé by a member of the armed forces. The authorities reportedly said Captain Azote had been mistaken for a terrorist as he was wearing a gun. Captain Azote was a member of the *Ligue togolaise des droits de l'homme*, Togolese Human Rights League. He had been dismissed from the army after the attempted coup in 1986 but reintegrated two months before the National Conference in 1991.

In March, Thomas Rupprecht, a German diplomat, was shot dead at a checkpoint by members of the armed forces when he refused to allow them to search his car.

TONGA

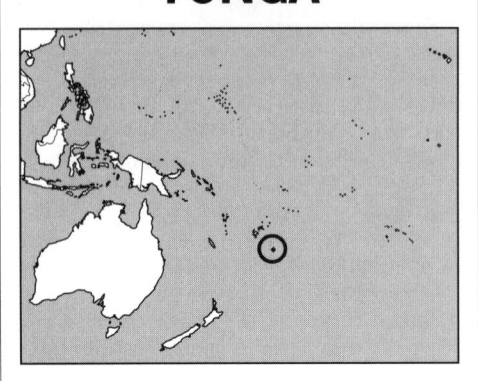

Three journalists and three pro-democracy activists were detained for the non-violent exercise of their right to freedom of expression.

In January, 'Akilisi Pohiva, leader of the pro-democracy movement, was elected "Number 1 People's Representative for Tongatapu" in the Legislative Assembly elections for the nine minority members who are elected by 99 per cent of the population. The majority of the Assembly's members are appointed by King Taufa 'Ahau Tupou IV or elected by the Nobles.

Filini Sikuea, a pro-democracy election candidate, Vaha'akolo Fonofehi, a writer for the *Times of Tonga* newspaper, and Filokalafi 'Akau'ola, the newspaper's deputy editor, were arrested in February for "inciting Police Minister Clive Edwards to anger". The arrests followed a police raid on the newspaper's office after the publication of a letter criticizing the Minister. Vaha'akolo Fonofehi and Filini Sikuea were reportedly detained by police for five days. Filokalafi 'Akau'ola was released after 26 hours. In March, a court decided to have the charges against Vaha'akolo Fonofehi dropped, but Filokalafi 'Akau'ola and Filini Sikuea were reportedly given 18- and 12-month prison terms, respectively. The sentences were suspended on good behaviour bonds.

In September, Filokalafi 'Akau'ola, who was still under the good behaviour bond, Kalafi Moala, editor of the *Times of Tonga*, and 'Akilisi Pohiva, were imprisoned by the Legislative Assembly for their role in peaceful public criticism of the Minister of Justice. The three had been charged by the Minister of Justice with "libelling the Legislative Assembly" following publication, in the *Times of Tonga* of 4 September, of an impeachment motion which accused the Minister of visiting the Olympic Games in Atlanta, USA, without parliament's authorization. The government claimed that the motion had not been formally submitted before publication, although the Secretary of the People's Representatives in parliament reportedly lodged the motion on 23 August. The Assembly, allegedly including the Minister of Justice, voted to pass the maximum sentence for the charge provided for in the Constitution – 30 days' imprisonment. In October, the Supreme Court ordered the early release of the three prisoners, stating that their detention resulted from an unfair trial in breach of the Constitution and the Rules of the House. However, the Court did not rescind their conviction, stating that only the Legislative Assembly could rule on whether there was a case of contempt to answer. The Legislative Assembly appealed to the Court of Appeal for examination of the Supreme Court's judgment, but no date for the hearing had been set by the of the year.

In November, police again detained 'Akilisi Pohiva and Filokalafi 'Akau'ola, and also detained Teisina Fuko, a member of the Legislative Assembly. They were questioned about newspaper articles criticizing the undemocratic nature of the system of government. Filokalafi 'Akau'ola was released the same day. Police threatened 'Akilisi Pohiva and Teisina Fuko with charges of sedition and defamation, but they were released after 24 hours following media reports of their detention. No formal charges had been laid against them by the end of the year.

In September, Amnesty International wrote to King Taufa 'Ahau Tupou IV, calling for the immediate and unconditional release of 'Akilisi Pohiva, Filokalafi 'Akau'ola and Kalafi Moala, whom it considered prisoners of conscience. In October, Amnesty International welcomed their release but expressed concern at the long-term issues raised by the government's moves to restrict the peaceful exercise of the right to freedom of expression guaranteed in Tonga's Constitution. In November, the organization expressed concern over the repeated detention of two of the men.

TRINIDAD AND TOBAGO

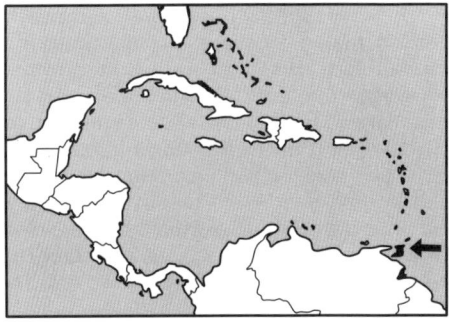

At least 36 people were sentenced to death and at least 116 prisoners remained under sentence of death. Five death warrants were signed, but no executions took place. At least nine people received sentences of flogging; these included the first woman sentenced to corporal punishment.

On 8 March, death warrants were issued for the execution of five prisoners. All five had been under sentence of death for longer than five years and should therefore have benefited from a 1993 ruling by the Judicial Committee of the Privy Council (JCPC) in London, the final court of appeal for Trinidad and Tobago, which states that any prisoner who has been under sentence of death for longer than five years has suffered "inhuman or degrading punishment or other treatment" and should have their death sentence commuted (see *Amnesty International Report 1994*). The executions were stayed by the Court of Appeals, and in June the death sentences of all five prisoners were commuted to 75 years' imprisonment with hard labour.

In May, in an attempt to expedite executions, the Attorney General announced that the government intended to seek a constitutional amendment to nullify the JCPC's ruling. The draft Constitutional (Amendment) Bill 1996 stated that neither the length of time a prisoner waits before execution nor the manner in which the execution is carried out can constitute cruel and unusual treatment or punishment. The Bill had not been presented to parliament by the end of the year.

At least nine people were sentenced to corporal punishment. Among them was Myra Bhagwansingh, a mother of four who was convicted of causing grievous bodily harm and sentenced in February to 12 years' imprisonment and 10 strokes with the cat-o'-nine-tails (a device consisting of nine knotted cords or thongs of rawhide attached to a handle). She was the first woman to receive a sentence of corporal punishment in Trinidad and Tobago. At the end of the year the conviction was under appeal and the flogging had not been carried out.

In March, Amnesty International appealed for clemency for the five prisoners facing execution. In June and October, the organization wrote to the government calling for the Constitutional (Amendment) Bill 1996 to be withdrawn and for no further limitations to be placed on the rights of those under sentence of death. In March, Amnesty International appealed for the sentence of corporal punishment imposed on Myra Bhagwansingh not to be carried out.

TUNISIA

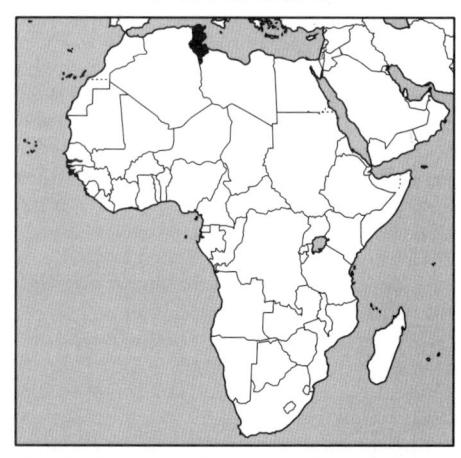

Hundreds of prisoners of conscience, including human rights defenders and people suspected of supporting unauthorized political opposition groups, were arrested. Up to 2,000 political prisoners, most of them prisoners of conscience, arrested in previous years remained imprisoned. Political trials fell short of international standards for fair trial. Torture and ill-treatment remained widespread, especially during *garde à vue* (incommunicado) detention, often in the Ministry of the Interior. Beatings and ill-treatment were increasingly reported in prisons.

Non-violent political opponents and critics of the government of President Zine el 'Abidine Ben 'Ali continued to be detained. Human rights defenders were increasingly targeted and further restrictions were imposed on the activities of local and international human rights organizations. In May, the President of the *Fédération internationale des droits de l'homme* (FIDH), International Federation of Human Rights, was expelled from Tunisia. Also in May, the European Parliament passed its first resolution expressing concern at the human rights situation in Tunisia.

In an unprecedented crack-down, several human rights defenders were detained and interrogated about their activities in Tunisia and abroad, and about their contacts with international human rights organizations. Khemais Chammari, member of parliament and Vice-President of the main legal opposition party, the *Mouvement des démocrates socialistes* (MDS), Movement of Socialist Democrats, also former Vice-President of the FIDH and former Secretary General of the *Ligue tunisienne des droits de l'homme* (LTDH), Tunisian League for Human Rights, was arrested in May. He was tried in July and sentenced to five years' imprisonment on charges of disclosing state secrets. He was accused of sending a Belgian lawyer information relating to the judicial investigation into the case of the MDS President, Mohamed Mou'adda, who was arrested in 1995 and sentenced in February 1996 to 11 years' imprisonment on charges including sharing intelligence with a foreign power (see *Amnesty International Report 1996*). Khemais Chammari and Mohamed Mou'adda were released by presidential decision in December. Five other prisoners of conscience benefited from the same measure and were released during the year.

A Tunisian staff member of the International Secretariat of Amnesty International was arrested in August, when he went to Tunisia on holiday. He was held for a week at the Ministry of the Interior and questioned about his work for the organization.

In October, Salah Zeghidi, Vice-President of the LTDH, was arrested on his return from Paris, France, where he and representatives of other human rights organizations, including Amnesty International and the FIDH, had participated in a public meeting on the human rights situation in Tunisia. He was interrogated about the meeting and was released the following day.

Hundreds more prisoners of conscience were detained on suspicion of supporting unauthorized political groups. Many were released after short-term detention and interrogation, but scores were sentenced to prison terms, including former prisoners who had already served prison sentences for similar charges. Most of them were accused of supporting the unauthorized Islamist group *al-Nahda*, and others of supporting the *Parti communiste des ouvriers tunisiens* (PCOT), Tunisian Workers' Communist Party, or the *Union de la jeunesse communiste*, Union of Communist Youth. Scores of wives and relatives of imprisoned and exiled supporters of *al-Nahda* were detained on suspicion of having received financial assistance or given such assistance to families of prisoners. Some were arrested in their homes and others were summoned to the Ministry of the Interior or to police and National Guard stations, and accused of unauthorized collection of funds.

In May, Salwa Dimassi and Ahlam Garat-Ali from Nabeul, mothers of three and five children respectively, were arrested with several other women on suspicion of links with Islamist groups. They remained detained without trial at the end of the year.

Bachir 'Abid, a student arrested in November 1995 and released on bail in March, was rearrested in May and detained for one month on suspicion of unauthorized political activity. Two other students who had been arrested with him the previous year, 'Ali Jallouli and 'Abdelmoumen Belanes, were released on bail in April (see *Amnesty International Report 1996*).

Tunisians living abroad were arrested and interrogated about their activities abroad when they returned to Tunisia. Some were imprisoned under a 1993 law which punishes activities outside Tunisia, including participation in peaceful meetings, demonstrations and criticism of the government (see *Amnesty International Report 1996*). 'Ali Hadfi, a Tunisian worker resident in Belgium and married to a Belgian national, was arrested in July when he visited Tunisia with his family. He was accused of supporting *al-Nahda*, and remained detained awaiting trial at the end of the year.

Prisoners of conscience were increasingly accused of supporting a "terrorist" or "criminal" organization (see *Amnesty International Reports 1994* and *1996*). Sou'ad Charbati, a mother of four from the Gabes region who was arrested in August 1995, was charged with supporting a "criminal" organization and sentenced to seven years' imprisonment in February. Bourhan Gasmi and Raja Chamekh were among seven students arrested in August on suspicion of activities on behalf of the PCOT and the *Union de la jeunesse communiste*. They were detained for up to a week on charges of belonging to a criminal association and were then released on bail. Bourhan Gasmi was sentenced to two years' imprisonment in October.

Former prisoners of conscience and relatives of imprisoned and exiled political opponents were increasingly detained for questioning. They were routinely required to report daily, and often two or even three times a day, to police stations, and prevented from leaving the country. After their release in January, 'Aicha Dhaouadi and Tourkia Hamadi (see *Amnesty International Report 1996*) were repeatedly questioned, required to report daily to police stations, and prevented from leaving the country.

Up to 2,000 political prisoners, most of them prisoners of conscience arrested in previous years, remained detained. 'Ali Ba'azaoui and 'Imed 'Ebdelli continued to serve their sentences. Sofiane Mourali and Hafedh Ben Gharbia (see *Amnesty International Report 1996*) were released by presidential pardon in May and were able to return to Germany. Mohamed Hedi Sassi and 'Adel Selmi were released in December.

Political trials continued to violate international standards for fair trials. The courts routinely failed to investigate allegations of torture and ill-treatment and accepted as evidence confessions retracted in court by the defendants, who stated that they had been forced to sign them under torture. Often the court convicted defendants even though no convincing evidence was produced to substantiate the charges.

Najib Hosni, a prominent human rights lawyer arrested in 1994, was sentenced to eight years' imprisonment in January 1996 on charges of forgery. There was no convincing evidence to substantiate the charges. He was also charged, in a separate trial, with possession of arms, but was acquitted in November. Amnesty International considers him a prisoner of conscience. No investigation was carried out into his complaint of torture the previous year (see *Amnesty International Report 1996*). He was released in December.

Amnesty International observers attended the trials of Mohamed Mou'adda, Khemais Chammari and Najib Hosni.

Torture and ill-treatment continued to be reported in the Ministry of the Interior and in police and National Guard stations. In May, Jalal al-'Ayachi was reportedly beaten and tortured in a police station in 'Ibn Khaldoun, Tunis. In September, a Swedish national of Algerian origin who had been visiting relatives was arrested at Tunis airport as he was leaving for Sweden. He was held for a week in the Ministry of the Interior in Tunis, where he was beaten and tortured. He was released without charge and went back to Sweden. A former prisoner of conscience, the wife of an Islamist refugee abroad and mother of four, was repeatedly detained and ill-treated throughout the year. She was usually released the same day, but on occasion she was held overnight. In July, she was reportedly undressed, sexually abused and told to divorce.

Beatings, denial of adequate medical care, and other forms of ill-treatment were increasingly reported in prisons. 'Ali al-'Asba'i, a 64-year-old man detained since February 1991 and sentenced to six years' imprisonment in August 1992 with 278 members and alleged supporters of *al-Nahda* (see *Amnesty International Report 1993*), was reportedly beaten and otherwise ill-treated in Bourj el-Roumi Prison and was denied the necessary medical care for a chronic eye infection. He was transferred to Mahdia Prison in August. Mohamed Hedi Sassi, released in December (see above), had reportedly been ill-treated in prison, especially at the beginning of the year.

No investigations were carried out into complaints of torture from previous years (see *Amnesty International Report 1996*).

In June, the Secretary General of Amnesty International visited Tunisia but was prevented from meeting prisoners of conscience. He conveyed the organization's serious human rights concerns to President Ben 'Ali in a meeting with presidential counsellors. In August, Amnesty International wrote to the President to protest at the detention of a Tunisian staff member of its International Secretariat, emphasizing that members of Amnesty International are not involved in research or campaigning on their own countries. In September, Amnesty International issued a joint open letter with the FIDH, Human Rights Watch, the Lawyers' Committee for Human Rights and *Reporters Sans Frontières* to President Ben 'Ali raising concerns regarding the human rights situation in Tunisia, and especially at the increasing targeting of human rights defenders. No response was received from the government.

TURKEY

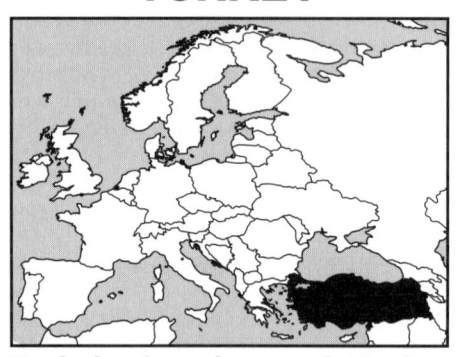

Hundreds of people were detained as prisoners of conscience. Most were released after short periods of detention, but others received prison sentences. Torture continued to be systematic and resulted in at least 25 deaths in custody. Twenty-three people reportedly "disappeared" in security force custody and scores of people were killed in the mainly Kurdish southeastern provinces in circumstances suggesting they had been extrajudicially executed by members of the security forces. For the 12th consecutive year, there were no judicial executions, although courts continued to pass death sentences and 14 people were sentenced to death during the year. Armed opposition groups were responsible for more than 40 deliberate and arbitrary killings of prisoners and other non-combatants.

State of emergency legislation was in force in 10 southeastern provinces, where the 12-year conflict between government forces and armed members of the Kurdish Workers' Party (PKK) claimed 2,500 lives during the year. In November, parliament lifted the state of emergency in Mardin province.

Trade unionists, students, and people suspected of supporting Kurdish separatism were frequently detained at peaceful public meetings or organizations' offices, and held for hours or days as prisoners of conscience. Most were released unconditionally or after being charged under various articles of the Turkish Penal Code (TPC). Article 8 of the Anti-Terror Law, which outlaws advocacy of separatism, continued to be used to prosecute and imprison people for peacefully expressing their opinions. Trials of 184 members of Turkey's literary and cultural elite for publishing a book, *Freedom of Thought*, continued at Istanbul State Security Court (SSC) under Article 8. The book republished texts which contained no advocacy of violence, but which had formed the basis of indictments against other authors who had been convicted by SSCs. New sentences were also handed down under Article 8. In September, Münir Ceylan, former President of Petrol-İş, the petroleum workers' trade union, was sentenced by Istanbul SSC to 16 months' imprisonment for an interview published in a monthly magazine. At the end of the year, Münir Ceylan was at liberty pending an appeal.

Prisoner of conscience İbrahim Aksoy, President of the banned Party for Democracy and Renewal and a former parliamentary deputy, remained in Ankara Central Closed Prison. In October 1995, he had begun serving 26 months in cumulative sentences received for his writings.

Articles 168, 169 and 312 of the TPC were used to prosecute writers, journalists and political activists who challenged the government's policies in the southeast. Human rights defenders were tried on manifestly fabricated charges of membership of, or support for, armed opposition groups. In May, Dr Seyfettin Kızılkan, President of Diyarbakır Medical Association, was arrested and charged with membership of the PKK, but it appeared that he had been imprisoned because of his statements on human rights to visiting foreign delegations. He was released in June, but his trial continued. In October,

Şanar Yurdatapan, spokesperson for *Barış İçin Biraraya* (BIBA), Together for Peace, an organization promoting reconciliation of the conflict in the southeast, was arrested and charged under Article 169 with supporting the PKK. The sole reason for Şanar Yurdatapan's imprisonment appeared to be his work to further peace and freedom of expression; he was a prisoner of conscience. He was released in November, but his trial continued.

Turkey does not recognize the right of conscientious objection to military service and there is no provision for alternative civilian service. Osman Murat Ülke, Chairperson of Izmir War Resisters' Association and a conscientious objector, was arrested in October on charges of alienating the people from military service, because he had burned his draft card. He was released in November at a hearing before the Military Court of General Staff in Ankara but was immediately taken under guard to a recruiting office where he was later arrested for "insubordination". He was temporarily released in December.

There were frequent, well-documented reports of torture by police and gendarmes (soldiers carrying out police duties in rural areas). The victims included those detained for common criminal offences as well as for offences under the Anti-Terror Law. Children and juveniles were among the victims. In January, 16 young people – seven of them teenage high-school students – reported that they had been blindfolded, stripped naked, hosed with cold water and subjected to electric shocks while held at Manisa Police Headquarters. Police officers reportedly raped the male detainees with truncheons and squeezed their testicles, while female detainees were compelled to undergo forced gynaecological tests and were threatened with rape and with being thrown from a window. Many of the allegations were corroborated by medical evidence. The youngest detainee, Mahir Göktaş, was 14 years old when detained. He said that police officers twisted his testicles and gave him electric shocks to his toe, sexual organs and stomach. On the basis of the torture allegations made by the young defendants, 10 police officers were brought to trial in June at Manisa Criminal Court. The trial continued at the end of the year.

Sevgi Kaya was 15 years old when she was detained with her elder brother in Istanbul in February. According to her account, during 12 days' detention at the Anti-Terror Branch of Istanbul Police Headquarters without access to her parents or a lawyer, she was beaten on her hands and feet, hosed with water, stripped and beaten in the presence of her brother. She was also suspended by the arms and told that she would be raped and killed. A medical report confirmed that Sevgi Kaya had injuries to her arms, traces of blows to her head, arms and legs, and bruising on her hands and feet. She was committed to prison on charges of membership of the Turkish Communist Labour Party/Leninist. She was released in November but her trial continued. No proceedings were known to have been taken against her alleged torturers.

At least eleven people died in custody apparently as a result of torture. Metin Göktepe, a photographer for the daily newspaper *Evrensel* (Universal), died in January after he had been detained by police while attempting to photograph the funeral of prisoners beaten to death in an Istanbul prison. Other detainees reported seeing Metin Göktepe being beaten by police officers at Eyüp Sports Centre, which was being used as a temporary interrogation centre, where Metin Göktepe's body was found one day later. An autopsy report confirmed that his death had been caused by severe beatings. During several days of official cover-up, the Istanbul Police Chief suggested that Metin Göktepe had died as a result of falling while trying to escape. In February, 11 police officers were indicted for murder, but prosecution of the Eyüp Police Chief for neglecting his duty and attempting to conceal a crime was blocked by the local Istanbul governor. The trial of the police officers continued at the end of the year.

In December, in its second public statement on Turkey, the European Committee for the Prevention of Torture and Inhuman or Degrading Treatment or Punishment described torture as "widespread ... a common occurrence" and reported that they had once again found instruments of torture. In 1992, they had found equipment in Diyarbakır and Ankara police headquarters (see *Amnesty International Report 1993*). When the Committee's delegates visited Istanbul police headquarters in September they found "an instrument adapted in a way which would facilitate the infliction of electric shocks and equipment which would facilitate the infliction of electric shocks and equipment which could be used to suspend a person by the arms".

In December, the European Court of Human Rights found that Turkish security forces were responsible for the torture of Zeki Aksoy in November 1992 (*Aksoy v Turkey*). He had been held in police custody for 14 days in Mardin, southeastern Turkey, where he was subjected to beatings, electric shocks, hosing with cold water and suspension by the arms. The Court ruled that this treatment amounted to torture, that the length of detention was excessive and that insufficient safeguards were provided. Zeki Aksoy was shot dead in April 1994 after complaining to his lawyer that he had been threatened with death unless he dropped his case. In September, the European Court of Human Rights found Turkish security forces guilty of burning houses in a village in southeastern Turkey, causing the Kurdish villagers to flee (*Akdivar v Turkey*).

There were further deaths in prison as a result of severe beatings administered when police and gendarmes were brought into prisons during unrest. In January, Orhan Özen, Rıza Boybaş and Abdülmecit Seçkin were beaten to death, and Gültekin Beyhan died later from head injuries, when police and gendarmes entered Ümraniye Special Type Prison to subdue a political prisoners' protest.

In September, 10 prisoners were beaten to death by gendarmes at Diyarbakır Prison. The circumstances, as outlined in a report prepared by the Diyarbakır Bar Association, strongly suggested that the killings were the consequence of a premeditated assault by security forces.

At least 23 people were reported to have "disappeared" while in the custody of police or soldiers. In April, Atilla Osmanoğlu "disappeared" after being abducted in Diyarbakır by two men, one of whom identified himself as a plainclothes police officer. The police authorities denied holding Atilla Osmanoğlu. In November, Fahriye Mordeniz and Mahmut Mordeniz "disappeared" after being detained in Diyarbakır. When relatives contacted a local police station they were informed that the couple had been detained by the Anti-Terror Branch. There has been no thorough and impartial investigation into the couple's "disappearance".

Scores of people were victims of political killings, many of which may have been extrajudicial executions. Abdullah Canan was reportedly seen being detained by the commander of Yüksekova Gendarmerie Headquarters and others at a check-point on the Hakkari-Van road in January. When his relatives appealed to the local gendarmerie, they denied that he was in custody. In February, Abdullah Canan's body was found bearing signs of gunshot wounds and torture. Abdullah Canan had reportedly received threats from local security forces because he had made a formal complaint about the forced evacuation and destruction of his village by gendarmes in November 1995.

Near the town of Güçlükonak in Şırnak province in January, 11 villagers were machine-gunned and the minibus in which they were travelling was set on fire. Seven of those killed were members of the government-appointed village guard corps. The authorities announced that the PKK were responsible for the killings. The Chief of General Staff flew journalists from all the major newspapers and broadcasting organizations to the site, and the Prime Minister condemned the PKK for the massacre. However, a broad-based delegation organized by BIBA spokesperson Şanar Yurdatapan found evidence that the villagers had been killed by the security forces, apparently in an attempt to discredit a unilateral cease-fire declared by the PKK in December 1995. Shortly before the killings in Güçlükonak, the European Parliament had passed a resolution encouraging the Turkish Government to respond to the PKK's cease-fire.

The forcible return to their country of origin of recognized refugees and asylum-seekers, including Iraqi and Iranian nationals, continued throughout the year. Amnesty International expressed grave concern to the government about these *refoulements* on several occasions. No response was received.

Armed members of the PKK were responsible for more than 40 deliberate and arbitrary killings. The victims included civilians, as well as captured soldiers and village guards. In May, Abdullah Ay and Masallah Lale were killed in Adana, allegedly by members of the PKK, on the grounds that they were "agents of the state". The Revolutionary People's Liberation Party-Front (DHKP-C) was also responsible for deliberate and arbitrary killings. In January, the DHKP-C carried out what they described as a "revenge" killing in retaliation for the deaths at Ümraniye Prison. DHKP-C members killed Özdemir Sabancı, a member of the family which owns the Sabancı industrial conglomerate, Haluk Görgün, a director, and Nilgün Hasef, a secretary. The three victims were in no way connected with the events at Ümraniye Prison.

The PKK, the DHKP-C and other armed organizations used the threat of murder as a form of party discipline. In August, Emine Yavuz was reportedly strangled by fellow PKK defendants in Diyarbakır Prison on the grounds that she was "an informer". In October, Fatma Özyurt, serving a prison sentence for alleged DHKP-C links, was reportedly killed by cellmates in Ankara Central Closed Prison on the grounds that she had "cooperated with the police". Ramız Şişman, serving a life sentence for membership of the Turkish Workers and Peasants' Liberation Army (TIKKO), was stabbed to death by cellmates in what appeared to be a "punishment" killing carried out on TIKKO party orders.

Amnesty International condemned these grave abuses and publicly called on armed opposition groups to instruct their members to respect humanitarian law and international human rights standards.

Throughout the year Amnesty International appealed for the release of prisoners of conscience and urged the government to initiate thorough, prompt and impartial investigations into allegations of torture, extrajudicial executions and "disappearances". Two Amnesty International researchers continued to be excluded from Turkey. In January, an Amnesty International delegate observed a hearing at Ankara SSC in the trial of Turkish Human Rights Foundation (TIHV) officials accused of insulting state institutions. They were subsequently acquitted. In May, Amnesty International delegates observed the trial on criminal charges of two doctors from the TIHV's Adana Treatment Centre for Torture Survivors. The authorities apparently improvised the charges to obstruct the functioning of the treatment centre. The trial continued at the end of the year. In June, Amnesty International delegates observed a hearing in the trial of Dr Seyfettin Kızılkan at Diyarbakır SSC. He was released but his trial continued. In October, an Amnesty International delegate observed the trial of the schoolchildren reportedly tortured at Manisa Police Headquarters. The children were released, but other defendants remained in custody, and the trial continued.

In October, 25 Amnesty International delegates from around the world, including relatives of victims of "disappearance" in Argentina, Bosnia-Herzegovina and Lebanon, participated in a vigil in Istanbul with relatives of Turkey's "disappeared".

Amnesty International published a number of reports, including *Turkey: Further information on continuing human rights abuses*, in February; *Turkey: No security without human rights*, in October; and *Turkey: Children at risk of torture, death in custody and "disappearance"*, in November.

TURKMENISTAN

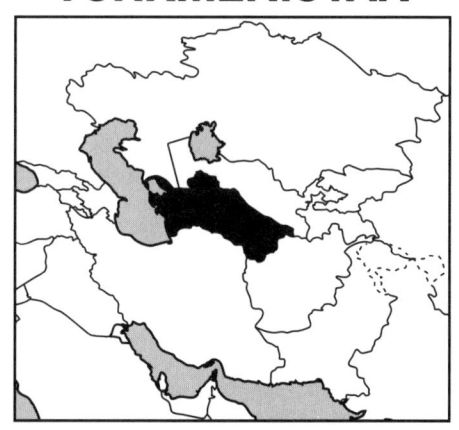

One prisoner of conscience convicted of privately criticizing the President was detained for three months. At least two possible prisoners of conscience who had been convicted of anti-state crimes were held throughout the year, and three other possible prisoners of conscience were held during the year in psychiatric hospitals on political rather than medical grounds. Two other possible prisoners of conscience were released. Anti-government demonstrators reportedly detained for short periods were at risk of ill-treatment; they included possible prisoners of conscience. Appalling prison conditions amounting to ill-treatment were reported.

The death penalty remained in force. At least 123 executions were reported.

Kakabay Aymamedov, a senior police officer, was arrested and put on trial in February after complaining about President Saparmurad Niyazov during a private conversation with two associates, one of whom apparently reported the conversation to the authorities. He was found guilty of "hooliganism" and was sentenced to four and a half years' imprisonment. He was a prisoner of conscience. He was released in May, reportedly as a result of a presidential pardon.

Possible prisoners of conscience Mukhamed Muradly and Yovshan Annakurban, who had been convicted of hooliganism in December 1995 in connection with an earlier anti-government demonstration (see *Amnesty International Report 1996*), were released under an amnesty in January with 18 of their co-defendants. The fate of seven other co-defendants who did not apparently benefit from the amnesty was unclear, and in the absence of a complete list of the defendants and any official information about them the fate of two other possible prisoners of conscience convicted in connection with the demonstration and previously identified as brothers Azhdar and Alamurad Amanmuradov (see *Amnesty International Report 1996*) could not be confirmed.

Mukhametkuli Aymuradov and Khoshali Garayev, possible prisoners of conscience serving long prison sentences for crimes including activities aimed at overthrowing the constitutional order and preparing terrorist acts (see *Amnesty International Report 1996*), remained in detention throughout the year. Mukhametkuli Aymuradov was reported to be in very poor health as a consequence of ill-treatment by law enforcement officials following an attempt in 1995 to escape from pre-trial detention.

Information emerged that possible prisoners of conscience Bayram Vellekov and Yevgenia Starikova (given as Yevgeny Starikov in *Amnesty International Report 1996*), who had been tried with Khoshali Garayev and Mukhametkuli Aymuradov and each sentenced to two years' imprisonment for "concealing a crime" in connection with Mukhametkuli Aymuradov's escape attempt, had been released under an amnesty in December 1995.

Rufina Arabova, who had a history of peaceful protest over violation of her employment rights, was reportedly confined to a psychiatric hospital in Ashgabat, the capital, from January to July. It was alleged that she was confined not on the basis of medical need, but because her protests were regarded by the authorities as an expression of political opposition. Similarly, in February, Durdymurad Khodzha-Mukhammed, co-chairman of the unregistered opposition Party of Democratic Development, was reported to have been confined to a psychiatric hospital for political reasons. He was believed to be still confined at the end of the year. Valentin Kopysov, a possible prisoner of conscience, who had reportedly been confined to a psychiatric hospital for political reasons since early 1994 (see *Amnesty International Report 1995*), was reported in late 1996 to no longer be confined, but the date and circumstances of his release were unclear.

In February and March, participants in anti-government demonstrations in various parts of the country against food shortages, wage arrears and house demolitions, were reportedly detained for short periods. There were fears that such detainees might be at risk of ill-treatment, in the light of previously reported cases of ill-treatment of anti-government protesters. Two of the three demonstrations which were reported to have taken place were described as having been entirely peaceful, and some of those detained may have been prisoners of conscience.

Appalling conditions in Turkmenistan's prisons amounting to ill-treatment were reported. In August, at least two prisoners were killed and seven wounded when law enforcement personnel put down a riot at a prison in the city of Mary. Atrocious living conditions at the prison were believed to have been among the factors which provoked the riot.

The death penalty remained in force. No official statistics for use of this punishment were published, but there were reports that 123 executions took place during the year solely for the offence of drug-trafficking. Given Turkmenistan's record of executing people for other offences, such as murder, it was feared that the total number of executions was even higher.

Amnesty International called for the immediate and unconditional release of

Kakabay Aymamedov. It continued to call for a judicial review of the case of Mukhametkuli Aymuradov and Khoshali Garayev, and sought further information about the detention of Valentin Kopysov, Rufina Arabova and Durdymurad Khodzha-Mukhammed. The organization raised concerns about the conduct of law enforcement officials towards participants in anti-government demonstrations.

Amnesty International called on Turkmenistan to comply with international standards for the treatment of prisoners. It continued to call for complete abolition of the death penalty.

In March, Amnesty International published *Turkmenistan: "Measures of persuasion" – recent concerns about possible prisoners of conscience and ill-treatment of political opponents*.

UGANDA

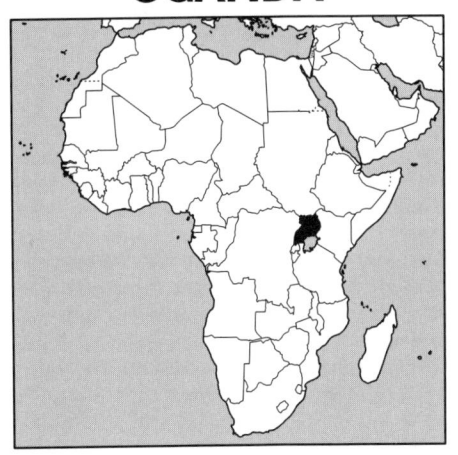

At least 17 prisoners of conscience were briefly held. Hundreds of people were detained without charge or trial and thousands were detained for several hours. Police, soldiers and a government militia were responsible for widespread torture and ill-treatment, in at least three cases resulting in death. Prison conditions amounted to cruel, inhuman and degrading treatment, and resulted in at least three deaths. Courts continued to impose sentences of caning. Police and soldiers carried out extrajudicial executions. At least 996 prisoners were under sentence of death at the end of the year, including at least 30 sentenced during the year, and three men were executed. Armed opposition groups were responsible for gross human rights abuses, including hundreds of deliberate and arbitrary killings and rape.

Continuing armed conflict between the Uganda People's Defence Forces (UPDF) and armed opposition groups displaced over 200,000 people. In the north, military activity by the Lord's Resistance Army (LRA) intensified in February after the group crossed into Uganda from bases in Sudan. In the northwest, the West Nile Bank Front (WNBF) attacked Uganda from Zaire and Sudan.

President Yoweri Museveni was re-elected in May and parliamentary elections were held in June.

At least 17 political activists briefly held at the time of the elections and during a traders' strike in October were prisoners of conscience. In May, Nsubuga Nsambu, a member of the Conservative Party, was held for two days and charged with sedition after insulting President Yoweri Museveni. Charges were dropped in September.

Hundreds of prisoners were detained without charge or trial and thousands of others were detained for several hours. In August and September, thousands of people were held for several hours and 240 detained for longer periods in the northern town of Gulu following army operations to "screen" suspected LRA rebels. In late August, more than 190 men were freed, but in September, 52 reportedly remained in detention without charge or trial in Gulu. Scores of men were detained for alleged involvement with the WNBF.

Dozens of other detainees had been arrested in previous years, among them 15 civilians and soldiers held for over two years in Lubiri barracks.

At least 39 suspected members of the WNBF were charged with treason after several months in illegal detention. In the past, treason charges – which preclude the granting of bail for 360 days – have been used to hold suspected government opponents for long periods without trial. At least 29 other men were charged with treason during the year. Over 150 men charged with treason in previous years remained in custody awaiting trial.

Police, soldiers and Local Defence Unit personnel were responsible for torture and ill-treatment. George Kaweesa, detained in Lubiri barracks, was reported to have died in January after being beaten by UPDF soldiers. In August, police in Tororo beat 71 prisoners, two of whom later died in custody.

Overcrowding and poor conditions amounting to cruel, inhuman or degrading treatment were reported in prisons throughout the country. In January, Local Administration prisons were taken over by the central prison authorities after repeated reports of torture, malnutrition and serious overcrowding. Three men died in a Local Administration Prison at Kangulumira in March as a result of the poor conditions in which they were held.

Courts continued to impose sentences of caning – a cruel, inhuman or degrading punishment; at least three men were caned following convictions for attempted sexual acts with children.

Police and soldiers were responsible for extrajudicial executions in northern Uganda. In August, UPDF officers in Gulu town threw four alleged LRA members to a waiting crowd, who killed them. Journalists and human rights activists based in northern Uganda received death threats both from UPDF soldiers and the armed opposition LRA.

At least 30 men were sentenced to death. In March, three men sentenced to death in previous years for murder were hanged. In August, prison officials reported that 996 prisoners were awaiting execution.

Armed opposition groups were responsible for gross human rights abuses. The LRA carried out hundreds of deliberate and arbitrary killings of civilians, including refugees. Over 110 Sudanese refugees were shot or hacked to death in July in an attack on Achol Pii camp and in August more than 60 civilians accused by the LRA of being informers were killed in Kilak.

Hundreds of people, in particular children, were abducted. Prisoners caught attempting to escape were tortured or killed. Captives were used as forced labour; boys were forcibly conscripted into the LRA and girls were raped.

The WNBF was responsible for deliberate and arbitrary killings in the northwest. Six Sudanese refugees were reported to have been beheaded in April in an attack on Koboko camp.

Amnesty International called on the President to commute all death sentences. In October, the organization called for a judicial inquiry into extrajudicial executions in Gulu and for journalists and human rights activists to be allowed to work without intimidation. In November, in a submission to a parliamentary commission of inquiry into the northern war, Amnesty International called for an end to detention without charge or trial. In July, Amnesty International condemned deliberate and arbitrary killings by the LRA and WNBF, and in October called on the LRA to free all captives.

UKRAINE

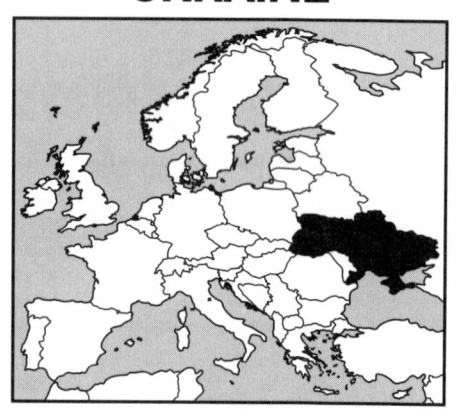

Executions continued despite the country's commitment to institute a moratorium. During the year, 167 death sentences were passed, 167 people were executed and two death-row prisoners were granted clemency. There were reports of ill-treatment and torture, including rape, in detention. One prisoner was allegedly tortured to death.

In June, the parliament approved Ukraine's first Constitution since returning to independence in August 1991, ending a long constitutional debate between the parliament, President Leonid Kuchma and the Communist Party. The new Constitution gives the Supreme Soviet of Crimea the right to adopt its own constitution, subject to approval by the Ukrainian parliament.

In May, official statistics issued by the Ministry of Justice showed that 112 people had been sentenced to death in 1991, 79 in 1992, 117 in 1993, 143 in 1994, and 191 in 1995. There had been 42 executions in 1991, 103 in 1992, 78 in 1993, 60 in 1994, and 149 in 1995. Two prisoners had their death sentence commuted in 1994, and one in 1995. This was the first time that Ukraine had published statistics on the use of the death penalty since its accession to the Council of Europe in November 1995.

Official statistics released by the Ministry of Justice stated that 167 death sentences were passed during 1996 and 167 prisoners were executed, some of whom had been sentenced to death in previous years. Two death-row prisoners were granted clemency by the President. On 28 June, the Parliamentary Assembly of the Council of Europe adopted a resolution on the abolition of the death penalty in Europe, in which it condemned Ukraine for violating its commitment to introduce a moratorium on executions and warned that further violation of its commitments would result in suspension of membership. In November, the Council of Europe revealed that over 100 people had been executed since the beginning of the year. The Council's rapporteur, speaking at an international seminar on the death penalty held in Ukraine, described the executions as "barbarism" and questioned the credibility of Ukraine's commitment to honour its international obligations. He also called on the authorities to disclose the names of those executed, which are considered a state secret.

Among those known to have been executed during the year were Yury Strukhov, Vladimir Ogoltsov, Aleksey Vedinedenko and Sergey Tekuchev, who was executed on 17 October. His parents were not informed about his death until 13 November.

Torture and ill-treatment in detention were reported and in at least one case may have resulted in death. Yury Mozola died in March, four days after his arrest, in the investigation isolation prison of the Lviv regional Security Services, where he had been detained on suspicion of multiple murder. He was allegedly tortured to death by law enforcement officials during interrogation. An investigation into Yury Mozola's death was opened by the office of the Military Procurator of Western Ukraine, but its conclusions were not known by the end of the year.

Also in March, a Roma woman, Eva H., was reportedly beaten and raped by two police officers in a street in Mukachevo in the Transcarpathian region of Ukraine. She was subsequently taken to hospital; she claimed that she was visited there by police officers who offered her money to stop mentioning the incident publicly, which she refused. Mukachevo's deputy head of the police department reportedly stated that the officers involved had been disciplined. Other sources, however, contradict this.

Amnesty International urged the President to grant clemency to all death-row prisoners and to institute a moratorium on executions. In March, Amnesty International received a communication from the Ukrainian Embassy in Canada, which stated: "On the national level neither official legislation was approved to abolish death penalty, nor moratorium on executions was imposed. Therefore, all accusations that Ukraine has violated its international obligations shall be deemed ungrounded and void."

Amnesty International urged the authorities to initiate prompt and impartial investigations into allegations of torture and ill-treatment in detention and police custody.

UNITED ARAB EMIRATES

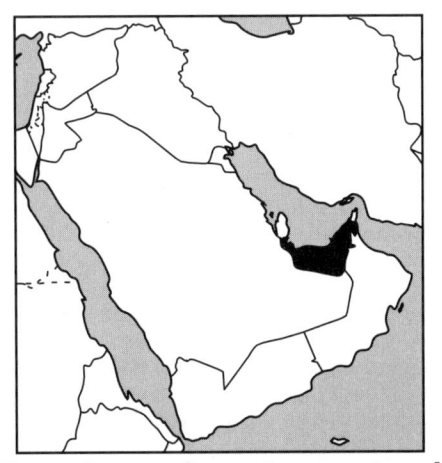

One prisoner of conscience sentenced during the year remained held beyond expiry of sentence. At least three possible prisoners of conscience were detained during the year. Torture and ill-treatment of detainees in police custody continued. At least three people were sentenced to flogging and a woman sentenced in 1995 was flogged. One person was executed and two others were believed to remain under sentence of death. At least nine Bahraini nationals were forcibly returned to Bahrain, where most were detained as possible prisoners of conscience.

One prisoner of conscience sentenced during the year remained held beyond expiry of his sentence. Elie Dib Ghalib, a Lebanese Christian, arrested in al-'Ain in Abu Dhabi in December 1995 and allegedly tortured (see below), was sentenced in October to one year's imprisonment and 39 lashes when a *Shari'a* court ruled that his marriage to a Muslim United Arab Emirates national was null and void and his relationship therefore a criminal offence under the country's law. He remained in detention in al-'Ain Central Prison although he had completed his sentence.

At least three possible prisoners of conscience were detained during the year. Two brothers, Jassim and Yassir 'Issa al-Yassi, and Ahmad 'Abdullah Makki were arrested in June in Dubai because of their relationship with Ja'far Hassan Sahwan (see below), a political opposition activist from Bahrain who had escaped to the United Arab Emirates to avoid arrest; they remained in detention without trial and possibly without charge at the end of the year. Two other possible prisoners of conscience detained in 1995 were released without charge. Sheikh 'Abd al-Mun'im al-'Ali, an Iraqi national arrested in January 1995 (see *Amnesty International Report 1996*), was released in November and deported to a third country. Hisham Fa'iq Muhammad Sha'sha', a Palestinian refugee under the protection of the UN High Commissioner for Refugees in the United Arab Emirates who had been held untried since September 1995 as a suspected government opponent, was expelled to Romania in May.

Torture and ill-treatment of political and other detainees in police custody continued. Elie Dib Ghalib (see above) was allegedly beaten and flogged repeatedly during pre-trial detention.

During the year, at least three people, including Elie Dib Ghalib, were sentenced to flogging and another, sentenced in 1995, was flogged. In June, a married couple were each sentenced to 210 lashes for theft. It was not known by the end of the year if the sentence had been carried out. Sarah Balabagan, sentenced to 100 lashes in October 1995, was flogged in January (see *Amnesty International Report 1996*). She was released in July and deported to the Philippines.

One person was executed and two others were believed to remain under sentence of death. Khalid Mohammad Moussaji, sentenced to death for murder, was executed in October. It remained unclear whether the death sentence on Mashal Badr al-Hamati, a Yemeni national, had been commuted by President Al-Sheikh Zayed bin Sultan Al-Nahyan (see previous *Amnesty International Reports*). In December, the Federal Supreme Court reportedly announced that it would uphold the death sentence on John Aquino, a Philippine national, unless he receives clemency from the family of the victim whom he was convicted of murdering in 1989 (see *Amnesty International Report 1996*).

At least nine Bahraini nationals, all possible asylum-seekers, were forcibly returned to Bahrain, where most of them were detained upon arrival as possible prisoners of conscience (see **Bahrain** entry). They included Ja'far Hassan Sahwan (see above), who was arrested in Dubai in June and handed over to the authorities in Bahrain. He remained in detention in Bahrain at the end of the year as a possible prisoner of conscience.

Amnesty International appealed for the release of detainees held for political or religious reasons if they were not charged with recognizably criminal offences and given fair trials. The organization sought assurances that those detained were being treated humanely and called for investigations into all allegations of torture and ill-treatment. It appealed for commutation of all death sentences and sentences of flogging. The government did not respond to Amnesty International's communications, or to its request to visit the country to investigate human rights violations.

UNITED KINGDOM

A few deaths in custody took place in disputed circumstances. No prosecutions were brought against police or prison officers in connection with deaths in custody which occurred in previous years, including in two cases where inquest juries

brought in verdicts of unlawful killings. There were allegations of ill-treatment in police custody and in prisons. The European Court of Human Rights established the primacy of the prohibition of torture in a deportation case. The summer "parade" season in Northern Ireland was marked by many human rights violations by the police. Armed opposition groups were responsible for human rights abuses.

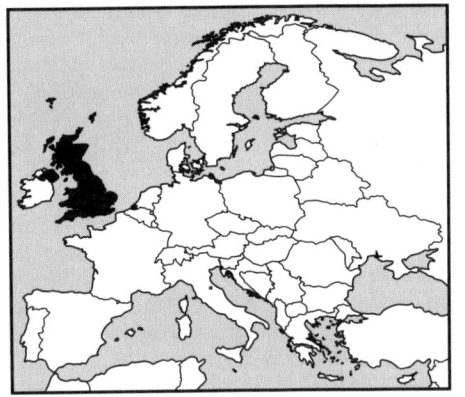

The cessation of military activities called by the Irish Republican Army (IRA) in September 1994 ended in February with a bomb attack in London. The Irish Continuity Army claimed responsibility for several bombings and attempted bombings in Northern Ireland. Loyalist armed groups, including the Ulster Defence Association (UDA) and the Ulster Volunteer Force (UVF), officially maintained their cessation of military activities. An internal feud within the Irish National Liberation Army led to six deaths, including that of nine-year-old Barbara McAlorum, before one of the two factions, the GHQ Staff, disbanded itself in September.

In July, the Asylum and Immigration Act 1996 became law, extending the "fast track" appeal procedures introduced in previous legislation to a broad range of asylum cases, including those where the applicant is from a country on a "white list", a list of countries where the authorities consider there to be no serious risk of persecution. Appeal rights in the majority of "safe third country" cases were effectively abolished. The Act also provided for the withdrawal of welfare benefits to the majority of asylum-seekers. This latter provision was legally challenged on several occasions.

In March the UN Committee on the Elimination of All Forms of Racial Discrimination expressed concerns, during its examination of the United Kingdom's Thirteenth Periodic Report, that a disproportionate number of members of minority groups were the victims of deaths in custody and ill-treatment.

There were a few deaths in custody in disputed circumstances during the year. Ibrahima Sey, a Gambian asylum-seeker, died on 16 March shortly after being restrained by police officers; he was sprayed with CS gas after being handcuffed. The introduction of CS gas as standard police equipment was approved in August, despite concern about its effects. Other deaths in custody being investigated by the police included those of Ziya Mustafa Birikim, Oscar Okoye, Ahmed El-Gammel and Bosey Davis.

In Northern Ireland, 36-year-old Jim McDonnell died, allegedly from a heart attack, after being forcibly restrained in Maghaberry Prison in March.

No prosecutions were brought against officers involved in the deaths of Brian Douglas or Wayne Douglas (see *Amnesty International Report 1996*). The inquest into the death of Brian Douglas ruled in August that he had died of "misadventure": the officers' conduct was lawful but events took a turn that led to death. The jury was told that Brian Douglas suffered six hairline fractures to the skull, consistent with his having been hit with a baton. In November, the inquest into the death of Wayne Douglas was told by eye-witnesses that a police officer knelt on Wayne Douglas' head while he was handcuffed and held face down on the ground by at least four other officers. The jury found that his death was accidentally caused by stress, exhaustion and positional asphyxia.

A police officer charged with a disciplinary offence in relation to the death of Joy Gardner during an attempted deportation was acquitted in January (see *Amnesty International Report 1996*). Another officer was acquitted in December on a charge of actual bodily harm in connection with the death of Gary Allsopp (see *Amnesty International Report 1996*).

No prosecutions were brought against police officers involved in the deaths of Richard O'Brien and Shiji Lapite, despite inquest jury verdicts of unlawful killing (see *Amnesty International Report 1996*). The January inquest was told that Shiji Lapite had sustained 36 to 45 separate injuries; he had been kicked and bitten, and died from a fractured cartilage in his voice-box caused by the neck-hold used by the officers in restraining him.

People held in police custody were allegedly ill-treated. In February, student Amer Rafiq was arrested in Manchester for public disorder and taken in a police van to the local police station. After his arrival he was taken to hospital because of his injuries; subsequent attempts to save his right eye failed. No prosecutions were brought against the officers involved in the arrest. In other cases, damages were awarded against the Metropolitan (London) Police for assault and other charges, including £220,000 for Kenneth Hsu; £302,000 for Danny Goswell; and £110,000 for Janet Scafe.

Category A prisoners (prisoners regarded as a high security risk) were held in conditions which led to serious deterioration in their physical and mental health. Róisín McAliskey, who was four months pregnant, was temporarily detained in a filthy cell in the special security unit of an all-male prison. She and other prisoners, including Patrick Kelly, who was suffering from cancer, received inadequate medical treatment.

Royal Ulster Constabulary conduct during the "parade" season of July and August in Northern Ireland led to claims of human rights violations by the police, including ill-treatment and beatings of peaceful protesters. Claims were also made of biased policing; evidence supporting the claims included the disproportionately high number of plastic bullets fired at Catholic crowds. Police investigated the death of Denis McShane who was run over by a police vehicle.

In September, Diarmuid O'Neill, an IRA member, was shot dead in disputed circumstances by police officers in London. Initial statements that he was killed during a shoot-out proved false, as he was unarmed. Questions were also raised about why Diarmuid O'Neill had been shot after CS gas had been sprayed into his room and what effect the gas might have had on his subsequent behaviour.

Inquests in Northern Ireland into disputed killings in previous years continued to be postponed due to legal challenges to the procedures. In June, the Court of Appeal upheld a coroner's decision, in the hearing into the death of Pearse Jordan (see *Amnesty International Reports 1993* and *1996*), to allow police officers to give evidence anonymously and to deny the family's lawyer access to witness statements at the outset of the inquest. This judicial decision was appealed against and other inquests into disputed killings were adjourned pending the outcome. The June inquest into the death of Patrick Shanaghan in 1991 was unable to investigate allegations that he had been killed as a result of collusion between the UDA and the security forces.

In February, the European Court of Human Rights ruled that the denial to John Murray of legal assistance while being interrogated under emergency legislation provisions in Northern Ireland violated his right to a fair trial. The Court also found that, in this particular case, his right of silence had not been violated (see *Amnesty International Reports 1995* and *1996*). The review of all emergency legislation in the United Kingdom, carried out by Lord Lloyd, was published in October. He recommended discontinuing some provisions, although this was premised on a situation of peace.

A 10-week trial began in October of four Palestinians charged in connection with the July 1994 bombings in London of the Israeli Embassy and a Jewish centre. Two defendants were acquitted, but Samar Alami and Jawad Botmeh were convicted of conspiracy to cause explosions and sentenced to 20 years' imprisonment each. The pre-trial investigation gave rise to concerns that the charges may have been politically motivated.

In Northern Ireland, some prisoners challenged the evidential basis for their convictions in the "Diplock Courts", leading to the acquittal of Stephen Larkin on a charge of murder in a retrial in May, and the quashing of the murder conviction of Colin Duffy by the Court of Appeal in September.

The European Court of Human Rights ruled in November that the government's attempt to deport Karamjit Singh Chahal to India was in violation of the European Convention for the Protection of Human Rights and Fundamental Freedoms. He had been detained pending deportation on "national security" grounds since 1990 (see *Amnesty International Reports 1992, 1995* and *1996*). The Court stated that the prohibition of torture was paramount and that allegations of national security risk were immaterial to a determination of whether a person faced "a real risk" of torture if returned. The Court further ruled that the hearing before an advisory panel of three people did not satisfy the right under the Convention to have one's detention scrutinized by a judicial authority, and that his detention had therefore been unlawful. Karamjit Singh Chahal was released on the day of the judgment. Subsequently, other people detained under the same provisions were released, including Sezai Ucar and Raghbir Singh.

Armed opposition groups committed human rights abuses. In February, a car bomb exploded in Docklands in London, killing two people; the IRA claimed responsibility for the attack. During that month another bomb exploded accidentally on a London bus, killing an IRA member and injuring eight people. In June, another IRA bomb destroyed a shopping centre in Manchester, injuring over 200 civilians. The IRA also claimed responsibility for two car bombs which exploded in Thiepval British Army Barracks in Lisburn, Northern Ireland, killing one soldier and injuring 30 others, including an eight-year-old girl.

There were several deliberate and arbitrary killings in Northern Ireland, including that of John Molloy, for which no organization claimed responsibility but which may have been carried out by Loyalists for sectarian reasons. In addition, Michael McGoldrick, a Catholic, was shot dead in his taxi in July, allegedly by the UVF. In December, a booby-trap exploded under a car, injuring a well-known Republican, Edward Copeland.

"Punishment" beatings and shootings continued. According to police figures, Republican armed groups were responsible for three shootings and 172 beatings, and Loyalist armed groups carried out 21 shootings and 130 beatings. It was more difficult than in previous years to ascertain which paramilitary groups were responsible for which actions, because such groups were less willing to claim responsibility.

The "punishment" shootings included the shooting of a young man in both legs in March by an organization called Loyalists against Thuggery. Tommy Sheppard was shot dead in March, allegedly by Loyalist paramilitaries, and Thomas Stewart, a UVF leader, was shot dead by Loyalists in October. The Republican organization Direct Action Against Drugs shot dead Ian Lyons in January, and Sean Devlin in October.

George Scott was beaten to death in September by masked men wielding baseball bats. Martin Doherty was bound, gagged and sustained puncture wounds and broken limbs when metal spikes were driven through his knees and elbows by Republican attackers. Republican attackers also tied people upside down to railings and beat them; among the victims was a 16-year-old boy. A woman was punched in the face and had a tin of paint thrown over her.

Amnesty International sent representatives to inquests into the deaths in custody of Shiji Lapite and Brian Douglas. The organization urged the authorities to carry out independent investigations into disputed cases, including the deaths of Ibrahima Sey and Diarmuid O'Neill.

Amnesty International urged the authorities to carry out a full and independent inquiry into the alleged ill-treatment of Amer Rafiq. The organization also wrote to government and prison authorities on several occasions concerning the treatment of prisoners.

In January, Amnesty International submitted written comments to the European Court of Human Rights in the case of Karamjit Singh Chahal. In February, Amnesty International published *United Kingdom: Wrongful detention of asylum-seeker Raghbir Singh*, which emphasized that the procedures for detaining and deporting people on national security grounds contravened international standards.

Amnesty International sent observers to trial proceedings in London and Belfast. The organization continued to urge the authorities to review the life sentences of Patrick Kane, Sean Kelly and Michael Timmons (see *Amnesty International Reports 1994* to *1996*).

In November, Amnesty International wrote to the Northern Ireland Secretary of State about a number of issues, including the events surrounding the summer parades, access to legal advice for suspects arrested under emergency legislation, inquests and the death in custody of Jim McDonnell.

Amnesty International expressed concern to the government about provisions in the Asylum and Immigration Act 1996. The organization opposed the withdrawal of welfare benefits from asylum-seekers because it could deny applicants access to asylum procedures, including a meaningful right of appeal.

Amnesty International continued to express concern about reports of human rights abuses by armed opposition groups.

UNITED STATES OF AMERICA

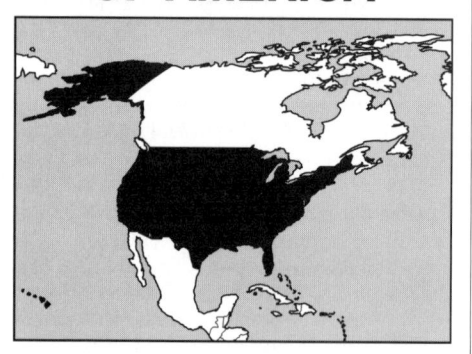

A total of 45 prisoners were executed in 19 states. One state carried out its first execution for more than 30 years. More than 3,150 prisoners were under sentence of death in 34 states and under federal law. There were reports of deaths in custody, police shootings in disputed circumstances, and torture and ill-treatment of prisoners. Chain-gangs, which constitute cruel, inhuman or degrading treatment, continued to be used and were introduced for women for the first time. There were legal developments in the cases of prisoners who had alleged that their prosecutions were politically motivated.

In November, Bill Clinton, the Democratic Party candidate, was re-elected President.

In April, President Clinton signed the Anti-Terrorism and Effective Death Penalty Act into law. The Act placed a limit on the number of *habeas corpus* appeals which death-row inmates could submit to federal courts, and set a time limit for filing appeals on behalf of death-row inmates.

The death penalty continued to be used extensively. In all, 45 prisoners were executed in 19 states, bringing the total number of executions since 1977 to 358. In Texas, most executions were stayed while the Court of Criminal Appeals considered whether a new law designed to shorten the time-frame for appeals in the state was constitutional. The Court upheld the law as constitutional at the end of the year.

Douglas Wright was executed in September. He was the first person to be executed in Oregon since 1962. He had chosen to drop his legal appeals.

In July, four men, two of whom had been sentenced to death, were released in Illinois after they were proved innocent. One of them, Verneal Jimerson, had had his 1978 conviction and death sentence overturned previously on appeal, after the only witness connecting him to the murder withdrew her testimony. However, in 1984, the same witness – in a deal with the prosecution to gain a reduction in her own a prison sentence – had changed her testimony again, and Verneal Jimerson was re-arrested, tried and sentenced to death for a second time. He was finally released on the basis of new forensic evidence which showed that he could not have committed the crime.

In January, Governor Jim Edgar of Illinois commuted the death sentence of Guinevere García to life imprisonment the day before her execution was scheduled to take place. Guinevere García, who was convicted of killing her estranged husband, had chosen to abandon her legal appeals and allow the state to carry out her execution. The Governor cited that this was "not the kind of case that typically results in a death sentence in Illinois" when granting clemency. In May, the Governor of Idaho granted clemency to Don Paradis, and in November the Governor of Virginia granted clemency to Joseph Payne. Both governors cited doubts concerning the guilt of the condemned men and commuted their sentences to life imprisonment without the possibility of parole.

Cases of deaths in custody, police shootings in disputed circumstances, and police ill-treatment continued to be reported. Victims included Frank Arzuega, an unarmed 15-year-old Puerto Rican, who was shot dead in January by an officer from the New York City Police Department (NYPD) while sitting in the back seat of a suspected stolen car; Hong Il Kim, a Korean man who died in February after being shot several times by four California police officers at the end of a car chase; and

Aswan Watson, an unarmed black man who died after being shot 18 times by NYPD officers while sitting in a parked car in June. In April, a police video showed two sheriff's deputies from the Riverside County Sheriff's Department, California, beating Mexican immigrants Leticia González and Enrique Funez-Flores after a car chase.

No officers were charged in connection with the above cases. However, a trial was pending in the case of an NYPD officer charged with manslaughter after fatally shooting an unarmed black man, Nathaniel Gaines Jr, in a New York subway in August. Three other NYPD officers were charged with serious offences committed while off duty. One officer was charged with an assault on a black man outside a night-club in May, which left the victim in a coma for eight days. Two were charged with second-degree murder: one for a shooting in January, which police initially claimed was a suicide, and one for the beating and shooting to death of Charles Campbell, an unarmed black man, during a dispute over parking in October.

A state of emergency was declared in St Petersburg, Florida, in October, when rioting took place after an unarmed black teenager, Tyrone Lewis, was shot dead by a white police officer. The US Justice Department started an investigation into the shooting, which was the sixth killing by the city's police in a year.

In May, a former New York City Transit Police Department officer was sentenced to five years' probation for shooting and wounding Desmond Robinson, a black, undercover police officer (see *Amnesty International Report 1996*). In October, an NYPD officer was acquitted by a non-jury court of criminally negligent homicide in the death of Anthony Baez (see *Amnesty International Report 1996*). In a controversial decision, the judge acknowledged that the officer had placed Anthony Baez in an illegal chokehold, but held that it had not been proved beyond reasonable doubt that this had caused his death. In November, one of three white police officers charged with manslaughter in the case of black motorist Johnny Gammage was acquitted by an all-white jury. The charges against the two other officers resulted in a mistrial in October; new trials were pending.

Torture and ill-treatment of prisoners were reported. There were allegations that prisoners in Georgia were systematically beaten in separate incidents by officers from an elite Tactical Squad responsible for conducting prison "shakedowns" (searches). The Commissioner of Corrections, Wayne Garner, is alleged to have personally supervised the searches and to have witnessed acts of ill-treatment – in which many prisoners sustained serious injuries – while taking no preventive action. Cases included an incident at Scott State Prison in January, in which unresisting prisoners allegedly received repeated beatings, and an incident in Hays Prison in July, in which several prisoners sustained serious injuries as a result of alleged beatings, both in the prison and later, during transfer.

In August, state disciplinary hearings opened into allegations that in June 1995 guards at California State Prison, Corcorcan, beat, kicked and forcibly sheared off the hair of some 36 shackled inmates who were transferred there following disturbances at another institution. The results of the hearings, which also considered appeals lodged by seven guards dismissed or demoted following the incident, were still pending at the end of the year. Meanwhile, the Federal Bureau of Investigation (FBI), was reported to be investigating other incidents in the prison, including the shooting by guards of several inmates since 1988 and allegations that guards had organized fights between rival prison gang members.

In October, 11 guards were charged with beating prisoners in a punitive segregation unit at Rikers Island prison complex in New York over a three-year period from 1992 to 1994 and with filing false reports to cover up their actions. The trial was pending at the end of the year.

According to reports, one of the guards charged with the 1994 murder of a prisoner in Terrell Unit, Texas (see *Amnesty International Report 1996*), who had been convicted of manslaughter and sentenced to 10 years' imprisonment, had been granted probation in September 1995 after serving only 99 days of his sentence. A second guard who had been sentenced to eight years' imprisonment was also released early on probation.

In May, the State of Wisconsin announced its intention to use a remote controlled electro-shock belt on prisoners. The Remote Electronically Activated

Control Technology (REACT) belt sends an electric current through the wearer's body, causing pain, incapacitation and sometimes involuntary bowel movements.

In June, Alabama agreed to end chain-gangs (the practice of shackling prisoners together in work crews) in settlement of a lawsuit (see *Amnesty International Report 1996*). A court ruling on the use of the "hitching rail" (a bar to which Alabama prisoners were chained for hours with their hands raised above their heads as punishment) was pending at the end of the year (see *Amnesty International Report 1996*). In September, the first chain-gangs for female prisoners were introduced in a jail in Arizona.

There were legal developments in the cases of prisoners whose prosecution had allegedly been politically motivated. In March, a motion was lodged for a retrial, based on alleged new evidence, in the case of Geronimo Pratt, the former Black Panther Party (BPP) leader, serving a life sentence for murder in California. Amnesty International had repeatedly called for a review of his case, on the basis that he may have been prosecuted because of his BPP activities as part of an FBI counter-intelligence program against the BPP in the 1970s (see previous *Amnesty International Reports*).

In March, the federal parole board refused to grant parole to Leonard Peltier, a member of the American Indian Movement serving two life sentences for murder. A petition for clemency in the case was still pending before President Clinton. Amnesty International had sent the parole board a copy of its 1995 communication to the Attorney General, in which the organization reiterated its concern that Leonard Peltier may have been denied a fair trial on political grounds and sought a review of the case (see previous *Amnesty International Reports*).

In June, Robert Norse Kahn began serving a 60-day prison term imposed for violating an injunction prohibiting the group Food Not Bombs (FNB) from distributing free food to the homeless in San Francisco, California (see previous *Amnesty International Reports*). He was released after a month. Meanwhile, the San Francisco authorities announced that they had reversed the previous city administration's policy of taking legal action against homeless people sleeping or drinking in public places in violation of local laws. Arrests of FNB activists declined.

Amnesty International made numerous appeals on behalf of prisoners sentenced to death, urging clemency in all cases. In June, the organization published a report, *The death penalty in Georgia: Racist, arbitrary and unfair*. In July, Amnesty International's Secretary General led a delegation which met Georgia's Attorney General and various civil rights organizations. In October, the US Government replied to Amnesty International's call for a Presidential Commission into the death penalty, denying that the death penalty was used in a racist manner and rejecting the request.

In June, Amnesty International published a report, *USA: Police brutality and excessive force in the New York City Police Department*. The report detailed widespread allegations of ill-treatment by police, deaths in custody and unjustified police shootings, dating from the mid-1980s to early 1996, mainly against members of ethnic minorities. The organization called on the New York City authorities to establish an independent inquiry to examine the extent of police ill-treatment and the effectiveness of measures taken to prevent or investigate abuses. The Mayor and the Police Commissioner declined to hold an inquiry, denying that ill-treatment was widespread and stating that complaints were already effectively investigated. Amnesty International continued to call for an inquiry and to raise new cases of unjustified police shootings of unarmed suspects and other allegations of ill-treatment, including the cases of Aswan Watson and Nathaniel Gaines Jr.

In June, Amnesty International published a report, *USA: Use of electro-shock stun belts*, condemning the introduction of the REACT belt, which the organization believed could be used to torture detainees. It called upon the US Government to ban the use and export of the belt. Amnesty International also wrote to the Governor of Wisconsin expressing concern that the proposed use of the belt on prison work crews in the state could constitute cruel, inhuman or degrading treatment, in violation of international standards. The authorities replied, defending the use of the belt in certain circumstances.

Amnesty International wrote to the authorities in Alabama, Arizona, California,

Florida, Georgia and New Jersey and to the federal authorities about other reported cases of ill-treatment and deaths in custody, including the cases of Hong Il Kim, Leticia González and Enrique Funez-Flores. Amnesty International expressed concern that the latter two cases appeared to fall within a pattern of ill-treatment of latinos by police in California. The organization also sought a full inquiry by the federal authorities into the case of Kenneth Trentadue, a prisoner who allegedly committed suicide by hanging in a federal prison in Oklahoma but whose body showed signs of numerous other injuries.

In June, Amnesty International wrote to the Governor of California and to the San Francisco authorities expressing concern that Robert Norse Kahn and other FNB members may have been targeted for their beliefs and activities on behalf of the homeless, and seeking further clarification on aspects of the case. No reply had been received by the end of the year.

URUGUAY

Two prisoners of conscience were imprisoned for 15 days. The "disappearance" and possible extrajudicial execution of a former agent of the Chilean military remained unclarified. The vast majority of human rights violations committed in past years remained uninvestigated.

In April, Uruguay ratified the Inter-American Convention on the Forced Disappearance of Persons.

The UN Committee against Torture, which reviewed Uruguay's second periodic report in November, urged the authorities to make provision for a clause which outlaws torture.

Prisoners of conscience Federico and Carlos Fasano, respectively director and editor of the national newspaper *La República*, were each sentenced to two years' imprisonment in May under an article of the Penal Code which restricts freedom of expression. Their conviction was based on the publication of newspaper articles about the alleged corruption of Juan Carlos Wasmosy, the President of Paraguay. The judge found that both journalists had infringed Article 138 of Uruguay's Penal Code, which stipulates that it is a criminal offence to question the "honour of foreign Heads of State and their diplomatic representatives". The offence is punishable by between two and nine years' imprisonment. Following national and international appeals, Federico and Carlos Fasano were released by an appeal court two weeks after their detention. However, their release was conditional, pending a hearing before the Supreme Court of Justice which had not taken place by the end of the year.

A body found in April 1995 was formally identified in June 1996 as that of Eugenio Berríos, a former Chilean military agent who "disappeared" in 1992. Allegations that Uruguayan military personnel had been responsible for his abduction and "disappearance" in 1992 and subsequent extrajudicial execution remained unclarified (see *Amnesty International Report 1994*).

Despite public statements by former members of the armed forces in February, April and May, which corroborated reports of human rights violations committed under past military governments, no official investigations were carried out into these allegations. In an open letter published in May, former navy captain Jorge Troccoli admitted responsibility for his part in the killing and "disappearance" of several opposition activists during the period of military rule between 1973 and 1985. The letter confirmed statements published in February and April by other former members of the Uruguayan armed forces. The statements also corroborated reports of human rights violations by Uruguayan military personnel and during combined military operations between the Uruguayan and Argentine security forces.

These unresolved cases of human rights violations included torture, killings and the "disappearance" after detention of at least 30 people in Uruguay and of more than 100 Uruguayan citizens in Argentina (see **Argentina** entry). The majority of human rights abuse cases reported after the end of military rule also remained unresolved.

In June, Amnesty International wrote to President Julio María Sanguinetti calling for the immediate and unconditional release of prisoners of conscience Federico and Carlos Fasano and for a review by the relevant authorities of Uruguay's Penal Code to ensure that future legislation does not permit the imprisonment of prisoners of conscience. President Sanguinetti replied that he did not have "the constitutional power to imprison or release any prisoner", and that "[w]hether rightly or wrongly, the Judiciary tried [Federico and Carlos Fasano] for having committed a common crime". The organization also urged the authorities to take the necessary steps to clarify the fate of all those who had been victims of "disappearance", and to ensure that all past human rights violations were investigated as required under international human rights standards.

UZBEKISTAN

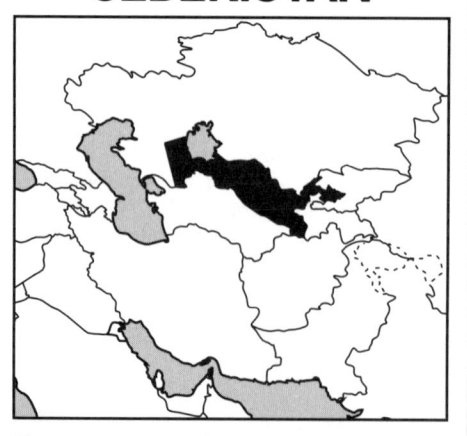

Three prisoners of conscience were held in police custody for short periods in connection with activities in defence of human rights. Three possible prisoners of conscience were detained for two months on a charge of libelling the President. Six possible prisoners of conscience arrested in 1994 were released. An opposition political activist was allegedly tortured in detention, and an international human rights monitor was ill-treated after being arbitrarily detained by police. The son of an opposition leader was assaulted by suspected government agents. Three Islamic religious activists remained "disappeared". At least twelve death sentences were passed and an unknown number of people were executed.

Addressing the *Oliy Majlis* (parliament) in August, President Islam Karimov called for the development of active opposition parties, a free press, and guarantees that the rights of citizens would be observed. The draft of a new law on political parties was published in September, but had not entered into force by the end of the year. During the year the authorities registered two human rights organizations, the Committee for the Defence of the Rights of the Individual and the Human Rights Society of Uzbekistan, the latter having formerly operated underground and in exile since its foundation in 1992. The Chairman of the Human Rights Society, former prisoner of conscience Abdumannob Pulatov (see *Amnesty International Report 1994*), returned from exile in the USA in August, at the personal invitation of President Karimov, to arrange the organization's registration.

Polina Braunerg, a lawyer and human rights activist, was detained three times during a three-day period in March by officers of the National Security Service in Almalyk, near the capital, Tashkent. She was held for questioning ostensibly about her alleged involvement in illegal commercial activity, but the real motive appeared to have been to investigate her human rights and political activities. Polina Braunerg's teenage son, Nikita Braunerg, was detained twice in the same period. Both were prisoners of conscience. In September, Akhmatzhan Abdulayev was detained for several hours after accompanying prominent human rights defender Mikhail Ardzinov to a meeting with a representative of Amnesty International during an international human rights seminar in Tashkent. Akhmatzhan Abdulayev was a prisoner of conscience.

Possible prisoners of conscience Kholiknazar Ganiyev and Bakhtiyor Burkhanov, university lecturers, and Nosim Boboyev, a tax inspector, were arrested in February in Samarkand and charged with "public defamation or slander of the President ... including by means of the press or other media". The charge apparently related to their possession of, and involvement in distributing, copies of several banned opposition publications. In April, the three men were released and the case against them was dropped.

Possible prisoners of conscience Abdulla Abdurazakov and Rashid Bekzhanov (see *Amnesty International Report 1996*) were released in May as part of a presidential amnesty. Possible prisoner of conscience Gaipnazar Koshchanov (see *Amnesty International Report 1996*), who was also released in May, was officially listed as a beneficiary of the amnesty, although he had apparently been due to complete his sentence at that time. A further amnesty in August resulted in the release of possible prisoners of conscience Mamadali Makhmudov (see *Amnesty International Report 1996*), Khoshim Suvanov and Shavkat Mamatov. The latter two had been part of a group of seven people tried in 1995 for serious crimes against the state (see *Amnesty International Report 1996*); the other four serving custodial sentences – Murad Dzhurayev, Erkin Ashurov, Nemat Akhmedov and Shavkat Kholbayev – remained in prison, but it was unclear whether they had also benefited from the amnesty by having their sentences reduced.

Reports of torture and ill-treatment continued to be received. Safar Bekzhanov, an activist with the outlawed *Erk* (Freedom) political party, who had been imprisoned in 1993 on a charge of fraud, which his supporters claimed had been fabricated for political reasons, was released under the May amnesty. He alleged that he had been tortured throughout his imprisonment. In August, John MacLeod, a British citizen and representative of the organization Human Rights Watch/Helsinki, was ill-treated by police in Tashkent who detained him for several hours.

Dmitry Fattakhov, who had allegedly been tortured in police custody in 1995 (see *Amnesty International Report 1996*), was released from confinement in a psychiatric hospital in February and allowed to travel to Israel with his mother for medical treatment.

In November, Khasan Mirsaidov, son of a prominent government opponent, Shukrulla Mirsaidov, was abducted by unknown men who beat him and detained him for around 12 hours. The attackers were believed to have been government agents. Khasan Mirsaidov's father and brother had suffered similar treatment in 1995 (see *Amnesty International Report 1996*).

There was no news about Islamic prayer leader Abduvali Mirzoyev and his assistant Ramazan Matkarimov, who "disappeared" in 1995 (see *Amnesty International Report 1996*). The Uzbek authorities continued to deny involvement in their "disappearance". The 1992 "disappearance" of Abdullo Utayev, leader of the unregistered Islamic Renaissance Party of Uzbekistan (see *Amnesty International Report 1994*), remained similarly unresolved; the Tashkent City Procurator's Office disclosed that they were treating his case as murder, albeit without indicating how they had concluded that he was dead.

The death penalty remained in force, but no official statistics on its application were made known. From unofficial sources it was known that at least twelve death sentences were passed for crimes including murder and drug-trafficking, but the true figures were probably much higher. It was reported that executions continued to take place, but reliable statistical data was unavailable. One death sentence passed in 1995 was changed on appeal to a term of imprisonment, but it also became known that two men sentenced to death in 1994, Bakhodir Sharipov and Sukhrob Sobirov, had been executed in September 1995 and the information withheld from their families for six months. Information received in 1996 showed that the number of death sentences passed in 1995 had been at least 20.

Amnesty International condemned the detention of Polina and Nikita Braunerg and Akhmatzhan Abdulayev and continued to urge an end to the practice of using short-term police custody to punish people for exercising fundamental human rights. The organization sought further information about the charges against Kholiknazar Ganiyev, Bakhtiyor Burkhanov and Nosim Boboyev. It welcomed the release of possible prisoners of conscience Abdulla Abdurazakov, Rashid Bekzhanov, Gaipnazar Koshchanov, Mamadali Makhmudov, Khoshim Suvanov and Shavkat Mamatov, but continued to call for a judicial review of the case of Murad

Dzhurayev, Erkin Ashurov, Nemat Akhmedov and Shavkat Kholbayev.

Amnesty International called for investigations into the allegations that Safar Bekzhanov had been tortured, the ill-treatment of John MacLeod and the beating of Khasan Mirsaidov, and for anyone found responsible to be brought to justice. The organization continued to call for clarification of the whereabouts of Abduvali Mirzoyev, Ramazan Matkarimov and Abdullo Utayev. It also called for the commutation of all death sentences and continued to press the authorities to abolish the death penalty.

VENEZUELA

Dozens of prisoners of conscience were detained during the year. Scores of people, including children, were extrajudicially executed in the context of police and army operations ostensibly aimed at combating crime. At least 25 prisoners burned to death in a prison in Caracas. Torture and ill-treatment by the security forces were widespread and some people died as a result of torture. Prison conditions remained extremely harsh. Most perpetrators of human rights violations continued to benefit from impunity.

Some constitutional guarantees, including the right not to be arrested without a warrant, remained suspended in areas bordering Colombia, where a growing military presence was accompanied by reports of systematic human rights violations by the Venezuelan security forces (see *Amnesty International Report 1996*). The Inter-American Commission on Human Rights and the UN Special Rapporteur on torture carried out their first visits to the country in May and June respectively. In September, the Inter-American Court of Human Rights required Venezuela to pay compensation to relatives of 14 fishermen killed by the army in El Amparo, Apure state, in 1988 (see *Amnesty International Report 1993*).

Dozens of prisoners of conscience were detained for short periods for their peaceful activities; many were tortured and ill-treated. In April, Antonio Espinoza, a community activist, was arrested without a warrant in Valencia, Carabobo state, by members of the *Dirección de los Servicios de Inteligencia y Prevención* (DISIP), Directorate of Intelligence and Prevention Services. He was detained for five days before being released without charge. Nelson Bracca, an activist in Caracas, was arrested in June by hooded members of the DISIP and the *Policía Técnica Judicial* (PTJ), Judicial Technical Police, who raided his home without search or arrest warrants. He was detained in a police station for seven days, where he was forced to stand for prolonged periods. In July, human rights defenders Jorge Nieves and Leticia Echenique, members of the *Comité para la Defensa de los Derechos Humanos* (CODEHUM), Committee for Human Rights Defence, a non-governmental organization based in Guasdualito, Apure state, were arbitrarily detained by members of the DISIP when they went to a local police station to enquire about the safety of a prisoner arrested the previous day. They remained in detention for a day before being released without charge. In October, Juan Bautista Moreno, president of CODEHUM, was arrested, together with four other human rights defenders, following a raid on his home by members of the DISIP. They were arrested for displaying a poster of the Universal Declaration of Human Rights and other human rights literature, which the officials claimed were "subversive". They were detained for seven days before being released without charge.

Scores of people, including children, were extrajudicially executed by the security forces. In January, Jesús Bladimir Lizardo Ortíz, an inmate in the *Retén de Catia*, a prison in Caracas, was shot dead by a prison warder. In April, José Antonio Clavijo Rodríguez and 17-year-old Alejandro Campos Orsini were shot dead in

Caracas in circumstances suggesting they may have been extrajudicially executed. They had received anonymous death threats because of their grass-roots activities. Eye-witnesses claimed that the perpetrators were linked to the security forces. In May, 13-year-old Lian Jonathan Cáseres Herrera was shot in the head at close range and killed by a member of the *Policía Metropolitana*, Metropolitan Police, while he was walking with two friends in a street in Caracas. Witnesses prevented the perpetrator from planting a weapon on the victim in order to claim he had died in a shoot-out. The police officer was suspended pending the outcome of his trial, which was continuing at the end of the year. In June, Carlos Perdomo and John Calderón were arrested during a Metropolitan Police operation in Caracas. Their arrest was filmed by a television crew. Both were seen, alive and unharmed, being taken away in a police vehicle. Hours later their bullet-riddled bodies were transferred to a morgue in Caracas. Those responsible were briefly detained before being released without charge.

On 22 October, at least 25 male inmates, including a 17-year-old, were burned to death in La Planta prison in Caracas, after members of the *Guardia Nacional* (GN), National Guard, locked them into an overcrowded cell and threw tear-gas canisters into it, which set it on fire. Three members of the GN were arrested and were awaiting trial at the end of the year.

The widespread use of torture and ill-treatment by the security forces, including the army, continued to be reported, and those responsible continued to benefit from impunity. Victims included men, women and children. Torture was systematic in the region bordering Colombia, where the Venezuelan security forces responded to incursions by Colombian armed opposition groups with widespread repression against the civilian population, whom they suspected of collaborating with such groups. Beatings, suspension from wrists or ankles for prolonged periods of time, near-asphyxiation with plastic bags, electric shocks and mock executions were used to extract confessions from suspects and to intimidate detainees. Confessions extracted under torture continued to be accepted as evidence by the courts. State attorneys regularly failed to act effectively on complaints of torture and official forensic doctors frequently avoided documenting cases of torture. Medical treatment for detainees who had suffered torture continued to be unavailable.

Five grass-roots activists – Miguel Antonio del Duca Mosquera, Jonathan Sojo Avilés, José Francisco Saavedra Ruza, José Manuel Fuentes and Araciel González – were tortured following their arrest on 13 June by members of the PTJ in Caracas. During the first three days of their detention they were held incommunicado in the *Comisaría del Oeste*, a police station, where high-ranking police officers subjected them to beatings, electric shocks and prolonged suspension by the wrists in order to extract confessions. They remained in detention, without medical care, until their release on bail between 21 June and 2 July.

Children were also tortured by the police and scores were detained in cruel, inhuman or degrading conditions. Arnold Blanco, aged 15, was arrested in July at his home in Petare, by the Municipal Police of Sucre, for alleged drug abuse. He was transferred to the *División de Menores de la PTJ*, a PTJ detention centre for young offenders in Cochecito, Caracas, where he was brutally beaten by warders, as a result of which he suffered fractured ribs. He received no medical care. Dozens of other children, some as young as 10, were also held in the PTJ detention centre and many of them were tortured by the police.

Some people died in custody reportedly as a result of torture. For example, Francis Zambrano was arbitrarily arrested by members of the Metropolitan Police in early April. He was transferred to a police station in Caracas, where he died following prolonged beatings and semi-asphyxiation. Those responsible were not brought to justice.

In the so-called "*zonas de seguridad fronteriza*", border security zones under military jurisdiction, where some constitutional guarantees remained suspended, scores of people were detained at random by the security forces and tortured during interrogation. In January, José Anicaso Rojas was arbitrarily arrested at his home in Guasdualito, Apure state, by members of the PTJ. He was taken to a local police station and subjected to prolonged suspension by the wrists, semi-asphyxiation and beatings in order to extract a confession. He was released without charge after eight days in detention and admitted to hospital. On 17 February, members of the GN investigating a Colombian guerrilla attack raided several houses in the community of La Victoria, Apure state, including that of Yosaida Martínez Rolón. She was arbitrarily detained, beaten, threatened with rape, and held in custody until 21 February. In April, Samuel García, Eleuterio Duque and José del Carmen Vergel were detained at an army road-block in Sector Balsal, Apure state. They were blindfolded and subjected to beatings, mock executions and electric shocks during interrogation. They were released without charge after four days in detention. In October, Laurentino Rolón Santander, a Colombian national, was arbitrarily arrested in Guasdualito, Apure state, by the *Dirección de Inteligencia Militar*, Military Intelligence Directorate. He was held incommunicado for four days and subjected to beatings and electric shocks during interrogation. He was then deported to Colombia. Those responsible for the torture of dozens of people in Cararabo, Amazonas state, in 1995 were not brought to justice (see *Amnesty International Report 1996*).

Prison conditions remained extremely harsh, often amounting to cruel, inhuman or degrading treatment. Despite the government's acknowledgment that systematic human rights violations were taking place in prisons throughout the country, the authorities failed to take steps to improve prison conditions. Serious overcrowding, extremely poor sanitary conditions and lack of adequate medical care led to a number of deaths from diseases such as tuberculosis. In October, several thousand inmates held in three prisons in Caracas carried out a peaceful demonstration, including a hunger-strike, demanding better prison conditions, a speeding up of their court proceedings and full investigations into the massacre of the 25 inmates of La Planta prison (see above).

The whereabouts of Julio Rafael Tovar and Juan Vicente Palmero, who "disappeared" in 1995 following their arrest by members of the security forces, remained unknown, and those responsible were not brought to justice (see *Amnesty International Report 1996*).

Scores of people continued to be imprisoned under the *Ley de Vagos y Maleantes*, Law of Vagrants and Crooks, despite government promises to repeal the law. The law permits administrative detention for periods of up to five years, without judicial appeal or review (see *Amnesty International Report 1996*). In July, José Antonio Landaeta Gatica was arrested without a warrant in Barquisimeto, Lara state. During his arrest he was brutally beaten by members of the state police, reportedly for coming from another state and being unemployed. He was denied medical treatment and remained imprisoned under the Law of Vagrants and Crooks.

An Amnesty International delegation, led by the organization's Secretary General, visited the country in July to present a memorandum to the Venezuelan Government, addressed to President Rafael Caldera, of the organization's concerns and recommendations. It included calls for the abolition of the Law of Vagrants and Crooks; an urgent improvement in prison conditions; the implementation of a law to prevent and punish torture; and an end to impunity for the perpetrators of human rights violations. The government dismissed Amnesty International's findings and concerns as "biased and unfounded".

VIET NAM

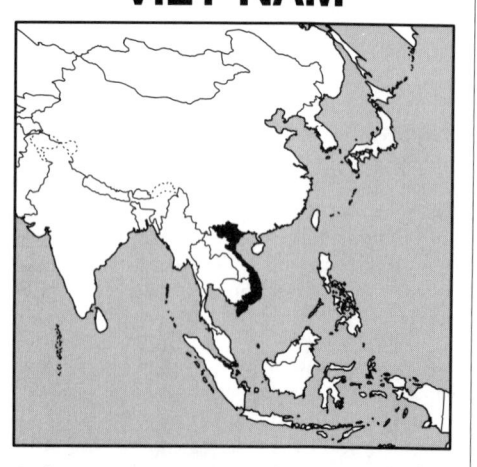

At least 54 prisoners of conscience and possible prisoners of conscience remained in detention throughout the year. Two prisoners of conscience were sentenced to prison terms after an unfair trial and two others were released. Twenty-two political prisoners, including possible prisoners of conscience, were arrested during the year. Death sentences were passed on 113 people. Five people were known to have been executed but the actual number was believed to be much higher.

The Communist Party of Viet Nam held its Eighth Congress in June, at which the country's senior leaders were confirmed in their positions, with President Le Duc Anh retaining his post as Head of State. Strict state control of the media, continuing restrictions on freedom of expression and lack of official information made it difficult to obtain details of human rights violations. Restrictions on visiting foreigners were imposed prior to the Party Congress, but a number of high-level delegations visited Viet Nam afterwards, including delegations from the Vatican and from Norway.

At least 54 prisoners of conscience and possible prisoners of conscience arrested in previous years were known to be detained throughout the year, although the true figures may have been higher. There was serious concern for the health of a number of prisoners of conscience serving long prison sentences. Doan Viet Hoat, a writer and academic arrested in 1990 and serving a 15-year sentence for his involvement with the *Freedom Forum* newsletter (see Amnesty International Reports 1993 to 1995), was held in solitary confinement in Thanh Cam prison in north Viet Nam. He was believed to be suffering from severe mental distress caused by total isolation. Pham Duc Kham, co-author of the *Freedom Forum* and serving a 12-year sentence, suffered from high blood pressure and a chronic ulcer. Nguyen Van Thuan, a writer, poet and former teacher involved in the High Tide of Humanism movement and with the *Freedom Forum*, serving an 18-year sentence, remained in poor health (see Amnesty International Report 1996). He had been hospitalized in 1994 following a stroke. In February, he was returned to Z30B prison camp where there were no medical facilities. Dong Tuy, who had been arrested in 1995 and sentenced to 11 years' imprisonment for his involvement in the Movement to Unite the People and Build Democracy (see *Amnesty International Report 1996*), was in very poor health and continued to be detained in a prison camp with minimal access to appropriate medical attention.

Prisoners of conscience detained for their religious beliefs continued to be held throughout the year. Thich Huyen Quang, the 77-year-old Supreme Patriarch of the unofficial Unified Buddhist Church of Viet Nam (see previous *Amnesty International Reports*), was detained without charge or trial in isolation in a remote part of the country. Brother Nguyen Chau Dat, a member of the Catholic Congregation of the Mother Co-Redemptrix, serving a 20-year sentence in K3 "re-education" camp (see *Amnesty International Report 1995*), suffered from poor health caused by hard labour, an inadequate diet and lack of medical treatment.

Two prisoners of conscience were sentenced to prison terms following an unfair trial in August; a third person received a suspended sentence. Le Hong Ha and Ha Si Phu had been detained without trial since their arrest in late 1995 (see *Amnesty International Report 1996*). Le Hong Ha, a former Interior Ministry official, had been a senior member of the Communist Party of Viet Nam until he was expelled in June 1995. He was reportedly charged with divulging national secrets under Article 92 of Viet Nam's Criminal Code, and sentenced to two years' imprisonment. Ha Si Phu, a scientist and well-known writer, received a one-year sentence, also for alleged offences under Article 92. He had been officially criticized in 1993 for the content of some of his essays which were frequently published in official Communist Party publications. It was believed that the men had been in possession of a letter written by Prime Minister Vo Van Kiet which called for greater political and economic reform. A third man, Nguyen Kien Giang, received a suspended sentence. The trial took place *in camera* and lasted less than one day.

Two prisoners of conscience were released. Doan Thanh Liem, a lawyer who was arrested in 1990 and sentenced after an unfair trial to 12 years' imprisonment in 1992 for allegedly "spreading anti-socialist propaganda" (see *Amnesty International Report 1993*), was unexpectedly released from a prison camp in February and immediately deported to the USA with his family. He had been suffering from serious health problems in detention, including tuberculosis. Tran Thanh Thuc, a medical doctor working in Ho Chi Minh City, who was arrested in 1987 and sentenced after an unfair trial the following year to 16 years' imprisonment on charges of espionage and working for the US Central Intelligence Agency, was released in August.

Three people, believed to have links with the Free Viet Nam Movement, were arrested in March when they were handed over by Cambodian officials at the Vietnamese border (see **Cambodia** entry). One of them, Ly Thara, remained in detention without charge or trial at the end of the year. He was a possible prisoner of conscience.

In December, 19 people, including possible prisoners of conscience, were arrested when they were deported to Viet Nam by the Cambodian authorities (see **Cambodia** entry). The 19, all believed to be members of a group called the People's Action Party, were detained by the Vietnamese authorities on arrival. There was no information as to their fate or whereabouts at the end of the year.

In April, Nguyen Ha Phan, Vice-President of the National Assembly and member of the Politburo was expelled from the Communist Party and later stripped of his posts for "having committed serious mistakes in the past". No further details were available on his case and reports that he may have been placed under house arrest remained unconfirmed.

One hundred and thirteen people were sentenced to death. In April, Duong The Tung was sentenced to death after having been convicted by the Ha Noi People's Court of the murder of a policeman. Duong The Tung, who had pleaded guilty to the charge and begged for clemency, was reportedly tortured by police officers armed with electric batons in an anteroom while awaiting the verdict of his trial. Also in April, Phung Thi Tho was sentenced to death after being found guilty of fraud by a court in Binh Dinh province. An official report stated that this was the first death sentence imposed in Viet Nam for fraud. Five executions were reported. However, this was believed to be only a small fraction of the number of people actually executed. Executions in Viet Nam are carried out by firing-squad. In August, Le Hong Bich was executed in An Giang province; he had been convicted of the rape and murder of a child. Three more people were executed in October. Increased publicity around death sentences and executions was believed to be part of an official crack-down on "social evils", including drug-related crime.

During the year Amnesty International continued to appeal for the release of all prisoners of conscience. In February, the organization published a report, *Socialist Republic of Viet Nam: The death penalty*, explaining its concerns about the increasing number of executions, and noting the 34 articles of the Criminal Code which carry the death penalty as an optional punishment. The organization urged the Vietnamese Government to commute all existing death sentences and to sign and ratify the Second Optional Protocol to the International Covenant on Civil and Political Rights, aiming at the abolition of the death penalty. In February, Amnesty International welcomed the release of Doan Thanh Liem. In August, the organization protested about the trial and sentencing of prisoners of conscience Le Hong Ha and Ha Si Phu, and in December it published a report, *Socialist Republic of Viet Nam: The case of Le Hong Ha and Ha Si Phu*, containing information about their trial. In October, a memorandum of Amnesty International's human rights concerns in Viet Nam was passed to Prime Minister Vo Van Kiet by Norwegian Prime Minister Gro Harlem Brundtland during her visit to the country. He reportedly accepted the memorandum and agreed to consider the contents. There was no official response to Amnesty International's appeals for the release of prisoners of conscience.

YEMEN

Twenty-one political prisoners remained in detention, most of them under sentence of death. They included a prisoner of conscience serving his 14th year under sentence of death. Scores of political suspects, including possible prisoners of conscience, were detained for brief periods during the year. Two political trials which began in 1995 continued during the year. Torture and ill-treatment were reported. The judicial punishment of flogging was widely imposed and the status of sentences of amputation passed in 1995 was unclear. At least one person died in custody. The fate and whereabouts of hundreds of people who "disappeared" in previous years remained unknown. At least eight people were sentenced to death and the cases of hundreds of others sentenced in previous years were at different stages of the appeal process. Executions were believed to have been carried out. Around 20 Saudi Arabian political or religious opponents of their government were forcibly returned to Saudi Arabia, apparently without being offered access to asylum procedures.

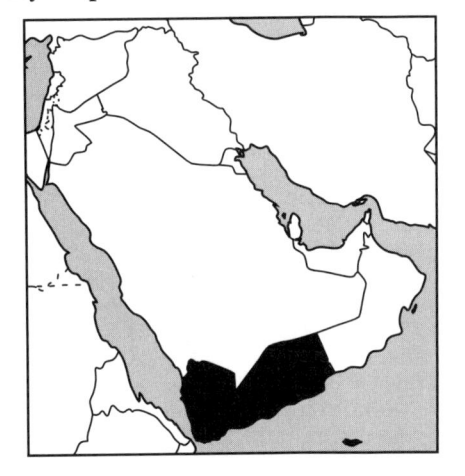

Contrary to the Constitution and the Code of Criminal Procedure, little action was taken during the year by the government of President 'Ali'Abdullah Saleh to bring to justice those responsible for arbitrary arrests, incommunicado detention and torture, or to impose institutional safeguards against these violations of human rights. Scores of political suspects, including possible prisoners of conscience, were subject to arbitrary arrest and detention, mainly by the Political Security (PS) office, in various parts of the country. Most of them were detained for short periods and denied access to lawyers before they were released without charge. Those targeted for arrest included government critics and members of opposition organizations. Idris al-Ma'khadi, a student at Sana'a University and member of *Hizb al-Haq*, a legal political party with two elected members of parliament, was arrested at the beginning of January with a group of students after they distributed statements condemning the beating of Dr 'Abu Bakr al-Saqaf, a university professor who was abducted and beaten in 1995 (see *Amnesty International Report 1996*). All those arrested with him were released after a few days in detention, but Idris al-Ma'khadi remained in incommunicado detention in the PS headquarters in Sana'a for several weeks before he was released without charge.

Many of those who were arrested or detained were suspected of having links with the *al-Jabha al-Wataniya Lilmu'ardha*, National Front for the Opposition, an opposition organization based abroad. It was not known whether any were still held at the end of the year, but some who were arrested in 1995 in connection with their links with political parties may have continued to be held without trial. They included 'Abdullah Muhammad Mustafa 'Ajina, reportedly a former member of the PS, who was believed to remain held without trial in the PS headquarters in Sana'a since his arrest in November 1995.

Twenty political prisoners, suspected members of the former *al-Jabha al-Wataniya al-Dimuqratiyya*, National Democratic Front, an opposition organization in the former Yemen Arab Republic, remained held (see *Amnesty International Report 1996*), most of them under sentence of death. However, new information came to light suggesting that the death sentences passed on two of them – Muhammad Nasser Sa'd al-Sabahi and Ahmad 'Abdullah Hussein al-Faqih – for murder had been commuted to payment of blood money. Some of these sentences had been upheld by the Supreme Court but had not been ratified by the President by the end of the year.

One prisoner of conscience, Mansur Rajih, a poet and writer under sentence of death, remained in prison for the 14th year (see *Amnesty International Report 1996*). He had been convicted of murder in 1983 after grossly unfair hearings. His sentence had not been ratified by the President at the end of the year. The government continued to insist that Mansur Rajih's release could only take place if he was pardoned by the family of the victim whom he was convicted of murdering. He remained held in Tai'z Central Prison suffering from ill health.

The hearings of two political trials which began in 1995 continued during the year. One trial, that of Adam Salah al-Din Mansur, an Algerian national (known also as 'Abu 'Abd al-Rahman), and 20 Yemeni nationals, remained in progress (see *Amnesty International Report 1996*). One session of the trial was attended by an Amnesty International observer. The other trial, that of three defendants charged with carrying out bomb attacks in 'Aden (see *Amnesty International Report 1996*), concluded. The defendants were convicted and sentenced to terms ranging from one and a half years' to three years' imprisonment. The court also ordered an investigation into the allegations of torture by the defendants (see below).

Throughout the year, there were frequent reports of torture and ill-treatment of political detainees as well as criminal suspects. Forms of torture included beatings with wooden or metal sticks, electric shocks, whipping, suspension from the wrists and the use of shackles. Muhammad Sa'd Tarmum, an engineer who was held in al-Sawlaban detention centre in 'Aden, was reportedly forced to place his hands on the floor and had his fingers repeatedly hit with a stone. Two women, Faiza Sa'id al-Mawsati and Samia 'Awadh Ba Najar, alleged that they had been raped while in the custody of the criminal investigation police in Hadhramout in March. They were charged with making false allegations and brought to trial. In August, the court acquitted the two women and sentenced one police officer to two and a half years' imprisonment on charges of deprivation of liberty. However, the court's verdict did not refer to the allegation of rape, and was subject to appeal by the end of the year.

During some trials, public prosecutors and judges referred torture victims for medical examinations and the findings were consistent with the allegations of torture. During the trial of the three defendants tried in connection with the bomb attacks in 'Aden (see above), the court ordered a medical examination of the victims and, in light of the findings, apparently ruled that legal proceedings against the alleged perpetrators should be initiated by the public prosecutor. No information was available regarding progress in the implementation of the ruling. However, in the cases of political suspects subjected to arbitrary arrest and short-term detention and released without charge or trial, no investigations into allegations of torture or ill-treatment were known to have resulted in any legal proceedings.

At least one person, 'Ahmad Sa'id Salmayn Bakhabira, died allegedly as a result of torture while in the custody of security forces in Si'un in June. His family appealed to the government for an investigation, but it was not known whether one had been initiated by the end of the year.

The judicial punishment of flogging was widely imposed and carried out, often with no real possibility for defendants to appeal against the sentence. No sentences of amputation were known to have been passed and the government assured Amnesty International that no such sentences had been carried out since 1993. It was unclear whether the sentences of amputation passed in 1995 had been commuted (see *Amnesty International Report 1996*).

The fate and whereabouts of hundreds of people who "disappeared" in previous years remained unknown (see previous *Amnesty International Reports*), but the government made an undertaking to investigate the cases brought to its attention by Amnesty International of people who had "disappeared" since 1994. These included Farazdaq Fuad Qaied, who "disappeared" in July 1994 from al-Qala Prison in Sana'a where he had been detained as a prisoner during the 1994 civil war.

At least eight people were sentenced to death, although the real figure may have been much higher. Three soldiers were convicted, one of them *in absentia*, of the murder of six civilians in Hudeida Province in August. They were convicted within a few days of the incident and their sentences were upheld by the appeal court a week later. It was not clear whether their sentences had been upheld by the Supreme Court and ratified by the President. Executions were believed to have been carried out, but the exact number was not known.

Hundreds of death sentences passed in previous years remained at different stages of the appeal process. For example, Sabah al-Difani was sentenced in December 1995 to death by stoning after she was convicted on murder charges. Her sentence was believed to be pending appeal before the Court of Appeal at the end of the year. The sentence of 'Ali Ahmad Qassim al-Khubayzan was also believed to be pending appeal before the Court of Appeal. He was sentenced in 1995 to cross-amputation, in addition to the gouging out of his eyes, crucifixion and death by starvation.

About 20 Saudi Arabian nationals, reportedly all political or religious opponents of their government, were forcibly returned to Saudi Arabia in October and November, apparently without being offered access to asylum procedures. They were reported to have been arrested upon arrival and were believed to be at serious risk of torture.

During the year, Amnesty International called for the immediate and unconditional release of prisoners of conscience and for prompt and fair trials for all political prisoners. The organization also called for investigations into allegations of torture and ill-treatment, and "disappearances", and for the bringing to justice of those found responsible. Appeals were sent to the authorities calling for the commutation of all outstanding death sentences.

An Amnesty International delegation visited Yemen in June and July and raised human rights concerns with government ministers and other officials. The government undertook to address specifically the issues of arbitrary arrest, torture, "disappearances" since 1994, and human rights violations against women.

Amnesty International called for urgent translation into practice of the commitments made by the government, but no actions were known to have been taken by the end of the year.

YUGOSLAVIA
(FEDERAL REPUBLIC OF)

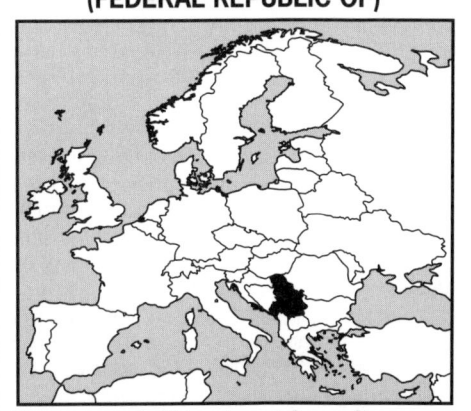

Torture and ill-treatment by police were widespread; most victims were ethnic Albanians in Kosovo province. At least two men died apparently as a result of torture by police, and the deaths of two others appeared to be connected with police beatings. Prisoners of conscience included several dozen men sentenced to up to 60 days' imprisonment for peacefully exercising their right to freedom of assembly and at least four conscientious objectors to military service. Around 60 political prisoners, ethnic Albanians, remained in prison; some were possible prisoners of conscience. At least five people were sentenced to death; no executions were reported.

In June, an amnesty was granted to men who in the period to December 1995 had evaded military service or deserted from the Yugoslav armed forces, with the exception of professional soldiers and commissioned officers. Press reports indicated that some 12,500 men had benefited from the amnesty, many of whom had gone abroad following the outbreak of armed conflict in the former Yugoslavia in 1991.

Following elections in Bosnia-Herzegovina, the UN Security Council lifted trade sanctions against Serbia and Montenegro in October, but did not lift the Federal Republic of Yugoslavia's suspension from the UN General Assembly. By the end of the year there were over 560,000 refugees in the country, the great majority of them Serbs from Croatia and Bosnia-Herzegovina.

The ruling Socialist Party of Serbia and its allies in Serbia and Montenegro won federal elections in November. However, in the same month the opposition coalition *Zajedno*, Together, won control of Belgrade and other major towns in a second round of local elections in Serbia. Attempts by the authorities to overturn these results led to mass demonstrations by opposition supporters and students in Belgrade and elsewhere. In December, a fact-finding mission from the Organization for Security and Co-operation in Europe invited by the government concluded that *Zajedno* had won in Belgrade and 13 other towns, but by the end of the year the government had not conceded most of the opposition victories, and demonstrations continued.

In August, the International Criminal Tribunal for the former Yugoslavia opened a liaison office in Belgrade, but the authorities offered only limited cooperation. Three officers of the former Yugoslav People's Army indicted in April for war crimes and crimes against humanity committed near the Croatian town of Vukovar in 1991, and for whom the Tribunal had issued international arrest warrants, had not been arrested by the end of the year (see **Croatia** entry).

In Serbia the first trial of a defendant accused of war crimes committed in Bosnia-Herzegovina ended in July. A court in Šabac convicted Duško Vučković, who had fought with Serbian paramilitary units, of killing 16 unarmed Muslims and wounding 20 others near Zvornik in 1992. He was also convicted of raping a Muslim woman on Serbian territory, just over the border. He was sentenced to seven years' imprisonment. In October, Nebojša Ranisavljević was arrested in Montenegro and charged with participating in the murder of some 20 men, most of them Muslims from Montenegro, abducted in 1993 by Serbian paramilitary forces (see *Amnesty International Report 1994*).

In Kosovo province, ethnic Albanian political leaders continued to call for independence by peaceful means for the province, predominantly inhabited by ethnic Albanians. However, between April and October, nine Serbs, including five police officers, were shot dead and six others were wounded; an organization calling itself the Liberation Army of Kosovo, about which little was known, claimed responsibility. The attacks started in April after a young ethnic Albanian was shot dead by a Serb civilian, who was arrested and charged. The next day, five Serbs, one of them a police officer, were shot dead, and four others, two of them police officers, were wounded.

The authorities responded with mass, and often apparently indiscriminate, arrests of ethnic Albanians in the area. Many of those arrested were physically ill-treated before being released without charge. In the days following the killing of a Serb police officer in Štimlje on 22 April, over 100 ethnic Albanians were detained for questioning. Most were released within hours, but some were held for up to three or four days. Some 35 people, including several children, were alleged to have been beaten by police. Among those ill-treated was Nazmi Kabashi, who was taken off a bus from Priština as it passed through Štimlje. He was reportedly so severely beaten that he required hospital treatment for internal injuries.

In early August, following explosions at police stations in Podujevo and three other towns in Kosovo, in which no one was injured, over 20 people reportedly sought medical treatment for injuries inflicted by police following mass arrests. Those arrested included Abdullah Murati and his 16-year-old son, Muharrem, who were detained for some hours in Podujevo police station. Police officers allegedly beat Abdullah Murati unconscious with rubber truncheons. When Abdullah Murati's son refused to beat his father, both men were further beaten.

In September, Osman Rama, Besim Rama and Avni Nura were arrested by plainclothes police. Osman Rama, who was released after six days, stated that he was forced into a car, blindfolded and taken to an unknown location, where he was questioned about the political activities of his brother, Besim, and severely beaten. Four days later he was again detained for six days and tortured. Besim Rama and Avni Nura were reportedly held incommunicado for over two weeks before being brought before an investigating judge, in violation of national law, which provides for a maximum of three days in police custody. They were charged with terrorism, and accused of killing three police officers and one civilian. Both were in detention awaiting trial at the end of the year.

Throughout the year there were almost daily reports of incidents – unrelated to armed attacks – in which police tortured and beat or otherwise ill-treated ethnic Albanians. The incidents often took place during house searches for arms; victims included the elderly, women and children. Many ethnic Albanians were arrested following these searches. Others were held for questioning about their political activities. Teachers who taught in privately organized schools which rejected the curricula laid down by the Serbian authorities and education in the Serbian language were also targeted. Detainees were usually held in police stations for periods ranging from a few hours to several days and were sometimes so severely tortured and ill-treated that they subsequently required medical care. In at least two cases it appeared that torture had directly caused, or contributed to, the victim's death. One case concerned Feriz Blakçori, a school teacher, who died on 10 December in hospital. The previous day he had been arrested by police who had discovered a rifle at his home in Priština. His death certificate reportedly attributed his death to cardiorespiratory insufficiency due to severe shock caused by bruising to his head and body.

Police searches for arms continued in the Sandžak area. In July, police in Sjenica reportedly arrested and severely beat six Slav Muslims in order to force them to admit to illegal possession of weapons.

During the mass demonstrations in November and December in protest against the annulment of local election results, over 50 demonstrators were arrested in Belgrade and other towns, some of whom were beaten and otherwise ill-treated by police. For example, following his arrest on 6 December, Dejan Bulatović was beaten by police in a Belgrade police station; he alleged that police also forced a rubber truncheon up his rectum and put a gun barrel in his mouth, threatening to shoot him. Dejan Bulatović was later sentenced to 25 days' imprisonment for disturbing the peace.

In two incidents in Vojvodina province, beatings appear to have led to the victim's death. Djuro Sudji, an ethnic Hungarian, died in March after throwing himself from the window of Novi Sad police station; an officer was later charged with beating and injuring him during questioning about a car theft. Two officers were arrested and charged after Nenad Pilipović, a Serb, died in June. They had reportedly arrested and beaten him after he was involved in a car accident.

Prisoners of conscience included over a dozen ethnic Albanians sentenced to up to 60 days' imprisonment, usually for organizing meetings, lessons outside the official schooling system or sports matches without official permission. They included Pal Krasniqi who in June began a 60-day prison sentence imposed in 1995 for holding a meeting of a school trade union branch.

Prisoners of conscience were among over 20 demonstrators sentenced in November and December, almost all in Belgrade, to up to 30 days' imprisonment on charges of disturbing the peace; some had been convicted of making symbolic gestures of protest, such as throwing eggs at the offices of the state media.

Other prisoners of conscience included an unknown number of conscientious objectors. Under Yugoslav law conscientious objector status must be applied for within 15 days of receiving the first summons for recruitment to military service. Conscientious objectors may do either unarmed military service or civilian service, which last 24 months – twice the length of armed service. They included at least four Jehovah's Witnesses serving prison sentences of between four and 12 months. One of them, Vladimir Lazar, was sentenced to a year's imprisonment for refusing, on religious grounds, to take up arms when called up to do reserve duties; he was not eligible for conscientious objector status because he had previously performed military service.

About 60 ethnic Albanians, most of them convicted in 1994 and 1995, after unfair trials, of seeking the secession of Kosovo province by violent means, remained in prison; some were possible prisoners of conscience. Among the 60 were Raif Çela and some of his 16 co-defendants (see *Amnesty International Report 1995*); their sentences were reduced in January to between six months and eight years' imprisonment by the Supreme Court of Serbia.

In March, six Slav Muslim political prisoners sentenced in October 1994 (see *Amnesty International Report 1995*) were released after the Supreme Court of Serbia ordered a retrial. Fifteen of their co-defendants had already been released in 1994. The retrial had not taken place by the end of the year.

The fate of some 20 Muslims from Serbia who "disappeared" after they were abducted from a bus in 1992 remained unknown (see *Amnesty International Report 1993* **Bosnia-Herzegovina** entry).

At least five people were sentenced to death. They included Aziz Musli, sentenced by a court in Zaječar for recidivist murder.

Amnesty International appealed to the authorities for independent and impartial investigations into all allegations of "disappearance", torture and ill-treatment and called for perpetrators of these violations to be brought to justice. It called for the immediate and unconditional release of prisoners of conscience and for other political prisoners to receive fair trials.

ZAIRE

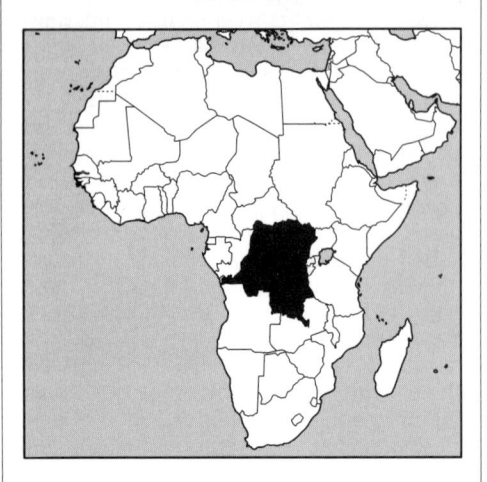

Prisoners of conscience and possible prisoners of conscience were among scores of people detained without charge or trial. Torture and ill-treatment continued to be reported. The security forces massacred unarmed civilians. Dozens of prisoners remained under sentence of death. Armed groups committed grave human rights abuses.

The transition to a multi-party political system continued to face setbacks and it remained unclear whether elections due to take place by July 1997 would be held. The President of the National Electoral Commission, established in January, denounced government interference in the Commission's work and its failure to provide funds. In August, the Supreme Court declared itself unable to rule on a submission presented by the opposition alliance, the *Union sacrée de l'opposition radicale, alliés et société civile*, Sacred Union of the Radical Opposition, Allies and Civil Society, challenging the legitimacy of Léon Kengo wa Dondo's appointment as Prime Minister (see *Amnesty International Report 1996*). Also in August, a coalition of parties supporting President Mobutu Sese Seko, known as the *Forces politiques du Conclave*, Political Forces of the Conclave, withdrew from the transitional parliament, which was deadlocked over two rival drafts of a new Constitution, essential to the holding of elections. In October, parliament adopted a draft Constitution, along federal lines, to be confirmed by referendum in February 1997. President Mobutu spent much of the second half of the year in Europe, receiving medical treatment.

Violence in eastern Zaire escalated into full-scale armed conflict. Large contingents of the *Forces armées zaïroises* (FAZ), Zairian Armed Forces, sent to eastern Zaire to carry out counter-insurgency operations, took part in widespread looting and human rights abuses. In early September, fighting broke out in South-Kivu region between the FAZ and a Tutsi-led armed group known as the *Alliance des forces démocratiques pour la libération du Congo-Zaïre* (AFDL), Alliance of Democratic Forces for the Liberation of Congo-Zaire, reportedly supported by the Rwandese Government. On 26 October, the Zairian Government declared a state of emergency in North and South-Kivu, but emergency measures were not implemented as most areas had been captured by the AFDL by the end of November.

During October, refugee camps housing more than one million largely Hutu refugees from Rwanda and Burundi came under attack. Refugees were attacked by the AFDL, apparently assisted by the Rwandese government forces, by forces of the former Rwandese government and allied *interahamwe* militias responsible for the 1994 genocide in Rwanda, and by Zairian troops. Virtually all refugee camps emptied, and more than one million refugees and displaced Zairians were deprived of all humanitarian aid by the fighting. In November, the UN Security Council called for a cease-fire and authorized the deployment of an international force to aid the refugees. In mid-November, some 500,000 refugees trekked back into Rwanda. Following the mass return of refugees, the multinational intervention force was not deployed, although hundreds of thousands of refugees and displaced Zairians remained dispersed inside Zaire.

After the conflict erupted in the east, the Zairian authorities publicly accused people of Tutsi or Hutu ethnic origin (locally known as Banyarwanda) of undermining the country. There were violent anti-Banyarwanda demonstrations in the capital, Kinshasa, and in the northern town of Kisangani, led by students, in which Banyarwanda were beaten and their homes looted or destroyed. In most cases the security forces did nothing to protect victims. Government forces deported hundreds of Tutsi to Rwanda and Burundi, while hundreds more fled to Congo.

In March, Zaire acceded to the UN Convention against Torture and Other Cruel, Inhuman or Degrading Treatment or Punishment. The mandate of the UN Special Rapporteur on Zaire was extended for one year. After visiting Zaire in November, the Special Rapporteur expressed concern at abuses committed by government forces and armed groups in eastern Zaire and the role played by the Government of Rwanda.

Scores of people were detained without charge or trial, some of whom appeared to be prisoners of conscience. Many were civilians who had been arrested by soldiers and held in military detention centres. Many were held incommunicado for far longer than the period allowed by law. For example, in July, Zairian jurists found one detainee, Mulalwe Karubandika, held without charge or trial in Uvira, South-Kivu, since January 1995.

Dozens of Tutsi and Hutu were arrested and detained without charge or trial, many of whom appeared to be prisoners of conscience. For example, five elderly Tutsi community leaders, three of them pastors, were arrested in September in South-Kivu and held incommunicado in a military camp. By the end of the year, there was no news of their fate, amid reports that many detainees had been extrajudicially executed before Zairian troops fled. Tutsi and Hutu were also arrested in Kinshasa and in Kisangani, apparently solely because of their ethnic origin.

Human rights activists who spoke out against persecution of Tutsi or made inquiries on behalf of Tutsi were accused of supporting the AFDL. Didi Mwati Bulambo and three other workers at the *Collectif d'action pour le développement des droits de l'homme*, Action Collective for Human Rights Development, were arrested in July after publicizing human rights abuses in South-Kivu. They were whipped and otherwise ill-treated in prison before being provisionally released. Three leading members of a human rights group, *La voix des sans voix* (Voice of the Voiceless), were arrested in November by members of the *Service d'action et de renseignements militaires* (SARM), Military Action and Intelligence Service. The three – Floribert Chebeya Bahizire, Harouna Mbongo and Bashi Nabukili – were held incommunicado for six days before being released without charge.

Several members of the international aid community working in North-Kivu region were subjected to arrests, threats and beatings in early July 1996. Opposition party leaders were also detained. Joseph Olengha N'Koy, a leading member of the *Union pour la démocratie et le progrès social*, Union for Democracy and Social Progress, was arrested in November after criticizing the government's handling of the armed conflict in eastern Zaire. He and another government opponent, Willy Mishiki, were released in mid-December, shortly before President Mobutu returned from Europe.

Torture, sometimes leading to death, was reported. For example, in January, nine young men of Hunde origin were arrested in eastern Zaire by soldiers. Kahima Baluku, a student, was reportedly shot dead and the others burned with heated machetes and severely beaten. Two – Biamungu Baroke and Kamulete Ngabo – died as a result.

On 9 May, a trader and mother of five children travelling by bus to Goma was arrested by members of SARM at a roadblock after failing to produce her identity card. She was stripped naked and stoned in front of the other passengers. She was taken to the SARM camp in Goma, where she was reportedly tortured, including by being gang-raped by soldiers. She was released without charge on 13 May.

In Kisangani, students and members of the *Service national d'intelligence et de protection*, National Intelligence and Protection Service, attacked members of the civilian population, especially people from Rwanda or Burundi, in October. Journalists and human rights activists were harassed and threatened. From early November onwards, heavily armed soldiers fleeing the conflict in the east arrived in Kisangani, adding to the general climate of insecurity and lawlessness. According to reports, they attacked Banyarwanda and Barundi families, beating them and raping the women, including girls as young as 12, in full view. They also beat Zairian citizens, such as Tshimbila, who were unable to give them money. At least seven schoolgirls reportedly died in early December, after soldiers gang-raped girls in a secondary school in Bunia, a town in northeastern Zaire.

Detainees were held by the security services in cramped and insanitary conditions amounting to cruel, inhuman or degrading treatment. Detainees who were sick or injured were denied medical care.

Government soldiers extrajudicially executed unarmed civilians in eastern Zaire throughout the year. Perpetrators enjoyed virtual impunity; none were known to have been brought to justice.

In February, government troops fired a mortar shell at Masisi hospital, killing a woman and a man. Soldiers subsequently pillaged the hospital.

Dozens of villagers were extrajudicially executed by soldiers during a counter-insurgency operation in May at Vichumbi, a fishing village on Lake Edward. Soldiers reportedly ordered all the villagers into Vichumbi's three churches and held them there for several days while they raided and burned houses. They then killed at least 37 men, whom they accused of being members of an armed opposition group, in front of the churches. Survivors reported that many others, including women and children, were shot as they tried to escape.

Hundreds of people were reportedly killed by soldiers during a counter-insurgency operation in May in Kanyabayonga, Rutshuru district, North-Kivu. One elderly man lost 24 members of his extended family including his son, Kambale Mutumu.

In some incidents, government soldiers collaborated with armed groups. For example, in July members of the *Division spéciale présidentielle*, Special Presidential Division, and Hunde armed groups attacked five Hutu villages in Bwito county, Rutshuru district. Several hundred civilians were reportedly killed.

Zairian soldiers were alleged to have extrajudicially executed 19 Rwandese refugees detained on suspicion of criminal activities in Masisi in July. Witnesses reported that the detainees were beaten to near unconsciousness by soldiers and then apparently killed at a remote spot near Kingi, on the edge of the National Park.

In early September, soldiers reportedly killed 35 Zairian Tutsi civilians; more than 50 others "disappeared". Soldiers extrajudicially executed four civilians in front of a crowd at Luberezi village, Uvira district, on 8 September.

As many as 60 prisoners were reported to be under sentence of death. No executions were reported during the year.

The AFDL, which gained control of much of North and South-Kivu, committed gross human rights abuses. Zairian doctors reported that Tutsi-led rebels had killed 34 patients and six staff at a hospital in Lemera town, south of Bukavu, on 6 October. On 13 October, rebel forces opened fire on a refugee camp at Runingo, northwest of Uvira, killing four refugees and wounding six.

After the town of Bukavu fell to the AFDL, the bodies of at least 83 people were found, most of whom appeared to have been unarmed civilians shot dead at close range. The Archbishop of Bukavu, Christophe Munzihirwa, was killed, allegedly because of his public criticism of the AFDL and its alleged support from the Rwandese Government.

About 500 Rwandese refugees and displaced Zairians were massacred by AFDL members in mid-November at Chimanga refugee camp, south of Bukavu. Jean-Claude Buhendwa, a Zairian Roman Catholic priest, was executed when he protested. The massacre followed clashes between the AFDL and members of the former Rwandese army and *interahamwe* militia at nearby Bilongo camp.

The AFDL also rounded up and forcibly expelled Burundi refugees, handing them over to Burundi government troops at the border. Hundreds of the returned refugees were subsequently killed by Burundian troops (see **Burundi** entry).

There were reports of killings by both the AFDL and Rwandese Hutu militia members at Mugunga camp, near Goma. Aid workers found and buried hundreds of bodies in Mugunga camp in late November. There were further reports of massacres of refugees by Rwandese militia members in November.

Amnesty International repeatedly called on the Zairian Government to prevent its forces committing human rights violations and to stop its officials from inciting ethnic hatred. In June, the organization publicly called for action to prevent further killings in eastern Zaire, and in September it condemned atrocities committed by Zairian soldiers and government officials against Tutsi in South-Kivu. In November, Amnesty International published *Zaire: Lawlessness and insecurity in North and South-Kivu*. As the crisis in eastern Zaire intensified, Amnesty International issued a detailed appeal for the protection of human rights. It called for an international presence in eastern Zaire, Burundi and Rwanda to protect civilians at risk, and for world governments to prevent further supplies of weapons to government forces and armed groups in the three countries until they demonstrated that the weapons would not be used to commit human rights abuses. The organization stressed that no one should be forced to return to a country where they might face human rights abuses. Amnesty International appealed to all combatants to stop attacks on civilians, and to officials in the region to stop inciting violence. It called for those responsible for abuses to be brought to justice and urged the international community to provide the resources to strengthen criminal justice systems in Zaire, Rwanda and Burundi, and to prosecute suspects in other countries. In November, Amnesty International delegates visited Zaire to gather information about human rights abuses and discuss the organization's concerns with government authorities. Amnesty International published a number of reports, including *Zaire: Violent persecution by state and armed groups* in November, and *Hidden from scrutiny: human rights abuses in eastern Zaire* in December.

ZAMBIA

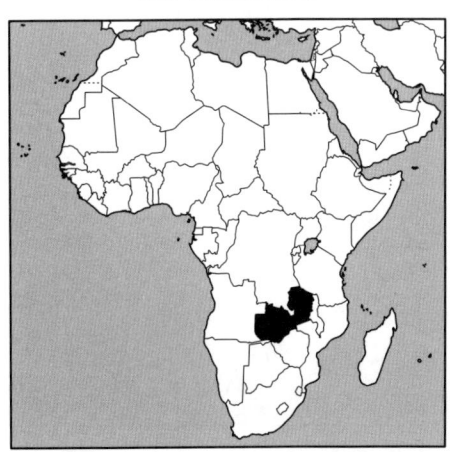

Journalists were held as prisoners of conscience. The trial of eight members of the political opposition ended in acquittal. There were reports of police shootings of unarmed suspects. At least five people were sentenced to death. No executions were carried out.

In January, the Supreme Court declared unconstitutional a colonial-era law restricting freedom of assembly that required police permits for public meetings, but parliament adopted legislation imposing similar restrictions weeks later.

In March, Zambia appeared before the UN Human Rights Committee, which examined Zambia's adherence to the International Covenant on Civil and Political Rights. The Committee addressed many of Amnesty International's concerns in its comments.

Parliament approved a new Constitution in May that disqualified former President Kenneth Kaunda of the United National Independence Party (UNIP) from contesting presidential elections because his parents were not Zambian and he had already served two terms as President (see *Amnesty International Report 1996*). Another constitutional clause excluded traditional chiefs from holding office. Two cabinet ministers resigned in protest and western donor countries suspended aid.

In September, the government published the findings of a 1995 commission of inquiry which investigated the death of opposition politician Baldwin Nkumbula. It concluded that he died from injuries sustained in an accidental car crash (see *Amnesty International Report 1996*).

In October, the government released the report of the 1993 Human Rights Commission of Inquiry which investigated prison conditions and allegations of human rights violations between 1972 and 1993. It concluded that human rights violations, including torture, by police, security and military personnel had occurred under the previous government and continued "on a significant scale". In response, the government accepted some of the Commission's recommendations, including the creation of a permanent human rights commission, but rejected other important reforms (see *Amnesty International Report 1996*).

President Frederick Chiluba was re-elected in November elections which were boycotted by seven opposition parties. There were allegations of electoral irregularities that favoured the ruling Movement for Multi-party Democracy. A week later, two election monitoring groups had their offices searched; their leaders were briefly detained and their assets frozen by the authorities after they accused the government of election rigging. In December, police sought to arrest opposition political leaders who had warned of violence, or a possible military coup, unless fresh elections were held.

Journalists at an independent newspaper were held as prisoners of conscience. In February, police detained three editors of an independent daily newspaper, *The Post*, for almost 48 hours for publishing cabinet ministers' discussions about holding a referendum on the proposed Constitution. A presidential decree banned that day's edition of the newspaper. An appeal to the Supreme Court was made against the charges of printing "classified documents" and against the ban, but no ruling had been made by the end of the year.

In March, police again detained two editors of *The Post* after parliament sentenced them *in absentia* to indefinite detention for "contempt of parliament". The High Court ordered their release after 24 days, ruling that the procedure followed by parliament was "incompatible with the rule of law".

Police arrested eight UNIP officials in June on treason charges in connection with bomb blasts and bomb threats carried out by a hitherto unknown group calling itself the "Black Mamba", which claimed to oppose the adoption of the new Constitution. Two of the officials were also charged with murder after a bomb killed a police explosives expert in June. Two defendants were released in September, and in November the High Court acquitted all eight, criticizing the lack of evidence and the prosecution witnesses' lack of credibility.

In June, UNIP members demonstrating outside the courtroom where the eight were on trial were confronted by riot police who fired live bullets into the crowd and beat protesters with clubs.

Reports were received of police shooting unarmed suspects. In January, a court sentenced a police officer to 15 months' imprisonment with hard labour for shooting and wounding two nightclub security guards. In August, the family of Mulyokela Yuyi alleged that he was fatally shot by policemen in Kitwe acting in collusion with criminal figures. An inquest into his death was continuing at the end of the year. Court proceedings initiated in several other cases of police shootings of unarmed people in 1994 and 1995 were continuing at the end of the year.

At least five people were sentenced to death during the year, including three men convicted of ritual child killings in 1995. At the end of the year at least 114 people awaited execution. No executions were carried out.

In February, Amnesty International called on the government to immediately and unconditionally release the two newspaper editors arrested for "contempt of parliament". In March, the organization published a report, *Zambia: A human rights review based on the International Covenant on Civil and Political Rights*. In June, the organization expressed concern about the detention of UNIP officials and wrote to the authorities about prison conditions and the ill health of the defendants. In July, Amnesty International wrote to the authorities inquiring about delays in investigating a fatal police shooting in 1992. No official reply was received. Also in July, Amnesty International wrote to President Chiluba asking about investigations into the 1995 killing of a villager and the razing of a village by some 300 Zambian soldiers. No response had been received from the government by the end of the year.

ZIMBABWE

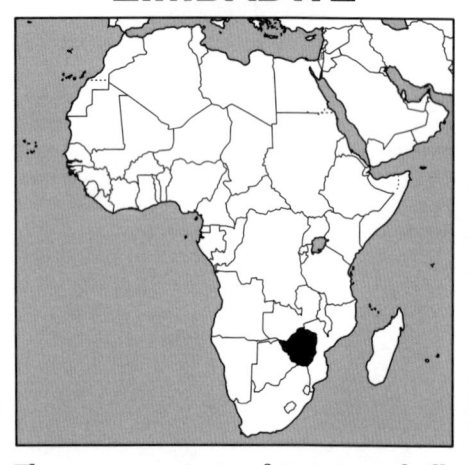

There were reports of torture and ill-treatment of people held in police custody. One person was killed and two others injured when police opened fire into crowds. Seven people were executed and at least five others were sentenced to death. Twenty-two people remained under sentence of death at the end of the year.

In July, the government attempted to prohibit a local gay and lesbian organization from participating in the Zimbabwe International Book Fair (see *Amnesty International Report 1996*). After a High Court ruling quashed the ban, the organization participated briefly in the book fair, despite threats of violence and death from protesters. In November, police briefly detained two trade unionists when riot police broke up a demonstration in support of striking state nurses and doctors, whose seven-week walk-out led to the closure of major hospitals until it ended in December.

In October, Parliament passed a 14th amendment to the Constitution, which limits foreigners' citizenship rights and eliminates the right to privacy, while nominally expanding the investigative powers of the Ombudsman.

The Reverend Ndabaningi Sithole, an opposition leader, remained on bail awaiting trial. His trial was postponed eight times during 1996 and had not begun by the end of the year. He had been arrested in October 1995 and charged with possessing arms, terrorism and conspiring to murder President Robert Mugabe (see *Amnesty International Report 1996*). In November, the Reverend Ndabaningi Sithole appealed to the Supreme Court on the constitutionality of the legislation under which the charges were brought against him, which requires him to prove his innocence. His appeal had not been heard by the end of the year.

There were reports of torture and ill-treatment of people held in police custody. In January, Abrahama Goletom Joseph Kinfe, an Eritrean national convicted of attempted murder in November 1995, claimed police officers beat him with fists, sticks and rubber batons until he confessed to trying to assassinate former Ethiopian Head of State Mengistu Haile Mariam, now living in exile in Zimbabwe. He appealed to the High Court against his conviction in October. Another man reported that he and a co-worker were beaten with sticks and whips by police in Gwanda town during an interrogation in June.

Police shot civilians while trying to disperse crowds, sparking civil unrest. In March, riots began in a Harare suburb after a police officer fired warning shots into a crowd that was trying to stop him from arresting a suspect, killing one person. In another incident in April, two bystanders were shot and injured by a police officer attempting to fire warning shots. In May, a police officer attempting to arrest a woman fired warning shots into a crowd of onlookers. Two people were hospitalized for gunshot wounds and submitted claims to the government for compensation.

Seven people were executed during the year, a significant increase over previous years. In February, a prisoner sentenced to death for a murder committed in 1992 was hanged. In September, five other prisoners sentenced to death for murder were executed. Piniel Sindiso Chiduza Ncube was hanged in December after his appeal was dismissed by the Supreme Court. At least five other people were sentenced to death after being convicted of murder. The government confirmed that 22 people remained under sentence of death at the end of the year.

Amnesty International appealed to Home Affairs Minister Dumiso Dabengwa to ensure police protection for members of the local lesbian and gay organization which participated in the international book fair. Following the five executions in September, Amnesty International appealed to President Mugabe and other officials to halt executions and commute all death sentences.

APPENDICES

APPENDIX I

AMNESTY INTERNATIONAL VISITS 1996

DATE	COUNTRY	PURPOSE
January	Gambia	Research
January	USA	Research
January	United Kingdom	Legal proceedings
January	Bulgaria	Research
January	Turkey	Research/Talks with government
January	Turkey	Legal proceedings
January/February	Hong Kong	Research on region
January/February	Israel	Talks with government
January/February	Palestinian Authority	Talks with government
January/February	Thailand	Research on region
February	Portugal	Research on region
February	Indonesia	Research
February	Spain	Research
February	Guyana	Legal proceedings
February	Tunisia	Legal proceedings
February/March	Kazakstan	Research/Talks with government
February/March	Australia	Research/Talks with government
February/March	Peru	Research
February/March	Guatemala	Research/Talks with government
February/March	Turkey	Research
March	Panama	Research
March	Sri Lanka	Research/Talks with government
March	Chile	Research/Talks with government
March	Suriname	Research
March	Jordan	Research
March	Germany	Research
March	Egypt	Research
March	Greece	Research/Legal proceedings
March	South Africa	Research/Legal proceedings
March	Thailand	Campaigning/Talks with government
March	Hong Kong	Campaigning/Talks with government
March	Japan	Campaigning/Talks with government
March/April	Burkina Faso	Intergovernmental meeting
March/April	France	Talks with government
April	Israel	Research/Talks with government
April	Palestinian Authority	Research
April	Chad	Research/Talks with government
April	Russian Federation	Research/Legal proceedings
April	Sierra Leone	Research/Talks with government
April	Kenya	Research
April	Sierra Leone	Research on region
April	Zimbabwe	Research
April	Botswana	Research
April/May	Suriname	Research

APPENDIX I

April/May	Argentina	Research/Talks with government
April/May	Bolivia	Research/Talks with government
April/May	Sudan	Research
April/May	USA	Research on region
April/May	Malaysia	Research
April/May	Zambia	Research
April/May	Brazil	Research/Talks with government/Legal proceedings
May	Peru	Research/Talks with government
May	Turkey	Legal proceedings
May	Sri Lanka	Research
May	Burundi	Research/Talks with government
May	USA	Research on region
May	Algeria	Research/Legal proceedings
May	Lebanon	Research/Talks with government/Legal proceedings
May	Colombia	Research/Talks with government
May	Turkey	Research
May	Benin	Research on region
May	Nigeria	Research
May	Pakistan	Talks with government
May	Kenya	Research on region
May	Costa Rica	Research
May/June	Austria	Research
May/June	Nicaragua	Research
May/June	USA	Research on region
May/June	Hong Kong	Research
May/June	Tanzania	Research/Talks with government
May/June	Kenya	Research on region/Talks with government/Intergovernmental meeting
May/June	Rwanda	Research/Talks with government
May/June	Mexico	Research/Talks with government
June	Taiwan	Research
June	Bosnia-Herzegovina	Research
June	Bulgaria	Talks with government
June	Ethiopia	Research/Legal proceedings
June	Yemen	Research
June	Turkey	Legal proceedings
June	USA	Talks with government
June/July	Angola	Research
June/July	Papua New Guinea	Research/Talks with government
June/July	Cameroon	Intergovernmental meeting
June/July	Tunisia	Research/Talks with government
June/July	Yemen	Talks with government
June/July	Bosnia-Herzegovina	Research
June/July	Russian Federation	Research
June/July	USA	Research on region
July	Tunisia	Legal proceedings
July	South Africa	Research
July	Pakistan	Research on region
July	Afghanistan	Research

July	Uzbekistan	Research on region
July	Thailand	Research on region
July	South Africa	Research/Talks with government
July	Turkey	Intergovernmental meeting
July	Venezuela	Talks with government
July/August	Zaire	Research
July/August	Palestinian Authority	Research/Talks with government
July/August	United Kingdom	Legal proceedings
July/August	India	Research
July/August	USA	Research/Talks with government
July/August	Guatemala	Research/Talks with government/Legal proceedings
July/August	Uganda	Research/Talks with government/Intergovernmental meeting
August	Nepal	Research
August	Russian Federation	Research on region
August	Chile	Legal proceedings
August	Indonesia	Research
August	Sri Lanka	Research
September	South Korea	Research
September	China	Talks with government/Intergovernmental meeting
September	Guatemala	Research
September	United Kingdom	Legal proceedings
September	Jordan	Research on region
September	USA	Research on region
September	Kenya	Research/Talks with government
September	Macedonia	Research
September	Uzbekistan	Research/Intergovernmental meeting
September	Romania	Research/Talks with government
September/October	Brazil	Research
September/October	Lebanon	Research/Talks with government/Legal proceedings
September to December	United Kingdom	Legal proceedings
October	Lesotho	Research
October	Tunisia	Legal proceedings
October	Lesotho	Legal proceedings
October	Federal Republic of Yugoslavia	Research
October	Turkey	Legal proceedings
October	United Kingdom	Research/Legal proceedings
October	Albania	Research
October	Turkey	Research
October	USA	Research
October	Turkey	Campaigning/Talks with government
October/November	Bosnia-Herzegovina	Research
October/November	Croatia	Research
October/November	Kenya	Research on region
October/November	Switzerland	Research/Intergovernmental meeting
October/November	Georgia	Research/Talks with government
November	Rwanda	Research/Talks with government
November	South Africa	Talks with government
November	Zaire	Research/Talks with government

APPENDIX I

November	Tunisia	Legal proceedings
November	South Africa	Intergovernmental meeting
November	Ethiopia	Intergovernmental meeting
November/December	Malawi	Research
November/December	Egypt	Research
November/December	Mexico	Research/Talks with government
November/December	Bosnia-Herzegovina	Research/Talks with government
November/December	Azerbaijan	Research on region/Intergovernmental meeting
November/December	Nepal	Research/Talks with government
November/December	Cambodia	Research
November/December	Philippines	Research
November/December	Tanzania	Research/Intergovernmental meeting
December	Portugal	Research/Talks with government
December	Germany	Research/Talks with government
December	Jordan	Research on region/Talks with government
December	Mongolia	Research/Talks with government
December	Bangladesh	Research
December	Pakistan	Research
December	Rwanda	Legal proceedings

STATUTE OF AMNESTY INTERNATIONAL
Articles 1 and 2

As amended by the 22nd International Council, meeting in Ljubljana, Slovenia, 12 to 20 August 1995

Object and Mandate

1. The object of AMNESTY INTERNATIONAL is to contribute to the observance throughout the world of human rights as set out in the Universal Declaration of Human Rights.

In pursuance of this object, and recognizing the obligation on each person to extend to others rights and freedoms equal to his or her own, AMNESTY INTERNATIONAL adopts as its mandate:

To promote awareness of and adherence to the Universal Declaration of Human Rights and other internationally recognized human rights instruments, the values enshrined in them, and the indivisibility and interdependence of all human rights and freedoms;

To oppose grave violations of the rights of every person freely to hold and to express his or her convictions and to be free from discrimination, and of the right of every person to physical and mental integrity, and, in particular, to oppose by all appropriate means irrespective of political considerations:

a) the imprisonment, detention or other physical restrictions imposed on any person by reason of his or her political, religious or other conscientiously held beliefs or by reason of his or her ethnic origin, sex, colour, language, national or social origin, economic status, birth or other status, provided that he or she has not used or advocated violence (hereinafter referred to as 'prisoners of conscience'; AMNESTY INTERNATIONAL shall work towards the release of and shall provide assistance to prisoners of conscience);

b) the detention of any political prisoner without fair trial within a reasonable time or any trial procedures relating to such prisoners that do not conform to internationally recognized norms;

c) the death penalty, and the torture or other cruel, inhuman or degrading treatment or punishment of prisoners or other detained or restricted persons, whether or not the persons affected have used or advocated violence;

d) the extrajudicial execution of persons whether or not imprisoned, detained or restricted, and "disappearances", whether or not the persons affected have used or advocated violence.

Methods

2. In order to achieve the aforesaid object and mandate, AMNESTY INTERNATIONAL shall:

a) at all times make clear its impartiality as regards countries adhering to the different world political ideologies and groupings;

b) promote as appears appropriate the adoption of constitutions, conventions, treaties and other measures which guarantee the rights contained in the provisions referred to in Article 1 hereof;

c) support and publicize the activities of and cooperate with international organizations and agencies which work for the implementation of the aforesaid provisions;

d) take all necessary steps to establish an effective organization of sections, affiliated groups and individual members;

e) secure the adoption by groups of members or supporters of individual prisoners of conscience or entrust to such groups other tasks in support of the object and mandate set out in Article 1;

APPENDIX II

f) provide financial and other relief to prisoners of conscience and their dependants and to persons who have lately been prisoners of conscience or who might reasonably be expected to be prisoners of conscience or to become prisoners of conscience if convicted or if they were to return to their own countries, to the dependants of such persons and to victims of torture in need of medical care as a direct result thereof;

g) provide legal aid, where necessary and possible, to prisoners of conscience and to persons who might reasonably be expected to be prisoners of conscience or to become prisoners of conscience if convicted or if they were to return to their own countries, and, where desirable, send observers to attend the trials of such persons;

h) publicize the cases of prisoners of conscience or persons who have otherwise been subjected to disabilities in violation of the aforesaid provisions;

i) investigate and publicize the disappearance of persons where there is reason to believe that they may be victims of violations of the rights set out in Article 1 hereof;

j) oppose the sending of persons from one country to another where they can reasonably be expected to become prisoners of conscience or to face torture or the death penalty;

k) send investigators, where appropriate, to investigate allegations that the rights of individuals under the aforesaid provisions have been violated or threatened;

l) make representations to international organizations and to governments whenever it appears that an individual is a prisoner of conscience or has otherwise been subjected to disabilities in violation of the aforesaid provisions;

m) promote and support the granting of general amnesties of which the beneficiaries will include prisoners of conscience;

n) adopt any other appropriate methods for the securing of its object and mandate.

The full text of the Statute of Amnesty International is available free upon request from: Amnesty International, International Secretariat, 1 Easton Street, London WC1X 8DJ, United Kingdom.

APPENDIX III

AMNESTY INTERNATIONAL AROUND THE WORLD

In 1996, there were 4,273 local Amnesty International groups registered with the International Secretariat, plus several thousand school, university, professional and other groups, in more than 80 countries and territories around the world. In 54 countries and territories these groups are coordinated by sections, whose addresses are given below. In addition, there are individual members, supporters and recipients of Amnesty International information (such as the bimonthly *Amnesty International News*) in more than 177 countries and territories.

SECTION ADDRESSES

Algeria:
Amnesty International,
Section Algérienne,
BP 377 Alger,
RP 16004

Argentina:
Amnistía Internacional,
Sección Argentina,
25 de Mayo 67, 4º Piso,
1002 Capital Federal,
Buenos Aires

Australia:
Amnesty International,
Australian Section,
Private Bag 23, Broadway,
New South Wales 2007

Austria:
Amnesty International,
Austrian Section,
Apostelgasse 25-27,
A-1030 Wien

Bangladesh:
Amnesty International,
Bangladesh Section,
100 Kalabagan,
1st Floor, 2nd Lane,
Dhaka-1205

Belgium:
Amnesty International,
Belgian Section (*Flemish branch*),
Kerkstraat 156,
2060 Antwerpen

Amnesty International,
Section belge francophone,
Rue Berckmans 9,
1060 Bruxelles

Benin:
Amnesty International,
BP 01 3536,
Cotonou

Bermuda:
Amnesty International,
Bermuda Section,
PO Box HM 2136,
Hamilton HM JX

Brazil:
Anistia Internacional,
Rua Jacinto Gomes 573,
Porto Alegre - RS,
CEP 90040-270,
São Paulo

Canada:
Amnesty International,
Canadian Section (*English-speaking branch*),
214 Montreal Rd, 4th Floor, Vanier,
Ontario, K1L 1A4

Amnistie Internationale,
Section canadienne francophone,
6250 boulevard Monk,
Montréal, Québec H4E 3H7

Chile:
Amnistía Internacional,
Sección Chilena,
Casilla 4062,
Santiago

Colombia:
Señores,
Apartado Aéreo 76350,
Bogotá

APPENDIX III

Côte d'Ivoire:
Amnesty International,
Section ivoirienne,
04 BP 895,
Abidjan 04

Denmark:
Amnesty International,
Danish Section,
Dyrkoeb 3,
1166 Copenhagen K

Ecuador:
Amnistía Internacional,
Sección Ecuatoriana,
Casilla 17-15-240-C,
Quito

Faroe Islands:
Amnesty International,
Faroe Islands Section,
PO Box 1075, FR-110,
Tórshavn

Finland:
Amnesty International,
Finnish Section,
Ruoholahdenkatu 24 D
00180 Helsinki

France:
Amnesty International,
Section française,
4 rue de la Pierre Levée,
75553 Paris, Cedex 11

Germany:
Amnesty International,
German Section,
Heerstrasse 178,
D-53108 Bonn

Ghana:
Amnesty International,
Ghanaian Section,
Private Mail Bag,
Kokomlemle
Accra - North

Greece:
Amnesty International,
Greek Section,
30 Sina Street,
106 72 Athens

Guyana:
Amnesty International,
Guyana Section,
c/o PO Box 10720,
Palm Court Building,
35 Main Street,
Georgetown

Hong Kong:
Amnesty International,
Hong Kong Section,
Unit C 3/F, Best-O-Best Commercial Centre,
32-36 Ferry Street,
Kowloon

Iceland:
Amnesty International,
Icelandic Section,
PO Box 618,
121 Reykjavík

India:
Amnesty International,
Indian Section,
13 Indra Prastha Building,
E-109 Pandav Nagar,
New Delhi-110092

Ireland:
Amnesty International,
Irish Section,
48 Fleet Street,
Dublin 2

Israel:
Amnesty International,
Israel Section,
PO Box 14179,
Tel Aviv 61141

Italy:
Amnesty International,
Italian Section,
Viale Mazzini, 146,
00195 Rome

Japan:
Amnesty International,
Japanese Section,
Sky Esta 2f,
2-18-23 Nishi Waseda,
Shinjuku-ku,
Tokyo 165

Korea (Republic of):
Amnesty International,
Kyeong Buk RCO Box 36,
706 600 Daegu

Luxembourg:
Amnesty International,
Luxembourg Section,
Boîte Postale 1914,
1019 Luxembourg

Mauritius:
Amnesty International,
Mauritius Section,
BP 69 Rose-Hill

Mexico:
Sección Mexicana
  de Amnistía Internacional,
Calle Aniceto Ortega 624,
  (paralela a Gabriel Mancera,
  esq. Angel Urraza-eje 6 Sur),
Col. del Valle,
México DF

Nepal:
Amnesty International,
Nepalese Section,
PO Box 135, Bagbazar,
Kathmandu

Netherlands:
Amnesty International,
Dutch Section,
Keizersgracht 620,
1017 ER Amsterdam

New Zealand:
Amnesty International,
New Zealand Section,
PO Box 793,
Wellington

Nigeria:
Amnesty International,
Nigerian Section,
PMB 3061, Suru-Lere,
Lagos

Norway:
Amnesty International,
Norwegian Section,
PO Box 702 Sentrum,
0106 Oslo

Peru:
Señores,
Casilla 659,
Lima 18

Philippines:
Amnesty International,
Philippines Section,
PO Box 286, Sta Mesa Post Office,
1008 Sta Mesa,
Manila

Portugal:
Amnistia Internacional,
Secção Portuguesa,
Rua Fialho de Almeida, Nº13, 1º,
1070 Lisboa

Puerto Rico:
Amnistía Internacional,
Sección de Puerto Rico,
Calle Robles No 54-Altos,
Oficina 11, Río Piedras,
Puerto Rico 00925

Senegal:
Amnesty International,
Senegalese Section,
No 74a, Zone A,
BP 21910,
Dakar

Sierra Leone:
Amnesty International,
Sierra Leone Section,
PMB 1021,
Freetown

Slovenia:
Amnesty International,
Komenskega 7,
1000 Ljubljana

Spain:
Amnesty International,
Sección Española,
PO Box 50318,
28080, Madrid

Sweden:
Amnesty International,
Swedish Section,
PO Box 23400,
S-104 35 Stockholm

Switzerland:
Amnesty International,
Swiss Section,
PO Box,
CH-3001, Bern

Tanzania:
Amnesty International,
Tanzanian Section,
PO Box 4331,
Dar es Salaam

Tunisia:
Amnesty International,
Section Tunisienne,
48 Avenue Farhat Hached, 3ème étage,
1001 Tunis

APPENDIX III/IV

United Kingdom:
Amnesty International,
United Kingdom Section,
99-119 Rosebery Avenue,
London EC1R 4RE

United States of America:
Amnesty International of the USA
 (AIUSA),
322 8th Ave,
New York, NY 10001

Uruguay:
Amnistía Internacional,
Sección Uruguaya,
Trist Narvaja 1624, Apto 2,
CP 11200 Montevideo

Venezuela:
Amnistía Internacional,
Sección Venezolana,
Apartado Postal 5110,
Carmelitas 1010-A,
Caracas

COUNTRIES AND TERRITORIES WITHOUT SECTIONS BUT WHERE LOCAL AMNESTY INTERNATIONAL GROUPS EXIST OR ARE BEING FORMED

Albania	Egypt	Morocco
Aruba	Gambia	Pakistan
Azerbaijan	Palestinian Authority/	Paraguay
Bahamas	Israeli Occupied	Poland
Barbados	Territories	Romania
Belarus	Georgia	Russia
Bolivia	Grenada	Slovakia
Botswana	Hungary	South Africa
Bulgaria	Jamaica	Taiwan
Burkina Faso	Jordan	Thailand
Cameroon	Kuwait	Togo
Costa Rica	Macao	Turkey
Croatia	Malaysia	Uganda
Curaçao	Mali	Ukraine
Cyprus	Malta	Yemen
Czech Republic	Moldova	Zambia
Dominican Republic	Mongolia	Zimbabwe

APPENDIX IV

INTERNATIONAL EXECUTIVE COMMITTEE

Ross Daniels/Australia
Celso Garbarz/Israel
Ian Gorvin/International Secretariat
Mary Gray/United States of America
Menno Kamminga/Netherlands
Gerry O'Connell/Italy
Robin Rickard/United Kingdom
Mahmoud Ben Romdhane/Tunisia
Susan Waltz/United States of America

APPENDIX V

SELECTED INTERNATIONAL HUMAN RIGHTS TREATIES

States which have ratified or acceded to a convention are party to the treaty and are bound to observe its provisions. States which have signed but not yet ratified have expressed their intention to become a party at some future date; meanwhile they are obliged to refrain from acts which would defeat the object and purpose of the treaty.

(AS OF 31 DECEMBER 1996)

	International Covenant on Civil and Political Rights (ICCPR)	Optional Protocol to ICCPR	Second Optional Protocol to ICCPR, aiming at the abolition of the death penalty	International Covenant on Economic, Social and Cultural Rights	Convention against Torture and Other Cruel, Inhuman or Degrading Treatment or Punishment	Convention relating to the Status of Refugees (1951)	Protocol relating to the Status of Refugees (1967)
Afghanistan	x			x	x(28)		
Albania	x			x	x	x	x
Algeria	x	x		x	x(22)	x	x
Andorra							
Angola	x	x		x		x	x
Antigua and Barbuda					x	x	x
Argentina	x	x		x	x(22)	x	x
Armenia	x	x		x	x	x	x
Australia	x	x	x	x	x(22)	x	x
Austria	x	x	x	x	x(22)	x	x
Azerbaijan	x			x	x*	x	x
Bahamas						x	x
Bahrain							
Bangladesh							
Barbados	x	x		x			
Belarus	x	x		x	x(28)		

APPENDIX V

	International Covenant on Civil and Political Rights (ICCPR)	Optional Protocol to ICCPR	Second Optional Protocol to ICCPR, aiming at the abolition of the death penalty	International Covenant on Economic, Social and Cultural Rights	Convention against Torture and Other Cruel, Inhuman or Degrading Treatment or Punishment	Convention relating to the Status of Refugees (1951)	Protocol relating to the Status of Refugees (1967)
Belgium	x	x	s	x	s	x	x
Belize	x*				x	x	x
Benin	x	x		x	x	x	x
Bhutan							
Bolivia	x	x		x	s	x	x
Bosnia-Herzegovina	x	x		x	x	x	x
Botswana						x	x
Brazil	x			x	x	x	x
Brunei Darussalam							
Bulgaria	x	x		x	x(22)(28)	x	x
Burkina Faso	x	x				x	x
Burundi	x			x	x	x	x
Cambodia	x			x	x	x	x
Cameroon	x	x		x	x	x	x
Canada	x	x		x	x(22)	x	x
Cape Verde	x			x	x	x	x
Central African Republic	x	x		x		x	x
Chad	x	x		x	x	x	x
Chile	x	x		x	x(28)	x	x
China					x(28)	x	x
Colombia	x	x		x	x	x	x
Comoros							
Congo	x	x		x		x	x
Costa Rica	x	x	s	x	x	x	x

APPENDIX V

	International Covenant on Civil and Political Rights (ICCPR)	Optional Protocol to ICCPR	Second Optional Protocol to ICCPR, aiming at the abolition of the death penalty	International Covenant on Economic, Social and Cultural Rights	Convention against Torture and Other Cruel, Inhuman or Degrading Treatment or Punishment	Convention relating to the Status of Refugees (1951)	Protocol relating to the Status of Refugees (1967)
Côte d'Ivoire	x			x	x	x	x
Croatia	x	x	x	x	x(22)	x	x
Cuba					x		
Cyprus	x	x		x	x(22)	x	x
Czech Republic	x	x		x	x(22)	x	x
Denmark	x	x	x	x	x(22)	x	x
Djibouti						x	x
Dominica	x			x		x	x
Dominican Republic	x	x		x	s	x	x
Ecuador	x	x	x	x	x(22)	x	x
Egypt	x			x	x	x	x
El Salvador	x	x		x	x*	x	x
Equatorial Guinea	x	x		x		x	x
Eritrea							
Estonia	x	x		x	x	x	x
Ethiopia	x			x	x	x	x
Fiji						x	x
Finland	x	x	x	x	x(22)	x	x
France	x	x		x	x(22)	x	x
Gabon	x			x	s	x	x
Gambia	x	x		x	s	x	x
Georgia	x	x		x	x		
Germany	x	x	x	x	x	x	x
Ghana						x	x

APPENDIX V

	International Covenant on Civil and Political Rights (ICCPR)	Optional Protocol to ICCPR	Second Optional Protocol to ICCPR, aiming at the abolition of the death penalty	International Covenant on Economic, Social and Cultural Rights	Convention against Torture and Other Cruel, Inhuman or Degrading Treatment or Punishment	Convention relating to the Status of Refugees (1951)	Protocol relating to the Status of Refugees (1967)
Greece				x	x(22)	x	x
Grenada	x			x			
Guatemala	x			x	x	x	x
Guinea	x	x		x	x	x	x
Guinea-Bissau				x		x	x
Guyana	x	x		x	x		
Haiti	x					x	x
Holy See						x	x
Honduras	s	s	s	x	x*	x	x
Hungary	x	x	x	x	x(22)	x	x
Iceland	x	x	x	x	x(22)*	x	x
India	x			x			
Indonesia					s		
Iran (Islamic Republic of)	x			x		x	x
Iraq	x			x			
Ireland	x	x	x	x	s	x	x
Israel	x			x	x(28)	x	x
Italy	x	x	x	x	x(22)	x	x
Jamaica	x	x		x		x	x
Japan	x			x		x	x
Jordan	x			x	x	x	x
Kazakstan							
Kenya	x			x		x	x
Kiribati							

AMNESTY INTERNATIONAL REPORT 1997

364

APPENDIX V

	International Covenant on Civil and Political Rights (ICCPR)	Optional Protocol to ICCPR	Second Optional Protocol to ICCPR, aiming at the abolition of the death penalty	International Covenant on Economic, Social and Cultural Rights	Convention against Torture and Other Cruel, Inhuman or Degrading Treatment or Punishment	Convention relating to the Status of Refugees (1951)	Protocol relating to the Status of Refugees (1967)
Korea (Democratic People's Republic)	x			x			
Korea (Republic of)	x	x		x	x	x	x
Kuwait	x*			x*	x*	x*	x*
Kyrgyzstan	x	x		x			
Lao People's Democratic Republic							
Latvia	x	x		x	x		
Lebanon	x			x			
Lesotho	x			x		x	x
Liberia	s			s		x	x
Libyan Arab Jamahiriya	x	x		x	x		
Liechtenstein					x(22)	x	x
Lithuania	x	x		x	x*		
Luxembourg	x	x	x	x	x(22)	x	x
Macedonia (former Yugoslav Republic)	x	x	x	x	x		x
Madagascar	x	x*		x		x	
Malawi	x	x*		x	x*	x	x
Malaysia							
Maldives							
Mali	x			x		x	x
Malta	x	x	x	x	x(22)	x	x
Marshall Islands							
Mauritania						x	x
Mauritius	x	x		x	x		
Mexico	x			x	x		

AMNESTY INTERNATIONAL REPORT 1997

APPENDIX V

	International Covenant on Civil and Political Rights (ICCPR)	Optional Protocol to ICCPR	Second Optional Protocol to ICCPR, aiming at the abolition of the death penalty	International Covenant on Economic, Social and Cultural Rights	Convention against Torture and Other Cruel, Inhuman or Degrading Treatment or Punishment	Convention relating to the Status of Refugees (1951)	Protocol relating to the Status of Refugees (1967)
Micronesia (Federated States of)							
Moldova	x			x	x		
Monaco		x			x(22)	x	
Mongolia	x			x			
Morocco	x			x	x(28)	x	x
Mozambique	x		x			x	x
Myanmar							
Namibia	x	x	x	x	x	x	
Nauru							
Nepal	x	x		x	x		
Netherlands	x	x	x	x	x(22)	x	x
New Zealand	x	x	x	x	x(22)	x	x
Nicaragua	x	x	s	x	s	x	x
Niger	x	x		x		x	x
Nigeria	x			x	s	x	x
Norway	x	x	x	x	x(22)	x	x
Oman							
Pakistan							
Palau							
Panama	x	x	x	x	x	x	x
Papua New Guinea						x	x
Paraguay	x	x		x	x	x	x
Peru	x	x		x	x	x	x
Philippines	x	x		x	x	x	x

APPENDIX V

	International Covenant on Civil and Political Rights (ICCPR)	Optional Protocol to ICCPR	Second Optional Protocol to ICCPR, aiming at the abolition of the death penalty	International Covenant on Economic, Social and Cultural Rights	Convention against Torture and Other Cruel, Inhuman or Degrading Treatment or Punishment	Convention relating to the Status of Refugees (1951)	Protocol relating to the Status of Refugees (1967)
Poland	x	x		x	x(22)	x	x
Portugal	x	x	x	x	x(22)	x	x
Qatar							
Romania	x	x	x	x	x	x	x
Russian Federation	x	x		x	x(22)	x	x
Rwanda	x			x		x	x
Saint Kitts and Nevis							
Saint Lucia							
Saint Vincent and the Grenadines	x	x		x		x	
Samoa						x	x
San Marino	x	x		x			
Sao Tome and Principe	s			s			
Saudi Arabia						x	x
Senegal	x	x		x	x(22)	x	x
Seychelles	x	x	x	x	x	x	x
Sierra Leone	x*	x*		x*	s	x	x
Singapore							
Slovakia	x	x		x	x	x	x
Slovenia	x	x	x	x	x(22)	x	x
Solomon Islands				x		x	
Somalia	x	x		x	x	x	x
South Africa	s			s	s	x*	x*
Spain	x	x	x	x	x(22)	x	x
Sri Lanka	x			x	x		

367

AMNESTY INTERNATIONAL REPORT 1997

APPENDIX V

	International Covenant on Civil and Political Rights (ICCPR)	Optional Protocol to ICCPR	Second Optional Protocol to ICCPR, aiming at the abolition of the death penalty	International Covenant on Economic, Social and Cultural Rights	Convention against Torture and Other Cruel, Inhuman or Degrading Treatment or Punishment	Convention relating to the Status of Refugees (1951)	Protocol relating to the Status of Refugees (1967)
Sudan	x			x	s	x	x
Suriname	x	x		x		x	x
Swaziland						x	x
Sweden	x	x	x	x	x(22)	x	x
Switzerland	x		x	x	x(22)	x	x
Syrian Arab Republic	x			x			
Tajikistan					x	x	x
Tanzania	x			x		x	x
Thailand	x*						
Togo	x	x		x	x(22)	x	x
Tonga							
Trinidad and Tobago	x	x		x			
Tunisia	x			x	x(22)	x	x
Turkey					x(22)	x	x
Turkmenistan							
Tuvalu						x	x
Uganda	x	x		x	x	x	x
Ukraine	x	x		x	x(28)		
United Arab Emirates							
United Kingdom	x			x	x	x	x
United States of America	x			s	x		
Uruguay	x	x	x	x	x(22)	x	x
Uzbekistan	x	x		x	x		
Vanuatu							

AMNESTY INTERNATIONAL REPORT 1997

APPENDIX V

	International Covenant on Civil and Political Rights (ICCPR)	Optional Protocol to ICCPR	Second Optional Protocol to ICCPR, aiming at the abolition of the death penalty	International Covenant on Economic, Social and Cultural Rights	Convention against Torture and Other Cruel, Inhuman or Degrading Treatment or Punishment	Convention relating to the Status of Refugees (1951)	Protocol relating to the Status of Refugees (1967)
Venezuela	x	x	x	x	x(22)		x
Viet Nam	x			x			
Yemen	x			x	x	x	x
Yugoslavia (Federal Republic of)	x	s		x	x(22)	x	x
Zaire	x	x		x	x*	x	x
Zambia	x	x		x		x	x
Zimbabwe	x			x		x	x

s – denotes that country has signed but not yet ratified

x – denotes that country is a party, either through ratification, accession or succession

* – denotes that country either signed or became a party in 1996

(22) denotes Declaration under Article 22 recognizing the competence of the Committee against Torture to consider individual complaints of violations of the Convention

(28) denotes that country has made a reservation under Article 28 that it does not recognize the competence of the Committee against Torture to examine reliable information which appears to indicate that torture is being systematically practised, and to undertake a confidential inquiry if warranted

SELECTED REGIONAL HUMAN RIGHTS TREATIES

(AS OF 31 DECEMBER 1996)

ORGANIZATION OF AFRICAN UNITY (OAU)
AFRICAN CHARTER ON HUMAN AND PEOPLES' RIGHTS (1981)

Country		Country	
Algeria	x	Madagascar	x
Angola	x	Malawi	x
Benin	x	Mali	x
Botswana	x	Mauritania	x
Burkina Faso	x	Mauritius	x
Burundi	x	Mozambique	x
Cameroon	x	Namibia	x
Cape Verde	x	Niger	x
Central African Republic	x	Nigeria	x
Chad	x	Rwanda	x
Comoros	x	Saharawi Arab Democratic Republic	x
Congo	x	Sao Tome and Principe	x
Côte d'Ivoire	x	Senegal	x
Djibouti	x	Seychelles	x
Egypt	x	Sierra Leone	x
Equatorial Guinea	x	Somalia	x
Eritrea		South Africa	x
Ethiopia		Sudan	x
Gabon	x	Swaziland	x
Gambia	x	Tanzania	x
Ghana	x	Togo	x
Guinea	x	Tunisia	x
Guinea-Bissau	x	Uganda	x
Kenya	x	Zaire	x
Lesotho	x	Zambia	x
Liberia	x	Zimbabwe	x
Libya	x		

x denotes that country is a party, either through ratification or accession

This chart lists countries which were members of the OAU at the end of 1996.

ORGANIZATION OF AMERICAN STATES (OAS)

	American Convention on Human Rights (1969)	Inter-American Convention to Prevent and Punish Torture (1985)	Inter-American Convention on the Forced Disappearance of Persons (1994)*
Antigua and Barbuda			
Argentina	x(62)	x	x
Bahamas			
Barbados	x		
Belize			
Bolivia	x(62)	s	s
Brazil	x	x	s
Canada			
Chile	x(62)	x	s
Colombia	x(62)	s	s
Costa Rica	x(62)	s	x
Cuba			
Dominica	x		
Dominican Republic	x	x	
Ecuador	x(62)	s	
El Salvador	x(62)	x	
Grenada	x		
Guatemala	x(62)	x	s
Guyana			
Haiti	x	s	
Honduras	x(62)	s	s
Jamaica	x		
Mexico	x	x	
Nicaragua	x(62)	s	s
Panama	x(62)	x	x
Paraguay	x(62)	x	x
Peru	x(62)	x	
Saint Kitts and Nevis			
Saint Lucia			
Saint Vincent and the Grenadines			
Suriname	x(62)	x	
Trinidad and Tobago	x(62)		
United States of America	s		
Uruguay	x(62)	x	x
Venezuela	x(62)	x	s

s   denotes that country has signed but not yet ratified
x   denotes that country is a party, either through ratification or accession
(62)   denotes Declaration under Article 62 recognizing as binding the jurisdiction of the Inter-American Court of Human Rights (on all matters relating to the interpretation or application of the American Convention)
* This Convention entered into force on 29 March 1996.

This chart lists countries which were members of the OAS at the end of 1996.

APPENDIX VI

COUNCIL OF EUROPE

	European Convention for the Protection of Human Rights and Fundamental Freedoms (1950)	Article 25	Article 46	Protocol No. 6*	European Convention for the Prevention of Torture and Inhuman or Degrading Treatment or Punishment (1987)
Albania	x	x	x		x
Andorra	x	x	x	x	s
Austria	x	x	x	x	x
Belgium	x	x	x	s	x
Bulgaria	x	x	x		x
Croatia	s			s	s
Cyprus	x	x	x		x
Czech Republic	x	x	x	x	x
Denmark	x	x	x	x	x
Estonia	x	x	x	s	x
Finland	x	x	x	x	x
France	x	x	x	x	x
Germany	x	x	x	x	x
Greece	x	x	x	s	x
Hungary	x	x	x	x	x
Iceland	x	x	x	x	x
Ireland	x	x	x	x	x
Italy	x	x	x	x	x
Latvia	s				
Liechtenstein	x	x	x	x	x
Lithuania	x	x	x		s
Luxembourg	x	x	x	x	x
Macedonia	s			s	s
Malta	x	x	x	x	x
Moldova	s			s	s
Netherlands	x	x	x	x	x
Norway	x	x	x	x	x
Poland	x	x	x		x
Portugal	x	x	x	x	x
Romania	x	x	x	x	x
Russian Federation	s				s
San Marino	x	x	x	x	x
Slovakia	x	x	x	x	x
Slovenia	x	x	x	x	x
Spain	x	x	x	x	x
Sweden	x	x	x	x	x
Switzerland	x	x	x	x	x
Turkey	x	x	x		x
Ukraine	s				s
United Kingdom	x	x	x		x

s denotes that country has signed but not yet ratified

x denotes that country is a party, either through ratification or accession

Article 25 denotes Declaration under Article 25 of the European Convention for the Protection of Human Rights and Fundamental Freedoms, recognizing the competence of the European Commission of Human Rights to consider individual complaints of violations of the Convention

Article 46 denotes Declaration under Article 46 of the European Convention for the Protection of Human Rights and Fundamental Freedoms, recognizing as compulsory the jurisdiction of the European Court of Human Rights in all matters concerning interpretation and application of the European Convention

* Protocol No. 6 to the European Convention for the Protection of Human Rights and Fundamental Freedoms concerning the abolition of the death penalty (1983)

This chart lists countries which were members of the Council of Europe at the end of 1996.

Amnesty International's Declaration on the Role of Health Professionals in the Exposure of Torture and Ill-treatment

As part of its 1996 campaign on the role of health professionals and the exposure of human rights violations, Amnesty International adopted the following Declaration which calls for action by individual health professionals, national and international professional associations, and the United Nations and its agencies. Amnesty International believes that the skills which health professionals can contribute to the investigation of human rights violations in general, and torture in particular, should be used in defence of human rights. This Declaration embodies concrete steps which will contribute to this aim if acted upon by health professionals, their professional organizations and by intergovernmental organizations.

Preamble

Human rights and medical ethics standards have evolved in recent years and, currently, strong legal and ethical prohibitions on torture and other human rights violations exist. These include the Universal Declaration of Human Rights, the United Nations Declaration on the Protection of All Persons from Being Subjected to Torture and Other Cruel, Inhuman or Degrading Treatment or Punishment, the Convention against Torture and Other Cruel, Inhuman or Degrading Treatment or Punishment, the Body of Principles for the Protection of All Persons under Any Form of Detention or Imprisonment, regional human rights treaties, and a number of statements adopted by doctors' and nurses' organizations. Torture and other cruel, inhuman or degrading treatment, however, continue and the need for positive action by health professionals to expose these abuses is as great as ever. The following Declaration articulates the steps – implicit in the ethics of medicine and nursing – which Amnesty International believes should be taken by health professionals to fulfil their role as protectors of the vulnerable, particularly those deprived of liberty.

Declaration

Amnesty International,

Recalling that the Declaration of Tokyo of the World Medical Association (1975) obliges doctors not to condone, countenance or participate in torture,

Recalling that the United Nations Principles of Medical Ethics relevant to the Role of Health Personnel, particularly Physicians, in the Protection of Prisoners and Detainees against Torture and Other Cruel, Inhuman or Degrading Treatment or Punishment (1982) state that it is a gross contravention of medical ethics for health personnel, particularly physicians, to assist, actively or passively, in acts of torture,

Further recalling that the International Council of Nurses has declared in The Role of the Nurse in the Care of Detainees and Prisoners (1975) that nurses having knowledge of physical or mental ill-treatment must take appropriate action including reporting the matter to appropriate national and/or international bodies,

Noting the fundamental obligation stemming from the Hippocratic oath and the World Medical Association's International Code of Medical Ethics (1949) for doctors to practise for the good of their patients and never to do harm,

Recalling the important role of health professionals in protecting particular vulnerable individuals such as children through exposing instances of serious abuses coming to their attention,

Recalling that torture and other cruel, inhuman or degrading treatment or punishment are contrary to international law,

Calls on health professionals witnessing torture or other cruel, inhuman or degrading treatment or punishment, or the effects of such violations, to report their observations to their immediate manager and to their professional association. In the event of inaction by the persons so informed (or where, in the judgment of the health professional, it would be too dangerous to report to these persons), the health professional should report his or her observations to an international professional, humanitarian or human rights organization,

Declares that the health professional making such a report should be given support by individual colleagues and by their national and international professional associations. Such associations should take firm action when a health professional is disciplined in any way or otherwise victimized for reporting human rights violations, including making strong representations to the authorities to quash such disciplinary measures and to provide legal assistance to the threatened individual,

Calls on national professional associations to adopt and publicize statements opposing professional involvement in human rights violations and to ensure that their members know of their ethical responsibility to report torture and ill-treatment and of the commitment of the association to support members reporting abuses,

Calls on international professional associations and the United Nations and its relevant agencies to publicize the ethical responsibility of health professionals to report human rights violations inflicted on their patients,

Calls on international professional bodies to make clear statements about the serious breach of professional ethics occasioned by a health professional's purposely omitting, modifying, or falsifying relevant information in the medical history of an alleged victim of torture or ill-treatment, such as to preclude or to make difficult the treatment of the patient, to prevent redress for the victim or to impede the bringing to justice of those responsible for the torture or ill-treatment,

Further calls on international professional bodies to investigate, and where appropriate, impose sanctions on, national associations which collude in the infliction of human rights violations in their countries.

This Declaration was adopted by Amnesty International in January 1996 as part of the organization's worldwide campaign for a more effective role to be played by health professionals in the exposure and investigation of torture and other human rights violations.

Amnesty International's Principles for the Medical Investigation of Torture and Other Cruel, Inhuman or Degrading Treatment

Torture continues to be a major preoccupation of Amnesty International in many countries around the world. An important element in the prevention of torture is the effective investigation of torture allegations and the prosecution of those responsible. Yet, in case after case, governments either carry out no investigation or preside over an inadequate, incompetent or deliberately misleading investigation. In view of the skills which health professionals can contribute to the investigation of human rights violations in general, and torture in particular, Amnesty International has adopted the following Principles for the Medical Investigation of Torture and Other Cruel, Inhuman or Degrading Treatment. The Principles are intended to provide a framework for the carrying out of medical evaluations of torture allegations and a standard for assessing the quality of investigations carried out by governments and courts. They do not provide detailed information about the precise examinations which should be carried out, but rather the key principles which ensure that an investigation is consistent with professional ethics and human rights.

Amnesty International calls on governments to ensure that all allegations of torture are investigated and that medical investigation of torture is carried out in conformity with the Principles set out below.

Preamble

A number of human rights standards call for the prompt investigation of allegations of torture or other cruel, inhuman or degrading treatment by relevant authorities. These include the United Nations Declaration on the Protection of All Persons from Being Subjected to Torture and Other Cruel, Inhuman or Degrading Treatment or Punishment, the Convention against Torture and Other Cruel, Inhuman or Degrading Treatment or Punishment, the Body of Principles for the Protection of All Persons under Any Form of Detention or Imprisonment, regional human rights treaties, and a number of statements adopted by doctors' and nurses' organizations. Such an investigation should be carried out by an appropriate individual or commission having powers to interview witnesses, review prison or police procedures and employ expert assistance. One of the important resources in such investigations is suitably qualified and experienced medical personnel. The principles set out below represent basic steps in the medical investigation of torture and ill-treatment.

1. Prompt access to a doctor

A detainee or prisoner should have prompt access to a doctor when an allegation of torture or ill-treatment is made or when there is suspicion that torture or ill-treatment has taken place. Such access should not be dependent on the institution of an official investigation into torture allegations.

2. Independence

The examining doctor should be independent of the authorities responsible for custody, interrogation and prosecution of the subject. He or she should, if possible, be experienced in the examination of individuals for legal purposes. The doctor's affiliation should be made clear to the prisoner and should be recorded in the final medical report. Where an independent doctor is not available, the doctor carrying out the examination should nevertheless comply with these principles.

3. Confidentiality of examination

The examination should take place in a room where confidentiality is ensured. The doctor should speak to and examine the subject alone. Where the subject is a female, a minor or a specially vulnerable person, examination should only take place in the presence of a witness acceptable to the subject. Where an interpreter is required, or the examining physician wishes to be assisted by a colleague, their presence should be dependent on the agreement of the subject. Any other third parties present should be asked to leave the examination room. If a third party refuses to leave, the doctor should note the name and affiliation of the person(s), and record his or her perception of the effect of this presence on the course of the examination. The doctor should use his or her judgment as to whether the examination can take place without further risk to the person being examined.

4. Consent to examination
The doctor should give his or her name and affiliation, explain the purpose of the examination and gain the consent of the subject to the examination if he or she is capable of giving consent. Before consent is obtained, the doctor should inform the subject of the names or posts of all recipients of the medical report.

5. Access to medical records
The doctor, and if necessary a translator, should have access to the subject's previous medical records.

6. Full examination
The physician's examination should include the elicitation of a full verbal medical history from the subject and the performance of a full clinical examination, including evaluation of the subject's mental state. Further medical, laboratory or psychological investigations, including evaluation of mental health status, should be arranged promptly as deemed necessary by the physician.

7. Report
The physician should promptly prepare an accurate written report. The report should include at least the following four parts:

i) Establishing details – name of the subject and names and affiliations of others present at the examination; the exact time and date, location, nature and address of the institution (including, where appropriate, the room) where the examination is being conducted (for example, detention centre, clinic, house etc) and the circumstances of the subject at the time of examination (for example, the nature of any restraints used, demeanour of those accompanying the prisoner); and any other relevant factor;

ii) A record of the subject's history as given during the interview, including the time when torture or ill-treatment is alleged to have occurred;

iii) A record of all abnormal physical and psychological findings on clinical examination including, where possible, colour photographs of all injuries;

iv) An interpretation as to the probable cause of all abnormal symptoms and all abnormal physical findings.

The report should clearly identify the doctor carrying out the examination and should be signed.

In the interpretation, the doctor should provide a general assessment of the consistency of the history and examination findings with the nature of the subject's allegations. A recommendation for any necessary medical treatment should also be given.

Where a doctor is unable to finalize the report, whether because of the unavailability of further examination or test results, or for any other reason, this should be stated.

8. Confidentiality of the report
The subject should be informed of the medical findings and be allowed to inspect the medical report. A copy of the doctor's report should be made available in full to the subject's nominated representative and, where appropriate, to the authority responsible for investigating the allegation of torture. It is the responsibility of the doctor to take reasonable steps to ensure that it is delivered securely to these persons. The report should not be made available to any other person except with the consent of the subject or on the authorization of a court empowered to enforce such a transfer.

9. Second examination
A second medical examination by an independent doctor should be permitted if requested by the victim of the alleged torture or ill-treatment and/or by his or her representative. The victim of the alleged torture and/or his or her representative should have the right to nominate the physician who will undertake the second examination. The second examination should be carried out in conformity with these principles.

10. Ethical duties
The doctor should bear in mind at all times that, in accordance with internationally accepted standards of medical ethics, his or her primary duty is to promote the wellbeing of the patient. In addition, he or she has a duty not to condone or participate in torture or other cruel, inhuman or degrading treatment. No aspect of the subject's character, physical characteristics, ethnic origin, or personal beliefs, nor the fact that an allegation of torture has been made by or on behalf of the subject, permits derogation from these duties.

These Principles were adopted by Amnesty International in January 1996 as part of the organization's worldwide campaign for a more effective role to be played by health professionals in the exposure and investigation of torture and other human rights violations.

SELECTED STATISTICS

AMNESTY INTERNATIONAL MEMBERSHIP
In 1996, there were about 1,000,000 Amnesty International members and subscribers in 162 countries and territories. There were 4,273 local Amnesty International groups registered with the International Secretariat, plus several thousand school, university, professional and other groups, in over 80 countries and territories.

PRISONER CASES
At the end of 1996, Amnesty International groups were working on over 2,000 different long-term assignments, concerning over 4,700 individuals, including prisoners of conscience and other victims of human rights violations. During the year action began on 612 new actions, many of which concerned more than one individual.

URGENT ACTION APPEALS
During 1996, Amnesty International initiated 500 actions which required urgent appeals from the Urgent Action Network. There were also 383 calls for further appeals on actions already issued. Members of the Urgent Action Network were therefore asked to send appeals on 883 occasions. These actions were issued on behalf of people in 92 countries.

The 500 new actions were issued on behalf of people who were either at risk or had been the victim of the following human rights violations: torture – 142 cases; "disappearance" – 68 cases; judicial execution – 124 cases; political killings and death threats – 163 cases; and legal concerns – 65 cases. (These categories are not mutually exclusive; more than one concern may have been featured in an action.) Other concerns included ill health, deaths in custody, *refoulement* (forcible repatriation) of asylum-seekers, corporal punishment and forcible exile.

REGIONAL ACTION NETWORKS
Amnesty International's Regional Action Networks deal with human rights abuses in every country of the world. During the year, approximately 2,247 Amnesty International local groups participated in the Regional Action Networks. They took action on more than 150 separate appeals involving thousands of victims of human rights violations.

AMNESTY INTERNATIONAL FUNDING
The international budget adopted by Amnesty International for 1996 was £17,205,000. This sum represents approximately one quarter of the estimated income likely to be raised during the year by the movement's national sections to finance their campaigning and other activities. Amnesty International's national sections and local volunteer groups are primarily responsible for funding the movement. An international fund-raising program is being developed. No money is sought or accepted from governments. The donations that sustain Amnesty International's work come from its members and the public.

RELIEF
During 1996, the International Secretariat of Amnesty International distributed £214,008 in relief (financial assistance) to victims of human rights violations such as prisoners of conscience and recently released prisoners of conscience and their dependants, and to provide medical treatment for torture victims. In addition, the organization's sections and groups distributed a further substantial amount, much of it in the form of modest payments by local groups to their adopted prisoners of conscience and dependent families.

Amnesty International's ultimate goal is to end human rights violations, but so long as they continue it tries to provide practical help to the victims. Relief is an important aspect of this work. Sometimes Amnesty International provides financial assistance directly to individuals. At other times, it works through local bodies such as local and national human rights organizations so as to ensure that resources are used as effectively as possible for those in most need. When Amnesty International asks an intermediary to distribute relief payments on its behalf, it stipulates precisely the intended purpose and beneficiaries, and requires the intermediary to report back fully on the expenditure of the funds.